Asymptotic Theory for Econometricians

Revised Edition

Asymptotic Theory for Econometricians

Revised Edition

Halbert White
Department of Economics
University of California, San Diego
La Jolla, California

ACADEMIC PRESS
An Imprint of Elsevier
San Diego San Francisco New York Boston London Sydney Tokyo

Cover photo credit: Copyright © 1999 Dynamic Graphics, Inc.

This book is printed on acid-free paper. ♾

Academic Press
An Imprint of Elsevier
525 B Street, Suite 1900, San Diego, California 92101-4495, USA
http://www.academicpress.com

Academic Press
Harcourt Place, 32 Jamestown Road, London NW1 7BY, UK
http://www.academicpress.com

Library of Congress Catalog Card Number: 00-107735

ISBN-13: 978-0-12-746652-1
ISBN-10: 0-12-746652-5

PRINTED IN THE UNITED STATES OF AMERICA
07 08 09 10 11 QW 9 8 7 6 5 4 3 2

This book is dedicated to the memory of my parents,

H. Lynn and Emily White.

Contents

Preface to the First Edition ix

Preface to the Revised Edition xi

References xiii

1 The Linear Model and Instrumental Variables Estimators 1

References 12

For Further Reading 12

2 Consistency 15

2.1 Limits 15

2.2 Almost Sure Convergence 18

2.3 Convergence in Probability 24

2.4 Convergence in rth Mean 28

References 30

3 Laws of Large Numbers 31

3.1 Independent Identically Distributed Observations 32

3.2 Independent Heterogeneously Distributed Observations . . . 35

3.3 Dependent Identically Distributed Observations 39

3.4 Dependent Heterogeneously Distributed Observations . . . 46

3.5 Martingale Difference Sequences 53

References 62

4 Asymptotic Normality **65**
4.1 Convergence in Distribution 65
4.2 Hypothesis Testing 74
4.3 Asymptotic Efficiency 83
References 111

5 Central Limit Theory **113**
5.1 Independent Identically Distributed Observations 114
5.2 Independent Heterogeneously Distributed Observations . . . 117
5.3 Dependent Identically Distributed Observations 122
5.4 Dependent Heterogeneously Distributed Observations . . . 130
5.5 Martingale Difference Sequences 133
References 136

6 Estimating Asymptotic Covariance Matrices **137**
6.1 General Structure of $\mathbf{V}_n$ 137
6.2 Case 1: $\{\mathbf{Z}_t\varepsilon_t\}$ Uncorrelated 139
6.3 Case 2: $\{\mathbf{Z}_t\varepsilon_t\}$ Finitely Correlated 147
6.4 Case 3: $\{\mathbf{Z}_t\varepsilon_t\}$ Asymptotically Uncorrelated 154
References 164

7 Functional Central Limit Theory and Applications **167**
7.1 Random Walks and Wiener Processes 167
7.2 Weak Convergence 171
7.3 Functional Central Limit Theorems 175
7.4 Regression with a Unit Root 178
7.5 Spurious Regression and Multivariate FCLTs 184
7.6 Cointegration and Stochastic Integrals 190
References 204

8 Directions for Further Study **207**
8.1 Extending the Data Generating Process 207
8.2 Nonlinear Models 209
8.3 Other Estimation Techniques 209
8.4 Model Misspecification 211
References 211

Solution Set 213
References 259

Index 261

Preface to the First Edition

Within the framework of the classical linear model it is a fairly straightforward matter to establish the properties of the ordinary least squares (OLS) and generalized least squares (GLS) estimators for samples of any size. Although the classical linear model is an excellent framework for developing a feel for the statistical techniques of estimation and inference that are central to econometrics, it is not particularly well adapted to the study of economic phenomena, because economists usually cannot conduct controlled experiments. Instead, the data usually exist as the outcome of a stochastic process outside the control of the investigator. For this reason, both the dependent and the explanatory variables may be stochastic, and equation disturbances may exhibit nonnormality or heteroskedasticity and serial correlation of unknown form, so that the classical assumptions are violated. Over the years a variety of useful techniques has evolved to deal with these difficulties. Many of these amount to straightforward modifications or extensions of the OLS techniques (e.g., the Cochrane-Orcutt technique, two-stage least squares, and three-stage least squares). However, the finite sample properties of these statistics are rarely easy to establish outside of somewhat limited special cases. Instead, their usefulness is justified primarily on the basis of their properties in large samples, because these properties can be fairly easily established using the powerful tools provided by laws of large numbers and central limit theory.

Despite the importance of large sample theory, it has usually received fairly cursory treatment in even the best econometrics textbooks. This is really no fault of the textbooks, however, because the field of asymptotic theory has been developing rapidly. It is only recently that econometricians have discovered or established methods for treating adequately and comprehensively the many different techniques available for dealing with the difficulties posed by economic data.

This book is intended to provide a somewhat more comprehensive and unified treatment of large sample theory than has been available previously and to relate the fundamental tools of asymptotic theory directly to many of the estimators of interest to econometricians. In addition, because economic data are generated in a variety of different contexts (time series, cross sections, time series-cross sections), we pay particular attention to the similarities and differences in the techniques appropriate to each of these contexts.

That it is possible to present our results in a fairly unified manner highlights the similarities among a variety of different techniques. It also allows us in specific instances to establish results that are somewhat more general than those previously available. We thus include some new results in addition to those that are better known.

This book is intended for use both as a reference and as a textbook for graduate students taking courses in econometrics beyond the introductory level. It is therefore assumed that the reader is familiar with the basic concepts of probability and statistics as well as with calculus and linear algebra and that the reader also has a good understanding of the classical linear model.

Because our goal here is to deal primarily with asymptotic theory, we do not consider in detail the meaning and scope of econometric models per se. Therefore, the material in this book can be usefully supplemented by standard econometrics texts, particularly any of those listed at the end of Chapter 1.

I would like to express my appreciation to all those who have helped in the evolution of this work. In particular, I would like to thank Charles Bates, Ian Domowitz, Rob Engle, Clive Granger, Lars Hansen, David Hendry, and Murray Rosenblatt. Particular thanks are due Jeff Wooldridge for his work in producing the solution set for the exercises. I also thank the students in various graduate classes at UCSD, who have served as unwitting and indispensable guinea pigs in the development of this material. I am deeply grateful to Annetta Whiteman, who typed this difficult manuscript with incredible swiftness and accuracy. Finally, I would like to thank the National Science Foundation for providing financial support for this work under grant SES81-07552.

Preface to the Revised Edition

It is a gratifying experience to be asked to revise and update a book written over fifteen years previously. Certainly, this request would be unnecessary had the book not exhibited an unusual tenacity in serving its purpose. Such tenacity had been my fond hope for this book, and it is always gratifying to see fond hopes realized.

It is also humbling and occasionally embarrassing to perform such a revision. Certain errors and omissions become painfully obvious. Thoughts of "How could I have thought that?" or "How could I have done that?" arise with regularity. Nevertheless, the opportunity is at hand to put things right, and it is satisfying to believe that one has succeeded in this. (I know, of course, that errors still lurk, but I hope that this time they are more benign or buried more deeply, or preferably both.)

Thus, the reader of this edition will find numerous instances where definitions have been corrected or clarified and where statements of results have been corrected or made more precise or complete. The exposition, too, has been polished in the hope of aiding clarity.

Not only is a revision of this sort an opportunity to fix prior shortcomings, but it is also an opportunity to bring the material covered up-to-date. In retrospect, the first edition of this book was more ambitious than originally intended. The fundamental research necessary to achieve the intended scope and cohesiveness of the overall vision for the work was by no means complete at the time the first edition was written. For example, the central limit theory for heterogeneous mixing processes had still not developed to the desired point at that time, nor had the theories of optimal instrumental variables estimation or asymptotic covariance estimation.

Indeed, the attempt made in writing the first edition to achieve its intended scope and coherence revealed a host of areas where work was needed, thus providing fuel for a great deal of my own research and (I like to think) that of others. In the years intervening, the efforts of the econometrics research community have succeeded wonderfully in delivering results in the areas needed and much more. Thus, the ambitions not realized in the first edition can now be achieved. If the theoretical vision presented here has not achieved a much better degree of unity, it can no longer be attributed to a lack of development of the field, but is now clearly identifiable as the author's own responsibility.

As a result of these developments, the reader of this second edition will now find much updated material, particularly with regard to central limit theory, asymptotically efficient instrumental variables estimation, and estimation of asymptotic covariance matrices. In particular, the original Chapter 7 (concerning efficient estimation with estimated error covariance matrices) and an entire section of Chapter 4 concerning efficient IV estimation have been removed and replaced with much more accessible and coherent results on efficient IV estimation, now appearing in Chapter 4.

There is also the progress of the field to contend with. When the first edition was written, cointegration was a subject in its infancy, and the tools needed to study the asymptotic behavior of estimators for models of cointegrated processes were years away from fruition. Indeed, results of DeJong and Davidson (2000) essential to placing estimation for cointegrated processes cohesively in place with the theory contained in the first six chapters of this book became available only months before work on this edition began.

Consequently, this second edition contains a completely new Chapter 7 devoted to functional central limit theory and its applications, specifically unit root regression, spurious regression, and regression with cointegrated processes. Given the explosive growth in this area, we cannot here achieve a broad treatment of cointegration. Nevertheless, in the new Chapter 7 the reader should find all the basic tools necessary for entrée into this fascinating area.

The comments, suggestions, and influence of numerous colleagues over the years have had effects both subtle and patent on the material presented here. With sincere apologies to anyone inadvertently omitted, I acknowledge with keen appreciation the direct and indirect contributions to the present state of this book by Takeshi Amemiya, Donald W. K. Andrews, Charles Bates, Herman Bierens, James Davidson, Robert DeJong,

Ian Domowitz, Graham Elliott, Robert Engle, A. Ronald Gallant, Arthur Goldberger, Clive W. J. Granger, James Hamilton, Bruce Hansen, Lars Hansen, Jerry Hausman, David Hendry, Søren Johansen, Edward Leamer, James Mackinnon, Whitney Newey, Peter C. B. Phillips, Eugene Savin, Chris Sims, Maxwell Stinchcombe, James Stock, Mark Watson, Kenneth West, and Jeffrey Wooldridge. Special thanks are due Mark Salmon, who originally suggested writing this book. UCSD graduate students who helped with the revision include Jin Seo Cho, Raffaella Giacomini, Andrew Patton, Sivan Ritz, Kevin Sheppard, Liangjun Su, and Nada Wasi. I also thank sincerely Peter Reinhard Hansen, who has assisted invaluably with the creation of this revised edition, acting as electronic amanuensis and editor, and who is responsible for preparation of the revised set of solutions to the exercises. Finally, I thank Michael J. Bacci for his invaluable logistical support and the National Science Foundation for providing financial support under grant SBR-9811562.

Del Mar, CA
July, 2000

References

DeJong R. M. and J. Davidson (2000). "The functional central limit theorem and weak convegence to stochastic integrals I: Weakly dependent processes," forthcoming in *Econometric Theory*, 16.

CHAPTER 1

The Linear Model and Instrumental Variables Estimators

The purpose of this book is to provide the reader with the tools and concepts needed to study the behavior of econometric estimators and test statistics in large samples. Throughout, attention will be directed to estimation and inference in the framework of a linear stochastic relationship such as

$$Y_t = \mathbf{X}_t'\boldsymbol{\beta}_o + \varepsilon_t, \quad t = 1, \ldots, n,$$

where we have n observations on the scalar dependent variable Y_t and the vector of explanatory variables $\mathbf{X}_t = (X_{t1}, X_{t2}, \ldots, X_{tk})'$. The scalar stochastic disturbance ε_t is unobserved, and $\boldsymbol{\beta}_o$ is an unknown $k \times 1$ vector of coefficients that we are interested in learning about, either through estimation or through hypothesis testing. In matrix notation this relationship is written as

$$\mathbf{Y} = \mathbf{X}\boldsymbol{\beta}_o + \boldsymbol{\varepsilon},$$

where $\mathbf{Y}$ is an $n \times 1$ vector, $\mathbf{X}$ is an $n \times k$ matrix with rows $\mathbf{X}_t'$, and $\boldsymbol{\varepsilon}$ is an $n \times 1$ vector with elements ε_t.

(Our notation embodies a convention we follow throughout: scalars will be represented in standard type, while vectors and matrices will be represented in boldface. Throughout, all vectors are column vectors.)

Most econometric estimators can be viewed as solutions to an optimization problem. For example, the ordinary least squares estimator is the value for $\boldsymbol{\beta}$ that minimizes the sum of squared residuals

$$\begin{aligned}\mathrm{SSR}(\boldsymbol{\beta}) &= (\mathbf{Y}-\mathbf{X}\boldsymbol{\beta})'(\mathbf{Y}-\mathbf{X}\boldsymbol{\beta}) \\ &= \sum_{t=1}^{n}(Y_t-\mathbf{X}_t'\boldsymbol{\beta})^2.\end{aligned}$$

The first-order conditions for a minimum are

$$\begin{aligned}\partial\mathrm{SSR}(\boldsymbol{\beta})/\partial\boldsymbol{\beta} &= -2\mathbf{X}'(\mathbf{Y}-\mathbf{X}\boldsymbol{\beta}) \\ &= -2\sum_{t=1}^{n}\mathbf{X}_t(Y_t-\mathbf{X}_t'\boldsymbol{\beta}) = \mathbf{0}.\end{aligned}$$

If $\mathbf{X}'\mathbf{X} = \sum_{t=1}^{n}\mathbf{X}_t\mathbf{X}_t'$ is nonsingular, this system of k equations in k unknowns can be uniquely solved for the ordinary least squares (OLS) estimator

$$\begin{aligned}\hat{\boldsymbol{\beta}}_n &= (\mathbf{X}'\mathbf{X})^{-1}\mathbf{X}'\mathbf{Y} \\ &= \left(\sum_{t=1}^{n}\mathbf{X}_t\mathbf{X}_t'\right)^{-1}\sum_{t=1}^{n}\mathbf{X}_tY_t.\end{aligned}$$

Our interest centers on the behavior of estimators such as $\hat{\boldsymbol{\beta}}_n$ as n grows larger and larger. We seek conditions that will allow us to draw conclusions about the behavior of $\hat{\boldsymbol{\beta}}_n$; for example, that $\hat{\boldsymbol{\beta}}_n$ has a particular distribution or certain first and second moments.

The assumptions of the *classical linear model* allow us to draw such conclusions for any n. These conditions and results can be formally stated as the following theorem.

Theorem 1.1 *The following are the assumptions of the classical linear model.*

(*i*) *The data are generated as* $Y_t = \mathbf{X}_t'\boldsymbol{\beta}_o + \varepsilon_t, \quad t = 1, \ldots, n,\ \boldsymbol{\beta}_o \in \mathbb{R}^k$.

(*ii*) $\mathbf{X}$ *is a nonstochastic and finite* $n \times k$ *matrix,* $n \geq k$.

(*iii*) $\mathbf{X}'\mathbf{X}$ *is nonsingular.*

(*iv*) $E(\boldsymbol{\varepsilon}) = \mathbf{0}$.

(*v*) $\boldsymbol{\varepsilon} \sim N(\mathbf{0}, \sigma_o^2\mathbf{I}), \quad \sigma_o^2 < \infty$.

(*a*) (*Existence*) *Given* (*i*)–(*iii*), $\hat{\boldsymbol{\beta}}_n$ *exists and is unique.*

(b) (*Unbiasedness*) *Given* (*i*)–(*iv*), $E(\hat{\boldsymbol{\beta}}_n) = \boldsymbol{\beta}_o$.

(c) (*Normality*) *Given* (*i*)–(*v*), $\hat{\boldsymbol{\beta}}_n \sim N(\boldsymbol{\beta}_o, \sigma_o^2(\mathbf{X}'\mathbf{X})^{-1})$.

(d) (*Efficiency*) *Given* (*i*)–(*v*), $\hat{\boldsymbol{\beta}}_n$ *is the maximum likelihood estimator and is the best unbiased estimator in the sense that the variance – covariance matrix of any other unbiased estimator exceeds that of* $\hat{\boldsymbol{\beta}}_n$ *by a positive semidefinite matrix, regardless of the value of* $\boldsymbol{\beta}_o$.

Proof. See Theil (1971, Ch. 3). ∎

In the statement of the assumptions above, $E(\cdot)$ denotes the expected value operator, and $\boldsymbol{\varepsilon} \sim N(\mathbf{0}, \sigma_o^2\mathbf{I})$ means that $\boldsymbol{\varepsilon}$ is distributed as ($\sim$) multivariate normal with mean vector zero and covariance matrix $\sigma_o^2\mathbf{I}$, where $\mathbf{I}$ is the identity matrix.

The properties of existence, unbiasedness, normality, and efficiency of an estimator are the small sample analogs of the properties that will be the focus of interest here. Unbiasedness tells us that the distribution of $\hat{\boldsymbol{\beta}}_n$ is centered around the unknown true value $\boldsymbol{\beta}_o$, whereas the normality property allows us to construct confidence intervals and test hypotheses using the t- or F-distributions (see Theil, 1971, pp. 130–146). The efficiency property guarantees that our estimator has the greatest possible precision within a given class of estimators and also helps ensure that tests of hypotheses have high power.

Of course, the classical assumptions are rather stringent and can easily fail in situations faced by economists. Since failures of assumptions (*iii*) and (*iv*) are easily remedied (exclude linearly dependent regressors if (*iii*) fails; include a constant in the model if (*iv*) fails), we will concern ourselves primarily with the failure of assumptions (*ii*) and (*v*). The possible failure of assumption (*i*) is a subject that requires a book in itself (see, e.g., White, 1994) and will not be considered here. Nevertheless, the tools developed in this book will be essential to understanding and treating the consequences of the failure of assumption (*i*).

Let us briefly examine the consequences of various failures of assumptions (*ii*) or (*v*). First, suppose that $\boldsymbol{\varepsilon}$ exhibits heteroskedasticity or serial correlation, so that $E(\boldsymbol{\varepsilon}\boldsymbol{\varepsilon}') = \boldsymbol{\Omega} \neq \sigma_0^2\mathbf{I}$. We have the following result for the OLS estimator.

Theorem 1.2 *Suppose the classical assumptions* (*i*)-(*iv*) *hold but replace* (*v*) *with* (*v'*) $\boldsymbol{\varepsilon} \sim N(\mathbf{0}, \boldsymbol{\Omega})$, $\boldsymbol{\Omega}$ *finite and nonsingular. Then* (*a*) *and* (*b*) *hold as before,* (*c*) *is replaced by*

(*c'*) (*Normality*) *Given* (*i*)–(*v'*),

$$\hat{\boldsymbol{\beta}}_n \sim N(\boldsymbol{\beta}_o, (\mathbf{X}'\mathbf{X})^{-1}\mathbf{X}'\boldsymbol{\Omega}\mathbf{X}(\mathbf{X}'\mathbf{X})^{-1}),$$

and (d) does not hold; that is, $\hat{\boldsymbol{\beta}}_n$ is no longer necessarily the best unbiased estimator.

Proof. By definition, $\hat{\boldsymbol{\beta}}_n = (\mathbf{X}'\mathbf{X})^{-1}\mathbf{X}'\mathbf{Y}$. Given (i),

$$\hat{\boldsymbol{\beta}}_n = \boldsymbol{\beta}_o + (\mathbf{X}'\mathbf{X})^{-1}\mathbf{X}'\boldsymbol{\varepsilon},$$

where $(\mathbf{X}'\mathbf{X})^{-1}\mathbf{X}'\boldsymbol{\varepsilon}$ is a linear combination of jointly normal random variables and is therefore jointly normal with

$$E((\mathbf{X}'\mathbf{X})^{-1}\mathbf{X}'\boldsymbol{\varepsilon}) = (\mathbf{X}'\mathbf{X})^{-1}\mathbf{X}'E(\boldsymbol{\varepsilon}) = \mathbf{0},$$

given (ii) and (iv) and

$$\begin{aligned} \text{var}(\mathbf{X}'\mathbf{X})^{-1}\mathbf{X}'\boldsymbol{\varepsilon} &= E((\mathbf{X}'\mathbf{X})^{-1}\mathbf{X}'\boldsymbol{\varepsilon}\boldsymbol{\varepsilon}'\mathbf{X}(\mathbf{X}'\mathbf{X})^{-1}) \\ &= (\mathbf{X}'\mathbf{X})^{-1}\mathbf{X}'E(\boldsymbol{\varepsilon}\boldsymbol{\varepsilon}')\mathbf{X}(\mathbf{X}'\mathbf{X})^{-1} \\ &= (\mathbf{X}'\mathbf{X})^{-1}\mathbf{X}'\boldsymbol{\Omega}\mathbf{X}(\mathbf{X}'\mathbf{X})^{-1}, \end{aligned}$$

given (ii) and (v'). Hence $\hat{\boldsymbol{\beta}}_n \sim N(\boldsymbol{\beta}_o, (\mathbf{X}'\mathbf{X})^{-1}\mathbf{X}'\boldsymbol{\Omega}\mathbf{X}(\mathbf{X}'\mathbf{X})^{-1})$. That (d) does not hold follows because there exists an unbiased estimator with a smaller covariance matrix than $\hat{\boldsymbol{\beta}}_n$, namely, $\boldsymbol{\beta}_n^* = (\mathbf{X}'\boldsymbol{\Omega}^{-1}\mathbf{X})^{-1}\mathbf{X}'\boldsymbol{\Omega}^{-1}\mathbf{Y}$. We examine its properties next. ■

As long as $\boldsymbol{\Omega}$ is known, the presence of serial correlation or heteroskedasticity does not cause problems for testing hypotheses or constructing confidence intervals. This can still be done using (c'), although the failure of (d) indicates that the OLS estimator may not be best for these purposes. However, if $\boldsymbol{\Omega}$ is unknown (apart from a factor of proportionality), testing hypotheses and constructing confidence intervals is no longer a simple matter. One might be able to construct tests based on estimates of $\boldsymbol{\Omega}$, but the resulting statistics may have very complicated distributions. As we shall see in Chapter 6, this difficulty is lessened in large samples by the availability of convenient approximations based on the central limit theorem and laws of large numbers.

If $\boldsymbol{\Omega}$ is known, efficiency can be regained by applying OLS to a linear transformation of the original model, i.e.,

$$\mathbf{C}^{-1}\mathbf{Y} = \mathbf{C}^{-1}\mathbf{X}\boldsymbol{\beta}_o + \mathbf{C}^{-1}\boldsymbol{\varepsilon}$$

or

$$\mathbf{Y}^* = \mathbf{X}^*\boldsymbol{\beta}_o + \boldsymbol{\varepsilon}^*,$$

where $\mathbf{Y}^* = \mathbf{C}^{-1}\mathbf{Y}$, $\mathbf{X}^* = \mathbf{C}^{-1}\mathbf{X}$, $\varepsilon^* = \mathbf{C}^{-1}\varepsilon$ and $\mathbf{C}$ is a nonsingular factorization of $\mathbf{\Omega}$ such that $\mathbf{CC}' = \mathbf{\Omega}$ so that $\mathbf{C}^{-1}\mathbf{\Omega}\mathbf{C}^{-1\prime} = \mathbf{I}$. This transformation ensures that $E(\varepsilon^*\varepsilon^{*\prime}) = E(\mathbf{C}^{-1}\varepsilon\varepsilon'\mathbf{C}^{-1\prime}) = \mathbf{C}^{-1}E(\varepsilon\varepsilon')\mathbf{C}^{-1\prime} = \mathbf{C}^{-1}\mathbf{\Omega}\mathbf{C}^{-1\prime} = \mathbf{I}$, so that assumption (v) once again holds. The least squares estimator for the transformed model is

$$\begin{aligned}\hat{\beta}_n^* &= (\mathbf{X}^{*\prime}\mathbf{X}^*)^{-1}\mathbf{X}^{*\prime}\mathbf{Y}^* \\ &= (\mathbf{X}'\mathbf{C}^{-1\prime}\mathbf{C}^{-1}\mathbf{X})^{-1}\mathbf{X}'\mathbf{C}^{-1\prime}\mathbf{C}^{-1}\mathbf{Y} \\ &= (\mathbf{X}'\mathbf{\Omega}^{-1}\mathbf{X})^{-1}\mathbf{X}'\mathbf{\Omega}^{-1}\mathbf{Y}.\end{aligned}$$

The estimator $\hat{\boldsymbol{\beta}}_n^*$ is called the generalized least squares (GLS) estimator, and its properties are given by the following result.

Theorem 1.3 *The following are the "generalized" classical assumptions.*

(i) *The data are generated as* $Y_t = \mathbf{X}_t'\boldsymbol{\beta}_o + \varepsilon_t, \quad t = 1, \ldots, n, \quad \boldsymbol{\beta}_o \in \mathbb{R}^k$.

(ii) $\mathbf{X}$ *is a nonstochastic and finite* $n \times k$ *matrix,* $n \geq k$.

(iii^*) $\mathbf{\Omega}$ *is finite and positive definite, and* $\mathbf{X}'\mathbf{\Omega}^{-1}\mathbf{X}$ *is nonsingular.*

(iv) $E(\varepsilon) = \mathbf{0}$.

(v^*) $\varepsilon \sim N(\mathbf{0},\mathbf{\Omega})$.

(a) *(Existence) Given* (i)–(iii^*), $\hat{\boldsymbol{\beta}}_n^*$ *exists and is unique.*

(b) *(Unbiasedness) Given* (i)–(iv), $E(\hat{\boldsymbol{\beta}}_n^*) = \boldsymbol{\beta}_o$.

(c) *(Normality) Given* (i)–(v^*), $\hat{\boldsymbol{\beta}}_n^* \sim N(\boldsymbol{\beta}_o, (\mathbf{X}'\mathbf{\Omega}^{-1}\mathbf{X})^{-1})$.

(d) *(Efficiency) Given* (i)–(v^*), $\hat{\boldsymbol{\beta}}_n^*$ *is the maximum likelihood estimator and is the best unbiased estimator.*

Proof. Apply Theorem 1.1 with $Y_t^* = \mathbf{X}_t^{*\prime}\boldsymbol{\beta}_o + \varepsilon_t^*$. ∎

If $\mathbf{\Omega}$ is known, we obtain efficiency by transforming the model "back" to a form in which OLS gives the efficient estimator. However, if $\mathbf{\Omega}$ is unknown, this transformation is not immediately available. It might be possible to estimate $\mathbf{\Omega}$, say by $\hat{\mathbf{\Omega}}$, but $\hat{\mathbf{\Omega}}$ is then random and so is the factorization $\hat{\mathbf{C}}$. Theorem 1.1 no longer applies. Nevertheless, it turns out that in large samples we can often proceed by replacing $\mathbf{\Omega}$ with a suitable estimator $\hat{\mathbf{\Omega}}$. We consider such situations in Chapter 4.

Hypothesis testing in the classical linear model relies heavily on being able to make use of the t- and F-distributions. However, it is quite possible that the normality assumption (v) or (v^*) may fail. When this happens, the classical t- and F-statistics generally no longer have the t- and F-distributions. Nevertheless, the central limit theorem can be applied when n is large to guarantee that $\hat{\boldsymbol{\beta}}_n$ or $\hat{\boldsymbol{\beta}}_n^*$ is distributed approximately as normal, as we shall see in Chapters 4 and 5.

Now consider what happens when assumption (ii) fails, so that the explanatory variables $\mathbf{X}_t$ are stochastic. In some cases, this causes no real problems because we can examine the properties of our estimators "conditional" on $\mathbf{X}$. For example, consider the unbiasedness property. To demonstrate unbiasedness we use (i) to write

$$\hat{\boldsymbol{\beta}}_n = \boldsymbol{\beta}_o + (\mathbf{X}'\mathbf{X})^{-1}\mathbf{X}'\boldsymbol{\varepsilon}.$$

If $\mathbf{X}$ is random, we can no longer write $E((\mathbf{X}'\mathbf{X})^{-1}\mathbf{X}'\boldsymbol{\varepsilon}) = (\mathbf{X}'\mathbf{X})^{-1}\mathbf{X}'E(\boldsymbol{\varepsilon})$. However, by taking conditional expectations, we can treat $\mathbf{X}$ as "fixed," so we have

$$\begin{aligned} E(\hat{\boldsymbol{\beta}}_n|\mathbf{X}) &= \boldsymbol{\beta}_o + E((\mathbf{X}'\mathbf{X})^{-1}\mathbf{X}'\boldsymbol{\varepsilon}|\mathbf{X}) \\ &= \boldsymbol{\beta}_o + (\mathbf{X}'\mathbf{X})^{-1}\mathbf{X}'E(\boldsymbol{\varepsilon}|\mathbf{X}). \end{aligned}$$

If we are willing to assume $E(\boldsymbol{\varepsilon}|\mathbf{X}) = \mathbf{0}$, then conditional unbiasedness follows, i.e.,

$$E(\hat{\boldsymbol{\beta}}_n|\mathbf{X}) = \boldsymbol{\beta}_o.$$

Unconditional unbiasedness follows from this as a consequence of the law of iterated expectations (given in Chapter 3), i.e.,

$$E(\hat{\boldsymbol{\beta}}_n) = E[E(\hat{\boldsymbol{\beta}}_n|\mathbf{X})] = E(\boldsymbol{\beta}_o) = \boldsymbol{\beta}_o.$$

The other properties can be similarly considered. However, the assumption that $E(\boldsymbol{\varepsilon}|\mathbf{X}) = \mathbf{0}$ is crucial. If $E(\boldsymbol{\varepsilon}|\mathbf{X}) \neq \mathbf{0}$, $\hat{\boldsymbol{\beta}}_n$ need not be unbiased, either conditionally or unconditionally.

Situations in which $E(\boldsymbol{\varepsilon}|\mathbf{X}) \neq \mathbf{0}$ can arise easily in economics. For example, $\mathbf{X}_t$ may contain errors of measurement. Suppose the data are generated as

$$Y_t = \mathbf{W}_t'\boldsymbol{\beta}_o + \nu_t, \quad E(\mathbf{W}_t\nu_t) = \mathbf{0},$$

but we measure $\mathbf{W}_t$ subject to errors $\boldsymbol{\eta}_t$, as $\mathbf{X}_t = \mathbf{W}_t + \boldsymbol{\eta}_t$, $E(\mathbf{W}_t\boldsymbol{\eta}_t') = \mathbf{0}$, $E(\boldsymbol{\eta}_t\boldsymbol{\eta}_t') \neq \mathbf{0}$, $E(\boldsymbol{\eta}_t\nu_t) = \mathbf{0}$. Then

$$Y_t = \mathbf{X}_t'\boldsymbol{\beta}_o + \nu_t - \boldsymbol{\eta}_t'\boldsymbol{\beta}_o = \mathbf{X}_t'\boldsymbol{\beta}_o + \varepsilon_t.$$

With $\varepsilon_t = \nu_t - \boldsymbol{\eta}_t'\boldsymbol{\beta}_o$, we have $E(\mathbf{X}_t\varepsilon_t) = E[(\mathbf{W}_t + \boldsymbol{\eta}_t)(\nu_t - \boldsymbol{\eta}_t'\boldsymbol{\beta}_o)] = -E(\boldsymbol{\eta}_t\boldsymbol{\eta}_t')\boldsymbol{\beta}_o \neq \mathbf{0}$. Now $E(\boldsymbol{\varepsilon}|\mathbf{X}) = \mathbf{0}$ implies that for all t, $E(\mathbf{X}_t\varepsilon_t) = \mathbf{0}$, since $E(\mathbf{X}_t\varepsilon_t) = E[E(\mathbf{X}_t\varepsilon_t|\mathbf{X})] = E[\mathbf{X}_tE(\varepsilon_t|\mathbf{X})] = \mathbf{0}$. Hence $E(\mathbf{X}_t\varepsilon_t) \neq \mathbf{0}$ implies $E(\boldsymbol{\varepsilon}|\mathbf{X}) \neq \mathbf{0}$. The OLS estimator will not be unbiased in the presence of measurement errors.

As another example, consider the data generating process

$$\begin{aligned} Y_t &= Y_{t-1}\alpha_o + \mathbf{W}_t'\boldsymbol{\delta}_o + \varepsilon_t, & E(\mathbf{W}_t\varepsilon_t) = \mathbf{0}; \\ \varepsilon_t &= \rho_o\varepsilon_{t-1} + \nu_t, & E(\varepsilon_{t-1}\nu_t) = 0. \end{aligned}$$

This is the case of *serially correlated errors* in the presence of a *lagged dependent variable* Y_{t-1}. Let $\mathbf{X}_t = (Y_{t-1}, \mathbf{W}_t')'$ and $\boldsymbol{\beta}_o = (\alpha_o, \boldsymbol{\delta}_o')'$. Again, we have

$$Y_t = \mathbf{X}_t'\boldsymbol{\beta}_o + \varepsilon_t,$$

but

$$E(\mathbf{X}_t\varepsilon_t) = E((Y_{t-1}, \mathbf{W}_t')'\varepsilon_t) = (E(Y_{t-1}\varepsilon_t), \mathbf{0})'.$$

If we also assume $E(Y_{t-1}\nu_t) = 0$, $E(Y_{t-1}\varepsilon_{t-1}) = E(Y_t\varepsilon_t)$, and $E(\varepsilon_t^2) = \sigma_o^2$, it can be shown that

$$E(Y_{t-1}\varepsilon_t) = \frac{\sigma_o^2\rho_o}{1 - \rho_o\alpha_o}.$$

Thus if $\rho_o \neq 0$, then $E(\mathbf{X}_t\varepsilon_t) \neq \mathbf{0}$ so that $E(\boldsymbol{\varepsilon}|\mathbf{X}) \neq \mathbf{0}$ and OLS is not generally unbiased.

As a final example, consider a system of simultaneous equations

$$\begin{aligned} Y_{t1} &= Y_{t2}\alpha_o + \mathbf{W}_{t1}'\boldsymbol{\delta}_o + \varepsilon_{t1}, & E(\mathbf{W}_{t1}\varepsilon_{t1}) = \mathbf{0}, \\ Y_{t2} &= \mathbf{W}_{t2}'\gamma_0 + \varepsilon_{t2}, & E(\mathbf{W}_{t2}\varepsilon_{t2}) = \mathbf{0}. \end{aligned}$$

Suppose we are only interested in the first equation, but we know $E(\varepsilon_{t1}\varepsilon_{t2}) = \sigma_{12} \neq 0$. Let $\mathbf{X}_{t1} = (Y_{t2}, \mathbf{W}_{t1}')'$ and $\boldsymbol{\beta}_o = (\alpha_o, \boldsymbol{\delta}_o')'$. The equation of interest is now

$$Y_{t1} = \mathbf{X}_{t1}'\boldsymbol{\beta}_o + \varepsilon_{t1}.$$

In this case $E(\mathbf{X}_{t1}\varepsilon_{t1}) = E((Y_{t2}, \mathbf{W}'_{t1})'\varepsilon_{t1}) = (E(Y_{t2}\varepsilon_{t1}), \mathbf{0})'$. Now

$$E(Y_{t2}\varepsilon_{t1}) = E((\mathbf{W}'_{t2}\gamma_0 + \varepsilon_{t2})\varepsilon_{t1}) = E(\varepsilon_{t1}\varepsilon_{t2}) = \sigma_{12} \neq 0,$$

assuming $E(\mathbf{W}_{t2}\varepsilon_{t1}) = \mathbf{0}$. Thus $E(\mathbf{X}_{t1}\varepsilon_{t1}) = (\sigma_{12}, \mathbf{0})' \neq \mathbf{0}$, so again OLS is not generally unbiased, either conditionally or unconditionally.

Not only is the OLS estimator generally biased in these circumstances, but it can be shown under reasonable conditions that this bias does not get smaller as n gets larger. Fortunately, there is an alternative to least squares that is better behaved, at least in large samples. This alternative, first used by P. G. Wright (1928) and his son S. Wright (1925) and formally developed by Reiersøl (1941, 1945) and Geary (1949), exploits the fact that even when $E(\mathbf{X}_t\varepsilon_t) \neq \mathbf{0}$, it is often possible to use economic theory to find other variables that are uncorrelated with the errors ε_t. Without such variables, correlations between the observables and unobservables (the errors ε_t) persistently contaminate our estimators, making it impossible to learn anything about $\boldsymbol{\beta}_o$. Hence, these variables are instrumental in allowing us to estimate $\boldsymbol{\beta}_o$, and we shall denote these "instrumental variables" as an $l \times 1$ vector $\mathbf{Z}_t$. The $n \times l$ matrix $\mathbf{Z}$ has rows $\mathbf{Z}'_t$.

To be useful, the instrumental variables must also be closely enough related to $\mathbf{X}_t$ so that $\mathbf{Z}'\mathbf{X}$ has full column rank. If we know from economic theory that $E(\mathbf{X}_t\varepsilon_t) = \mathbf{0}$, then $\mathbf{X}_t$ can serve directly as the set of instrumental variables. As we saw previously, $\mathbf{X}_t$ may be correlated with ε_t so we cannot always choose $\mathbf{Z}_t = \mathbf{X}_t$. Nevertheless, in each of those examples, the structure of the data generating process suggests some reasonable choices for $\mathbf{Z}$. In the case of errors of measurement, a useful set of instrumental variables would be another set of measurements on $\mathbf{W}_t$ subject to errors $\boldsymbol{\xi}_t$ uncorrelated with $\boldsymbol{\eta}_t$ and ν_t, say $\mathbf{Z}_t = \mathbf{W}_t + \boldsymbol{\xi}_t$. Then $E(\mathbf{Z}_t\varepsilon_t) = E[(\mathbf{W}_t + \boldsymbol{\xi}_t)(\nu_t - \boldsymbol{\eta}'_t\boldsymbol{\beta}_o)] = \mathbf{0}$. In the case of serial correlation in the presence of lagged dependent variables, a useful choice is $\mathbf{Z}_t = (\mathbf{W}'_t, \mathbf{W}'_{t-1})'$ provided $E(\mathbf{W}_{t-1}\varepsilon_t) = \mathbf{0}$, which is not unreasonable. Note that the relation $Y_{t-1} = Y_{t-2}\alpha_o + \mathbf{W}'_{t-1}\boldsymbol{\delta}_o + \varepsilon_{t-1}$ ensures that $\mathbf{W}_{t-1}$ will be related to Y_{t-1}. In the case of simultaneous equations, a useful choice is $\mathbf{Z}_t = (\mathbf{W}'_{t1}, \mathbf{W}'_{t2})'$. The relation $Y_{t2} = \mathbf{W}'_{t2}\gamma_0 + \varepsilon_{2t}$ ensures that $\mathbf{W}_{t2}$ will be related to Y_{t2}.

In what follows, we shall simply assume that such instrumental variables are available. However, in Chapter 4 we shall be able to specify precisely how best to choose the instrumental variables.

Earlier, we stated the important fact that most econometric estimators can be viewed as solutions to an optimization problem. In the present context, the zero correlation property $E(\mathbf{Z}_t\varepsilon_t) = \mathbf{0}$ provides the fundamental basis for estimating $\boldsymbol{\beta}_o$. Because $\varepsilon_t = Y_t - \mathbf{X}'_t\boldsymbol{\beta}_o$, $\boldsymbol{\beta}_o$ is a solution of the equations $E(\mathbf{Z}_t(Y_t - \mathbf{X}_t'\boldsymbol{\beta}_o)) = \mathbf{0}$. However, we usually do not know the expectations $E(\mathbf{Z}_t Y_t)$ and $E(\mathbf{Z}_t\mathbf{X}_t')$ needed to find a solution to these equations, so we replace expectations with sample averages, which we hope will provide a close enough approximation. Thus, consider finding a solution to the equations

$$n^{-1}\sum_{t=1}^{n}\mathbf{Z}_t(Y_t - \mathbf{X}_t'\boldsymbol{\beta}_o) = \mathbf{Z}'(\mathbf{Y} - \mathbf{X}\boldsymbol{\beta}_o)/n = \mathbf{0}.$$

This is a system of l equations in k unknowns. If $l < k$, there is a multiplicity of solutions; if $l = k$, the unique solution is $\tilde{\boldsymbol{\beta}}_n = (\mathbf{Z}'\mathbf{X})^{-1}\mathbf{Z}'\mathbf{Y}$, provided that $\mathbf{Z}'\mathbf{X}$ is nonsingular; and if $l > k$, these equations need have no solution, although there may be a value for $\boldsymbol{\beta}$ that makes $\mathbf{Z}'(\mathbf{Y} - \mathbf{X}\boldsymbol{\beta})$ "closest" to zero.

This provides the basis for solving an optimization problem. Because economic theory typically leads to situations in which $l \geq k$, we can estimate $\boldsymbol{\beta}_o$ by finding that value of $\boldsymbol{\beta}$ that minimizes the quadratic distance from zero of $\mathbf{Z}'(\mathbf{Y} - \mathbf{X}\boldsymbol{\beta})$,

$$d_n(\boldsymbol{\beta}) = (\mathbf{Y} - \mathbf{X}\boldsymbol{\beta})'\mathbf{Z}\hat{\mathbf{P}}_n\mathbf{Z}'(\mathbf{Y} - \mathbf{X}\boldsymbol{\beta}),$$

where $\hat{\mathbf{P}}_n$ is a symmetric $l \times l$ positive definite norming matrix which may be stochastic. For now, $\hat{\mathbf{P}}_n$ can be any symmetric positive definite matrix. In Chapter 4 we shall see how the choice of $\hat{\mathbf{P}}_n$ affects the properties of our estimator and how $\hat{\mathbf{P}}_n$ can best be chosen.

We choose the quadratic distance measure because the minimization problem "minimize $d_n(\boldsymbol{\beta})$ with respect to $\boldsymbol{\beta}$" has a convenient linear solution and yields many well-known econometric estimators. Other distance measures yield other families of estimators that we will not consider here.

The first-order conditions for a minimum are

$$\partial d_n(\boldsymbol{\beta})/\partial\boldsymbol{\beta} = -2\mathbf{X}'\mathbf{Z}\hat{\mathbf{P}}_n\mathbf{Z}'(\mathbf{Y} - \mathbf{X}\boldsymbol{\beta}) = \mathbf{0}.$$

Provided that $\mathbf{X}'\mathbf{Z}\hat{\mathbf{P}}_n\mathbf{Z}'\mathbf{X}$ is nonsingular (for which it is necessary that $\mathbf{Z}'\mathbf{X}$ have full column rank), the resulting solution is the *instrumental variables* (IV) estimator (also known as the "method of moments" estimator)

$$\tilde{\boldsymbol{\beta}}_n = (\mathbf{X}'\mathbf{Z}\hat{\mathbf{P}}_n\mathbf{Z}'\mathbf{X})^{-1}\mathbf{X}'\mathbf{Z}\hat{\mathbf{P}}_n\mathbf{Z}'\mathbf{Y}.$$

All of the estimators considered in this book have this form, and by choosing $\mathbf{Z}$ or $\hat{\mathbf{P}}_n$ appropriately, we can obtain a large number of the estimators of interest to econometricians. For example, with $\mathbf{Z} = \mathbf{X}$ and $\hat{\mathbf{P}}_n = (\mathbf{X}'\mathbf{X}/n)^{-1}$,

$\tilde{\boldsymbol{\beta}}_n = \hat{\boldsymbol{\beta}}_n$; that is, the IV estimator equals the OLS estimator. Given any $\mathbf{Z}$, choosing $\hat{\mathbf{P}}_n = (\mathbf{Z}'\mathbf{Z}/n)^{-1}$ gives an estimator known as *two-stage least squares* (2SLS). The tools developed in the following chapters will allow us to pick $\mathbf{Z}$ and $\hat{\mathbf{P}}_n$ in ways appropriate to many of the situations encountered in economics.

Now consider the problem of determining whether $\tilde{\boldsymbol{\beta}}_n$ is unbiased. If the data generating process is $\mathbf{Y} = \mathbf{X}\boldsymbol{\beta}_o + \boldsymbol{\varepsilon}$, we have

$$\begin{aligned}\tilde{\boldsymbol{\beta}}_n &= (\mathbf{X}'\mathbf{Z}\hat{\mathbf{P}}_n\mathbf{Z}'\mathbf{X})^{-1}\mathbf{X}'\mathbf{Z}\hat{\mathbf{P}}_n\mathbf{Z}'\mathbf{Y} \\ &= (\mathbf{X}'\mathbf{Z}\hat{\mathbf{P}}_n\mathbf{Z}'\mathbf{X})^{-1}\mathbf{X}'\mathbf{Z}\hat{\mathbf{P}}_n\mathbf{Z}'(\mathbf{X}\boldsymbol{\beta}_o + \boldsymbol{\varepsilon}) \\ &= \boldsymbol{\beta}_o + (\mathbf{X}'\mathbf{Z}\hat{\mathbf{P}}_n\mathbf{Z}'\mathbf{X})^{-1}\mathbf{X}'\mathbf{Z}\hat{\mathbf{P}}_n\mathbf{Z}'\boldsymbol{\varepsilon},\end{aligned}$$

so that

$$E(\tilde{\boldsymbol{\beta}}_n) = \boldsymbol{\beta}_o + E((\mathbf{X}'\mathbf{Z}\hat{\mathbf{P}}_n\mathbf{Z}'\mathbf{X})^{-1}\mathbf{X}'\mathbf{Z}\hat{\mathbf{P}}_n\mathbf{Z}'\boldsymbol{\varepsilon}).$$

In general, it is not possible to guarantee that the second term above vanishes, even when $E(\boldsymbol{\varepsilon}|\mathbf{Z}) = \mathbf{0}$. In fact, the expectation in the second term above may not even be defined. For this reason, the concept of unbiasedness is not particularly relevant to the study of IV estimators. Instead, we shall make use of the weaker concept of *consistency*. Loosely speaking, an estimator is "consistent" for $\boldsymbol{\beta}_o$ if it gets closer and closer to $\boldsymbol{\beta}_o$ as n grows. In Chapters 2 and 3 we make this concept precise and explore the consistency properties of OLS and IV estimators. For the examples above in which $E(\boldsymbol{\varepsilon}|\mathbf{X}) \neq \mathbf{0}$, it turns out that OLS is not consistent, whereas consistent IV estimators are available under general conditions.

Although we only consider linear stochastic relationships in this book, this still covers a wide range of situations. For example, suppose we have several equations that describe demand for a group of p commodities:

$$\begin{aligned}Y_{t1} &= \mathbf{X}_{t1}'\boldsymbol{\beta}_1 + \varepsilon_{t1} \\ Y_{t2} &= \mathbf{X}_{t2}'\boldsymbol{\beta}_2 + \varepsilon_{t2} \\ &\vdots \\ Y_{tp} &= \mathbf{X}_{tp}'\boldsymbol{\beta}_p + \varepsilon_{tp}, \quad t = 1, \dots, n.\end{aligned}$$

Now let $\mathbf{Y}_t$, be a $p \times 1$ vector, $\mathbf{Y}_t = (Y_{t1}, Y_{t2}, \dots, Y_{tp})'$, let $\boldsymbol{\varepsilon}_t' = (\varepsilon_{t1}, \varepsilon_{t2}, \dots, \varepsilon_{tp})$, let $\boldsymbol{\beta}_o = (\boldsymbol{\beta}_1', \boldsymbol{\beta}_2' \dots, \boldsymbol{\beta}_p')'$, and let

$$\mathbf{X}_t = \begin{bmatrix} \mathbf{X}_{t1} & \mathbf{0} & \cdots & \mathbf{0} \\ \mathbf{0} & \mathbf{X}_{t2} & & \mathbf{0} \\ \vdots & \vdots & \ddots & \vdots \\ \mathbf{0} & \mathbf{0} & \cdots & \mathbf{X}_{tp} \end{bmatrix}.$$

Now $\mathbf{X}_t$ is a $k \times p$ matrix, where $k = \sum_{i=1}^{p} k_i$ and $\mathbf{X}_{ti}$ is a $k_i \times 1$ vector.

The system of equations can be written as

$$\begin{bmatrix} Y_{t1} \\ Y_{t2} \\ \vdots \\ Y_{tp} \end{bmatrix} = \begin{bmatrix} \mathbf{X}_{t1} & \mathbf{0} & \cdots & \mathbf{0} \\ \mathbf{0} & \mathbf{X}_{t2} & & \mathbf{0} \\ \vdots & \vdots & \ddots & \vdots \\ \mathbf{0} & \mathbf{0} & \cdots & \mathbf{X}_{tp} \end{bmatrix}' \begin{bmatrix} \boldsymbol{\beta}_1 \\ \boldsymbol{\beta}_2 \\ \vdots \\ \boldsymbol{\beta}_p \end{bmatrix} + \begin{bmatrix} \varepsilon_{t1} \\ \varepsilon_{t2} \\ \vdots \\ \varepsilon_{tp} \end{bmatrix}$$

or

$$\mathbf{Y}_t = \mathbf{X}_t' \boldsymbol{\beta}_o + \boldsymbol{\varepsilon}_t.$$

Letting $\mathbf{Y} = (\mathbf{Y}_1', \mathbf{Y}_2' \dots, \mathbf{Y}_n')'$, $\mathbf{X} = (\mathbf{X}_1, \mathbf{X}_2, \dots, \mathbf{X}_n)'$, and $\boldsymbol{\varepsilon} = (\boldsymbol{\varepsilon}_1', \boldsymbol{\varepsilon}_2', \dots, \boldsymbol{\varepsilon}_n')'$, we can write this system as

$$\mathbf{Y} = \mathbf{X}\boldsymbol{\beta}_o + \boldsymbol{\varepsilon}.$$

Now $\mathbf{Y}$ is $pn \times 1$, $\boldsymbol{\varepsilon}$ is $pn \times 1$, and $\mathbf{X}$ is $pn \times k$. This allows us to consider simultaneous systems of equations in the present framework.

Alternatively, suppose that we have observations on an individual t in each of p time periods,

$$\begin{aligned} Y_{t1} &= \mathbf{X}_{t1}' \boldsymbol{\beta}_o + \varepsilon_{t1}, \\ Y_{t2} &= \mathbf{X}_{t2}' \boldsymbol{\beta}_o + \varepsilon_{t2}, \\ &\vdots \\ Y_{tp} &= \mathbf{X}_{tp}' \boldsymbol{\beta}_o + \varepsilon_{tp}, \quad t = 1, \dots, n. \end{aligned}$$

Define $\mathbf{Y}_t$ and $\boldsymbol{\varepsilon}_t$ as above, and let

$$\mathbf{X}_t = [\mathbf{X}_{t1}, \mathbf{X}_{t2}, \dots, \mathbf{X}_{tp}]$$

be a $k \times p$ matrix. The observations can now be written as

$$\mathbf{Y}_t = \mathbf{X}_t' \boldsymbol{\beta}_o + \boldsymbol{\varepsilon}_t,$$

or equivalently as

$$\mathbf{Y} = \mathbf{X}\boldsymbol{\beta}_o + \boldsymbol{\varepsilon},$$

with $\mathbf{Y}$, $\mathbf{X}$, and $\boldsymbol{\varepsilon}$ as defined above. This allows us to consider panel data in the present framework. Further, by adopting appropriate definitions, the case of simultaneous systems of equations for panel data can also be considered.

Recall that the GLS estimator was obtained by considering a linear transformation of a linear stochastic relationship, i.e.,

$$\mathbf{Y}^* = \mathbf{X}^*\beta_o + \varepsilon^*,$$

where $\mathbf{Y}^* = \mathbf{C}^{-1}\mathbf{Y}$, $\mathbf{X}^* = \mathbf{C}^{-1}\mathbf{X}$, and $\varepsilon^* = \mathbf{C}^{-1}\varepsilon$ for some nonsingular matrix $\mathbf{C}$. It follows that any such linear transformation can be considered within the present framework.

The reason for restricting our attention to linear models and IV estimators is to provide clear motivation for the concepts and techniques introduced while also maintaining a relatively simple focus for the discussion. Nevertheless, the tools presented have a much wider applicability and are directly relevant to many other models and estimation techniques.

References

Geary, R. C. (1949). "Determination of linear relations between systematic parts of variables with errors in observation, the variances of which are unknown." *Econometrica*, 17, 30–59.

Reiersøl, O. (1941). "Confluence analysis by means of lag moments and other methods of confluence analysis." *Econometrica*, 9, 1–24.

——— (1945). "Confluence analysis by means of instrumental sets of variables." *Akiv för Matematik, Astronomi och Fysik*, 32a, 1–119.

Theil, H. (1971). *Principles of Econometrics*. Wiley, New York.

White, H. (1994). *Estimation, Inference and Specification Analysis*. Cambridge University Press, New York.

Wright, P. G. (1928). *The Tariff on Animal and Vegetable Oils*. Macmillan, New York.

Wright, S. (1925). "Corn and Hog Correlations," *U.S. Department of Agriculture, Bulletin No. 1300*, Washington D.C.

For Further Reading

The references given below provide useful background and detailed discussion of many of the issues touched upon in this chapter.

Chow, G. C. (1983). *Econometrics*, Chapters 1, 2. McGraw-Hill, New York.

Dhrymes, P. (1978). *Introductory Econometrics*, Chapters 1–3, 6.1–6.3. Springer-Verlag, New York.

Goldberger, A. S. (1964). *Econometric Theory*, Chapters 4, 5.1–5.4, 7.1–7.4. Wiley, New York.

Hamilton, J. D. (1994). *Time Series Analysis.* Princeton University Press, Princeton.

Harvey, A. C. (1981). *The Econometric Analysis of Time Series*, Chapters 1.2, 1.3, 1.5, 1.6, 2.1–2.4, 2.7–2.10, 7.1–7.2, 8.1, 9.1–9.2. Wiley, New York.

Intriligator, M. (1978). *Econometric Models, Techniques and Applications*, Chapters 2, 4, 5, 6.1–6.5, 10. Prentice-Hall, Englewood Cliffs, New Jersey.

Johnston, J. and J. DiNardo (1997). *Econometric Methods.* 4th ed. Chapters 5–8. McGraw-Hill, New York.

Kmenta, J. (1971). *Elements of Econometrics*, Chapters 7, 8, 10.1–10.3. Macmillan, New York.

Maddala, G. S. (1977). *Econometrics*, Chapters 7, 8, 11.1–11.4, 14, 16.1–16.3. McGraw-Hill, New York.

Malinvaud, E. (1970). *Statistical Methods of Econometrics*, Chapters 1–5, 6.1–6.7. North-Holland, Amsterdam.

Theil, H. (1971). *Principles of Econometrics*, Chapters 3, 6, 7.1–7.2, 9. Wiley, New York.

CHAPTER 2

Consistency

In this chapter we introduce the concepts needed to analyze the behavior of $\hat{\boldsymbol{\beta}}_n$ and $\tilde{\boldsymbol{\beta}}_n$ as $n \to \infty$.

2.1 Limits

The most fundamental concept is that of a limit.

Definition 2.1 *Let $\{b_n\}$ be a sequence of real numbers. If there exists a real number b and if for every real $\delta > 0$ there exists an integer $N(\delta)$ such that for all $n \geq N(\delta)$, $|b_n - b| < \delta$, then b is the* limit *of the sequence $\{b_n\}$.*

In this definition the constant δ can take on any real value, but it is the very small values of δ that provide the definition with its impact. By choosing a very small δ, we ensure that b_n gets arbitrarily close to its limit b for all n that are sufficiently large. When a limit exists, we say that the sequence $\{b_n\}$ *converges* to b as n tends to infinity, written $b_n \to b$ as $n \to \infty$. We also write $b = \lim_{n\to\infty} b_n$. When no ambiguity is possible, we simply write $b_n \to b$ or $b = \lim b_n$. If for any $a \in \mathbb{R}$, there exists an integer $N(a)$ such that $b_n > a$ for all $n \geq N(a)$, we write $b_n \to \infty$ and we write $b_n \to -\infty$ if $-b_n \to \infty$.

Example 2.2 (*i*) *Let* $b_n = 1-1/n$. *Then* $b_n \to 1$. (*ii*) *Let* $b_n = (1+a/n)^n$. *Then* $b_n \to e^a$. (*iii*) *Let* $b_n = n^2$. *Then* $b_n \to \infty$. (*iv*) *Let* $b_n = (-1)^n$. *Then no limit exists.*

The concept of a limit extends directly to sequences of real vectors. Let $\mathbf{b}_n$ be a $k \times 1$ vector with real elements b_{ni}, $i = 1, \ldots, k$. If $b_{ni} \to b_i$, $i = 1, \ldots, k$, then $\mathbf{b}_n \to \mathbf{b}$, where $\mathbf{b}$ has elements b_i, $i = 1, \ldots, k$. An analogous extension applies to matrices.

Often we wish to consider the limit of a continuous function of a sequence. For this, either of the following equivalent definitions of continuity suffices.

Definition 2.3 *Given* $\mathbf{g} : \mathbb{R}^k \to \mathbb{R}^l$ $(k, l \in \mathbb{N})$ *and* $\mathbf{b} \in \mathbb{R}^k$, (*i*) *the function* $\mathbf{g}$ *is* continuous at $\mathbf{b}$ *if for any sequence* $\{\mathbf{b}_n\}$ *such that* $\mathbf{b}_n \to \mathbf{b}$, $\mathbf{g}(\mathbf{b}_n) \to \mathbf{g}(\mathbf{b})$; *or equivalently* (*ii*) *the function* $\mathbf{g}$ *is* continuous at $\mathbf{b}$ *if for every* $\varepsilon > 0$ *there exists* $\delta(\varepsilon) > 0$ *such that if* $\mathbf{a} \in \mathbb{R}^k$ *and* $|a_i - b_i| < \delta(\varepsilon)$, $i = 1, \ldots, k$, *then* $|g_j(\mathbf{a}) - g_j(\mathbf{b})| < \varepsilon$, $j = 1, \ldots, l$. *Further, if* $B \subset \mathbb{R}^k$, *then* $\mathbf{g}$ *is* continuous on B *if it is continuous at every point of* B.

Example 2.4 (*i*) *From this it follows that if* $\mathbf{a}_n \to \mathbf{a}$ *and* $\mathbf{b}_n \to \mathbf{b}$, *then* $\mathbf{a}_n + \mathbf{b}_n \to \mathbf{a} + \mathbf{b}$ *and* $\mathbf{a}_n \mathbf{b}'_n \to \mathbf{ab}'$. (*ii*) *The matrix inverse function is continuous at every point that represents a nonsingular matrix, so that if* $\mathbf{X}'\mathbf{X}/n \to \mathbf{M}$, *a finite nonsingular matrix, then* $(\mathbf{X}'\mathbf{X}/n)^{-1} \to \mathbf{M}^{-1}$.

Often it is useful to have a measure of the order of magnitude of a particular sequence without particularly worrying about its convergence. The following definition compares the behavior of a sequence $\{b_n\}$ with the behavior of a power of n, say n^λ, where λ is chosen so that $\{b_n\}$ and $\{n^\lambda\}$ behave similarly.

Definition 2.5 (*i*) *The sequence* $\{b_n\}$ *is* at most of order n^λ, *denoted* $b_n = O(n^\lambda)$, *if for some finite real number* $\Delta > 0$, *there exists a finite integer* N *such that for all* $n \geq N$, $|n^{-\lambda} b_n| < \Delta$. (*ii*) *The sequence* $\{b_n\}$ *is* of order smaller than n^λ, *denoted* $b_n = o(n^\lambda)$, *if for every real number* $\delta > 0$ *there exists a finite integer* $N(\delta)$ *such that for all* $n \geq N(\delta)$, $|n^{-\lambda} b_n| < \delta$, *i.e.,* $n^{-\lambda} b_n \to 0$.

In this definition we adopt a convention that we utilize repeatedly in the material to follow; specifically, we let Δ represent a real positive constant that we may take to be as large as necessary, and we let δ (and similarly ε) represent a real positive constant that we may take to be as small as necessary. In any two different places Δ (or δ) need not represent the same value, although there is no loss of generality in supposing that it does. (Why?)

As we have defined these notions, $b_n = O(n^\lambda)$ if $\{n^{-\lambda} b_n\}$ is eventually bounded, whereas $b_n = o(n^\lambda)$ if $n^{-\lambda} b_n \to 0$. Obviously, if $b_n = o(n^\lambda)$, then $b_n = O(n^\lambda)$. Further, if $b_n = O(n^\lambda)$, then for every $\delta > 0$, $b_n = O(n^{\lambda+\delta})$. When $b_n = O(n^0)$, it is simply (eventually) bounded and may or may not have a limit. We often write $O(1)$ in place of $O(n^0)$. Similarly, $b_n = o(1)$ means $b_n \to 0$.

Example 2.6 *(i) Let $b_n = 4 + 2n + 6n^2$. Then $b_n = O(n^2)$ and $b_n = o(n^{2+\delta})$ for every $\delta > 0$. (ii) Let $b_n = (-1)^n$. Then $b_n = O(1)$ and $b_n = O(n^\delta)$ for every $\delta > 0$. (iii) Let $b_n = \exp(-n)$. Then $b_n = o(n^{-\delta})$ for every $\delta > 0$ and $b_n = O(n^{-\delta})$ for every $\delta > 0$. (iv) Let $b_n = \exp(n)$. Then $b_n \neq O(n^\kappa)$ for any $\kappa \in \mathbb{R}$.*

If each element of a vector or matrix is $O(n^\lambda)$ or $o(n^\lambda)$, then that vector or matrix is $O(n^\lambda)$ or $o(n^\lambda)$.

Some elementary facts about the orders of magnitude of sums and products of sequences are given by the next result.

Proposition 2.7 *Let a_n and b_n be scalars. (i) If $a_n = O(n^\lambda)$ and $b_n = O(n^\mu)$, then $a_n b_n = O(n^{\lambda+\mu})$ and $a_n + b_n = O(n^\kappa)$, where $\kappa = \max[\lambda, \mu]$. (ii) If $a_n = o(n^\lambda)$ and $b_n = o(n^\mu)$, then $a_n b_n = o(n^{\lambda+\mu})$ and $a_n + b_n = o(n^\kappa)$. (iii) If $a_n = O(n^\lambda)$ and $b_n = o(n^\mu)$, then $a_n b_n = o(n^{\lambda+\mu})$ and $a_n + b_n = O(n^\kappa)$.*

Proof. *(i)* Since $a_n = O(n^\lambda)$ and $b_n = O(n^\mu)$, there exist a finite $\Delta > 0$ and $N \in \mathbb{N}$ such that, for all $n \geq N$, $|n^{-\lambda} a_n| < \Delta$ and $|n^{-\mu} b_n| < \Delta$. Consider $a_n b_n$. Now $|n^{-\lambda-\mu} a_n b_n| = |n^{-\lambda} a_n n^{-\mu} b_n| = |n^{-\lambda} a_n| \cdot |n^{-\mu} b_n| < \Delta^2$ for all $n \geq N$. Hence $a_n b_n = O(n^{\lambda+\mu})$. Consider $a_n + b_n$. Now $|n^{-\kappa}(a_n + b_n)| = |n^{-\kappa} a_n + n^{-\kappa} b_n| \leq |n^{-\kappa} a_n| + |n^{-\kappa} b_n|$ by the triangle inequality. Since $\kappa \geq \lambda$ and $\kappa \geq \mu$, $|n^{-\kappa}(a_n + b_n)| \leq |n^{-\kappa} a_n| + |n^{-\kappa} b_n| \leq |n^{-\lambda} a_n| + |n^{-\mu} b_n| < 2\Delta$ for all $n \geq N$. Hence $a_n + b_n = O(n^\kappa)$, $\kappa = \max[\lambda, \mu]$.

(ii) The proof is identical to that of *(i)*, replacing Δ with every $\delta > 0$ and N with $N(\delta)$.

(iii) Since $a_n = O(n^\lambda)$ there exist a finite $\Delta > 0$ and $N' \in \mathbb{N}$ such that for all $n \geq N'$, $|n^{-\lambda} a_n| < \Delta$. Given $\delta > 0$, let $\delta'' = \delta/\Delta$. Then since $b_n = o(n^\mu)$ there exists $N''(\delta'')$ such that $|n^{-\mu} b_n| < \delta''$ for $n \geq N''(\delta'')$. Now $|n^{-\lambda-\mu} a_n b_n| = |n^{-\lambda} a_n n^{-\mu} b_n| = |n^{-\lambda} a_n| \cdot |n^{-\mu} b_n| < \Delta\delta'' = \delta$ for $n \geq N = \max(N', N''(\delta))$. Hence $a_n b_n = o(n^{\lambda+\mu})$. Since $b_n = o(n^\mu)$, it is also $O(n^\mu)$. That $a_n + b_n = O(n^\kappa)$ follows from *(i)*. ∎

A particularly important special case is illustrated by the following exercise.

Exercise 2.8 *Let $\mathbf{A}_n$ be a $k \times k$ matrix and let $\mathbf{b}_n$ be a $k \times 1$ vector. If $\mathbf{A}_n = o(1)$ and $\mathbf{b}_n = O(1)$, verify that $\mathbf{A}_n \mathbf{b}_n = o(1)$.*

For the most part, econometrics is concerned not simply with sequences of real numbers, but rather with sequences of real-valued *random* scalars or vectors. Very often these are either averages, for example, $\bar{Z}_n = \sum_{t=1}^n Z_t/n$, or functions of averages, such as $\bar{Z}_n^2$, where $\{Z_t\}$ is, for example, a sequence of random scalars. Since the Z_t's are random variables, we have to allow for a possibility that would not otherwise occur, that is, that different realizations of the sequence $\{Z_t\}$ can lead to different limits for $\bar{Z}_n$. Convergence to a particular value must now be considered as a random event and our interest centers on cases in which nonconvergence occurs only rarely in some appropriately defined sense.

2.2 Almost Sure Convergence

The stochastic convergence concept most closely related to the limit notions previously discussed is that of almost sure convergence. Sequences that converge almost surely can be manipulated in almost exactly the same ways as nonrandom sequences.

Random variables are best viewed as functions from an underlying space Ω to the real line. Thus, when discussing a real-valued random variable b_n, we are in fact talking about a mapping $b_n : \Omega \to \mathbb{R}$. We let ω be a typical element of Ω and call the real number $b_n(\omega)$ a *realization* of the random variable. Subsets of Ω, for example $\{\omega \in \Omega : b_n(\omega) \leq a\}$, are *events* and we will assign a probability to these, e.g., $P\{\omega \in \Omega : b_n(\omega) \leq a\}$. We write $P[b_n \leq a]$ as a shorthand notation. There are additional details that we will consider more carefully in subsequent chapters, but this understanding will suffice for now.

Interest will often center on averages such as

$$b_n(\cdot) = n^{-1} \sum_{t=1}^{n} Z_t(\cdot).$$

We write the parentheses with dummy argument $(\cdot)$ to emphasize that b_n and Z_t are functions.

Definition 2.9 *Let $\{b_n(\cdot)\}$ be a sequence of real-valued random variables. We say that $b_n(\cdot)$* converges almost surely *to b, written $b_n(\cdot) \xrightarrow{a.s.} b$ if there exists a real number b such that $P\{\omega : b_n(\omega) \to b\} = 1$.*

The probability measure P determines the joint distribution of the entire sequence $\{Z_t\}$. A sequence b_n converges almost surely if the probability of obtaining a realization of the sequence $\{Z_t\}$ for which convergence to b occurs is unity. Equivalently, the probability of observing a realization of $\{Z_t\}$ for which convergence to b does not occur is zero. Failure to converge is possible but will almost never happen under this definition. Obviously, then, nonstochastic convergence implies almost sure convergence.

Because the set of ω's for which $b_n(\omega) \to b$ has probability one, b_n is sometimes said to converge to b *with probability* 1, (w.p.1). Other common terminology is that b_n converges *almost everywhere* (a.e.) in Ω or that b_n is *strongly consistent* for b. When no ambiguity is possible, we drop the notation $(\cdot)$ and simply write $b_n \xrightarrow{a.s.} b$ instead of $b_n(\cdot) \xrightarrow{a.s.} b$.

Example 2.10 *Let $\bar{Z}_n \equiv n^{-1} \sum_{t=1}^{n} Z_t$, where $\{Z_t\}$ is a sequence of independent identically distributed (i.i.d.) random variables with $\mu \equiv E(Z_t) < \infty$. Then $\bar{Z}_n \xrightarrow{a.s.} \mu$, by the Kolmogorov strong law of large numbers (Theorem 3.1).*

The almost sure convergence of the sample mean illustrated by this example occurs under a wide variety of conditions on the sequence $\{Z_t\}$. A discussion of these conditions is the subject of the next chapter.

As with nonstochastic limits, the almost sure convergence concept extends immediately to vectors and matrices of finite dimension. Almost sure convergence element by element suffices for almost sure convergence of vectors and matrices.

The behavior of continuous functions of almost surely convergent sequences is analogous to the nonstochastic case.

Proposition 2.11 *Given $\mathbf{g} : \mathbb{R}^k \to \mathbb{R}^l$ $(k, l \in \mathbb{N})$ and any sequence of random $k \times 1$ vectors $\{\mathbf{b}_n\}$ such that $\mathbf{b}_n \xrightarrow{a.s.} \mathbf{b}$, where $\mathbf{b}$ is $k \times 1$, if $\mathbf{g}$ is continuous at $\mathbf{b}$, then $\mathbf{g}(\mathbf{b}_n) \xrightarrow{a.s.} \mathbf{g}(\mathbf{b})$.*

Proof. Since $\mathbf{b}_n(\omega) \to \mathbf{b}$ implies $\mathbf{g}(\mathbf{b}_n(\omega)) \to \mathbf{g}(\mathbf{b})$,

$$\{\omega : \mathbf{b}_n(\omega) \to \mathbf{b}\} \subset \{\omega : \mathbf{g}(\mathbf{b}_n(\omega)) \to \mathbf{g}(\mathbf{b})\}.$$

Hence

$$1 = P\{\omega : \mathbf{b}_n(\omega) \to \mathbf{b}\} \leq P\{\omega : \mathbf{g}(\mathbf{b}_n(\omega)) \to \mathbf{g}(\mathbf{b})\} \leq 1,$$

so that $\mathbf{g}(\mathbf{b}_n) \xrightarrow{a.s.} \mathbf{g}(\mathbf{b})$. ∎

This result is one of the most important in this book, because consistency results for many of our estimators follow by simply applying Proposition 2.11.

Theorem 2.12 *Suppose*

(*i*) $\mathbf{Y}_t = \mathbf{X}_t'\boldsymbol{\beta}_o + \varepsilon_t, \quad t = 1, 2, \ldots, \boldsymbol{\beta}_o \in \mathbb{R}^k$;

(*ii*) $\mathbf{X}'\boldsymbol{\varepsilon}/n \xrightarrow{a.s.} \mathbf{0}$;

(*iii*) $\mathbf{X}'\mathbf{X}/n \xrightarrow{a.s.} \mathbf{M}$, *finite and positive definite.*

Then $\hat{\boldsymbol{\beta}}_n$ *exists for all n sufficiently large a.s., and* $\hat{\boldsymbol{\beta}}_n \xrightarrow{a.s.} \boldsymbol{\beta}_o$.

Proof. Since $\mathbf{X}'\mathbf{X}/n \xrightarrow{a.s.} \mathbf{M}$, it follows from Proposition 2.11 that

$$\det(\mathbf{X}'\mathbf{X}/n) \xrightarrow{a.s.} \det(\mathbf{M}).$$

Because $\mathbf{M}$ is positive definite by (*iii*), $\det(\mathbf{M}) > 0$. It follows that for all n sufficiently large $\det(\mathbf{X}'\mathbf{X}/n) > 0$ *a.s.*, so $(\mathbf{X}'\mathbf{X}/n)^{-1}$ exists for all n sufficiently large *a.s.* Hence $\hat{\boldsymbol{\beta}}_n = \boldsymbol{\beta}_o + (\mathbf{X}'\mathbf{X}/n)^{-1}\mathbf{X}'\boldsymbol{\varepsilon}/n$ exists for all n sufficiently large *a.s.*

Now $\hat{\boldsymbol{\beta}}_n = \boldsymbol{\beta}_o + (\mathbf{X}'\mathbf{X}/n)^{-1}\mathbf{X}'\boldsymbol{\varepsilon}/n$ by (*i*). It follows from Proposition 2.11 that $\hat{\boldsymbol{\beta}}_n \xrightarrow{a.s.} \boldsymbol{\beta}_o + \mathbf{M}^{-1} \cdot \mathbf{0} = \boldsymbol{\beta}_o$, given (*ii*) and (*iii*). ■

In the proof, we refer to events that occur *a.s.* Any event that occurs with probability one is said to occur almost surely (*a.s.*) (e.g., convergence to a limit or existence of the inverse).

Theorem 2.12 is a fundamental consistency result for least squares estimation in many commonly encountered situations. Whether this result applies in a given situation depends on the nature of the data. For example, if our observations are randomly drawn from a population, as in a pure cross section, they may be taken to be i.i.d. The conditions of Theorem 2.12 hold for i.i.d. observations provided $E(\mathbf{X}_t\mathbf{X}_t') = \mathbf{M}$, finite and positive definite, and $E(\mathbf{X}_t\varepsilon_t) = \mathbf{0}$, since Kolmogorov's strong law of large numbers (Example 2.10) ensures that $\mathbf{X}'\mathbf{X}/n = n^{-1}\sum_{t=1}^n \mathbf{X}_t\mathbf{X}_t' \xrightarrow{a.s.} \mathbf{M}$ and $\mathbf{X}'\boldsymbol{\varepsilon}/n = n^{-1}\sum_{t=1}^n \mathbf{X}_t\varepsilon_t \xrightarrow{a.s.} \mathbf{0}$. If the observations are dependent (as in a time series), different laws of large numbers must be applied to guarantee that the appropriate conditions hold. These are given in the next chapter.

A result for the IV estimator can be proven analogously.

Exercise 2.13 *Prove the following result. Suppose*

(*i*) $\mathbf{Y}_t = \mathbf{X}_t'\boldsymbol{\beta}_o + \varepsilon_t, \quad t = 1, 2, \ldots, \boldsymbol{\beta}_o \in \mathbb{R}^k$;

(*ii*) $\mathbf{Z}'\boldsymbol{\varepsilon}/n \xrightarrow{a.s.} \mathbf{0}$;

(*iii*) (*a*) $\mathbf{Z}'\mathbf{X}/n \xrightarrow{a.s.} \mathbf{Q}$, *finite with full column rank;*

(*b*) $\hat{\mathbf{P}}_n \xrightarrow{a.s.} \mathbf{P}$, *finite and positive definite.*

Then $\tilde{\boldsymbol{\beta}}_n$ *exists for all* n *sufficiently large a.s., and* $\tilde{\boldsymbol{\beta}}_n \xrightarrow{a.s.} \boldsymbol{\beta}_o$.

This consistency result for the IV estimator precisely specifies the conditions that must be satisfied for a sequence of random vectors $\{\mathbf{Z}_t\}$ to act as a set of instrumental variables. They must be unrelated to the errors, as specified by assumption *(ii)*, and they must be closely enough related to the explanatory variables that $\mathbf{Z}'\mathbf{X}/n$ converges to a matrix with full column rank, as required by assumption *(iii.a)*. Note that a necessary condition for this is that the order condition for identification holds (see Fisher, 1966, Chapter 2); that is, that $l \geq k$. (Recall that $\mathbf{Z}$ is $pn \times l$ and $\mathbf{X}$ is $pn \times k$.) For now, we simply treat the instrumental variables as given. In Chapter 4 we see how the instrumental variables may be chosen optimally.

A potentially restrictive aspect of the consistency results just given for the least squares and IV estimators is that the matrices $\mathbf{X}'\mathbf{X}/n$, $\mathbf{Z}'\mathbf{X}/n$, and $\hat{\mathbf{P}}_n$ are each required to converge to a fixed limiting value. When the observations are not identically distributed (as in a stratified cross section, a panel, or certain time-series cases), these matrices need not converge, and the results of Theorem 2.12 and Exercise 2.13 do not necessarily apply.

Nevertheless, it is possible to obtain more general versions of these results that do not require the convergence of $\mathbf{X}'\mathbf{X}/n$, $\mathbf{Z}'\mathbf{X}/n$, or $\hat{\mathbf{P}}_n$ by generalizing Proposition 2.11. To do this we make use of the notion of uniform continuity.

Definition 2.14 *Given* $\mathbf{g} : \mathbb{R}^k \to \mathbb{R}^l$ $(k, l \in \mathbb{N})$, *we say that* $\mathbf{g}$ *is* uniformly continuous *on a set* $B \subset \mathbb{R}^k$ *if for each* $\varepsilon > 0$ *there is a* $\delta(\varepsilon) > 0$ *such that if* $\mathbf{a}$ *and* $\mathbf{b}$ *belong to* B *and* $|a_i - b_i| < \delta(\varepsilon)$, $i = 1, \ldots, k$, *then* $|g_j(\mathbf{a}) - g_j(\mathbf{b})| < \varepsilon$, $j = 1, \ldots, l$.

Note that uniform continuity implies continuity on B but that continuity on B does not imply uniform continuity. The essential aspect of uniform continuity that distinguishes it from continuity is that δ depends only on ε and not on $\mathbf{b}$. However, when B is compact, continuity does imply uniform continuity, as formally stated in the next result.

Theorem 2.15 (Uniform continuity theorem) *Suppose* $\mathbf{g} : \mathbb{R}^k \to \mathbb{R}^l$ *is a continuous function on* $C \subset \mathbb{R}^k$. *If* C *is compact, then* $\mathbf{g}$ *is uniformly continuous on* C.

Proof. See Bartle (1976, p. 160). ■

Now we extend Proposition 2.11 to cover situations where a random sequence $\{b_n\}$ does not necessarily converge to a fixed point but instead "follows" a nonrandom sequence $\{c_n\}$, in the sense that $b_n - c_n \xrightarrow{a.s.} 0$, where the sequence of real numbers $\{c_n\}$ does not necessarily converge.

Proposition 2.16 *Let* $\mathbf{g} : \mathbb{R}^k \to \mathbb{R}^l$ *be continuous on a compact set* $C \subset \mathbb{R}^k$. *Suppose that* $\{\mathbf{b}_n\}$ *is a sequence of random* $k \times 1$ *vectors and* $\{\mathbf{c}_n\}$ *is a sequence of* $k \times 1$ *vectors such that* $\mathbf{b}_n(\cdot) - \mathbf{c}_n \xrightarrow{a.s.} \mathbf{0}$ *and there exists* $\eta > 0$ *such that for all* n *sufficiently large* $\{\mathbf{c} : |c_i - c_{ni}| < \eta, \ i = 1, \ldots, k\} \subset C$, *i.e., for all* n *sufficiently large,* $\mathbf{c}_n$ *is interior to* C *uniformly in* n. *Then* $\mathbf{g}(\mathbf{b}_n(\cdot)) - \mathbf{g}(\mathbf{c}_n) \xrightarrow{a.s.} \mathbf{0}$.

Proof. Let g_j be the jth element of $\mathbf{g}$. Since C is compact, g_j is uniformly continuous on C by Theorem 2.15. Let $F = \{\omega : \mathbf{b}_n(\omega) - \mathbf{c}_n \to \mathbf{0}\}$; then $P(F) = 1$ since $\mathbf{b}_n - \mathbf{c}_n \xrightarrow{a.s.} \mathbf{0}$. Choose $\omega \in F$. Since $\mathbf{c}_n$ is interior to C for all n sufficiently large uniformly in n and $\mathbf{b}_n(\omega) - \mathbf{c}_n \to \mathbf{0}$, $\mathbf{b}_n(\omega)$ is also interior to C for all n sufficiently large. By uniform continuity, for any $\varepsilon > 0$ there exists $\delta(\varepsilon) > 0$ such that if $|b_{ni}(\omega) - c_{ni}| < \delta(\varepsilon)$, $i = 1, \ldots, k$, then $|g_j(\mathbf{b}_n(\omega)) - g_j(\mathbf{c}_n)| < \varepsilon$. Hence $\mathbf{g}(\mathbf{b}_n(\omega)) - \mathbf{g}(\mathbf{c}_n) \to \mathbf{0}$. Since this is true for any $\omega \in F$ and $P(F) = 1$, then $\mathbf{g}(\mathbf{b}_n) - \mathbf{g}(\mathbf{c}_n) \xrightarrow{a.s.} \mathbf{0}$. ■

To state the results for the OLS and IV estimators below concisely, we define the following concepts, as given by White (1982, pp. 484–485).

Definition 2.17 *A sequence of* $k \times k$ *matrices* $\{\mathbf{A}_n\}$ *is said to be* uniformly nonsingular *if for some* $\delta > 0$ *and all* n *sufficiently large* $|\det(\mathbf{A}_n)| > \delta$. *If* $\{\mathbf{A}_n\}$ *is a sequence of positive semidefinite matrices, then* $\{\mathbf{A}_n\}$ *is* uniformly positive definite *if* $\{\mathbf{A}_n\}$ *is uniformly nonsingular. If* $\{\mathbf{A}_n\}$ *is a sequence of* $l \times k$ *matrices, then* $\{\mathbf{A}_n\}$ *has* uniformly full column rank *if there exists a sequence of* $k \times k$ *submatrices* $\{\mathbf{A}_n^*\}$ *which is uniformly nonsingular.*

If a sequence of matrices is uniformly nonsingular, the elements of the sequence are prevented from getting "too close" to singularity. Similarly, if a sequence of matrices has uniformly full column rank, the elements of the sequence are prevented from getting "too close" to a matrix with less than full column rank.

Next we state the desired extensions of Theorem 2.12 and Exercise 2.13.

Theorem 2.18 *Suppose*

(*i*) $\mathbf{Y}_t = \mathbf{X}_t'\boldsymbol{\beta}_o + \varepsilon_t, \quad t = 1, 2, \ldots, \ \boldsymbol{\beta}_o \in \mathbb{R}^k$;

(*ii*) $\mathbf{X}'\boldsymbol{\varepsilon}/n \xrightarrow{a.s.} \mathbf{0}$;

(*iii*) $\mathbf{X}'\mathbf{X}/n - \mathbf{M}_n \xrightarrow{a.s.} \mathbf{0}$, *where* $\mathbf{M}_n = O(1)$ *and is uniformly positive definite.*

Then $\hat{\boldsymbol{\beta}}_n$ *exists for all* n *sufficiently large a.s., and* $\hat{\boldsymbol{\beta}}_n \xrightarrow{a.s.} \boldsymbol{\beta}_o$.

Proof. Because $\mathbf{M}_n = O(1)$, it is bounded for all n sufficiently large, and it follows from Proposition 2.16 that $\det(\mathbf{X}'\mathbf{X}/n) - \det(\mathbf{M}_n) \xrightarrow{a.s.} 0$. Since $\det(\mathbf{M}_n) > \delta > 0$ for all n sufficiently large by Definition 2.17, it follows that $\det(\mathbf{X}'\mathbf{X}/n) > \delta/2 > 0$ for all n sufficiently large $a.s.$, so that $(\mathbf{X}'\mathbf{X}/n)^{-1}$ exists for all n sufficiently large $a.s.$ Hence $\hat{\boldsymbol{\beta}}_n \equiv (\mathbf{X}'\mathbf{X}/n)^{-1}\mathbf{X}'\mathbf{Y}/n$ exists for all n sufficiently large $a.s.$

Now $\hat{\boldsymbol{\beta}}_n = \boldsymbol{\beta}_o + (\mathbf{X}'\mathbf{X}/n)^{-1}\mathbf{X}'\boldsymbol{\varepsilon}/n$ by (i). It follows from Proposition 2.16 that $\hat{\boldsymbol{\beta}}_n - (\boldsymbol{\beta}_o + \mathbf{M}_n^{-1} \cdot \mathbf{0}) \xrightarrow{a.s.} \mathbf{0}$ or $\hat{\boldsymbol{\beta}}_n \xrightarrow{a.s.} \boldsymbol{\beta}_o$, given (ii) and (iii). ■

Compared with Theorem 2.12, the present result relaxes the requirement that $\mathbf{X}'\mathbf{X}/n \xrightarrow{a.s.} \mathbf{M}$ and instead requires that $\mathbf{X}'\mathbf{X}/n - \mathbf{M}_n \xrightarrow{a.s.} \mathbf{0}$, allowing for the possibility that $\mathbf{X}'\mathbf{X}/n$ may not converge to a fixed limit. Note that the requirement $\det(\mathbf{M}_n) > \delta > 0$ ensures the uniform continuity of the matrix inverse function.

The proof of the IV result requires a demonstration that $\{\mathbf{Q}_n'\mathbf{P}_n\mathbf{Q}_n\}$ is uniformly positive definite under appropriate conditions. These conditions are provided by the following result.

Lemma 2.19 *If $\{\mathbf{A}_n\}$ is a $O(1)$ sequence of $l \times k$ matrices with uniformly full column rank and $\{\mathbf{B}_n\}$ is a $O(1)$ sequence of uniformly positive definite $l \times l$ matrices, then $\{\mathbf{A}_n'\mathbf{B}_n\mathbf{A}_n\}$ and $\{\mathbf{A}_n'\mathbf{B}_n^{-1}\mathbf{A}_n\}$ are $O(1)$ sequences of uniformly positive definite $k \times k$ matrices.*

Proof. See White (1982, Lemma A.3). ■

Exercise 2.20 *Prove the following result. Suppose*

(i) $\mathbf{Y}_t = \mathbf{X}_t'\boldsymbol{\beta}_o + \varepsilon_t, \quad t = 1, 2, \ldots, \ \boldsymbol{\beta}_o \in \mathbb{R}^k$;

(ii) $\mathbf{Z}'\boldsymbol{\varepsilon}/n \xrightarrow{a.s.} \mathbf{0}$;

(iii) (a) $\mathbf{Z}'\mathbf{X}/n - \mathbf{Q}_n \xrightarrow{a.s.} \mathbf{0}$, *where* $\mathbf{Q}_n = O(1)$ *and has uniformly full column rank;*

(b) $\hat{\mathbf{P}}_n - \mathbf{P}_n \xrightarrow{a.s.} \mathbf{0}$, *where* $\mathbf{P}_n = O(1)$ *and is symmetric and uniformly positive definite.*

Then $\tilde{\boldsymbol{\beta}}_n$ exists for all n sufficiently large a.s., and $\tilde{\boldsymbol{\beta}}_n \xrightarrow{a.s.} \boldsymbol{\beta}_o$.

The notion of orders of magnitude extends to almost surely convergent sequences in a straightforward way.

Definition 2.21 (i) *The random sequence $\{b_n\}$ is* at most of order n^λ almost surely *denoted $b_n = O_{a.s.}(n^\lambda)$, if there exist $\Delta < \infty$ and $N < \infty$ such that $P[|n^{-\lambda}b_n| < \Delta$ for all $n \geq N] = 1$. (ii) The sequence $\{b_n\}$ is* of order smaller than n^λ almost surely *denoted $b_n = o_{a.s.}(n^\lambda)$ if $n^{-\lambda}b_n \xrightarrow{a.s.} 0$.*

A sufficient condition that $b_n = O_{a.s.}(n^{-\lambda})$ is that $n^{-\lambda} b_n - a_n \xrightarrow{a.s.} 0$, where $a_n = O(1)$. The algebra of $O_{a.s.}$ and $o_{a.s.}$ is analogous to that for O and o.

Exercise 2.22 *Prove the following. Let a_n and b_n be random scalars. (i) If $a_n = O_{a.s.}(n^{\lambda})$ and $b_n = O_{a.s.}(n^{\mu})$, then $a_n b_n = O_{a.s.}(n^{\lambda+\mu})$ and $\{a_n + b_n\}$ is $O_{a.s.}(n^{\kappa})$, $\kappa = \max[\lambda, \mu]$. (ii) If $a_n = o_{a.s.}(n^{\lambda})$ and $b_n = o_{a.s.}(n^{\mu})$, then $a_n b_n = o_{a.s.}(n^{\lambda+\mu})$ and $a_n + b_n = o_{a.s.}(n^{\kappa})$. (iii) If $a_n = O_{a.s.}(n^{\lambda})$ and $b_n = o_{a.s.}(n^{\mu})$, then $a_n b_n = o_{a.s.}(n^{\lambda+\mu})$ and $\{a_n + b_n\}$ is $O_{a.s.}(n^{\kappa})$.*

2.3 Convergence in Probability

A weaker stochastic convergence concept is that of convergence in probability.

Definition 2.23 *Let $\{b_n\}$ be a sequence of real-valued random variables. If there exists a real number b such that for every $\varepsilon > 0$, $P(\omega : |b_n(\omega) - b| < \varepsilon) \to 1$ as $n \to \infty$, then b_n* converges in probability *to b, written $b_n \xrightarrow{p} b$.*

With almost sure convergence, the probability measure P takes into account the joint distribution of the entire sequence $\{Z_t\}$, but with convergence in probability, we only need concern ourselves sequentially with the joint distribution of the elements of $\{Z_t\}$ that actually appear in b_n, typically the first n. When a sequence converges in probability, it becomes less and less likely that an element of the sequence lies beyond any specified distance ε from b as n increases. The constant b is called the *probability limit of* b_n. A common notation is $\text{plim}\, b_n = b$.

Convergence in probability is also referred to as *weak consistency*, and since this has been the most familiar stochastic convergence concept in econometrics, the word "weak" is often simply dropped. The relationship between convergence in probability and almost sure convergence is specified by the following result.

Theorem 2.24 *Let $\{b_n\}$ be a sequence of random variables. If $b_n \xrightarrow{a.s.} b$, then $b_n \xrightarrow{p} b$. If $b_n \xrightarrow{p} b$, then there exists a subsequence $\{b_{n_j}\}$ such that $b_{n_j} \xrightarrow{a.s.} b$.*

Proof. See Lukacs (1975, p. 480). ■

Thus, almost sure convergence implies convergence in probability, but the converse does not hold. Nevertheless, a sequence that converges in probability always contains a subsequence that converges almost surely. Essentially, convergence in probability allows more erratic behavior in the converging sequence than almost sure convergence, and by simply disregarding the erratic elements of the sequence we can obtain an almost surely convergent subsequence. For an example of a sequence that converges in probability but not almost surely, see Lukacs (1975, pp. 34–35).

Example 2.25 *Let* $\bar{\mathcal{Z}}_n \equiv n^{-1}\sum_{t=1}^{n}\mathcal{Z}_t$, *where* $\{\mathcal{Z}_t\}$ *is a sequence of random variables such that* $E(\mathcal{Z}_t) = \mu$, $\text{var}(\mathcal{Z}_t) = \sigma^2 < \infty$ *for all* t *and* $\text{cov}(\mathcal{Z}_t, \mathcal{Z}_\tau) = 0$ *for* $t \neq \tau$. *Then* $\bar{\mathcal{Z}}_n \xrightarrow{p} \mu$ *by the Chebyshev weak law of large numbers, (see Rao, 1973, p. 112).*

Note that, in contrast to Example 2.10, the random variables here are not assumed either to be independent (simply uncorrelated) or identically distributed (except for having identical mean and variance). However, second moments are restricted by the present result, whereas they are completely unrestricted in Example 2.10.

Note also that, under the conditions of Example 2.10, convergence in probability follows immediately from the almost sure convergence. In general, most weak consistency results have strong consistency analogs that hold under identical or closely related conditions. For example, strong consistency also obtains under the conditions of Example 2.25. These analogs typically require somewhat more sophisticated techniques for their proof.

Vectors and matrices are said to converge in probability provided each element converges in probability.

To show that continuous functions of weakly consistent sequences converge to the functions evaluated at the probability limit, we use the following result.

Proposition 2.26 (The implication rule) *Consider events* E *and* F_i, $i = 1, \ldots, k$, *such that* $\left(\bigcap_{i=1}^{k} F_i\right) \subset E$. *Then* $\sum_{i=1}^{k} P(F_i^c) \geq P(E^c)$.

Proof. See Lukacs (1975, p. 7). ∎

Proposition 2.27 *Given* $\mathbf{g} : \mathbb{R}^k \to \mathbb{R}^l$ *and any sequence* $\{\mathbf{b}_n\}$ *of* $k \times 1$ *random vectors such that* $\mathbf{b}_n \xrightarrow{p} \mathbf{b}$, *where* $\mathbf{b}$ *is a* $k \times 1$ *vector, if* $\mathbf{g}$ *is continuous at* $\mathbf{b}$, *then* $\mathbf{g}(\mathbf{b}_n) \xrightarrow{p} \mathbf{g}(\mathbf{b})$.

Proof. Let g_j be an element of $\mathbf{g}$. For every $\varepsilon > 0$, the continuity of $\mathbf{g}$ implies that there exists $\delta(\varepsilon) > 0$ such that if $|b_{ni}(\omega) - b_i| < \delta(\varepsilon)$, $i = 1, \ldots, k$, then $|g_j(\mathbf{b}_n(\omega)) - g_j(\mathbf{b})| < \varepsilon$. Define the events $F_{ni} \equiv \{\omega : |b_{ni}(\omega) - b_i| < \delta(\varepsilon)\}$ and $E_n \equiv \{\omega : |g_j(\mathbf{b}_n(\omega)) - g_j(\mathbf{b})| < \varepsilon\}$. Then $\left(\bigcap_{i=1}^{k} F_{ni}\right) \subset E_n$. By the implication rule, $\sum_{i=1}^{k} P(F_{ni}^c) \geq P(E_n^c)$. Since

$\mathbf{b}_n \xrightarrow{p} \mathbf{b}$, for arbitrary $\eta > 0$, and all n sufficiently large, $P(F_{ni}^c) \leq \eta$. Hence $P(E_n^c) \leq k\eta$, or $P(E_n) \geq 1 - k\eta$. Since $P(E_n) \leq 1$ and η is arbitrary, $P(E_n) \to 1$ as $n \to \infty$, hence $g_j(\mathbf{b}_n) \xrightarrow{p} g_j(\mathbf{b})$. Since this holds for all $j = 1, \ldots, l$, $\mathbf{g}(\mathbf{b}_n) \xrightarrow{p} \mathbf{g}(\mathbf{b})$. ∎

This result allows us to establish direct analogs of Theorem 2.12 and Exercise 2.13.

Theorem 2.28 *Suppose*

(*i*) $\mathbf{Y}_t = \mathbf{X}_t'\boldsymbol{\beta}_o + \varepsilon_t, \quad t = 1, 2, \ldots, \boldsymbol{\beta}_o \in \mathbb{R}^k$;

(*ii*) $\mathbf{X}'\boldsymbol{\varepsilon}/n \xrightarrow{p} \mathbf{0}$;

(*iii*) $\mathbf{X}'\mathbf{X}/n \xrightarrow{p} \mathbf{M}$, *finite and positive definite.*

Then $\hat{\boldsymbol{\beta}}_n$ *exists in probability, and* $\hat{\boldsymbol{\beta}}_n \xrightarrow{p} \boldsymbol{\beta}_o$.

Proof. The proof is identical to that of Theorem 2.12 except that Proposition 2.27 is used instead of Proposition 2.11 and convergence in probability replaces convergence almost surely. ∎

The statement that $\hat{\boldsymbol{\beta}}_n$ "exists in probability" is understood to mean that there exists a subsequence $\{\hat{\boldsymbol{\beta}}_{n_j}\}$ such that $\hat{\boldsymbol{\beta}}_{n_j}$ exists for all n_j sufficiently large *a.s.*, by Theorem 2.24. In other words, $\mathbf{X}'\mathbf{X}/n$ can converge to $\mathbf{M}$ in such a way that $\mathbf{X}'\mathbf{X}/n$ does not have an inverse for each n, so that $\hat{\boldsymbol{\beta}}_n$ may fail to exist for particular values of n. However, a subsequence of $\{\mathbf{X}'\mathbf{X}/n\}$ converges almost surely, and for that subsequence, $\hat{\boldsymbol{\beta}}_{n_j}$ will exist for all n_j sufficiently large, almost surely.

Exercise 2.29 *Prove the following result. Suppose*

(*i*) $\mathbf{Y}_t = \mathbf{X}_t'\boldsymbol{\beta}_o + \varepsilon_t, \quad t = 1, 2, \ldots, \boldsymbol{\beta}_o \in \mathbb{R}^k$;

(*ii*) $\mathbf{Z}'\boldsymbol{\varepsilon}/n \xrightarrow{p} \mathbf{0}$;

(*iii*) (*a*) $\mathbf{Z}'\mathbf{X}/n \xrightarrow{p} \mathbf{Q}$, *finite with full column rank;*

(*b*) $\hat{\mathbf{P}}_n \xrightarrow{p} \mathbf{P}$, *finite, symmetric, and positive definite.*

Then $\tilde{\boldsymbol{\beta}}_n$ *exists in probability, and* $\tilde{\boldsymbol{\beta}}_n \xrightarrow{p} \boldsymbol{\beta}_o$.

Whether or not these results apply in particular situations depends on the nature of the data. As we mentioned before, for certain kinds of data it is restrictive to assume that $\mathbf{X}'\mathbf{X}/n$, $\mathbf{Z}'\mathbf{X}/n$, and $\hat{\mathbf{P}}_n$ converge to constant limits. We can relax this restriction by using an analog of Proposition 2.16. This result is also used heavily in later chapters.

Proposition 2.30 *Let* $\mathbf{g} : \mathbb{R}^k \to \mathbb{R}^l$ *be continuous on a compact set* $C \subset \mathbb{R}^k$. *Suppose that* $\{\mathbf{b}_n\}$ *is a sequence of random* $k \times 1$ *vectors and* $\{\mathbf{c}_n\}$ *is a sequence of* $k \times 1$ *vectors such that* $\mathbf{b}_n - \mathbf{c}_n \xrightarrow{p} \mathbf{0}$, *and for all* n *sufficiently large,* $\mathbf{c}_n$ *is interior to* C, *uniformly in* n. *Then* $\mathbf{g}(\mathbf{b}_n) - \mathbf{g}(\mathbf{c}_n) \xrightarrow{p} \mathbf{0}$.

Proof. Let g_j be an element of $\mathbf{g}$. Since C is compact, g_j is uniformly continuous by Theorem 2.15, so that for every $\varepsilon > 0$ there exists $\delta(\varepsilon) > 0$ such that if $|b_{ni} - c_{ni}| < \delta(\varepsilon)$, $i = 1, \ldots, k$, then $|g_j(\mathbf{b}_n) - g_j(\mathbf{c}_n)| < \varepsilon$. Define the events $F_{ni} \equiv \{\omega : |b_{ni}(\omega) - c_{ni}| < \delta(\varepsilon)\}$ and $E_n \equiv \{\omega : |g_j(\mathbf{b}_n(\omega)) - g_j(\mathbf{c}_n)| < \varepsilon\}$. Then $\left(\bigcap_{i=1}^k F_{ni}\right) \subset E_n$. By the implication rule, $\sum_{i=1}^k P\left(F_{ni}^c\right) \geq P(E_n^c)$. Since $\mathbf{b}_n - \mathbf{c}_n \xrightarrow{p} \mathbf{0}$, for arbitrary $\eta > 0$ and all n sufficiently large, $P(F_{ni}^c) \leq \eta$. Hence $P(E_n^c) \leq k\eta$, or $P(E_n) \geq 1 - k\eta$. Since $P(E_n) \leq 1$ and η is arbitrary, $P(E_n) \to 1$ as $n \to \infty$, hence $g_j(\mathbf{b}_n) - g_j(\mathbf{c}_n) \xrightarrow{p} 0$. As this holds for all $j = 1, \ldots, l$, $\mathbf{g}(\mathbf{b}_n) - \mathbf{g}(\mathbf{c}_n) \xrightarrow{p} \mathbf{0}$. ∎

Theorem 2.31 *Suppose*

(*i*) $\mathbf{Y}_t = \mathbf{X}_t'\boldsymbol{\beta}_o + \varepsilon_t, \quad t = 1, 2, \ldots, \ \boldsymbol{\beta}_o \in \mathbb{R}^k$;

(*ii*) $\mathbf{X}'\boldsymbol{\varepsilon}/n \xrightarrow{p} \mathbf{0}$;

(*iii*) $\mathbf{X}'\mathbf{X}/n - \mathbf{M}_n \xrightarrow{p} \mathbf{0}$, *where* $\mathbf{M}_n = O(1)$ *and is uniformly positive definite.*

Then $\hat{\boldsymbol{\beta}}_n$ *exists in probability, and* $\hat{\boldsymbol{\beta}}_n \xrightarrow{p} \boldsymbol{\beta}_o$.

Proof. The proof is identical to that of Theorem 2.18 except that Proposition 2.30 is used instead of Proposition 2.16 and convergence in probability replaces convergence almost surely. ∎

Exercise 2.32 *Prove the following result. Suppose*

(*i*) $\mathbf{Y}_t = \mathbf{X}_t'\boldsymbol{\beta}_o + \varepsilon_t, \quad t = 1, 2, \ldots, \ \boldsymbol{\beta}_o \in \mathbb{R}^k$;

(*ii*) $\mathbf{Z}'\boldsymbol{\varepsilon}/n \xrightarrow{p} \mathbf{0}$;

(*iii*) (*a*) $\mathbf{Z}'\mathbf{X}/n - \mathbf{Q}_n \xrightarrow{p} \mathbf{0}$, *where* $\mathbf{Q}_n = O(1)$ *and has uniformly full column rank;*

(*b*) $\hat{\mathbf{P}}_n - \mathbf{P}_n \xrightarrow{p} \mathbf{0}$, *where* $\mathbf{P}_n = O(1)$ *and is symmetric and uniformly positive definite.*

Then $\tilde{\boldsymbol{\beta}}_n$ *exists in probability, and* $\tilde{\boldsymbol{\beta}}_n \xrightarrow{p} \boldsymbol{\beta}_o$.

As with convergence almost surely, the notion of orders of magnitude extends directly to convergence in probability.

Definition 2.33 *(i) The sequence* $\{b_n\}$ *is* at most of order n^λ in probability, *denoted* $b_n = O_p(n^\lambda)$, *if for every* $\varepsilon > 0$ *there exist a finite* $\Delta_\varepsilon > 0$ *and* $N_\varepsilon \in \mathbb{N}$, *such that* $P\{\omega : |n^{-\lambda} b_n(\omega)| > \Delta_\varepsilon\} < \varepsilon$ *for all* $n \geq N_\varepsilon$. *(ii) The sequence* $\{b_n\}$ *is* of order smaller than n^λ in probability, *denoted* $b_n = o_p(n^\lambda)$, *if* $n^{-\lambda} b_n \xrightarrow{p} 0$.

When $b_n = O_p(1)$, we say $\{b_n\}$ is *bounded in probability* and when $b_n = o_p(1)$ we have $b_n \xrightarrow{p} 0$.

Example 2.34 *Let* $b_n = Z_n$, *where* $\{Z_t\}$ *is a sequence of identically distributed* $N(0,1)$ *random variables. Then* $P(\omega : |b_n(\omega)| > \Delta) = P(|Z_n| > \Delta) = 2\Phi(-\Delta)$ *for all* $n \geq 1$, *where* Φ *is the standard normal cumulative distribution function (c.d.f.). By making* Δ *sufficiently large, we have* $2\Phi(-\Delta) < \delta$ *for arbitrary* $\delta > 0$. *Hence,* $b_n = Z_n = O_p(1)$.

Note that Φ in this example can be replaced by any c.d.f. F and the result still holds, i.e., any random variable Z with c.d.f. F is $O_p(1)$.

Exercise 2.35 *Prove the following. Let* a_n *and* b_n *be random scalars. (i) If* $a_n = O_p(n^\lambda)$ *and* $b_n = O_p(n^\mu)$, *then* $a_n b_n = O_p(n^{\lambda+\mu})$ *and* $a_n + b_n = O_p(n^\kappa)$, $\kappa = \max(\lambda, \mu)$. *(ii) If* $a_n = o_p(n^\lambda)$ *and* $b_n = o_p(n^\mu)$, *then* $a_n b_n = o_p(n^{\lambda+\mu})$ *and* $a_n + b_n = o_p(n^\kappa)$. *(iii) If* $a_n = O_p(n^\lambda)$ *and* $b_n = o_p(n^\mu)$, *then* $a_n b_n = o_p(n^{\lambda+\mu})$ *and* $a_n + b_n = O_p(n^\kappa)$. *(Hint: Apply Proposition 2.30.)*

One of the most useful results in this chapter is the following corollary to this exercise, which is applied frequently in obtaining the asymptotic normality results of Chapter 4.

Corollary 2.36 (Product rule) *Let* $\mathbf{A}_n$ *be* $l \times k$ *and let* $\mathbf{b}_n$ *be* $k \times 1$. *If* $\mathbf{A}_n = o_p(1)$ *and* $\mathbf{b}_n = O_p(1)$, *then* $\mathbf{A}_n \mathbf{b}_n = o_p(1)$.

Proof. Let $\mathbf{a}_n \equiv \mathbf{A}_n \mathbf{b}_n$ with $\mathbf{A}_n = [A_{nij}]$. Then $a_{ni} = \sum_{j=1}^{k} A_{nij} b_{nj}$. As $A_{nij} = o_p(1)$ and $b_{nj} = O_p(1)$, $A_{nij} b_{nj} = o_p(1)$ by Exercise 2.35 *(iii)*. Hence, $a_n = o_p(1)$, since it is the sum of k terms each of which is $o_p(1)$. It follows that $\mathbf{a}_n \equiv \mathbf{A}_n \mathbf{b}_n = o_p(1)$. ∎

2.4 Convergence in rth Mean

The convergence notions of limits, almost sure limits, and probability limits are those most frequently encountered in econometrics, and most of the results in the literature are stated in these terms. Another convergence concept often encountered in the context of time series data is that of convergence in the rth mean.

Definition 2.37 *Let $\{b_n\}$ be a sequence of real-valued random variables such that for some $r > 0$, $E|b_n|^r < \infty$. If there exists a real number b such that $E(|b_n - b|^r) \to 0$ as $n \to \infty$, then b_n* converges in the rth mean *to b, written $b_n \xrightarrow{r.m.} b$.*

The most commonly encountered situation is that in which $r = 2$, in which case convergence is said to occur in quadratic mean, denoted $b_n \xrightarrow{q.m.} b$. Alternatively, b is said to be the *limit in mean square* of b_n, denoted $\text{l.i.m.}\, b_n = b$.

A useful property of convergence in the rth mean is that it implies convergence in the sth mean for $s < r$. To prove this, we use Jensen's inequality, which we now state.

Proposition 2.38 (Jensen's inequality) *Let $g : \mathbb{R} \to \mathbb{R}$ be a convex function on an interval $B \subset \mathbb{R}$ and let $\mathcal{Z}$ be a random variable such that $P(\mathcal{Z} \in B) = 1$. Then $g(E(\mathcal{Z})) \leq E(g(\mathcal{Z}))$. If g instead is concave on B, then $g(E(\mathcal{Z})) \geq E(g(\mathcal{Z}))$.*

Proof. See Rao (1973, pp. 57–58). ∎

Example 2.39 *Let $g(z) = |z|$. It follows from Jensen's inequality that $|E(\mathcal{Z})| \leq E(|\mathcal{Z}|)$. Let $g(z) = z^2$. It follows from Jensen's inequality that $(E(\mathcal{Z}))^2 \leq E(\mathcal{Z}^2)$.*

Theorem 2.40 *If $b_n \xrightarrow{r.m.} b$ and $r > s$, then $b_n \xrightarrow{s.m.} b$.*

Proof. Let $g(z) = z^q$, $q < 1$, $z \geq 0$. Then g is concave. Set $z = |b_n - b|^r$ and $q = s/r$. From Jensen's inequality,

$$E(|b_n - b|^s) = E(\{|b_n - b|^r\}^q) \leq \{E(|b_n - b|^r)\}^q .$$

Since $E(|b_n - b|^r) \to 0$ it follows that $E(\{|b_n - b|^r\}^q) = E(|b_n - b|^s) \to 0$ and hence $b_n \xrightarrow{s.m.} b$. ∎

Convergence in the rth mean is a stronger convergence concept than convergence in probability, and in fact implies convergence in probability. To show this, we use the generalized Chebyshev inequality.

Proposition 2.41 (Generalized Chebyshev inequality) *Let $\mathcal{Z}$ be a random variable such that $E|\mathcal{Z}|^r < \infty$, $r > 0$. Then for every $\varepsilon > 0$,*

$$P(|\mathcal{Z}| \geq \varepsilon) \leq E(|\mathcal{Z}|^r)/\varepsilon^r .$$

Proof. See Lukacs (1975, pp. 8-9). ■

When $r = 1$ we have Markov's inequality and when $r = 2$ we have the familiar Chebyshev inequality.

Theorem 2.42 *If* $b_n \xrightarrow{r.m.} b$ *for some* $r > 0$, *then* $b_n \xrightarrow{p} b$.

Proof. Since $E(|b_n - b|^r) \to 0$ as $n \to \infty$, $E(|b_n - b|^r) < \infty$ for all n sufficiently large. It follows from the generalized Chebyshev inequality that, for every $\varepsilon > 0$,

$$P(\omega : |b_n(\omega) - b| \geq \varepsilon) \leq E(|b_n - b|^r)/\varepsilon^r.$$

Hence $P(\omega : |b_n(\omega) - b| < \varepsilon) \geq 1 - E(|b_n - b|^r)/\varepsilon^r \to 1$ as $n \to \infty$, since $b_n \xrightarrow{r.m.} b$. It follows that $b_n \xrightarrow{p} b$. ■

Without further conditions, no necessary relationship holds between convergence in the rth mean and almost sure convergence. For further discussion, see Lukacs (1975, Ch. 2).

Since convergence in the rth mean will be used primarily in specifying conditions for later results rather than in stating their conclusions, we provide no analogs to the previous consistency results for the least squares or IV estimators.

References

Bartle, R. G. (1976). *The Elements of Real Analysis.* Wiley, New York.

Fisher, F. M. (1966). *The Identification Problem in Econometrics.* McGraw-Hill, New York.

Lukacs, E. (1975). *Stochastic Convergence.* Academic Press, New York.

Rao, C. R. (1973). *Linear Statistical Inference and Its Applications.* Wiley, New York.

White, H. (1982). "Instrumental variables regression with independent observations." *Econometrica*, 50, 483–500.

CHAPTER 3

Laws of Large Numbers

In this chapter we study laws of large numbers, which provide conditions guaranteeing the stochastic convergence (e.g., of $\mathbf{Z}'\mathbf{X}/n$ and $\mathbf{Z}'\varepsilon/n$), required for the consistency results of the previous chapter. Since different conditions will apply to different kinds of economic data (e.g., time series or cross section), we shall pay particular attention to the kinds of data these conditions allow. Only strong consistency results will be stated explicitly, since strong consistency implies convergence in probability (by Theorem 2.24).

The laws of large numbers we consider are all of the following form.

Proposition 3.0 *Given restrictions on the dependence, heterogeneity, and moments of a sequence of random variables* $\{Z_t\}$, $\bar{Z}_n - \bar{\mu}_n \xrightarrow{a.s.} 0$, *where* $\bar{Z}_n \equiv n^{-1} \sum_{t=1}^{n} Z_t$ *and* $\bar{\mu}_n \equiv E(\bar{Z}_n)$.

The results that follow specify precisely which restrictions on the dependence, heterogeneity (i.e., the extent to which the distributions of the Z_t may differ across t), and moments are sufficient to allow the conclusion $\bar{Z}_n - E(\bar{Z}_n) \xrightarrow{a.s.} 0$ to hold. As we shall see, there are sometimes trade-offs among these restrictions; for example, relaxing dependence or heterogeneity restrictions may require strengthening moment restrictions.

3.1 Independent Identically Distributed Observations

The simplest case is that of independent identically distributed (i.i.d.) random variables.

Theorem 3.1 (Kolmogorov) *Let* $\{Z_t\}$ *be a sequence of i.i.d. random variables. Then* $\bar{Z}_n \xrightarrow{a.s.} \mu$ *if and only if* $E|Z_t| < \infty$ *and* $E(Z_t) = \mu$.

Proof. See Rao (1973, p. 115). ■

An interesting feature of this result is that the condition given is sufficient as well as necessary for $\bar{Z}_n \xrightarrow{a.s.} \mu$. Also note that since $\{Z_t\}$ is i.i.d., $E(\bar{Z}_n) = \mu$.

To apply this result to econometric estimators we have to know that the summands of $\mathbf{Z}'\mathbf{X}/n = n^{-1}\sum_{t=1}^{n} \mathbf{Z}_t\mathbf{X}_t'$ and $\mathbf{Z}'\varepsilon/n = n^{-1}\sum_{t=1}^{n} \mathbf{Z}_t\varepsilon_t$ are i.i.d. This occurs when the elements of $\{(\mathbf{Z}_t', \mathbf{X}_t', \varepsilon_t)\}$ are i.i.d. To prove this, we use the following result.

Proposition 3.2 *Let* $\mathbf{g} : \mathbb{R}^k \to \mathbb{R}^l$ *be a continuous*[1] *function.* (*i*) *Let* $\mathcal{Z}_t$ *and* $\mathcal{Z}_\tau$ *be identically distributed. Then* $\mathbf{g}(\mathcal{Z}_t)$ *and* $\mathbf{g}(\mathcal{Z}_\tau)$ *are identically distributed.* (*ii*) *Let* $\mathcal{Z}_t$ *and* $\mathcal{Z}_\tau$ *be independent. Then* $\mathbf{g}(\mathcal{Z}_t)$ *and* $\mathbf{g}(\mathcal{Z}_\tau)$ *are independent.*

Proof. (*i*) Let $\mathcal{Y}_t = \mathbf{g}(\mathcal{Z}_t)$, $\mathcal{Y}_\tau = \mathbf{g}(\mathcal{Z}_\tau)$. Let $A = [\mathbf{z} : \mathbf{g}(\mathbf{z}) \leq \mathbf{a}]$. Then $F_t(\mathbf{a}) \equiv P[\mathcal{Y}_t \leq \mathbf{a}] = P[\mathcal{Z}_t \in A] = P[\mathcal{Z}_\tau \in A] = P[\mathcal{Y}_\tau \leq \mathbf{a}] \equiv F_\tau(\mathbf{a})$ for all $\mathbf{a} \in \mathbb{R}^l$. Hence $\mathbf{g}(\mathcal{Z}_t)$ and $\mathbf{g}(\mathcal{Z}_\tau)$ are identically distributed. (*ii*) Let $A_1 = [\mathbf{z} : \mathbf{g}(\mathbf{z}) \leq \mathbf{a}_1]$, $A_2 = [\mathbf{z} : \mathbf{g}(\mathbf{z}) \leq \mathbf{a}_2]$. Then $F_{t\tau}(\mathbf{a}_1, \mathbf{a}_2) \equiv P[\mathcal{Y}_t \leq \mathbf{a}_1, \mathcal{Y}_\tau \leq \mathbf{a}_2] = P[\mathcal{Z}_t \in A_1, \mathcal{Z}_\tau \in A_2] = P[\mathcal{Z}_t \in A_1]P[\mathcal{Z}_\tau \in A_2] = P[\mathcal{Y}_t \leq \mathbf{a}_1]P[\mathcal{Y}_\tau \leq \mathbf{a}_2] = F_t(\mathbf{a}_1)F_\tau(\mathbf{a}_2)$ for all $\mathbf{a}_1$, $\mathbf{a}_2 \in \mathbb{R}^l$. Hence $\mathbf{g}(\mathcal{Z}_t)$ and $\mathbf{g}(\mathcal{Z}_\tau)$ are independent. ■

Proposition 3.3 *If* $\{(\mathbf{Z}_t', \mathbf{X}_t', \varepsilon_t)\}$ *is an i.i.d. random sequence, then* $\{\mathbf{X}_t\mathbf{X}_t'\}$, $\{\mathbf{X}_t\varepsilon_t\}$, $\{\mathbf{Z}_t\mathbf{X}_t'\}$, $\{\mathbf{Z}_t\varepsilon_t\}$, *and* $\{\mathbf{Z}_t\mathbf{Z}_t'\}$ *are also i.i.d. sequences.*

Proof. Immediate from Proposition 3.2 (*i*) and (*ii*). ■

To write the moment conditions on the explanatory variables in compact form, we make use of the Cauchy-Schwarz inequality, which follows as a corollary to the following result.

---

[1] This result also holds for measurable functions, defined in Definition 3.21.

Proposition 3.4 (Hölder's inequality) *If $p > 1$ and $1/p + 1/q = 1$ and if $E|\mathcal{Y}|^p < \infty$ and $E|\mathcal{Z}|^q < \infty$, then $E|\mathcal{Y}\mathcal{Z}| \leq [E|\mathcal{Y}|^p]^{1/p}[E|\mathcal{Z}|^q]^{1/q}$.*

Proof. See Lukacs (1975, p. 11). ■

If $p = q = 2$, we have the Cauchy-Schwarz inequality,

$$E|\mathcal{Y}\mathcal{Z}| \leq E(\mathcal{Y}^2)^{1/2}E(\mathcal{Z}^2)^{1/2}.$$

The i, jth element of $\mathbf{X}_t\mathbf{X}_t'$ is given by $\sum_{h=1}^p X_{thi}X_{thj}$ and it follows from the triangle inequality that

$$\left|\sum_{h=1}^p X_{thi}X_{thj}\right| \leq \sum_{h=1}^p |X_{thi}X_{thj}|.$$

Hence,

$$\begin{aligned} E|\sum_{h=1}^p X_{thi}X_{thj}| &\leq \sum_{h=1}^p E|X_{thi}X_{thj}| \\ &\leq \sum_{h=1}^p (E\,|X_{thi}|^2)^{1/2}(E|X_{thj}|^2)^{1/2} \end{aligned}$$

by the Cauchy-Schwarz inequality. It follows that the elements of $\mathbf{X}_t\mathbf{X}_t'$ will have $E|\sum_{h=1}^p X_{thi}X_{thj}| < \infty$ (as we require to apply Kolmogorov's law of large numbers), provided simply that $E|X_{thi}|^2 < \infty$ for all h and i.

Combining Theorems 3.1 and 2.12, we have the following OLS consistency result for i.i.d. observations.

Theorem 3.5 *Suppose*

(*i*) $\mathbf{Y}_t = \mathbf{X}_t'\boldsymbol{\beta}_o + \varepsilon_t, \quad t = 1, 2, \ldots, \boldsymbol{\beta}_o \in \mathbb{R}^k$;

(*ii*) $\{(\mathbf{X}_t', \varepsilon_t)\}$ *is an i.i.d. sequence;*

(*iii*) (*a*) $E(\mathbf{X}_t\varepsilon_t) = \mathbf{0}$;

(*b*) $E|X_{thi}\varepsilon_{th}| < \infty$, $h = 1, \ldots, p$, $i = 1, \ldots, k$;

(*iv*) (*a*) $E|X_{thi}|^2 < \infty$, $h = 1, \ldots, p$, $i = 1, \ldots, k$;

(*b*) $\mathbf{M} \equiv E(\mathbf{X}_t\mathbf{X}_t')$ *is positive definite.*

Then $\hat{\boldsymbol{\beta}}_n$ exists for all n sufficiently large a.s., and $\hat{\boldsymbol{\beta}}_n \xrightarrow{a.s.} \boldsymbol{\beta}_o$.

Proof. Given (*ii*), $\{\mathbf{X}_t\varepsilon_t\}$ and $\{\mathbf{X}_t\mathbf{X}_t'\}$ are i.i.d. sequences. The elements of $\mathbf{X}_t\varepsilon_t$ and $\mathbf{X}_t\mathbf{X}_t'$ have finite expected absolute values, given (*iii*) and (*iv*) and applying the Cauchy-Schwarz inequality as above. By Theorem 3.1,

$\mathbf{X}'\boldsymbol{\varepsilon}/n = n^{-1}\sum_{t=1}^{n}\mathbf{X}_t\varepsilon_t \xrightarrow{a.s.} \mathbf{0}$, and $n^{-1}\sum_{t=1}^{n}\mathbf{X}_t\mathbf{X}_t' \xrightarrow{a.s.} \mathbf{M}$, finite and positive definite, so the conditions of Theorem 2.12 are satisfied and the result follows. ∎

This result is useful in situations in which we have observations from a random sample, as in a simple cross section. The result does not apply to stratified cross sections since there the observations are not identically distributed across strata, and generally will not apply to time-series data since there the observations $(\mathbf{X}_t\varepsilon_t)$ generally are not independent. For these situations, we need laws of large numbers that do not impose the i.i.d. assumption. Since (i) is assumed, we could equally well have specified (ii) as requiring that $\{(\mathbf{X}_t', \mathbf{Y}_t)\}$ is an i.i.d. sequence and then applied Proposition 3.2, which implies that $\{(\mathbf{X}_t', \varepsilon_t)\}$ is an i.i.d. sequence. Next, note that conditions sufficient to ensure $E(\mathbf{X}_t\varepsilon_t) = \mathbf{0}$ would be $\mathbf{X}_t$ independent of ε_t for all t and $E(\varepsilon_t) = 0$; alternatively, it would suffice that $E(\varepsilon_t|\mathbf{X}_t) = \mathbf{0}$. This latter condition follows if $E(\mathbf{Y}_t|\mathbf{X}_t) = \mathbf{X}_t'\boldsymbol{\beta}_o$ and we define ε_t as $\varepsilon_t \equiv \mathbf{Y}_t - E(\mathbf{Y}_t|\mathbf{X}_t) = \mathbf{Y}_t - \mathbf{X}_t'\boldsymbol{\beta}_o$. Both of these alternatives to (iii) are stronger than the simple requirement that $E(\mathbf{X}_t\varepsilon_t) = \mathbf{0}$.

In fact, by defining $\boldsymbol{\beta}_o \equiv E(\mathbf{X}_t\mathbf{X}_t')^{-1}E(\mathbf{X}_t\mathbf{Y}_t)$ and $\varepsilon_t \equiv \mathbf{Y}_t - \mathbf{X}_t'\boldsymbol{\beta}_o$, it is guaranteed that $E(\mathbf{X}_t\varepsilon_t) = \mathbf{0}$ (verify this). Thus, we are not making strong assumptions about how $\mathbf{Y}_t$ is generated. Note that no restrictions are placed on the second moment of ε_t in obtaining consistency for $\hat{\boldsymbol{\beta}}_n$. In fact, ε_t can have infinite variance without affecting the consistency of $\hat{\boldsymbol{\beta}}_n$ for $\boldsymbol{\beta}_o$.

The result for the IV estimator is analogous.

Exercise 3.6 *Prove the following result. Given*

(i) $\mathbf{Y}_t = \mathbf{X}_t'\boldsymbol{\beta}_o + \varepsilon_t, \quad t = 1, 2, \ldots, \boldsymbol{\beta}_o \in \mathbb{R}^k$;

(ii) $\{(\mathbf{Z}_t', \mathbf{X}_t', \varepsilon_t)\}$ *an i.i.d. sequence;*

(iii) (a) $E(\mathbf{Z}_t\varepsilon_t) = \mathbf{0}$;

(b) $E|Z_{thi}\varepsilon_{th}| < \infty$, $h = 1, \ldots, p$, $i = 1, \ldots, l$;

(iv) (a) $E|Z_{thi}X_{thj}| < \infty$, $h = 1, \ldots, p$, $i = 1, \ldots, l$, $j = 1, \ldots, k$;

(b) $\mathbf{Q} \equiv E(\mathbf{Z}_t\mathbf{X}_t')$ *has full column rank;*

(c) $\hat{\mathbf{P}}_n \xrightarrow{a.s.} \mathbf{P}$, *finite, symmetric, and positive definite.*

Then $\tilde{\boldsymbol{\beta}}_n$ *exists for all* n *sufficiently large a.s., and* $\tilde{\boldsymbol{\beta}}_n \xrightarrow{a.s.} \boldsymbol{\beta}_o$

3.2 Independent Heterogeneously Distributed Observations

For cross-sectional data, it is often appropriate to assume that the observations are independent but not identically distributed. The failure of the identical distribution assumption results from stratifying (grouping) the population in some way. The independence assumption remains valid provided that sampling within and across the strata is random. A law of large numbers useful in these situations is the following.

Theorem 3.7 (Markov) *Let $\{\mathcal{Z}_t\}$ be a sequence of independent random variables, with finite means $\mu_t \equiv E(\mathcal{Z}_t)$. If for some $\delta > 0$, $\sum_{t=1}^{\infty}(E|\mathcal{Z}_t - \mu_t|^{1+\delta})/t^{1+\delta} < \infty$, then $\bar{\mathcal{Z}}_n - \bar{\mu}_n \xrightarrow{a.s.} 0$.*

Proof. See Chung (1974, pp. 125–126). ∎

In this result the random variables are allowed to be heterogeneous (i.e., not identically distributed), but the moments are restricted by the condition that $\sum_{t=1}^{\infty} E|\mathcal{Z}_t - \mu_t|^{1+\delta}/t^{1+\delta} < \infty$, known as Markov's condition. If $\delta = 1$, we have a law of large numbers due to Kolmogorov (e.g., see Rao, 1973, p. 114). But *Markov's condition* allows us to choose δ arbitrarily small, thus reducing the restrictions imposed on $\mathcal{Z}_t$.

By making use of Jensen's inequality and the following useful inequality, it is possible to state a corollary with a simpler moment condition.

Proposition 3.8 (The c_r inequality) *Let $\mathcal{Y}$ and $\mathcal{Z}$ be random variables with $E|\mathcal{Y}|^r < \infty$ and $E|\mathcal{Z}|^r < \infty$ for some $r > 0$. Then $E|\mathcal{Y}+\mathcal{Z}|^r \leq c_r(E|\mathcal{Y}|^r + E|\mathcal{Z}|^r)$, where $c_r = 1$ if $r \leq 1$ and $c_r = 2^{r-1}$ if $r > 1$.*

Proof. See Lukacs (1975, p. 13). ∎

Corollary 3.9 *Let $\{\mathcal{Z}_t\}$ be a sequence of independent random variables such that $E|\mathcal{Z}_t|^{1+\delta} < \Delta < \infty$ for some $\delta > 0$ and all t. Then $\bar{\mathcal{Z}}_n - \bar{\mu}_n \xrightarrow{a.s.} 0$.*

Proof. By Proposition 3.8,

$$E|\mathcal{Z}_t - \mu_t|^{1+\delta} \leq 2^{\delta}(E|\mathcal{Z}_t|^{1+\delta} + |\mu_t|^{1+\delta}).$$

By assuming that $E|\mathcal{Z}_t|^{1+\delta} < \Delta$ and using Jensen's inequality,

$$|\mu_t| \leq E|\mathcal{Z}_t| \leq (E|\mathcal{Z}_t|^{1+\delta})^{1/1+\delta}.$$

It follows that for all t,

$$|\mu_t|^{1+\delta} < \Delta.$$

Hence, for all t, $E|\mathcal{Z}_t - \mu_t|^{1+\delta} < 2^{1+\delta}\Delta$. Verifying the moment condition of Theorem 3.7, we have

$$\sum_{t=1}^{\infty} E|\mathcal{Z}_t - \mu_t|^{1+\delta}/t^{1+\delta} < 2^{1+\delta}\Delta \sum_{t=1}^{\infty} 1/t^{1+\delta} < \infty,$$

since $\sum_{t=1}^{\infty} 1/t^{1+\delta} < \infty$ for any $\delta > 0$. Hence the conditions of Theorem 3.7 are satisfied and the result follows. ■

Compared with Theorem 3.1, this corollary imposes slightly more in the way of moment restrictions but allows the observations to be rather heterogeneous.

It is useful to point out that a nonstochastic sequence can be viewed as a sequence of independent, not identically distributed random variables, where the distribution function of these random variables places probability one at the observed value. Hence, Corollary 3.9 can be applied to situations in which we have fixed regressors, provided they are uniformly bounded, as the condition $E|\mathcal{Z}_t|^{1+\delta} < \Delta < \infty$ requires. Situations with unbounded fixed regressors can be treated using Theorem 3.7. To apply Corollary 3.9 to the linear model, we use the following fact.

Proposition 3.10 *If $\{(\mathbf{Z}_t', \mathbf{X}_t', \varepsilon_t)\}$ is an independent sequence, then $\{\mathbf{X}_t\mathbf{X}_t'\}$, $\{\mathbf{X}_t\varepsilon_t\}$, $\{\mathbf{Z}_t\mathbf{X}_t'\}$, $\{\mathbf{Z}_t\varepsilon_t\}$, and $\{\mathbf{Z}_t\mathbf{Z}_t'\}$ are also independent sequences.*

Proof. Immediate from Proposition 3.2 (*ii*). ■

To simplify the moment conditions that we impose, we use the following consequence of Hölder's inequality.

Proposition 3.11 (Minkowski's inequality) *Let $q \geq 1$. If $E|\mathcal{Y}|^q < \infty$ and $E|\mathcal{Z}|^q < \infty$, then $(E|\mathcal{Y} + \mathcal{Z}|^q)^{1/q} \leq (E|\mathcal{Y}|^q)^{1/q} + (E|\mathcal{Z}|^q)^{1/q}$.*

Proof. See Lukacs (1975, p. 11). ■

To apply Corollary 3.9 to $\mathbf{X}_t\mathbf{X}_t'$, we need to ensure that

$$E|\sum_{h=1}^{p} X_{thi}X_{thj}|^{1+\delta}$$

is bounded uniformly in t. This is accomplished by the following corollary.

Corollary 3.12 *Suppose $E|X_{thi}^2|^{1+\delta} < \Delta < \infty$ for some $\delta > 0$, all $h = 1, \ldots, p$, $i = 1, \ldots, k$, and all t. Then each element of $\mathbf{X}_t\mathbf{X}_t'$ satisfies $E|\sum_{h=1}^{p} X_{thi}X_{thj}|^{1+\delta} < \Delta' < \infty$ for some $\delta > 0$, all $i, j = 1, \ldots, k$, and all t, where $\Delta' \equiv p^{1+\delta}\Delta$.*

Proof. By Minkowski's inequality,

$$E\left|\sum_{h=1}^{p} X_{thi}X_{thj}\right|^{1+\delta} \leq \left[\sum_{h=1}^{p}(E|X_{thi}X_{thj}|^{1+\delta})^{1/(1+\delta)}\right]^{1+\delta}.$$

By the Cauchy-Schwarz inequality,

$$E|X_{thi}X_{thj}|^{1+\delta} \leq [E|X_{thi}^2|^{1+\delta}]^{1/2}[E|X_{thj}^2|^{1+\delta}]^{1/2}.$$

Since $E|X_{thi}^2|^{1+\delta} < \Delta < \infty$, $h = 1, \ldots, p$, $i = 1, \ldots, k$, it follows that for all $h = 1, \ldots, p$ and $i, j = 1, \ldots, k$,

$$E|X_{thi}X_{thj}|^{1+\delta} \leq \Delta^{1/2}\Delta^{1/2} = \Delta,$$

so that

$$\begin{aligned} E\left|\sum_{h=1}^{p} X_{thi}X_{thj}\right|^{1+\delta} &\leq \left[\sum_{h=1}^{p}\Delta^{1/(1+\delta)}\right]^{1+\delta} \\ &= p^{1+\delta}\Delta = \Delta'. \end{aligned}$$

■

The requirement that $E|X_{thi}^2|^{1+\delta} < \Delta < \infty$ means that all the explanatory variables have moments slightly greater than 2 uniformly bounded. A similar requirement is imposed on the elements of $\mathbf{X}_t\varepsilon_t$.

Exercise 3.13 *Show that if* $E|X_{thi}\varepsilon_{th}|^{1+\delta} < \Delta < \infty$ *for some* $\delta > 0$, *all* $h = 1, \ldots, p$, $i = 1, \ldots, k$, *and all* t, *then each element of* $\mathbf{X}_t\varepsilon_t$ *satisfies* $E|\sum_{h=1}^{p} X_{thi}\varepsilon_{th}|^{1+\delta} < \Delta' < \infty$ *for some* $\delta > 0$, *all* $i = 1, \ldots, k$, *and all* t, *where* $\Delta' = p^{1+\delta}\Delta$.

We now have all the results needed to obtain a consistency theorem for the ordinary least squares estimator. Since the argument is analogous to that of Theorem 3.5 we state the result as an exercise.

Exercise 3.14 *Prove the following result. Suppose*

(*i*) $\mathbf{Y}_t = \mathbf{X}_t'\boldsymbol{\beta}_o + \boldsymbol{\varepsilon}_t, \quad t = 1, 2, \ldots, \boldsymbol{\beta}_o \in \mathbb{R}^k$;

(*ii*) $\{(\mathbf{X}_t', \boldsymbol{\varepsilon}_t)\}$ *is an independent sequence;*

(*iii*) (*a*) $E(\mathbf{X}_t\boldsymbol{\varepsilon}_t) = \mathbf{0}, \quad t = 1, 2, \ldots$;

(*b*) $E|X_{thi}\varepsilon_{th}|^{1+\delta} < \Delta < \infty$ *for some* $\delta > 0$, *all* $h = 1, \ldots, p$, $i = 1, \ldots, k$, *and all* t;

(*iv*) (*a*) $E|X_{thi}^2|^{1+\delta} < \Delta < \infty$ *for some* $\delta > 0$, *all* $h = 1, \ldots, p$, $i = 1, \ldots, k$, *and all* t;

(*b*) $\mathbf{M}_n \equiv E(\mathbf{X}'\mathbf{X}/n)$ *is uniformly positive definite.*

Then $\hat{\boldsymbol{\beta}}_n$ *exists for all* n *sufficiently large a.s., and* $\hat{\boldsymbol{\beta}}_n \xrightarrow{a.s.} \boldsymbol{\beta}_o$.

Compared with Theorem 3.5, we have relaxed the identical distribution assumption at the expense of imposing slightly greater moment restrictions in (*iii.b*) and (*iv.a*). Also note that (*iv.a*) implies that $\mathbf{M}_n = O(1)$. (Why?)

The extra generality we have gained now allows treatment of situations with fixed regressors, or observations from a stratified cross section, and also applies to models with (unconditionally) heteroskedastic errors. None of these cases is covered by Theorem 3.5.

The result for the IV estimator is analogous.

Theorem 3.15 *Suppose*

(*i*) $\mathbf{Y}_t = \mathbf{X}_t'\boldsymbol{\beta}_o + \varepsilon_t, \quad t = 1, 2, \ldots, \boldsymbol{\beta}_o \in \mathbb{R}^k$;

(*ii*) $\{(\mathbf{Z}_t', \mathbf{X}_t', \varepsilon_t)\}$ *is an independent sequence;*

(*iii*) (*a*) $E(\mathbf{Z}_t\varepsilon_t) = \mathbf{0}, \quad t = 1, 2, \ldots$;

(*b*) $E|Z_{thi}\varepsilon_{th}|^{1+\delta} < \Delta < \infty$, *for some* $\delta > 0$, *all* $h = 1, \ldots, p$, $i = 1, \ldots, l$, *and all* t;

(*iv*) (*a*) $E|Z_{thi}X_{thj}|^{1+\delta} < \Delta < \infty$, *for some* $\delta > 0$, *all* $h = 1, \ldots, p$, $i = 1, \ldots, l$, $j = 1, \ldots, k$ *and all* t;

(*b*) $\mathbf{Q}_n \equiv E(\mathbf{Z}'\mathbf{X}/n)$ *has uniformly full column rank;*

(*c*) $\hat{\mathbf{P}}_n - \mathbf{P}_n \xrightarrow{a.s.} \mathbf{0}$, *where* $\mathbf{P}_n = O(1)$ *and is symmetric and uniformly positive definite.*

Then $\tilde{\boldsymbol{\beta}}_n$ *exists for all* n *sufficiently large a.s., and* $\tilde{\boldsymbol{\beta}}_n \xrightarrow{a.s.} \boldsymbol{\beta}_o$.

Proof. By Proposition 3.10, $\{\mathbf{Z}_t\varepsilon_t\}$ and $\{\mathbf{Z}_t\mathbf{X}_t'\}$ are independent sequences with elements satisfying the moment condition of Corollary 3.9, given (*iii.b*) and (*iv.a*), by arguments analogous to those of Corollary 3.12 and Exercise 3.13. It follows from Corollary 3.9 that $\mathbf{Z}'\boldsymbol{\varepsilon}/n \xrightarrow{a.s.} \mathbf{0}$ and $\mathbf{Z}'\mathbf{X}/n - \mathbf{Q}_n \xrightarrow{a.s.} \mathbf{0}$, where $\mathbf{Q}_n = O(1)$ given (*iv.a*) as a consequence of Jensen's inequality. Hence, the conditions of Exercise 2.20 are satisfied and the results follow. ∎

3.3 Dependent Identically Distributed Observations

The assumption of independence is inappropriate for economic time series, which typically exhibit considerable dependence. To cover these cases, we need laws of large numbers that allow the random variables to be dependent. To speak precisely about the kinds of dependence allowed, we need to make explicit some fundamental notions of probability theory that we have so far used implicitly.

Definition 3.16 *A family (collection) $\mathcal{F}$ of subsets of a set Ω is a* σ-field (σ-algebra) *provided*

(i) *$\emptyset$ and Ω belong to $\mathcal{F}$;*

(ii) *if F belongs to $\mathcal{F}$, then F^c (the complement of F in Ω) belongs to $\mathcal{F}$;*

(iii) *if $\{F_i\}$ is a sequence of sets in $\mathcal{F}$, then $\bigcup_{i=1}^{\infty} F_i$ belongs to $\mathcal{F}$.*

For example, let $\mathcal{F} = \{\emptyset, \Omega\}$. Then $\mathcal{F}$ is easily verified to be a σ-field (try it!). Or let F be a subset of Ω and put $\mathcal{F} = \{\emptyset, \Omega, F, F^c\}$. Again $\mathcal{F}$ is easily verified to be a σ-field. We consider further examples below.

The pair $(\Omega, \mathcal{F})$ is called a *measurable space* when $\mathcal{F}$ is a σ-field of Ω.

The sets in a σ-field $\mathcal{F}$ are sets for which it is possible to assign well-defined probabilities. Thus, we can think of the sets in $\mathcal{F}$ as *events*. We are now in a position to give a formal definition of the concept of a probability or, more formally, a probability measure.

Definition 3.17 *Let $\{\Omega, \mathcal{F}\}$ be a measurable space. A mapping $P : \mathcal{F} \to [0, 1]$ is a* probability measure *on $\{\Omega, \mathcal{F}\}$ provided that:*

(i) *$P(\emptyset) = 0$.*

(ii) *For any $F \in \mathcal{F}$, $P(F^c) = 1 - P(F)$.*

(iii) *For any disjoint sequence $\{F_i\}$ of sets in $\mathcal{F}$ (i.e., $F_i \cap F_j = \emptyset$ for all $i \neq j$), $P\left(\bigcup_{i=1}^{\infty} F_i\right) = \sum_{i=1}^{\infty} P(F_i)$.*

When $(\Omega, \mathcal{F})$ is a measurable space and P is a probability measure on $(\Omega, \mathcal{F})$, we call the triple $(\Omega, \mathcal{F}, P)$ a *probability space*. When the underlying measurable space is clear, we just call P a probability measure. Thus, a probability measure P assigns a number between zero and one to every event ($F \in \mathcal{F}$) in a way that coincides with our intuitive notion of how probabilities should behave. This powerful way of understanding probabilities is one of Kolmogorov's many important contributions (Kolmogorov 1933).

Now that we have formally defined probability measures, let us return our attention to the various collections of events (σ-fields) that are relevant for econometrics.

Recall that an open set is a set containing only interior points, where a point x in the set B is *interior* provided that all points in a sufficiently small neighborhood of x ($\{y : |y - x| < \varepsilon\}$ for some $\varepsilon > 0$) are also in B. Thus (a, b) is open, while $(a, b]$ is not.

Definition 3.18 *The* Borel σ-field $\mathcal{B}$ *is the smallest collection of sets (called the Borel sets) that includes*

(*i*) *all open sets of* $\mathbb{R}$;

(*ii*) *the complement* B^c *of any set* B *in* $\mathcal{B}$;

(*iii*) *the union* $\bigcup_{i=1}^{\infty} B_i$ *of any sequence* $\{B_i\}$ *of sets in* $\mathcal{B}$.

The Borel sets of $\mathbb{R}$ just defined are said to be *generated* by the open sets of $\mathbb{R}$. The same Borel sets would be generated by all the open half-lines of $\mathbb{R}$, all the closed half-lines of $\mathbb{R}$, all the open intervals of $\mathbb{R}$, or all the closed intervals of $\mathbb{R}$. The Borel sets are a "rich" collection of events for which probabilities can be defined. Nevertheless, there do exist subsets of the real line not in $\mathcal{B}$ for which probabilities are not defined; constructing such sets is very complicated (see Billingsley, 1979, p. 37).

Thus, we can think of the Borel σ-field as consisting of all the events on the real line to which we can assign a probability. Sets not in $\mathcal{B}$ will not define events.

The Borel σ-field just defined relates to real-valued random variables. A simple extension covers vector-valued random variables.

Definition 3.19 *The* Borel σ-field $\mathcal{B}^q$, $q < \infty$, *is the smallest collection of sets that includes*

(*i*) *all open sets of* $\mathbb{R}^q$;

(*ii*) *the complement* B^c *of any set* B *in* $\mathcal{B}^q$;

(*iii*) *the union* $\bigcup_{i=1}^{\infty} B_i$ *of any sequence* $\{B_i\}$ *in* $\mathcal{B}^q$.

In our notation, $\mathcal{B}$ and $\mathcal{B}^1$ mean the same thing.

Generally, we are interested in infinite sequences $\{(\mathbf{Z}_t', \mathbf{X}_t', \varepsilon_t)\}$. If $p = 1$, this is a sequence of random $1 \times (l + k + 1)$ vectors, whereas if $p > 1$, this is a sequence of $p \times (l + k + 1)$ matrices. Nevertheless, we can convert these matrices into vectors by simply stacking the columns of a matrix, one on top of the other, to yield a $p(l + k + 1) \times 1$ vector, denoted $\text{vec}((\mathbf{Z}_t', \mathbf{X}_t', \varepsilon_t))$. (In what follows, we drop the vec operator and understand that it is implicit in this context.) Generally, then, we are interested in infinite sequences of q-dimensional random vectors, where $q = p(l + k + 1)$. Corresponding to these are the Borel sets of $\mathbb{R}^q_\infty$, defined as the Cartesian products of a countable infinity of copies of $\mathbb{R}^q$, $\mathbb{R}^q_\infty \equiv \mathbb{R}^q \times \mathbb{R}^q \times \ldots$. In what follows we can think of ω taking its values in $\Omega = \mathbb{R}^q_\infty$. The events in which we are interested are the Borel sets of $\mathbb{R}^q_\infty$, which we define as follows.

Definition 3.20 *The* Borel sets *of* $\mathbb{R}^q_\infty$, *denoted* $\mathcal{B}^q_\infty$, *are the smallest collection of sets that includes*

(*i*) *all sets of the form* $\times_{i=1}^\infty B_i$, *where each* $B_i \in \mathcal{B}^q$ *and* $B_i = \mathbb{R}^q$ *except for finitely many* i;

(*ii*) *the complement* F^c *of any set* F *in* $\mathcal{B}^q_\infty$;

(*iii*) *the union* $\bigcup_{i=1}^\infty F_i$ *of any sequence* $\{F_i\}$ *in* $\mathcal{B}^q_\infty$.

A set of the form specified by (i) is called a *measurable finite-dimensional product cylinder*, so $\mathcal{B}^q_\infty$ is the Borel σ-field generated by all the measurable finite-dimensional product cylinders. When $(\mathbb{R}^q_\infty, \mathcal{B}^q_\infty)$ is the specific measurable space, a probability measure P on $(\mathbb{R}^q_\infty, \mathcal{B}^q_\infty)$ will govern the behavior of events involving infinite sequences of finite dimensional vectors, just as we require. In particular, when $q = 1$, the elements $\mathcal{Z}_t(\cdot)$ of the sequence $\{\mathcal{Z}_t\}$ can be thought of as functions from $\Omega = \mathbb{R}^1_\infty$ to the real line $\mathbb{R}$ that simply pick off the tth coordinate of $\omega \in \Omega$; with $\omega = \{z_t\}$, $\mathcal{Z}_t(\omega) = z_t$. When $q > 1$, $\mathcal{Z}_t(\cdot)$ maps $\Omega = \mathbb{R}^q_\infty$ into $\mathbb{R}^q$.

The following definition plays a key role in our analysis.

Definition 3.21 *A function* g *on* Ω *to* $\mathbb{R}$ *is* $\mathcal{F}$-measurable *if for every real number* a *the set* $[\omega : g(\omega) \leq a] \in \mathcal{F}$.

Example 3.22 *Let* $(\Omega, \mathcal{F}) = (\mathbb{R}^q_\infty, \mathcal{B}^q_\infty)$ *and set* $q = 1$. *Then* $\mathcal{Z}_t(\cdot)$ *as just defined is* $\mathcal{B}^q_\infty$*-measurable because* $[\omega : \mathcal{Z}_t(\omega) \leq a] = [z_1, \ldots, z_{t-1}, z_t, z_{t+1}, \ldots : z_1 < \infty, \ldots, z_{t-1} < \infty, z_t \leq a, z_{t+1} < \infty, \ldots] \in \mathcal{B}^q_\infty$ *for any* $a \in \mathbb{R}$.

When a function is $\mathcal{F}$-measurable, it means that we can express the probability of an event, say, $[\mathcal{Z}_t \leq a]$, in terms of the probability of an event in $\mathcal{F}$, say, $[\omega : \mathcal{Z}_t(\omega) \leq a]$. In fact, a random variable is precisely an $\mathcal{F}$-measurable function from Ω to $\mathbb{R}$.

In Definition 3.21, when the σ-field is taken to be $\mathcal{B}^q_\infty$, the Borel sets of $\mathbb{R}^q_\infty$, we shall drop explicit reference to $\mathcal{B}^q_\infty$ and simply say that the function g is measurable. Otherwise, the relevant σ-field will be explicitly identified.

Proposition 3.23 *Let* f *and* g *be* $\mathcal{F}$*-measurable real-valued functions, and let* c *be a real number. Then the functions* cf, $f + g$, fg, *and* $|f|$ *are also* $\mathcal{F}$*-measurable.*

Proof. See Bartle (1966, Lemma 2.6). ■

Example 3.24 *If $\mathcal{Z}_t$ is measurable, then $\mathcal{Z}_t/n$ is measurable, so that $\bar{\mathcal{Z}}_n = \sum_{t=1}^n \mathcal{Z}_t/n$ is measurable.*

A function from Ω to $\mathbb{R}^q$ is measurable if and only if each component of the vector valued function is measurable. The notion of measurability extends to transformations from Ω to Ω in the following way.

Definition 3.25 *Let $(\Omega, \mathcal{F})$ be a measurable space. A one-to-one transformation*[2] *$T : \Omega \to \Omega$ is* measurable *provided that $T^{-1}(\mathcal{F}) \subset \mathcal{F}$.*

In other words, the transformation T is measurable provided that any set taken by the transformation (or its inverse) into $\mathcal{F}$ is itself a set in $\mathcal{F}$. This ensures that sets that are not events cannot be transformed into events, nor can events be transformed into sets that are not events.

Example 3.26 *For any $\omega = (\ldots, z_{t-2}, z_{t-1}, z_t, z_{t+1}, z_{t+2}, \ldots)$ let $\omega' = T\omega = (\ldots, z_{t-1}, z_t, z_{t+1}, z_{t+2}, z_{t+3}, \ldots)$, so that T transforms ω by shifting each of its coordinates back one location. Then T is measurable since $T(F)$ is in $\mathcal{F}$ and $T^{-1}(F)$ is in $\mathcal{F}$, for all $F \in \mathcal{F}$.*

The transformation of this example is often called the *shift*, or the *backshift* operator. By using such transformations, it is possible to define a corresponding transformation of a random variable. For example, set $\mathcal{Z}_1(\omega) = \mathcal{Z}(\omega)$, where $\mathcal{Z}$ is a measurable function from Ω to $\mathbb{R}$; then we can define the random variables $\mathcal{Z}_2(\omega) = \mathcal{Z}(T\omega)$, $\mathcal{Z}_3(\omega) = \mathcal{Z}(T^2\omega)$, and so on, provided that T is a measurable transformation. The random variables constructed in this way are said to be random variables *induced* by a measurable transformation.

Definition 3.27 *Let $(\Omega, \mathcal{F}, P)$ be a probability space. The transformation $T : \Omega \to \Omega$ is* measure preserving *if it is measurable and if $P(T^{-1}F) = P(F)$ for all F in $\mathcal{F}$.*

The random variables induced by measure-preserving transformations then have the property that $P[\mathcal{Z}_1 \leq a] = P[\omega : \mathcal{Z}(\omega) \leq a] = P[\omega : \mathcal{Z}(T\omega) \leq a] = P[\mathcal{Z}_2 \leq a]$; that is, they are identically distributed. In fact,

---

[2] The transformation T maps an element of Ω, say ω, into another element of Ω, say $\omega' = T\omega$. When T operates on a set F, it should be understood as operating on each element of F. Similarly, when T operates on a family $\mathcal{F}$, it should be understood as operating on each set in the family.

such random variables have an even stronger property. We use the following definition.

Definition 3.28 *Let G_1 be the joint distribution function of the sequence $\{\boldsymbol{Z}_1, \boldsymbol{Z}_2, \ldots\}$, where $\boldsymbol{Z}_t$ is a $q \times 1$ vector, and let $G_{\tau+1}$ be the joint distribution function of the sequence $\{\boldsymbol{Z}_{\tau+1}, \boldsymbol{Z}_{\tau+2}, \ldots\}$. The sequence $\{\boldsymbol{Z}_t\}$ is* stationary *if $G_1 = G_{\tau+1}$ for each $\tau \geq 1$.*

In other words, a sequence is stationary if the *joint* distribution of the variables in the sequence is identical, regardless of the date of the first observation.

Proposition 3.29 *Let $\mathcal{Z}$ be a random variable (i.e., $\mathcal{Z}$ is a measurable function) and T be a measure-preserving transformation. Let $\mathcal{Z}_1(\omega) = \mathcal{Z}(\omega)$, $\mathcal{Z}_2(\omega) = \mathcal{Z}(T\omega)$, ... , $\mathcal{Z}_n(\omega) = \mathcal{Z}(T^{n-1}\omega)$ for each ω in Ω. Then $\{\mathcal{Z}_t\}$ is a stationary sequence.*

Proof. Stout (1974, p. 169). ∎

A converse to this result is also available.

Proposition 3.30 *Let $\{\mathcal{Z}_t\}$ be a stationary sequence. Then there exists a measure-preserving transformation T defined on $(\Omega, \mathcal{F}, P)$ such that $\mathcal{Z}_1(\omega) = \mathcal{Z}_1(\omega)$, $\mathcal{Z}_2(\omega) = \mathcal{Z}_1(T\omega)$, $\mathcal{Z}_3(\omega) = \mathcal{Z}_1(T^2\omega)$, ... , $\mathcal{Z}_n(\omega) = \mathcal{Z}_1(T^{n-1}\omega)$ for all ω in Ω.*

Proof. Stout (1974, p. 170). ∎

Example 3.31 *Let $\{\mathcal{Z}_t\}$ be a sequence of i.i.d. $N(0,1)$ random variables. Then $\{\mathcal{Z}_t\}$ is stationary.*

The independence imposed in this example is crucial. If the elements of $\{\mathcal{Z}_t\}$ are simply identically distributed $N(0,1)$, the sequence is not necessarily stationary, because it is possible to construct different joint distributions that all have normal marginal distributions. By changing the joint distributions with t, we could violate the stationarity condition while preserving marginal normality. Thus stationarity is a strengthening of the identical distribution assumption, since it applies to joint and not simply marginal distributions. On the other hand, stationarity is weaker than the i.i.d. assumption, since i.i.d. sequences are stationary, but stationary sequences do not have to be independent.

Does a version of the law of large numbers, Theorem 3.1, hold if the i.i.d. assumption is simply replaced by the stationarity assumption? The answer is no, unless additional restrictions are imposed.

Example 3.32 *Let $\mathcal{U}_t$ be a sequence of i.i.d. random variables uniformly distributed on* $[0, 1]$ *and let* $\mathcal{Z}$ *be* $N(0, 1)$, *independent of* $\mathcal{U}_t$, $t = 1, 2, \ldots$. *Define* $\mathcal{Y}_t \equiv \mathcal{Z} + \mathcal{U}_t$. *Then* $\{\mathcal{Y}_t\}$ *is stationary (why?), but* $\bar{\mathcal{Y}}_n \equiv \sum_{t=1}^{n} \mathcal{Y}_t / n$ *does not converge to* $E(\mathcal{Y}_t) = \frac{1}{2}$. *Instead,* $\bar{\mathcal{Y}}_n - \mathcal{Z} \xrightarrow{a.s.} \frac{1}{2}$.

In this example, $\bar{\mathcal{Y}}_n$ converges to a random variable, $\mathcal{Z} + \frac{1}{2}$, rather than to a constant. The problem is that there is too much dependence in the sequence $\{\mathcal{Y}_t\}$. No matter how far into the future we take an observation on $\mathcal{Y}_t$, the initial value $\mathcal{Y}_1$ still determines to some extent what $\mathcal{Y}_t$ will be, as a result of the common component $\mathcal{Z}$. In fact, the correlation between $\mathcal{Y}_1$ and $\mathcal{Y}_t$ is always positive for any value of t.

To obtain a law of large numbers, we have to impose a restriction on the dependence or "memory" of the sequence. One such restriction is the concept of *ergodicity*.

Definition 3.33 *Let* $(\Omega, \mathcal{F}, P)$ *be a probability space. Let* $\{\mathcal{Z}_t\}$ *be a stationary sequence and let* T *be the measure-preserving transformation of Proposition 3.30. Then* $\{\mathcal{Z}_t\}$ *is* ergodic *if*

$$\lim_{n\to\infty} n^{-1} \sum_{t=1}^{n} P(F \cap T^t G) = P(F)P(G)$$

for all events $F, G \in \mathcal{F}$,

If F and G were independent, then we would have $P(F \cap G) = P(F)P(G)$. We can think of $T^t G$ as being the event G shifted t periods into the future, and since $P(T^t G) = P(G)$ when T is measure preserving, this definition says that an ergodic process (sequence) is one such that for any events F and G, F and $T^t G$ are independent on average in the limit. Thus ergodicity can be thought of as a form of "average asymptotic independence." For more on measure-preserving transformations, stationarity, and ergodicity the reader may consult Doob (1953, pp. 167–185) and Rosenblatt (1978).

The desired law of large numbers can now be stated.

Theorem 3.34 (Ergodic theorem) *Let* $\{\mathcal{Z}_t\}$ *be a stationary ergodic scalar sequence with* $E|\mathcal{Z}_t| < \infty$. *Then* $\bar{\mathcal{Z}}_n \xrightarrow{a.s.} \mu \equiv E(\mathcal{Z}_t)$.

Proof. See Stout (1974, p. 181). ∎

To apply this result, we make use of the following theorem.

Theorem 3.35 *Let* $\mathbf{g}$ *be an* $\mathcal{F}$*-measurable function into* $\mathbb{R}^k$ *and define* $\boldsymbol{\mathcal{Y}}_t \equiv \mathbf{g}(\ldots, \boldsymbol{\mathcal{Z}}_{t-1}, \boldsymbol{\mathcal{Z}}_t, \boldsymbol{\mathcal{Z}}_{t+1}, \ldots)$, *where* $\boldsymbol{\mathcal{Z}}_t$ *is* $q \times 1$. *(i) If* $\{\boldsymbol{\mathcal{Z}}_t\}$ *is stationary, then* $\{\boldsymbol{\mathcal{Y}}_t\}$ *is stationary. (ii) If* $\{\boldsymbol{\mathcal{Z}}_t\}$ *is stationary and ergodic, then* $\{\boldsymbol{\mathcal{Y}}_t\}$ *is stationary and ergodic.*

Proof. See Stout (1974, pp. 170, 182). ∎

Note that $\mathbf{g}$ depends on the present and infinite past and future of the sequence $\{\mathcal{Z}_t\}$. As stated by Stout, $\mathbf{g}$ only depends on the present and future of $\mathcal{Z}_t$, but the result is valid as given here.

Proposition 3.36 *If* $\{(\mathbf{Z}_t', \mathbf{X}_t', \varepsilon_t)\}$ *is a stationary ergodic sequence, then* $\{\mathbf{X}_t\mathbf{X}_t'\}$, $\{\mathbf{X}_t\varepsilon_t\}$, $\{\mathbf{Z}_t\mathbf{X}_t'\}$, $\{\mathbf{Z}_t\varepsilon_t\}$, *and* $\{\mathbf{Z}_t\mathbf{Z}_t'\}$ *are stationary ergodic sequences.*

Proof. Immediate from Theorem 3.35 and Proposition 3.23. ∎

Now we can state a result applicable to time-series data.

Theorem 3.37 *Suppose*

(*i*) $\mathbf{Y}_t = \mathbf{X}_t'\boldsymbol{\beta}_o + \varepsilon_t, \quad t = 1, 2, \ldots, \boldsymbol{\beta}_o \in \mathbb{R}^k$;

(*ii*) $\{(\mathbf{X}_t', \varepsilon_t)\}$ *is a stationary ergodic sequence;*

(*iii*) (*a*) $E(\mathbf{X}_t\varepsilon_t) = \mathbf{0}$;

(*b*) $E\,|X_{thi}\varepsilon_{th}| < \infty$, $h = 1, \ldots, p$, $i = 1, \ldots, k$;

(*iv*) (*a*) $E|X_{thi}|^2 < \infty$, $h = 1, \ldots, p$, $i = 1, \ldots, k$;

(*b*) $\mathbf{M} \equiv E(\mathbf{X}_t\mathbf{X}_t')$ *is positive definite.*

Then $\hat{\boldsymbol{\beta}}_n$ *exists for all* n *sufficiently large a.s., and* $\hat{\boldsymbol{\beta}}_n \xrightarrow{a.s.} \boldsymbol{\beta}_o$.

Proof. We verify the conditions of Theorem 2.12. Given (*ii*), $\{\mathbf{X}_t\varepsilon_t\}$ and $\{\mathbf{X}_t\mathbf{X}_t'\}$ are stationary ergodic sequences by Proposition 3.36, with elements having finite expected absolute values (given (*iii*) and (*iv*)). By the ergodic theorem (Theorem 3.34), $\mathbf{X}'\varepsilon/n \xrightarrow{a.s.} \mathbf{0}$ and $\mathbf{X}'\,\mathbf{X}/n \xrightarrow{a.s.} \mathbf{M}$, finite and positive definite. Hence, the conditions of Theorem 2.12 hold and the results follow. ∎

Compared with Theorem 3.5, we have replaced the i.i.d. assumption with the strictly weaker condition that the regressors and errors are stationary and ergodic. In both results, only the finiteness of second-order moments and cross moments is imposed. Thus Theorem 3.5 is a corollary of Theorem 3.37.

A direct generalization of Exercise 3.6 for the IV estimator is also available.

Exercise 3.38 *Prove the following result. Suppose*

(*i*) $\mathbf{Y}_t = \mathbf{X}_t'\boldsymbol{\beta}_o + \varepsilon_t, \quad t = 1, 2, \ldots, \boldsymbol{\beta}_o \in \mathbb{R}^k$;

(*ii*) $\{(\mathbf{Z}_t', \mathbf{X}_t', \varepsilon_t)\}$ *is a stationary ergodic sequence;*

(*iii*) (*a*) $E(\mathbf{Z}_t\varepsilon_t) = \mathbf{0}$;

(*b*) $E|Z_{thi}\varepsilon_{th}| < \infty$, $h = 1, \ldots, p$, $i = 1, \ldots, k$;

(*iv*) (*a*) $E|Z_{thi}X_{thj}| < \infty$, $h = 1, \ldots, p$, $i = 1, \ldots, l$, $j = 1, \ldots, k$;

(*b*) $\mathbf{Q} \equiv E(\mathbf{Z}_t\mathbf{X}_t')$ *has full column rank;*

(*c*) $\hat{\mathbf{P}}_n \xrightarrow{a.s.} \mathbf{P}$, *finite, symmetric, and positive definite.*

Then $\tilde{\boldsymbol{\beta}}_n$ *exists for all n sufficiently large a.s., and* $\tilde{\boldsymbol{\beta}}_n \xrightarrow{a.s.} \boldsymbol{\beta}_o$.

Economic applications of Theorem 3.37 and Exercise 3.38 depend on whether it is reasonable to suppose that economic time series are stationary and ergodic. Ergodicity is often difficult to ascertain theoretically (although it does hold for certain Markov sequences; see Stout (1974, pp. 185–200) and is impossible to verify empirically (since this requires an infinite sample), although it can be tested and rejected (see, for example, Domowitz and El-Gamal, 1993; and Corradi, Swanson, and White, 2000). Further, many important economic time series seem not to be stationary but heterogeneous, exhibiting means, variances, and covariances that change over time.

3.4 Dependent Heterogeneously Distributed Observations

To apply the consistency results of the preceding chapter to dependent heterogeneously distributed observations, we need to find conditions that ensure that the law of large numbers continues to hold. This can be done by replacing the ergodicity assumption with somewhat stronger conditions. Useful in this context are conditions on the dependence of a sequence known as *mixing conditions.*

To specify these conditions, we use the following definition.

Definition 3.39 *The* Borel σ-field generated *by* $\{\mathcal{Z}_t, t = n, \ldots, n+m\}$, *denoted* $\mathcal{B}_n^{n+m} = \sigma(\mathcal{Z}_n, \ldots, \mathcal{Z}_{n+m})$, *is the smallest* σ*-algebra of* Ω *that includes*

(*i*) *all sets of the form* $\times_{i=1}^{n-1}\mathbb{R}^q \times_{i=n}^{n+m} B_i \times_{i=n+m+1}^{\infty} \mathbb{R}^q$, *where each* $B_i \in \mathcal{B}^q$;

(*ii*) *the complement* A^c *of any set* A *in* $\mathcal{B}_n^{n+m}$;

(*iii*) *the union* $\bigcup_{i=1}^{\infty} A_i$ *of any sequence* $\{A_i\}$ *in* $\mathcal{B}_n^{n+m}$.

The σ-field $\mathcal{B}_n^{n+m}$ is the smallest σ-field of subsets of Ω with respect to which $\mathbf{Z}_t$, $t = n, \ldots, n+m$ are measurable. In other words, $\mathcal{B}_n^{n+m}$ is the smallest collection of events that allows us to express the probability of an event, say, $[\mathbf{Z}_n < \mathbf{a}_1, \mathbf{Z}_{n+1} < \mathbf{a}_2]$, in terms of the probability of an event in $\mathcal{B}_n^{n+m}$, say $[\omega : \mathbf{Z}_n(\omega) < \mathbf{a}_1, \mathbf{Z}_{n+1}(\omega) < \mathbf{a}_2]$. The definition of mixing is given in terms of the Borel σ-fields generated by subsets of the history of a process extending infinitely far into both the past and future, $\{\mathbf{Z}_t\}_{t=-\infty}^{\infty}$. For our purposes, we can think of $\mathbf{Z}_1$ as generating the first observation available to us, so realizations of $\mathbf{Z}_t$ are unobservable for $t \leq 0$. In what follows, this does not matter. All that does matter is the behavior of $\mathbf{Z}_t$, $t \leq 0$, if we could observe its realizations.

Definition 3.40 *Let $\mathcal{B}_{-\infty}^n \equiv \sigma(\ldots, \mathbf{Z}_n)$ be the smallest collection of subsets of Ω that contains the union of the σ-fields $\mathcal{B}_a^n$ as $a \to -\infty$; let $\mathcal{B}_{n+m}^{\infty} = \sigma(\mathbf{Z}_{n+m}, \ldots)$ be the smallest collection of subsets of Ω that contains the union of the σ-fields $\mathcal{B}_{n+m}^a$ as $a \to \infty$.*

Intuitively, we can think of $\mathcal{B}_{-\infty}^n$ as representing all the information contained in the past of the sequence $\{\mathbf{Z}_t\}$ up to time n, whereas $\mathcal{B}_{n+m}^{\infty}$ represents all the information contained in the future of the sequence $\{\mathbf{Z}_t\}$ from time $n+m$ on.

We now define two measures of dependence between σ-fields.

Definition 3.41 *Let $\mathcal{G}$ and $\mathcal{H}$ be σ-fields and define*

$$\begin{aligned}\phi(\mathcal{G}, \mathcal{H}) &\equiv \sup_{\{G \in \mathcal{G}, H \in \mathcal{H} : P(G) > 0)\}} |P(H|G) - P(H)|,\\ \alpha(\mathcal{G}, \mathcal{H}) &\equiv \sup_{\{G \in \mathcal{G}, H \in \mathcal{H}\}} |P(G \cap H) - P(G)P(H)|.\end{aligned}$$

Intuitively, ϕ and α measure the dependence of the events in $\mathcal{H}$ on those in $\mathcal{G}$ in terms of how much the probability of the joint occurrence of an event in each σ-algebra differs from the product of the probabilities of each event occurring. The events in $\mathcal{G}$ and $\mathcal{H}$ are independent if and only if $\phi(\mathcal{G}, \mathcal{H})$ and $\alpha(\mathcal{G}, \mathcal{H})$ are zero. The function α provides an absolute measure of dependence and ϕ a relative measure of dependence

Definition 3.42 *For a sequence of random vectors $\{\mathbf{Z}_t\}$, with $\mathcal{B}_{-\infty}^n$ and $\mathcal{B}_{n+m}^{\infty}$ as in Definition 3.40, define the* mixing coefficients

$$\phi(m) \equiv \sup_n \phi(\mathcal{B}_{-\infty}^n, \mathcal{B}_{n+m}^{\infty}) \quad \textit{and} \quad \alpha(m) \equiv \sup_n \alpha(\mathcal{B}_{-\infty}^n, \mathcal{B}_{n+m}^{\infty}).$$

If, for the sequence $\{\mathbf{Z}_t\}$, $\phi(m) \to 0$ as $m \to \infty$, $\{\mathbf{Z}_t\}$ is called ϕ-mixing. *If, for the sequence $\{\mathbf{Z}_t\}$, $\alpha(m) \to 0$ as $m \to \infty$, $\{\mathbf{Z}_t\}$ is called* α-mixing.

The quantities $\phi(m)$ and $\alpha(m)$ measure how much dependence exists between events separated by at least m time periods. Hence, if $\phi(m) = 0$ or $\alpha(m) = 0$ for some m, events m periods apart are independent. By allowing $\phi(m)$ or $\alpha(m)$ to approach zero as $m \to \infty$, we allow consideration of situations in which events are independent asymptotically. In the probability literature, ϕ-mixing sequences are also called *uniform mixing* (see Iosifescu and Theodorescu, 1969), whereas α-mixing sequences are called *strong mixing* (see Rosenblatt, 1956). Because $\phi(m) \geq \alpha(m)$, ϕ-mixing implies α-mixing.

Example 3.43 *(i) Let $\{Z_t\}$ be a γ-dependent sequence (i.e., Z_t is independent of $Z_{t-\tau}$ for all $\tau > \gamma$). Then $\phi(m) = \alpha(m) = 0$ for all $m > \gamma$. (ii) Let $\{Z_t\}$ be a nonstochastic sequence. Then it is an independent sequence, so $\phi(m) = \alpha(m) = 0$ for all $m > 0$. (iii) Let $Z_t = \rho_o Z_{t-1} + \varepsilon_t$, $t = 1, \ldots, n$, where $|\rho_o| < 1$ and ε_t is i.i.d. $N(0,1)$. (This is called the* Gaussian $AR(1)$ process.) *Then $\alpha(m) \to 0$ as $m \to \infty$, although $\phi(m) \nrightarrow 0$ as $m \to \infty$ (Ibragimov and Linnik, 1971, pp. 312–313).*

The concept of mixing has a meaningful physical interpretation. Adapting an example due to Halmos (1956), we imagine a dry martini initially poured so that 99% is gin and 1% is vermouth (placed in a layer at the top). The martini is steadily stirred by a swizzle stick; t increments with each stir. We observe the proportions of gin and vermouth in any measurable set (i.e., volume of martini). If these proportions tend to 99% and 1% after many stirs, regardless of which volume we observe, then the process is mixing. In this example, the stochastic process corresponds to the position of a given particle at each point in time, which can be represented as a sequence of three-dimensional vectors $\{\mathbf{Z}_t\}$.

The notion of mixing is a stronger memory requirement than that of ergodicity for stationary sequences, since given stationarity, mixing implies ergodicity, as the next result makes precise.

Proposition 3.44 *Let $\{Z_t\}$ be a stationary sequence. If $\alpha(m) \to 0$ as $m \to \infty$, then $\{Z_t\}$ is ergodic.*

Proof. See Rosenblatt (1978). ■

Note that if $\phi(m) \to 0$ as $m \to \infty$, then $\alpha(m) \to 0$ as $m \to \infty$, so that ϕ-mixing processes are also ergodic. Ergodic processes are not necessarily mixing, however. On the other hand, mixing is defined for sequences that are not necessarily strictly stationary, so mixing is more general in this sense. For more on mixing and ergodicity, see Rosenblatt (1972, 1978).

To state the law of large numbers for mixing sequences we use the following definition.

Definition 3.45 *Let $a \in \mathbb{R}$. (i) If $\phi(m) = O(m^{-a-\varepsilon})$ for some $\varepsilon > 0$, then ϕ is* of size *$-a$. (ii) If $\alpha(m) = O(m^{-a-\varepsilon})$ for some $\varepsilon > 0$, then α is* of size *$-a$.*

This definition allows precise statements about the memory of a random sequence that we shall relate to moment conditions expressed in terms of a. As a gets smaller, the sequence exhibits more and more dependence, while as $a \rightarrow \infty$, the sequence exhibits less dependence.

Example 3.46 *(i) Let $\{Z_t\}$ be independent $Z_t \sim N(0, \sigma_t^2)$. Then $\{Z_t\}$ has ϕ of size -1. (This is not the smallest size that could be invoked.) (ii) Let Z_t be a Gaussian $AR(1)$ process. It can be shown that $\{Z_t\}$ has α of size $-a$ for any $a \in \mathbb{R}$, since $\alpha(m)$ decreases exponentially with m.*

The result of this example extends to many finite autoregressive moving average (ARMA) processes. Under general conditions, finite ARMA processes have exponentially decaying memories.

Using the concept of mixing, we can state a law of large numbers, due to McLeish (1975), which applies to heterogeneous dependent sequences.

Theorem 3.47 (McLeish) *Let $\{Z_t\}$ be a sequence of scalars with finite means $\mu_t \equiv E(Z_t)$ and suppose that $\sum_{t=1}^{\infty}(E|Z_t - \mu_t|^{r+\delta}/t^{r+\delta})^{1/r} < \infty$ for some δ, $0 < \delta \leq r$ where $r \geq 1$. If ϕ is of size $-r/(2r-1)$ or α is of size $-r/(r-1)$, $r > 1$, then $\bar{Z}_n - \bar{\mu}_n \xrightarrow{a.s.} 0$.*

Proof. See McLeish (1975, Theorem 2.10). ∎

This result generalizes the Markov law of large numbers, Theorem 3.7. (There we have $r = 1$.)

Using an argument analogous to that used in obtaining Corollary 3.9, we obtain the following corollary.

Corollary 3.48 *Let $\{Z_t\}$ be a sequence with ϕ of size $-r/(2r-1)$, $r \geq 1$, or α of size $-r/(r-1)$, $r > 1$, such that $E|Z_t|^{r+\delta} < \Delta < \infty$ for some $\delta > 0$ and all t. Then $\bar{Z}_n - \bar{\mu}_n \xrightarrow{a.s.} 0$.*

Setting r arbitrarily close to unity yields a generalization of Corollary 3.9 that would apply to sequences with exponential memory decay. For sequences with longer memories, r is greater, and the moment restrictions increase accordingly. Here we have a clear trade-off between the amount of allowable dependence and the sufficient moment restrictions.

To apply this result, we use the following theorem.

Theorem 3.49 *Let* $\mathbf{g}$ *be a measurable function into* $\mathbb{R}^k$ *and define* $\mathcal{Y}_t \equiv \mathbf{g}(\mathcal{Z}_t, \mathcal{Z}_{t+1}, \ldots, \mathcal{Z}_{t+\tau})$, *where* τ *is finite. If the sequence of* $q \times 1$ *vectors* $\{\mathcal{Z}_t\}$ *is* ϕ*-mixing* (α*-mixing*) *of size* $-a$, $a > 0$, *then* $\{\mathcal{Y}_t\}$ *is* ϕ*-mixing* (α*-mixing*) *of size* $-a$.

Proof. See White and Domowitz (1984, Lemma 2.1). ∎

In other words, measurable functions of mixing processes are mixing and of the same size. Note that whereas functions of ergodic processes retain ergodicity for any τ, finite or infinite, mixing is guaranteed only for finite τ.

Proposition 3.50 *If* $\{(\mathbf{Z}_t', \mathbf{X}_t', \varepsilon_t)\}$ *is a mixing sequence of size* $-a$, *then* $\{\mathbf{X}_t\mathbf{X}_t'\}$, $\{\mathbf{X}_t\varepsilon_t\}$, $\{\mathbf{Z}_t\mathbf{X}_t'\}$, $\{\mathbf{Z}_t\varepsilon_t\}$, *and* $\{\mathbf{Z}_t\mathbf{Z}_t'\}$ *are mixing sequences of size* $-a$.

Proof. Immediate from Theorem 3.49 and Proposition 3.23. ∎

Now we can generalize the results of Exercise 3.14 to allow for dependence as well as heterogeneity.

Exercise 3.51 *Prove the following result. Suppose*

(*i*) $\mathbf{Y}_t = \mathbf{X}_t'\boldsymbol{\beta}_o + \varepsilon_t, \quad t = 1, 2, \ldots, \boldsymbol{\beta}_o \in \mathbb{R}^k$;

(*ii*) $\{(\mathbf{X}_t', \varepsilon_t)\}$ *is a mixing sequence with* ϕ *of size* $-r/(2r-1)$, $r \geq 1$ *or* α *of size* $-r/(r-1)$, $r > 1$;

(*iii*) (*a*) $E(\mathbf{X}_t\varepsilon_t) = \mathbf{0}, \quad t = 1, 2, \ldots$;

(*b*) $E|X_{thi}\varepsilon_{th}|^{r+\delta} < \Delta < \infty$, *for some* $\delta > 0$, $h = 1, \ldots, p$, $i = 1, \ldots, k$ *and for all* t;

(*iv*) (*a*) $E|X_{thi}^2|^{r+\delta} < \Delta < \infty$, *for some* $\delta > 0$, $h = 1, \ldots, p$, $i = 1, \ldots, k$ *and for all* t;

(*b*) $\mathbf{M}_n \equiv E(\mathbf{X}'\mathbf{X}/n)$ *is uniformly positive definite.*

Then $\hat{\boldsymbol{\beta}}_n$ *exists for all* n *sufficiently large a.s., and* $\hat{\boldsymbol{\beta}}_n \xrightarrow{a.s.} \boldsymbol{\beta}_o$.

From this result, we can obtain the result of Exercise 3.14 as a direct corollary by setting $r = 1$. Compared to our first consistency result, Theorem 3.5, we have relaxed the independence and identical distribution assumptions, but strengthened the moment requirements somewhat. Among the many different possibilities that this result allows, we can have lagged dependent variables and nonstochastic variables both appearing in the explanatory variables $\mathbf{X}_t$. The regression errors ε_t may be heteroskedastic or may be serially correlated.

In fact, Exercise 3.51 is a powerful result that can be applied to a wide range of situations faced by economists. For further discussion of linear models with mixing observations, see Domowitz (1983).

Applications of Exercise 3.51 often use the following result, which allows the interchange of expectation and infinite sums.

Proposition 3.52 *Let* $\{Z_t\}$ *be a sequence of random variables such that* $\sum_{t=1}^{\infty} E|Z_t| < \infty$. *Then* $\sum_{t=1}^{\infty} Z_t$ *converges a.s. and*

$$E(\sum_{t=1}^{\infty} Z_t) = \sum_{t=1}^{\infty} E(Z_t) < \infty.$$

Proof. See Billingsley (1979, p. 181). ∎

This result is useful in verifying the conditions of Exercise 3.51 for the following exercise.

Exercise 3.53 (*i*) *State conditions that are sufficient to ensure the consistency of the OLS estimator when* $Y_t = \alpha_o Y_{t-1} + \beta_o X_t + \varepsilon_t$, *where* Y_t, X_t *and* ε_t *are scalars. (Hint: The Minkowski inequality applies to infinite sums; that is, given* $\{Z_t\}$ *such that* $\sum_{t=1}^{\infty}(E|Z_t|^p)^{1/p} < \infty$ *with* $p \geq 1$, *then* $E|\sum_{t=1}^{\infty} Z_t|^p \leq (\sum_{t=1}^{\infty}(E|Z_t|^p)^{1/p})^p$.) (*ii*) *Find a simple example to which Exercise 3.51 does not apply.*

Conditions for the consistency of the IV estimator are given by the next result.

Theorem 3.54 *Suppose*

(*i*) $\mathbf{Y}_t = \mathbf{X}_t'\boldsymbol{\beta}_o + \varepsilon_t, \quad t = 1, 2, \ldots, \boldsymbol{\beta}_o \in \mathbb{R}^k$;

(*ii*) $\{(\mathbf{Z}_t', \mathbf{X}_t', \varepsilon_t)\}$ *is a mixing sequence with* ϕ *of size* $-r/(2r-1)$, $r \geq 1$, *or* α *of size* $-r/(r-1)$, $r > 1$;

(*iii*) (*a*) $E(\mathbf{Z}_t\varepsilon_t) = \mathbf{0}, \quad t = 1, 2, \ldots$;

(*b*) $E|Z_{thi}\varepsilon_{th}|^{r+\delta} < \Delta < \infty$, *for some* $\delta > 0$, *all* $h = 1, \ldots, p$, $i = 1, \ldots, l$, *and all* t;

(*iv*) (*a*) $E|Z_{thi}X_{thj}|^{r+\delta} < \Delta < \infty$, *for some* $\delta > 0$, *all* $h = 1, \ldots, p$, $i = 1, \ldots, l$, $j = 1, \ldots, k$ *and all* t;

(*b*) $\mathbf{Q}_n \equiv E(\mathbf{Z}'\mathbf{X}/n)$ *has uniformly full column rank;*

(*c*) $\hat{\mathbf{P}}_n - \mathbf{P}_n \xrightarrow{a.s.} \mathbf{0}$, *where* $\mathbf{P}_n = O(1)$ *and is symmetric and uniformly positive definite.*

Then $\tilde{\boldsymbol{\beta}}_n$ *exists for all n sufficiently large a.s., and* $\tilde{\boldsymbol{\beta}}_n \xrightarrow{a.s.} \boldsymbol{\beta}_o$.

Proof. By Proposition 3.50, $\{\mathbf{Z}_t\varepsilon_t\}$ and $\{\mathbf{Z}_t\mathbf{X}_t'\}$ are mixing sequences with elements satisfying the conditions of Corollary 3.48 (given (*iii.b*) and (*iv.a*)). It follows from Corollary 3.48 that $\mathbf{Z}'\varepsilon/n \xrightarrow{a.s.} \mathbf{0}$ and $\mathbf{Z}'\mathbf{X}/n - \mathbf{Q}_n \xrightarrow{a.s.} \mathbf{0}$, where $\mathbf{Q}_n = O(1)$, given (*iv.a*) as a consequence of Jensen's inequality. Hence the conditions of Exercise 2.20 are satisfied and the results follow. ■

Although mixing is an appealing dependence concept, it shares with ergodicity the property that it can be somewhat difficult to verify theoretically and is impossible to verify empirically. An alternative dependence concept that is easier to verify theoretically is a form of asymptotic non-correlation.

Definition 3.55 *The scalar sequence* $\{Z_t\}$ *has* asymptotically uncorrelated elements (*or is* asymptotically uncorrelated) *if there exist constants* $\{\rho_\tau, \tau \geq 0\}$ *such that* $0 \leq \rho_\tau \leq 1$, $\sum_{\tau=0}^{\infty} \rho_\tau < \infty$ *and* $\text{cov}(Z_t, Z_{t+\tau}) \leq \rho_\tau(\text{var}(Z_t)\text{var}(Z_{t+\tau}))^{1/2}$ *for all* $\tau > 0$, *where* $\text{var}(Z_t) < \infty$ *for all* t.

Note that ρ_τ is only an upper bound on the correlation between Z_t and $Z_{t+\tau}$ and that the actual correlation may depend on t. Further, only positive correlation matters, so that if Z_t and $Z_{t+\tau}$ are negatively correlated, we can set $\rho_\tau = 0$. Also note that for $\sum_{\tau=0}^{\infty} \rho_\tau < \infty$, it is necessary that $\rho_\tau \to 0$ as $\tau \to \infty$, and it is sufficient that for all τ sufficiently large, $\rho_\tau < \tau^{-1-\delta}$ for some $\delta > 0$.

Example 3.56 *Let* $Z_t = \rho_o Z_{t-1} + \varepsilon_t$, *where* ε_t *is i.i.d.,* $E(\varepsilon_t) = 0$, $\text{var}(\varepsilon_t) = \sigma_o^2$, $E(Z_{t-1}\varepsilon_t) = 0$. *Then* $\text{corr}(Z_t, Z_{t+\tau}) = \rho_o^\tau$. *If* $0 \leq \rho_o < 1$, $\sum_{\tau=0}^{\infty} \rho_o^\tau = 1/(1 - \rho_o) < \infty$, *so the sequence* $\{Z_t\}$ *is asymptotically uncorrelated.*

If a sequence has constant finite variance and has covariances that depend only on the time lag between Z_t and $Z_{t+\tau}$, the sequence is said to be *covariance stationary*. (This is implied by stationarity but is weaker because a sequence can be covariance stationary without being stationary.) Verifying that a covariance stationary sequence has asymptotically uncorrelated elements is straightforward when the process has a finite ARMA representation (see Granger and Newbold, 1977, Ch. 1). In this case, ρ_τ can be determined from well-known formulas (see, e.g., Granger and Newbold, 1977, Ch. 1) and the condition $\sum_{\tau=0}^{\infty} \rho_\tau < \infty$ can be directly evaluated. Thus, covariance stationary sequences as well as stationary ergodic sequences can often be shown to be asymptotically uncorrelated, although an asymptotically uncorrelated sequence need not be stationary and ergodic or covariance stationary. Under general conditions on the size of ϕ

or α, mixing processes can be shown to be asymptotically uncorrelated. Asymptotically uncorrelated sequences need not be mixing, however.

A law of large numbers for asymptotically uncorrelated sequences is the following.

Theorem 3.57 *Let* $\{\mathcal{Z}_t\}$ *be a scalar sequence with asymptotically uncorrelated elements with means* $\mu_t \equiv E(\mathcal{Z}_t)$ *and* $\sigma_t^2 \equiv \text{var}(\mathcal{Z}_t) < \Delta < \infty$. *Then* $\bar{\mathcal{Z}}_n - \bar{\mu}_n \xrightarrow{a.s.} 0$.

Proof. Immediate from Stout (1974, Theorem 3.7.2). ∎

Compared with Corollary 3.48, we have relaxed the dependence restriction from asymptotic independence (mixing) to asymptotic uncorrelation, but we have altered the moment requirements from restrictions on moments of order $r + \delta$ ($r \geq 1$, $\delta > 0$) to second moments. Typically, this is a strengthening of the moment restrictions.

Since taking functions of random variables alters their correlation properties, there is no simple analog of Proposition 3.2, Theorem 3.35, or Theorem 3.49. To obtain consistency results for the OLS or IV estimators, one must directly assume that all the appropriate sequences are asymptotically uncorrelated so that the almost sure convergence assumed in Theorem 2.18 or Exercise 2.20 holds. Since asymptotically uncorrelated sequences will not play an important role in the rest of this book, we omit stating and proving results for such sequences.

3.5 Martingale Difference Sequences

In all of the consistency results obtained so far, there has been the explicit requirement that either $E(\mathbf{X}_t\varepsilon_t) = \mathbf{0}$ or $E(\mathbf{Z}_t\varepsilon_t) = \mathbf{0}$. Economic theory can play a key role in justifying this assumption. In fact, it often occurs that economic theory is used to justify the stronger assumption that $E(\varepsilon_t|\mathbf{X}_t) = \mathbf{0}$ or $E(\varepsilon_t|\mathbf{Z}_t) = \mathbf{0}$, which then implies $E(\mathbf{X}_t\varepsilon_t) = \mathbf{0}$ or $E(\mathbf{Z}_t\varepsilon_t) = \mathbf{0}$. In particular, this occurs when $\mathbf{X}_t'\boldsymbol{\beta}_o$ is viewed as the value of $\mathbf{Y}_t$ we expect to observe when $\mathbf{X}_t$ occurs, so that $\mathbf{X}_t'\boldsymbol{\beta}_o$ is the conditional expectation of $\mathbf{Y}_t$ given $\mathbf{X}_t$, i.e., $E(\mathbf{Y}_t|\mathbf{X}_t) = \mathbf{X}_t'\boldsymbol{\beta}_o$. Then we define $\varepsilon_t = \mathbf{Y}_t - E(\mathbf{Y}_t|\mathbf{X}_t) = \mathbf{Y}_t - \mathbf{X}_t'\boldsymbol{\beta}_o$. Using the algebra of conditional expectations given below, it is straightforward to show that $E(\varepsilon_t|\mathbf{X}_t) = \mathbf{0}$.

One of the more powerful economic theories (powerful in the sense of imposing a great deal of structure on the way in which the data behave) is the theory of rational expectations. Often this theory can be used not only to justify the assumption that $E(\varepsilon_t|\mathbf{X}_t) = \mathbf{0}$ but also that

$$E(\varepsilon_t|\mathbf{X}_t, \mathbf{X}_{t-1}, \ldots; \varepsilon_{t-1}, \varepsilon_{t-2}, \ldots) = \mathbf{0},$$

i.e., that the conditional expectation of ε_t, given the entire past history of the errors ε_t and the current and past values of the explanatory variables $\mathbf{X}_t$, is zero. This assumption allows us to apply laws of large numbers for martingale difference sequences that are convenient and powerful.

To define what martingale difference sequences are and to state the associated results, we need to provide a more complete background on the properties of conditional expectations.

So far we have relied on the reader's intuitive understanding of what a conditional expectation is. A precise definition is the following.

Definition 3.58 *Let $\mathcal{Y}$ be an $\mathcal{F}$-measurable random variable, $E(|\mathcal{Y}|) < \infty$, and let $\mathcal{G}$ be a σ-field contained in $\mathcal{F}$. Then there exists a random variable $E(\mathcal{Y}|\mathcal{G})$ called the* conditional expectation of $\mathcal{Y}$ given $\mathcal{G}$, *such that*

(*i*) *$E(\mathcal{Y}|\mathcal{G})$ is $\mathcal{G}$-measurable and $E(|E(\mathcal{Y}|\mathcal{G})|) < \infty$.*

(*ii*) *$E(\mathcal{Y}|\mathcal{G})$ satisfies*

$$E(1_{[G]}E(\mathcal{Y}|\mathcal{G})) = E(1_{[G]}\mathcal{Y})$$

for all sets G in $\mathcal{G}$, where $1_{[G]}$ is the indicator function equal to unity on the set G and zero elsewhere.

As Doob (1953, p. 18) notes, this definition actually defines an entire class of random variables each of which satisfies the above definition, because any random variable that equals $E(\mathcal{Y}|\mathcal{G})$ with probability one satisfies this definition. However, any member of the class of random variables specified by the definition can be used in any expression involving a conditional expectation, so we will not distinguish between members of this class.

To put the conditional expectation in more familiar terms, we relate this definition to the expectation of $\mathcal{Y}_t$ conditional on other random variables $\mathcal{Z}_t$, $t = a, \ldots, b$, as follows.

Definition 3.59 *Let $\mathcal{Y}_t$ be a random variable such that $E(|\mathcal{Y}_t|) < \infty$ and let $\mathcal{B}_a^b = \sigma(\mathcal{Z}_a, \mathcal{Z}_{a+1}, \ldots, \mathcal{Z}_b)$ be the σ-algebra generated by the random vectors $\mathcal{Z}_t$, $t = a, \ldots, b$. Then the* conditional expectation of Y_t given $\mathcal{Z}_t$, *$t = a, \ldots, b$, is defined as*

$$E(\mathcal{Y}_t|\mathcal{Z}_a, \ldots, \mathcal{Z}_b) \equiv E(\mathcal{Y}_t|\mathcal{B}_a^b).$$

The conditional expectation $E(\mathcal{Y}_t|\mathcal{B}_a^b)$ can be expressed as a measurable function of $\mathbf{Z}_t$, $t = a, \ldots, b$, as the following result shows.

Proposition 3.60 *Let* $\mathcal{B}_a^b = \sigma(\mathbf{Z}_a, \mathbf{Z}_{a+1}, \ldots, \mathbf{Z}_b)$. *Then there exists a measurable function* g *such that*

$$E(\mathcal{Y}_t|\mathbf{Z}_a, \ldots, \mathbf{Z}_b) = g(\mathbf{Z}_a, \ldots, \mathbf{Z}_b).$$

Proof. Immediate from Doob (1953, Theorem 1.5, p. 603). ∎

Example 3.61 *Let* $\mathcal{Y}$ *and* $\mathcal{Z}$ *be jointly normal with* $E(\mathcal{Y}) = E(\mathcal{Z}) = 0$, $\text{var}(\mathcal{Y}) = \sigma_{\mathcal{Y}}^2$, $\text{var}(\mathcal{Z}) = \sigma_{\mathcal{Z}}^2$, $\text{cov}(\mathcal{Y}, \mathcal{Z}) = \sigma_{\mathcal{YZ}}$. *Then*

$$E(\mathcal{Y}|\mathcal{Z}) = (\sigma_{\mathcal{YZ}}/\sigma_{\mathcal{Z}}^2)\mathcal{Z}.$$

The role of economic theory can now be interpreted as specifying a particular form for the function g in Proposition 3.60, although, as we can see from Example 3.61, the g function is in fact a direct consequence of the form of the joint distribution of the random variables involved. For an economic theory to be valid, the g function specified by that economic theory must be identical to that implied by the joint distribution of the random variables; otherwise the economic theory provides only an approximation to the statistical relationship between the random variables under consideration.

We now state some useful properties of conditional expectations.

Proposition 3.62 (Linearity of conditional expectation) *Let* $a_1, \ldots, a_k$ *be finite constants and suppose* $\mathcal{Y}_1, \ldots, \mathcal{Y}_k$ *are random variables such that* $E|\mathcal{Y}_j| < \infty$, $j = 1, \ldots, k$. *Then* $E(a_j|\mathcal{G}) = a_j$ *and*

$$E(\sum_{j=1}^{k} a_j \mathcal{Y}_j|\mathcal{G}) = \sum_{j=1}^{k} a_j E(\mathcal{Y}_j|\mathcal{G}).$$

Proof. See Doob (1953, p. 23). ∎

Proposition 3.63 *If* $\mathcal{Y}$ *is a random variable and* $\mathcal{Z}$ *is a random variable measurable with respect to* $\mathcal{G}$ *such that* $E|\mathcal{Y}| < \infty$ *and* $E|\mathcal{ZY}| < \infty$, *then with probability one*

$$E(\mathcal{ZY}|\mathcal{G}) = \mathcal{Z}E(\mathcal{Y}|\mathcal{G})$$

and

$$E([\mathcal{Y} - E(\mathcal{Y}|\mathcal{G})]\mathcal{Z}) = 0.$$

Proof. See Doob (1953, p. 22). ■

Example 3.64 *Let $\mathcal{G} = \sigma(\mathbf{X}_t)$. Then $E(\mathbf{X}_t \mathbf{Y}_t|\mathbf{X}_t) = \mathbf{X}_t E(\mathbf{Y}_t|\mathbf{X}_t)$. Define $\varepsilon_t = \mathbf{Y}_t - E(\mathbf{Y}_t|\mathbf{X}_t)$. Then $E(\mathbf{X}_t\varepsilon_t) = E(\mathbf{X}_t[\mathbf{Y}_t - E(\mathbf{Y}_t|\mathbf{X}_t)]) = \mathbf{0}$.*

If we set $E(\mathbf{Y}_t|\mathbf{X}_t) = \mathbf{X}_t'\boldsymbol{\beta}_o$, the result of this example justifies the orthogonality condition for the OLS estimator, $E(\mathbf{X}_t\varepsilon_t) = \mathbf{0}$.

A version of Jensen's inequality also holds for conditional expectations.

Proposition 3.65 (Conditional Jensen's inequality) *Let $g : \mathbb{R} \to \mathbb{R}$ be a convex function on an interval $B \subset \mathbb{R}$ and let $\mathcal{Y}$ be a random variable such that $P[\mathcal{Y} \in B] = 1$. If $E|\mathcal{Y}| < \infty$ and $E|g(\mathcal{Y})| < \infty$, then*

$$g[E(\mathcal{Y}|\mathcal{G})] \leq E(g(\mathcal{Y})|\mathcal{G})$$

for any σ-field $\mathcal{G}$ of sets in Ω. If g is concave, then

$$g[E(\mathcal{Y}|\mathcal{G})] \geq E(g(\mathcal{Y})|\mathcal{G}).$$

Proof. See Doob (1953, p. 33). ■

Example 3.66 *Let $g(y) = |y|$. It follows from the conditional Jensen's inequality that $|E(\mathcal{Y}|\mathcal{G})| \leq E(|\mathcal{Y}||\mathcal{G})$.*

Proposition 3.67 *Let $\mathcal{G}$ and $\mathcal{H}$ be σ-fields and suppose $\mathcal{G} \subset \mathcal{H}$ and that some version of $E(\mathcal{Y}|\mathcal{H})$ is measurable with respect to $\mathcal{G}$. Then*

$$E(\mathcal{Y}|\mathcal{H}) = E(\mathcal{Y}|\mathcal{G}),$$

with probability one.

Proof. See Doob (1953, p. 21). ■

In other words, conditional expectations with respect to two different σ-fields, one contained in the other, coincide provided that the expectation conditioned on the larger σ-field is measurable with respect to the smaller σ-field. Otherwise, no necessary relation holds between the two conditional expectations.

Example 3.68 *Suppose that $E(\mathcal{Y}_t|\mathcal{H}_{t-1}) = 0$, where $\mathcal{H}_{t-1} = \sigma(\ldots, \mathcal{Y}_{t-2}, \mathcal{Y}_{t-1})$. Then $E(\mathcal{Y}_t|\mathcal{Y}_{t-1}) = 0$, since $E(\mathcal{Y}_t|\mathcal{Y}_{t-1}) = E(\mathcal{Y}_t|\mathcal{G}_{t-1})$, where $\mathcal{G}_{t-1} = \sigma(\mathcal{Y}_{t-1})$ satisfies $\mathcal{G}_{t-1} \subset \mathcal{H}_{t-1}$ and $E(\mathcal{Y}_t|\mathcal{H}_{t-1}) = 0$ is measurable with respect to $\mathcal{G}_{t-1}$.*

One of the most useful properties of the conditional expectation is given by the law of iterated expectations.

Proposition 3.69 (Law of iterated expectations) *Let $E|\mathcal{Y}| < \infty$ and let $\mathcal{G}$ be a σ-field of sets in Ω. Then*

$$E[E(\mathcal{Y}|\mathcal{G})] = E(\mathcal{Y}).$$

Proof. Set $G = \Omega$ in Definition 3.58. ∎

Example 3.70 *Suppose $E(\varepsilon_t|\mathbf{X}_t) = \mathbf{0}$. Then by Proposition 3.69, $E(\varepsilon_t) = E(E(\varepsilon_t|\mathbf{X}_t)) = \mathbf{0}$.*

A more general result is the following.

Proposition 3.71 (Law of iterated expectations) *Let $\mathcal{G}$ and $\mathcal{H}$ be σ-fields of sets in Ω with $\mathcal{H} \subset \mathcal{G}$, and suppose $E(|\mathcal{Y}|) < \infty$. Then*

$$E[E(\mathcal{Y}|\mathcal{G})|\mathcal{H}] = E(\mathcal{Y}|\mathcal{H}).$$

Proof. See Doob (1953, p. 37). ∎

Proposition 3.69 is the special case of Proposition 3.71 in which $\mathcal{H} = \{\emptyset, \Omega\}$, the trivial σ-field.

With the law of iterated expectations available, it is straightforward to show that the conditional expectation has an optimal prediction property, in the sense that in predicting a random variable $\mathcal{Y}$, the prediction mean squared error of the conditional expectation of $\mathcal{Y}$ is smaller than that of any other predictor of $\mathcal{Y}$ measurable with respect to the same σ-field.

Theorem 3.72 *Let $\mathcal{Y}$ be a random variable with $E(\mathcal{Y}^2) < \infty$ and let $\hat{\mathcal{Y}} \equiv E(\mathcal{Y}|\mathcal{G})$. Then for any other $\mathcal{G}$-measurable random variable $\tilde{\mathcal{Y}}$, $E((\mathcal{Y} - \hat{\mathcal{Y}})^2) \leq E((\mathcal{Y} - \tilde{\mathcal{Y}})^2)$.*

Proof. Adding and subtracting $\hat{\mathcal{Y}}$ in $(\mathcal{Y} - \tilde{\mathcal{Y}})^2$ gives

$$\begin{aligned} E((\mathcal{Y} - \tilde{\mathcal{Y}})^2) &= E((\mathcal{Y} - \hat{\mathcal{Y}} + \hat{\mathcal{Y}} - \tilde{\mathcal{Y}})^2) \\ &= E((\mathcal{Y} - \hat{\mathcal{Y}})^2 + 2E((\mathcal{Y} - \hat{\mathcal{Y}})(\hat{\mathcal{Y}} - \tilde{\mathcal{Y}})) \\ &\quad + E((\hat{\mathcal{Y}} - \tilde{\mathcal{Y}})^2). \end{aligned}$$

By the law of iterated expectations and Proposition 3.63,

$$\begin{aligned} E((\mathcal{Y} - \hat{\mathcal{Y}})(\hat{\mathcal{Y}} - \tilde{\mathcal{Y}})) &= E[E((\mathcal{Y} - \hat{\mathcal{Y}})(\hat{\mathcal{Y}} - \tilde{\mathcal{Y}})|\mathcal{G})] \\ &= E[E(\mathcal{Y} - \hat{\mathcal{Y}}|\mathcal{G})(\hat{\mathcal{Y}} - \tilde{\mathcal{Y}})]. \end{aligned}$$

But $E(\mathcal{Y} - \hat{\mathcal{Y}}|\mathcal{G}) = 0$, so $E((\mathcal{Y} - \hat{\mathcal{Y}})(\hat{\mathcal{Y}} - \tilde{\mathcal{Y}})) = 0$ and

$$E((\mathcal{Y} - \tilde{\mathcal{Y}})^2) = E((\mathcal{Y} - \hat{\mathcal{Y}})^2 + E((\hat{\mathcal{Y}} - \tilde{\mathcal{Y}})^2),$$

and the result follows, because the final term on the right is nonnegative. ■

This result provides us with another interpretation for the conditional expectation. The conditional expectation of $\mathcal{Y}$ given $\mathcal{G}$ gives the minimum mean squared error prediction of $\mathcal{Y}$ based on a specified information set (σ-field) $\mathcal{G}$.

With the next definition (from Stout, 1974, p. 30) we will have sufficient background to define the concept of a martingale difference sequence.

Definition 3.73 *Let $\{\mathcal{Y}_t\}$ be a sequence of random scalars, and let $\{\mathcal{F}_t\}$ be a sequence of σ-fields $\mathcal{F}_t \subset \mathcal{F}$ such that $\mathcal{F}_{t-1} \subset \mathcal{F}_t$ for all t (i.e., $\{\mathcal{F}_t\}$ is an* increasing sequence of σ-fields, *also called a* filtration). *If $\mathcal{Y}_t$ is measurable with respect to $\mathcal{F}_t$, then $\{\mathcal{F}_t\}$ is said to be* adapted *to the sequence $\{\mathcal{Y}_t\}$ and $\{\mathcal{Y}_t, \mathcal{F}_t\}$ is called an* adapted stochastic sequence.

One way of generating an adapted stochastic sequence is to let $\mathcal{F}_t$ be the σ-field generated by current and past $\mathcal{Y}_t$, i.e., $\mathcal{F}_t = \sigma(\ldots, \mathcal{Y}_{t-1}, \mathcal{Y}_t)$. Then $\{\mathcal{F}_t\}$ is increasing and $\mathcal{Y}_t$ is always measurable with respect to $\mathcal{F}_t$. However, $\mathcal{F}_t$ can contain more than just the present and past of $\mathcal{Y}_t$; it can also contain the present and past of other random variables as well. For example, let $\mathcal{Y}_t = \mathcal{Z}_{t1}$, where $\boldsymbol{\mathcal{Z}}_t' = (\mathcal{Z}_{t1}, \ldots, \mathcal{Z}_{tq})$, and let $\mathcal{F}_t = \sigma(\ldots, \boldsymbol{\mathcal{Z}}_{t-1}, \boldsymbol{\mathcal{Z}}_t)$. Then $\mathcal{F}_t$ is again increasing and $\mathcal{Y}_t$ is again measurable with respect to $\mathcal{F}_t$, so $\{\mathcal{Y}_t, \mathcal{F}_t\}$ is an adapted stochastic sequence. This is the situation most relevant for our purposes.

Definition 3.74 *Let $\{\mathcal{Y}_t, \mathcal{F}_t\}$ be an adapted stochastic sequence. Then $\{\mathcal{Y}_t, \mathcal{F}_t\}$ is a* martingale difference sequence *if*

$$E(\mathcal{Y}_t|\mathcal{F}_{t-1}) = 0, \quad \text{for all } t \geq 1.$$

Example 3.75 *(i) Let $\{\mathcal{Y}_t\}$ be a sequence of i.i.d. random variables with $E(\mathcal{Y}_t) = 0$, and let $\mathcal{F}_t = \sigma(\ldots, \mathcal{Y}_{t-1}, \mathcal{Y}_t)$. Then $\{\mathcal{Y}_t, \mathcal{F}_t\}$ is a martingale difference sequence. (ii) (The Lévy device) Let $\{\mathcal{Y}_t, \mathcal{F}_t\}$ be any adapted stochastic sequence such that $E|\mathcal{Y}_t| < \infty$ for all t. Then*

$$\{\mathcal{Y}_t - E(\mathcal{Y}_t|\mathcal{F}_{t-1}), \mathcal{F}_t\}$$

is a martingale difference sequence because $\mathcal{Y}_t - E(\mathcal{Y}_t|\mathcal{F}_{t-1})$ is measurable with respect to $\mathcal{F}_t$ and, by linearity,

$$E[\mathcal{Y}_t - E(\mathcal{Y}_t|\mathcal{F}_{t-1})|\mathcal{F}_{t-1}] = E(\mathcal{Y}_t|\mathcal{F}_{t-1}) - E(\mathcal{Y}_t|\mathcal{F}_{t-1}) = 0.$$

The device of Example 3.75 (*ii*) is useful in certain circumstances because it reduces the study of the behavior of an arbitrary sequence of random variables to the study of the behavior of a martingale difference sequence and a sequence of conditional expectations (Stout, 1974, p. 33).

The martingale difference assumption is often justified in economics by the efficient markets theory or rational expectations theory, e.g., Samuelson (1965). In these theories the random variable $\mathcal{Y}_t$ is the price change of an asset or a commodity traded in a competitive market and $\mathcal{F}_t$ is the σ-field generated by all current and past information available to market participants, $\mathcal{F}_t = \sigma(\ldots, \mathcal{Z}_{t-1}, \mathcal{Z}_t)$, where $\mathcal{Z}_t$ is a finite-dimensional vector of observable information, including information on $\mathcal{Y}_t$. A zero profit (no arbitrage) condition then ensures that $E(\mathcal{Y}_t|\mathcal{F}_{t-1}) = 0$. Note that if $\mathcal{G}_t = \sigma(\ldots, \mathcal{Y}_{t-1}, \mathcal{Y}_t)$, then $\{\mathcal{Y}_t, \mathcal{G}_t\}$ is also an adapted stochastic sequence, and because $\mathcal{G}_t \subset \mathcal{F}_t$, it follows from Proposition 3.71 that

$$E(\mathcal{Y}_t|\mathcal{G}_{t-1}) = E[E(\mathcal{Y}_t|\mathcal{F}_{t-1})|\mathcal{G}_{t-1}] = 0,$$

so $\{\mathcal{Y}_t, \mathcal{G}_t\}$ is also a martingale difference sequence.

The martingale difference assumption often arises in a regression context in the following way. Suppose we have observations on a scalar Y_t (set $p = 1$ for now) that we are interested in explaining or forecasting on the basis of variables $\mathbf{Z}_t$ as well as on the basis of the past values of Y_t. Let $\mathcal{F}_{t-1}$ be the σ-field containing the information used to explain or forecast Y_t, i.e., $\mathcal{F}_{t-1} = \sigma(\ldots, (\mathbf{Z}'_{t-1}, Y_{t-2})', (\mathbf{Z}'_t, Y_{t-1})')$. Then by Proposition 3.60,

$$E(Y_t|\mathcal{F}_{t-1}) = g(\ldots, (\mathbf{Z}'_{t-1}, Y_{t-2})', (\mathbf{Z}'_t, Y_{t-1})'),$$

where g is some function of current and past values of $\mathbf{Z}_t$ and past values of Y_t. Let $\mathbf{X}_t$ contain a finite number of current and lagged values of $(\mathbf{Z}'_t, Y_{t-1})$, e.g., $\mathbf{X}_t = ((\mathbf{Z}'_{t-\tau}, Y_{t-\tau-1})', \ldots, (\mathbf{Z}'_t, Y_{t-1})')'$ for some $\tau < \infty$. Economic theory is then often used in an attempt to justify the assumption that for some $\boldsymbol{\beta}_o < \infty$,

$$g(\ldots, (\mathbf{Z}'_{t-1}, Y_{t-2})', (\mathbf{Z}'_t, Y_{t-1})') = \mathbf{X}'_t\boldsymbol{\beta}_o.$$

If this is true, we then have

$$E(Y_t|\mathcal{F}_{t-1}) = \mathbf{X}'_t\boldsymbol{\beta}_o.$$

Note that by definition, Y_t is measurable with respect to $\mathcal{F}_t$, so that $\{Y_t, \mathcal{F}_t\}$ is an adapted stochastic sequence. Hence, by the Lévy device, we find that $\{Y_t - E(Y_t|\mathcal{F}_{t-1}), \mathcal{F}_t\}$ is a martingale difference sequence. If we let

$$\varepsilon_t = Y_t - \mathbf{X}'_t\boldsymbol{\beta}_o$$

and it is true that $E(Y_t|\mathcal{F}_{t-1}) = \mathbf{X}_t'\boldsymbol{\beta}_o$, then $\varepsilon_t = Y_t - E(Y_t|\mathcal{F}_{t-1})$, so $\{\varepsilon_t, \mathcal{F}_t\}$ is a martingale difference sequence. Of direct importance for least squares estimation is the fact that $\{\mathcal{F}_t\}$ is also adapted to each sequence of cross products between regressors and errors $\{X_{ti}\varepsilon_t\}$, $i = 1, \ldots, k$. It is then easily shown that $\{X_{ti}\varepsilon_t, \mathcal{F}_t\}$ is also a martingale difference sequence, since by Proposition 3.63

$$E(X_{ti}\varepsilon_t|\mathcal{F}_{t-1}) = X_{ti}E(\varepsilon_t|\mathcal{F}_{t-1}) = 0.$$

A law of large numbers for martingale difference sequences is the following theorem.

Theorem 3.76 (Chow) *Let $\{Z_t, \mathcal{F}_t\}$ be a martingale difference sequence. If for some $r \geq 1$, $\sum_{t=1}^{\infty}(E|Z_t|^{2r})/t^{1+r} < \infty$, then $\bar{Z}_n \xrightarrow{a.s.} 0$.*

Proof. See Stout (1974, pp. 154–155). ■

Note the similarity of the present result to the Markov law of large numbers, Theorem 3.7. There the stronger assumption of independence replaces the martingale difference assumption, whereas the required moment conditions are weaker with independence than they are here. A corollary analogous to Corollary 3.9 also holds.

Exercise 3.77 *Prove the following. Let $\{Z_t, \mathcal{F}_t\}$ be a martingale difference sequence such that $E|Z_t|^{2r} < \Delta < \infty$ for some $r \geq 1$ and all t. Then $\bar{Z}_n \xrightarrow{a.s.} 0$.*

Using this result and the law of large numbers for mixing sequences, we can state the following consistency result for the OLS estimator.

Theorem 3.78 *Suppose*

(*i*) $\mathbf{Y}_t = \mathbf{X}_t'\boldsymbol{\beta}_o + \varepsilon_t, \quad t = 1, 2, \ldots, \boldsymbol{\beta}_o \in \mathbb{R}^k$;

(*ii*) $\{\mathbf{X}_t\}$ *is a sequence of mixing random variables with ϕ of size $-r/(2r-1)$, $r \geq 1$, or α of size $-r/(r-1)$, $r > 1$;*

(*iii*) (*a*) $\{X_{thi}\varepsilon_{th}, \mathcal{F}_{t-1}\}$ *is a martingale difference sequence, $h = 1, \ldots, p$, $i = 1, \ldots, k$;*

(*b*) $E\,|X_{thi}\varepsilon_{th}|^{2r} < \Delta < \infty$, *for all $h = 1, \ldots, p$, $i = 1, \ldots, k$ and t;*

(*iv*) (*a*) $E|X_{thi}^2|^{r+\delta} < \Delta < \infty$, *for some $\delta > 0$ and all $h = 1, \ldots, p$, $i = 1, \ldots, k$ and t;*

(*b*) $\mathbf{M}_n \equiv E(\mathbf{X}'\mathbf{X}/n)$ *is uniformly positive definite.*

Then $\hat{\boldsymbol{\beta}}_n$ *exists for all n sufficiently large a.s., and* $\hat{\boldsymbol{\beta}}_n \xrightarrow{a.s.} \boldsymbol{\beta}_o$.

Proof. To verify that the conditions of Theorem 2.18 hold, we note first that $\mathbf{X}'\boldsymbol{\varepsilon}/n = \sum_{h=1}^{p} \mathbf{X}_h' \boldsymbol{\varepsilon}_h/n$ where $\mathbf{X}_h$ is the $n \times k$ matrix with rows $\mathbf{X}_{th}$ and $\boldsymbol{\varepsilon}_h$ is the $n \times 1$ vector with elements ε_{th}. By assumption $(iii.a)$, $\{X_{thi}\varepsilon_{th}, \mathcal{F}_t\}$ is a martingale difference sequence. Because the moment conditions of Exercise 3.77 are satisfied by $(iii.b)$, we have $n^{-1}\sum X_{thi}\varepsilon_{th} \xrightarrow{a.s.} 0$, $h = 1, \ldots, p$, $i = 1, \ldots, k$, so $\mathbf{X}'\boldsymbol{\varepsilon}/n \xrightarrow{a.s.} \mathbf{0}$ by Proposition 2.11. Next, Proposition 3.50 ensures that $\{\mathbf{X}_t\mathbf{X}_t'\}$ is a mixing sequence (given (ii)) that satisfies the conditions of Corollary 3.48 (given $(iv.a)$). It follows that $\mathbf{X}'\mathbf{X}/n - \mathbf{M}_n \xrightarrow{a.s.} \mathbf{0}$, and $\mathbf{M}_n = O(1)$ (given $(iv.a)$) by Jensen's inequality. Hence the conditions of Theorem 2.18 are satisfied and the result follows. ■

Note that the conditions placed on $\mathbf{X}_t$ by (ii) and $(iv.a)$ ensure that $\mathbf{X}'\mathbf{X}/n - \mathbf{M}_n \xrightarrow{a.s.} \mathbf{0}$ and that these conditions can be replaced by any other conditions that ensure the same conclusion.

A result for the IV estimator can be obtained analogously.

Exercise 3.79 *Prove the following result. Given*

(i) $\mathbf{Y}_t = \mathbf{X}_t'\boldsymbol{\beta}_o + \boldsymbol{\varepsilon}_t, \quad t = 1, 2, \ldots, \boldsymbol{\beta}_o \in \mathbb{R}^k$;

(ii) $\{(\mathbf{Z}_t', \mathbf{X}_t', \boldsymbol{\varepsilon}_t)\}$ *is a mixing sequence with* ϕ *of size* $-r/(2r-1)$, $r \geq 1$, *or* α *of size* $-r/(r-1)$, $r > 1$;

(iii) (a) $\{Z_{thi}\varepsilon_{th}, \mathcal{F}_t\}$ *is a martingale difference sequence,* $h = 1, \ldots, p$, $i = 1, \ldots, l$;

(b) $E|Z_{thi}\varepsilon_{th}|^{2r} < \Delta < \infty$, *for all* $h = 1, \ldots, p$, $i = 1, \ldots, l$ *and* t;

(iv) (a) $E|Z_{thi}X_{thj}|^{r+\delta} < \Delta < \infty$, *for some* $\delta > 0$ *and all* $h = 1, \ldots, p$, $i = 1, \ldots, l$, $j = 1 \ldots, k$ *and* t;

(b) $\mathbf{Q}_n \equiv E(\mathbf{Z}'\mathbf{X}/n)$ *has uniformly full column rank;*

(c) $\hat{\mathbf{P}}_n - \mathbf{P}_n \xrightarrow{a.s.} \mathbf{0}$, *where* $\mathbf{P}_n = O(1)$ *and is symmetric and uniformly positive definite.*

Then $\tilde{\boldsymbol{\beta}}_n$ *exists for all n sufficiently large a.s., and* $\tilde{\boldsymbol{\beta}}_n \xrightarrow{a.s.} \boldsymbol{\beta}_o$.

As with results for the OLS estimator, (ii) and $(iv.a)$ can be replaced by any other conditions that ensure $\mathbf{Z}'\mathbf{X}/n - \mathbf{Q}_n \xrightarrow{a.s.} \mathbf{0}$. Note that assumption (ii) is stronger than absolutely necessary here. Instead, it suffices that $\{(\mathbf{Z}_t', \mathbf{X}_t')\}$ is appropriately mixing. However, assumption (ii) is used later to ensure the consistency of estimated covariance matrices.

References

Bartle, R. G. (1966). *The Elements of Integration.* Wiley, New York.

Billingsley, P. (1979). *Probability and Measure.* Wiley, New York.

Chung, K. L. (1974). *A Course in Probability Theory.* Harcourt, New York.

Corradi, V., N. Swanson, and H. White (2000). "Testing for stationarity-ergodicity and for comovement between nonlinear discrete time Markov processes." *Journal of Econometrics*, 96, 39–73.

Domowitz, I. (1983). "The linear model with stochastic regressors and heteroskedastic dependent errors." Discussion Paper, Center for Mathematical Studies in Economics and Management Sciences, Northwestern University, Evanston, Illinois.

——— and M. A. El-Gamal (1993). "A consistent test of stationary-ergodicity." *Econometric Theory*, 9, 589–601.

Doob, J. L. (1953). *Stochastic Processes.* Wiley, New York.

Granger, C. W. J. and P. Newbold (1977). *Forecasting Economic Time Series.* Academic Press, New York.

Halmos, P. R. (1956). *Lectures in Ergodic Theory.* Chelsea Publishing, New York.

Ibragimov, I. A. and Y. V. Linnik (1971). *Independent and Stationary Sequences of Random Variables.* Wolters-Noordhoff, The Netherlands.

Iosifescu, M. and R. Theodorescu (1969). *Random Processes and Learning.* Springer-Verlag, New York.

Kolmogorov, A. N. (1933). *Grundbegriffe der Wahrscheinlichkeitsrechnung.* Ergebnisse der Mathematik und ihrer Grenzgebiete, Vol. 2, No. 3. Springer-Verlag, Berlin.

Lukacs, E. (1975). *Stochastic Convergence.* Academic Press, New York.

McLeish, D. L. (1975). "A maximal inequality and dependent strong laws." *Annals of Probability*, 3, 826–836.

Rao, C. R. (1973). *Linear Statistical Inference and Its Applications.* Wiley, New York.

Rosenblatt, M. (1956). "A central limit theorem and a strong mixing condition." *Proc. Nat. Acad. Sci. U.S.A.*, 42, 43–47.

——— (1972). "Uniform ergodicity and strong mixing." *Z. Wahrsch. Verw. Gebiete*, 24, 79–84.

——— (1978). "Dependence and asymptotic independence for random processes." In *Studies in Probability Theory*, M. Rosenblatt, ed., Mathematical Association of America, Washington, D.C.

Samuelson, P. (1965). "Proof that properly anticipated prices fluctuate randomly." *Industrial Management Review.* 6, 41–49.

Stout, W. F. (1974). *Almost Sure Convergence.* Academic Press, New York.

White, H. and I. Domowitz (1984). "Nonlinear regression with dependent observations." *Econometrica*, 52, 143–162.

CHAPTER 4

Asymptotic Normality

In the classical linear model with fixed regressors and normally distributed i.i.d. errors, the least squares estimator $\hat{\boldsymbol{\beta}}_n$ is distributed as a multivariate normal with $E(\hat{\boldsymbol{\beta}}_n) = \boldsymbol{\beta}_o$ and $\text{var}(\hat{\boldsymbol{\beta}}_n) = \sigma_o^2(\mathbf{X}'\mathbf{X})^{-1}$ for any sample size n. This fact forms the basis for statistical tests of hypotheses, based typically on t- and F-statistics. When the sample size is large, econometric estimators such as $\hat{\boldsymbol{\beta}}_n$ have a distribution that is approximately normal under much more general conditions, and this fact forms the basis for large sample statistical tests of hypotheses. In this chapter we study the tools used in determining the asymptotic distribution of $\hat{\boldsymbol{\beta}}_n$, how this asymptotic distribution can be used to test hypotheses in large samples, and how asymptotic efficiency can be obtained.

4.1 Convergence in Distribution

The most fundamental concept is that of convergence in distribution.

Definition 4.1 *Let $\{\mathbf{b}_n\}$ be a sequence of random finite-dimensional vectors with joint distribution functions $\{F_n\}$. If $F_n(\mathbf{z}) \to F(\mathbf{z})$ as $n \to \infty$ for every continuity point $\mathbf{z}$, where F is the distribution function of a random variable $\mathcal{Z}$, then $\mathbf{b}_n$* converges in distribution *to the random variable $\mathcal{Z}$, denoted $\mathbf{b}_n \xrightarrow{d} \mathcal{Z}$.*

Heuristically, the distribution of $\mathbf{b}_n$ gets closer and closer to that of the random variable $\mathcal{Z}$, so the distribution F can be used as an approximation to the distribution of $\mathbf{b}_n$. When $\mathbf{b}_n \xrightarrow{d} \mathcal{Z}$, we also say that $\mathbf{b}_n$ *converges in law* to $\mathcal{Z}$ (written $\mathbf{b}_n \xrightarrow{L} \mathcal{Z}$), or that $\mathbf{b}_n$ is *asymptotically distributed* as F, denoted $\mathbf{b}_n \overset{A}{\sim} F$. Then F is called the *limiting distribution* of $\mathbf{b}_n$. Note that the convergence specified by this definition is pointwise and only has to occur at points $\mathbf{z}$ where F is continuous (the "continuity points").

Example 4.2 *Let $\{\mathbf{b}_n\}$ be a sequence of i.i.d. random variables with distribution function F. Then (trivially) F is the limiting distribution of $\mathbf{b}_n$.*

This illustrates the fact that convergence in distribution is a very weak convergence concept and by itself implies nothing about the convergence of the sequence of random variables.

Example 4.3 *Let $\{Z_t\}$ be i.i.d. random variables with mean μ and finite variance $\sigma^2 > 0$. Define*

$$b_n \equiv \frac{\bar{Z}_n - E(\bar{Z}_n)}{(\text{var}(\bar{Z}_n))^{1/2}} = n^{-1/2} \sum_{t=1}^{n} (Z_t - \mu)/\sigma.$$

Then by the Lindeberg-Lévy central limit theorem (Theorem 5.2), $b_n \overset{A}{\sim} N(0,1)$.

In other words, the sample mean $\bar{Z}_n$ of i.i.d. observations, when standardized, has a distribution that approaches the standard normal distribution. This result actually holds under rather general conditions on the sequence $\{Z_t\}$. The conditions under which this convergence occurs are studied at length in the next chapter. In this chapter, we simply assume that such conditions are satisfied, so convergence in distribution is guaranteed.

Convergence in distribution is meaningful even when the limiting distribution is that of a degenerate random variable.

Lemma 4.4 *Suppose $b_n \xrightarrow{p} b$ (a constant). Then $b_n \overset{A}{\sim} F_b$, where F_b is the distribution function of a random variable Z that takes the value b with probability one (i.e., $b_n \xrightarrow{d} b$). Also, if $b_n \overset{A}{\sim} F_b$, then $b_n \xrightarrow{p} b$.*

Proof. See Rao (1973, p. 120). ∎

In other words, convergence in probability to a constant implies convergence in distribution to that constant. The converse is also true.

A useful implication of convergence in distribution is the following lemma.

Lemma 4.5 *If* $b_n \xrightarrow{d} \mathcal{Z}$, *then* b_n *is* $O_p(1)$.

Proof. Recall that b_n is $O_p(1)$ if, given any $\delta > 0$, $P\left[|b_n| > \Delta_\delta\right] < \delta$ for some $\Delta_\delta < \infty$ and all $n \geq N_\delta$. Because $b_n \to \mathcal{Z}$, $P\left[|b_n| > \Delta_\delta\right] \to P\left[|\mathcal{Z}| > \Delta_\delta\right]$, provided (without loss of generality) that Δ_δ and $-\Delta_\delta$ are continuity points of the distribution of $\mathcal{Z}$. Thus $|P[|b_n| > \Delta_\delta] - P[|\mathcal{Z}| > \Delta_\delta]| < \delta$ for all $n \geq N_\delta$, so that $P[|b_n| > \Delta_\delta] < \delta + P[|\mathcal{Z}| > \Delta_\delta]$ for all $n \geq N_\delta$. Because $P[|\mathcal{Z}| > \Delta_\delta] < \delta$ for Δ_δ sufficiently large, we have $P[|b_n| > \Delta_\delta] < 2\delta$ for Δ_δ sufficiently large and all $n \geq N_\delta$. ∎

This allows us to establish the next useful lemma.

Lemma 4.6 (Product rule) *Recall from Corollary 2.36 that if* $\mathbf{A}_n = o_p(1)$ *and* $\mathbf{b}_n = O_p(1)$, *then* $\mathbf{A}_n\mathbf{b}_n = o_p(1)$. *Hence, if* $\mathbf{A}_n \xrightarrow{p} \mathbf{0}$ *and* $\mathbf{b}_n \xrightarrow{d} \boldsymbol{\mathcal{Z}}$, *then* $\mathbf{A}_n\mathbf{b}_n \xrightarrow{p} \mathbf{0}$.

In turn, this result is often used in conjunction with the following result, which is one of the most useful of those relating convergence in probability and convergence in distribution.

Lemma 4.7 (Asymptotic equivalence) *Let* $\{\mathbf{a}_n\}$ *and* $\{\mathbf{b}_n\}$ *be two sequences of random vectors. If* $\mathbf{a}_n - \mathbf{b}_n \xrightarrow{p} \mathbf{0}$ *and* $\mathbf{b}_n \xrightarrow{d} \boldsymbol{\mathcal{Z}}$, *then* $\mathbf{a}_n \xrightarrow{d} \boldsymbol{\mathcal{Z}}$.

Proof. See Rao (1973, p. 123). ∎

This result is helpful in situations in which we wish to find the asymptotic distribution of $\mathbf{a}_n$ but cannot easily do so directly. Often, however, it is easy to find a $\mathbf{b}_n$ that has a known asymptotic distribution and that satisfies $\mathbf{a}_n - \mathbf{b}_n \xrightarrow{p} \mathbf{0}$. Lemma 4.7 then ensures that $\mathbf{a}_n$ has the same limiting distribution as $\mathbf{b}_n$ and we say that $\mathbf{a}_n$ is "asymptotically equivalent" to $\mathbf{b}_n$. The joint use of Lemmas 4.6 and 4.7 is the key to the proof of the asymptotic normality results for the OLS and IV estimators.

Another useful tool in the study of convergence in distribution is the characteristic function.

Definition 4.8 *Let* $\boldsymbol{\mathcal{Z}}$ *be a* $k \times 1$ *random vector with distribution function* F. *The* characteristic function *of* $\boldsymbol{\mathcal{Z}}$ *is defined as* $f(\boldsymbol{\lambda}) \equiv E(\exp(i\boldsymbol{\lambda}'\boldsymbol{\mathcal{Z}}))$, *where* $i^2 = -1$ *and* $\boldsymbol{\lambda}$ *is a* $k \times 1$ *real vector.*

Example 4.9 *Let* $\mathcal{Z}$ *be a nonstochastic real number,* $\mathcal{Z} = c$. *Then* $f(\lambda) = E(\exp(i\lambda\mathcal{Z})) = E(\exp(i\lambda c)) = \exp(i\lambda c)$.

Example 4.10 (*i*) *Let* $\mathcal{Z} \sim N(\mu, \sigma^2)$. *Then* $f(\lambda) = \exp(i\lambda\mu - \lambda^2\sigma^2/2)$. (*ii*) *Let* $\boldsymbol{\mathcal{Z}} \sim N(\boldsymbol{\mu}, \boldsymbol{\Sigma})$, *where* $\boldsymbol{\mu}$ *is* $k \times 1$ *and* $\boldsymbol{\Sigma}$ *is* $k \times k$. *Then* $f(\boldsymbol{\lambda}) = \exp(i\boldsymbol{\lambda}'\boldsymbol{\mu} - \boldsymbol{\lambda}'\boldsymbol{\Sigma}\boldsymbol{\lambda}/2)$.

A useful table of characteristic functions is given by Lukacs (1970, p. 18).

Because the characteristic function is the Fourier transformation of the probability density function, it has the property that any characteristic function uniquely determines a distribution function, as formally expressed by the next result.

Theorem 4.11 (Uniqueness theorem) *Two distribution functions are identical if and only if their characteristic functions are identical.*

Proof. See Lukacs (1974, p. 14). ■

Thus the behavior of a random variable can be studied either through its distribution function or its characteristic function, whichever is more convenient.

Example 4.12 *The distribution of a linear transformation of a random variable is easily found using the characteristic function. Consider* $\boldsymbol{\mathcal{Y}} = \mathbf{A}\boldsymbol{\mathcal{Z}}$*, where* $\mathbf{A}$ *is a* $q \times k$ *matrix and* $\boldsymbol{\mathcal{Z}}$ *is a random k-vector. Let* $\boldsymbol{\theta}$ *be* $q \times 1$*. Then*

$$\begin{aligned} f_{\boldsymbol{\mathcal{Y}}}(\boldsymbol{\theta}) &= E(\exp(i\boldsymbol{\theta}'\boldsymbol{\mathcal{Y}})) = E(\exp(i\boldsymbol{\theta}'\mathbf{A}\boldsymbol{\mathcal{Z}})) \\ &= E(\exp(i\boldsymbol{\lambda}'\boldsymbol{\mathcal{Z}})) = f_{\boldsymbol{\mathcal{Z}}}(\boldsymbol{\lambda}), \end{aligned}$$

defining $\boldsymbol{\lambda} = \mathbf{A}'\boldsymbol{\theta}$*. Hence if* $\boldsymbol{\mathcal{Z}} \sim N(\boldsymbol{\mu},\boldsymbol{\Sigma})$*,*

$$\begin{aligned} f_{\boldsymbol{\mathcal{Y}}}(\boldsymbol{\theta}) &= f_{\boldsymbol{\mathcal{Z}}}(\boldsymbol{\lambda}) = \exp(i\boldsymbol{\lambda}'\boldsymbol{\mu} - \boldsymbol{\lambda}'\boldsymbol{\Sigma}\boldsymbol{\lambda}/2) \\ &= \exp(i\boldsymbol{\theta}'\mathbf{A}\boldsymbol{\mu} - \boldsymbol{\theta}'\mathbf{A}\boldsymbol{\Sigma}\mathbf{A}'\boldsymbol{\theta}/2), \end{aligned}$$

so that $\boldsymbol{\mathcal{Y}} \sim N(\mathbf{A}\boldsymbol{\mu}, \mathbf{A}\boldsymbol{\Sigma}\mathbf{A}')$ *by the uniqueness theorem.*

Other useful facts regarding characteristic functions are the following.

Proposition 4.13 *Let* $\mathcal{Y} = a\mathcal{Z} + b$*,* $a, b \in \mathbb{R}$*. Then*

$$f_{\mathcal{Y}}(\lambda) = f_{\mathcal{Z}}(a\lambda)\exp(i\lambda b).$$

Proof.

$$\begin{aligned} f_{\mathcal{Y}}(\lambda) &= E(\exp(i\lambda\mathcal{Y})) = E(\exp(i\lambda(a\mathcal{Z} + b))) \\ &= E(\exp(i\lambda a\mathcal{Z})\exp(i\lambda b)) \\ &= E(\exp(i\lambda a\mathcal{Z}))\exp(i\lambda b) = f_{\mathcal{Z}}(\lambda a)\exp(i\lambda b). \end{aligned}$$

■

Proposition 4.14 *Let $\mathcal{Y}$ and $\mathcal{Z}$ be independent. Then if $\mathcal{X} = \mathcal{Y} + \mathcal{Z}$, $f_{\mathcal{X}}(\lambda) = f_{\mathcal{Y}}(\lambda) f_{\mathcal{Z}}(\lambda)$.*

Proof.

$$\begin{aligned} f_{\mathcal{X}}(\lambda) &= E(\exp(i\lambda\mathcal{X})) = E(\exp(i\lambda(\mathcal{Y}+\mathcal{Z}))) \\ &= E(\exp(i\lambda\mathcal{Y})\exp(i\lambda\mathcal{Z})) \\ &= E(\exp(i\lambda\mathcal{Y}))E(\exp(i\lambda\mathcal{Z})) \end{aligned}$$

by independence. Hence $f_{\mathcal{X}}(\lambda) = f_{\mathcal{Y}}(\lambda) f_{\mathcal{Z}}(\lambda)$. ∎

Proposition 4.15 *If the kth moment μ_k of a distribution function F exists, then the characteristic function f of F can be differentiated k times and $f^{(k)}(0) = i^k \mu_k$, where $f^{(k)}$ is the kth derivative of f.*

Proof. This is an immediate corollary of Lukacs (1970, Corollary 3 to Theorem 2.3.1, p. 22). ∎

Example 4.16 *Suppose that $\mathcal{Z} \sim N(0, \sigma^2)$. Then $f'(0) = 0$, $f''(0) = -\sigma^2$, $f'''(0) = 0$, etc.*

The main result of use in studying convergence in distribution is the following.

Theorem 4.17 (Continuity theorem) *Let $\{\mathbf{b}_n\}$ be a sequence of random $k \times 1$ vectors with characteristic functions $\{f_n(\boldsymbol{\lambda})\}$. If $\mathbf{b}_n \xrightarrow{d} \boldsymbol{\mathcal{Z}}$, then for every $\boldsymbol{\lambda}$, $f_n(\boldsymbol{\lambda}) \to f(\boldsymbol{\lambda})$, where $f(\boldsymbol{\lambda}) = E(\exp(i\boldsymbol{\lambda}'\boldsymbol{\mathcal{Z}}))$. Further, if for every $\boldsymbol{\lambda}$, $f_n(\boldsymbol{\lambda}) \to f(\boldsymbol{\lambda})$ and f is continuous at $\boldsymbol{\lambda} = \mathbf{0}$, then $\mathbf{b}_n \xrightarrow{d} \boldsymbol{\mathcal{Z}}$, where $f(\boldsymbol{\lambda}) = E(\exp(i\boldsymbol{\lambda}'\boldsymbol{\mathcal{Z}}))$.*

Proof. See Lukacs (1970, pp. 49–50). ∎

This result essentially says that convergence in distribution is equivalent to convergence of characteristic functions. The usefulness of the result is that often it is much easier to study the limiting behavior of characteristic functions than distribution functions. If the sequence of characteristic functions f_n converges to a function f that is continuous at $\boldsymbol{\lambda} = \mathbf{0}$, this theorem guarantees that the function f is a characteristic function and that the limiting distribution F of $\mathbf{b}_n$ is that corresponding to the characteristic function $f(\boldsymbol{\lambda})$.

In all the cases that follow, the limiting distribution F will be either that of a degenerate random variable (following from convergence in probability to a constant) or a multivariate normal distribution (following from an appropriate central limit theorem). In the latter case, it is often convenient to standardize the random variables so that the asymptotic distribution is unit multivariate normal. To do this we can use the matrix square root.

Exercise 4.18 *Prove the following. Let* $\mathbf{V}$ *be a positive (semi) definite symmetric matrix. Then there exists a positive (semi) definite symmetric matrix square root* $\mathbf{V}^{1/2}$ *such that the elements of* $\mathbf{V}^{1/2}$ *are continuous functions of* $\mathbf{V}$ *and* $\mathbf{V}^{1/2}\mathbf{V}^{1/2} = \mathbf{V}$. *(Hint: Express* $\mathbf{V}$ *as* $\mathbf{V} = \mathbf{Q}'\mathbf{D}\mathbf{Q}$, *where* $\mathbf{Q}$ *is an orthogonal matrix and* $\mathbf{D}$ *is diagonal with the eigenvalues of* $\mathbf{V}$ *along the diagonal.)*

Exercise 4.19 *Show that if* $\mathcal{Z} \sim N(\mathbf{0}, \mathbf{V})$, *then* $\mathbf{V}^{-1/2}\mathcal{Z} \sim N(\mathbf{0}, \mathbf{I})$, *provided* $\mathbf{V}$ *is positive definite, where* $\mathbf{V}^{-1/2} = (\mathbf{V}^{1/2})^{-1}$.

Definition 4.20 *Let* $\{\mathbf{b}_n\}$ *be a sequence of random vectors. If there exists a sequence of matrices* $\{\mathbf{V}_n\}$ *such that* $\mathbf{V}_n$ *is nonsingular for all* n *sufficiently large and* $\mathbf{V}_n^{-1/2}\mathbf{b}_n \overset{A}{\sim} N(\mathbf{0}, \mathbf{I})$, *then* $\mathbf{V}_n$ *is called the* asymptotic covariance matrix *of* $\mathbf{b}_n$, *denoted* $\text{avar}(\mathbf{b}_n)$.

When $\text{var}(\mathbf{b}_n)$ is finite, we can usually define $\mathbf{V}_n = \text{var}(\mathbf{b}_n)$. Note that the behavior of $\mathbf{b}_n$ is not restricted to require that $\mathbf{V}_n$ converge to any limit, although it may. Generally, however, we will at least require that the smallest eigenvalues of $\mathbf{V}_n$ and $\mathbf{V}_n^{-1}$ are uniformly bounded away from zero for all n sufficiently large. Even when $\text{var}(\mathbf{b}_n)$ is not finite, the asymptotic covariance matrix can exist, although in such cases we cannot set $\mathbf{V}_n = \text{var}(\mathbf{b}_n)$.

Example 4.21 *Define* $b_n = \mathcal{Z} + \mathcal{Y}/n$, *where* $\mathcal{Z} \sim N(0, 1)$ *and* $\mathcal{Y}$ *is Cauchy, independent of* $\mathcal{Z}$. *Then* $\text{var}(b_n)$ *is infinite for every* n, *but* $b_n \overset{A}{\sim} N(0, 1)$ *as a consequence of Lemma 4.7. Hence* $\text{avar}(b_n) = 1$.

Given a sequence $\{\mathbf{V}_n^{-1/2}\mathbf{b}_n\}$ that converges in distribution, we shall often be interested in the behavior of linear combinations of $\mathbf{b}_n$, say, $\{\mathbf{A}_n\mathbf{b}_n\}$, where $\mathbf{A}_n$, like $\mathbf{V}_n^{-1/2}$, is not required to converge to a particular limit. We can use characteristic functions to study the behavior of these sequences by making use of the following corollary to the continuity theorem.

Corollary 4.22 *If* $\boldsymbol{\lambda} \in \mathbb{R}^k$ *and a sequence* $\{f_n(\boldsymbol{\lambda})\}$ *of characteristic functions converges to a characteristic function* $f(\boldsymbol{\lambda})$, *then the convergence is uniform in every compact subset of* $\mathbb{R}^k$.

Proof. This is a straightforward extension of Lukacs (1970, p. 50). ■

This result says that in any compact subset of $\mathbb{R}^k$ the distance between $f_n(\boldsymbol{\lambda})$ and $f(\boldsymbol{\lambda})$ does not depend on $\boldsymbol{\lambda}$, but only on n. This fact is crucial to establishing the next result.

Lemma 4.23 *Let $\{\mathbf{b}_n\}$ be a sequence of random $k \times 1$ vectors with characteristic functions $\{f_n(\boldsymbol{\lambda})\}$, and suppose $f_n(\boldsymbol{\lambda}) \to f(\boldsymbol{\lambda})$. If $\{\mathbf{A}_n\}$ is any sequence of $q \times k$ nonstochastic matrices such that $\mathbf{A}_n = O(1)$, then the sequence $\{\mathbf{A}_n\mathbf{b}_n\}$ has characteristic functions $\{f_n^*(\boldsymbol{\theta})\}$, where $\boldsymbol{\theta}$ is $q \times 1$, such that for every $\boldsymbol{\theta}$, $f_n^*(\boldsymbol{\theta}) - f(\mathbf{A}_n'\boldsymbol{\theta}) \to 0$.*

Proof. From Example 4.12, $f_n^*(\boldsymbol{\theta}) = f_n(\mathbf{A}_n'\boldsymbol{\theta})$. For fixed $\boldsymbol{\theta}$, $\boldsymbol{\lambda}_n \equiv \mathbf{A}_n'\boldsymbol{\theta}$ takes values in a compact region of $\mathbb{R}^k$, say, $\mathcal{N}_\theta$, for all n sufficiently large because $\mathbf{A}_n = O(1)$. Because $f_n(\boldsymbol{\lambda}) \to f(\boldsymbol{\lambda})$, we have $f_n(\boldsymbol{\lambda}_n) - f(\boldsymbol{\lambda}_n) \to 0$ uniformly for all $\boldsymbol{\lambda}_n$ in $\mathcal{N}_\theta$, by Corollary 4.22. Hence for fixed $\boldsymbol{\theta}$, $f_n(\mathbf{A}_n'\boldsymbol{\theta}) - f(\mathbf{A}_n'\boldsymbol{\theta}) = f_n^*(\boldsymbol{\theta}) - f(\mathbf{A}_n'\boldsymbol{\theta}) \to 0$ for any $O(1)$ sequence $\{\mathbf{A}_n\}$. Because $\boldsymbol{\theta}$ is arbitrary, the result follows. ∎

The following consequence of this result is used many times below.

Corollary 4.24 *Let $\{\mathbf{b}_n\}$ be a sequence of random $k \times 1$ vectors such that $\mathbf{V}_n^{-1/2}\mathbf{b}_n \stackrel{A}{\sim} N(\mathbf{0}, \mathbf{I})$, where $\{\mathbf{V}_n\}$ and $\{\mathbf{V}_n^{-1}\}$ are $O(1)$. Let $\{\mathbf{A}_n\}$ be a $O(1)$ sequence of (nonstochastic) $q \times k$ matrices with full row rank q for all n sufficiently large, uniformly in n. Then the sequence $\{\mathbf{A}_n\mathbf{b}_n\}$ is such that $\boldsymbol{\Gamma}_n^{-1/2}\mathbf{A}_n\mathbf{b}_n \stackrel{A}{\sim} N(\mathbf{0}, \mathbf{I})$, where $\boldsymbol{\Gamma}_n \equiv \mathbf{A}_n\mathbf{V}_n\mathbf{A}_n'$ and $\boldsymbol{\Gamma}_n$ and $\boldsymbol{\Gamma}_n^{-1}$ are $O(1)$.*

Proof. $\boldsymbol{\Gamma}_n = O(1)$ by Lemma 2.19. $\boldsymbol{\Gamma}_n^{-1} = O(1)$ because $\boldsymbol{\Gamma}_n = O(1)$ and $\det(\boldsymbol{\Gamma}_n) > \delta > 0$ for all n sufficiently large, given the conditions on $\{\mathbf{A}_n\}$ and $\{\mathbf{V}_n\}$. Let $f_n^*(\boldsymbol{\theta})$ be the characteristic function of $\boldsymbol{\Gamma}_n^{-1/2}\mathbf{A}_n\mathbf{b}_n = \boldsymbol{\Gamma}_n^{-1/2}\mathbf{A}_n\mathbf{V}_n^{1/2}\mathbf{V}_n^{-1/2}\mathbf{b}_n$. Because $\boldsymbol{\Gamma}_n^{-1/2}\mathbf{A}_n\mathbf{V}_n^{1/2} = O(1)$, Lemma 4.23 applies, implying $f_n^*(\boldsymbol{\theta}) - f(\mathbf{V}_n^{1/2}\mathbf{A}_n'\boldsymbol{\Gamma}_n^{-1/2}\boldsymbol{\theta}) \to 0$, where $f(\boldsymbol{\lambda}) = \exp(-\boldsymbol{\lambda}'\boldsymbol{\lambda}/2)$, the limiting characteristic function of $\mathbf{V}_n^{-1/2}\mathbf{b}_n$. Now $f(\mathbf{V}_n^{1/2}\mathbf{A}_n'\boldsymbol{\Gamma}_n^{-1/2}\boldsymbol{\theta}) = \exp(-\boldsymbol{\theta}'\boldsymbol{\Gamma}_n^{-1/2}\mathbf{A}_n\mathbf{V}_n\mathbf{A}_n'\boldsymbol{\Gamma}_n^{-1/2}\boldsymbol{\theta}/2) = \exp(-\boldsymbol{\theta}'\boldsymbol{\theta}/2)$ by definition of $\boldsymbol{\Gamma}_n^{-1/2}$. Hence $f_n^*(\boldsymbol{\lambda}) - \exp(-\boldsymbol{\theta}'\boldsymbol{\theta}/2) \to 0$, so $\boldsymbol{\Gamma}_n^{-1/2}\mathbf{A}_n\mathbf{b}_n \stackrel{A}{\sim} N(\mathbf{0}, \mathbf{I})$ by the continuity theorem (Theorem 4.17). ∎

This result allows us to complete the proof of the following general asymptotic normality result for the least squares estimator.

Theorem 4.25 *Given*

(i) $\mathbf{Y}_t = \mathbf{X}_t'\boldsymbol{\beta}_o + \varepsilon_t, \quad t = 1, 2, \ldots, \boldsymbol{\beta}_o \in \mathbb{R}^k$;

(ii) $\mathbf{V}_n^{-1/2}n^{-1/2}\mathbf{X}'\boldsymbol{\varepsilon} \stackrel{A}{\sim} N(\mathbf{0}, \mathbf{I})$, *where* $\mathbf{V}_n \equiv \text{var}(n^{-1/2}\mathbf{X}'\boldsymbol{\varepsilon})$ *is* $O(1)$ *and uniformly positive definite;*

(*iii*) $\mathbf{X}'\mathbf{X}/n - \mathbf{M}_n \xrightarrow{p} \mathbf{0}$, *where* $\mathbf{M}_n = E(\mathbf{X}'\mathbf{X}/n)$ *is* $O(1)$ *and uniformly positive definite.*

Then

$$\mathbf{D}_n^{-1/2}\sqrt{n}(\hat{\boldsymbol{\beta}}_n - \boldsymbol{\beta}_o) \overset{A}{\sim} N(\mathbf{0}, \mathbf{I}),$$

where $\mathbf{D}_n \equiv \mathbf{M}_n^{-1}\mathbf{V}_n\mathbf{M}_n^{-1}$ *and* $\mathbf{D}_n^{-1}$ *are* $O(1)$. *Suppose in addition that*

(*iv*) *there exists a matrix* $\hat{\mathbf{V}}_n$ *positive semidefinite and symmetric such that* $\hat{\mathbf{V}}_n - \mathbf{V}_n \xrightarrow{p} \mathbf{0}$. *Then* $\hat{\mathbf{D}}_n - \mathbf{D}_n \xrightarrow{p} \mathbf{0}$, *where*

$$\hat{\mathbf{D}}_n \equiv (\mathbf{X}'\mathbf{X}/n)^{-1}\hat{\mathbf{V}}_n(\mathbf{X}'\mathbf{X}/n)^{-1}.$$

Proof. Because $\mathbf{X}'\mathbf{X}/n - \mathbf{M}_n \xrightarrow{p} \mathbf{0}$ and $\mathbf{M}_n$ is finite and nonsingular by (*iii*), $(\mathbf{X}'\mathbf{X}/n)^{-1}$ and $\hat{\boldsymbol{\beta}}_n$ exist in probability. Given (*i*) and the existence of $(\mathbf{X}'\mathbf{X}/n)^{-1}$,

$$\sqrt{n}(\hat{\boldsymbol{\beta}}_n - \boldsymbol{\beta}_o) = (\mathbf{X}'\mathbf{X}/n)^{-1}n^{-1/2}\mathbf{X}'\boldsymbol{\varepsilon}.$$

Hence, given (*ii*),

$$\sqrt{n}(\hat{\boldsymbol{\beta}}_n - \boldsymbol{\beta}_o) - \mathbf{M}_n^{-1}n^{-1/2}\mathbf{X}'\boldsymbol{\varepsilon} = [(\mathbf{X}'\mathbf{X}/n)^{-1} - \mathbf{M}_n^{-1}]\mathbf{V}_n^{1/2}\mathbf{V}_n^{-1/2}n^{-1/2}\mathbf{X}'\boldsymbol{\varepsilon},$$

or, premultiplying by $\mathbf{D}_n^{-1/2}$,

$$\mathbf{D}_n^{-1/2}\sqrt{n}(\hat{\boldsymbol{\beta}}_n - \boldsymbol{\beta}_o) - \mathbf{D}_n^{-1/2}\mathbf{M}_n^{-1}n^{-1/2}\mathbf{X}'\boldsymbol{\varepsilon} = \mathbf{D}_n^{-1/2}[(\mathbf{X}'\mathbf{X}/n)^{-1} - \mathbf{M}_n^{-1}]\mathbf{V}_n^{1/2}\mathbf{V}_n^{-1/2}n^{-1/2}\mathbf{X}'\boldsymbol{\varepsilon}.$$

The desired result will follow by applying the product rule Lemma 4.6 to the line immediately above, and the asymptotic equivalence Lemma 4.7 to the preceding line. Now $\mathbf{V}_n^{-1/2}n^{-1/2}\mathbf{X}'\boldsymbol{\varepsilon} \overset{A}{\sim} N(\mathbf{0}, \mathbf{I})$ by (*ii*); further, $\mathbf{D}_n^{-1/2}[(\mathbf{X}'\mathbf{X}/n)^{-1} - \mathbf{M}_n^{-1}]\mathbf{V}_n^{1/2}$ is $o_p(1)$ because $\mathbf{D}_n^{-1/2}$ and $\mathbf{V}_n^{1/2}$ are $O(1)$ given (*ii*) and (*iii*), and $[(\mathbf{X}'\mathbf{X}/n)^{-1} - \mathbf{M}_n^{-1}]$ is $o_p(1)$ by Proposition 2.30 given (*iii*). Hence, by Lemma 4.5,

$$\mathbf{D}_n^{-1/2}\sqrt{n}(\hat{\boldsymbol{\beta}}_n - \boldsymbol{\beta}_o) - \mathbf{D}_n^{-1/2}\mathbf{M}_n^{-1}n^{-1/2}\mathbf{X}'\boldsymbol{\varepsilon} \xrightarrow{p} \mathbf{0}.$$

By Lemma 4.7, the asymptotic distribution of $\mathbf{D}_n^{-1/2}\sqrt{n}(\hat{\boldsymbol{\beta}}_n - \boldsymbol{\beta}_o)$ is the same as that of $\mathbf{D}_n^{-1/2}\mathbf{M}_n^{-1}n^{-1/2}\mathbf{X}'\boldsymbol{\varepsilon}$. We find the asymptotic distribution of this random variable by applying Corollary 4.24, which immediately yields $\mathbf{D}_n^{-1/2}\mathbf{M}_n^{-1}n^{-1/2}\mathbf{X}'\boldsymbol{\varepsilon} \overset{A}{\sim} N(\mathbf{0}, \mathbf{I})$.

Because (*ii*), (*iii*), and (*iv*) hold, $\hat{\mathbf{D}}_n - \mathbf{D}_n \xrightarrow{p} \mathbf{0}$ is an immediate consequence of Proposition 2.30. ■

The structure of this result is very straightforward. Given the linear data generating process, we require only that $(\mathbf{X}'\mathbf{X}/n)$ and $(\mathbf{X}'\mathbf{X}/n)^{-1}$ are $O_p(1)$ and that $n^{-1/2}\mathbf{X}'\boldsymbol{\varepsilon}$ is asymptotically unit normal after standardizing by the inverse square root of its asymptotic covariance matrix. The asymptotic covariance (dispersion) matrix of $\sqrt{n}(\hat{\boldsymbol{\beta}}_n - \boldsymbol{\beta}_o)$ is $\mathbf{D}_n$, which can be consistently estimated by $\hat{\mathbf{D}}_n$. Note that this result allows the regressors to be stochastic and imposes no restriction on the serial correlation or heteroskedasticity of ε_t, except that needed to ensure that (*ii*) holds. As we shall see in the next chapter, only mild restrictions need to be imposed in guaranteeing (*ii*).

In special cases, it may be known that $\mathbf{V}_n$ has a special form. For example, when ε_t is an i.i.d. scalar with $E(\varepsilon_t) = 0$, $E(\varepsilon_t^2) = \sigma_o^2$, and $\mathbf{X}_t$ is nonstochastic, then $\mathbf{V}_n = \sigma_o^2\mathbf{X}'\mathbf{X}/n$. Finding a consistent estimator for $\mathbf{V}_n$ then requires no more than finding a consistent estimator for σ_o^2.

In more general cases considered below it is often possible to write

$$\mathbf{V}_n = E(\mathbf{X}'\boldsymbol{\varepsilon}\boldsymbol{\varepsilon}'\mathbf{X}/n) = E(\mathbf{X}'\boldsymbol{\Omega}_n\mathbf{X}/n).$$

Finding a consistent estimator for $\mathbf{V}_n$ in these cases is made easier by the knowledge of the structure of $\boldsymbol{\Omega}_n$. However, even when $\boldsymbol{\Omega}_n$ is unknown, it turns out that consistent estimators for $\mathbf{V}_n$ are generally available. The conditions under which $\mathbf{V}_n$ can be consistently estimated are treated in Chapter 6.

A result analogous to Theorem 4.25 is available for instrumental variables estimators. Because the proof follows that of Theorem 4.25 very closely, proof of the following result is left as an exercise.

Exercise 4.26 *Prove the following result. Given*

(*i*) $\mathbf{Y}_t = \mathbf{X}_t'\boldsymbol{\beta}_o + \varepsilon_t, \quad t = 1, 2, \ldots, \ \boldsymbol{\beta}_o \in \mathbb{R}^k$;

(*ii*) $\mathbf{V}_n^{-1/2}n^{-1/2}\mathbf{Z}'\boldsymbol{\varepsilon} \overset{A}{\sim} N(\mathbf{0}, \mathbf{I})$, *where* $\mathbf{V}_n \equiv \text{var}(n^{-1/2}\mathbf{Z}'\boldsymbol{\varepsilon})$ *is* $O(1)$ *and uniformly positive definite;*

(*iii*) (*a*) $\mathbf{Z}'\mathbf{X}/n - \mathbf{Q}_n \xrightarrow{p} \mathbf{0}$, *where* $\mathbf{Q}_n \equiv E(\mathbf{Z}'\mathbf{X}/n)$ *is* $O(1)$ *with uniformly full column rank;*

(*b*) *There exists* $\hat{\mathbf{P}}_n$ *such that* $\hat{\mathbf{P}}_n - \mathbf{P}_n \xrightarrow{p} \mathbf{0}$ *and* $\mathbf{P}_n = O(1)$ *and is symmetric and uniformly positive definite.*

Then $\mathbf{D}_n^{-1/2}\sqrt{n}(\tilde{\boldsymbol{\beta}}_n - \boldsymbol{\beta}_o) \overset{A}{\sim} N(\mathbf{0}, \mathbf{I})$, *where*

$$\mathbf{D}_n \equiv (\mathbf{Q}_n'\mathbf{P}_n\mathbf{Q}_n)^{-1}\mathbf{Q}_n'\mathbf{P}_n\mathbf{V}_n\mathbf{P}_n\mathbf{Q}_n(\mathbf{Q}_n'\mathbf{P}_n\mathbf{Q}_n)^{-1}$$

and $\mathbf{D}_n^{-1}$ *are* $O(1)$.

Suppose in addition that

(*iv*) *There exists a matrix* $\hat{\mathbf{V}}_n$ *positive semidefinite and symmetric such that* $\hat{\mathbf{V}}_n - \mathbf{V}_n \xrightarrow{p} \mathbf{0}$.

Then $\hat{\mathbf{D}}_n - \mathbf{D}_n \xrightarrow{p} \mathbf{0}$, *where*

$$\hat{\mathbf{D}}_n = (\mathbf{X}'\mathbf{Z}\hat{\mathbf{P}}_n\mathbf{Z}'\mathbf{X}/n^2)^{-1}(\mathbf{X}'\mathbf{Z}/n)\hat{\mathbf{P}}_n\hat{\mathbf{V}}_n\hat{\mathbf{P}}_n(\mathbf{Z}'\mathbf{X}/n)(\mathbf{X}'\mathbf{Z}\hat{\mathbf{P}}_n\mathbf{Z}'\mathbf{X}/n^2)^{-1}.$$

4.2 Hypothesis Testing

A direct and very important use of the asymptotic normality of a given estimator is in hypothesis testing. Often, hypotheses of interest can be expressed in terms of linear combinations of the parameters as

$$\mathbf{R}\boldsymbol{\beta}_o = \mathbf{r},$$

where $\mathbf{R}$ is a given $q \times k$ matrix and $\mathbf{r}$ is a given $q \times 1$ vector that, through $\mathbf{R}\boldsymbol{\beta}_o = \mathbf{r}$, specify the hypotheses of interest. For example, if the hypothesis is that the elements of $\boldsymbol{\beta}_o$ sum to unity, $\mathbf{R} = [1, \ldots, 1]$ and $\mathbf{r} = 1$.

Several different approaches can be taken in computing a statistic to test the null hypothesis $\mathbf{R}\boldsymbol{\beta}_o = \mathbf{r}$ versus the alternative $\mathbf{R}\boldsymbol{\beta}_o \neq \mathbf{r}$. The methods that we consider here involve the use of Wald, Lagrange multiplier, and quasi-likelihood ratio statistics.

Although the approaches to forming the test statistics differ, the way that we determine their asymptotic distributions is the same. In each case we exploit an underlying asymptotic normality property to obtain a statistic distributed asymptotically as chi-squared (χ^2). To do this we use the following results.

Lemma 4.27 *Let* $\mathbf{g} : \mathbb{R}^k \to \mathbb{R}^l$ *be continuous on* $\mathbb{R}^k$ *and let* $\mathbf{b}_n \xrightarrow{d} \boldsymbol{\mathcal{Z}}$, *a* $k \times 1$ *random vector. Then* $\mathbf{g}(\mathbf{b}_n) \to \mathbf{g}(\boldsymbol{\mathcal{Z}})$.

Proof. See Rao (1973, p. 124). ∎

Corollary 4.28 *Let* $\mathbf{V}_n^{-1/2}\mathbf{b}_n \overset{A}{\sim} N(\mathbf{0}, \mathbf{I}_k)$. *Then*

$$\mathbf{b}_n'\mathbf{V}_n^{-1}\mathbf{b}_n = \mathbf{b}_n'\mathbf{V}_n^{-1/2}\mathbf{V}_n^{-1/2}\mathbf{b}_n \overset{A}{\sim} \chi_k^2,$$

where χ_k^2 *is a chi-squared random variable with* k *degrees of freedom.*

Proof. By hypothesis, $\mathbf{V}_n^{-1/2}\mathbf{b}_n \xrightarrow{d} \mathcal{Z} \sim N(\mathbf{0}, \mathbf{I}_k)$. The function $g(\mathbf{z}) = \mathbf{z}'\mathbf{z}$ is continuous on $\mathbb{R}^k$. Hence,

$$\mathbf{b}_n'\mathbf{V}_n^{-1}\mathbf{b}_n = g(\mathbf{V}^{-1/2}\mathbf{b}_n) \xrightarrow{d} g(\mathcal{Z}) = \mathcal{Z}'\mathcal{Z} \sim \chi_k^2.$$

■

Typically, $\mathbf{V}_n$ will be unknown, but there will be a consistent estimator $\hat{\mathbf{V}}_n$ such that $\hat{\mathbf{V}}_n - \mathbf{V}_n \xrightarrow{p} \mathbf{0}$. To replace $\mathbf{V}_n$ in Corollary 4.28 with $\hat{\mathbf{V}}_n$, we use the following result.

Lemma 4.29 *Let* $\mathbf{g} : \mathbb{R}^k \to \mathbb{R}^l$ *be continuous on* $\mathbb{R}^k$. *If* $\mathbf{a}_n - \mathbf{b}_n \xrightarrow{p} \mathbf{0}$ *and* $\mathbf{b}_n \xrightarrow{d} \mathcal{Z}$, *then* $\mathbf{g}(\mathbf{a}_n) - \mathbf{g}(\mathbf{b}_n) \xrightarrow{p} \mathbf{0}$ *and* $\mathbf{g}(\mathbf{a}_n) \xrightarrow{d} \mathbf{g}(\mathcal{Z})$.

Proof. Rao (1973, p. 124) proves that $\mathbf{g}(\mathbf{a}_n) - \mathbf{g}(\mathbf{b}_n) \xrightarrow{p} \mathbf{0}$. That $\mathbf{g}(\mathbf{a}_n) \xrightarrow{d} \mathbf{g}(\mathcal{Z})$ follows from Lemmas 4.7 and 4.27. ■

Now we can prove the result that is the basis for finding the asymptotic distribution of the Wald, Lagrange multiplier, and quasi-likelihood ratio tests.

Theorem 4.30 *Let* $\mathbf{V}_n^{-1/2}\mathbf{b}_n \overset{A}{\sim} N(\mathbf{0}, \mathbf{I}_k)$, *and suppose there exists* $\hat{\mathbf{V}}_n$ *positive semidefinite and symmetric such that* $\hat{\mathbf{V}}_n - \mathbf{V}_n \xrightarrow{p} \mathbf{0}$, *where* $\mathbf{V}_n$ *is* $O(1)$, *and for all n sufficiently large,* $\det(\mathbf{V}_n) > \delta > 0$. *Then* $\mathbf{b}_n'\hat{\mathbf{V}}_n^{-1}\mathbf{b}_n \overset{A}{\sim} \chi_k^2$.

Proof. We apply Lemma 4.29. Consider $\hat{\mathbf{V}}_n^{-1/2}\mathbf{b}_n - \mathbf{V}_n^{-1/2}\mathbf{b}_n$, where $\hat{\mathbf{V}}_n^{-1/2}$ exists in probability for all n sufficiently large. Now

$$\hat{\mathbf{V}}_n^{-1/2}\mathbf{b}_n - \mathbf{V}_n^{-1/2}\mathbf{b}_n = (\hat{\mathbf{V}}_n^{-1/2}\mathbf{V}_n^{1/2} - \mathbf{I})\mathbf{V}_n^{-1/2}\mathbf{b}_n.$$

By hypothesis $\mathbf{V}_n^{-1/2}\mathbf{b}_n \overset{A}{\sim} N(\mathbf{0}, \mathbf{I}_k)$ and $\hat{\mathbf{V}}_n^{-1/2}\mathbf{V}_n^{1/2} - \mathbf{I} \xrightarrow{p} \mathbf{0}$ by Proposition 2.30. It follows from the product rule Lemma 4.6 that $\hat{\mathbf{V}}_n^{-1/2}\mathbf{b}_n - \mathbf{V}_n^{-1/2}\mathbf{b}_n \xrightarrow{p} \mathbf{0}$. Because $\mathbf{V}_n^{-1/2}\mathbf{b}_n \xrightarrow{d} \mathcal{Z} \sim N(\mathbf{0}, \mathbf{I}_k)$, it follows from Lemma 4.29 that $\mathbf{b}_n'\hat{\mathbf{V}}_n^{-1}\mathbf{b}_n \overset{A}{\sim} \chi_k^2$. ■

The Wald statistic allows the simplest analysis, although it may or may not be the easiest statistic to compute in a given situation. The motivation for the Wald statistic is that when the null hypothesis is correct, $\mathbf{R}\hat{\boldsymbol{\beta}}_n$ should be close to $\mathbf{R}\boldsymbol{\beta}_o = \mathbf{r}$, so a value of $\mathbf{R}\hat{\boldsymbol{\beta}}_n - \mathbf{r}$ far from zero is evidence against the null hypothesis. To tell how far from zero $\mathbf{R}\hat{\boldsymbol{\beta}}_n - \mathbf{r}$ must be before we reject the null hypothesis, we need to determine its asymptotic distribution.

Theorem 4.31 (Wald test) *Let the conditions of Theorem 4.25 hold and let* $\text{rank}(\mathbf{R}) = q \leq k$. *Then under* H_0: $\mathbf{R}\boldsymbol{\beta}_o = \mathbf{r}$,

(*i*) $\boldsymbol{\Gamma}_n^{-1/2}\sqrt{n}(\mathbf{R}\hat{\boldsymbol{\beta}}_n - \mathbf{r}) \overset{A}{\sim} N(\mathbf{0}, \mathbf{I})$, *where*

$$\boldsymbol{\Gamma}_n \equiv \mathbf{R}\mathbf{D}_n\mathbf{R}' = \mathbf{R}\mathbf{M}_n^{-1}\mathbf{V}_n\mathbf{M}_n^{-1}\mathbf{R}'.$$

(*ii*) *The Wald statistic* $\mathcal{W}_n \equiv n(\mathbf{R}\hat{\boldsymbol{\beta}}_n - \mathbf{r})'\hat{\boldsymbol{\Gamma}}_n^{-1}(\mathbf{R}\hat{\boldsymbol{\beta}}_n - \mathbf{r}) \overset{A}{\sim} \chi_q^2$, *where*

$$\hat{\boldsymbol{\Gamma}}_n \equiv \mathbf{R}\hat{\mathbf{D}}_n\mathbf{R}' = \mathbf{R}(\mathbf{X}'\mathbf{X}/n)^{-1}\hat{\mathbf{V}}_n(\mathbf{X}'\mathbf{X}/n)^{-1}\mathbf{R}'.$$

Proof. (*i*) Under H_0, $\mathbf{R}\hat{\boldsymbol{\beta}}_n - \mathbf{r} = \mathbf{R}(\hat{\boldsymbol{\beta}}_n - \boldsymbol{\beta}_o)$, so

$$\boldsymbol{\Gamma}_n^{-1/2}\sqrt{n}(\mathbf{R}\hat{\boldsymbol{\beta}}_n - \mathbf{r}) = \boldsymbol{\Gamma}_n^{-1/2}\mathbf{R}\mathbf{D}_n^{1/2}\mathbf{D}_n^{-1/2}\sqrt{n}(\hat{\boldsymbol{\beta}}_n - \boldsymbol{\beta}_o).$$

It follows from Corollary 4.24 that $\boldsymbol{\Gamma}_n^{-1/2}\sqrt{n}(\mathbf{R}\hat{\boldsymbol{\beta}}_n - \mathbf{r}) \overset{A}{\sim} N(\mathbf{0}, \mathbf{I})$.

(*ii*) Because $\hat{\mathbf{D}}_n - \mathbf{D}_n \xrightarrow{p} \mathbf{0}$ from Theorem 4.25, it follows from Proposition 2.30 that $\hat{\boldsymbol{\Gamma}}_n - \boldsymbol{\Gamma}_n \xrightarrow{p} \mathbf{0}$. Given the result in (*i*), (*ii*) follows from Theorem 4.30. ∎

This version of the Wald statistic is useful regardless of the presence of heteroskedasticity or serial correlation in the error terms because a consistent estimator ($\hat{\mathbf{V}}_n$) for $\mathbf{V}_n$ is used in computing $\hat{\boldsymbol{\Gamma}}_n$. In the special case when $\mathbf{V}_n$ can be consistently estimated by $\hat{\sigma}_n^2(\mathbf{X}'\mathbf{X}/n)$, the Wald test has the form

$$\mathcal{W}_n = n(\mathbf{R}\hat{\boldsymbol{\beta}}_n - \mathbf{r})'[\mathbf{R}(\mathbf{X}'\mathbf{X}/n)^{-1}\mathbf{R}']^{-1}(\mathbf{R}\hat{\boldsymbol{\beta}}_n - \mathbf{r})/\hat{\sigma}_n^2,$$

which is simply q times the standard F-statistic for testing the hypothesis $\mathbf{R}\boldsymbol{\beta}_o = \mathbf{r}$. The validity of the asymptotic χ_q^2 distribution for this statistic depends crucially on the consistency of $\hat{\mathbf{V}}_n = \hat{\sigma}_n^2(\mathbf{X}'\mathbf{X}/n)$ for $\mathbf{V}_n$; if this $\hat{\mathbf{V}}_n$ is not consistent for $\mathbf{V}_n$, the asymptotic distribution of this form for $\mathcal{W}_n$ is not χ_q^2 in general.

The Wald statistic is most convenient in situations in which the restrictions $\mathbf{R}\boldsymbol{\beta}_o = \mathbf{r}$ are not easy to impose in estimating $\boldsymbol{\beta}_o$. When these restrictions are easily imposed (say, $\mathbf{R}\boldsymbol{\beta}_o = \mathbf{r}$ specifies that the last element of $\boldsymbol{\beta}_o$ is zero), the Lagrange multiplier statistic is more easily computed.

The motivation for the Lagrange multiplier statistic is that a constrained least squares estimator can be obtained by solving the problem

$$\min_{\boldsymbol{\beta}}(\mathbf{Y} - \mathbf{X}\boldsymbol{\beta})'(\mathbf{Y} - \mathbf{X}\boldsymbol{\beta})/n, \qquad \text{s.t. } \mathbf{R}\boldsymbol{\beta} = \mathbf{r},$$

which is equivalent to finding the saddle point of the Lagrangian

$$\mathcal{L} = (\mathbf{Y} - \mathbf{X}\boldsymbol{\beta})'(\mathbf{Y} - \mathbf{X}\boldsymbol{\beta})/n + (\mathbf{R}\boldsymbol{\beta} - \mathbf{r})'\boldsymbol{\lambda}.$$

The Lagrange multipliers $\boldsymbol{\lambda}$ can be thought of as giving the shadow price of the constraint and should therefore be small when the constraint is valid and large otherwise. (See Engle, 1981, for a general discussion.) The Lagrange multiplier test can be thought of as testing the hypothesis that $\boldsymbol{\lambda} = \mathbf{0}$.

The first order conditions are

$$\begin{aligned} \partial\mathcal{L}/\partial\boldsymbol{\beta} &= 2(\mathbf{X}'\mathbf{X}/n)\boldsymbol{\beta} - 2\mathbf{X}'\mathbf{Y}/n + \mathbf{R}'\boldsymbol{\lambda} = \mathbf{0} \\ \partial\mathcal{L}/\partial\boldsymbol{\lambda} &= \mathbf{R}\boldsymbol{\beta} - \mathbf{r} = \mathbf{0}. \end{aligned}$$

To solve for the estimate of the Lagrange multiplier, premultiply the first equation by $\mathbf{R}(\mathbf{X}'\mathbf{X}/n)^{-1}$ and set $\mathbf{R}\boldsymbol{\beta} = \mathbf{r}$. This yields

$$\begin{aligned} \ddot{\boldsymbol{\lambda}}_n &= 2(\mathbf{R}(\mathbf{X}'\mathbf{X}/n)^{-1}\mathbf{R}')^{-1}(\mathbf{R}\hat{\boldsymbol{\beta}}_n - \mathbf{r}) \\ \ddot{\boldsymbol{\beta}}_n &= \hat{\boldsymbol{\beta}}_n - (\mathbf{X}'\mathbf{X}/n)^{-1}\mathbf{R}'\ddot{\boldsymbol{\lambda}}_n/2, \end{aligned}$$

where $\ddot{\boldsymbol{\beta}}_n$ is the constrained least squares estimator (which automatically satisfies $\mathbf{R}\ddot{\boldsymbol{\beta}}_n = \mathbf{r}$). In this form, $\ddot{\boldsymbol{\lambda}}_n$ is simply a nonsingular transformation of $\mathbf{R}\hat{\boldsymbol{\beta}}_n - \mathbf{r}$. This allows the following result to be proved very simply.

Theorem 4.32 (Lagrange multiplier test) *Let the conditions of Theorem 4.25 hold and let* $\operatorname{rank}(\mathbf{R}) = q \le k$. *Then under* H_0: $\mathbf{R}\boldsymbol{\beta}_o = \mathbf{r}$,

(*i*) $\boldsymbol{\Lambda}_n^{-1/2}\sqrt{n}\ddot{\boldsymbol{\lambda}}_n \overset{A}{\sim} N(\mathbf{0}, \mathbf{I})$, *where*

$$\boldsymbol{\Lambda}_n \equiv 4(\mathbf{R}\mathbf{M}_n^{-1}\mathbf{R}')^{-1}\boldsymbol{\Gamma}_n(\mathbf{R}\mathbf{M}_n^{-1}\mathbf{R}')^{-1}$$

and $\boldsymbol{\Gamma}_n$ *is as defined in Theorem 4.31.*

(*ii*) *The Lagrange multiplier statistic* $\mathcal{LM}_n \equiv n\ddot{\boldsymbol{\lambda}}_n'\hat{\boldsymbol{\Lambda}}_n^{-1}\ddot{\boldsymbol{\lambda}}_n \overset{A}{\sim} \chi^2_q$, *where*

$$\begin{aligned} \hat{\boldsymbol{\Lambda}}_n \equiv\ & 4(\mathbf{R}(\mathbf{X}'\mathbf{X}/n)^{-1}\mathbf{R}')^{-1}\mathbf{R}(\mathbf{X}'\mathbf{X}/n)^{-1}\ddot{\mathbf{V}}_n(\mathbf{X}'\mathbf{X}/n)^{-1}\mathbf{R}' \\ & \times(\mathbf{R}(\mathbf{X}'\mathbf{X}/n)^{-1}\mathbf{R}')^{-1} \end{aligned}$$

and $\ddot{\mathbf{V}}_n$ *is computed from the constrained regression such that* $\ddot{\mathbf{V}}_n - \mathbf{V}_n \xrightarrow{p} \mathbf{0}$ *under* H_0.

Proof. (*i*) Consider the difference

$$\begin{aligned} &\boldsymbol{\Lambda}_n^{-1/2}\sqrt{n}\ddot{\boldsymbol{\lambda}}_n - 2\boldsymbol{\Lambda}_n^{-1/2}(\mathbf{R}\mathbf{M}_n^{-1}\mathbf{R}')^{-1}\sqrt{n}(\mathbf{R}\hat{\boldsymbol{\beta}}_n - \mathbf{r}) \\ &= 2\boldsymbol{\Lambda}_n^{-1/2}[(\mathbf{R}(\mathbf{X}'\mathbf{X}/n)^{-1}\mathbf{R}')^{-1} - (\mathbf{R}\mathbf{M}_n^{-1}\mathbf{R}')^{-1}]\boldsymbol{\Gamma}_n^{1/2}\boldsymbol{\Gamma}_n^{-1/2}\sqrt{n}(\mathbf{R}\hat{\boldsymbol{\beta}}_n - \mathbf{r}). \end{aligned}$$

From Theorem 4.31, $\mathbf{\Gamma}_n^{-1/2}\sqrt{n}(\mathbf{R}\hat{\boldsymbol{\beta}}_n - \mathbf{r}) \overset{A}{\sim} N(\mathbf{0}, \mathbf{I})$. Because $(\mathbf{X}'\mathbf{X}/n) - \mathbf{M}_n \xrightarrow{p} \mathbf{0}$, it follows from Proposition 2.30 and the fact that $\mathbf{\Lambda}_n^{-1/2}$ and $\mathbf{\Gamma}_n^{-1/2}$ are $O(1)$ that $\mathbf{\Lambda}_n^{-1/2}[(\mathbf{R}(\mathbf{X}'\mathbf{X}/n)^{-1}\mathbf{R}')^{-1} - (\mathbf{R}\mathbf{M}_n\mathbf{R}')^{-1}]\mathbf{\Gamma}_n^{1/2} \xrightarrow{p} \mathbf{0}$. Hence by the product rule Lemma 4.6,

$$\mathbf{\Lambda}_n^{-1/2}\sqrt{n}\ddot{\boldsymbol{\lambda}}_n - 2\mathbf{\Lambda}_n^{-1/2}(\mathbf{R}\mathbf{M}_n^{-1}\mathbf{R}')^{-1}\sqrt{n}(\mathbf{R}\hat{\boldsymbol{\beta}}_n - \mathbf{r}) \xrightarrow{p} \mathbf{0}.$$

It follows from Lemma 4.7 that $\mathbf{\Lambda}_n^{-1/2}\sqrt{n}\ddot{\boldsymbol{\lambda}}_n$ has the same asymptotic distribution as $2\mathbf{\Lambda}_n^{-1/2}(\mathbf{R}\mathbf{M}_n^{-1}\mathbf{R}')^{-1}\sqrt{n}(\mathbf{R}\hat{\boldsymbol{\beta}}_n - \mathbf{r})$. It follows immediately from Corollary 4.24 that $2\mathbf{\Lambda}_n^{-1/2}(\mathbf{R}\mathbf{M}_n^{-1}\mathbf{R}')^{-1}\sqrt{n}(\mathbf{R}\boldsymbol{\beta}_n - \mathbf{r}) \overset{A}{\sim} N(\mathbf{0}, \mathbf{I})$; hence $\mathbf{\Lambda}_n^{-1/2}\sqrt{n}\ddot{\boldsymbol{\lambda}}_n \overset{A}{\sim} N(\mathbf{0}, \mathbf{I})$.

(*ii*) Because $\ddot{\mathbf{V}}_n - \mathbf{V}_n \xrightarrow{p} \mathbf{0}$ by hypothesis and $(\mathbf{X}'\mathbf{X}/n) - \mathbf{M}_n \xrightarrow{p} \mathbf{0}$, $\hat{\mathbf{\Lambda}}_n - \mathbf{\Lambda}_n \xrightarrow{p} \mathbf{0}$ by Proposition 2.30, given the result in (*i*), (*ii*) follows from Theorem 4.30. ∎

Note that the Wald and Lagrange multiplier statistics would be identical if $\hat{\mathbf{V}}_n$ were used in place of $\ddot{\mathbf{V}}_n$. This suggests that the two statistics should be asymptotically equivalent.

Exercise 4.33 *Prove that under the conditions of Theorems 4.31 and 4.32,* $\mathcal{W}_n - \mathcal{LM}_n \xrightarrow{p} 0$.

Although the fact that $\ddot{\boldsymbol{\lambda}}_n$ is a linear combination of $\mathbf{R}\hat{\boldsymbol{\beta}}_n - \mathbf{r}$ simplifies the proof of Theorem 4.32, the whole point of using the Lagrange multiplier statistic is to avoid computing $\hat{\boldsymbol{\beta}}_n$ and to compute only the simpler $\ddot{\boldsymbol{\beta}}_n$. Computation of $\ddot{\boldsymbol{\beta}}_n$ is particularly simple when the data are generated as $\mathbf{Y} = \mathbf{X}_1\boldsymbol{\beta}_1 + \mathbf{X}_2\boldsymbol{\beta}_2 + \boldsymbol{\varepsilon}$ and H_0 specifies that $\boldsymbol{\beta}_2$ (a $q \times 1$ vector) is zero. Then

$$\mathbf{R} = [\underset{(q\times(k-q))}{\mathbf{0}} \;:\; \underset{(q\times q)}{\mathbf{I}}], \qquad \underset{(q\times 1)}{\mathbf{r} = \mathbf{0}},$$

and $\ddot{\boldsymbol{\beta}}_n' = (\ddot{\boldsymbol{\beta}}_{1n}', \mathbf{0})$ where $\ddot{\boldsymbol{\beta}}_{1n} = (\mathbf{X}_1'\mathbf{X}_1)^{-1}\mathbf{X}_1'\mathbf{Y}$.

Exercise 4.34 *Define* $\ddot{\boldsymbol{\varepsilon}} = \mathbf{Y} - \mathbf{X}_1\ddot{\boldsymbol{\beta}}_{1n}$. *Show that under* H_0: $\boldsymbol{\beta}_2 = \mathbf{0}$,

$$\begin{aligned}\ddot{\boldsymbol{\lambda}}_n &= 2\mathbf{X}_2'(\mathbf{I} - \mathbf{X}_1(\mathbf{X}_1'\mathbf{X}_1)^{-1}\mathbf{X}_1')\boldsymbol{\varepsilon}/n \\ &= 2\mathbf{X}_2'\ddot{\boldsymbol{\varepsilon}}/n.\end{aligned}$$

(*Hint:* $\mathbf{R}\hat{\boldsymbol{\beta}}_n - \mathbf{r} = \mathbf{R}(\mathbf{X}'\mathbf{X}/n)^{-1}\mathbf{X}'(\mathbf{Y} - \mathbf{X}\ddot{\boldsymbol{\beta}}_n)/n$).

By applying the particular form of $\mathbf{R}$ to the result of Theorem 4.32 (*ii*), we obtain

$$\mathcal{LM}_n = n\ddot{\boldsymbol{\lambda}}_n'[(-\mathbf{X}_2'\mathbf{X}_1(\mathbf{X}_1'\mathbf{X}_1)^{-1} : \mathbf{I}_q)\ddot{\mathbf{V}}_n(-\mathbf{X}_2'\mathbf{X}_1(\mathbf{X}_1'\mathbf{X}_1)^{-1} : \mathbf{I}_q)']^{-1}\ddot{\boldsymbol{\lambda}}_n/4.$$

When $\mathbf{V}_n$ can be consistently estimated by $\ddot{\mathbf{V}}_n = \ddot{\sigma}_n^2(\mathbf{X}'\mathbf{X}/n)$, where $\ddot{\sigma}_n^2 = \ddot{\varepsilon}'\ddot{\varepsilon}/n$, the $\mathcal{LM}_n$ statistic simplifies even further.

Exercise 4.35 *If* $\ddot{\sigma}_n^2(\mathbf{X}'\mathbf{X}/n) - \mathbf{V}_n \xrightarrow{p} \mathbf{0}$ *and* $\boldsymbol{\beta}_2 = \mathbf{0}$, *show that* $\mathcal{LM}_n = n\ddot{\varepsilon}'\mathbf{X}(\mathbf{X}'\mathbf{X})^{-1}\mathbf{X}'\ddot{\varepsilon}/(\ddot{\varepsilon}'\ddot{\varepsilon})$, *which is n times the simple* R^2 *of the regression of* $\ddot{\varepsilon}$ *on* $\mathbf{X}$.

The result of this exercise implies a very simple procedure for testing $\boldsymbol{\beta}_2 = \mathbf{0}$ when $\mathbf{V}_n = \sigma_o^2\mathbf{M}_n$. First, regress $\mathbf{Y}$ on $\mathbf{X}_1$ and form the constrained residuals $\ddot{\varepsilon}$. Then regress $\ddot{\varepsilon}$ on $\mathbf{X}$. The product of the sample size n and the simple R^2 (i.e., without adjustment for the presence of a constant in the regression) from this regression is the $\mathcal{LM}_n$ test statistic, which has the χ_q^2 distribution asymptotically. As Engle (1981) showed, many interesting diagnostic statistics can be computed in this way.

When the errors ε_t are scalar i.i.d. $N(0, \sigma_o^2)$ random variables, the OLS estimator is also the maximum likelihood estimator (MLE) because $\hat{\boldsymbol{\beta}}_n$ solves the problem

$$\max \mathcal{L}(\boldsymbol{\beta}, \sigma; \mathbf{Y}) = \exp[-n \log \sqrt{2\pi} - n \log \sigma - \frac{1}{2}\sum_{t=1}^{n}(Y_t - \mathbf{X}_t'\boldsymbol{\beta})^2/\sigma^2],$$

where $\mathcal{L}(\boldsymbol{\beta}, \sigma; \mathbf{Y})$ is the sample likelihood based on the normality assumption. When ε_t is not i.i.d. $N(0, \sigma_o^2)$, $\hat{\boldsymbol{\beta}}_n$ is said to be a quasi-maximum likelihood estimator (QMLE).

When $\hat{\boldsymbol{\beta}}_n$ is the MLE, hypothesis tests can be based on the log-likelihood ratio

$$\mathcal{LR}_n = \log\left[\frac{\mathcal{L}(\ddot{\boldsymbol{\beta}}_n, \ddot{\sigma}_n; \mathbf{Y})}{\mathcal{L}(\hat{\boldsymbol{\beta}}_n \hat{\sigma}_n; \mathbf{Y})}\right],$$

where $\hat{\sigma}_n^2 = n^{-1}\sum_{t=1}^{n}(Y_t - \mathbf{X}_t'\hat{\boldsymbol{\beta}}_n)^2$ as before and $\ddot{\boldsymbol{\beta}}_n$, $\ddot{\sigma}_n$ solve

$$\max \mathcal{L}(\boldsymbol{\beta}, \sigma; \mathbf{Y}), \qquad \text{s.t. } \mathbf{R}\boldsymbol{\beta} = \mathbf{r}.$$

It is easy to show that $\ddot{\boldsymbol{\beta}}_n$ is the constrained OLS estimator and $\ddot{\sigma}_n^2 = \ddot{\varepsilon}'\ddot{\varepsilon}/n$ as before. The likelihood ratio is nonnegative and always less than or equal to 1. Simple algebra yields

$$\mathcal{LR}_n = (n/2)\log(\hat{\sigma}_n^2/\ddot{\sigma}_n^2).$$

Because $\ddot{\sigma}_n^2 = \hat{\sigma}_n^2 + (\hat{\boldsymbol{\beta}}_n - \ddot{\boldsymbol{\beta}}_n)'(\mathbf{X}'\mathbf{X}/n)(\hat{\boldsymbol{\beta}}_n - \ddot{\boldsymbol{\beta}}_n)$ (verify this),

$$\mathcal{LR}_n = -(n/2)\log[1 + (\hat{\boldsymbol{\beta}}_n - \ddot{\boldsymbol{\beta}}_n)'(\mathbf{X}'\mathbf{X}/n)(\hat{\boldsymbol{\beta}}_n - \ddot{\boldsymbol{\beta}}_n)/\hat{\sigma}_n^2].$$

To find the asymptotic distribution of this statistic, we make use of the mean value theorem of calculus.

Theorem 4.36 (Mean value theorem) *Let $s : \mathbb{R}^k \to \mathbb{R}$ be defined on an open convex set $\Theta \subset \mathbb{R}^k$ such that s is continuously differentiable on Θ with $k \times 1$ gradient ∇s. Then for any points $\boldsymbol{\theta}$ and $\boldsymbol{\theta}_o \in \Theta$ there exists $\bar{\boldsymbol{\theta}}$ on the segment connecting $\boldsymbol{\theta}$ and $\boldsymbol{\theta}_o$ such that $s(\boldsymbol{\theta}) = s(\boldsymbol{\theta}_o) + \nabla s(\bar{\boldsymbol{\theta}})'(\boldsymbol{\theta} - \boldsymbol{\theta}_o)$.*

Proof. See Bartle (1976, p. 365). ∎

For the present application, we choose $s(\theta) = \log(1+\theta)$. If we also choose $\theta_o = 0$, we have $s(\theta) = \log(1) + (1/(1+\bar{\theta}))\theta = \theta/(1+\bar{\theta})$, where $\bar{\theta}$ lies between θ and zero. Let $\theta_n = (\hat{\boldsymbol{\beta}}_n - \ddot{\boldsymbol{\beta}}_n)'(\mathbf{X}'\mathbf{X}/n)(\hat{\boldsymbol{\beta}}_n - \ddot{\boldsymbol{\beta}}_n)/\ddot{\sigma}_n^2$ so that under H_0, $|\bar{\theta}_n| < |\theta_n| \xrightarrow{p} 0$; hence $\bar{\theta}_n \xrightarrow{p} 0$. Applying the mean value theorem now gives

$$\mathcal{LR}_n = -(n/2)(1+\bar{\theta}_n)^{-1}(\hat{\boldsymbol{\beta}}_n - \ddot{\boldsymbol{\beta}}_n)'(\mathbf{X}'\mathbf{X}/n)(\hat{\boldsymbol{\beta}}_n - \ddot{\boldsymbol{\beta}}_n)/\ddot{\sigma}_n^2.$$

Because $(1+\bar{\theta}_n)^{-1} \xrightarrow{p} 1$, it follows from Lemma 4.6 that

$$-2\mathcal{LR}_n - n(\hat{\boldsymbol{\beta}}_n - \ddot{\boldsymbol{\beta}}_n)'(\mathbf{X}'\mathbf{X}/n)(\hat{\boldsymbol{\beta}}_n - \ddot{\boldsymbol{\beta}}_n)/\hat{\sigma}_n^2 \xrightarrow{p} 0,$$

provided the second term has a limiting distribution. Now

$$\hat{\boldsymbol{\beta}}_n - \ddot{\boldsymbol{\beta}}_n = (\mathbf{X}'\mathbf{X}/n)^{-1}\mathbf{R}'(\mathbf{R}(\mathbf{X}'\mathbf{X}/n)^{-1}\mathbf{R}')^{-1}(\mathbf{R}\hat{\boldsymbol{\beta}}_n - \mathbf{r}).$$

Thus

$$-2\mathcal{LR}_n - n(\mathbf{R}\hat{\boldsymbol{\beta}}_n - \mathbf{r})'[\mathbf{R}(\mathbf{X}'\mathbf{X}/n)^{-1}\mathbf{R}']^{-1}(\mathbf{R}\hat{\boldsymbol{\beta}}_n - \mathbf{r})/\hat{\sigma}_n^2 \xrightarrow{p} 0.$$

This second term is the Wald statistic formed with $\hat{\mathbf{V}}_n = \hat{\sigma}_n^2(\mathbf{X}'\mathbf{X}/n)$, so $-2\mathcal{LR}_n$ is asymptotically equivalent to the Wald statistic and has the χ_q^2 distribution asymptotically, provided $\hat{\sigma}_n^2(\mathbf{X}'\mathbf{X}/n)$ is a consistent estimator for $\mathbf{V}_n$. If this is not true, then $-2\mathcal{LR}_n$ does not in general have the χ_q^2 distribution asymptotically. It does have a limiting distribution, but not a simple one that has been tabulated or is easily computable (see White, 1994, Ch. 6, for further details). Note that it is not violation of the normality assumption per se, but the failure of $\mathbf{V}_n$ to equal $\sigma_o^2\mathbf{M}_n$ that results in $-2\mathcal{LR}_n$ not having the χ_q^2 distribution asymptotically.

The formal statement of the result for the $\mathcal{LR}_n$ statistic is the following.

Theorem 4.37 (Likelihood ratio test) *Let the conditions of Theorem 4.25 hold, let* $\text{rank}(\mathbf{R}) = q \leq k$, *and let* $\hat{\sigma}_n^2(\mathbf{X}'\mathbf{X}/n) - \mathbf{V}_n \xrightarrow{p} \mathbf{0}$. *Then under* H_0: $\mathbf{R}\boldsymbol{\beta}_o = \mathbf{r}$, $-2\mathcal{LR}_n \overset{A}{\sim} \chi_q^2$.

Proof. Set $\hat{\mathbf{V}}_n$ in Theorem 4.31 to $\hat{\mathbf{V}}_n = \hat{\sigma}_n^2(\mathbf{X}'\mathbf{X}/n)$. Then from the argument preceding the theorem above $-2\mathcal{LR}_n - \mathcal{W}_n \xrightarrow{p} 0$. Because $\mathcal{W}_n \overset{A}{\sim} \chi_q^2$, it follows from Lemma 4.7 that $-2\mathcal{LR}_n \overset{A}{\sim} \chi_q^2$. ■

The mean value theorem just introduced provides a convenient way to find the asymptotic distribution of statistics used to test nonlinear hypotheses. In general, nonlinear hypotheses can be conveniently represented as

$$H_0: \ \mathbf{s}(\boldsymbol{\beta}_o) = \mathbf{0},$$

where $\mathbf{s}$: $\mathbb{R}^k \to \mathbb{R}^q$ is a continuously differentiable function of $\boldsymbol{\beta}$.

Example 4.38 *Suppose* $\mathbf{Y} = \mathbf{X}_1\beta_1 + \mathbf{X}_2\beta_2 + \mathbf{X}_3\beta_3 + \boldsymbol{\varepsilon}$, *where* $\mathbf{X}_1$, $\mathbf{X}_2$, *and* $\mathbf{X}_3$ *are* $n \times 1$ *and* β_1, β_2, *and* β_3 *are scalars. Further, suppose we hypothesize that* $\beta_3 = \beta_1\beta_2$. *Then* $s(\boldsymbol{\beta}_o) = \beta_3 - \beta_1\beta_2 = 0$ *expresses the null hypothesis.*

Just as with linear restrictions, we can construct a Wald test based on the asymptotic distribution of $\mathbf{s}(\hat{\boldsymbol{\beta}}_n)$; we can construct a Lagrange multiplier test based on the Lagrange multipliers derived from minimizing the least squares (or other estimation) objective function subject to the constraint; or we can form a log-likelihood ratio.

To illustrate the approach, consider the Wald test based on $\mathbf{s}(\hat{\boldsymbol{\beta}}_n)$. As before, a value of $\mathbf{s}(\hat{\boldsymbol{\beta}}_n)$ far from zero is evidence against H_0. To tell how far $\mathbf{s}(\hat{\boldsymbol{\beta}}_n)$ must be from zero to reject H_0, we need to determine its asymptotic distribution. This is provided by the next result.

Theorem 4.39 (Wald test) *Let the conditions of Theorem 4.25 hold and let rank* $\nabla\mathbf{s}(\boldsymbol{\beta}_o) = q \leq k$, *where* $\nabla\mathbf{s}$ *is the* $k \times q$ *gradient matrix of* $\mathbf{s}$. *Then under* H_0: $\mathbf{s}(\boldsymbol{\beta}_o) = \mathbf{0}$,

(*i*) $\boldsymbol{\Gamma}_n^{-1/2}\sqrt{n}\mathbf{s}(\hat{\boldsymbol{\beta}}_n) \overset{A}{\sim} N(\mathbf{0}, \mathbf{I})$, *where*

$$\boldsymbol{\Gamma}_n \equiv \nabla\mathbf{s}(\boldsymbol{\beta}_o)'\mathbf{D}_n\nabla\mathbf{s}(\boldsymbol{\beta}_o).$$

(*ii*) *The Wald statistic* $\mathcal{W}_n \equiv n\mathbf{s}(\hat{\boldsymbol{\beta}}_n)'\hat{\boldsymbol{\Gamma}}_n^{-1}\mathbf{s}(\hat{\boldsymbol{\beta}}_n) \overset{A}{\sim} \chi_q^2$, *where*

$$\begin{aligned}\hat{\boldsymbol{\Gamma}}_n &= \nabla\mathbf{s}(\hat{\boldsymbol{\beta}}_n)'\hat{\mathbf{D}}_n\nabla\mathbf{s}(\hat{\boldsymbol{\beta}}_n) \\ &= \nabla\mathbf{s}(\hat{\boldsymbol{\beta}}_n)'(\mathbf{X}'\mathbf{X}/n)^{-1}\hat{\mathbf{V}}_n(\mathbf{X}'\mathbf{X}/n)^{-1}\nabla\mathbf{s}(\hat{\boldsymbol{\beta}}_n).\end{aligned}$$

Proof. (i) Because $\mathbf{s}(\boldsymbol{\beta})$ is a vector function, we apply the mean value theorem to each element $s_i(\boldsymbol{\beta})$, $i = 1, \ldots, q$, to get

$$s_i(\hat{\boldsymbol{\beta}}_n) = s_i(\boldsymbol{\beta}_o) + \nabla s_i(\bar{\boldsymbol{\beta}}_n^{(i)})'(\hat{\boldsymbol{\beta}}_n - \boldsymbol{\beta}_o),$$

where $\bar{\boldsymbol{\beta}}_n^{(i)}$ is a $k \times 1$ vector lying on the segment connecting $\hat{\boldsymbol{\beta}}_n$ and $\boldsymbol{\beta}_o$. The superscript (i) reflects the fact that the mean value may be different for each element $s_i(\boldsymbol{\beta})$ of $\mathbf{s}(\boldsymbol{\beta})$.

Under H_0, $s_i(\boldsymbol{\beta}_o) = 0$, $i = 1, \ldots, q$, so

$$\sqrt{n} s_i(\hat{\boldsymbol{\beta}}_n) = \nabla s_i(\bar{\boldsymbol{\beta}}_n^{(i)})' \sqrt{n}(\hat{\boldsymbol{\beta}}_n - \boldsymbol{\beta}_o).$$

This suggests considering the difference

$$\begin{aligned} & \sqrt{n} s_i(\hat{\boldsymbol{\beta}}_n) - \nabla s_i(\boldsymbol{\beta}_o)' \sqrt{n}(\hat{\boldsymbol{\beta}}_n - \boldsymbol{\beta}_o) \\ = \; & (\nabla s_i(\bar{\boldsymbol{\beta}}_n^{(i)}) - \nabla s_i(\boldsymbol{\beta}_o))' \sqrt{n}(\hat{\boldsymbol{\beta}}_n - \boldsymbol{\beta}_o) \\ = \; & (\nabla s_i(\bar{\boldsymbol{\beta}}_n^{(i)}) - \nabla s_i(\boldsymbol{\beta}_o))' \mathbf{D}_n^{1/2} \mathbf{D}_n^{-1/2} \sqrt{n}(\hat{\boldsymbol{\beta}}_n - \boldsymbol{\beta}_o). \end{aligned}$$

By Theorem 4.25, $\mathbf{D}_n^{-1/2}\sqrt{n}(\hat{\boldsymbol{\beta}}_n - \boldsymbol{\beta}_o) \overset{A}{\sim} N(\mathbf{0}, \mathbf{I})$. Because $\hat{\boldsymbol{\beta}}_n \xrightarrow{p} \boldsymbol{\beta}_o$, it follows that $\bar{\boldsymbol{\beta}}_n^{(i)} \xrightarrow{p} \boldsymbol{\beta}_o$ so $\nabla s_i(\bar{\boldsymbol{\beta}}_n^{(i)}) - \nabla s_i(\boldsymbol{\beta}_o) \xrightarrow{p} \mathbf{0}$ by Proposition 2.27. Because $\mathbf{D}_n^{1/2}$ is $O(1)$, we have $(\nabla s_i(\bar{\boldsymbol{\beta}}_n^{(i)}) - \nabla s_i(\boldsymbol{\beta}_o))'\mathbf{D}_n^{1/2} \xrightarrow{p} \mathbf{0}$. It follows from Lemma 4.6 that

$$\sqrt{n} s_i(\hat{\boldsymbol{\beta}}_n) - \nabla s_i(\boldsymbol{\beta}_o)' \sqrt{n}(\hat{\boldsymbol{\beta}}_n - \boldsymbol{\beta}_o) \xrightarrow{p} \mathbf{0}, \; i = 1, \ldots, q.$$

In vector form this becomes

$$\sqrt{n} \mathbf{s}(\hat{\boldsymbol{\beta}}_n) - \nabla \mathbf{s}(\boldsymbol{\beta}_o)' \sqrt{n}(\hat{\boldsymbol{\beta}}_n - \boldsymbol{\beta}_o) \xrightarrow{p} \mathbf{0},$$

and because $\boldsymbol{\Gamma}_n^{-1/2}$ is $O(1)$,

$$\boldsymbol{\Gamma}_n^{-1/2} \sqrt{n} \mathbf{s}(\hat{\boldsymbol{\beta}}_n) - \boldsymbol{\Gamma}_n^{-1/2} \nabla \mathbf{s}(\boldsymbol{\beta}_o)' \sqrt{n}(\hat{\boldsymbol{\beta}}_n - \boldsymbol{\beta}_o) \xrightarrow{p} \mathbf{0}.$$

Corollary 4.24 immediately yields

$$\boldsymbol{\Gamma}_n^{-1/2} \nabla \mathbf{s}(\boldsymbol{\beta}_o)' \sqrt{n}(\hat{\boldsymbol{\beta}}_n - \boldsymbol{\beta}_o) \overset{A}{\sim} N(\mathbf{0}, \mathbf{I}),$$

so by Lemma 4.7, $\boldsymbol{\Gamma}_n^{-1/2}\sqrt{n}\mathbf{s}(\hat{\boldsymbol{\beta}}_n) \overset{A}{\sim} N(\mathbf{0}, \mathbf{I})$.

(ii) Because $\hat{\mathbf{D}}_n - \mathbf{D}_n \xrightarrow{p} \mathbf{0}$ from Theorem 4.25 and $\nabla \mathbf{s}(\hat{\boldsymbol{\beta}}_n) - \nabla \mathbf{s}(\boldsymbol{\beta}_o) \xrightarrow{p} \mathbf{0}$ by Proposition 2.27, $\hat{\boldsymbol{\Gamma}}_n - \boldsymbol{\Gamma}_n \xrightarrow{p} \mathbf{0}$ by Proposition 2.30. Given the result in (i), (ii) follows from Theorem 4.30. ∎

Note the similarity of this result to Theorem 4.31 which gives the Wald test for the linear hypothesis $\mathbf{R}\boldsymbol{\beta}_o = \mathbf{r}$. In the present context, $\mathbf{s}(\boldsymbol{\beta}_o)$ plays the role of $\mathbf{R}\boldsymbol{\beta}_o - \mathbf{r}$, whereas $\nabla\mathbf{s}(\boldsymbol{\beta}_o)'$ plays the role of $\mathbf{R}$ in computing the covariance matrix.

Exercise 4.40 *Write down the Wald statistic for testing the hypothesis of Example 4.38.*

Exercise 4.41 *Give the Lagrange multiplier statistic for testing the hypothesis* H_0: $\mathbf{s}(\boldsymbol{\beta}_o) = \mathbf{0}$ *versus* H_1: $\mathbf{s}(\boldsymbol{\beta}_o) \neq \mathbf{0}$, *and derive its limiting distribution under the conditions of Theorem 4.25.*

Exercise 4.42 *Give the Wald and Lagrange multiplier statistics for testing the hypotheses* $\mathbf{R}\boldsymbol{\beta}_o = \mathbf{r}$ *and* $\mathbf{s}(\boldsymbol{\beta}_o) = \mathbf{0}$ *on the basis of the IV estimator* $\tilde{\boldsymbol{\beta}}_n$ *and derive their limiting distributions under the conditions of Exercise 4.26.*

4.3 Asymptotic Efficiency

Given a class of estimators (e.g., the class of instrumental variables estimators), it is desirable to choose that member of the class that has the smallest asymptotic covariance matrix (assuming that this member exists and can be computed). The reason for this is that such estimators are obviously more precise, and in general allow construction of more powerful test statistics. In what follows, we shall abuse notation slightly and write $\text{avar}(\tilde{\boldsymbol{\beta}}_n)$ instead of $\text{avar}\left(\sqrt{n}(\tilde{\boldsymbol{\beta}}_n - \boldsymbol{\beta}_o)\right)$. A definition of asymptotic efficiency adequate for our purposes here is the following.

Definition 4.43 *Let* $\mathcal{P}$ *be a set of data generating processes such that each data generating process* $P^o \in \mathcal{P}$ *has a corresponding coefficient vector* $\boldsymbol{\beta}^o \in \mathbb{R}^k$ *and let* $\mathcal{E}$ *be a class of estimators* $\{\tilde{\boldsymbol{\beta}}_n\}$ *such that for each* $P^o \in \mathcal{P}$, $\mathbf{D}_n^{o-1/2}\sqrt{n}\left(\tilde{\boldsymbol{\beta}}_n - \boldsymbol{\beta}^o\right) \xrightarrow{d^o} N(\mathbf{0}, \mathbf{I})$ *for* $\{\text{avar}^o(\tilde{\boldsymbol{\beta}}_n) \equiv \mathbf{D}_n^o\}$ *nonstochastic,* $O(1)$ *and uniformly nonsingular. Then* $\{\boldsymbol{\beta}_n^*\} \in \mathcal{E}$ is asymptotically efficient relative to $\{\tilde{\boldsymbol{\beta}}_n\} \in \mathcal{E}$ for $\mathcal{P}$ *if for every* $P^o \in \mathcal{P}$ *the matrix* $\text{avar}^o(\tilde{\boldsymbol{\beta}}_n) - \text{avar}^o(\boldsymbol{\beta}_n^*)$ *is positive semidefinite for all n sufficiently large. The estimator* $\{\boldsymbol{\beta}_n^*\} \in \mathcal{E}$ is asymptotically efficient in $\mathcal{E}$ for $\mathcal{P}$ *if it is asymptotically efficient relative to every other member of its class,* $\mathcal{E}$, *for* $\mathcal{P}$.

We write $\boldsymbol{\beta}^o$ instead of $\boldsymbol{\beta}_o$ to emphasize that $\boldsymbol{\beta}^o$ corresponds to (at least) one possible data generating process (P^o) among many ($\mathcal{P}$).

The class of estimators we consider is the class $\mathcal{E}$ of instrumental variables estimators

$$\tilde{\beta}_n = (\mathbf{X}'\mathbf{Z}\hat{\mathbf{P}}_n\mathbf{Z}'\mathbf{X})^{-1}\mathbf{X}'\mathbf{Z}\hat{\mathbf{P}}_n\mathbf{Z}'\mathbf{Y},$$

where different members of the class are defined by the different possible choices for $\hat{\mathbf{P}}_n$ and $\mathbf{Z}$. For any data generating process P^o satisfying the conditions of Exercise 4.26, we have that the asymptotic covariance matrix of $\tilde{\boldsymbol{\beta}}_n$ is

$$\mathbf{D}_n = (\mathbf{Q}_n'\mathbf{P}_n\mathbf{Q}_n)^{-1}\mathbf{Q}_n'\mathbf{P}_n\mathbf{V}_n\mathbf{P}_n\mathbf{Q}_n(\mathbf{Q}_n'\mathbf{P}_n\mathbf{Q}_n)^{-1}.$$

We leave the dependence of $\mathbf{D}_n$ (and other quantities) on P^o implicit for now, and begin our analysis by considering how to choose $\hat{\mathbf{P}}_n$ to make $\mathbf{D}_n$ as small as possible.

Until now, we have let $\hat{\mathbf{P}}_n$ be any positive definite matrix. It turns out, however, that by choosing $\hat{\mathbf{P}}_n = \hat{\mathbf{V}}_n^{-1}$, one obtains an asymptotically efficient estimator for the class of IV estimators with given instrumental variables $\mathbf{Z}$. To prove this, we make use of the following proposition.

Proposition 4.44 *Let* $\mathbf{A}$ *and* $\mathbf{B}$ *be positive definite matrices of order* k. *Then* $\mathbf{A} - \mathbf{B}$ *is positive semidefinite if and only if* $\mathbf{B}^{-1} - \mathbf{A}^{-1}$ *is positive semidefinite.*

Proof. This follows from Goldberger (1964, Theorem 1.7.21, p. 38). ∎

This result is useful because in the cases of interest to us it will often be much easier to determine whether $\mathbf{B}^{-1} - \mathbf{A}^{-1}$ is positive semidefinite than to examine the positive semidefiniteness of $\mathbf{A} - \mathbf{B}$ directly.

Proposition 4.45 *Given instrumental variables* $\mathbf{Z}$, *let* $\mathcal{P}$ *be the collection of probability measures satisfying the conditions of Exercise 4.26. Then the choice* $\hat{\mathbf{P}}_n = \hat{\mathbf{V}}_n^{-1}$ *gives the IV estimator*

$$\beta_n^* = (\mathbf{X}'\mathbf{Z}\hat{\mathbf{V}}_n^{-1}\mathbf{Z}'\mathbf{X})^{-1}\mathbf{X}'\mathbf{Z}\hat{\mathbf{V}}_n^{-1}\mathbf{Z}'\mathbf{Y},$$

which is asymptotically efficient for $\mathcal{P}$ *within the class* $\mathcal{E}$ *of instrumental variables estimators of the form*

$$\tilde{\beta}_n = (\mathbf{X}'\mathbf{Z}\hat{\mathbf{P}}_n\mathbf{Z}'\mathbf{X})^{-1}\mathbf{X}'\mathbf{Z}\hat{\mathbf{P}}_n\mathbf{Z}'\mathbf{Y}.$$

Proof. From Exercise 4.26, we have

$$\text{avar}(\beta_n^*) = (\mathbf{Q}_n'\mathbf{V}_n^{-1}\mathbf{Q}_n)^{-1}.$$

From Proposition 4.44, $\text{avar}(\tilde{\boldsymbol{\beta}}_n) - \text{avar}(\boldsymbol{\beta}_n^*)$ is p.s.d. if and only if

$$(\text{avar}(\boldsymbol{\beta}_n^*))^{-1} - (\text{avar}(\tilde{\boldsymbol{\beta}}_n))^{-1}$$

is p.s.d. Now for all n sufficiently large,

$$\begin{aligned}
&(\text{avar}(\boldsymbol{\beta}_n^*))^{-1} - (\text{avar}(\hat{\boldsymbol{\beta}}))^{-1}\\
= \;& \mathbf{Q}_n'\mathbf{V}_n^{-1}\mathbf{Q}_n - \mathbf{Q}_n'\mathbf{P}_n\mathbf{Q}_n(\mathbf{Q}_n'\mathbf{P}_n\mathbf{V}_n\mathbf{P}_n\mathbf{Q}_n)^{-1}\mathbf{Q}_n'\mathbf{P}_n\mathbf{Q}_n\\
= \;& \mathbf{Q}_n'\mathbf{V}_n^{-1/2}(\mathbf{I}\\
& -\mathbf{V}_n^{1/2}\mathbf{P}_n\mathbf{Q}_n(\mathbf{Q}_n'\mathbf{P}_n\mathbf{V}_n^{1/2}\mathbf{V}_n^{1/2}\mathbf{P}_n\mathbf{Q}_n)^{-1}\mathbf{Q}_n'\mathbf{P}_n\mathbf{V}_n^{1/2})\mathbf{V}_n^{-1/2}\mathbf{Q}_n\\
= \;& \mathbf{Q}_n'\mathbf{V}_n^{-1/2}(\mathbf{I} - \mathbf{G}_n(\mathbf{G}_n'\mathbf{G}_n)^{-1}\mathbf{G}_n')\mathbf{V}_n^{-1/2}\mathbf{Q}_n,
\end{aligned}$$

where $\mathbf{G}_n \equiv \mathbf{V}_n^{-1/2}\mathbf{P}_n\mathbf{Q}_n$. This is a quadratic form in an idempotent matrix and is therefore p.s.d. As this holds for all P^o in $\mathcal{P}$, the result follows. ∎

Hansen (1982) considers estimators for coefficients $\boldsymbol{\beta}_o$ implicitly defined by moment conditions of the form $E(\mathbf{g}(\mathbf{X}_t, \mathbf{Y}_t, \mathbf{Z}_t, \boldsymbol{\beta}_o)) = \mathbf{0}$, where $\mathbf{g}$ is an $l \times 1$ vector-valued function. Analogous to our construction of the IV estimator, Hansen's estimator is constructed by attempting to make the sample moment

$$n^{-1}\sum_{t=1}^{n}\mathbf{g}(\mathbf{X}_t, \mathbf{Y}_t, \mathbf{Z}_t, \boldsymbol{\beta})$$

as close to zero as possible by solving the problem

$$\min_{\boldsymbol{\beta}} \left[n^{-1}\sum_{t=1}^{n}\mathbf{g}(\mathbf{X}_t, \mathbf{Y}_t, \mathbf{Z}_t, \boldsymbol{\beta})\right]' \hat{\mathbf{P}}_n \left[n^{-1}\sum_{t=1}^{n}\mathbf{g}(\mathbf{X}_t, \mathbf{Y}_t, \mathbf{Z}_t, \boldsymbol{\beta})\right].$$

Hansen establishes that the resulting "method of moments" estimator is consistent and asymptotically normal and that the choice $\hat{\mathbf{P}}_n = \hat{\mathbf{V}}_n^{-1}$, $\hat{\mathbf{V}}_n - \mathbf{V}_n \xrightarrow{p} \mathbf{0}$, where

$$\mathbf{V}_n = \text{var}(n^{-1/2}\sum_{t=1}^{n}\mathbf{g}(\mathbf{X}_t, \mathbf{Y}_t, \mathbf{Z}_t, \boldsymbol{\beta}_o))$$

delivers the asymptotically efficient estimator in the class of method of moment estimators. Hansen calls the method of moments estimator with $\hat{\mathbf{P}}_n = \hat{\mathbf{V}}_n^{-1}$ the *generalized method of moments* (GMM) estimator.

Thus, the estimator $\boldsymbol{\beta}_n^*$ of Proposition 4.45 is the GMM estimator for the case in which

$$\mathbf{g}(\mathbf{X}_t, \mathbf{Y}_t, \mathbf{Z}_t, \boldsymbol{\beta}_o) = \mathbf{Z}_t(\mathbf{Y}_t - \mathbf{X}_t'\boldsymbol{\beta}_o).$$

We call $\boldsymbol{\beta}_n^*$ a "linear" GMM estimator because the defining moment condition $E(\mathbf{Z}_t(\mathbf{Y}_t - \mathbf{X}_t'\boldsymbol{\beta}_o)) = \mathbf{0}$ is linear in $\boldsymbol{\beta}_o$.

Exercise 4.46 *Given instrumental variables* $\mathbf{X}$, *suppose that*

$$\mathbf{V}_n^{-1/2} \sum \mathbf{X}_t \varepsilon_t \overset{A}{\sim} N(\mathbf{0}, \mathbf{I}),$$

where $\mathbf{V}_n = \sigma_o^2 \mathbf{M}_n$. *Show that the asymptotically efficient IV estimator is the least squares estimator,* $\hat{\boldsymbol{\beta}}_n$, *according to Proposition 4.45.*

Exercise 4.47 *Given instrumental variables* $\mathbf{Z}$, *suppose that*

$$\mathbf{V}_n^{-1/2} \sum \mathbf{Z}_t \varepsilon_t \overset{A}{\sim} N(\mathbf{0}, \mathbf{I}),$$

where $\mathbf{V}_n = \sigma_o^2 \mathbf{L}_n$ *and* $\mathbf{L}_n \equiv E(\mathbf{Z}'\mathbf{Z}/n)$. *Show that the asymptotically efficient IV estimator is the* two-stage least squares estimator

$$\tilde{\boldsymbol{\beta}}_{2SLS} = (\mathbf{X}'\mathbf{Z}(\mathbf{Z}'\mathbf{Z})^{-1}\mathbf{Z}'\mathbf{X})^{-1}\mathbf{X}'\mathbf{Z}(\mathbf{Z}'\mathbf{Z})^{-1}\mathbf{Z}'\mathbf{Y}$$

according to Proposition 4.45.

Note that the value of σ_o^2 plays no role in either Exercise 4.46 or Exercise 4.47 as long as it is finite. In what follows, we shall simply ignore σ_o^2, and proceed as if $\sigma_o^2 = 1$.

If instead of testing the restrictions $\mathbf{s}(\boldsymbol{\beta}_o) = \mathbf{0}$, as considered in the previous section, we believe or know these restrictions to be true (because, for example, they are dictated by economic theory), then, as we discuss next, we can further improve asymptotic efficiency by imposing these restrictions. (Of course, for this to really work, the restrictions must in fact be true.)

Thus, suppose we are given constraints $\mathbf{s}(\boldsymbol{\beta}_o) = \mathbf{0}$, where $\mathbf{s} : \mathbb{R}^k \to \mathbb{R}^q$ is a known continuously differentiable function, such that $\text{rank}(\nabla \mathbf{s}(\boldsymbol{\beta}_o)) = q$ and $\nabla \mathbf{s}(\boldsymbol{\beta}_o)$ $(k \times q)$ is finite; The *constrained instrumental variables estimator* can be found as the solution to the problem

$$\min_{\boldsymbol{\beta}} (\mathbf{Y} - \mathbf{X}\boldsymbol{\beta})'\mathbf{Z}\hat{\mathbf{P}}_n\mathbf{Z}'(\mathbf{Y} - \mathbf{X}\boldsymbol{\beta}), \quad \text{s.t. } \mathbf{s}(\boldsymbol{\beta}) = \mathbf{0},$$

which is equivalent to finding the saddle point of the Lagrangian

$$\mathcal{L} = (\mathbf{Y} - \mathbf{X}\boldsymbol{\beta})'\mathbf{Z}\hat{\mathbf{P}}_n\mathbf{Z}'(\mathbf{Y} - \mathbf{X}\boldsymbol{\beta}) + \mathbf{s}(\boldsymbol{\beta})'\boldsymbol{\lambda}.$$

The first-order conditions are

$$\begin{aligned}
\frac{\partial \mathcal{L}}{\partial \boldsymbol{\beta}} &= 2(\mathbf{X}'\mathbf{Z}\hat{\mathbf{P}}_n\mathbf{Z}'\mathbf{X})\boldsymbol{\beta} - 2\mathbf{X}'\mathbf{Z}\hat{\mathbf{P}}_n\mathbf{Z}'\mathbf{Y} + \nabla \mathbf{s}(\boldsymbol{\beta})\boldsymbol{\lambda} = \mathbf{0} \\
\frac{\partial \mathcal{L}}{\partial \boldsymbol{\lambda}} &= \mathbf{s}(\boldsymbol{\beta}) = \mathbf{0}.
\end{aligned}$$

Setting $\tilde{\boldsymbol{\beta}}_n = (\mathbf{X}'\mathbf{Z}\hat{\mathbf{P}}_n\mathbf{Z}'\mathbf{X})^{-1}\mathbf{X}'\mathbf{Z}\hat{\mathbf{P}}_n\mathbf{Z}'\mathbf{Y}$ and taking a mean value expansion of $\mathbf{s}(\boldsymbol{\beta})$ around $\mathbf{s}(\hat{\boldsymbol{\beta}})$ yields the equations

$$\begin{aligned}\frac{\partial \mathcal{L}}{\partial \boldsymbol{\beta}} &= 2(\mathbf{X}'\mathbf{Z}\hat{\mathbf{P}}_n\mathbf{Z}'\mathbf{X})(\boldsymbol{\beta} - \tilde{\boldsymbol{\beta}}_n) + \nabla\mathbf{s}(\boldsymbol{\beta})\boldsymbol{\lambda} = \mathbf{0},\\ \frac{\partial \mathcal{L}}{\partial \boldsymbol{\lambda}} &= \mathbf{s}(\tilde{\boldsymbol{\beta}}_n) + \nabla\bar{\mathbf{s}}'(\boldsymbol{\beta} - \tilde{\boldsymbol{\beta}}_n) = \mathbf{0},\end{aligned}$$

where $\nabla\bar{\mathbf{s}}'$ is the $q \times k$ Jacobian matrix with ith row evaluated at a mean value $\bar{\boldsymbol{\beta}}_n^{(i)}$. To solve for $\boldsymbol{\lambda}$ in the first equation, premultiply by $\nabla\bar{\mathbf{s}}'(\mathbf{X}'\mathbf{Z}\hat{\mathbf{P}}_n\mathbf{Z}'\mathbf{X})^{-1}$ to get

$$2\nabla\bar{\mathbf{s}}(\boldsymbol{\beta} - \tilde{\boldsymbol{\beta}}_n) + \nabla\bar{\mathbf{s}}'(\mathbf{X}'\mathbf{Z}\hat{\mathbf{P}}_n\mathbf{Z}'\mathbf{X})^{-1}\nabla\mathbf{s}(\boldsymbol{\beta})\boldsymbol{\lambda} = \mathbf{0},$$

substitute $-\mathbf{s}(\tilde{\boldsymbol{\beta}}_n) = \nabla\bar{\mathbf{s}}'(\boldsymbol{\beta} - \tilde{\boldsymbol{\beta}}_n)$, and invert $\nabla\bar{\mathbf{s}}'(\mathbf{X}'\mathbf{Z}\hat{\mathbf{P}}_n\mathbf{Z}'\mathbf{X})^{-1}\nabla\mathbf{s}(\boldsymbol{\beta})$ to obtain

$$\boldsymbol{\lambda} = 2[\nabla\bar{\mathbf{s}}'(\mathbf{X}'\mathbf{Z}\hat{\mathbf{P}}_n\mathbf{Z}'\mathbf{X})^{-1}\nabla\mathbf{s}(\boldsymbol{\beta})]^{-1}\mathbf{s}(\tilde{\boldsymbol{\beta}}_n).$$

The expression for $\partial\mathcal{L}/\partial\boldsymbol{\beta}$ above yields

$$\boldsymbol{\beta} - \tilde{\boldsymbol{\beta}}_n = -(\mathbf{X}'\mathbf{Z}\hat{\mathbf{P}}_n\mathbf{Z}'\mathbf{X})^{-1}\nabla\mathbf{s}(\boldsymbol{\beta})\boldsymbol{\lambda}/2$$

so we obtain the solution for $\boldsymbol{\beta}$ by substituting for $\boldsymbol{\lambda}$:

$$\boldsymbol{\beta} = \tilde{\boldsymbol{\beta}}_n - (\mathbf{X}'\mathbf{Z}\hat{\mathbf{P}}_n\mathbf{Z}'\mathbf{X})^{-1}\nabla\mathbf{s}(\boldsymbol{\beta})[\nabla\bar{\mathbf{s}}'(\mathbf{X}'\mathbf{Z}\hat{\mathbf{P}}_n\mathbf{Z}'\mathbf{X})^{-1}\nabla\mathbf{s}(\boldsymbol{\beta})]^{-1}\mathbf{s}(\tilde{\boldsymbol{\beta}}_n).$$

The difficulty with this solution is that it is not in closed form, because the unknown $\boldsymbol{\beta}$ appears on both sides of the equation. Further, appearing in this expression is $\nabla\bar{\mathbf{s}}$, which has q rows each of which depends on a mean value lying between $\boldsymbol{\beta}$ and $\tilde{\boldsymbol{\beta}}_n$.

Nevertheless, a computationally practical and asymptotically equivalent result can be obtained by replacing $\nabla\bar{\mathbf{s}}$ and $\nabla\mathbf{s}(\boldsymbol{\beta})$ by $\nabla\mathbf{s}(\tilde{\boldsymbol{\beta}}_n)$ on the right-hand side of the expression above, which yields

$$\begin{aligned}\boldsymbol{\beta}_n^* &= \tilde{\boldsymbol{\beta}}_n - (\mathbf{X}'\mathbf{Z}\hat{\mathbf{P}}_n\mathbf{Z}'\mathbf{X})^{-1}\nabla\mathbf{s}(\tilde{\boldsymbol{\beta}}_n)[\nabla\mathbf{s}(\tilde{\boldsymbol{\beta}}_n)'\\ &\quad\times(\mathbf{X}'\mathbf{Z}\hat{\mathbf{P}}_n\mathbf{Z}'\mathbf{X})^{-1}\nabla\mathbf{s}(\tilde{\boldsymbol{\beta}}_n)]^{-1}\mathbf{s}(\tilde{\boldsymbol{\beta}}_n).\end{aligned}$$

This gives us a convenient way of computing a constrained IV estimator. First we compute the unconstrained estimator, and then we "impose" the constraints by subtracting a "correction factor"

$$(\mathbf{X}'\mathbf{Z}\hat{\mathbf{P}}_n\mathbf{Z}'\mathbf{X})^{-1}\nabla\mathbf{s}(\tilde{\boldsymbol{\beta}}_n)[\nabla\mathbf{s}(\tilde{\boldsymbol{\beta}}_n)'(\mathbf{X}'\mathbf{Z}\hat{\mathbf{P}}_n\mathbf{Z}'\mathbf{X})^{-1}\nabla\mathbf{s}(\tilde{\boldsymbol{\beta}}_n)]^{-1}\mathbf{s}(\tilde{\boldsymbol{\beta}}_n)$$

from the unconstrained estimator. We say "impose" because $\boldsymbol{\beta}_n^*$ will not satisfy the constraints exactly for any finite n. However, an estimator that does satisfy the constraints to any desired degree of accuracy can be obtained by iterating the procedure just described, that is, by replacing $\tilde{\boldsymbol{\beta}}_n$ by $\boldsymbol{\beta}_n^*$ in the formula above to get a second round estimator, say, $\boldsymbol{\beta}_n^{**}$. This process could continue until the change in the resulting estimator was sufficiently small. Nevertheless, this iteration process has no effect on the asymptotic covariance matrix of the resulting estimator.

Exercise 4.48 *Define*

$$\begin{aligned}\boldsymbol{\beta}_n^{**} &= \boldsymbol{\beta}_n^* - (\mathbf{X}'\mathbf{Z}\hat{\mathbf{P}}_n\mathbf{Z}'\mathbf{X})^{-1}\nabla \mathbf{s}(\boldsymbol{\beta}_n^*) \\ &\quad \times [\nabla \mathbf{s}(\boldsymbol{\beta}_n^*)'(\mathbf{X}'\mathbf{Z}\hat{\mathbf{P}}_n\mathbf{Z}'\mathbf{X})^{-1}\nabla \mathbf{s}(\boldsymbol{\beta}_n^*)]^{-1}\mathbf{s}(\boldsymbol{\beta}_n^*).\end{aligned}$$

Show that under the conditions of Exercise 4.26 and the conditions on $\mathbf{s}$ *that* $\sqrt{n}(\boldsymbol{\beta}_n^{**} - \boldsymbol{\beta}_n^*) \xrightarrow{p} \mathbf{0}$, *so that* $\sqrt{n}(\boldsymbol{\beta}_n^* - \boldsymbol{\beta}_o)$ *has the same asymptotic distribution as* $\sqrt{n}(\boldsymbol{\beta}_n^{**} - \boldsymbol{\beta}_o)$. *(Hint: Show that* $\sqrt{n}\mathbf{s}(\boldsymbol{\beta}_n^*) \xrightarrow{p} \mathbf{0}$.*)*

Thus, in considering the effect of imposing the restriction $\mathbf{s}(\boldsymbol{\beta}_o) = \mathbf{0}$, we can just compare the asymptotic behavior of $\boldsymbol{\beta}_n^*$ to $\tilde{\boldsymbol{\beta}}_n$

As we saw in Proposition 4.45, the asymptotically efficient IV estimator takes $\hat{\mathbf{P}}_n = \hat{\mathbf{V}}_n^{-1}$. We therefore consider the effect of imposing constraints on the IV estimator with $\hat{\mathbf{P}}_n = \hat{\mathbf{V}}_n^{-1}$.

Theorem 4.49 *Suppose the conditions of Exercise 4.26 hold for* $\hat{\mathbf{P}}_n = \hat{\mathbf{V}}_n^{-1}$ *and that* $\mathbf{s} : \mathbb{R}^k \to \mathbb{R}^q$ *is a continuously differentiable function such that* $\mathbf{s}(\boldsymbol{\beta}_o) = \mathbf{0}$, $\nabla \mathbf{s}(\boldsymbol{\beta}_o)$ *is finite and* $\operatorname{rank}(\nabla \mathbf{s}(\boldsymbol{\beta}_o)) = q$. *Define* $\tilde{\boldsymbol{\beta}}_n = (\mathbf{X}'\mathbf{Z}\hat{\mathbf{V}}_n^{-1}\mathbf{Z}'\mathbf{X})^{-1}\mathbf{X}'\mathbf{Z}\hat{\mathbf{V}}_n^{-1}\mathbf{Z}'\mathbf{Y}$ *and define* $\boldsymbol{\beta}_n^*$ *as the constrained IV estimator above with* $\hat{\mathbf{P}}_n = \hat{\mathbf{V}}_n^{-1}$. *Then*

$$\begin{aligned}&\operatorname{avar}(\tilde{\boldsymbol{\beta}}_n) - \operatorname{avar}(\boldsymbol{\beta}_n^*) \\ &\quad = \operatorname{avar}(\tilde{\boldsymbol{\beta}}_n)\nabla \mathbf{s}(\boldsymbol{\beta}_o)[\nabla \mathbf{s}(\boldsymbol{\beta}_o)'\operatorname{avar}(\tilde{\boldsymbol{\beta}}_n)\nabla \mathbf{s}(\boldsymbol{\beta}_o)]^{-1}\nabla \mathbf{s}(\boldsymbol{\beta}_o)'\operatorname{avar}(\tilde{\boldsymbol{\beta}}_n),\end{aligned}$$

which is a positive semidefinite matrix.

Proof. From Exercise 4.26 it follows that

$$\operatorname{avar}(\tilde{\boldsymbol{\beta}}_n) = (\mathbf{Q}_n'\mathbf{V}_n^{-1}\mathbf{Q}_n)^{-1}.$$

Taking a mean value expansion of $\mathbf{s}(\tilde{\boldsymbol{\beta}}_n)$ around $\boldsymbol{\beta}_o$ gives $\mathbf{s}(\tilde{\boldsymbol{\beta}}_n) = \mathbf{s}(\boldsymbol{\beta}_o) + \nabla \bar{\mathbf{s}}'(\tilde{\boldsymbol{\beta}}_n - \boldsymbol{\beta}_o)$, and because $\mathbf{s}(\boldsymbol{\beta}_o) = \mathbf{0}$, we have $\mathbf{s}(\tilde{\boldsymbol{\beta}}_n) = \nabla \bar{\mathbf{s}}'(\tilde{\boldsymbol{\beta}}_n - \boldsymbol{\beta}_o)$. Substituting this in the formula for $\boldsymbol{\beta}_n^*$ allows us to write

$$\sqrt{n}(\boldsymbol{\beta}_n^* - \boldsymbol{\beta}_o) = \tilde{\mathbf{A}}_n\sqrt{n}(\tilde{\boldsymbol{\beta}}_n - \boldsymbol{\beta}_o),$$

where

$$\begin{aligned}\tilde{\mathbf{A}}_n &= \mathbf{I} - (\mathbf{X}'\mathbf{Z}\hat{\mathbf{V}}_n^{-1}\mathbf{Z}'\mathbf{X})^{-1}\nabla\mathbf{s}(\tilde{\boldsymbol{\beta}}_n)[\nabla\mathbf{s}(\tilde{\boldsymbol{\beta}}_n)' \\ &\quad\times(\mathbf{X}'\mathbf{Z}\hat{\mathbf{V}}_n^{-1}\mathbf{Z}'\mathbf{X})^{-1}\nabla\mathbf{s}(\tilde{\boldsymbol{\beta}}_n)]^{-1}\nabla\bar{\mathbf{s}}'.\end{aligned}$$

Under the conditions of Exercise 4.26, $\tilde{\boldsymbol{\beta}}_n \xrightarrow{p} \boldsymbol{\beta}_o$ and Proposition 2.30 applies to ensure that $\tilde{\mathbf{A}}_n - \mathbf{A}_n \xrightarrow{p} \mathbf{0}$, where

$$\mathbf{A}_n = \mathbf{I} - \text{avar}(\tilde{\boldsymbol{\beta}}_n)\nabla\mathbf{s}(\boldsymbol{\beta}_0)[\nabla\mathbf{s}(\boldsymbol{\beta}_o)'\text{avar}(\tilde{\boldsymbol{\beta}}_n)\nabla\mathbf{s}(\boldsymbol{\beta}_0)]^{-1}\nabla\mathbf{s}(\boldsymbol{\beta}_o)'.$$

Hence, by Lemma 4.6,

$$\sqrt{n}(\boldsymbol{\beta}_n^* - \boldsymbol{\beta}_o) - \mathbf{A}_n\sqrt{n}(\tilde{\boldsymbol{\beta}}_n - \boldsymbol{\beta}_o) = (\tilde{\mathbf{A}}_n - \mathbf{A}_n)\sqrt{n}(\tilde{\boldsymbol{\beta}}_n - \boldsymbol{\beta}_o) \xrightarrow{p} \mathbf{0},$$

because $\sqrt{n}(\tilde{\boldsymbol{\beta}}_n - \boldsymbol{\beta}_o)$ is $O_p(1)$ as a consequence of Exercise 4.26. From the asymptotic equivalence Lemma 4.7 it follows that $\sqrt{n}(\boldsymbol{\beta}_n^* - \boldsymbol{\beta}_o)$ has the same asymptotic distribution as $\mathbf{A}_n\sqrt{n}(\tilde{\boldsymbol{\beta}}_n - \boldsymbol{\beta}_o)$. It follows from Lemma 4.23 that $\sqrt{n}(\boldsymbol{\beta}_n^* - \boldsymbol{\beta}_o)$ is asymptotically normal with mean zero and

$$\text{avar}(\boldsymbol{\beta}_n^*) = \boldsymbol{\Gamma}_n = \mathbf{A}_n\text{avar}(\tilde{\boldsymbol{\beta}}_n)\mathbf{A}_n'.$$

Straightforward algebra yields

$$\begin{aligned}\text{avar}(\boldsymbol{\beta}_n^*) &= \text{avar}(\tilde{\boldsymbol{\beta}}_n) - \text{avar}(\tilde{\boldsymbol{\beta}}_n)\nabla\mathbf{s}(\boldsymbol{\beta}_o) \\ &\quad\times[\nabla\mathbf{s}(\boldsymbol{\beta}_o)'\text{avar}(\tilde{\boldsymbol{\beta}}_n)\nabla\mathbf{s}(\boldsymbol{\beta}_o)]^{-1}\nabla\mathbf{s}(\boldsymbol{\beta}_o)'\text{avar}(\tilde{\boldsymbol{\beta}}_n),\end{aligned}$$

and the result follows immediately. ■

This result guarantees that imposing correct a priori restrictions leads to an efficiency improvement over the efficient IV estimator that does not impose these restrictions. Interestingly, imposing the restrictions using the formula for $\boldsymbol{\beta}_n^*$ with an inefficient estimator $\tilde{\boldsymbol{\beta}}_n$ for given instrumental variables may or may not lead to efficiency gains relative to $\tilde{\boldsymbol{\beta}}_n$.

A feature of this result worth noting is that the asymptotic distribution of the constrained estimator $\boldsymbol{\beta}_n^*$ is concentrated in a $k - q$-dimensional subspace of $\mathbb{R}^k$, so that $\text{avar}(\boldsymbol{\beta}_n^*)$ will not be nonsingular. Instead, it has rank $k - q$. In particular, observe that

$$\sqrt{n}(\boldsymbol{\beta}_n^* - \boldsymbol{\beta}_o) = \sqrt{n}\mathbf{A}_n(\tilde{\boldsymbol{\beta}}_n - \boldsymbol{\beta}_o).$$

But

$$\begin{aligned}\nabla\mathbf{s}(\boldsymbol{\beta}_o)'\mathbf{A}_n &= \nabla\mathbf{s}(\boldsymbol{\beta}_o)'\Big(\mathbf{I} - \text{avar}(\tilde{\boldsymbol{\beta}}_n)\nabla\mathbf{s}(\boldsymbol{\beta}_o) \\ &\quad\times[\nabla\mathbf{s}(\boldsymbol{\beta}_o)'\text{avar}(\tilde{\boldsymbol{\beta}}_n)\nabla\mathbf{s}(\boldsymbol{\beta}_o)]^{-1}\nabla\mathbf{s}(\boldsymbol{\beta}_o)'\Big) \\ &= \nabla\mathbf{s}(\boldsymbol{\beta}_o)' - \nabla\mathbf{s}(\boldsymbol{\beta}_o)' \\ &= \mathbf{0}.\end{aligned}$$

Consequently, we have

$$\text{avar}(\sqrt{n}\,\nabla \mathbf{s}(\boldsymbol{\beta}_o)'(\boldsymbol{\beta}_n^* - \boldsymbol{\beta}_o)) = \mathbf{0}.$$

An alternative way to improve the asymptotic efficiency of the IV estimator is to include additional valid instrumental variables. To establish this, we make use of the formula for the inverse of a partitioned matrix, which we now state for convenience.

Proposition 4.50 *Define the $k \times k$ nonsingular symmetric matrix*

$$\mathbf{A} = \begin{bmatrix} \mathbf{B} & \mathbf{C}' \\ \mathbf{C} & \mathbf{D} \end{bmatrix},$$

where $\mathbf{B}$ is $k_1 \times k_1$, $\mathbf{C}$ is $k_2 \times k_1$ and $\mathbf{D}$ is $k_2 \times k_2$. Then, defining $\mathbf{E} \equiv \mathbf{D} - \mathbf{C}\mathbf{B}^{-1}\mathbf{C}'$,

$$\mathbf{A}^{-1} = \begin{bmatrix} \mathbf{B}^{-1}(\mathbf{I} + \mathbf{C}'\mathbf{E}^{-1}\mathbf{C}\mathbf{B}^{-1}) & -\mathbf{B}^{-1}\mathbf{C}'\mathbf{E}^{-1} \\ -\mathbf{E}^{-1}\mathbf{C}\mathbf{B}^{-1} & \mathbf{E}^{-1} \end{bmatrix}.$$

Proof. See Goldberger (1964, p. 27). ∎

Proposition 4.51 *Partition $\mathbf{Z}$ as $\mathbf{Z} = (\mathbf{Z}_1, \mathbf{Z}_2)$ and let $\mathcal{P}$ be the collection of all probability measures such that the conditions of Exercise 4.26 hold for both $\mathbf{Z}_1$ and $\mathbf{Z}_2$. Define $\mathbf{V}_{1n} = E(\mathbf{Z}_1'\boldsymbol{\varepsilon}\boldsymbol{\varepsilon}'\mathbf{Z}_1/n)$, and the estimators*

$$\begin{aligned} \tilde{\boldsymbol{\beta}}_n &= (\mathbf{X}'\mathbf{Z}_1\hat{\mathbf{V}}_{1n}^{-1}\mathbf{Z}_1'\mathbf{X})^{-1}\mathbf{X}'\mathbf{Z}_1\hat{\mathbf{V}}_{1n}^{-1}\mathbf{Z}_1'\mathbf{Y}, \\ \boldsymbol{\beta}_n^* &= (\mathbf{X}'\mathbf{Z}\hat{\mathbf{V}}_n^{-1}\mathbf{Z}'\mathbf{X})^{-1}\mathbf{X}'\mathbf{Z}\hat{\mathbf{V}}_n^{-1}\mathbf{Z}'\mathbf{Y}. \end{aligned}$$

Then for each P^o in $\mathcal{P}$, $\text{avar}(\tilde{\boldsymbol{\beta}}_n) - \text{avar}(\boldsymbol{\beta}_n^*)$ is a positive semidefinite matrix for all n sufficiently large.

Proof. Partition $\mathbf{Q}_n$ as $\mathbf{Q}_n' = (\mathbf{Q}_{1n}', \mathbf{Q}_{2n}')$, where $\mathbf{Q}_{1n} = E(\mathbf{Z}_1'\mathbf{X}/n)$, $\mathbf{Q}_{2n} = E(\mathbf{Z}_2'\mathbf{X}/n)$, and partition $\mathbf{V}_n$ as

$$\mathbf{V}_n = \begin{bmatrix} \mathbf{V}_{1n} & \mathbf{V}_{12n} \\ \mathbf{V}_{21n} & \mathbf{V}_{2n} \end{bmatrix}.$$

The partitioned inverse formula gives

$$\mathbf{V}_n^{-1} = \begin{bmatrix} \mathbf{V}_{1n}^{-1}(\mathbf{I} + \mathbf{V}_{12n}\mathbf{E}_n^{-1}\mathbf{V}_{21n})\mathbf{V}_{1n}^{-1} & -\mathbf{V}_{1n}^{-1}\mathbf{V}_{12n}\mathbf{E}_n^{-1} \\ -\mathbf{E}_n^{-1}\mathbf{V}_{21n}\mathbf{V}_{1n}^{-1} & \mathbf{E}_n^{-1} \end{bmatrix},$$

where $\mathbf{E}_n = \mathbf{V}_{2n} - \mathbf{V}_{21n}\mathbf{V}_{1n}^{-1}\mathbf{V}_{12n}$. From Exercise 4.26, we have

$$\begin{aligned}\text{avar}(\tilde{\boldsymbol{\beta}}_n) &= \left(\mathbf{Q}_{1n}'\mathbf{V}_{1n}^{-1}\mathbf{Q}_{1n}\right)^{-1}, \\ \text{avar}(\boldsymbol{\beta}_n^*) &= \left(\mathbf{Q}_n'\mathbf{V}_n^{-1}\mathbf{Q}_n\right)^{-1}.\end{aligned}$$

We apply Proposition 4.44 and consider

$$\begin{aligned}&\left(\text{avar}(\boldsymbol{\beta}_n^*)\right)^{-1} - \left(\text{avar}(\tilde{\boldsymbol{\beta}}_n)\right)^{-1} \\ &= \mathbf{Q}_n'\mathbf{V}_n^{-1}\mathbf{Q}_n - \mathbf{Q}_{1n}'\mathbf{V}_{1n}^{-1}\mathbf{Q}_{1n} \\ &= [\mathbf{Q}_{1n}', \mathbf{Q}_{2n}']\,\mathbf{V}_n^{-1}\,[\mathbf{Q}_{1n}', \mathbf{Q}_{2n}']' - \mathbf{Q}_{1n}'\mathbf{V}_{1n}^{-1}\mathbf{Q}_{1n} \\ &= \mathbf{Q}_{1n}'\left(\mathbf{V}_{1n}^{-1} + \mathbf{V}_{1n}^{-1}\mathbf{V}_{12n}\mathbf{E}_n^{-1}\mathbf{V}_{21n}\mathbf{V}_{1n}^{-1}\right)\mathbf{Q}_{1n} \\ &\quad -\mathbf{Q}_{2n}'\mathbf{E}_n^{-1}\mathbf{V}_{21n}\mathbf{V}_{1n}^{-1}\mathbf{Q}_{1n} - \mathbf{Q}_{1n}'\mathbf{V}_{1n}^{-1}\mathbf{V}_{12n}\mathbf{E}_n^{-1}\mathbf{Q}_{2n} \\ &\quad +\mathbf{Q}_{2n}'\mathbf{E}_n^{-1}\mathbf{Q}_{2n} - \mathbf{Q}_{1n}'\mathbf{V}_{1n}^{-1}\mathbf{Q}_{1n} \\ &= \left(\mathbf{Q}_{1n}'\mathbf{V}_{1n}^{-1}\mathbf{V}_{12n} - \mathbf{Q}_{2n}'\right)\mathbf{E}_n^{-1}\left(\mathbf{V}_{21n}\mathbf{V}_{1n}^{-1}\mathbf{Q}_{1n} - \mathbf{Q}_{2n}\right).\end{aligned}$$

Because $\mathbf{E}_n^{-1}$ is a symmetric positive definite matrix (why?), we can write $\mathbf{E}_n^{-1} = \mathbf{E}_n^{-1/2}\mathbf{E}_n^{-1/2}$, so that

$$\begin{aligned}&\left(\text{avar}(\boldsymbol{\beta}_n^*)\right)^{-1} - \left(\text{avar}(\tilde{\boldsymbol{\beta}}_n)\right)^{-1} \\ &\quad = \left(\mathbf{Q}_{1n}'\mathbf{V}_{1n}^{-1}\mathbf{V}_{12n} - \mathbf{Q}_{2n}'\right)\mathbf{E}_n^{-1/2}\mathbf{E}_n^{-1/2}\left(\mathbf{V}_{21n}\mathbf{V}_{1n}^{-1}\mathbf{Q}_{1n} - \mathbf{Q}_{2n}\right).\end{aligned}$$

Because this is the product of a matrix and its transpose, we immediately have $(\text{avar}(\boldsymbol{\beta}_n^*))^{-1} - (\text{avar}(\tilde{\boldsymbol{\beta}}_n))^{-1}$ is p.s.d. As this holds for all P^o in $\mathcal{P}$ the result follows, which by Proposition 4.44 implies that $\text{avar}(\tilde{\boldsymbol{\beta}}_n) - \text{avar}(\boldsymbol{\beta}_n^*)$ is p.s.d. ∎

This result states essentially that the asymptotic precision of the IV estimator cannot be worsened by including additional instrumental variables. We can be more specific, however, and specify situations in which $\text{avar}(\boldsymbol{\beta}_n^*) = \text{avar}(\tilde{\boldsymbol{\beta}}_n)$, so that nothing is gained by adding an extra instrumental variable.

Proposition 4.52 *Let the conditions of Proposition 4.51 hold. Then we have* $\text{avar}(\tilde{\boldsymbol{\beta}}_n) = \text{avar}(\boldsymbol{\beta}_n^*)$ *if and only if*

$$E(\mathbf{X}'\mathbf{Z}_1/n)E(\mathbf{Z}_1'\boldsymbol{\varepsilon}\boldsymbol{\varepsilon}'\mathbf{Z}_1/n)^{-1}E(\mathbf{Z}_1'\boldsymbol{\varepsilon}\boldsymbol{\varepsilon}'\mathbf{Z}_2/n) - E(\mathbf{X}'\mathbf{Z}_2/n) = \mathbf{0}.$$

Proof. Immediate from the final line of the proof of Proposition 4.51. ∎

To interpret this condition, consider the special case in which

$$E(\mathbf{Z}'\varepsilon\varepsilon'\mathbf{Z}/n) = E(\mathbf{Z}'\mathbf{Z}/n).$$

In this case the difference in Proposition 4.52 can be consistently estimated by

$$n^{-1}(\mathbf{X}'\mathbf{Z}_1(\mathbf{Z}_1'\mathbf{Z}^1)^{-1}\mathbf{Z}_1'\mathbf{Z}_2 - \mathbf{X}'\mathbf{Z}_2) = n^{-1}\mathbf{X}\left[\mathbf{Z}_1(\mathbf{Z}_1'\mathbf{Z}_1)^{-1}\mathbf{Z}_1' - \mathbf{I}\right]\mathbf{Z}_2.$$

This quantity is recognizable as the cross product of $\mathbf{Z}_2$ and the projection of $\mathbf{X}$ onto the space orthogonal to that spanned by the columns of $\mathbf{Z}_1$. If we write $\tilde{\mathbf{X}} = \mathbf{X}(\mathbf{Z}_1(\mathbf{Z}_1'\mathbf{Z}_1)^{-1}\mathbf{Z}_1' - \mathbf{I})$, the difference in Proposition 4.52 is consistently estimated by $\tilde{\mathbf{X}}'\mathbf{Z}_2/n$, so that $\text{avar}(\tilde{\beta}_n) = \text{avar}(\beta_n^*)$ if and only if $\tilde{\mathbf{X}}'\mathbf{Z}_2/n \xrightarrow{p} \mathbf{0}$, which can be interpreted as saying that adding $\mathbf{Z}_2$ to the list of instrumental variables is of no use if it is uncorrelated with $\tilde{\mathbf{X}}$, the matrix of residuals of the regression of $\mathbf{X}$ on $\mathbf{Z}_1$.

One of the interesting consequences of Propositions 4.51 and 4.52 is that in the presence of heteroskedasticity or serial correlation of unknown form, there may exist estimators for the linear model more efficient than OLS. This result has been obtained independently by Cragg (1983) and Chamberlain (1982). To construct these estimators, it is necessary to find additional instrumental variables uncorrelated with ε_t. If $E(\varepsilon_t|\mathbf{X}_t) = \mathbf{0}$, such instrumental variables are easily found because any measurable function of $\mathbf{X}_t$ will be uncorrelated with ε_t. Hence, we can set $\mathbf{Z}_t = (\mathbf{X}_t', \mathbf{z}(\mathbf{X}_t)')'$, where $\mathbf{z}(\mathbf{X}_t)$ is a $(l-k)\times 1$ vector of measurable functions of $\mathbf{X}_t$.

Example 4.53 *Let $p = k = 1$ so $Y_t = X_t\beta_o + \varepsilon_t$, where Y_t, X_t and ε_t are scalars. Suppose that X_t is nonstochastic, and for convenience suppose $M_n \equiv n^{-1}\sum X_t^2 \to 1$. Let ε_t be independent heterogeneously distributed such that $E(\varepsilon_t) = 0$ and $E(\varepsilon_t^2) = \sigma_t^2$. Further, suppose $X_t > \delta > 0$ for all t, and take $z(X_t) = X_t^{-1}$ so that $\mathbf{Z}_t = (X_t, X_t^{-1})'$. We consider $\hat{\beta}_n = (\mathbf{X}'\mathbf{X})^{-1}\mathbf{X}'\mathbf{Y}$ and $\beta_n^* = (\mathbf{X}'\mathbf{Z}\hat{\mathbf{V}}_n^{-1}\mathbf{Z}\mathbf{X})^{-1}\mathbf{X}'\mathbf{Z}\hat{\mathbf{V}}_n^{-1}\mathbf{Z}'\mathbf{Y}$, and suppose that sufficient other assumptions guarantee that the result of Exercise 4.26 holds for both estimators. By Propositions 4.51 and 4.52, it follows that* $\text{avar}(\hat{\beta}_n) > \text{avar}(\beta_n^*)$ *if and only if*

$$\left(n^{-1}\sum_{t=1}^{n}\sigma_t^2X_t^2\right)^{-1}\left(n^{-1}\sum_{t=1}^{n}\sigma_t^2\right) - 1 \neq 0$$

or equivalently, if and only if $n^{-1}\sum_{t=1}^{n}\sigma_t^2X_t^2 \neq n^{-1}\sum_{t=1}^{n}\sigma_t^2$. This would certainly occur if $\sigma_t = X_t^{-1}$. (Verify this using Jensen's inequality.)

It also follows from Propositions 4.51 and 4.52 that when $\mathbf{V}_n \neq \mathbf{L}_n$, there may exist estimators more efficient than two-stage least squares. If $l > k$, additional instrumental variables are not necessarily required to improve efficiency over 2SLS (see White, 1982); but as the result of Proposition 4.51 indicates, additional instrumental variables (e.g., functions of $\mathbf{Z}_t$) can nevertheless generate further improvements.

The results so far suggest that in particular situations efficiency may or may not be improved by using additional instrumental variables. This leads us to ask whether there exists an optimal set of instrumental variables, that is, a set of instrumental variables that one could not improve upon by using additional instrumental variables. If so, we could in principle definitively know whether or not a given set of instrumental variables is best.

To address this question, we introduce an approach developed by Bates and White (1993) that permits direct construction of the optimal instrumental variables. This is in sharp contrast to the approach taken when we considered the best choice for $\hat{\mathbf{P}}_n$. There, we seemingly pulled the best choice, $\hat{\mathbf{V}}_n^{-1}$, out of a hat (as if by magic!), and simply verified its optimality. There was no hint of how we arrived at this choice. (This is a common feature of the efficiency literature, a feature that has endowed it with no little mystery.) With the Bates–White method, however, we will be able to see how to construct the optimal (most efficient) instrumental variables estimators, step-by-step.

Bates and White consider classes of estimators $\mathcal{E}$ indexed by a parameter γ such that for each data generating process P^o in a set $\mathcal{P}$,

$$\sqrt{n}(\hat{\boldsymbol{\theta}}_n(\gamma) - \boldsymbol{\theta}^o) = \mathbf{H}_n^o(\gamma)^{-1}\sqrt{n}\mathbf{s}_n^o(\gamma) + o_{p^o}(1), \tag{4.1}$$

where: $\hat{\boldsymbol{\theta}}_n(\gamma)$ is an estimator indexed by γ taking values in a set Γ; $\boldsymbol{\theta}^o = \boldsymbol{\theta}(P^o)$ is the $k \times 1$ parameter vector corresponding to the data generating process P^o; $\mathbf{H}_n^o(\gamma)$ is a nonstochastic nonsingular $k \times k$ matrix depending on γ and P^o; $\mathbf{s}_n^o(\gamma)$ is a random $k \times 1$ vector depending on γ and P^o such that $\mathbf{I}_n^o(\gamma)^{-1/2}\sqrt{n}\mathbf{s}_n^o(\gamma) \xrightarrow{d^o} N(\mathbf{0}, \mathbf{I})$, where $\mathbf{I}_n^o(\gamma) \equiv \text{var}^o(\sqrt{n}\mathbf{s}_n^o(\gamma))$, $\xrightarrow{d^o}$ denotes convergence in distribution under P^o, and var^o denotes variance under P^o; and $o_{p^o}(1)$ denotes terms vanishing in probability-P^o. Bates and White consider how to choose γ in Γ to obtain an asymptotically efficient estimator.

Bates and White's method is actually formulated for a more general setting but (4.1) will suffice for us here.

To relate the Bates–White method to our instrumental variables estimation framework, we begin by writing the process generating the dependent variables in a way that makes explicit the role of P^o. Specifically, we write

$$\mathbf{Y}_t^o = \mathbf{X}_t^{o\prime}\boldsymbol{\beta}^o + \varepsilon_t, \quad t = 1, 2, \ldots .$$

The rationale for this is as follows. The data generating process P^o governs the probabilistic behavior of all of the random variables (measurable mappings from the underlying measurable space $(\Omega, \mathcal{F})$) in our system. Given the way our data are generated, the probabilistic behavior of the mapping ε_t is governed by P^o, but the mapping itself is not determined by P^o. We thus do not give a ^{o} superscript to ε_t.

On the other hand, different values $\boldsymbol{\beta}^o$ (corresponding to $\boldsymbol{\theta}^o$ in the Bates–White setting) result in different mappings for the dependent variables; we acknowledge this by writing $\mathbf{Y}_t^o$, and we view $\boldsymbol{\beta}^o$ as determined by P^o, i.e., $\boldsymbol{\beta}^o = \boldsymbol{\beta}(P^o)$. Further, because lags of $\mathbf{Y}_t^o$ or elements of $\mathbf{Y}_t^o$ itself (recall the simultaneous equations framework) may appear as elements of the explanatory variable matrix, different values for $\boldsymbol{\beta}^o$ may also result in different mappings for the explanatory variables. We acknowledge this by writing $\mathbf{X}_t^o$.

Next, consider the instrumental variables. These also are measurable mappings from $\{\Omega, \mathcal{F}\}$ whose probabilistic behavior is governed by P^o. As we will see, it is useful to permit these mappings to depend on P^o as well. Consequently, we write $\mathbf{Z}_t^o$. Because our goal is the choice of optimal instrumental variables, we let $\mathbf{Z}_t^o$ depend on γ and write $\mathbf{Z}_t^o(\gamma)$ to emphasize this dependence. The optimal choice of γ will then deliver the optimal choice of instrumental variables. Later, we will revisit and extend this interpretation of γ.

In Exercise 4.26 (*ii*), we assume $\mathbf{V}_n^{-1/2} n^{-1/2}\mathbf{Z}'\varepsilon \xrightarrow{d} N(\mathbf{0}, \mathbf{I})$, where $\mathbf{V}_n \equiv \text{var}(n^{-1/2}\mathbf{Z}'\varepsilon)$. For the Bates–White framework with $\mathbf{Z}_t^o(\gamma)$, this becomes $\mathbf{V}_n^o(\gamma)^{-1/2} n^{-1/2}\mathbf{Z}^o(\gamma)'\varepsilon \xrightarrow{d^o} N(\mathbf{0}, \mathbf{I})$, where $\mathbf{V}_n^o(\gamma) \equiv \text{var}^o(n^{-1/2}$ $\mathbf{Z}^o(\gamma)'\varepsilon)$, and $\mathbf{Z}^o(\gamma)$ is the $np \times l$ matrix with blocks $\mathbf{Z}_t^o(\gamma)'$. In (*iii.a*) we assume $\mathbf{Z}'\mathbf{X}/n - \mathbf{Q}_n = o_p(1)$, where $\mathbf{Q}_n \equiv E(\mathbf{Z}'\mathbf{X}/n)$ is $O(1)$ with uniformly full column rank. This becomes $\mathbf{Z}^o(\gamma)'\mathbf{X}^o/n - \mathbf{Q}_n^o = o_{p^o}(1)$, where $\mathbf{Q}_n^o \equiv E^o(\mathbf{Z}^o(\gamma)'\mathbf{X}^o/n)$ is $O(1)$ with uniformly full column rank; $E^o(\cdot)$ denotes expectation with respect to P^o. In (*iii.b*) we assume $\hat{\mathbf{P}}_n - \mathbf{P}_n = o_p(1)$, where $\mathbf{P}_n$ is $O(1)$ and uniformly positive definite. This becomes $\hat{\mathbf{P}}_n(\gamma) - \mathbf{P}_n^o(\gamma) = o_{p^o}(1)$, where $\mathbf{P}_n^o(\gamma)$ is $O(1)$ and uniformly positive definite. Finally, the instrumental variables estimator has the form

$$\tilde{\boldsymbol{\beta}}_n(\gamma) = \left(\mathbf{X}^{o\prime}\mathbf{Z}^o(\gamma)\hat{\mathbf{P}}_n(\gamma)\mathbf{Z}^o(\gamma)'\mathbf{X}^o\right)^{-1}\mathbf{X}^{o\prime}\mathbf{Z}^o(\gamma)\hat{\mathbf{P}}_n(\gamma)\mathbf{Z}^o(\gamma)'\mathbf{Y}^o.$$

We will use the following further extension of Exercise 4.26.

Theorem 4.54 *Let $\mathcal{P}$ be a set of probability measures P^o on $(\Omega, \mathcal{F})$, and let Γ be a set with elements γ. Suppose that for each P^o in $\mathcal{P}$*

(i) $\mathbf{Y}_t^o = \mathbf{X}_t^{o\prime}\boldsymbol{\beta}^o + \varepsilon_t, \quad t = 1, 2, \ldots, \boldsymbol{\beta}^o \in \mathbb{R}^k$.

For each γ in Γ and each P^o in $\mathcal{P}$, let $\{\mathbf{Z}_{nt}^o(\gamma)\}$ be a double array of random $p \times l$ matrices, such that

(ii) $n^{-1/2}\sum_{t=1}^n \mathbf{Z}_{nt}^o(\gamma)\varepsilon_t - n^{1/2}\mathbf{m}_n^o(\gamma) = o_{p^o}(1)$, *where*

$$\mathbf{V}_n^o(\gamma)^{-1/2} n^{1/2}\mathbf{m}_n^o(\gamma) \xrightarrow{d^o} N(\mathbf{0}, \mathbf{I}),$$

and $\mathbf{V}_n^o(\gamma) \equiv \text{var}^o(n^{1/2}\mathbf{m}_n^o(\gamma))$ is $O(1)$ and uniformly positive definite;

(iii) (a) $n^{-1}\sum_{t=1}^n \mathbf{Z}_{nt}^o(\gamma)\mathbf{X}_t^{o\prime} - \mathbf{Q}_n^o(\gamma) = o_{p^o}(1)$, *where $\mathbf{Q}_n^o(\gamma)$ is $O(1)$ with uniformly full column rank;*

(b) *There exists $\hat{\mathbf{P}}_n(\gamma)$ such that $\hat{\mathbf{P}}_n(\gamma) - \mathbf{P}_n^o(\gamma) = o_{p^o}(1)$ and $\mathbf{P}_n^o(\gamma) = O(1)$ and is symmetric and uniformly positive definite.*

Then for each P^o in $\mathcal{P}$ and γ in Γ

$$\mathbf{D}_n^o(\gamma)^{-1/2}\sqrt{n}\left(\tilde{\boldsymbol{\beta}}_n(\gamma) - \boldsymbol{\beta}^o\right) \xrightarrow{d^o} N(\mathbf{0}, \mathbf{I}),$$

where

$$\begin{aligned}\mathbf{D}_n^o(\gamma) \;\equiv\; & \left(\mathbf{Q}_n^o(\gamma)'\mathbf{P}_n^o(\gamma)\mathbf{Q}_n^o(\gamma)\right)^{-1} \\ & \times \mathbf{Q}_n^o(\gamma)'\mathbf{P}_n^o(\gamma)\mathbf{V}_n^o(\gamma)\mathbf{P}_n^o(\gamma)\mathbf{Q}_n^o(\gamma)\left(\mathbf{Q}_n^o(\gamma)'\mathbf{P}_n^o(\gamma)\mathbf{Q}_n^o(\gamma)\right)^{-1}\end{aligned}$$

and $\mathbf{D}_n^o(\gamma)^{-1}$ are $O(1)$.

Proof. Apply the proof of Exercise 4.26 for each P^o in $\mathcal{P}$ and γ in Γ. ∎

This result is stated with features that permit fairly general applications, discussed further next. In particular, we let $\{\mathbf{Z}_{nt}^o(\gamma)\}$ be a double array of matrices. In some cases a single array (sequence) $\{\mathbf{Z}_t^o(\gamma)\}$ suffices. In such cases we can simply put $\mathbf{m}_n^o(\gamma) = n^{-1}\mathbf{Z}^o(\gamma)'\boldsymbol{\varepsilon}$, so that $\mathbf{V}_n^o(\gamma) \equiv \text{var}^o(n^{-1/2}\mathbf{Z}^o(\gamma)'\boldsymbol{\varepsilon})$, parallel to Exercise 4.26. In this case we also have $\mathbf{Q}_n^o(\gamma) = E^o(\mathbf{Z}^o(\gamma)'\mathbf{X}^o/n)$. These identifications will suffice for now, but the additional flexibility permitted in Theorem 4.54 will become useful shortly. Recall that the proof of Exercise 4.26 gives

$$\begin{aligned}\sqrt{n}\left(\tilde{\boldsymbol{\beta}}_n(\gamma) - \boldsymbol{\beta}^o\right) \;=\; & \left(\mathbf{Q}_n^o(\gamma)'\mathbf{V}_n^o(\gamma)^{-1}\mathbf{Q}_n^o(\gamma)\right)^{-1} \\ & \times \mathbf{Q}_n^o(\gamma)'\mathbf{V}_n^o(\gamma)^{-1} n^{-1/2}\mathbf{Z}^o(\gamma)'\boldsymbol{\varepsilon} + o_{p^o}(1)\end{aligned}$$

when we choose $\hat{\mathbf{P}}_n(\gamma)$ so that $\mathbf{P}_n^o(\gamma) = \mathbf{V}_n^o(\gamma)^{-1}$, the asymptotically efficient choice. Comparing this expression to (4.1) we see that $\tilde{\boldsymbol{\beta}}_n(\gamma)$ corresponds to $\hat{\theta}_n(\gamma)$, $\mathcal{E}$ is the set of estimators $\mathcal{E} \equiv \{\{\tilde{\boldsymbol{\beta}}_n(\gamma)\},\ \gamma \in \Gamma\}$, $\boldsymbol{\beta}^o$ corresponds to $\boldsymbol{\theta}^o$, and we can put

$$\begin{aligned}
\mathbf{H}_n^o(\gamma) &= \mathbf{Q}_n^o(\gamma)'\mathbf{V}_n^o(\gamma)^{-1}\mathbf{Q}_n^o(\gamma) \\
\mathbf{s}_n^o(\gamma) &= \mathbf{Q}_n^o(\gamma)'\mathbf{V}_n^o(\gamma)^{-1}n^{-1}\mathbf{Z}^o(\gamma)'\varepsilon \\
\mathbf{I}_n^o(\gamma) &= \mathbf{H}_n^o(\gamma).
\end{aligned}$$

Our consideration of the construction of the optimal instrumental variables estimator makes essential use of these correspondences.

The key to applying the Bates–White constructive method here is the following result, a version of Theorem 2.6 of Bates and White (1993).

Proposition 4.55 *Let $\hat{\theta}_n(\gamma)$ satisfy (4.1) for all γ in a nonempty set Γ and all P^o in $\mathcal{P}$, and suppose there exists γ^* in Γ such that*

$$\mathbf{H}_n^o(\gamma) = \text{cov}^o\left(\sqrt{n}\mathbf{s}_n^o(\gamma), \sqrt{n}\mathbf{s}_n^o(\gamma^*)\right) \tag{4.2}$$

for all $\gamma \in \Gamma$ and all P^o in $\mathcal{P}$. Then for all $\gamma \in \Gamma$ and all P^o in $\mathcal{P}$

$$\text{avar}^o\left(\hat{\theta}_n(\gamma)\right) - \text{avar}^o\left(\hat{\theta}_n(\gamma^*)\right)$$

is positive semidefinite for all n sufficiently large.

Proof. Given (4.1), we have that for all γ in Γ, all P^o in $\mathcal{P}$, and all n sufficiently large

$$\begin{aligned}
\text{avar}^o\left(\hat{\theta}_n(\gamma)\right) &= \mathbf{H}_n^o(\gamma)^{-1}\mathbf{I}_n^o(\gamma)\mathbf{H}_n^o(\gamma)^{-1} \\
\text{avar}^o\left(\hat{\theta}_n(\gamma^*)\right) &= \mathbf{H}_n^o(\gamma^*)^{-1}\mathbf{I}_n^o(\gamma^*)\mathbf{H}_n^o(\gamma^*)^{-1} = \mathbf{H}_n^o(\gamma^*)^{-1},
\end{aligned}$$

so

$$\text{avar}^o\left(\hat{\theta}_n(\gamma)\right) - \text{avar}^o\left(\hat{\theta}_n(\gamma^*)\right) = \mathbf{H}_n^o(\gamma)^{-1}\mathbf{I}_n^o(\gamma)\mathbf{H}_n^o(\gamma)^{-1} - \mathbf{H}_n^o(\gamma^*)^{-1}.$$

We now show that this quantity equals

$$\text{var}^o(\mathbf{H}_n^o(\gamma)^{-1}\sqrt{n}\mathbf{s}_n^o(\gamma) - \mathbf{H}_n^o(\gamma^*)^{-1}\sqrt{n}\mathbf{s}_n^o(\gamma^*)).$$

Note that (4.2) implies

$$\text{var}^o\begin{pmatrix} \sqrt{n}\mathbf{s}_n^o(\gamma) \\ \sqrt{n}\mathbf{s}_n^o(\gamma^*) \end{pmatrix} = \begin{pmatrix} \mathbf{I}_n^o(\gamma) & \mathbf{H}_n^o(\gamma) \\ \mathbf{H}_n^o(\gamma) & \mathbf{H}_n^o(\gamma^*) \end{pmatrix},$$

So the variance of $\mathbf{H}_n^o(\gamma)^{-1}\sqrt{n}\mathbf{s}_n^o(\gamma) - \mathbf{H}_n^o(\gamma^*)^{-1}\sqrt{n}\mathbf{s}_n^o(\gamma^*)$ is given by

$$\begin{aligned}\mathbf{H}_n^o(\gamma)^{-1}\mathbf{I}_n^o(\gamma)\mathbf{H}_n^o(\gamma)^{-1} + \mathbf{H}_n^o(\gamma^*)^{-1}\mathbf{H}_n^o(\gamma^*)\mathbf{H}_n^o(\gamma^*)^{-1} \\ - \mathbf{H}_n^o(\gamma)^{-1}\mathbf{H}_n^o(\gamma)\mathbf{H}_n^o(\gamma^*)^{-1} - \mathbf{H}_n^o(\gamma^*)^{-1}\mathbf{H}_n^o(\gamma)\mathbf{H}_n^o(\gamma)^{-1} \\ = \mathbf{H}_n^o(\gamma)^{-1}\mathbf{I}_n^o(\gamma)\mathbf{H}_n^o(\gamma)^{-1} - \mathbf{H}_n^o(\gamma^*)^{-1},\end{aligned}$$

as claimed. Since this quantity is a variance–covariance matrix it is positive semidefinite, and the proof is complete. ∎

The key to finding the asymptotically efficient estimator in a given class is thus to find γ^* such that for all P^o in $\mathcal{P}$ and γ in Γ

$$\mathbf{H}_n^o(\gamma) = \text{cov}^o\left(\sqrt{n}\mathbf{s}_n^o(\gamma), \sqrt{n}\mathbf{s}_n^o(\gamma^*)\right).$$

Finding the optimal instrumental variables turns out to be somewhat involved, but key insight can be gained by initially considering $\mathbf{Z}_t^o(\gamma)$ as previously suggested and by requiring that the errors $\{\varepsilon_t\}$ be sufficiently well behaved. Thus, consider applying (4.2) with $\mathbf{Z}_t^o(\gamma)$. The correspondences previously identified give

$$\begin{aligned}&\mathbf{Q}_n^o(\gamma)'\mathbf{V}_n^o(\gamma)^{-1}\mathbf{Q}_n^o(\gamma) = \\ &\text{cov}^o\left(\mathbf{Q}_n^o(\gamma)'\mathbf{V}_n^o(\gamma)^{-1}n^{-1/2}\mathbf{Z}^o(\gamma)'\varepsilon, \mathbf{Q}_n^o(\gamma^*)'\mathbf{V}_n^o(\gamma^*)^{-1}n^{-1/2}\mathbf{Z}^o(\gamma^*)'\varepsilon\right).\end{aligned}$$

Defining $\mathbf{C}_n^o(\gamma, \gamma^*) \equiv \text{cov}^o(n^{-1/2}\mathbf{Z}^o(\gamma)'\varepsilon, n^{-1/2}\mathbf{Z}^o(\gamma^*)'\varepsilon)$, we have the simpler expression

$$\begin{aligned}\mathbf{Q}_n^o(\gamma)'\mathbf{V}_n^o(\gamma)^{-1}\mathbf{Q}_n^o(\gamma) &= \mathbf{Q}_n^o(\gamma)'\mathbf{V}_n^o(\gamma)^{-1} \\ &\quad \times\mathbf{C}_n^o(\gamma, \gamma^*)\,\mathbf{V}_n^o(\gamma^*)^{-1}\mathbf{Q}_n^o(\gamma^*).\end{aligned}$$

It therefore suffices to find γ^* such that for all γ

$$\mathbf{Q}_n^o(\gamma) = \mathbf{C}_n^o(\gamma, \gamma^*)\,\mathbf{V}_n^o(\gamma^*)^{-1}\mathbf{Q}_n^o(\gamma^*).$$

To make this choice tractable, we impose plausible structure on ε_t. Specifically, we suppose there is an increasing sequence of σ-fields $\{\mathcal{F}_t\}$ adapted to $\{\varepsilon_t\}$ such that for each P^o in $\mathcal{P}$ $\{\varepsilon_t, \mathcal{F}_t\}$ is a martingale difference sequence. That is, $E^o(\varepsilon_t|\mathcal{F}_{t-1}) = 0$. Recall that the instrumental variables $\{\mathbf{Z}_t^o\}$ must be uncorrelated with ε_t. It is therefore natural to restrict attention to instrumental variables $\mathbf{Z}_t^o(\gamma)$ that are measurable-$\mathcal{F}_{t-1}$, as then

$$\begin{aligned}E^o(\mathbf{Z}_t^o(\gamma)\varepsilon_t) &= E^o(E^o(\mathbf{Z}_t^o(\gamma)\varepsilon_t|\mathcal{F}_{t-1})) \\ &= E^o(\mathbf{Z}_t^o(\gamma)E^o(\varepsilon_t|\mathcal{F}_{t-1})) = \mathbf{0}.\end{aligned}$$

Imposing these requirements on $\{\varepsilon_t\}$ and $\{\mathbf{Z}_t^o(\gamma)\}$, we have that

$$\begin{aligned}
\mathbf{C}_n^o(\gamma,\gamma^*) &= \text{cov}^o\left(n^{-1/2}\mathbf{Z}^o(\gamma)'\varepsilon, n^{-1/2}\mathbf{Z}^o(\gamma^*)'\varepsilon\right) \\
&= n^{-1}\sum_{t=1}^n E^o\left(\mathbf{Z}_t^o(\gamma)\varepsilon_t\varepsilon_t'\mathbf{Z}_t^o(\gamma^*)'\right) \\
&= n^{-1}\sum_{t=1}^n E^o\left(E^o(\mathbf{Z}_t^o(\gamma)\varepsilon_t\varepsilon_t'\mathbf{Z}_t^o(\gamma^*)'|\mathcal{F}_{t-1})\right) \\
&= n^{-1}\sum_{t=1}^n E^o\left(\mathbf{Z}_t^o(\gamma)E^o(\varepsilon_t\varepsilon_t'|\mathcal{F}_{t-1})\mathbf{Z}_t^o(\gamma^*)'\right) \\
&= n^{-1}\sum_{t=1}^n E^o\left(\mathbf{Z}_t^o(\gamma)\,\boldsymbol{\Omega}_t^o\,\mathbf{Z}_t^o(\gamma^*)'\right),
\end{aligned}$$

where $\boldsymbol{\Omega}_t^o \equiv E^o(\varepsilon_t\varepsilon_t'|\mathcal{F}_{t-1})$. The first equality is by definition, the second follows from the martingale difference property of ε_t, the third uses the law of iterated expectations, and the fourth applies Proposition 3.63.

Consequently, we seek γ^* such that

$$n^{-1}\sum_{t=1}^n E^o(\mathbf{Z}_t^o(\gamma)\mathbf{X}_t^{o\prime}) = n^{-1}\sum_{t=1}^n E^o(\mathbf{Z}_t^o(\gamma)\,\boldsymbol{\Omega}_t^o\,\mathbf{Z}_t^o(\gamma^*)')\mathbf{V}_n^o(\gamma^*)^{-1}\mathbf{Q}_n^o(\gamma^*),$$

or, by the law of iterated expectations,

$$\begin{aligned}
&n^{-1}\sum_{t=1}^n E^o(E^o\left(\mathbf{Z}_t^o(\gamma)\mathbf{X}_t^{o\prime}|\mathcal{F}_{t-1}\right)) \\
&\qquad = n^{-1}\sum_{t=1}^n E^o(\mathbf{Z}_t^o(\gamma)E^o\left(\mathbf{X}_t^{o\prime}|\mathcal{F}_{t-1}\right)) \\
&\qquad = n^{-1}\sum_{t=1}^n E^o(\mathbf{Z}_t^o(\gamma)\tilde{\mathbf{X}}_t^{o\prime}) \\
&\qquad = n^{-1}\sum_{t=1}^n E^o(\mathbf{Z}_t^o(\gamma)\,\boldsymbol{\Omega}_t^o\,\mathbf{Z}_t^o(\gamma^*)')\mathbf{V}_n^o(\gamma^*)^{-1}\mathbf{Q}_n^o(\gamma^*),
\end{aligned}$$

where we define $\tilde{\mathbf{X}}_t^o \equiv E^o\left(\mathbf{X}_t^o|\mathcal{F}_{t-1}\right)$.

Inspecting the last equation, we see that equality holds provided we choose γ^* such that

$$\mathbf{Q}_n^o(\gamma^*)'\mathbf{V}_n^o(\gamma^*)^{-1}\mathbf{Z}_t^o(\gamma^*)\boldsymbol{\Omega}_t^o = \tilde{\mathbf{X}}_t^o. \tag{4.3}$$

If $\mathbf{\Omega}_t^o \equiv E^o(\varepsilon_t \varepsilon_t' | \mathcal{F}_{t-1})$ is nonsingular, as is plausible, this becomes

$$\mathbf{Q}_n^o(\gamma^*)'\mathbf{V}_n^o(\gamma^*)^{-1}\mathbf{Z}_t^o(\gamma^*) = \tilde{\mathbf{X}}_t^o \mathbf{\Omega}_t^{o-1}$$

which looks promising, as both sides are measurable-$\mathcal{F}_{t-1}$. We must therefore choose $\mathbf{Z}_t^o(\gamma^*)$ so that a particular linear combination of $\mathbf{Z}_t^o(\gamma^*)$ equals $\tilde{\mathbf{X}}_t^o \mathbf{\Omega}_t^{o-1}$.

This still looks challenging, however, because γ^* also appears in $\mathbf{Q}_n^o(\gamma^*)$ and $\mathbf{V}_n^o(\gamma^*)$. Nevertheless, consider the simplest possible choice for $\mathbf{Z}_t^o(\gamma^*)$,

$$\mathbf{Z}_t^o(\gamma^*) = \tilde{\mathbf{X}}_t^o \mathbf{\Omega}_t^{o-1}.$$

For this to be valid, it must happen that $\mathbf{Q}_n^o(\gamma^*)' = \mathbf{V}_n^o(\gamma^*)$, so that $\mathbf{Q}_n^o(\gamma^*)'\mathbf{V}_n^o(\gamma^*)^{-1} = \mathbf{I}$. Now with this choice for $\mathbf{Z}_t^o(\gamma^*)$

$$\begin{aligned}
\mathbf{V}_n^o(\gamma^*) &= \operatorname{var}^o\left(n^{-1/2}\sum_{t=1}^n \mathbf{Z}_t^o(\gamma^*)\varepsilon_t\right) \\
&= n^{-1}\sum_{t=1}^n E^o\left(\mathbf{Z}_t^o(\gamma^*)\varepsilon_t\varepsilon_t'\mathbf{Z}_t^o(\gamma^*)'\right) \\
&= n^{-1}\sum_{t=1}^n E^o\left(\mathbf{Z}_t^o(\gamma^*)\mathbf{\Omega}_t^o\mathbf{Z}_t^o(\gamma^*)'\right) \\
&= n^{-1}\sum_{t=1}^n E^o\left(\tilde{\mathbf{X}}_t^o\mathbf{\Omega}_t^{o-1}\mathbf{\Omega}_t^o\mathbf{\Omega}_t^{o-1}\tilde{\mathbf{X}}_t^{o\prime}\right) \\
&= n^{-1}\sum_{t=1}^n E^o\left(\tilde{\mathbf{X}}_t^o\mathbf{\Omega}_t^{o-1}\tilde{\mathbf{X}}_t^{o\prime}\right) \\
&= n^{-1}\sum_{t=1}^n E^o\left(\mathbf{Z}_t^o(\gamma^*)\tilde{\mathbf{X}}_t^{o\prime}\right) \\
&= n^{-1}\sum_{t=1}^n E^o\left(\mathbf{Z}_t^o(\gamma^*)E^o\left(\mathbf{X}_t^{o\prime}|\mathcal{F}_{t-1}\right)\right) \\
&= n^{-1}\sum_{t=1}^n E^o\left(\mathbf{Z}_t^o(\gamma^*)\mathbf{X}_t^{o\prime}\right) \\
&= \mathbf{Q}_n^o(\gamma^*).
\end{aligned}$$

The choice $\mathbf{Z}_t^o(\gamma^*) = \tilde{\mathbf{X}}_t^o\mathbf{\Omega}_t^{o-1}$ thus satisfies the sufficient condition (4.2), and therefore delivers the optimal instrumental variables.

Nevertheless, using these optimal instrumental variables presents apparent obstacles in that neither $\mathbf{\Omega}_t^o \equiv E^o(\varepsilon_t\varepsilon_t'|\mathcal{F}_{t-1})$ nor $\tilde{\mathbf{X}}_t^o = E^o(\mathbf{X}_t^o|\mathcal{F}_{t-1})$

are necessarily known or observable. We shall see that these obstacles can be overcome under reasonable assumptions. Before dealing with the general case, however, we consider two important special cases in which these obstacles are removed. This provides insight useful in dealing with the general case, and leads us naturally to procedures having general applicability.

Thus, suppose for the moment

$$E^o(\varepsilon_t \varepsilon_t' | \mathcal{F}_{t-1}) = \mathbf{\Omega}_t, \quad t = 1, 2, \ldots ,$$

where $\mathbf{\Omega}_t$ is a known $p \times p$ matrix. (We consider the consequences of not knowing $\mathbf{\Omega}_t$ later.) Although this restricts $\mathcal{P}$, it does not restrict it completely — different choices for P^o can imply different distributions for ε_t, even though $\mathbf{\Omega}_t$ is identical.

If we then also require that $\mathbf{X}_t^o$ is measurable-$\mathcal{F}_{t-1}$ it follows that

$$\begin{aligned} \tilde{\mathbf{X}}_t^o &= E^o(\mathbf{X}_t^o | \mathcal{F}_{t-1}) \\ &= \mathbf{X}_t^o, \end{aligned}$$

so that $\tilde{\mathbf{X}}_t^o = \mathbf{X}_t^o$ is observable. Note that this also implies

$$E^o(\mathbf{Y}_t^o | \mathcal{F}_{t-1}) = E^o(\mathbf{X}_t^{o\prime} \boldsymbol{\beta}^o + \varepsilon_t | \mathcal{F}_{t-1}) = \mathbf{X}_t^{o\prime} \boldsymbol{\beta}^o,$$

so that the conditional mean of $\mathbf{Y}_t^o$ still depends on P^o through $\boldsymbol{\beta}^o$, but we can view (i') as defining a relation useful for prediction. This requirement rules out a system of simultaneous equations, but still permits $\mathbf{X}_t^o$ to contain lags of elements of $\mathbf{Y}_t^o$.

With these restrictions on $\mathcal{P}$ we have that $\mathbf{Z}_t^o(\gamma^*) = \tilde{\mathbf{X}}_t^o \mathbf{\Omega}_t^{o-1} = \mathbf{X}_t^o \mathbf{\Omega}_t^{-1}$ delivers a usable set of optimal instrumental variables. Observe that this clearly illustrates the way in which the existence of an optimal IV estimator depends on the collection $\mathcal{P}$ of candidate data generating processes.

Let us now examine the estimator resulting from choosing the optimal instrumental variables in this setting.

Exercise 4.56 *Let $\mathbf{X}_t$ be $\mathcal{F}_{t-1}$-measurable and suppose that $\mathbf{\Omega}_t = E^o(\varepsilon_t \varepsilon_t' | \mathcal{F}_{t-1})$ for all P^o in $\mathcal{P}$. Show that with the choice $\mathbf{Z}_t^o(\gamma^*) = \mathbf{X}_t^o \mathbf{\Omega}_t^{-1}$ then $\mathbf{V}_n(\gamma^*) = E(n^{-1} \sum_{t=1}^n \mathbf{X}_t^o \mathbf{\Omega}_t^{-1} \mathbf{X}_t^{o\prime})$ and show that with $\hat{\mathbf{V}}_n(\gamma^*) = n^{-1} \sum_{t=1}^n \mathbf{X}_t^o \mathbf{\Omega}_t^{-1} \mathbf{X}_t^{o\prime}$ this yields the GLS estimator*

$$\begin{aligned} \boldsymbol{\beta}_n^* &= \left(n^{-1} \sum_{t=1}^n \mathbf{X}_t^o \mathbf{\Omega}_t^{-1} \mathbf{X}_t^{o\prime} \right)^{-1} n^{-1} \sum_{t=1}^n \mathbf{X}_t^o \mathbf{\Omega}_t^{-1} \mathbf{Y}_t^o \\ &= (\mathbf{X}' \mathbf{\Omega}^{-1} \mathbf{X})^{-1} \mathbf{X}' \mathbf{\Omega}^{-1} \mathbf{Y}, \end{aligned}$$

where $\mathbf{\Omega}$ *is the* $np \times np$ *block diagonal matrix with* $p \times p$ *diagonal blocks* $\mathbf{\Omega}_t$, $t = 1, \ldots, n$ *and zeroes elsewhere, and we drop the* ^{o} *superscript in writing* $\mathbf{X}$ *and* $\mathbf{Y}$.

This is the generalized least squares estimator whose finite sample efficiency properties we discussed in Chapter 1. Our current discussion shows that these finite sample properties have large sample analogs in a setting that neither requires normality for the errors ε_t nor requires that the regressors $\mathbf{X}_t^o$ be nonstochastic.

In fact, we have now proven part (a) of the following asymptotic efficiency result for the generalized least squares estimator.

Theorem 4.57 (Efficiency of GLS) *Suppose the conditions of Theorem 4.54 hold and that in addition* $\mathcal{P}$ *is such that for each* P^o *in* $\mathcal{P}$

(*i*) $\mathbf{Y}_t^o = \mathbf{X}_t^{o\prime}\boldsymbol{\beta}^o + \varepsilon_t, \quad t = 1, 2, \ldots, \boldsymbol{\beta}^o \in \mathbb{R}^k$,
where $\{(\mathbf{X}_{t+1}^o, \varepsilon_t), \mathcal{F}_t\}$ *is an adapted stochastic sequence with* $E^o(\varepsilon_t | \mathcal{F}_{t-1}) = \mathbf{0}$, $t = 1, 2, \ldots$; *and*

(*ii*) $E^o(\varepsilon_t \varepsilon_t' | \mathcal{F}_{t-1}) = \mathbf{\Omega}_t$ *is a known finite and nonsingular* $p \times p$ *matrix* $t = 1, 2, \ldots$.

(*iii*) *For each* $\gamma \in \Gamma$, $\mathbf{Z}_t^o(\gamma)$ *is* $\mathcal{F}_{t-1}$*-measurable,* $t = 1, 2, \ldots$, *and* $\mathbf{Q}_n^o(\gamma) = n^{-1}\sum_{t=1}^n E(\mathbf{Z}_t^o(\gamma)\mathbf{X}_t^{o\prime})$.

Then

(*a*) $\mathbf{Z}_t^o(\gamma^*) = \mathbf{X}_t^o \mathbf{\Omega}_t^{-1}$ *delivers*

$$\boldsymbol{\beta}_n^* = \left(n^{-1}\sum_{t=1}^n \mathbf{X}_t^o \mathbf{\Omega}_t^{-1} \mathbf{X}_t^{o\prime}\right)^{-1} n^{-1}\sum_{t=1}^n \mathbf{X}_t^o \mathbf{\Omega}_t^{-1} \mathbf{Y}_t^o,$$

which is asymptotically efficient in $\mathcal{E}$ *for* $\mathcal{P}$.

(*b*) *Further, the asymptotic covariance matrix of* $\boldsymbol{\beta}_n^*$ *is given by*

$$\text{avar}^o(\boldsymbol{\beta}_n^*) = \left[n^{-1}\sum_{t=1}^n E^o\left(\mathbf{X}_t^o \mathbf{\Omega}_t^{-1} \mathbf{X}_t^{o\prime}\right)\right]^{-1},$$

which is consistently estimated by

$$\hat{\mathbf{D}}_n = \left[n^{-1}\sum_{t=1}^n \mathbf{X}_t^o \mathbf{\Omega}_t^{-1} \mathbf{X}_t^{o\prime}\right]^{-1},$$

i.e., $\hat{\mathbf{D}}_n - \text{avar}^o(\boldsymbol{\beta}_n^*) \xrightarrow{p^o} \mathbf{0}$.

We leave the proof of (*b*) as an exercise:

Exercise 4.58 *Prove Theorem 4.57 (b).*

As we remarked in Chapter 1, the GLS estimator typically is not feasible because the conditional covariances $\{\mathbf{\Omega}_t\}$ are usually unknown. Nevertheless, we might be willing to model $\mathbf{\Omega}_t$ based on an assumed data generating process for $\boldsymbol{\varepsilon}_t\boldsymbol{\varepsilon}_t'$, say

$$E^o(\boldsymbol{\varepsilon}_t\boldsymbol{\varepsilon}_t'|\mathcal{F}_{t-1}) = \mathbf{h}(\mathbf{W}_t^o, \boldsymbol{\alpha}^o),$$

where $\mathbf{h}$ is a known function mapping $\mathcal{F}_{t-1}$-measurable random variables $\mathbf{W}_t^o$ and unknown parameters $\boldsymbol{\alpha}^o$ into $p \times p$ matrices. Note that different P^o's can now be accommodated by different values for $\boldsymbol{\alpha}^o$, and that $\mathbf{W}_t^o$ may depend on P^o.

An example is the ARCH(q) data generating process of Engle (1982) in which $\mathbf{h}(\mathbf{W}_t^o, \boldsymbol{\alpha}^o) = \alpha_0^o + \alpha_1^o\varepsilon_{t-1}^2 + \cdots + \alpha_q^o\varepsilon_{t-q}^2$ for the scalar ($p = 1$) case. Here, $\mathbf{W}_t^o = (\varepsilon_{t-1}^2, \ldots, \varepsilon_{t-q}^2)$. The popular GARCH(1,1) DGP of Bollerslev (1986) can be similarly treated by viewing it as an ARCH(∞) DGP, in which case $\mathbf{W}_t^o = (\varepsilon_{t-1}^2, \varepsilon_{t-2}^2, \ldots)$.

If we can obtain an estimator, say $\hat{\boldsymbol{\alpha}}_n$, consistent for $\boldsymbol{\alpha}^o$ regardless of which P^o in $\mathcal{P}$ generated the data, then we can hope that replacing the unknown $\mathbf{\Omega}_t = \mathbf{h}(\mathbf{W}_t^o, \boldsymbol{\alpha}^o)$ with the estimator $\hat{\mathbf{\Omega}}_{nt} = \mathbf{h}(\mathbf{W}_t^o, \hat{\boldsymbol{\alpha}}_n)$ might still deliver an efficient estimator of the form

$$\boldsymbol{\beta}_n^* = \left(n^{-1}\sum_{t=1}^n \mathbf{X}_t^o\hat{\mathbf{\Omega}}_{nt}^{-1}\mathbf{X}_t^{o\prime}\right)^{-1} n^{-1}\sum_{t=1}^n \mathbf{X}_t^o\hat{\mathbf{\Omega}}_{nt}^{-1}\mathbf{Y}_t^o.$$

Such estimators are called "feasible" GLS (FGLS) estimators, because they can feasibly be computed whereas, in the absence of knowledge of $\mathbf{\Omega}_t$, GLS cannot.

Inspecting the FGLS estimator, we see that it is also an IV estimator with

$$\begin{aligned} \mathbf{Z}_{nt}^o &= \mathbf{X}_t^o\hat{\mathbf{\Omega}}_{nt}^{-1} \\ \hat{\mathbf{P}}_n &= n^{-1}\sum_{t=1}^n \mathbf{X}_t^o\hat{\mathbf{\Omega}}_{nt}^{-1}\mathbf{X}_t^{o\prime}. \end{aligned}$$

Observe that $\mathbf{Z}_{nt}^o = \mathbf{X}_t^o\hat{\mathbf{\Omega}}_{nt}^{-1}$ is now double subscripted to make explicit its dependence on both n and t. This double subscripting is explicitly allowed for in Theorem 4.54, and we can now see the usefulness of the flexibility this affords. To accommodate this choice as well as other similar choices, we now elaborate our specifications of $\mathbf{Z}_{nt}^o$ and γ. Specifically, we put

$$\mathbf{Z}_{nt}^o(\gamma) = \mathbf{Z}_{t2}^o(\gamma_2)\zeta(\mathbf{Z}_{t1}^o(\gamma_1), \gamma_{3n}).$$

Now γ has three components: $\gamma = (\gamma_1, \gamma_2, \gamma_3)$, where $\gamma_3 = \{\gamma_{3n}\}$ is a sequence of $\mathcal{F}_{t-1}$-measurable mappings, ζ is a known function such that $\zeta(\mathbf{Z}_{t1}^o(\gamma_1), \gamma_{3n})$ is a $p \times p$ matrix, and $\mathbf{Z}_{t1}^o(\gamma_1)$ and $\mathbf{Z}_{t2}^o(\gamma_2)$ are $\mathcal{F}_{t-1}$-measurable for all γ_1, γ_2, where $\mathbf{Z}_{t1}^o(\gamma_1)$ is an $l \times p$ random matrix.

By putting $\mathbf{Z}_{t1}^o(\gamma_1) = \mathbf{X}_t^o$, $\mathbf{Z}_{t2}^o(\gamma_2) = \mathbf{W}_t^o$, $\gamma_{3n} = \hat{\alpha}_n$, and $\zeta = (\mathbf{h})^{-1}$ we obtain

$$\begin{aligned} \mathbf{Z}_{nt}^o(\gamma) &= \mathbf{X}_t^o(\mathbf{h}(\mathbf{W}_t^o, \hat{\alpha}_n))^{-1} \\ &= \mathbf{X}_t^o\hat{\mathbf{\Omega}}_{nt}^{-1}. \end{aligned}$$

Many other choices that yield consistent asymptotically normal IV estimators are also permitted.

The requirement that ζ be known is not restrictive; in particular, we can choose ζ such that $\zeta(\mathbf{z}_1, \gamma_{3n}) = \gamma_{3n}(\mathbf{z}_1)$ (the evaluation functional) which allows consideration of nonparametric estimators of the inverse covariance matrix, $\mathbf{\Omega}_t^{o-1}$, as well as parametric estimators such as ARCH (set $\gamma_{3n}(\cdot) = [h(\cdot, \hat{\alpha}_n)]^{-1}$).

To see what choices for γ are permitted, it suffices to apply Theorem 4.54 with $\mathbf{Z}^o(\gamma)$ interpreted as the $np \times l$ matrix with blocks $\mathbf{Z}_{nt}^o(\gamma)'$. We expand $\mathcal{P}$ to include data generating processes such that $\mathbf{\Omega}_t^{o-1}$ can be sufficiently well estimated by $\zeta(\mathbf{Z}_{t1}^o(\gamma_1), \gamma_{3n})$ for some choice of (γ_1, γ_3). (What is meant by "sufficiently well" is that conditions *(ii)* and *(iii)* of Theorem 4.54 hold.) It is here that the generality afforded by Theorem 4.54 *(ii)* is required, as we can no longer necessarily take $\mathbf{m}_n^o(\gamma) = n^{-1}\sum_{t=1}^n \mathbf{Z}_{nt}^o(\gamma)\varepsilon_t$. The presence of γ_{3n} and the nature of the function ζ may cause $n^{-1/2}\sum_{t=1}^n \mathbf{Z}_{nt}^o(\gamma)\varepsilon_t$ to fail to have a finite second moment, even though $n^{-1/2}\sum_{t=1}^n \mathbf{Z}_{nt}^o(\gamma)\varepsilon_t - n^{1/2}\mathbf{m}_n^o(\gamma) = o_{p^o}(1)$ for well behaved $\mathbf{m}_n^o(\gamma)$. Similarly, there is no guarantee that $E^o(\mathbf{Z}_{nt}^o(\gamma)\mathbf{X}_t^{o\prime})$ exists, although the sample average $n^{-1}\sum_{t=1}^n \mathbf{Z}_{nt}^o(\gamma)\mathbf{X}_t^{o\prime}$ may have a well defined probability limit $\mathbf{Q}_n^o(\gamma)$.

Consider first the form of $\mathbf{m}_n^o$. For notational economy, let $\gamma_{t1}^o \equiv \mathbf{Z}_{t1}^o(\gamma_1)$ and $\gamma_{t2}^o \equiv \mathbf{Z}_{t2}^o(\gamma_2)$. Then with

$$\mathbf{Z}_{nt}^o(\gamma) = \mathbf{Z}_{t2}^o(\gamma_2)\zeta(\mathbf{Z}_{t1}^o(\gamma_1), \gamma_{3n}) \equiv \gamma_{t2}^o\zeta(\gamma_{t1}^o, \gamma_{3n})$$

we have

$$\begin{aligned} n^{-1/2}\sum_{t=1}^{n} \mathbf{Z}_{nt}^{o}(\gamma)\varepsilon_t &= n^{-1/2}\sum_{t=1}^{n} \gamma_{t2}^{o}\zeta(\gamma_{t1}^{o},\gamma_{3n})\varepsilon_t \\ &= n^{-1/2}\sum_{t=1}^{n} \gamma_{t2}^{o}\zeta(\gamma_{t1}^{o},\gamma_{3}^{o})\varepsilon_t \\ &\quad + n^{-1/2}\sum_{t=1}^{n} \gamma_{t2}^{o}\left[\zeta(\gamma_{t1}^{o},\gamma_{3n}) - \zeta(\gamma_{t1}^{o},\gamma_{3}^{o})\right]\varepsilon_t, \end{aligned}$$

where we view γ_3^o as the probability limit of γ_{3n} under P^o. If sufficient regularity is available to ensure that the second term vanishes in probability, i.e.,

$$n^{-1/2}\sum_{t=1}^{n} \gamma_{t2}^{o}\left[\zeta(\gamma_{t1}^{o},\gamma_{3n}) - \zeta(\gamma_{t1}^{o},\gamma_{3}^{o})\right]\varepsilon_t = o_{p^o}(1),$$

then we can take

$$n^{1/2}\mathbf{m}_n^o(\gamma) = n^{-1/2}\sum_{t=1}^{n} \gamma_{t2}^{o}\zeta(\gamma_{t1}^{o},\gamma_{3}^{o})\varepsilon_t.$$

We ensure "sufficient regularity" simply by assuming that Γ and $\mathcal{P}$ are chosen so that the desired convergence holds for all $\gamma \in \Gamma$ and P^o in $\mathcal{P}$.

The form of $\mathbf{Q}_n^o$ follows similarly. With $\mathbf{Z}_{nt}^o(\gamma) = \gamma_{t2}^o\zeta(\gamma_{t1}^o,\gamma_{3n})$ we have

$$\begin{aligned} n^{-1}\sum_{t=1}^{n} \mathbf{Z}_{nt}^{o}(\gamma)\mathbf{X}_t^{o\prime} &= n^{-1}\sum_{t=1}^{n} \gamma_{t2}^{o}\zeta(\gamma_{t1}^{o},\gamma_{3n})\mathbf{X}_t^{o\prime} \\ &= n^{-1}\sum_{t=1}^{n} \gamma_{t2}^{o}\zeta(\gamma_{t1}^{o},\gamma_{3}^{o})\mathbf{X}_t^{o\prime} \\ &\quad + n^{-1}\sum_{t=1}^{n} \gamma_{t2}^{o}\left[\zeta(\gamma_{t1}^{o},\gamma_{3n}) - \zeta(\gamma_{t1}^{o},\gamma_{3}^{o})\right]\mathbf{X}_t^{o\prime}. \end{aligned}$$

If Γ and $\mathcal{P}$ are assumed chosen such that

$$n^{-1}\sum_{t=1}^{n} \gamma_{t2}^{o}\zeta(\gamma_{t1}^{o},\gamma_{3}^{o})\mathbf{X}_t^{o\prime} - n^{-1}\sum_{t=1}^{n} E^o[\gamma_{t2}^{o}\zeta(\gamma_{t1}^{o},\gamma_{3}^{o})\mathbf{X}_t^{o\prime}] = o_{p^o}(1)$$

and

$$n^{-1}\sum_{t=1}^{n} \gamma_{t2}^{o}\left[\zeta(\gamma_{t1}^{o},\gamma_{3n}) - \zeta(\gamma_{t1}^{o},\gamma_{3}^{o})\right]\mathbf{X}_t^{o\prime} = o_{p^o}(1),$$

then we can take

$$\mathbf{Q}_n^o(\gamma) = n^{-1} \sum_{t=1}^{n} E^o[\gamma_{t2}^o \zeta(\gamma_{t1}^o, \gamma_3^o)\mathbf{X}_t^{o\prime}].$$

With $\mathbf{V}_n^o(\gamma) \equiv \text{var}^o(n^{1/2}\mathbf{m}_n^o(\gamma))$, the Bates–White correspondences are now

$$\begin{aligned}
\mathbf{H}_n^o(\gamma) &= \mathbf{Q}_n^o(\gamma)'\mathbf{V}_n^o(\gamma)^{-1}\mathbf{Q}_n^o(\gamma) \\
\mathbf{s}_n^o(\gamma) &= \mathbf{Q}_n^o(\gamma)'\mathbf{V}_n^o(\gamma)^{-1}\mathbf{m}_n^o(\gamma) \\
\mathbf{I}_n^o(\gamma) &= \mathbf{H}_n^o(\gamma).
\end{aligned}$$

(As before, we set $\mathbf{P}_n^o = \mathbf{V}_n^{o-1}$.) By argument parallel to that following Proposition 4.55, the sufficient condition for efficiency is

$$\mathbf{Q}_n^o(\gamma) = \mathbf{C}_n^o\,(\gamma, \gamma^*)\,\mathbf{V}_n^o(\gamma^*)^{-1}\mathbf{Q}_n^o(\gamma^*),$$

where now $\mathbf{C}_n^o\,(\gamma, \gamma^*) = \text{cov}^o(n^{1/2}\mathbf{m}_n^o(\gamma), n^{1/2}\mathbf{m}_n^o(\gamma^*))$.

Following arguments exactly parallel to those leading to Equation (4.3), we find that the sufficient condition holds if

$$\mathbf{Q}_n^o(\gamma^*)'\mathbf{V}_n^o(\gamma^*)^{-1}\mathbf{Z}_{t2}^o(\gamma_2^*)\zeta(\mathbf{Z}_{t1}^o(\gamma_1^*), \gamma_3^{*o})\mathbf{\Omega}_t^o = \mathbf{X}_t^o.$$

Choosing $\mathbf{Z}_{t2}^o(\gamma_2^*) = \mathbf{X}_t^o$ and $\zeta(\mathbf{Z}_{t1}^o(\gamma_1^*), \gamma_3^{*o}) = \mathbf{\Omega}_t^{o-1}$ can be verified to ensure $\mathbf{Q}_n^o(\gamma^*)' = \mathbf{V}_n^o(\gamma^*)$ as before, so optimality follows. Thus, the optimal choice for $\mathbf{Z}_{nt}^o(\gamma)$ is

$$\mathbf{Z}_{nt}^o(\gamma^*) = \mathbf{X}_t^o\hat{\mathbf{\Omega}}_{nt}^{-1},$$

where $\hat{\mathbf{\Omega}}_{nt}^{-1} = \zeta(\mathbf{Z}_{t1}^o(\gamma_1^*), \gamma_{3n}^*)$ is such that $\zeta(\mathbf{Z}_{t1}^o(\gamma_1^*), \gamma_3^{*o}) = \mathbf{\Omega}_t^{o-1}$. In particular, if $\mathbf{\Omega}_t^o = \mathbf{h}(\mathbf{W}_t^o, \alpha^o)$, then taking $\zeta(\mathbf{z}_1, \gamma_{3n}) = \gamma_{3n}(\mathbf{z}_1)$, $\mathbf{Z}_{t1}^o(\gamma_1^*) = \mathbf{W}_t^o$ and $\gamma_3^{*o} = [\mathbf{h}(\cdot, \alpha^o)]^{-1}$ gives the optimal choice of instrumental variables.

We formalize this result as follows.

Theorem 4.59 (Efficiency of FGLS) *Suppose the conditions of Theorem 4.54 hold and that in addition $\mathcal{P}$ is such that for each P^o in $\mathcal{P}$*

(*i*) $\mathbf{Y}_t^o = \mathbf{X}_t^{o\prime}\beta^o + \varepsilon_t, \quad t = 1, 2, \ldots, \; \beta^o \in \mathbb{R}^k$,
where $\{(\mathbf{X}_{t+1}^o, \varepsilon_t), \mathcal{F}_t\}$ is an adapted stochastic sequence with $E^o(\varepsilon_t | \mathcal{F}_{t-1}) = \mathbf{0}$, $t = 1, 2, \ldots$; and

(*ii*) *$E^o(\varepsilon_t\varepsilon_t' | \mathcal{F}_{t-1}) = \mathbf{\Omega}_t^o$ is an unknown finite and nonsingular $p \times p$ matrix* $t = 1, 2, \ldots$.

(*iii*) *For each* $\gamma \in \Gamma$,

$$\mathbf{Z}_{nt}^{o}(\gamma) = \mathbf{Z}_{t2}^{o}(\gamma_2)\gamma_{3n}(\mathbf{Z}_{t1}^{o}(\gamma_1)),$$

where $\gamma \equiv (\gamma_1, \gamma_2, \gamma_3)$, *and* $\gamma_3 \equiv \{\gamma_{3n}\}$ *is such that* γ_{3n} *is* $\mathcal{F}$-*measurable for all* $n = 1, 2, \ldots$, *and* $\mathbf{Z}_{t1}^{o}(\gamma_1)$ *and* $\mathbf{Z}_{t2}^{o}(\gamma_2)$ *are* $\mathcal{F}_{t-1}$-*measurable for all* γ_1 *and* γ_2, $t = 1, 2, \ldots$; *and there exists* γ_3^o *such that*

$$\mathbf{m}_n^o(\gamma) = n^{-1}\sum_{t=1}^{n} \mathbf{Z}_{t2}^{o}(\gamma_2)\gamma_3^o(\mathbf{Z}_{t1}^{o}(\gamma_1))\varepsilon_t$$

and

$$\mathbf{Q}_n^o(\gamma) = n^{-1}\sum_{t=1}^{n} E(\mathbf{Z}_{t2}^{o}(\gamma_2)\gamma_3^o(\mathbf{Z}_{t1}^{o}(\gamma_1))\mathbf{X}_t^{o\prime});$$

(*iv*) *for some* γ_1^*, γ_3^*, $\hat{\boldsymbol{\Omega}}_{nt}^{-1} = \gamma_{3n}^*(\mathbf{Z}_{t1}^{o}(\gamma_1^*))$, *where* $\gamma_3^{*o}(\mathbf{Z}_{t1}^{o}(\gamma_1^*)) = \boldsymbol{\Omega}_t^{o-1}$.

Then

(*a*) $\mathbf{Z}_{nt}(\gamma^*) = \mathbf{X}_t^o\hat{\boldsymbol{\Omega}}_{nt}^{-1}$ *delivers*

$$\boldsymbol{\beta}_n^* = \left(n^{-1}\sum_{t=1}^{n}\mathbf{X}_t^o\hat{\boldsymbol{\Omega}}_{nt}^{-1}\mathbf{X}_t^{o\prime}\right)^{-1} n^{-1}\sum_{t=1}^{n}\mathbf{X}_t^o\hat{\boldsymbol{\Omega}}_{nt}^{-1}\mathbf{Y}_t^o,$$

which is asymptotically efficient in $\mathcal{E}$ *for* $\mathcal{P}$;

(*b*) *the asymptotic covariance matrix of* $\boldsymbol{\beta}_n^*$ *is given by*

$$\text{avar}^o(\boldsymbol{\beta}_n^*) = \left[n^{-1}\sum_{t=1}^{n}E^o\left(\mathbf{X}_t^o\boldsymbol{\Omega}_t^{o-1}\mathbf{X}_t^{o\prime}\right)\right]^{-1},$$

which is consistently estimated by

$$\hat{\mathbf{D}}_n = \left[n^{-1}\sum_{t=1}^{n}\mathbf{X}_t^o\hat{\boldsymbol{\Omega}}_{nt}^{-1}\mathbf{X}_t^{o\prime}\right]^{-1},$$

i.e., $\hat{\mathbf{D}}_n - \text{avar}^o(\boldsymbol{\beta}_n^*) \xrightarrow{p^o} \mathbf{0}$.

Proof. (*a*) Apply Proposition 4.55 and the argument preceding the statement of Theorem 4.59. We leave the proof of part (*b*) as an exercise. ∎

Exercise 4.60 *Prove part (b) of Theorem 4.59.*

The arguments needed to verify that

$$n^{-1}\sum_{t=1}^{n}\gamma_{t2}^{o}\left[\gamma_{3n}(\gamma_{t1}^{o})-\gamma_{3}^{o}(\gamma_{t1}^{o})\right]\varepsilon_t = o_{p^o}(1)$$

and

$$n^{-1}\sum_{t=1}^{n}\gamma_{t2}^{o}\left[\gamma_{3n}(\gamma_{t1}^{o})-\gamma_{3}^{o}(\gamma_{t1}^{o})\right]\mathbf{X}_t^{o\prime} = o_{p^o}(1)$$

depend on what is known about $\boldsymbol{\Omega}_t^o$ and how it is estimated. The next exercise illustrates one possibility.

Exercise 4.61 *Suppose that conditions 4.59 (i) and 4.59 (ii) hold with $p = 1$ and that*

$$\Omega_t^o = \alpha_1^o + \alpha_2^o W_t^o, \quad t = 1, 2, \dots,$$

where $W_t^o = 1$ during recessions and $W_t^o = 0$ otherwise.

(*i*) *Let $\hat{\varepsilon}_t = Y_t^o - \mathbf{X}_t^{o\prime}\hat{\boldsymbol{\beta}}_n$, where $\hat{\boldsymbol{\beta}}_n$ is the OLS estimator, and let $\hat{\boldsymbol{\alpha}}_n = (\hat{\alpha}_{1n}, \hat{\alpha}_{2n})'$ be the OLS estimator from the regression of $\hat{\varepsilon}_t^2$ on a constant and W_t^o. Prove that $\hat{\boldsymbol{\alpha}}_n = \boldsymbol{\alpha}^o + o_{p^o}(1)$, where $\boldsymbol{\alpha}^o = (\alpha_1^o, \alpha_2^o)'$, providing any needed additional conditions.*

(*ii*) *Next, verify that conditions 4.59 (iii) and (iv) hold for*

$$\mathbf{Z}_{nt}^o(\gamma^*) = \mathbf{X}_t^o(\hat{\alpha}_{1n} + \hat{\alpha}_{2n}W_t^o)^{-1}.$$

When less is known about the structure of $\boldsymbol{\Omega}_t^o$, nonparametric estimators can be used. See, for example, White and Stinchcombe (1991). The notion of stochastic equicontinuity (see Andrews, 1994a,b) plays a key role in such situations, but will not be explored here.

We are now in a position to see how to treat the general situation in which $\tilde{\mathbf{X}}_t^o \equiv E(\mathbf{X}_t^o|\mathcal{F}_{t-1})$ appears instead of $\mathbf{X}_t^o$. By taking

$$\mathbf{Z}_{nt}^o(\gamma) = \underset{l\times p}{\gamma_{4n}(\mathbf{Z}_{t2}^o(\gamma_2))}\,\underset{p\times p}{\gamma_{3n}(\mathbf{Z}_{t1}^o(\gamma_1))}$$

we can accommodate the choice

$$\mathbf{Z}_{nt}(\gamma) = \hat{\mathbf{X}}_t\hat{\boldsymbol{\Omega}}_{nt}^{-1},$$

where $\hat{\mathbf{X}}_{nt} = \gamma_{4n}(\mathbf{Z}^o_{t2}(\gamma_2)) = \gamma_{4n}(\gamma^o_{t2})$ is an estimator of $\tilde{\mathbf{X}}^o_t$. As we might now expect, this choice delivers the optimal IV estimator.

To see this, we examine $\mathbf{m}^o_n$ and $\mathbf{Q}^o_n$. We have

$$\begin{aligned} n^{-1/2}\sum_{t=1}^n \mathbf{Z}^o_{nt}(\gamma)\varepsilon_t &= n^{-1/2}\sum_{t=1}^n \gamma_{4n}(\gamma^o_{t2})\gamma_{3n}(\gamma^o_{t1})\varepsilon_t \\ &= n^{-1/2}\sum_{t=1}^n \gamma^o_4(\gamma^o_{t2})\gamma^o_3(\gamma^o_{t1})\varepsilon_t \\ &\quad + n^{-1/2}\sum_{t=1}^n [\gamma_{4n}(\gamma^o_{t2})\gamma_{3n}(\gamma^o_{t1}) - \gamma^o_4(\gamma^o_{t2})\gamma^o_3(\gamma^o_{t1})]\varepsilon_t \\ &= n^{1/2}\mathbf{m}^o_n(\gamma) + o_{p^o}(1), \end{aligned}$$

provided we set $\mathbf{m}^o_n(\gamma) = n^{-1}\sum_{t=1}^n \gamma^o_4(\gamma^o_{t2})\gamma^o_3(\gamma^o_{t1})\varepsilon_t$ and

$$n^{-1}\sum_{t=1}^n [\gamma_{4n}(\gamma^o_{t2})\gamma_{3n}(\gamma^o_{t1}) - \gamma^o_4(\gamma^o_{t2})\gamma^o_3(\gamma^o_{t1})]\varepsilon_t = o_{p^o}(1).$$

Similarly,

$$\begin{aligned} n^{-1}\sum_{t=1}^n \mathbf{Z}^o_{nt}(\gamma)\mathbf{X}^{o\prime}_t &= n^{-1}\sum_{t=1}^n \gamma_{4n}(\gamma^o_{t2})\gamma_{3n}(\gamma^o_{t1})\mathbf{X}^{o\prime}_t \\ &= n^{-1}\sum_{t=1}^n \gamma^o_4(\gamma^o_{t2})\gamma^o_3(\gamma^o_{t1})\mathbf{X}^{o\prime}_t \\ &\quad + n^{-1}\sum_{t=1}^n [\gamma_{4n}(\gamma^o_{t2})\gamma_{3n}(\gamma^o_{t1}) - \gamma^o_4(\gamma^o_{t2})\gamma^o_3(\gamma^o_{t1})]\mathbf{X}^{o\prime}_t. \end{aligned}$$

Provided the second term vanishes in probability ($-P^o$) and a law of large numbers applies to the first term, we can take

$$\mathbf{Q}^o_n(\gamma) = n^{-1}\sum_{t=1}^n E^o(\gamma^o_4(\gamma^o_{t2})\gamma^o_3(\gamma^o_{t1})\mathbf{X}^{o\prime}_t).$$

With $\mathbf{V}^o_n(\gamma) \equiv \text{var}^o(n^{1/2}\mathbf{m}^o_n(\gamma))$, the Bates–White correspondences are again

$$\begin{aligned} \mathbf{H}^o_n(\gamma) &= \mathbf{Q}^o_n(\gamma)'\mathbf{V}^o_n(\gamma)^{-1}\mathbf{Q}^o_n(\gamma), \\ \mathbf{s}^o_n(\gamma) &= \mathbf{Q}^o_n(\gamma)'\mathbf{V}^o_n(\gamma)^{-1}\mathbf{m}^o_n(\gamma), \\ \mathbf{I}^o_n(\gamma) &= \mathbf{H}^o_n(\gamma), \end{aligned}$$

and the sufficient condition for asymptotic efficiency is again

$$\mathbf{Q}_n^o(\gamma) = \mathbf{C}_n^o(\gamma, \gamma^*)\,\mathbf{V}_n^o(\gamma^*)^{-1}\mathbf{Q}_n^o(\gamma^*).$$

Arguments parallel to those leading to Equation (4.3) show that the sufficient condition holds if

$$\mathbf{Q}_n^o(\gamma^*)'\mathbf{V}_n^o(\gamma^*)^{-1}\gamma_4^{*o}(\mathbf{Z}_{t2}^o(\gamma_2^*))\gamma_3^{*o}(\mathbf{Z}_{t1}^o(\gamma_1^*))\boldsymbol{\Omega}_t^o = \tilde{\mathbf{X}}_t^o.$$

It suffices that $\gamma_3^{*o}(\mathbf{Z}_{t1}^o(\gamma_1^*)) = \boldsymbol{\Omega}_t^{o-1}$ and $\gamma_4^{*o}(\mathbf{Z}_{t2}^o(\gamma_2^*)) = \tilde{\mathbf{X}}_t^o$, as this ensures $\mathbf{Q}_n^o(\gamma^*)' = \mathbf{V}_n^o(\gamma^*)^{-1}$.

We can now state our asymptotic efficiency result for the IV estimator.

Theorem 4.62 (Efficient IV) *Suppose the conditions of Theorem 4.54 hold and that in addition $\mathcal{P}$ is such that for each P^o in $\mathcal{P}$*

(*i*) $\mathbf{Y}_t^o = \mathbf{X}_t^{o\prime}\beta^o + \varepsilon_t, \quad t = 1, 2, \ldots, \ \beta^o \in \mathbb{R}^k$,
where $\{\varepsilon_t, \mathcal{F}_t\}$ is an adapted stochastic sequence with $E^o(\varepsilon_t|\mathcal{F}_{t-1}) = \mathbf{0}$, $t = 1, 2, \ldots$; and

(*ii*) *$E^o(\varepsilon_t\varepsilon_t'|\mathcal{F}_{t-1}) = \boldsymbol{\Omega}_t^o$ is an unknown finite and nonsingular $p \times p$ matrix $t = 1, 2, \ldots$.*

(*iii*) *For each $\gamma \in \Gamma$,*

$$\mathbf{Z}_{nt}^o(\gamma) = \gamma_{4n}(\mathbf{Z}_{t2}^o(\gamma_2))\gamma_{3n}(\mathbf{Z}_{t1}^o(\gamma_1)),$$

where $\gamma \equiv (\gamma_1, \gamma_2, \gamma_3, \gamma_4)$, and $\gamma_3 \equiv \{\gamma_{3n}\}$ and $\gamma_4 \equiv \{\gamma_{4n}\}$, are such that γ_{3n} and γ_{4n} are $\mathcal{F}$-measurable for all $n = 1, 2, \ldots$ and $\mathbf{Z}_{t1}^o(\gamma_1)$ and $\mathbf{Z}_{t2}^o(\gamma_2)$ are $\mathcal{F}_{t-1}$-measurable for all γ_1 and γ_2, $t = 1, 2, \ldots$; and there exist γ_3^o and γ_4^o such that

$$\mathbf{m}_n^o(\gamma) = n^{-1}\sum_{t=1}^{n}\gamma_4^o(\mathbf{Z}_{t2}^o(\gamma_2))\gamma_3^o(\mathbf{Z}_{t1}^o(\gamma_1))\varepsilon_t$$

and

$$\mathbf{Q}_n^o(\gamma) = n^{-1}\sum_{t=1}^{n}E^o(\gamma_4^o(\mathbf{Z}_{t2}^o(\gamma_2))\gamma_3^o(\mathbf{Z}_{t1}^o(\gamma_1))\mathbf{X}_t^{o\prime});$$

(*iv*) *for some γ_1^* and γ_3^*, $\hat{\boldsymbol{\Omega}}_{nt}^{-1} = \gamma_{3n}^*(\mathbf{Z}_{t1}^o(\gamma_1^*))$, where $\gamma_3^{*o}(\mathbf{Z}_{t1}^o(\gamma_1^*)) = \boldsymbol{\Omega}_t^{o-1}$ and for some γ_2^* and γ_4^*, $\hat{\mathbf{X}}_t = \gamma_{4n}^*(\mathbf{Z}_{t2}^o(\gamma_2^*))$, where $\gamma_4^{*o}(\mathbf{Z}_{t2}^o(\gamma_2^*)) = E^o(\mathbf{X}_t^o|\mathcal{F}_{t-1})$.*

Then

(*a*) $\mathbf{Z}^o_{nt}(\gamma^*) = \hat{\mathbf{X}}_{nt}\hat{\boldsymbol{\Omega}}_{nt}^{-1}$ *delivers*

$$\boldsymbol{\beta}^*_n = \left(n^{-1}\sum_{t=1}^{n}\hat{\mathbf{X}}_{nt}\hat{\boldsymbol{\Omega}}_{nt}^{-1}\mathbf{X}^{o\prime}_t\right)^{-1} n^{-1}\sum_{t=1}^{n}\hat{\mathbf{X}}_{nt}\hat{\boldsymbol{\Omega}}_{nt}^{-1}\mathbf{Y}^o_t,$$

which is asymptotically efficient in $\mathcal{E}$ for $\mathcal{P}$;

(*b*) *the asymptotic covariance matrix of $\boldsymbol{\beta}^*_n$ is given by*

$$\text{avar}^o(\boldsymbol{\beta}^*_n) = \left[n^{-1}\sum_{t=1}^{n}E^o\left(\tilde{\mathbf{X}}^o_t\boldsymbol{\Omega}^{o-1}_t\tilde{\mathbf{X}}^{o\prime}_t\right)\right]^{-1},$$

which is consistently estimated by

$$\hat{\mathbf{D}}_n = 2\left[n^{-1}\sum_{t=1}^{n}\hat{\mathbf{X}}_{nt}\hat{\boldsymbol{\Omega}}_{nt}^{-1}\mathbf{X}^{o\prime}_t + n^{-1}\sum_{t=1}^{n}\mathbf{X}^o_t\hat{\boldsymbol{\Omega}}_{nt}^{-1}\hat{\mathbf{X}}'_{nt}\right]^{-1},$$

i.e., $\hat{\mathbf{D}}_n - \text{avar}^o(\boldsymbol{\beta}^*_n) \xrightarrow{p^o} \mathbf{0}$.

Proof. (*a*) Apply Proposition 4.55 and the argument preceding the statement of Theorem 4.62. We leave the proof of part (*b*) as an exercise. ∎

Exercise 4.63 *Prove Theorem 4.62 (b).*

Other consistent estimators for $\text{avar}^o(\boldsymbol{\beta}^*_n)$ are available, for example

$$\tilde{\mathbf{D}}_n = \left[n^{-1}\sum_{t=1}^{n}\hat{\mathbf{X}}_{nt}\hat{\boldsymbol{\Omega}}_{nt}^{-1}\hat{\mathbf{X}}'_{nt}\right]^{-1}.$$

This requires additional conditions, however. The estimator $\hat{\mathbf{D}}_n$ above is consistent without further assumptions.

Exercise 4.64 *Suppose condition 4.62 (i) and (ii) hold and that*

$$\begin{aligned}\boldsymbol{\Omega}^o_t &= \boldsymbol{\Sigma}^o,\\ E^o(\mathbf{X}^{o\prime}_t|\mathcal{F}_{t-1}) &= \mathbf{Z}^{o\prime}_t\boldsymbol{\pi}^o, \quad t = 1,2,\ldots,\end{aligned}$$

where $\boldsymbol{\pi}^o$ is an $l \times k$ matrix.

(*i*) (*a*) *Let* $\hat{\boldsymbol{\pi}}_n = (n^{-1}\sum_{t=1}^n \mathbf{Z}^o_t\mathbf{Z}^{o\prime}_t)^{-1}n^{-1}\sum_{t=1}^n \mathbf{Z}^o_t\mathbf{X}^{o\prime}_t$.
Give simple conditions under which $\hat{\boldsymbol{\pi}}_n = \boldsymbol{\pi}^o + o_{p^o}(1)$.

(*b*) *Let* $\hat{\boldsymbol{\Sigma}}_n = n^{-1}\sum_{t=1}^{n} \hat{\varepsilon}_t\hat{\varepsilon}_t'$, *where* $\hat{\varepsilon}_t = \mathbf{Y}_t^o - \mathbf{X}_t^{o\prime}\tilde{\boldsymbol{\beta}}_n$,

$$\tilde{\boldsymbol{\beta}}_n = (\mathbf{X}'\mathbf{Z}(\mathbf{Z}'\mathbf{Z})^{-1}\mathbf{Z}'\mathbf{X})^{-1}\mathbf{X}'\mathbf{Z}(\mathbf{Z}'\mathbf{Z})^{-1}\mathbf{Z}'\mathbf{Y}$$

(*the 2SLS estimator*). *Give simple conditions under which* $\hat{\boldsymbol{\Sigma}}_n = \boldsymbol{\Sigma}^o + o_{p^o}(1)$.

(*ii*) *Next, verify that conditions 4.62 (iii) and 4.62 (iv) hold for* $\mathbf{Z}_{nt}^o(\gamma^*) = \hat{\pi}_n'\mathbf{Z}_t^o\hat{\boldsymbol{\Sigma}}_n^{-1}$. *The resulting estimator is the three stage least squares (3SLS) estimator.*

References

Andrews, A. (1994a). "Asymptotics for semiparametric econometric-models via stochastic equicontinuity." *Econometrica*, 62, 43–72.

——— (1994b). "Empirical process methods in econometrics." In *Handbook of Econometrics*, 4. Engle, R. F. and D. L. McFadden, eds., pp. 2247–2294. North Holland, Amsterdam.

Bartle, R. G. (1976). *The Elements of Real Analysis.* Wiley, New York.

Bates C. E. and H. White (1993). "Determination of estimtors with minimum asymptotic covariance matrices." *Econometric Theory*, 9, 633–648.

Bollerslev, T. (1986). "Generalized autoregressive conditional heteroskedasticity." *Journal of Econometrics*, 31, 307–327.

Chamberlain, G. (1982). "Multivariate regression models for panel data." *Journal of Econometrics*, 18, 5–46.

Cragg, J. (1983). "More efficient estimation in the presence of heteroskedasticity of unknown form." *Econometrica*, 51, 751–764.

Engle, R. F. (1981). "Wald, likelihood ratio, and Lagrange multiplier tests in econometrics." In *Handbook of Econometrics*, 2, Z. Griliches and M. Intrilligator, eds., North Holland, Amsterdam.

——— (1982). "Autoregressive conditional heteroskedasticity with estimates of the variance of United Kingdom inflation." *Econometrica*, 50, 987–1008.

Goldberger, A. S. (1964). *Econometric Theory.* Wiley, New York.

Hansen, L. P. (1982). "Large Sample Properties of Generalized Method of Moments Estimators." *Econometrica*, 50, 1029–1054.

Lukacs, E. (1970). *Characteristic Functions.* Griffin, London.

——— (1975). *Stochastic Convergence.* Academic Press, New York.

Rao, C. R. (1973). *Linear Statistical Inference and Its Applications.* Wiley, New York.

White, H. (1982). "Instrumental variables regression with independent observations." *Econometrica*, 50, 483–500.

——— (1994). *Estimation, Inference and Specification Analysis.* Cambridge University Press, New York.

——— and M. Stinchcombe (1991). "Adaptive efficient weighted least squares with dependent observations." In *Directions in Robust Statistics and Diagnostics*, W. Stahel and S. Weisberg, eds., pp. 337–364. IMA Volumes in Mathemaics and Its Applications. Springer-Verlag, New York.

CHAPTER 5

Central Limit Theory

In this chapter we study different versions of the central limit theorem that provide conditions guaranteeing the asymptotic normality of $n^{-1/2}\mathbf{X}'\varepsilon$ or $n^{-1/2}\mathbf{Z}'\varepsilon$ required for the results of the previous chapter. As with laws of large numbers, different conditions will apply to different kinds of economic data. Central limit results are generally available for each of the situations considered in Chapter 3, and we shall pay particular attention to the parallels involved.

The central limit theorems we consider are all of the following form.

Proposition 5.0 *Given restrictions on the moments, dependence, and heterogeneity of a scalar sequence* $\{Z_t\}$, $(\bar{Z}_n - \bar{\mu}_n)/(\bar{\sigma}_n/\sqrt{n}) = \sqrt{n}(\bar{Z}_n - \bar{\mu}_n)/\bar{\sigma}_n \overset{A}{\sim} N(0,1)$, *where* $\bar{\mu}_n \equiv E(\bar{Z}_n)$ *and* $\bar{\sigma}_n^2/n \equiv \text{var}(\bar{Z}_n)$.

In other words, under general conditions the sample average of a sequence has a limiting unit normal distribution when appropriately standardized. The results that follow specify precisely the restrictions that are sufficient to imply asymptotic normality. As with the laws of large numbers, there are natural trade-offs among these restrictions. Typically, greater dependence or heterogeneity is allowed at the expense of imposing more stringent moment requirements.

Although the results of the preceding chapter imposed the asymptotic normality requirement on the joint distribution of vectors such as $n^{-1/2}\mathbf{X}'\varepsilon$ or $n^{-1/2}\mathbf{Z}'\varepsilon$, it is actually only necessary to study central limit theory for sequences of scalars. This simplicity is a consequence of the following result.

Proposition 5.1 (Cramér-Wold device) *Let $\{\mathbf{b}_n\}$ be a sequence of random $k \times 1$ vectors and suppose that for any real $k \times 1$ vector $\boldsymbol{\lambda}$ such that $\boldsymbol{\lambda}'\boldsymbol{\lambda} = 1$, $\boldsymbol{\lambda}'\mathbf{b}_n \overset{A}{\sim} \boldsymbol{\lambda}'\mathcal{Z}$, where $\mathcal{Z}$ is a $k \times 1$ vector with joint distribution function F. Then the limiting distribution function of $\mathbf{b}_n$ exists and equals F.*

Proof. See Rao (1973, p. 123). ■

We shall apply this result by showing that under general conditions,

$$n^{-1/2} \sum_{t=1}^{n} \boldsymbol{\lambda}'\mathbf{V}_n^{-1/2}\mathbf{X}_t\varepsilon_t \overset{A}{\sim} \boldsymbol{\lambda}'\mathcal{Z}$$

or

$$n^{-1/2} \sum_{t=1}^{n} \boldsymbol{\lambda}'\mathbf{V}_n^{-1/2}\mathbf{Z}_t\varepsilon_t \overset{A}{\sim} \boldsymbol{\lambda}'\mathcal{Z},$$

where $\mathcal{Z} \sim N(\mathbf{0}, \mathbf{I})$, which, by Proposition 5.1, allows us to obtain the desired conclusion, i.e.,

$$\mathbf{V}_n^{-1/2} n^{-1/2}\mathbf{X}'\varepsilon \overset{A}{\sim} N(\mathbf{0}, \mathbf{I}) \text{ or } \mathbf{V}_n{}^{-1/2} n^{-1/2}\mathbf{Z}'\varepsilon \overset{A}{\sim} N(\mathbf{0}, \mathbf{I}).$$

When used in this context below, the vector $\boldsymbol{\lambda}$ will always be understood to have unit norm, i.e., $\boldsymbol{\lambda}'\boldsymbol{\lambda} = 1$.

5.1 Independent Identically Distributed Observations

As with laws of large numbers, the case of independent identically distributed observations is the simplest.

Theorem 5.2 (Lindeberg-Lévy) *Let $\{\mathcal{Z}_t\}$ be a sequence of i.i.d. random scalars, with $\mu \equiv E(\mathcal{Z}_t)$ and $\sigma^2 \equiv \text{var}(\mathcal{Z}_t) < \infty$. If $\sigma^2 \neq 0$, then*

$$\begin{aligned} \sqrt{n}(\bar{\mathcal{Z}}_n - \bar{\mu}_n)/\bar{\sigma}_n &= \sqrt{n}(\bar{\mathcal{Z}}_n - \mu)/\sigma \\ &= n^{-1/2} \sum_{t=1}^{n} (\mathcal{Z}_t - \mu)/\sigma \overset{A}{\sim} N(0, 1). \end{aligned}$$

Proof. Let $f(\lambda)$ be the characteristic function of $\mathcal{Z}_t - \mu$ and let $f_n(\lambda)$ be the characteristic function of $\sqrt{n}(\bar{\mathcal{Z}}_n - \bar{\mu}_n)/\bar{\sigma}_n = n^{-1/2}\sum_{t=1}^{n}(\mathcal{Z}_t - \mu)/\sigma$. From Propositions 4.13 and 4.14 we have

$$f_n(\lambda) = f(\lambda/(\sigma\sqrt{n}))^n$$

or

$$\log f_n(\lambda) = n \log f(\lambda/(\sigma\sqrt{n})).$$

Taking a Taylor expansion of $f(\lambda)$ around $\lambda = 0$ gives $f(\lambda) = 1 - \sigma^2\lambda^2/2 + o(\lambda^2)$ since $\sigma^2 < \infty$, by Proposition 4.15. Hence

$$\log f_n(\lambda) = n \log[1 - \lambda^2/(2n) + o(\lambda^2/n)] \to -\lambda^2/2$$

as $n \to \infty$. Hence $f_n(\lambda) \to \exp(-\lambda^2/2)$. Since this is continuous at zero, it follows from the continuity theorem (Theorem 4.17), the uniqueness theorem (Theorem 4.11), and Example 4.10 (*i*) that $\sqrt{n}(\bar{\mathcal{Z}}_n - \bar{\mu}_n)/\bar{\sigma}_n \overset{A}{\sim} N(0,1)$. ■

Compared with the law of large numbers for i.i.d. observations, we impose a single additional requirement, i.e., that $\sigma^2 \equiv \text{var}(\mathcal{Z}_t) < \infty$. Note that this implies $E|\mathcal{Z}_t| < \infty$. (Why?) Also note that without loss of generality, we can set $E(\mathcal{Z}_t) = 0$.

We can apply Theorem 5.2 to give conditions that ensure that the conditions of Theorem 4.25 and Exercise 4.26 are satisfied.

Theorem 5.3 *Given*

(*i*) $\mathbf{Y}_t = \mathbf{X}_t'\boldsymbol{\beta}_o + \varepsilon_t, \quad t = 1, 2, \ldots, \boldsymbol{\beta}_o \in \mathbb{R}^k$;

(*ii*) $\{(\mathbf{X}_t', \varepsilon_t)\}$ *is an i.i.d. sequence;*

(*iii*) (*a*) $E(\mathbf{X}_t\varepsilon_t) = \mathbf{0}$;

(*b*) $E|X_{thi}\varepsilon_{th}|^2 < \infty$, $h = 1, \ldots, p$, $i = l, \ldots, k$;

(*c*) $\mathbf{V}_n \equiv \text{var}(n^{-1/2}\mathbf{X}'\varepsilon) = \mathbf{V}$ *is positive definite;*

(*iv*) (*a*) $E|X_{thi}|^2 < \infty$, $h = 1, \ldots, p$, $i = 1, \ldots, k$;

(*b*) $\mathbf{M} \equiv E(\mathbf{X}_t\mathbf{X}_t')$ *is positive definite.*

Then $\mathbf{D}^{-1/2}\sqrt{n}(\hat{\boldsymbol{\beta}}_n - \boldsymbol{\beta}_o) \overset{A}{\sim} N(\mathbf{0}, \mathbf{I})$, *where* $\mathbf{D} = \mathbf{M}^{-1}\mathbf{V}\mathbf{M}^{-1}$. *Suppose in addition that*

(*v*) *there exists* $\hat{\mathbf{V}}_n$ *symmetric and positive semidefinite such that* $\hat{\mathbf{V}}_n - \mathbf{V} \xrightarrow{p} \mathbf{0}$.

Then $\hat{\mathbf{D}}_n - \mathbf{D} \xrightarrow{p} \mathbf{0}$, *where* $\hat{\mathbf{D}}_n = (\mathbf{X}'\mathbf{X}/n)^{-1}\hat{\mathbf{V}}_n(\mathbf{X}'\mathbf{X}/n)^{-1}$.

Proof. We verify the conditions of Theorem 4.25. We apply Theorem 5.2 and set $\mathcal{Z}_t = \boldsymbol{\lambda}'\mathbf{V}^{-1/2}\mathbf{X}_t\varepsilon_t$. The summands $\boldsymbol{\lambda}'\mathbf{V}^{-1/2}\mathbf{X}_t\varepsilon_t$ are i.i.d. given (*ii*), with $E(\mathcal{Z}_t) = 0$ given (*iii.a*), and $\text{var}(\mathcal{Z}_t) = 1$ given (*iii.b*) and (*iii.c*). Hence $n^{-1/2}\sum_{t=1}^n \mathcal{Z}_t = n^{-1/2}\sum_{t=1}^n \boldsymbol{\lambda}'\mathbf{V}^{-1/2}\mathbf{X}_t\varepsilon_t \overset{A}{\sim} N(0,1)$

by the Lindeberg-Lévy Theorem 5.2. It follows from Proposition 5.1 that $\mathbf{V}^{-1/2}n^{-1/2}\mathbf{X}'\boldsymbol{\varepsilon} \overset{A}{\sim} N(\mathbf{0}, \mathbf{I})$, where $\mathbf{V}$ is $O(1)$ given $(iii.b)$ and positive definite given $(iii.c)$. It follows from Kolmogorov's strong law of large numbers, Theorem 3.1, and from Theorem 2.24 that $\mathbf{X}'\mathbf{X}/n - \mathbf{M} \xrightarrow{p} \mathbf{0}$ given (ii) and (iv). Since the rest of the conditions of Theorem 4.25 are satisfied by assumption, the result follows. ■

In many cases $\mathbf{V}$ may simplify. For example, it may be known that $E(\varepsilon_t^2|\mathbf{X}_t) = \sigma_o^2$ $(p = 1)$. If so,

$$\begin{aligned}\mathbf{V} &\equiv E(\mathbf{X}_t\varepsilon_t\varepsilon_t\mathbf{X}_t') = E(\varepsilon_t^2\mathbf{X}_t\mathbf{X}_t') = E(E(\varepsilon_t^2\mathbf{X}_t\mathbf{X}_t'|\mathbf{X}_t)) \\ &= E(E(\varepsilon_t^2|\mathbf{X}_t)\mathbf{X}_t\mathbf{X}_t') = \sigma_o^2 E(\mathbf{X}_t\mathbf{X}_t') = \sigma_o^2\mathbf{M}.\end{aligned}$$

The obvious estimator for $\mathbf{V}$ is then $\hat{\mathbf{V}}_n = \hat{\sigma}_n^2(\mathbf{X}'\mathbf{X}/n)$, where $\hat{\sigma}_n^2$ is consistent for σ_o^2. A similar result holds for systems of equations in which it is known that $E(\boldsymbol{\varepsilon}_t\boldsymbol{\varepsilon}_t'|\mathbf{X}_t) = \mathbf{I}$ (after suitable transformation of an underlying DGP). Then $\mathbf{V} = \mathbf{M}$ and a consistent estimator is $\hat{\mathbf{V}}_n = (\mathbf{X}'\mathbf{X}/n)$. Consistency results for more general cases are studied in the next chapter.

In comparison with the consistency result for the OLS estimator, we have obtained the asymptotic normality result by imposing the additional second moment conditions of $(iii.b)$ and $(iii.c)$. Otherwise, the conditions are identical. A similar result holds for the IV estimator.

Exercise 5.4 *Prove the following result. Given*

(i) $\mathbf{Y}_t = \mathbf{X}_t'\boldsymbol{\beta}_o + \boldsymbol{\varepsilon}_t, \quad t = 1, 2, \ldots, \boldsymbol{\beta}_o \in \mathbb{R}^k$;

(ii) $\{(\mathbf{Z}_t', \mathbf{X}_t', \boldsymbol{\varepsilon}_t)\}$ *is an i.i.d. sequence;*

(iii) (a) $E(\mathbf{Z}_t\boldsymbol{\varepsilon}_t) = \mathbf{0}$;

(b) $E|Z_{thi}\varepsilon_{th}|^2 < \infty$, $h = 1, \ldots, p$, $i = 1, \ldots, l$;

(c) $\mathbf{V}_n \equiv \text{var}(n^{-1/2}\mathbf{Z}'\boldsymbol{\varepsilon}) = \mathbf{V}$ *is positive definite;*

(iv) (a) $E|Z_{thi}X_{thj}| < \infty$, $h = 1, \ldots, p$, $i = 1, \ldots, l$, *and* $j = 1, \ldots, k$;

(b) $\mathbf{Q} \equiv E(\mathbf{Z}_t\mathbf{X}_t')$ *has full column rank;*

(c) $\hat{\mathbf{P}}_n \xrightarrow{p} \mathbf{P}$, *finite, symmetric, and positive definite.*

Then $\mathbf{D}^{-1/2}\sqrt{n}(\tilde{\boldsymbol{\beta}}_n - \boldsymbol{\beta}_o) \overset{A}{\sim} N(\mathbf{0}, \mathbf{I})$, *where*

$$\mathbf{D} \equiv (\mathbf{Q}'\mathbf{P}\mathbf{Q})^{-1}\mathbf{Q}'\mathbf{P}\mathbf{V}\mathbf{P}\mathbf{Q}(\mathbf{Q}'\mathbf{P}\mathbf{Q})^{-1}.$$

Suppose further that

(v) *there exists* $\hat{\mathbf{V}}_n$ *symmetric and positive semidefinite such that* $\hat{\mathbf{V}}_n - \mathbf{V} \xrightarrow{p} \mathbf{0}$.

Then $\hat{\mathbf{D}}_n - \mathbf{D} \xrightarrow{p} \mathbf{0}$, *where*

$$\hat{\mathbf{D}}_n \equiv (\mathbf{X}'\mathbf{Z}\hat{\mathbf{P}}_n\mathbf{Z}'\mathbf{X}/n^2)^{-1}(\mathbf{X}'\mathbf{Z}/n)\hat{\mathbf{P}}_n\hat{\mathbf{V}}_n\hat{\mathbf{P}}_n(\mathbf{Z}'\mathbf{X}/n)(\mathbf{X}'\mathbf{Z}\hat{\mathbf{P}}_n\mathbf{Z}'\mathbf{X}/n^2)^{-1}.$$

Exercise 5.5 *If* $p = 1$ *and* $E(\varepsilon_t^2|\mathbf{Z}_t) = \sigma_o^2$, *what is the efficient IV estimator? What is the natural estimator for* $\mathbf{V}$? *What additional conditions ensure that* $\hat{\mathbf{P}}_n - \mathbf{P} \xrightarrow{p} \mathbf{0}$ *and* $\hat{\mathbf{V}}_n - \mathbf{V} \xrightarrow{p} \mathbf{0}$?

These results apply to observations from a random sample. However, they do not apply to situations such as the standard regression model with fixed regressors, or to stratified cross sections, because in these situations the elements of the sum $n^{-1/2}\sum_{t=1}^n \mathbf{X}_t\varepsilon_t$ are no longer identically distributed. For example, with $\mathbf{X}_t$ fixed and $E(\varepsilon_t^2) = \sigma_o^2$, $\text{var}(\mathbf{X}_t\varepsilon_t) = \sigma_o^2\mathbf{X}_t\mathbf{X}_t'$, which depends on $\mathbf{X}_t\mathbf{X}_t'$ and hence differs from observation to observation. For these cases we need to relax the identical distribution assumption.

5.2 Independent Heterogeneously Distributed Observations

Several different central limit theorems are available for the case in which our observations are not identically distributed. The most general result is in fact the centerpiece of all asymptotic distribution theory.

Theorem 5.6 (Lindeberg-Feller) *Let* $\{Z_t\}$ *be a sequence of independent random scalars with* $\mu_t \equiv E(Z_t)$, $\sigma_t^2 \equiv \text{var}(Z_t) < \infty$, $\sigma_t^2 \neq 0$ *and distribution functions* F_t, $t = 1, 2, \ldots$. *Then*

$$\sqrt{n}(\bar{Z}_n - \bar{\mu}_n)/\bar{\sigma}_n \overset{A}{\sim} N(0,1)$$

and

$$\lim_{n\to\infty} \max_{1\le t\le n} n^{-1}(\sigma_t^2/\bar{\sigma}_n^2) = 0,$$

if and only if for every $\varepsilon > 0$,

$$\lim_{n\to\infty} \bar{\sigma}_n^{-2} n^{-1} \sum_{t=1}^n \int_{(z-\mu_t)^2 > \varepsilon n \bar{\sigma}_n^2} (z-\mu_t)^2 dF_t(z) = 0.$$

Proof. See Loeve (1977, pp. 292–294). ∎

The last condition of this result is called the Lindeberg condition. It essentially requires the average contribution of the extreme tails to the variance of Z_t to be zero in the limit. When the Lindeberg condition holds, not only does asymptotic normality follow, but the *uniform asymptotic negligibility* condition $\max_{1\le t\le n} n^{-1}(\sigma_t^2/\bar{\sigma}_n^2) \to 0$ as $n \to \infty$ also holds. This condition says that none of the Z_t has a variance so great that it dominates the variance of $\bar{Z}_n$. Further, the case $\sigma_t^2 = 0$ for all t is ruled out by the Lindeberg condition. Thus $\max_{1\le t\le n} \sigma_t^2 > 0$, which by the Lindeberg conditions implies that $n\bar{\sigma}_n^2 \to \infty$, so $n\bar{\sigma}_n^2 = \sum_{t=1}^n \sigma_t^2$ is prevented from converging to some finite value. Together, asymptotic normality and uniform asymptotic negligibility imply the Lindeberg condition.

Example 5.7 *Let $\sigma_t^2 = \rho^t$, $0 < \rho < 1$. Then $n\bar{\sigma}_n^2 = \sum_{t=1}^n \rho^t \to \rho/(1-\rho)$ as $n \to \infty$, and*

$$\max_{1\le t\le n} n^{-1}(\sigma_t^2/\bar{\sigma}_n^2) = \rho/[\rho/(1-\rho)] = 1-\rho \neq 0.$$

Hence $\{Z_t\}$ is not uniformly asymptotically negligible. It follows that the Lindeberg condition is not satisfied, so asymptotic normality may or may not hold for such a sequence.

Example 5.8 *Let $\{Z_t\}$ be i.i.d. with $\sigma^2 \equiv \text{var}(Z_t) < \infty$. By Theorem 5.2, $\sqrt{n}(\bar{Z}_n - \bar{\mu}_n)/\bar{\sigma}_n \overset{A}{\sim} N(0,1)$. Further, $\bar{\sigma}_n^2 = \sigma^2$, so*

$$\max_{1\le t\le n} n^{-1}(\sigma_t^2/\bar{\sigma}_n^2) = n^{-1}(\sigma^2/\sigma^2) \to 0.$$

It follows that the Lindeberg condition is satisfied.

Exercise 5.9 *Give a direct demonstration that the Lindeberg condition is satisfied for identically distributed $\{Z_t\}$ with $\sigma^2 \equiv \text{var}(Z_t) < \infty$, so that Theorem 5.2 follows as a corollary to Theorem 5.6. Hint: apply the Monotone Convergence Theorem (Rao, 1973, p. 135).*

In general, the Lindeberg condition can be somewhat difficult to verify, so it is convenient to have a simpler condition that implies the Lindeberg condition. This is provided by the following result.

Theorem 5.10 (Liapounov[1]) *Let $\{Z_t\}$ be a sequence of independent random scalars with $\mu_t \equiv E(Z_t)$, $\sigma_t^2 \equiv \text{var}(Z_t)$, and $E|Z_t - \mu_t|^{2+\delta} < \Delta < \infty$ for some $\delta > 0$ and all t. If $\bar{\sigma}_n^2 > \delta' > 0$ for all n sufficiently large, then $\sqrt{n}(\bar{Z}_n - \bar{\mu}_n)/\bar{\sigma}_n \overset{A}{\sim} N(0,1)$.*

---

[1] As stated, this result is actually a corollary to Liapounov's original theorem. See Loeve (1977, p. 287).

Proof. We verify that the Lindeberg condition is satisfied. Define $A = \{z : (z-\mu_t)^2 > \varepsilon n\bar{\sigma}_n^2\}$; then

$$\int_A (z-\mu_t)^2 dF_t(z) = \int_A |z-\mu_t|^\delta |z-\mu_t|^{-\delta}(z-\mu_t)^2 dF_t(z).$$

Whenever $(z-\mu_t)^2 > \varepsilon n\bar{\sigma}_n^2$, it follows that $|z-\mu_t|^{-\delta} < (\varepsilon n\bar{\sigma}_n^2)^{-\delta/2}$, so

$$\begin{aligned}\int_A (z-\mu_t)^2 dF_t(z) &< (\varepsilon n\bar{\sigma}_n^2)^{-\delta/2}\int_A |z-\mu_t|^{2+\delta} dF_t(z)\\ &\leq (\varepsilon n\bar{\sigma}_n^2)^{-\delta/2} E|Z_t-\mu_t|^{2+\delta}\\ &< (\varepsilon n\bar{\sigma}_n^2)^{-\delta/2}\Delta.\end{aligned}$$

Hence for any $\varepsilon > 0$,

$$\bar{\sigma}_n^{-2} n^{-1}\sum_{t=1}^n \int_A (z-\mu_t)^2 dF_t(z) < \bar{\sigma}_n^{-2}(\varepsilon n\bar{\sigma}_n^2)^{-\delta/2}\Delta = n^{-\delta/2}\bar{\sigma}_n^{-2-\delta}\varepsilon^{-\delta/2}\Delta.$$

Since $\bar{\sigma}_n^2 > \delta'$, $\bar{\sigma}_n^{-2-\delta} < (\delta')^{-1-\delta/2}$ for all n sufficiently large. It follows that

$$\bar{\sigma}_n^{-2} n^{-1}\sum_{t=1}^n \int_A (z-\mu_t)^2 dF_t(z) < n^{-\delta/2}(\delta')^{-1-\delta/2}\varepsilon^{-\delta/2}\Delta \to 0 \quad \text{as } n\to\infty.$$

■

This result allows us to substitute the requirement that some moment of order slightly greater than two is uniformly bounded in place of the more complicated Lindeberg condition. Note that $E|Z_t|^{2+\delta} < \Delta$ also implies that $E|Z_t-\mu_t|^{2+\delta}$ is uniformly bounded. Note also the analogy with Corollary 3.9. There we obtained a law of large numbers for independent random variables by imposing a uniform bound on $E|Z_t|^{1+\delta}$. Now we can obtain a central limit theorem imposing a uniform bound on $E|Z_t|^{2+\delta}$.

We seek an asymptotic normality result analogous to Theorem 5.3 for independent heterogeneous random variables. If we apply Theorem 5.10 instead of Theorem 5.2, we run into a small difficulty. Recall that we applied the Cramér-Wold device to the sums $n^{-1/2}\sum_{t=1}^n \boldsymbol{\lambda}'\mathbf{V}^{-1/2}\mathbf{X}_t\varepsilon_t$, where $\mathbf{V} = \text{var}(n^{-1/2}\mathbf{X}'\boldsymbol{\varepsilon})$. In the present case the random variables $\mathbf{X}_t\varepsilon_t$ are no longer identically distributed, and there is now no reason to suppose that $\mathbf{V}_n$ is a constant or has a constant limit, in general. By analogy, we would like to apply the Cramér-Wold device to $n^{-1/2}\sum_{t=1}^n \boldsymbol{\lambda}'\mathbf{V}_n^{-1/2}\mathbf{X}_t\varepsilon_t$. But the summands $\boldsymbol{\lambda}'\mathbf{V}_n^{-1/2}\mathbf{X}_t\varepsilon_t$ now depend explicitly on n, a possibility not covered by Theorem 5.10. Nevertheless, the needed generalization is readily available.

Theorem 5.11 *Let* $\{Z_{nt}\}$ *be a sequence of independent random scalars with* $\mu_{nt} \equiv E(Z_{nt})$, $\sigma_{nt}^2 \equiv \text{var}(Z_{nt})$, *and* $E|Z_{nt}|^{2+\delta} < \Delta < \infty$ *for some* $\delta > 0$ *and all* n *and* t. *Define* $\bar{Z}_n \equiv n^{-1}\sum_{t=1}^n Z_{nt}$, $\bar{\mu}_n \equiv n^{-1}\sum_{t=1}^n \mu_{nt}$ *and* $\bar{\sigma}_n^2 \equiv \text{var}(\sqrt{n}\bar{Z}_n) = n^{-1}\sum_{t=1}^n \sigma_{nt}^2$. *If* $\bar{\sigma}_n^2 > \delta' > 0$ *for all* n *sufficiently large, then* $\sqrt{n}(\bar{Z}_n - \bar{\mu}_n)/\bar{\sigma}_n \overset{A}{\sim} N(0,1)$.

Proof. See Loeve (1977, pp. 287–290). ■

Exercise 5.12 *Prove the following result. Given*

(*i*) $\mathbf{Y}_t = \mathbf{X}_t'\boldsymbol{\beta}_o + \varepsilon_t, \quad t = 1, 2, \ldots, \boldsymbol{\beta}_o \in \mathbb{R}^k$;

(*ii*) $\{(\mathbf{X}_t', \varepsilon_t)\}$ *is an independent sequence;*

(*iii*) (*a*) $E(\mathbf{X}_t\varepsilon_t) = \mathbf{0}, \quad t = 1, 2, \ldots$;

(*b*) $E|X_{thi}\varepsilon_{th}|^{2+\delta} < \Delta < \infty$ *for some* $\delta > 0$ *and all* $h = 1, \ldots, p$, $i = 1, \ldots, k$, *and* t;

(*c*) $\mathbf{V}_n \equiv \text{var}(n^{-1/2}\mathbf{X}'\varepsilon)$ *is uniformly positive definite;*

(*iv*) (*a*) $E|X_{thi}^2|^{1+\delta} < \Delta < \infty$ *for some* $\delta > 0$ *and all* $h = 1, \ldots, p$, $i = 1, \ldots, k$, *and* t;

(*b*) $\mathbf{M}_n \equiv E(\mathbf{X}'\mathbf{X}/n)$ *is uniformly positive definite.*

Then $\mathbf{D}_n^{-1/2}\sqrt{n}(\hat{\boldsymbol{\beta}}_n - \boldsymbol{\beta}_o) \overset{A}{\sim} N(\mathbf{0}, \mathbf{I})$, *where* $\mathbf{D}_n \equiv \mathbf{M}_n^{-1}\mathbf{V}_n\mathbf{M}_n^{-1}$. *Suppose in addition that*

(*v*) *there exists* $\hat{\mathbf{V}}_n$ *symmetric and positive semidefinite such that* $\hat{\mathbf{V}}_n - \mathbf{V}_n \xrightarrow{p} \mathbf{0}$.

Then $\hat{\mathbf{D}}_n - \mathbf{D}_n \xrightarrow{p} \mathbf{0}$, *where* $\hat{\mathbf{D}}_n \equiv (\mathbf{X}'\mathbf{X}/n)^{-1}\hat{\mathbf{V}}_n(\mathbf{X}'\mathbf{X}/n)^{-1}$.

Note the general applicability of this result. We can let $\mathbf{X}_t$ be fixed or stochastic (although independence is required), and the errors may be homoskedastic or heteroskedastic. A similarly general result holds for instrumental variables estimators.

Theorem 5.13 *Given*

(*i*) $\mathbf{Y}_t = \mathbf{X}_t'\boldsymbol{\beta}_o + \varepsilon_t, \quad t = 1, 2, \ldots, \boldsymbol{\beta}_o \in \mathbb{R}^k$;

(*ii*) $\{(\mathbf{Z}_t', \mathbf{X}_t', \varepsilon_t)\}$ *is an independent sequence;*

(*iii*) (*a*) $E(\mathbf{Z}_t\varepsilon_t) = \mathbf{0}, \quad t = 1, 2, \ldots$;

(*b*) $E|Z_{thi}\varepsilon_{th}|^{2+\delta} < \Delta < \infty$ *for some* $\delta > 0$ *and all* $h = 1, \ldots, p$, $i = 1, \ldots, l$, *and* t;

(*c*) $\mathbf{V}_n \equiv \text{var}(n^{-1/2}\mathbf{Z}'\varepsilon)$ *is uniformly positive definite;*

(*iv*) (*a*) $E|Z_{thi}X_{thj}|^{1+\delta} < \Delta < \infty$ *for some* $\delta > 0$ *and all* $h = 1, \ldots, p$, $i = 1, \ldots, l$, $j = 1, \ldots, k$, *and* t;

(*b*) $\mathbf{Q}_n \equiv E(\mathbf{Z}'\mathbf{X}/n)$ *has uniformly full column rank*;

(*c*) $\hat{\mathbf{P}}_n - \mathbf{P}_n \xrightarrow{p} \mathbf{0}$, *where* $\mathbf{P}_n = O(1)$ *and is symmetric and uniformly positive definite.*

Then $\mathbf{D}_n^{-1/2}\sqrt{n}(\tilde{\boldsymbol{\beta}}_n - \boldsymbol{\beta}_o) \overset{A}{\sim} N(\mathbf{0}, \mathbf{I})$, *where*

$$\mathbf{D}_n \equiv (\mathbf{Q}_n'\mathbf{P}_n\mathbf{Q}_n)^{-1}\mathbf{Q}_n'\mathbf{P}_n\mathbf{V}_n\mathbf{P}_n\mathbf{Q}_n(\mathbf{Q}_n'\mathbf{P}_n\mathbf{Q}_n)^{-1}.$$

Suppose in addition that

(*v*) *there exists* $\hat{\mathbf{V}}_n$ *symmetric and positive semidefinite such that* $\hat{\mathbf{V}}_n - \mathbf{V}_n \xrightarrow{p} \mathbf{0}$.

Then $\hat{\mathbf{D}}_n - \mathbf{D}_n \xrightarrow{p} \mathbf{0}$, *where*

$$\mathbf{D}_n \equiv (\mathbf{X}'\mathbf{Z}\hat{\mathbf{P}}_n\mathbf{Z}'\mathbf{X}/n^2)^{-1}(\mathbf{X}'\mathbf{Z}/n)\hat{\mathbf{P}}_n\hat{\mathbf{V}}_n\hat{\mathbf{P}}_n(\mathbf{Z}'\mathbf{X}/n)(\mathbf{X}'\mathbf{Z}\hat{\mathbf{P}}_n\mathbf{Z}'\mathbf{X}/n^2)^{-1}.$$

Proof. We verify the conditions of Exercise 4.26. To apply Theorem 5.11, let $\mathcal{Z}_{nt} \equiv \boldsymbol{\lambda}'\mathbf{V}_n^{-1/2}\mathbf{Z}_t\varepsilon_t$ and consider $n^{-1/2}\sum_{t=1}^n \boldsymbol{\lambda}'\mathbf{V}_n^{-1/2}\mathbf{Z}_t\varepsilon_t$. The summands $\mathcal{Z}_{nt}$ are independent given (*ii*) with $E(\mathcal{Z}_{nt}) = 0$ given (*iii.a*), $\bar{\sigma}_n^2 = 1$ given (*iii.c*), and $E|\mathcal{Z}_{nt}|^{2+\delta}$ uniformly bounded (apply Minkowski's inequality) given (*iii.b*). Hence

$$n^{-1/2}\sum_{t=1}^n \mathcal{Z}_{nt} = n^{-1/2}\sum_{t=1}^n \boldsymbol{\lambda}'\mathbf{V}_n^{-1/2}\mathbf{Z}_t\varepsilon_t \overset{A}{\sim} N(0,1)$$

by Theorem 5.11 and $\mathbf{V}_n^{-1/2}n^{-1/2}\mathbf{Z}'\boldsymbol{\varepsilon} \overset{A}{\sim} N(\mathbf{0}, \mathbf{I})$ by the Cramér-Wold device, Proposition 5.1.

Assumptions (*ii*), (*iv.a*), and (*iv.b*) ensure that $\mathbf{Z}'\mathbf{X}/n - \mathbf{Q}_n \xrightarrow{p} \mathbf{0}$ by Corollary 3.9 and Theorem 2.24. Since the remaining conditions of Exercise 4.26 are satisfied by assumption, the result follows. ∎

Note the close similarity of the present result to that of Exercise 5.4. We have dropped the identical distribution assumption made there at the expense of imposing just slightly more in the way of moment requirements in (*iii.b*) and (*iv.a*). Otherwise, the conditions are identical. This relatively minor trade-off has greatly increased the applicability of the results. Not only do the present results apply to situations with fixed regressors and either homoskedastic or heteroskedastic disturbances, but they also apply to cross-sectional data with either homoskedastic or heteroskedastic disturbances. Further, by setting $1 < p < \infty$, the present results apply to panel data (i.e., time-series cross-sectional data) when p observations are available for each individual.

As previously discussed, the independence assumption is not generally appropriate in time-series applications, so we now turn to central limit results applicable to time-series data.

5.3 Dependent Identically Distributed Observations

In the last two sections we saw that obtaining central limit theorems for independent processes typically required strengthening the moment restrictions beyond what was sufficient for obtaining laws of large numbers. In the case of stationary ergodic processes, not only will we strengthen the moment requirements, but we will also impose stronger conditions on the memory of the process.

To motivate the memory conditions that we add, consider a random scalar $\mathcal{Z}_t$, and let $\mathcal{F}_t$ be a σ-algebra such that $\{\mathcal{Z}_t, \mathcal{F}_t\}$ is an adapted stochastic sequence ($\mathcal{Z}_t$ is measurable with respect to $\mathcal{F}_t$ and $\mathcal{F}_{t-1} \subset \mathcal{F}_t \subset \mathcal{F}$.) We can think of $\mathcal{F}_t$ as being the σ–algebra generated by the entire current and past history of $\mathcal{Z}_t$ or, more generally, as the σ-algebra generated by the entire current and past history of $\mathcal{Z}_t$ as well as other random variables, say $\mathcal{Y}_t$. Given $E|\mathcal{Z}_t| < \infty$, we can write

$$\mathcal{Z}_t = \mathcal{Z}_t - E(\mathcal{Z}_t|\mathcal{F}_{t-1}) + E(\mathcal{Z}_t|\mathcal{F}_{t-1}).$$

Similarly,

$$\mathcal{Z}_t = \mathcal{Z}_t - E(\mathcal{Z}_t|\mathcal{F}_{t-1}) + E(\mathcal{Z}_t|\mathcal{F}_{t-1}) - E(\mathcal{Z}_t|\mathcal{F}_{t-2}) + E(\mathcal{Z}_t|\mathcal{F}_{t-2}).$$

Proceeding in this way we can write

$$\mathcal{Z}_t = \sum_{j=0}^{m-1} \mathcal{R}_{tj} + E(\mathcal{Z}_t|\mathcal{F}_{t-m}), \ m = 1, 2, \dots ,$$

where $\mathcal{R}_{tj}$ is the revision made in forecasting $\mathcal{Z}_t$ when information becomes available at time $t - j$:

$$\mathcal{R}_{tj} \equiv E(\mathcal{Z}_t|\mathcal{F}_{t-j}) - E(\mathcal{Z}_t|\mathcal{F}_{t-j-1}).$$

Note that for fixed j, $\{\mathcal{R}_{tj}, \mathcal{F}_{t-j}\}$ is a martingale difference sequence, because it is an adapted stochastic sequence and

$$\begin{aligned} E(\mathcal{R}_{tj}|\mathcal{F}_{t-j-1}) &= E[E(\mathcal{Z}_t|\mathcal{F}_{t-j}) - E(\mathcal{Z}_t|\mathcal{F}_{t-j-1})|\mathcal{F}_{t-j-1}] \\ &= E[E(\mathcal{Z}_t|\mathcal{F}_{t-j})|\mathcal{F}_{t-j-1}] - E[E(\mathcal{Z}_t|\mathcal{F}_{t-j-1})|\mathcal{F}_{t-j-1}] \\ &= E(\mathcal{Z}_t|\mathcal{F}_{t-j-1}) - E(\mathcal{Z}_t|\mathcal{F}_{t-j-1}) = 0, \end{aligned}$$

where we have applied the linearity property and the law of iterated expectations, Proposition 3.71.

Thus we have written $\mathcal{Z}_t$ as a sum of martingale differences plus a remainder. The validity of the central limit theorem we discuss rests on the ability to write

$$\mathcal{Z}_t = \sum_{j=0}^{\infty} \mathcal{R}_{tj}.$$

In this form, $\mathcal{Z}_t$ is expressed as a "telescoping sum," because adjacent elements of $\mathcal{R}_{tj}$ cancel out. Among other things, the validity of this expression requires that $E(\mathcal{Z}_t|\mathcal{F}_{t-m})$ tend appropriately to zero as $m \to \infty$. Remember that $E(\mathcal{Z}_t|\mathcal{F}_{t-m})$ is a random variable, so the convergence to zero must be stochastic. In fact, the condition we impose will imply that

$$E([E(\mathcal{Z}_t|\mathcal{F}_{t-m})]^2) \to 0 \text{ as } m \to \infty,$$

which can be stated in terms of convergence in quadratic mean as defined in Chapter 2, i.e.,

$$E(\mathcal{Z}_t|\mathcal{F}_{t-m}) \xrightarrow{q.m.} 0 \text{ as } m \to \infty.$$

One way of interpreting this condition is that as we forecast $\mathcal{Z}_t$ based only on the information available at more and more distant points in the past, our forecast approaches zero (in a mean squared error sense). Further, this condition actually implies that $E(\mathcal{Z}_t) = 0$ as we prove next, so that as our forecast becomes based on less and less information, it approaches the forecast we would make with no information, i.e., the unconditional expectation $E(\mathcal{Z}_t)$.

Lemma 5.14 *Let $\{\mathcal{Z}_t, \mathcal{F}_t\}$ be an adapted stochastic sequence such that $E(\mathcal{Z}_t^2) < \infty$, $t = 1, 2 \ldots$, and suppose $E(\mathcal{Z}_t|\mathcal{F}_{t-m}) \xrightarrow{q.m.} 0$ as $m \to \infty$. Then $E(\mathcal{Z}_t) = 0$.*

Proof. By Theorem 2.40 $E(\mathcal{Z}_t|\mathcal{F}_{t-m}) \xrightarrow{q.m.} 0$ as $m \to \infty$ implies that $E(|E(\mathcal{Z}_t|\mathcal{F}_{t-m})|) \xrightarrow{q.m.} 0$ as $m \to \infty$. Hence, for every $\varepsilon > 0$ there exists

$M(\varepsilon)$ such that $0 \leq E(|E(\mathcal{Z}_t|\mathcal{F}_{t-m})|) < \varepsilon$ for all $m > M(\varepsilon)$. By Jensen's inequality, $|E[E(\mathcal{Z}_t|\mathcal{F}_{t-m})]| \leq E(|E(\mathcal{Z}_t|\mathcal{F}_{t-m})|)$, so $0 \leq |E[E(\mathcal{Z}_t|\mathcal{F}_{t-m})]| < \varepsilon$ for all $m > M(\varepsilon)$. But by the law of iterated expectations, $E(\mathcal{Z}_t) = E[E(\mathcal{Z}_t|\mathcal{F}_{t-m})]$, so $0 \leq |E(\mathcal{Z}_t)| < \varepsilon$. Since ε is arbitrary, it follows that $E(\mathcal{Z}_t) = 0$. ∎

In establishing the central limit result, it is necessary to have $\bar{\sigma}_n^2 = \text{var}(\sqrt{n}\bar{\mathcal{Z}}_n)$ finite. However, for this it does not suffice simply to have $\sigma^2 = \text{var}(\mathcal{Z}_t)$ finite. Inspecting $\bar{\sigma}_n^2$, we see that

$$\begin{aligned}
\bar{\sigma}_n^2 &= n\,\text{var}(\bar{\mathcal{Z}}_n) \\
&= nE\left(\left(n^{-1}\sum_{t=1}^{n}\mathcal{Z}_t\right)^2\right) \\
&= n^{-1}\sum_{t=1}^{n}E(\mathcal{Z}_t^2) + 2n^{-1}\sum_{\tau=1}^{n-1}\sum_{t=\tau+1}^{n}E(\mathcal{Z}_t\mathcal{Z}_{t-\tau}).
\end{aligned}$$

When $\mathcal{Z}_t$ is stationary, $\rho_\tau \equiv E(\mathcal{Z}_t\mathcal{Z}_{t-\tau})/\sigma^2$ does not depend on t. Hence,

$$\begin{aligned}
\bar{\sigma}_n^2 &= \sigma^2 + 2\sigma^2 n^{-1}\sum_{\tau=1}^{n-1}(n-\tau)\rho_\tau \\
&= \sigma^2 + 2\sigma^2\sum_{\tau=1}^{n-1}\rho_\tau(1-\tau/n).
\end{aligned}$$

This last term contains a growing number of terms as $n \to \infty$, and without further conditions is not guaranteed to converge. It turns out that the condition

$$\sum_{m=0}^{\infty}(E[E(\mathcal{Z}_0|\mathcal{F}_{-m})^2])^{1/2} < \infty$$

is sufficient to ensure that ρ_τ declines fast enough that $\bar{\sigma}_n^2$ converges to a finite limit, say, $\bar{\sigma}^2$, as $n \to \infty$ and that this, together with stationarity and ergodicity, provides enough structure to obtain a central limit result.

In order to give a convenient statement of an ergodic central limit theorem, we introduce the notion of an *adapted mixingale* process.

Definition 5.15 *Let $\{\mathcal{Z}_t, \mathcal{F}_t\}$ be an adapted stochastic sequence with $E(\mathcal{Z}_t^2) < \infty$. Then $\{\mathcal{Z}_t, \mathcal{F}_t\}$ is an* adapted mixingale *if there exist finite nonnegative sequences $\{c_t\}$ and $\{\gamma_m\}$ such that $\gamma_m \to 0$ as $m \to \infty$ and*

$$\left(E\left(E(\mathcal{Z}_t|\mathcal{F}_{t-m})^2\right)\right)^{1/2} \leq c_t\gamma_m.$$

We say γ_m is of size $-a$ if $\gamma_m = O(m^{-a-\varepsilon})$ for some $\varepsilon > 0$.

The notion of a mixingale is due to McLeish (1974). Note that in this definition $\{\mathcal{Z}_t\}$ need not be stationary or ergodic, but may be heterogeneous. In the mixingale definition of McLeish, $\mathcal{F}_t$ need not be adapted to $\mathcal{Z}_t$. Nevertheless, we impose this because it simplifies matters nicely and is sufficient for all our applications. As the name is intended to suggest, mixingale processes have attributes of both mixing processes and martingale difference processes. They can be thought of as processes that behave "asymptotically" like martingale difference processes, analogous to mixing processes, which behave "asymptotically" like independent processes.

Theorem 5.16 (Scott) *Let $\{\mathcal{Z}_t, \mathcal{F}_t\}$ be a stationary ergodic adapted mixingale with γ_m of size -1. Then $\bar{\sigma}_n^2 \equiv \text{var}(n^{-1/2}\sum_{t=1}^n \mathcal{Z}_t) \to \bar{\sigma}^2 < \infty$ as $n \to \infty$ and if $\bar{\sigma}^2 > 0$, then $n^{-1/2}\bar{\mathcal{Z}}_n/\bar{\sigma} \overset{A}{\sim} N(0,1)$.*

Proof. Under the conditions given, the result follows from Theorem 3 of Scott (1973), provided that

$$\sum_{m=1}^{\infty} \left\{ \left(E\left[E\left(\mathcal{Z}_0|\mathcal{F}_{-m}\right)^2 \right] \right)^{1/2} + \left(E\left[\mathcal{Z}_0 - E\left(\mathcal{Z}_0|\mathcal{F}_m\right)\right]^2 \right)^{1/2} \right\} < \infty.$$

Because $\mathcal{Z}_0$ is $\mathcal{F}_m$-measurable for each $m \geq 1$, $E(\mathcal{Z}_0|\mathcal{F}_m) = \mathcal{Z}_0$ and the second term in the summation vanishes. It suffices then that

$$\sum_{m=1}^{\infty} \left(E\left[E\left(\mathcal{Z}_0|\mathcal{F}_{-m}\right)^2 \right] \right)^{1/2} < \infty.$$

Applying the mixingale and stationarity conditions we have

$$\begin{aligned}
\sum_{m=1}^{\infty} \left(E\left[E\left(\mathcal{Z}_0|\mathcal{F}_{-m}\right)^2 \right] \right)^{1/2} &\leq c_0 \sum_{m=1}^{\infty} \gamma_m \\
&\leq c_0 \Delta \sum_{m=1}^{\infty} m^{-(1+\varepsilon)} \\
&< \infty
\end{aligned}$$

with $\Delta < \infty$, as γ_m is of size -1. ∎

A related but more general result is given by Heyde (1975), where the interested reader can find further details of the underlying mathematics.

Applying Theorem 5.16 and Proposition 5.1 we obtain the following result for the OLS estimator.

Theorem 5.17 *Given*

(*i*) $\mathbf{Y}_t = \mathbf{X}_t'\boldsymbol{\beta}_o + \varepsilon_t, \quad t = 1, 2, \ldots, \boldsymbol{\beta}_o \in \mathbb{R}^k$;

(*ii*) $\{(\mathbf{X}_t', \varepsilon_t)\}$ *is a stationary ergodic sequence;*

(*iii*) (*a*) $\{X_{thi}\varepsilon_{th}, \mathcal{F}_t\}$ *is an adapted mixingale of size* -1, $h = 1, \ldots, p$, $i = 1, \ldots, k$;

(*b*) $E|X_{thi}\varepsilon_{th}|^2 < \infty$, $h = 1, \ldots, p$, $i = 1, \ldots, k$;

(*c*) $\mathbf{V}_n \equiv \text{var}(n^{-1/2}\mathbf{X}'\boldsymbol{\varepsilon})$ *is uniformly positive definite;*

(*iv*) (*a*) $E|X_{thi}|^2 < \infty$, $h = 1, \ldots, p$, $i = 1, \ldots, k$;

(*b*) $\mathbf{M} \equiv E(\mathbf{X}_t\mathbf{X}_t')$ *is positive definite;*

Then $\mathbf{V}_n \to \mathbf{V}$ *finite and positive definite as* $n \to \infty$, *and* $\mathbf{D}^{-1/2}\sqrt{n}(\hat{\boldsymbol{\beta}}_n - \boldsymbol{\beta}_o) \overset{A}{\sim} N(\mathbf{0}, \mathbf{I})$, *where* $\mathbf{D} = \mathbf{M}^{-1}\mathbf{V}\mathbf{M}^{-1}$.

Suppose in addition that

(*v*) *there exists* $\hat{\mathbf{V}}_n$ *symmetric and positive semidefinite such that* $\hat{\mathbf{V}}_n - \mathbf{V}_n \xrightarrow{p} \mathbf{0}$.

Then $\hat{\mathbf{D}}_n - \mathbf{D} \xrightarrow{p} \mathbf{0}$, *where* $\hat{\mathbf{D}}_n = (\mathbf{X}'\mathbf{X}/n)^{-1}\hat{\mathbf{V}}_n(\mathbf{X}'\mathbf{X}/n)^{-1}$.

Proof. We verify the conditions of Theorem 4.25. First we apply Theorem 5.16 and Proposition 5.1 to show that $\mathbf{V}_n^{-1/2}n^{-1/2}\mathbf{X}'\boldsymbol{\varepsilon} \overset{A}{\sim} N(\mathbf{0}, \mathbf{I})$. Consider $n^{-1/2}\sum_{t=1}^{n} \boldsymbol{\lambda}'\mathbf{V}^{-1/2}\mathbf{X}_t\boldsymbol{\varepsilon}_t$, where $\mathbf{V}$ is any finite positive definite matrix. By Theorem 3.35, $\{\mathcal{Z}_t \equiv \boldsymbol{\lambda}'\mathbf{V}^{-1/2}\mathbf{X}_t\boldsymbol{\varepsilon}_t\}$ is a stationary ergodic sequence given (*ii*), and $\{\mathcal{Z}_t, \mathcal{F}_t\}$ is an adapted stochastic sequence because $\mathcal{Z}_t$ is measurable with respect to $\mathcal{F}_t$ by Proposition 3.23, and $\mathcal{F}_{t-1} \subset \mathcal{F}_t \subset \mathcal{F}$. To see that $E(\mathcal{Z}_t^2) < \infty$, note that we can write

$$\begin{aligned} \mathcal{Z}_t &= \boldsymbol{\lambda}'\mathbf{V}^{-1/2}\mathbf{X}_t\boldsymbol{\varepsilon}_t \\ &= \sum_{h=1}^{p} \boldsymbol{\lambda}'\mathbf{V}^{-1/2}\mathbf{X}_{th}\varepsilon_{th} \\ &= \sum_{h=1}^{p}\sum_{i=1}^{k} \tilde{\lambda}_i X_{thi}\varepsilon_{th}, \end{aligned}$$

where $\tilde{\lambda}_i$ is the ith element of the $k \times 1$ vector $\tilde{\boldsymbol{\lambda}} \equiv \mathbf{V}^{-1/2}\boldsymbol{\lambda}$. By definition of $\boldsymbol{\lambda}$ and $\mathbf{V}$, there exists $\Delta < \infty$ such that $|\tilde{\lambda}_i| < \Delta$ for all i. It follows from

Minkowski's inequality that

$$\begin{aligned} E(\mathcal{Z}_t^2) &\leq \left[\sum_{h=1}^{p}\sum_{i=1}^{k}\left(E|\tilde{\lambda}_i X_{thi}\varepsilon_{th}|^2\right)^{1/2}\right]^2 \\ &\leq \left[\Delta\sum_{h=1}^{p}\sum_{i=1}^{k}\left(E|X_{thi}\varepsilon_{th}|^2\right)^{1/2}\right]^2 \\ &\leq [\Delta pk\Delta^{1/2}]^2 < \infty, \end{aligned}$$

since for Δ sufficiently large, $E|X_{thi}\varepsilon_{th}|^2 < \Delta < \infty$ given (*iii.b*) and the stationarity assumption. Next, we show $\{\mathcal{Z}_t, \mathcal{F}_t\}$ is a mixingale of size -1. Using the expression for $\mathcal{Z}_t$ just given, we can write

$$\begin{aligned} E([E(\mathcal{Z}_0|\mathcal{F}_{-m})]^2) &= E\left(\left[E\left(\sum_{h=1}^{p}\sum_{i=1}^{k}\tilde{\lambda}_i X_{0hi}\varepsilon_{0h}|\mathcal{F}_{-m}\right)\right]^2\right) \\ &= E\left(\left[\sum_{h=1}^{p}\sum_{i=1}^{k}E\left(\tilde{\lambda}_i X_{0hi}\varepsilon_{0h}|\mathcal{F}_{-m}\right)\right]^2\right). \end{aligned}$$

Applying Minkowski's inequality it follows that

$$\begin{aligned} E([E(\mathcal{Z}_0|\mathcal{F}_{-m})]^2) &\leq \left[\sum_{h=1}^{p}\sum_{i=1}^{k}\left(E\left[E(\tilde{\lambda}_i X_{0hi}\varepsilon_{0h}|\mathcal{F}_{-m})^2\right]\right)^{1/2}\right]^2 \\ &\leq \left[\Delta\sum_{h=1}^{p}\sum_{i=1}^{k}\left(E\left[E(X_{0hi}\varepsilon_{0h}|\mathcal{F}_{-m})^2\right]\right)^{1/2}\right]^2 \\ &\leq \left[\Delta\sum_{h=1}^{p}\sum_{i=1}^{k}c_{0hi}\gamma_{mhi}\right]^2 \\ &\leq [\Delta pk\bar{c}_0\bar{\gamma}_m]^2, \end{aligned}$$

where $\bar{c}_0 = \max_{h,i} c_{0hi} < \infty$ and $\bar{\gamma}_m = \max_{h,i}\gamma_{mhi}$ is of size -1. Thus, $\{\mathcal{Z}_t, \mathcal{F}_t\}$ is a mixingale of size -1 as required.

By Theorem 5.16, it follows that

$$\begin{aligned} \text{var}(\sqrt{n}\bar{\mathcal{Z}}_n) &= \text{var}\left(n^{-1/2}\sum_{t=1}^{n}\boldsymbol{\lambda}'\mathbf{V}^{-1/2}\mathbf{X}_t\varepsilon_t\right) \\ &= \boldsymbol{\lambda}'\mathbf{V}^{-1/2}\mathbf{V}_n\mathbf{V}^{-1/2}\boldsymbol{\lambda} \to \bar{\sigma}^2 < \infty. \end{aligned}$$

Hence $\mathbf{V}_n$ converges to a finite matrix. Now set $\mathbf{V} = \lim_{n\to\infty}\mathbf{V}_n$, which is positive definite given (*iii.c*). Then $\bar{\sigma}^2 = \boldsymbol{\lambda}'\mathbf{V}^{-1/2}\mathbf{V}\mathbf{V}^{-1/2}\boldsymbol{\lambda} = 1$. It then follows from Theorem 5.16 that $n^{-1/2}\sum_{t=1}^n \boldsymbol{\lambda}'\mathbf{V}^{-1/2}\mathbf{X}_t\varepsilon_t \overset{A}{\sim} N(0,1)$. Since this holds for every $\boldsymbol{\lambda}$ such that $\boldsymbol{\lambda}'\boldsymbol{\lambda} = 1$, it follows from Proposition 5.1 that $\mathbf{V}^{-1/2}n^{-1/2}\sum_{t=1}^n \mathbf{X}_t\varepsilon_t \overset{A}{\sim} N(\mathbf{0},\mathbf{I})$. Now

$$\begin{aligned} & \mathbf{V}_n^{-1/2}n^{-1/2}\sum_{t=1}^n \mathbf{X}_t\varepsilon_t - \mathbf{V}^{-1/2}n^{-1/2}\sum_{t=1}^n \mathbf{X}_t\varepsilon_t \\ = \ & (\mathbf{V}_n^{-1/2}\mathbf{V}^{1/2} - \mathbf{I})\mathbf{V}^{-1/2}n^{-1/2}\sum_{t=1}^n \mathbf{X}_t\varepsilon_t \xrightarrow{p} \mathbf{0}, \end{aligned}$$

since $\mathbf{V}_n^{-1/2}\mathbf{V}^{1/2} - \mathbf{I}$ is $o(1)$ by Definition 2.5 and

$$\mathbf{V}^{-1/2}n^{-1/2}\sum_{t=1}^n \mathbf{X}_t\varepsilon_t \overset{A}{\sim} N(\mathbf{0},\mathbf{I}),$$

which allows application of Lemma 4.6. Hence by Lemma 4.7,

$$\mathbf{V}_n^{-1/2}n^{-1/2}\mathbf{X}'\boldsymbol{\varepsilon} \overset{A}{\sim} N(\mathbf{0},\mathbf{I}).$$

Next, $\mathbf{X}'\mathbf{X}/n - \mathbf{M} \xrightarrow{p} \mathbf{0}$ by the ergodic theorem (Theorem 3.34) and Theorem 2.24 given (*ii*) and (*iv*), where $\mathbf{M}$ is finite and positive definite. Since the conditions of Theorem 4.25 are satisfied, it follows that $\mathbf{D}_n^{-1/2}\sqrt{n}(\hat{\boldsymbol{\beta}}_n - \boldsymbol{\beta}_o) \overset{A}{\sim} N(\mathbf{0},\mathbf{I})$, where $\mathbf{D}_n \equiv \mathbf{M}^{-1}\mathbf{V}_n\mathbf{M}^{-1}$. Because $\mathbf{D}_n - \mathbf{D} \to \mathbf{0}$ as $n \to \infty$, it follows that

$$\begin{aligned} & \mathbf{D}^{-1/2}\sqrt{n}(\hat{\boldsymbol{\beta}}_n - \boldsymbol{\beta}_o) - \mathbf{D}_n^{-1/2}\sqrt{n}(\hat{\boldsymbol{\beta}}_n - \boldsymbol{\beta}_o) \\ = \ & (\mathbf{D}^{-1/2}\mathbf{D}_n^{1/2} - \mathbf{I})\mathbf{D}_n^{-1/2}\sqrt{n}(\hat{\boldsymbol{\beta}}_n - \boldsymbol{\beta}_o) \xrightarrow{p} \mathbf{0} \end{aligned}$$

by Lemma 4.6. Hence, by Lemma 4.7,

$$\mathbf{D}^{-1/2}\sqrt{n}(\hat{\boldsymbol{\beta}}_n - \boldsymbol{\beta}_o) \overset{A}{\sim} N(\mathbf{0},\mathbf{I}).$$

■

Comparing this result with the OLS result in Theorem 5.3 for i.i.d. regressors, we have replaced the i.i.d. assumption with stationarity, ergodicity, and the mixingale requirements of (*iii.a*). Because these conditions are always satisfied for i.i.d. sequences, Theorem 5.3 is in fact a direct corollary of Theorem 5.16. (Condition (*iii.a*) is satisfied because for i.i.d. sequences

$E(X_{0hi}\varepsilon_{0h}|\mathcal{F}_{-m}) = 0$ for all $m > 0$.) Note that these conditions impose the restrictions placed on Z_t in Theorem 5.16 for each regressor-error cross product $X_{thi}\varepsilon_{th}$.

Although the present result now allows for the possibility that $\mathbf{X}_t$ contains lagged dependent variables $Y_{t-1}, Y_{t-2}, \ldots$, it does not allow ε_t to be serially correlated at the same time. This is ruled out by (*iii.a*) which implies $E(\mathbf{X}_t\varepsilon_t) = \mathbf{0}$ by Lemma 5.14. This condition will be violated if lagged dependent variables are present when ε_t is serially correlated. Also note that if lagged dependent variables are present in $\mathbf{X}_t$, condition (*iv.a*) requires that $E(Y_t^2)$ is finite. This in turn places restrictions on the possible values allowed for $\boldsymbol{\beta}_o$.

Exercise 5.18 *Suppose that the data are generated as* $Y_t = \beta_{o1}Y_{t-1} + \beta_{o2}Y_{t-2} + \varepsilon_t$. *State general conditions on* $\{Y_t\}$ *and* (β_{o1}, β_{o2}) *which ensure the consistency and asymptotic normality of the OLS estimator for* β_{o1} *and* β_{o2}.

As just mentioned, OLS is inappropriate when the model contains lagged dependent variables in the presence of serially correlated errors. However, useful instrumental variables estimators are often available.

Exercise 5.19 *Prove the following result. Given*

(*i*) $\mathbf{Y}_t = \mathbf{X}_t'\boldsymbol{\beta}_o + \varepsilon_t, \quad t = 1, 2, \ldots, \boldsymbol{\beta}_o \in \mathbb{R}^k$;

(*ii*) $\{(\mathbf{Z}_t', \mathbf{X}_t', \varepsilon_t)\}$ *is a stationary ergodic sequence;*

(*iii*) (*a*) $\{Z_{thi}\varepsilon_{th}, \mathcal{F}_t\}$ *is an adapted mixingale of size* -1, $h = 1, \ldots, p$, $i = 1, \ldots, l$;

(*b*) $E\,|Z_{thi}\varepsilon_{th}|^2 < \infty$, $h = 1, \ldots, p$, $i = 1, \ldots, l$;

(*c*) $\mathbf{V}_n \equiv \text{var}(n^{-1/2}\mathbf{Z}'\boldsymbol{\varepsilon})$ *is uniformly positive definite;*

(*iv*) (*a*) $E|Z_{thi}X_{thj}| < \infty$, $h = 1, \ldots, p$, $i = 1, \ldots, l$, *and* $j = 1, \ldots, k$;

(*b*) $\mathbf{Q} \equiv E(\mathbf{Z}_t\mathbf{X}_t')$ *has full column rank;*

(*c*) $\hat{\mathbf{P}}_n \xrightarrow{p} \mathbf{P}$ *finite, symmetric, and positive definite.*

Then $\mathbf{V}_n \to \mathbf{V}$ *finite and positive definite as* $n \to \infty$, *and* $\mathbf{D}^{-1/2}\sqrt{n}(\tilde{\boldsymbol{\beta}}_n - \boldsymbol{\beta}_o) \stackrel{A}{\sim} N(\mathbf{0}, \mathbf{I})$, *where*

$$\mathbf{D} \equiv (\mathbf{Q}'\mathbf{P}\mathbf{Q})^{-1}\mathbf{Q}'\mathbf{P}\mathbf{V}\mathbf{P}\mathbf{Q}(\mathbf{Q}'\mathbf{P}\mathbf{Q})^{-1}.$$

Suppose further that

(*v*) *there exists* $\hat{\mathbf{V}}_n$ *symmetric and positive semidefinite such that* $\hat{\mathbf{V}}_n - \mathbf{V} \xrightarrow{p} \mathbf{0}$.

Then $\hat{\mathbf{D}}_n - \mathbf{D} \xrightarrow{p} \mathbf{0}$, *where*

$$\hat{\mathbf{D}}_n \equiv (\mathbf{X}'\mathbf{Z}\hat{\mathbf{P}}_n\mathbf{Z}'\mathbf{X}/n^2)^{-1}(\mathbf{X}'\mathbf{Z}/n)\hat{\mathbf{P}}_n\hat{\mathbf{V}}_n\hat{\mathbf{P}}_n(\mathbf{Z}'\mathbf{X}/n)(\mathbf{X}'\mathbf{Z}\hat{\mathbf{P}}_n\mathbf{Z}'\mathbf{X}/n^2)^{-1}.$$

This result follows as a corollary to a more general theorem for nonlinear equations given by Hansen (1982). However, all the essential features of his assumptions are illustrated in the present result.

Since the results of this section are based on a stationarity assumption, unconditional heteroskedasticity is explicitly ruled out. However, conditional heteroskedasticity is nevertheless a possibility, so efficiency improvements along the lines of Theorem 4.55 may be obtained by accounting for conditional heteroskedasticity.

5.4 Dependent Heterogeneously Distributed Observations

To allow for situations in which the errors exhibit unconditional heteroskedasticity, or the explanatory variables contain fixed as well as lagged dependent variables, we apply central limit results for sequences of mixing random variables. A convenient version of the Liapounov theorem for mixing processes is the following.

Theorem 5.20 (Wooldridge-White) *Let* $\{Z_{nt}\}$ *be a double array of scalars with* $\mu_{nt} \equiv E(Z_{nt}) = 0$ *and* $\sigma_{nt}^2 \equiv \text{var}(Z_{nt})$ *such that* $E|Z_{nt}|^r < \Delta < \infty$ *for some* $r \geq 2$, *and all* n *and* t, *and having mixing coefficients* ϕ *of size* $-r/2(r-1)$, *or* α *of size* $-r/(r-2)$, $r > 2$. *If* $\bar{\sigma}_n^2 \equiv \text{var}\left(n^{-1/2}\sum_{t=1}^n Z_t\right) > \delta > 0$ *for all* n *sufficiently large, then* $\sqrt{n}(\bar{Z}_n - \bar{\mu}_n)/\bar{\sigma}_n \overset{A}{\sim} N(0,1)$.

Proof. The result follows from Corollary 3.1 of Wooldridge and White (1988) applied to the random variables $\tilde{Z}_{nt} \equiv Z_{nt}/\bar{\sigma}_n$. See also Wooldridge (1986, Ch. 3, Corollary 4.4.) ∎

Compared with Theorem 5.11, the moment requirements are now potentially stronger to allow for considerably more dependence in Z_t. Note, however, that if $\phi(m)$ or $\alpha(m)$ decrease exponentially in m, we can set r arbitrarily close to two, implying essentially the same moment restrictions as in the independent case.

The analog to Exercise 5.12 is as follows.

Exercise 5.21 *Prove the following result. Given*

(*i*) $\mathbf{Y}_t = \mathbf{X}_t'\boldsymbol{\beta}_o + \varepsilon_t, \quad t = 1, 2, \ldots, \boldsymbol{\beta}_o \in \mathbb{R}^k$;

(*ii*) $\{(\mathbf{X}_t', \varepsilon_t)\}$ *is a mixing sequence with either* ϕ *of size* $-r/2(r-1)$, $r \geq 2$ *or* α *of size* $-r/(r-2), r > 2$;

(*iii*) (*a*) $E(\mathbf{X}_t\varepsilon_t) = \mathbf{0}, \quad t = 1, 2, \ldots$;

(*b*) $E|X_{thi}\varepsilon_{th}|^r < \Delta < \infty$ *for* $h = 1, \ldots, p$, $i = 1, \ldots, k$, *and all* t;

(*c*) $\mathbf{V}_n \equiv \text{var}\left(n^{-1/2}\sum_{t=1}^n \mathbf{X}_t\varepsilon_t\right)$ *is uniformly positive definite;*

(*iv*) (*a*) $E|X_{thi}^2|^{(r/2)+\delta} < \Delta < \infty$ *for some* $\delta > 0$ *and all* $h = 1, \ldots, p$, $i = 1, \ldots, k$, *and* t;

(*b*) $\mathbf{M}_n \equiv E(\mathbf{X}'\mathbf{X}/n)$ *is uniformly positive definite.*

Then $\mathbf{D}_n^{-1/2}\sqrt{n}(\hat{\boldsymbol{\beta}}_n - \boldsymbol{\beta}_o) \overset{A}{\sim} N(\mathbf{0}, \mathbf{I})$, *where* $\mathbf{D}_n = \mathbf{M}_n^{-1}\mathbf{V}_n\mathbf{M}_n^{-1}$. *Suppose in addition that*

(*v*) *there exists* $\hat{\mathbf{V}}_n$ *symmetric and positive semidefinite such that* $\hat{\mathbf{V}}_n - \mathbf{V}_n \xrightarrow{p} \mathbf{0}$.

Then $\hat{\mathbf{D}}_n - \mathbf{D}_n \xrightarrow{p} \mathbf{0}$, *where* $\hat{\mathbf{D}}_n \equiv (\mathbf{X}'\mathbf{X}/n)^{-1}\hat{\mathbf{V}}_n(\mathbf{X}'\mathbf{X}/n)^{-1}$.

Compared with Exercise 5.12, we have relaxed the memory requirement from independence to mixing (asymptotic independence). Depending on the amount of dependence the observations exhibit, the moment conditions may or may not be stronger than those of Exercise 5.12.

The flexibility gained by dispensing with the stationarity assumption of Theorem 5.17 is that the present result can accommodate the inclusion of fixed regressors as well as lagged dependent variables in the explanatory variables of the model. The price paid is an increase in the moment restrictions, as well as an increase in the strength of the memory conditions.

Exercise 5.22 *Suppose the data are generated as* $Y_t = \beta_{o1}Y_{t-1} + \beta_{o2}W_t + \varepsilon_t$, *where* W_t *is a fixed scalar. Let* $\mathbf{X}_t = (Y_{t-1}, W_t)$ *and provide conditions on* $\{(\mathbf{X}_t, \varepsilon_t)'\}$ *and* (β_{o1}, β_{o2}) *that ensure that the OLS estimator of* β_{o1} *and* β_{o2} *is consistent and asymptotically normal.*

The result for the instrumental variables estimator is the following.

Theorem 5.23 *Given*

(*i*) $\mathbf{Y}_t = \mathbf{X}_t'\boldsymbol{\beta}_o + \varepsilon_t$, $t = 1, 2, \ldots, \boldsymbol{\beta}_o \in \mathbb{R}^k$;

(*ii*) $\{(\mathbf{Z}_t', \mathbf{X}_t', \varepsilon_t)\}$ *is a mixing sequence with either* ϕ *of size* $-r/2(r-1)$, $r \geq 2$ *or* α *of size* $-r/(r-2)$, $r > 2$;

(iii) (*a*) $E(\mathbf{Z}_t\varepsilon_t) = \mathbf{0}, \quad t = 1, 2, \ldots;$

(*b*) $E|Z_{thi}\varepsilon_{th}|^r < \Delta < \infty$ *for* $h = 1, \ldots, p$, $i = 1, \ldots, l$, *and all* t;

(*c*) $\mathbf{V}_n \equiv \text{var}\left(n^{-1/2}\sum_{t=1}^n \mathbf{Z}_t\varepsilon_t\right)$, *is uniformly positive definite;*

(iv) (*a*) $E|Z_{thi}X_{thj}|^{(r/2)+\delta} < \Delta < \infty$ *for* $\delta > 0$ *and all* $h = 1, \ldots, p$, $i = 1, \ldots, l$, $j = 1, \ldots, k$, *and* t;

(*b*) $\mathbf{Q}_n \equiv E(\mathbf{Z}'\mathbf{X}/n)$ *has uniformly full column rank;*

(*c*) $\hat{\mathbf{P}}_n - \mathbf{P}_n \xrightarrow{p} \mathbf{0}$, *where* $\mathbf{P}_n = O(1)$ *and is symmetric and uniformly positive definite.*

Then $\mathbf{D}_n^{-1/2}\sqrt{n}(\tilde{\boldsymbol{\beta}}_n - \boldsymbol{\beta}_o) \overset{A}{\sim} N(\mathbf{0}, \mathbf{I})$, *where*

$$\mathbf{D}_n \equiv (\mathbf{Q}_n'\mathbf{P}_n\mathbf{Q}_n)^{-1}\mathbf{Q}_n'\mathbf{P}_n\mathbf{V}_n\mathbf{P}_n\mathbf{Q}_n(\mathbf{Q}_n'\mathbf{P}_n\mathbf{Q}_n)^{-1}.$$

Suppose further that

(v) *there exists* $\hat{\mathbf{V}}_n$ *symmetric and positive semidefinite such that* $\hat{\mathbf{V}}_n - \mathbf{V}_n \xrightarrow{p} \mathbf{0}$.

Then $\hat{\mathbf{D}}_n - \mathbf{D}_n \xrightarrow{p} \mathbf{0}$, *where*

$$\hat{\mathbf{D}}_n \equiv (\mathbf{X}'\mathbf{Z}\hat{\mathbf{P}}_n\mathbf{Z}'\mathbf{X}/n^2)^{-1}(\mathbf{X}'\mathbf{Z}/n)\hat{\mathbf{P}}_n\hat{\mathbf{V}}_n\hat{\mathbf{P}}_n(\mathbf{Z}'\mathbf{X}/n)(\mathbf{X}'\mathbf{Z}\hat{\mathbf{P}}_n\mathbf{Z}'\mathbf{X}/n^2)^{-1}.$$

Proof. We verify that the conditions of Exercise 4.26 hold. First we apply Proposition 5.1 to show $\mathbf{V}_n^{-1/2}n^{-1/2}\mathbf{Z}'\boldsymbol{\varepsilon} \overset{A}{\sim} N(\mathbf{0}, \mathbf{I})$. Consider

$$n^{-1/2}\sum_{t=1}^n \boldsymbol{\lambda}'\mathbf{V}_n^{-1/2}\mathbf{Z}_t\varepsilon_t.$$

By Theorem 3.49, $\boldsymbol{\lambda}'\mathbf{V}_n^{-1/2}\mathbf{Z}_t\varepsilon_t$ is a sequence of mixing random variables with either ϕ of size $-r/2(r-1)$, $r \geq 2$ or α of size $-r/(r-1)$, $r > 2$, given (*ii*). Further, $E(\boldsymbol{\lambda}'\mathbf{V}_n^{-1/2}\mathbf{Z}_t\varepsilon_t) = 0$ given (*iii.a*), $E|\boldsymbol{\lambda}'\mathbf{V}_n^{-1/2}\mathbf{Z}_t\varepsilon_t|^r < \Delta < \infty$ for all t given (*iii.b*), and

$$\bar{\sigma}_n^2 \equiv \text{var}\left(n^{-1/2}\sum_{t=1}^n \boldsymbol{\lambda}'\mathbf{V}_n^{-1/2}\mathbf{Z}_t\varepsilon_t\right) = \boldsymbol{\lambda}'\mathbf{V}_n^{-1/2}\mathbf{V}_n\mathbf{V}_n^{-1/2}\boldsymbol{\lambda} = 1.$$

It follows from Theorem 5.20 that $n^{-1/2}\sum_{t=1}^n \boldsymbol{\lambda}'\mathbf{V}_n^{-1/2}\mathbf{Z}_t\varepsilon_t \overset{A}{\sim} N(\mathbf{0}, \mathbf{I})$. Since this holds for every $\boldsymbol{\lambda}$, $\boldsymbol{\lambda}'\boldsymbol{\lambda} = 1$, it follows from Proposition 5.1 that $\mathbf{V}_n^{-1/2}n^{-1/2}\sum_{t=1}^n \mathbf{Z}_t\varepsilon_t \overset{A}{\sim} N(\mathbf{0}, \mathbf{I})$.

Next, $\mathbf{Z}'\mathbf{X}/n - \mathbf{Q}_n \xrightarrow{p} \mathbf{0}$ by Corollary 3.48 given (*iv.a*), where $\{\mathbf{Q}_n\}$ is $O(1)$ and has uniformly full column rank by (*iv.a*) and (*iv.b*). Since (*iv.c*) also holds, the desired result now follows from Exercise 4.26. ■

This result is in a sense the most general of all the results that we have obtained, because it contains so many special cases. Specifically, it covers every situation previously considered (i.i.d., i.h.d., and d.i.d. observations), although at the explicit cost of imposing slightly stronger conditions in various respects. Note, too, this result applies to systems of equations or panel data since we can choose $p > 1$.

5.5 Martingale Difference Sequences

In Chapter 3 we discussed laws of large numbers for martingale difference sequences and mentioned that economic theory is often used to justify the martingale difference assumption. If the martingale difference assumption is valid, then it often allows us to simplify or weaken some of the other conditions imposed in establishing the asymptotic normality of our estimators.

There are a variety of central limit theorems available for martingale difference sequences. One version that is relatively convenient is an extension of the Lindeberg-Feller theorem (Theorem 5.6). In stating it, we consider sequences of random variables $\{Z_{nt}\}$ and associated σ-algebras $\{\mathcal{F}_{nt}, 1 \leq t \leq n\}$, where $\mathcal{F}_{nt-1} \subset \mathcal{F}_{nt}$ and Z_{nt} is measurable with respect to $\mathcal{F}_{nt}$. We can think of $\mathcal{F}_{nt}$ as being the σ-field generated by the current and past of Z_{nt} as well as any other relevant random variables.

Theorem 5.24 *Let $\{Z_{nt}, \mathcal{F}_{nt}\}$ be a martingale difference sequence such that $\sigma_{nt}^2 \equiv E(Z_{nt}^2) < \infty$, $\sigma_{nt}^2 \neq 0$, and let F_{nt} be the distribution function of Z_{nt}. Define $\bar{Z}_n \equiv n^{-1}\sum_{t=1}^{n} Z_{nt}$ and $\bar{\sigma}_n^2 \equiv \text{var}\left(\sqrt{n}\bar{Z}_n\right) = n^{-1}\sum_{t=1}^{n} \sigma_{nt}^2$. If for every $\varepsilon > 0$*

$$\lim_{n\to\infty} \bar{\sigma}_n^{-2} n^{-1} \sum_{t=1}^{n} \int_{z^2 > \varepsilon n \bar{\sigma}_n^2} z^2 dF_{nt}(z) = 0,$$

and

$$n^{-1}\sum_{t=1}^{n} Z_{nt}^2/\bar{\sigma}_n^2 - 1 \xrightarrow{p} 0,$$

then $\sqrt{n}\bar{Z}_n/\bar{\sigma}_n \overset{A}{\sim} N(0,1)$.

Proof. This follows immediately as a corollary to Theorem 2.3 of McLeish (1974). ■

Comparing this result with the Lindeberg-Feller theorem, we see that both impose the Lindeberg condition, whereas the independence assumption has here been weakened to the martingale difference assumption. The present result also imposes a condition not explicit in the Lindeberg-Feller theorem, i.e., essentially that the sample variance $n^{-1}\sum_{t=1}^{n} Z_{nt}^2$ is a consistent estimator for $\bar{\sigma}_n^2$. This condition is unnecessary in the independent case because it is implied there by the Lindeberg condition. Without independence, we make use of additional conditions, e.g., stationarity and ergodicity or mixing, to ensure that the sample variance is indeed consistent for $\bar{\sigma}_n^2$.

To illustrate how use of the martingale difference assumption allows us to simplify our results, consider the IV estimator in the case of stationary observations. We have the following result.

Theorem 5.25 *Suppose conditions (i), (ii), (iv) and (v) of Exercise 5.19 hold, and replace condition (iii) with*

(*iii'*) (*a*) $E(Z_{thi}\varepsilon_{th}|\mathcal{F}_{t-1}) = 0$ *for all* t, *where* $\{\mathcal{F}_t\}$ *is adapted to* $\{Z_{thi}\varepsilon_{th}\}$, $h = 1, \dots, p$, $i = 1, \dots, l$;

(*b*) $E|Z_{thi}\varepsilon_{th}|^2 < \infty$, $h = 1, \dots, p$, $i = 1, \dots, l$;

(*c*) $\mathbf{V}_n \equiv \text{var}(n^{-1/2}\mathbf{Z}'\varepsilon) = \text{var}(\mathbf{Z}_t\varepsilon_t) \equiv \mathbf{V}$ *is nonsingular.*

Then the conclusions of Exercise 5.19 hold.

Proof. One way to prove this is to show that (*iii'*) implies (*iii*). This is direct, and it is left to the reader to verify.

Alternatively, we can apply Proposition 5.1 and Theorem 5.24 to verify that $\mathbf{V}_n^{-1/2} n^{-1/2}\mathbf{Z}'\varepsilon \overset{A}{\sim} N(\mathbf{0}, \mathbf{I})$. Since $\{\mathbf{Z}_t\varepsilon_t\}$ is a stationary martingale difference sequence,

$$\text{var}\left(n^{-1/2}\mathbf{Z}'\varepsilon\right) = n^{-1}\sum_{t=1}^{n} E(\mathbf{Z}_t\varepsilon_t\varepsilon_t'\mathbf{Z}_t') = \mathbf{V},$$

finite by (*iii'.b*) and positive definite by (*iii'.c*). Hence, consider

$$n^{-1/2}\sum_{t=1}^{n} \boldsymbol{\lambda}'\mathbf{V}^{-1/2}\mathbf{Z}_t\varepsilon_t.$$

By Proposition 3.23, $\boldsymbol{\lambda}'\mathbf{V}^{-1/2}\ \mathbf{Z}_t\varepsilon_t$ is measurable with respect to $\mathcal{F}_t$ given (*iii'.a*). Writing $\boldsymbol{\lambda}'\mathbf{V}^{-1/2}\mathbf{Z}_t\varepsilon_t = \sum_{h=1}^{p}\sum_{i=1}^{l} \tilde{\lambda}_i Z_{thi}\varepsilon_{th}$, it follows from the linearity of condition expectations that

$$E(\boldsymbol{\lambda}'\mathbf{V}^{-1/2}\mathbf{Z}_t\boldsymbol{\varepsilon}_t|\mathcal{F}_{t-1}) = \sum_{h=1}^{p}\sum_{i=1}^{l}\tilde{\lambda}_i E(Z_{thi}\varepsilon_{th}|\mathcal{F}_{t-1}) = 0$$

given $(iii'.a)$. Hence $\{\boldsymbol{\lambda}'\mathbf{V}^{-1/2}\mathbf{Z}_t\boldsymbol{\varepsilon}_t, \mathcal{F}_t\}$ is a martingale difference sequence. As a consequence of stationarity, $\text{var}(\boldsymbol{\lambda}'\mathbf{V}^{-1/2}\mathbf{Z}_t\boldsymbol{\varepsilon}_t) = \boldsymbol{\lambda}'\mathbf{V}^{-1/2}\mathbf{V}\mathbf{V}^{-1/2}\boldsymbol{\lambda} = 1$ for all t, and for all t, $F_{nt} = F$, the distribution function of $\boldsymbol{\lambda}'\mathbf{V}^{-1/2}\mathbf{Z}_t\boldsymbol{\varepsilon}_t$. It follows from Exercise 5.9 that the Lindeberg condition is satisfied. Since $\{\boldsymbol{\lambda}'\mathbf{V}^{-1/2}\mathbf{Z}_t\boldsymbol{\varepsilon}_t\boldsymbol{\varepsilon}_t'\mathbf{Z}_t'\mathbf{V}^{-1/2}\boldsymbol{\lambda}\}$ is a stationary and ergodic sequence by Proposition 3.30 with finite expected absolute values given $(iii'.b)$ and $(iii'.c)$, the ergodic theorem (Theorem 3.34) and Theorem 2.24 imply

$$\begin{aligned} & n^{-1}\sum_{t=1}^{n}\boldsymbol{\lambda}'\mathbf{V}^{-1/2}\mathbf{Z}_t\boldsymbol{\varepsilon}_t\boldsymbol{\varepsilon}_t'\mathbf{Z}_t'\mathbf{V}^{-1/2}\boldsymbol{\lambda} - \boldsymbol{\lambda}'\mathbf{V}^{-1/2}\mathbf{V}\mathbf{V}^{-1/2}\boldsymbol{\lambda} \\ = \; & n^{-1}\sum_{t=1}^{n}\boldsymbol{\lambda}'\mathbf{V}^{-1/2}\mathbf{Z}_t\boldsymbol{\varepsilon}_t\boldsymbol{\varepsilon}_t'\mathbf{Z}_t'\mathbf{V}^{-1/2}\boldsymbol{\lambda} - 1 \xrightarrow{p} 0. \end{aligned}$$

Hence, by Theorem 5.24 $n^{-1/2}\sum_{t=1}^{n}\boldsymbol{\lambda}'\mathbf{V}^{-1/2}\mathbf{Z}_t\boldsymbol{\varepsilon}_t \overset{A}{\sim} N(0,1)$. It follows from Proposition 5.1 that $\mathbf{V}^{-1/2}n^{-1/2}\mathbf{Z}'\boldsymbol{\varepsilon} \overset{A}{\sim} N(\mathbf{0},\mathbf{I})$, and since $\mathbf{V} = \mathbf{V}_n$, $\mathbf{V}_n^{-1/2}n^{-1/2}\mathbf{Z}'\boldsymbol{\varepsilon} \overset{A}{\sim} N(\mathbf{0},\mathbf{I})$. The rest of the results follow as before. ∎

Whereas use of the martingale difference assumption allows us to state simpler conditions for stationary ergodic processes, it also allows us to state weaker conditions on certain aspects of the behavior of mixing processes. To do this conveniently, we apply a Liapounov-like corollary to the central limit theorem just given.

Corollary 5.26 *Let $\{Z_{nt}, \mathcal{F}_{nt}\}$ be a martingale difference sequence such that $E|Z_{nt}|^{2+\delta} < \Delta < \infty$ for some $\delta > 0$ and all n and t. If $\bar{\sigma}_n^2 > \delta' > 0$ for all n sufficiently large and $n^{-1}\sum_{t=1}^{n} Z_{nt}^2 - \bar{\sigma}_n^2 \xrightarrow{p} 0$, then $\sqrt{n}\bar{Z}_n/\bar{\sigma}_n \overset{A}{\sim} N(0,1)$.*

Proof. Given $E|Z_{nt}|^{2+\delta} < \Delta < \infty$, the Lindeberg condition holds as shown in the proof of Theorem 5.10. Since $\bar{\sigma}_n^2 > \delta' > 0$, $\bar{\sigma}_n^{-2}$ is $O(1)$, so $n^{-1}\sum_{t=1}^{n} Z_{nt}^2/\bar{\sigma}_n^2 - 1 = \bar{\sigma}_n^{-2}(n^{-1}\sum_{t=1}^{n} Z_{nt}^2 - \bar{\sigma}_n^2) \xrightarrow{p} 0$ by Exercise 2.35. The conditions of Theorem 5.24 hold and the result follows. ∎

We use this result to obtain an analog to Theorem 5.25.

Exercise 5.27 *Prove the following. Suppose conditions (i), (ii), (iv), and (v) of Theorem 5.23 hold, and replace (iii) with* (*iii'*) (*a*) $E(Z_{thi}\varepsilon_{th}|\mathcal{F}_{t-1}) = 0$ *for all* t, *where* $\{\mathcal{F}_t\}$ *is adapted to* $\{Z_{thi}\varepsilon_{th}\}$, $h = 1, \ldots, p$, $i = 1, \ldots, l$;

(*b*) $E\,|Z_{thi}\varepsilon_{th}|^r < \Delta < \infty$ *for all* $h = 1, \ldots, p$, $i = 1, \ldots, l$ *and all* t;

(*c*) $\mathbf{V}_n \equiv \text{var}(n^{-1/2}\mathbf{Z}'\boldsymbol{\varepsilon})$ *is uniformly positive definite.*

Then the conclusions of Theorem 5.23 hold.

Note that although the assumption (*iii.a*) has been strengthened from $E(\mathbf{Z}_t\boldsymbol{\varepsilon}_t) = \mathbf{0}$ to the martingale difference assumption, we have maintained the moment requirements of (*iii.b*).

References

Hansen, L. P. (1982). "Large sample properties of generalized method of moments estimators." *Econometrica*, 50, 1029–1054.

Heyde, C. C. (1975). "On the central limit theorem and iterated logarithm law for stationary processes." *Bulletin of the Australian Mathematical Society*, 12, 1–8.

Loeve, M. (1977). *Probability Theory.* Springer-Verlag, New York.

McLeish, D. L. (1974). "Dependent central limit theorems and invariance principles." *Annals of Probability*, 2, 620–628.

Rao, C. R. (1973). *Linear Statistical Inference and Its Applications.* Wiley, New York.

Scott, D. J. (1973). "Central limit theorems for martingales and for processes with stationary increments using a Skorokhod representation approach." *Advances in Applied Probability*, 5, 119–137.

Wooldridge, J. M. (1986). *Asymptotic Properties of Econometric Estimators.* Unpublished Ph.D. dissertation. University of California, San Diego.

——— and H. White (1988). "Some invariance principles and central limit theorems for dependent heterogeneous processes." *Econometric Theory*, 4, 210–230.

CHAPTER 6

Estimating Asymptotic Covariance Matrices

In all the preceding chapters, we defined $\mathbf{V}_n \equiv \text{var}(n^{-1/2}\mathbf{X}'\boldsymbol{\varepsilon})$ or $\mathbf{V}_n \equiv \text{var}(n^{-1/2}\mathbf{Z}'\boldsymbol{\varepsilon})$ and assumed that a consistent estimator $\hat{\mathbf{V}}_n$ for $\mathbf{V}_n$ is available. In this chapter we obtain conditions that allow us to find convenient consistent estimators $\hat{\mathbf{V}}_n$. Because the theory of estimating $\text{var}(n^{-1/2}\mathbf{X}'\boldsymbol{\varepsilon})$ is identical to that of estimating $\text{var}(n^{-1/2}\mathbf{Z}'\boldsymbol{\varepsilon})$, we consider only the latter. Further, because the optimal choice for $\mathbf{P}_n$ is $\mathbf{V}_n^{-1}$, as we saw in Chapter 4, conditions that permit consistent estimation of $\mathbf{V}_n$ will also permit consistent estimation of $\mathbf{P}_n = \mathbf{V}_n^{-1}$ by $\hat{\mathbf{P}}_n = \hat{\mathbf{V}}_n^{-1}$.

6.1 General Structure of $\mathbf{V}_n$

Before proceeding to look at special cases, it is helpful to examine the general form of $\mathbf{V}_n$. We have

$$\mathbf{V}_n \equiv \text{var}(n^{-1/2}\mathbf{Z}'\boldsymbol{\varepsilon}) = E(\mathbf{Z}'\boldsymbol{\varepsilon}\boldsymbol{\varepsilon}'\mathbf{Z}/n),$$

because we assume that $E(n^{-1/2}\mathbf{Z}'\boldsymbol{\varepsilon}) = \mathbf{0}$. In terms of individual observations, this can be expressed as

$$\mathbf{V}_n = E\left(n^{-1}\sum_{t=1}^{n}\sum_{\tau=1}^{n}\mathbf{Z}_t\boldsymbol{\varepsilon}_t\boldsymbol{\varepsilon}_\tau'\mathbf{Z}_\tau'\right).$$

An equivalent way of writing the summation on the right is helpful in obtaining further insight. We can also write

$$\begin{aligned}\mathbf{V}_n &= n^{-1}\sum_{t=1}^{n} E(\mathbf{Z}_t\varepsilon_t\varepsilon_t'\mathbf{Z}_t') \\ &\quad + n^{-1}\sum_{\tau=1}^{n-1}\sum_{t=\tau+1}^{n} E(\mathbf{Z}_t\varepsilon_t\varepsilon_{t-\tau}'\mathbf{Z}_{t-\tau}' + \mathbf{Z}_{t-\tau}\varepsilon_{t-\tau}\varepsilon_t'\mathbf{Z}_t') \\ &= n^{-1}\sum_{t=1}^{n} \mathrm{var}(\mathbf{Z}_t\varepsilon_t) \\ &\quad + n^{-1}\sum_{\tau=1}^{n-1}\sum_{t=\tau+1}^{n} \mathrm{cov}(\mathbf{Z}_t\varepsilon_t, \mathbf{Z}_{t-\tau}\varepsilon_{t-\tau}) + \mathrm{cov}(\mathbf{Z}_{t-\tau}\varepsilon_{t-\tau}, \mathbf{Z}_t\varepsilon_t).\end{aligned}$$

The last expression reveals that $\mathbf{V}_n$ is the average of the variances of $\mathbf{Z}_t\varepsilon_t$ plus a term that takes into account the covariances between $\mathbf{Z}_t\varepsilon_t$ and $\mathbf{Z}_{t-\tau}\varepsilon_{t-\tau}$ for all t and τ. We consider three important special cases.

Case 1. The first case we consider occurs when $\{\mathbf{Z}_t\varepsilon_t\}$ is uncorrelated, so that

$$\mathrm{cov}(\mathbf{Z}_t\varepsilon_t, \mathbf{Z}_{t-\tau}\varepsilon_{t-\tau}) = \mathrm{cov}(\mathbf{Z}_{t-\tau}\varepsilon_{t-\tau}, \mathbf{Z}_t\varepsilon_t)' = \mathbf{0}$$

for all $t \neq \tau$, so

$$\mathbf{V}_n = n^{-1}\sum_{t=1}^{n} E(\mathbf{Z}_t\varepsilon_t\varepsilon_t'\mathbf{Z}_t').$$

This occurs when $\{(\mathbf{Z}_t', \varepsilon_t)\}$ is an independent sequence or when $\{\mathbf{Z}_t\varepsilon_t, \mathcal{F}_t\}$ is a martingale difference sequence for some adapted σ-fields $\mathcal{F}_t$.

Case 2. The next case we consider occurs when $\{\mathbf{Z}_t\varepsilon_t\}$ is "finitely correlated," so that

$$\mathrm{cov}(\mathbf{Z}_t\varepsilon_t, \mathbf{Z}_{t-\tau}\varepsilon_{t-\tau}) = \mathrm{cov}(\mathbf{Z}_{t-\tau}\varepsilon_{t-\tau}, \mathbf{Z}_t\varepsilon_t)' = \mathbf{0}$$

for all $\tau > m$, $1 \leq m < \infty$, so

$$\begin{aligned}\mathbf{V}_n &= n^{-1}\sum_{t=1}^{n} E(\mathbf{Z}_t\varepsilon_t\varepsilon_t'\mathbf{Z}_t') \\ &\quad + n^{-1}\sum_{\tau=1}^{m}\sum_{t=\tau+1}^{n} E(\mathbf{Z}_t\varepsilon_t\varepsilon_{t-\tau}'\mathbf{Z}_{t-\tau}') + E(\mathbf{Z}_{t-\tau}\varepsilon_{t-\tau}\varepsilon_t'\mathbf{Z}_t').\end{aligned}$$

This case arises when $E(\mathbf{Z}_t\varepsilon_t|\mathcal{F}_{t-\tau}) = \mathbf{0}$ for some τ, $1 < \tau < \infty$ and adapted σ-fields $\mathcal{F}_t$. A simple example of this case arises when $\mathbf{Z}_t$ is nonstochastic and ε_t is a scalar MA(1) process, i.e.,

$$\varepsilon_t = \alpha v_t + v_{t-1},$$

where $\{v_t\}$ is an i.i.d. sequence with $E(v_t) = 0$. Setting $\mathcal{F}_t = \sigma(\ldots, \varepsilon_t)$, we readily verify that $E(\mathbf{Z}_t\varepsilon_t|\mathcal{F}_{t-\tau}) = \mathbf{Z}_t E(\varepsilon_t|\mathcal{F}_{t-\tau}) = \mathbf{0}$ for $\tau \geq 2$, implying that

$$\begin{aligned}\mathbf{V}_n &= n^{-1}\sum_{t=1}^{n} E(\mathbf{Z}_t\varepsilon_t\varepsilon_t\mathbf{Z}_t') \\ &\quad + n^{-1}\sum_{t=2}^{n} E(\mathbf{Z}_t\varepsilon_t\varepsilon_{t-1}\mathbf{Z}_{t-1}') + E(\mathbf{Z}_{t-1}\varepsilon_{t-1}\varepsilon_t\mathbf{Z}_t').\end{aligned}$$

Case 3. The last case that we consider occurs when $\{\mathbf{Z}_t\varepsilon_t\}$ is an asymptotically uncorrelated sequence so that

$$\operatorname{cov}(\mathbf{Z}_t\varepsilon_t, \mathbf{Z}_{t-\tau}\varepsilon_{t-\tau}) = \operatorname{cov}(\mathbf{Z}_{t-\tau}\varepsilon_{t-\tau}, \mathbf{Z}_t\varepsilon_t)' \to \mathbf{0} \quad \text{as } \tau \to \infty.$$

Rather than making direct use of the assumption that $\{(\mathbf{Z}_t', \varepsilon_t)\}$ is asymptotically uncorrelated, we shall assume that $\{(\mathbf{Z}_t', \varepsilon_t)\}$ is a mixing sequence, which will suffice for asymptotic uncorrelatedness.

In what follows, we typically assume that nothing more is known about the correlation structure of $\{\mathbf{Z}_t\varepsilon_t\}$ beyond that it falls in one of these three cases. If additional knowledge were available, then it could be used to estimate $\mathbf{V}_n$; more importantly, however, it could be used to obtain efficient estimators as discussed in Chapter 4. The analysis of this chapter is thus relevant in the common situation in which this knowledge is absent.

6.2 Case 1: $\{\mathbf{Z}_t\varepsilon_t\}$ Uncorrelated

In this section, we treat the case in which

$$\mathbf{V}_n = n^{-1}\sum_{t=1}^{n} E(\mathbf{Z}_t\boldsymbol{\varepsilon}_t\boldsymbol{\varepsilon}_t'\mathbf{Z}_t').$$

A special case of major importance arises when

$$E(\boldsymbol{\varepsilon}_t\boldsymbol{\varepsilon}_t'|\mathbf{Z}_t) = \sigma_o^2\mathbf{I},$$

so that

$$\mathbf{V}_n = n^{-1} \sum_{t=1}^{n} \sigma_o^2 E(\mathbf{Z}_t \mathbf{Z}_t') = \sigma_o^2 \mathbf{L}_n.$$

Our first result applies to this case.

Theorem 6.1 *Suppose* $\mathbf{V}_n = \sigma_o^2 \mathbf{L}_n$, *where* $\sigma_o^2 < \infty$ *and* $\mathbf{L}_n$ *is* $O(1)$. *If there exists* $\tilde{\sigma}_n^2$ *such that* $\tilde{\sigma}_n^2 \xrightarrow{p} \sigma_o^2$ *and if* $\mathbf{Z}'\mathbf{Z}/n - \mathbf{L}_n \xrightarrow{p} \mathbf{0}$, *then* $\hat{\mathbf{V}}_n \equiv \tilde{\sigma}_n^2 \mathbf{Z}'\mathbf{Z}/n$ *is such that* $\hat{\mathbf{V}}_n - \mathbf{V}_n \xrightarrow{p} \mathbf{0}$.

Proof. Immediate from Proposition 2.30. ∎

Exercise 6.2 *Using Exercise 3.79, find conditions that ensure that* $\tilde{\sigma}_n^2 \xrightarrow{p} \sigma_o^2$ *and* $\mathbf{Z}'\mathbf{Z}/n - \mathbf{L}_n \xrightarrow{p} \mathbf{0}$, *where* $\tilde{\sigma}_n^2 = (\mathbf{Y} - \mathbf{X}\tilde{\boldsymbol{\beta}}_n)'(\mathbf{Y} - \mathbf{X}\tilde{\boldsymbol{\beta}}_n)/(np)$.

Conditions under which $\tilde{\sigma}_n^2 \to \sigma_o^2$ and $\mathbf{Z}'\mathbf{Z}/n - \mathbf{L}_n \xrightarrow{p} \mathbf{0}$ are easily found from the results of Chapter 3.

In the remainder of this section we consider the cases in which the sequence $\{(\mathbf{Z}_t', \mathbf{X}_t', \boldsymbol{\varepsilon}_t)\}$ is stationary or $\{(\mathbf{Z}_t', \mathbf{X}_t', \boldsymbol{\varepsilon}_t)\}$ is a heterogeneous sequence. We invoke the martingale difference assumption in each case, which allows results for independent observations to follow as direct corollaries.

The results that we obtain next are motivated by the following considerations. We are interested in estimating

$$\mathbf{V}_n = n^{-1} \sum_{t=1}^{n} E(\mathbf{Z}_t \boldsymbol{\varepsilon}_t \boldsymbol{\varepsilon}_t' \mathbf{Z}_t').$$

If both $\mathbf{Z}_t$ and $\boldsymbol{\varepsilon}_t$ were observable, a consistent estimator is easily available from the results of Chapter 3, say,

$$\tilde{\mathbf{V}}_n \equiv n^{-1} \sum_{t=1}^{n} \mathbf{Z}_t \boldsymbol{\varepsilon}_t \boldsymbol{\varepsilon}_t' \mathbf{Z}_t'.$$

For example, if $\{(\mathbf{Z}_t', \boldsymbol{\varepsilon}_t)\}$ were a stationary ergodic sequence, then as long as the elements of $\mathbf{Z}_t \boldsymbol{\varepsilon}_t \boldsymbol{\varepsilon}_t' \mathbf{Z}_t'$ have finite expected absolute value, it follows from the ergodic theorem that $\tilde{\mathbf{V}}_n - \mathbf{V}_n \xrightarrow{a.s.} \mathbf{0}$. Of course, $\boldsymbol{\varepsilon}_t$ is not observable. However, it can be estimated by

$$\tilde{\boldsymbol{\varepsilon}}_t \equiv \mathbf{Y}_t - \mathbf{X}_t' \tilde{\boldsymbol{\beta}}_n,$$

where $\tilde{\boldsymbol{\beta}}_n$ is consistent for $\boldsymbol{\beta}_o$. This leads us to consider estimators of the form

$$\hat{\mathbf{V}}_n \equiv n^{-1}\sum_{t=1}^{n}\mathbf{Z}_t\tilde{\varepsilon}_t\tilde{\varepsilon}_t'\mathbf{Z}_t'.$$

As we prove next, replacing ε_t with $\tilde{\varepsilon}_t$ makes no difference asymptotically under general conditions, so $\hat{\mathbf{V}}_n - \mathbf{V}_n \xrightarrow{a.s.} \mathbf{0}$. These conditions are precisely specified for stationary sequences by the next result.

Theorem 6.3 *Suppose that*

(*i*) $\mathbf{Y}_t = \mathbf{X}_t'\boldsymbol{\beta}_o + \varepsilon_t, \quad t = 1, 2, \ldots, \quad \boldsymbol{\beta}_o \in \mathbb{R}^k$;

(*ii*) $\{(\mathbf{Z}_t', \mathbf{X}_t', \varepsilon_t)\}$ *is a stationary ergodic sequence;*

(*iii*) (*a*) $\{\mathbf{Z}_t\varepsilon_t, \mathcal{F}_t\}$ *is a martingale difference sequence;*

(*b*) $E|Z_{thi}\varepsilon_{th}|^2 < \infty$, $h = 1, \ldots, p$, $i = 1, \ldots, l$;

(*c*) $\mathbf{V}_n \equiv \text{var}(n^{-1/2}\mathbf{Z}'\varepsilon) = \text{var}(\mathbf{Z}_t\varepsilon_t) \equiv \mathbf{V}$ *is positive definite;*

(*iv*) (*a*) $E|Z_{thi}X_{thj}|^2 < \infty$, $h = 1, \ldots, p$, $i = 1, \ldots, l$, $j = 1, \ldots, k$;

(*b*) $\mathbf{Q} \equiv E(\mathbf{Z}_t\mathbf{X}_t')$ *has full column rank;*

(*c*) $\hat{\mathbf{P}}_n \xrightarrow{p} \mathbf{P}$, *finite, symmetric, and positive definite.*

Then $\hat{\mathbf{V}}_n - \mathbf{V} \xrightarrow{p} \mathbf{0}$, *and* $\hat{\mathbf{V}}_n^{-1} - \mathbf{V}^{-1} \xrightarrow{p} \mathbf{0}$.

Proof. By definition and assumption (*iii.a*),

$$\hat{\mathbf{V}}_n - \mathbf{V} = n^{-1}\sum_{t=1}^{n}\mathbf{Z}_t\tilde{\varepsilon}_t\tilde{\varepsilon}_t'\mathbf{Z}_t' - E(\mathbf{Z}_t\varepsilon_t\varepsilon_t'\mathbf{Z}_t').$$

Now $\tilde{\varepsilon}_t \equiv \mathbf{Y}_t - \mathbf{X}_t'\tilde{\boldsymbol{\beta}}_n = \mathbf{Y}_t - \mathbf{X}_t'\boldsymbol{\beta}_o - \mathbf{X}_t'(\tilde{\boldsymbol{\beta}}_n - \boldsymbol{\beta}_o) = \varepsilon_t - \mathbf{X}_t'(\tilde{\boldsymbol{\beta}}_n - \boldsymbol{\beta}_o)$, given assumption (i). Substituting for $\tilde{\varepsilon}_t$, we have

$$\begin{aligned}
\hat{\mathbf{V}}_n - \mathbf{V} &= n^{-1}\sum_{t=1}^{n} \mathbf{Z}_t(\varepsilon_t - \mathbf{X}_t'(\tilde{\boldsymbol{\beta}}_n - \boldsymbol{\beta}_o))(\varepsilon_t - \mathbf{X}_t'(\tilde{\boldsymbol{\beta}}_n - \boldsymbol{\beta}_o))'\mathbf{Z}_t' \\
&\quad - E(\mathbf{Z}_t\varepsilon_t\varepsilon_t'\mathbf{Z}_t') \\
&= n^{-1}\sum_{t=1}^{n} \mathbf{Z}_t\varepsilon_t\varepsilon_t'\mathbf{Z}_t' - E(\mathbf{Z}_t\varepsilon_t\varepsilon_t'\mathbf{Z}_t') \\
&\quad - n^{-1}\sum_{t=1}^{n} \mathbf{Z}_t\mathbf{X}_t'(\tilde{\boldsymbol{\beta}}_n - \boldsymbol{\beta}_o)\varepsilon_t'\mathbf{Z}_t' \\
&\quad - n^{-1}\sum_{t=1}^{n} \mathbf{Z}_t\varepsilon_t(\tilde{\boldsymbol{\beta}}_n - \boldsymbol{\beta}_o)'\mathbf{X}_t\mathbf{Z}_t' \\
&\quad + n^{-1}\sum_{t=1}^{n} \mathbf{Z}_t\mathbf{X}_t'(\tilde{\boldsymbol{\beta}}_n - \boldsymbol{\beta}_o)(\tilde{\boldsymbol{\beta}}_n - \boldsymbol{\beta}_o)'\mathbf{X}_t\mathbf{Z}_t'.
\end{aligned}$$

Given (ii) and $(iii.b)$, the ergodic theorem ensures that $n^{-1}\sum_{t=1}^{n} \mathbf{Z}_t\varepsilon_t\varepsilon_t'\mathbf{Z}_t' - E(\mathbf{Z}_t\varepsilon_t\varepsilon_t'\mathbf{Z}_t') \xrightarrow{a.s.} \mathbf{0}$, and therefore also vanishes in probability. It suffices that the remaining terms also vanish in probability, by Exercise 2.35.

To analyze the remaining terms, recall that $\text{vec}(\mathbf{ABC}) = (\mathbf{C}' \otimes \mathbf{A})\text{vec}(\mathbf{B})$, and apply this to the second summation with $\mathbf{A}$, $\mathbf{B}$, and $\mathbf{C}$ chosen to give

$$\begin{aligned}
\text{vec}\left(n^{-1}\sum_{t=1}^{n} \mathbf{Z}_t\mathbf{X}_t'(\tilde{\boldsymbol{\beta}}_n - \boldsymbol{\beta}_o)\varepsilon_t'\mathbf{Z}_t'\right) &= n^{-1}\sum_{t=1}^{n} \text{vec}\left(\mathbf{Z}_t\mathbf{X}_t'(\tilde{\boldsymbol{\beta}}_n - \boldsymbol{\beta}_o)\varepsilon_t'\mathbf{Z}_t'\right) \\
&= n^{-1}\sum_{t=1}^{n} (\mathbf{Z}_t\varepsilon_t \otimes \mathbf{Z}_t\mathbf{X}_t')\,\text{vec}(\tilde{\boldsymbol{\beta}}_n - \boldsymbol{\beta}_o).
\end{aligned}$$

The conditions of the theorem ensure that $\tilde{\boldsymbol{\beta}}_n \xrightarrow{p} \boldsymbol{\beta}_o$ by Exercise 3.38. To conclude that this term vanishes in probability, it suffices that $n^{-1}\sum_{t=1}^{n} (\mathbf{Z}_t\varepsilon_t \otimes \mathbf{Z}_t\mathbf{X}_t')$ is $O_p(1)$ by Corollary 2.36. But this is guaranteed by the ergodic theorem, provided that $E\left(\mathbf{Z}_t\varepsilon_t \otimes \mathbf{Z}_t\mathbf{X}_t'\right)$ is finite. Conditions $(iii.b)$ and $(iv.a)$ ensure this, as can be verified by repeated application of the Cauchy-Schwarz inequality.

Thus,

$$n^{-1}\sum_{t=1}^{n} (\mathbf{Z}_t\varepsilon_t \otimes \mathbf{Z}_t\mathbf{X}_t')\,\text{vec}(\tilde{\boldsymbol{\beta}}_n - \boldsymbol{\beta}_o) \xrightarrow{p} \mathbf{0}.$$

Similarly, apply $\text{vec}(\mathbf{ABC}) = (\mathbf{C}' \otimes \mathbf{A})\text{vec}(\mathbf{B})$ to obtain

$$\begin{aligned} &\text{vec}\left(n^{-1}\sum_{t=1}^{n}\mathbf{Z}_t\mathbf{X}_t'(\tilde{\boldsymbol{\beta}}_n - \boldsymbol{\beta}_o)(\tilde{\boldsymbol{\beta}}_n - \boldsymbol{\beta}_o)'\mathbf{X}_t\mathbf{Z}_t'\right) \\ &= n^{-1}\sum_{t=1}^{n}(\mathbf{Z}_t\mathbf{X}_t' \otimes \mathbf{Z}_t\mathbf{X}_t')\,\text{vec}\left((\tilde{\boldsymbol{\beta}}_n - \boldsymbol{\beta}_o)(\tilde{\boldsymbol{\beta}}_n - \boldsymbol{\beta}_o)'\right). \end{aligned}$$

Again we have $\tilde{\boldsymbol{\beta}}_n - \boldsymbol{\beta}_o \xrightarrow{p} \mathbf{0}$, so this term vanishes provided that $E(\mathbf{Z}_t\mathbf{X}_t' \otimes \mathbf{Z}_t\mathbf{X}_t')$ is finite. This is true given (*iv.a*), as can be verified by Cauchy-Schwarz. The desired result $\hat{\mathbf{V}}_n - \mathbf{V} \xrightarrow{p} \mathbf{0}$ now follows by Exercise 2.35. As $\mathbf{V}$ is positive definite given (*iii.c*), it follows from Proposition 2.30 that $\hat{\mathbf{V}}_n^{-1} - \mathbf{V}^{-1} \xrightarrow{p} \mathbf{0}$. ■

Comparing the conditions of this result with those of Theorem 5.25,we see that we have strengthened moment condition (*iv.a*) and that this, together with the other assumptions, implies assumption (*v*) of Theorem 5.25. An immediate corollary of this fact is that the conclusions of Theorem 5.25 hold under the conditions of Theorem 6.3.

Corollary 6.4 *Suppose conditions (i)–(iv) of Theorem 6.3 hold. Then*

$$\mathbf{D}^{-1}\sqrt{n}(\tilde{\boldsymbol{\beta}}_n - \boldsymbol{\beta}_o) \overset{A}{\sim} N(\mathbf{0}, \mathbf{I})$$

where

$$\mathbf{D} \equiv (\mathbf{Q}'\mathbf{PQ})^{-1}\mathbf{Q}'\mathbf{PVPQ}(\mathbf{Q}'\mathbf{PQ})^{-1}.$$

Further, $\hat{\mathbf{D}}_n - \mathbf{D} \xrightarrow{p} \mathbf{0}$*, where*

$$\hat{\mathbf{D}}_n = (\mathbf{X}'\mathbf{Z}\hat{\mathbf{P}}_n\mathbf{Z}'\mathbf{X}/n^2)^{-1}(\mathbf{X}'\mathbf{Z}/n)\hat{\mathbf{P}}_n\hat{\mathbf{V}}_n\hat{\mathbf{P}}_n(\mathbf{Z}'\mathbf{X}/n)(\mathbf{X}'\mathbf{Z}\hat{\mathbf{P}}_n\mathbf{Z}'\mathbf{X}/n^2)^{-1}.$$

Proof. Immediate from Theorem 5.25 and Theorem 6.3. ■

The usefulness of this result arises in situations in which it is inappropriate to assume that

$$E(\boldsymbol{\varepsilon}_t\boldsymbol{\varepsilon}_t'|\mathbf{Z}_t) = \sigma_o^2\mathbf{I},$$

that is, when the errors $\boldsymbol{\varepsilon}_t$ exhibit heteroskedasticity of unknown form. The present results thus provide an instrumental variables analog of the heteroskedasticity-consistent covariance matrix estimator of White (1980).

The results of Theorem 6.3 and Corollary 6.4 suggest a simple two-step procedure for obtaining the efficient estimator of Proposition 4.45, i.e.,

$$\boldsymbol{\beta}_n^* = (\mathbf{X}'\mathbf{Z}\hat{\mathbf{V}}_n^{-1}\mathbf{Z}'\mathbf{X})^{-1}\mathbf{X}'\mathbf{Z}\hat{\mathbf{V}}_n^{-1}\mathbf{Z}'\mathbf{Y}.$$

First, one obtains a consistent estimator for $\boldsymbol{\beta}_o$, for example, the 2SLS estimator,

$$\tilde{\boldsymbol{\beta}}_n = (\mathbf{X}'\mathbf{Z}(\mathbf{Z}'\mathbf{Z})^{-1}\mathbf{Z}'\mathbf{X})^{-1}\mathbf{X}'\mathbf{Z}(\mathbf{Z}'\mathbf{Z})^{-1}\mathbf{Z}'\mathbf{Y},$$

and forms

$$\hat{\mathbf{V}}_n = n^{-1}\sum_{t=1}^{n}\mathbf{Z}_t\tilde{\varepsilon}_t\tilde{\varepsilon}_t'\mathbf{Z}_t',$$

where $\tilde{\varepsilon}_t \equiv \mathbf{Y}_t - \mathbf{X}_t'\tilde{\boldsymbol{\beta}}_n$. Second, this estimator is then used to compute the efficient estimator $\boldsymbol{\beta}_n^*$. Because $\boldsymbol{\beta}_n^*$ can be computed in this way, it is called the *two-stage instrumental variables* (2SIV) estimator, introduced by White (1982). Formally, we have the following result.

Corollary 6.5 *Suppose that*

(i) $\mathbf{Y}_t = \mathbf{X}_t'\boldsymbol{\beta}_o + \varepsilon_t, \quad t = 1, 2, \ldots, \quad \boldsymbol{\beta}_o \in \mathbb{R}^k$;

(ii) $\{(\mathbf{Z}_t', \mathbf{X}_t', \varepsilon_t)\}$ *is a stationary ergodic sequence;*

(iii) (a) $\{\mathbf{Z}_t\varepsilon_t, \mathcal{F}_t\}$ *is a martingale difference sequence;*
(b) $E\,|Z_{thi}\varepsilon_{th}|^2 < \infty, h = 1, \ldots, p, \; i = 1, \ldots, l$;
(c) $\mathbf{V}_n \equiv \text{var}(n^{-1/2}\mathbf{Z}'\varepsilon) = \text{var}(\mathbf{Z}_t\varepsilon_t) \equiv \mathbf{V}$ *is positive definite;*

(iv) (a) $E|Z_{thi}X_{thj}|^2 < \infty$, $h = 1, \ldots, p$, $i = 1, \ldots, l$, $j = 1, \ldots, k$, *and* $E|\mathbf{Z}_{thi}|^2 < \infty$, $h = 1, \ldots, p$, $i = 1, \ldots, l$;
(b) $\mathbf{Q} \equiv E(\mathbf{Z}_t\mathbf{X}_t')$ *has full column rank;*
(c) $\mathbf{L} \equiv E(\mathbf{Z}_t\mathbf{Z}_t')$ *is positive definite.*

Define

$$\hat{\mathbf{V}}_n \equiv n^{-1}\sum_{t=1}^{n}\mathbf{Z}_t\tilde{\varepsilon}_t\tilde{\varepsilon}_t'\mathbf{Z}_t',$$

where $\tilde{\varepsilon}_t \equiv \mathbf{Y}_t - \mathbf{X}_t\tilde{\boldsymbol{\beta}}_n$, $\tilde{\boldsymbol{\beta}}_n \equiv (\mathbf{X}'\mathbf{Z}(\mathbf{Z}'\mathbf{Z})^{-1}\mathbf{Z}'\mathbf{X})^{-1}\mathbf{X}'\mathbf{Z}(\mathbf{Z}'\mathbf{Z})^{-1}\mathbf{Z}'\mathbf{Y}$, *and define*

$$\boldsymbol{\beta}_n^* \equiv (\mathbf{X}'\mathbf{Z}\hat{\mathbf{V}}_n^{-1}\mathbf{Z}'\mathbf{X})^{-1}\mathbf{X}'\mathbf{Z}\hat{\mathbf{V}}_n^{-1}\mathbf{Z}'\mathbf{Y}.$$

Then $\mathbf{D}^{-1/2}\sqrt{n}(\boldsymbol{\beta}_n^* - \boldsymbol{\beta}_o) \overset{A}{\sim} N(\mathbf{0}, \mathbf{I})$, *where*

$$\mathbf{D} = (\mathbf{Q}'\mathbf{V}^{-1}\mathbf{Q})^{-1}.$$

Further, $\hat{\mathbf{D}}_n - \mathbf{D} \xrightarrow{p} \mathbf{0}$, *where*

$$\hat{\mathbf{D}}_n = (\mathbf{X}'\mathbf{Z}\hat{\mathbf{V}}_n^{-1}\mathbf{Z}'\mathbf{X}/n^2)^{-1}.$$

Proof. Conditions (i)–(iv) ensure that Theorem 6.3 holds for $\tilde{\boldsymbol{\beta}}_n$. (Note that the second part of $(iv.a)$ is redundant if $\mathbf{X}_t$ contains a constant.) Next set $\hat{\mathbf{P}}_n = \hat{\mathbf{V}}_n^{-1}$ in Corollary 6.4. Then $\mathbf{P} = \mathbf{V}^{-1}$, and the result follows. ∎

This result is the most explicit asymptotic normality result obtained so far, because all of the conditions are stated directly in terms of the stochastic properties of the instrumental variables, regressors, and errors. The remainder of the asymptotic normality results stated in this chapter will also share this convenient feature.

We note that results for the OLS estimator follow as a special case upon setting $\mathbf{Z}_t = \mathbf{X}_t$ and that results for the i.i.d. case follow as immediate corollaries, since an i.i.d. sequence is a stationary ergodic martingale difference sequence when $E(\mathbf{Z}_t\varepsilon_t) = \mathbf{0}$.

Analogous results hold for heterogeneous sequences. Because the proofs are completely parallel to those just given, they are left as an exercise for the reader.

Exercise 6.6 *Prove the following result. Suppose*

(i) $\mathbf{Y}_t = \mathbf{X}_t'\boldsymbol{\beta}_0 + \varepsilon_t, \quad t = 1, 2, \ldots, \quad \boldsymbol{\beta}_o \in \mathbb{R}^k$;

(ii) $\{(\mathbf{Z}_t', \mathbf{X}_t', \varepsilon_t)\}$ *is a mixing sequence with either* ϕ *of size* $-r/(2r-1), r \geq 1$, *or* α *of size* $-r/(r-1), r > 1$;

(iii) (a) $\{\mathbf{Z}_t\varepsilon_t, \mathcal{F}_t\}$ *is a martingale difference sequence*;

(b) $E|Z_{thi}\varepsilon_{th}|^{2(r+\delta)} < \Delta < \infty$ *for some* $\delta > 0$ *and all* $h = 1, \ldots, p$, $i = 1, \ldots, l$, *and* t;

(c) $\mathbf{V}_n \equiv \text{var}(n^{-1/2}\mathbf{Z}'\boldsymbol{\varepsilon})$ *is uniformly positive definite*;

(iv) (a) $E|Z_{thi}X_{thj}|^{2(r+\delta)} < \Delta < \infty$ *for some* $\delta > 0$ *and all* $h = 1, \ldots, p$, $i = 1, \ldots, l$, $j = 1, \ldots, k$, *and* t;

(b) $\mathbf{Q}_n \equiv E(\mathbf{Z}'\mathbf{X}/n)$ *has uniformly full column rank;*

(c) $\hat{\mathbf{P}}_n - \mathbf{P}_n \xrightarrow{p} \mathbf{0}$, *where* $\mathbf{P}_n = O(1)$ *is symmetric and uniformly positive definite.*

Then $\hat{\mathbf{V}}_n - \mathbf{V}_n \xrightarrow{p} \mathbf{0}$ *and* $\hat{\mathbf{V}}_n^{-1} - \mathbf{V}_n^{-1} \xrightarrow{p} \mathbf{0}$.

Exercise 6.7 *Prove the following result. Suppose conditions* (i)–(iv) *of Exercise 6.6 hold. Then* $\mathbf{D}_n^{-1/2}\sqrt{n}(\tilde{\boldsymbol{\beta}}_n - \boldsymbol{\beta}_o) \overset{A}{\sim} N(\mathbf{0}, \mathbf{I})$, *where*

$$\mathbf{D}_n \equiv (\mathbf{Q}_n'\mathbf{P}_n\mathbf{Q}_n)^{-1}\mathbf{Q}_n'\mathbf{P}_n\mathbf{V}_n\mathbf{P}_n\mathbf{Q}_n(\mathbf{Q}_n'\mathbf{P}_n\mathbf{Q}_n)^{-1}.$$

Further, $\hat{\mathbf{D}}_n - \mathbf{D}_n \xrightarrow{p} \mathbf{0}$, *where*

$$\hat{\mathbf{D}}_n = (\mathbf{X}'\mathbf{Z}\hat{\mathbf{P}}_n\mathbf{Z}'\mathbf{X}/n^2)^{-1}(\mathbf{X}'\mathbf{Z}/n)\hat{\mathbf{P}}_n\hat{\mathbf{V}}_n\hat{\mathbf{P}}_n(\mathbf{Z}'\mathbf{X}/n)(\mathbf{X}'\mathbf{Z}\hat{\mathbf{P}}_n\mathbf{Z}'\mathbf{X}/n^2)^{-1}.$$

Exercise 6.8 *Prove the following result. Suppose*

(i) $\mathbf{Y}_t = \mathbf{X}_t'\boldsymbol{\beta}_o + \varepsilon_t, \quad t = 1, 2, \ldots, \quad \boldsymbol{\beta}_o \in \mathbb{R}^k$;

(ii) $\{(\mathbf{Z}_t', \mathbf{X}_t', \varepsilon_t)\}$ *is a mixing sequence with either* ϕ *of size* $-r/(2r-1)$, $r \geq 1$, *or* α *of size* $-r/(r-1), r > 1$;

(iii) (a) $\{\mathbf{Z}_t\varepsilon_t, \mathcal{F}_t\}$ *is a martingale difference sequence;*

(b) $E|Z_{thi}\varepsilon_{th}|^{2(r+\delta)} < \Delta < \infty$ *for some* $\delta > 0$ *and all* $h = 1, \ldots, p$, $i = 1, \ldots, l$, *and* t;

(c) $\mathbf{V}_n \equiv \text{var}(n^{-1/2}\mathbf{Z}'\boldsymbol{\varepsilon})$ *is uniformly positive definite;*

(iv) (a) $E|Z_{thi}X_{thj}|^{2(r+\delta)} < \Delta < \infty$ *and* $E|Z_{thi}|^{2(r+\delta)} < \Delta < \infty$, *for some* $\delta > 0$ *and all* $h = 1, \ldots, p$, $i = 1, \ldots, l$, $j = 1, \ldots, k$, *and* t;

(b) $\mathbf{Q}_n \equiv E(\mathbf{Z}'\mathbf{X}/n)$ *has uniformly full column rank;*

(c) $\mathbf{L}_n \equiv E(\mathbf{Z}'\mathbf{Z}/n)$ *is uniformly positive definite.*

Define

$$\hat{\mathbf{V}}_n = n^{-1}\sum_{t=1}^{n} \mathbf{Z}_t\tilde{\boldsymbol{\varepsilon}}_t\tilde{\boldsymbol{\varepsilon}}_t'\mathbf{Z}_t',$$

where $\tilde{\boldsymbol{\varepsilon}}_t = \mathbf{Y}_t - \mathbf{X}_t'\tilde{\boldsymbol{\beta}}_n$, $\tilde{\boldsymbol{\beta}}_n \equiv (\mathbf{X}'\mathbf{Z}(\mathbf{Z}'\mathbf{Z})^{-1}\mathbf{Z}'\mathbf{X})^{-1}\mathbf{X}'\mathbf{Z}(\mathbf{Z}'\mathbf{Z})^{-1}\mathbf{Z}'\mathbf{Y}$, *and*

$$\boldsymbol{\beta}_n^* \equiv (\mathbf{X}'\mathbf{Z}\hat{\mathbf{V}}_n^{-1}\mathbf{Z}'\mathbf{X})^{-1}\mathbf{X}'\mathbf{Z}\hat{\mathbf{V}}_n^{-1}\mathbf{Z}'\mathbf{Y}.$$

Then $\mathbf{D}_n^{-1/2}\sqrt{n}(\boldsymbol{\beta}_n^* - \boldsymbol{\beta}_o) \overset{A}{\sim} N(\mathbf{0}, \mathbf{I})$, *where*

$$\mathbf{D}_n = (\mathbf{Q}_n'\mathbf{V}_n^{-1}\mathbf{Q}_n)^{-1}.$$

Further, $\hat{\mathbf{D}}_n - \mathbf{D}_n \xrightarrow{p} \mathbf{0}$, *where*

$$\hat{\mathbf{D}}_n = (\mathbf{X}'\mathbf{Z}\hat{\mathbf{V}}_n^{-1}\mathbf{Z}'\mathbf{X}/n^2)^{-1}.$$

This result allows for unconditional heterogeneity not allowed by Corollary 6.5, at the expense of imposing somewhat stronger memory and moment conditions. Results for the independent case follow as corollaries because independent sequences are ϕ-mixing sequences for which we can set $r = 1$. Thus the present result contains the result of White (1982) as a special case but also allows for the presence of dynamic effects (lagged dependent or predetermined variables) not permitted there, as well as applying explicitly to systems of equations or panel data.

6.3 Case 2: $\{\mathbf{Z}_t\boldsymbol{\varepsilon}_t\}$ Finitely Correlated

Here we treat the case in which, for $m < \infty$,

$$\begin{aligned}
\mathbf{V}_n &= n^{-1}\sum_{t=1}^{n} E(\mathbf{Z}_t\boldsymbol{\varepsilon}_t\boldsymbol{\varepsilon}_t'\mathbf{Z}_t') \\
&\quad + n^{-1}\sum_{t=2}^{n} E(\mathbf{Z}_t\boldsymbol{\varepsilon}_t\boldsymbol{\varepsilon}_{t-1}'\mathbf{Z}_{t-1}') + E(\mathbf{Z}_{t-1}\boldsymbol{\varepsilon}_{t-1}\boldsymbol{\varepsilon}_t'\mathbf{Z}_t') \\
&\quad \vdots \\
&\quad + n^{-1}\sum_{t=m+1}^{n} E(\mathbf{Z}_t\boldsymbol{\varepsilon}_t\boldsymbol{\varepsilon}_{t-m}'\mathbf{Z}_{t-m}') + E(\mathbf{Z}_{t-m}\boldsymbol{\varepsilon}_{t-m}\boldsymbol{\varepsilon}_t'\mathbf{Z}_t') \\
&= n^{-1}\sum_{t=1}^{n} E(\mathbf{Z}_t\boldsymbol{\varepsilon}_t\boldsymbol{\varepsilon}_t'\mathbf{Z}_t') \\
&\quad + n^{-1}\sum_{\tau=1}^{m}\sum_{t=\tau+1}^{n} E(\mathbf{Z}_t\boldsymbol{\varepsilon}_t\boldsymbol{\varepsilon}_{t-\tau}'\mathbf{Z}_{t-\tau}') + E(\mathbf{Z}_{t-\tau}\boldsymbol{\varepsilon}_{t-\tau}\boldsymbol{\varepsilon}_t'\mathbf{Z}_t').
\end{aligned}$$

Throughout, we shall assume that this structure is generated by a knowledge that $E(\mathbf{Z}_t\boldsymbol{\varepsilon}_t|\mathcal{F}_{t-\tau}) = \mathbf{0}$ for $\tau = m+1 < \infty$ and adapted σ-fields $\mathcal{F}_t$. The other conditions imposed and methods of proof will be nearly identical to those of the preceding section.

First we consider the estimator

$$\begin{aligned}
\hat{\mathbf{V}}_n &= n^{-1}\sum_{t=1}^{n} \mathbf{Z}_t\tilde{\boldsymbol{\varepsilon}}_t\tilde{\boldsymbol{\varepsilon}}_t'\mathbf{Z}_t' \\
&\quad + n^{-1}\sum_{\tau=1}^{m}\sum_{t=\tau+1}^{n} \mathbf{Z}_t\tilde{\boldsymbol{\varepsilon}}_t\tilde{\boldsymbol{\varepsilon}}_{t-\tau}'\mathbf{Z}_{t-\tau}' + \mathbf{Z}_{t-\tau}\tilde{\boldsymbol{\varepsilon}}_{t-\tau}\tilde{\boldsymbol{\varepsilon}}_t'\mathbf{Z}_t'.
\end{aligned}$$

It turns out that $\hat{\mathbf{V}}_n - \mathbf{V}_n \xrightarrow{p} \mathbf{0}$ under general conditions, as we now demonstrate.

Theorem 6.9 *Suppose that*

(*i*) $\mathbf{Y}_t = \mathbf{X}_t'\boldsymbol{\beta}_o + \boldsymbol{\varepsilon}_t, \quad t = 1, 2, \ldots, \quad \boldsymbol{\beta}_o \in \mathbb{R}^k$;

(*ii*) $\{(\mathbf{Z}_t', \mathbf{X}_t', \boldsymbol{\varepsilon}_t)\}$ *is a stationary ergodic sequence;*

(*iii*) (*a*) $E(\mathbf{Z}_t\boldsymbol{\varepsilon}_t|\mathcal{F}_{t-\tau}) = \mathbf{0}$ *for* $\tau = m+1 < \infty$ *and adapted* σ*-fields* $\mathcal{F}_t$;

(*b*) $E|Z_{thi}\varepsilon_{th}|^2 < \infty$, $h = 1, \ldots, p$, $i = 1, \ldots, l$;

(*c*) $\mathbf{V}_n \equiv \text{var}(n^{-1/2}\mathbf{Z}'\boldsymbol{\varepsilon}) = \mathbf{V}$ *is positive definite;*

(iv) *(a)* $E\,|Z_{thi}X_{thj}|^2 < \infty$, $h = 1, \ldots, p$, $i = 1, \ldots, l$, $j = 1, \ldots, k$;

(b) $\mathbf{Q} \equiv E(\mathbf{Z}_t\mathbf{X}_t')$ *has full column rank;*

(c) $\hat{\mathbf{P}}_n \xrightarrow{p} \mathbf{P}$, *finite, symmetric, and positive definite.*

Then $\hat{\mathbf{V}}_n - \mathbf{V} \xrightarrow{p} \mathbf{0}$ *and* $\hat{\mathbf{V}}_n^{-1} - \mathbf{V}^{-1} \xrightarrow{p} \mathbf{0}$.

Proof. By definition and assumption *(iii.a)*,

$$\begin{aligned}\hat{\mathbf{V}}_n - \mathbf{V} = {}& n^{-1}\sum_{t=1}^{n} \mathbf{Z}_t\tilde{\varepsilon}_t\tilde{\varepsilon}_t'\mathbf{Z}_t' - E(\mathbf{Z}_t\varepsilon_t\varepsilon_t'\mathbf{Z}_t') \\ &+ n^{-1}\sum_{\tau=1}^{m}\sum_{t=\tau+1}^{n} [\mathbf{Z}_t\tilde{\varepsilon}_t\tilde{\varepsilon}_{t-\tau}'\mathbf{Z}_{t-\tau}' - E(\mathbf{Z}_t\varepsilon_t\varepsilon_{t-\tau}'\mathbf{Z}_{t-\tau}') \\ &\qquad + \mathbf{Z}_{t-\tau}\tilde{\varepsilon}_{t-\tau}\tilde{\varepsilon}_t'\mathbf{Z}_t' - E(\mathbf{Z}_{t-\tau}\varepsilon_{t-\tau}\varepsilon_t'\mathbf{Z}_t')].\end{aligned}$$

If we can show that

$$n^{-1}\sum_{t=\tau+1}^{n} \mathbf{Z}_t\tilde{\varepsilon}_t\tilde{\varepsilon}_{t-\tau}'\mathbf{Z}_{t-\tau}' - E(\mathbf{Z}_t\varepsilon_t\varepsilon_{t-\tau}'\mathbf{Z}_{t-\tau}') \xrightarrow{p} \mathbf{0}, \quad \tau = 0, \ldots, m,$$

then the desired result follows by Exercise 2.35.

Now

$$\begin{aligned}&n^{-1}\sum_{t=\tau+1}^{n} \mathbf{Z}_t\tilde{\varepsilon}_t\tilde{\varepsilon}_{t-\tau}'\mathbf{Z}_{t-\tau}' - E(\mathbf{Z}_t\varepsilon_t\varepsilon_{t-\tau}'\mathbf{Z}_{t-\tau}') \\ &\quad = ((n-\tau)/n)(n-\tau)^{-1}\sum_{t=\tau+1}^{n} \mathbf{Z}_t\tilde{\varepsilon}_t\tilde{\varepsilon}_{t-\tau}'\mathbf{Z}_{t-\tau}' - E(\mathbf{Z}_t\varepsilon_t\varepsilon_{t-\tau}'\mathbf{Z}_{t-\tau}').\end{aligned}$$

For $\tau = 0, \ldots, m$, we have $((n-\tau)/n) \to 1$ as $n \to \infty$, so it suffices to show that for $\tau = 0, \ldots, m$,

$$(n-\tau)^{-1}\sum_{t=\tau+1}^{n} \mathbf{Z}_t\tilde{\varepsilon}_t\tilde{\varepsilon}_{t-\tau}'\mathbf{Z}_{t-\tau}' - E(\mathbf{Z}_t\varepsilon_t\varepsilon_{t-\tau}'\mathbf{Z}_{t-\tau}') \xrightarrow{p} \mathbf{0}.$$

As before, replace $\tilde{\boldsymbol{\varepsilon}}_t$ with $\tilde{\boldsymbol{\varepsilon}}_t = \boldsymbol{\varepsilon}_t - \mathbf{X}_t'(\tilde{\boldsymbol{\beta}}_n - \boldsymbol{\beta}_o)$, to obtain

$$\begin{aligned}
(n-\tau)^{-1} \sum_{t=\tau+1}^{n} &\mathbf{Z}_t\tilde{\boldsymbol{\varepsilon}}_t\tilde{\boldsymbol{\varepsilon}}_{t-\tau}'\mathbf{Z}_{t-\tau}' - E(\mathbf{Z}_t\boldsymbol{\varepsilon}_t\boldsymbol{\varepsilon}_{t-\tau}'\mathbf{Z}_{t-\tau}') \\
&= (n-\tau)^{-1} \sum_{t=\tau+1}^{n} \mathbf{Z}_t\boldsymbol{\varepsilon}_t\boldsymbol{\varepsilon}_{t-\tau}'\mathbf{Z}_{t-\tau}' - E(\mathbf{Z}_t\boldsymbol{\varepsilon}_t\boldsymbol{\varepsilon}_{t-\tau}'\mathbf{Z}_{t-\tau}') \\
&\quad - (n-\tau)^{-1} \sum_{t=\tau+1}^{n} \mathbf{Z}_t\mathbf{X}_t'(\tilde{\boldsymbol{\beta}}_n - \boldsymbol{\beta}_o)\boldsymbol{\varepsilon}_{t-\tau}'\mathbf{Z}_{t-\tau}' \\
&\quad - (n-\tau)^{-1} \sum_{t=\tau+1}^{n} \mathbf{Z}_t\boldsymbol{\varepsilon}_t(\tilde{\boldsymbol{\beta}}_n - \boldsymbol{\beta}_o)'\mathbf{X}_{t-\tau}\mathbf{Z}_{t-\tau}' \\
&\quad + (n-\tau)^{-1} \sum_{t=\tau+1}^{n} \mathbf{Z}_t\mathbf{X}_t'(\tilde{\boldsymbol{\beta}}_n - \boldsymbol{\beta}_o)(\tilde{\boldsymbol{\beta}}_n - \boldsymbol{\beta}_o)'\mathbf{X}_{t-\tau}\mathbf{Z}_{t-\tau}'.
\end{aligned}$$

The desired result follows by Exercise 2.35 if each of the terms above vanishes in probability.

The first term vanishes almost surely (in probability) by the ergodic theorem given (*ii*) and (*iii.b*). For the second, use $\text{vec}(\mathbf{ABC}) = (\mathbf{C}' \otimes \mathbf{A})\text{vec}(\mathbf{B})$ to write

$$\begin{aligned}
\text{vec}&\left((n-\tau)^{-1} \sum_{t=\tau+1}^{n} \mathbf{Z}_t\mathbf{X}_t'(\tilde{\boldsymbol{\beta}}_n - \boldsymbol{\beta}_o)\boldsymbol{\varepsilon}_{t-\tau}'\mathbf{Z}_{t-\tau}' \right) \\
&= (n-\tau)^{-1} \sum_{t=\tau+1}^{n} (\mathbf{Z}_{t-\tau}\boldsymbol{\varepsilon}_{t-\tau} \otimes \mathbf{Z}_t\mathbf{X}_t')\, \text{vec}(\tilde{\boldsymbol{\beta}}_n - \boldsymbol{\beta}_o).
\end{aligned}$$

The conditions of the theorem ensure $\tilde{\boldsymbol{\beta}}_n \xrightarrow{p} \boldsymbol{\beta}_o$ by Exercise 3.38, so it suffices that $(n-\tau)^{-1}\sum_{t=\tau+1}^{n} (\mathbf{Z}_{t-\tau}\boldsymbol{\varepsilon}_{t-\tau} \otimes \mathbf{Z}_t\mathbf{X}_t')$ is $O_p(1)$ by Corollary 2.36. But this follows by the ergodic theorem, given (*iii.b*) and (*iv.a*) upon application of Cauchy-Schwarz's inequality.

Similar argument establishes that

$$\begin{aligned}
\text{vec}&\left((n-\tau)^{-1} \sum_{t=\tau+1}^{n} \mathbf{Z}_t\boldsymbol{\varepsilon}_t(\tilde{\boldsymbol{\beta}}_n - \boldsymbol{\beta}_o)'\mathbf{X}_{t-\tau}\mathbf{Z}_{t-\tau}' \right) \\
&= (n-\tau)^{-1} \sum_{t=\tau+1}^{n} (\mathbf{Z}_{t-\tau}\mathbf{X}_{t-\tau}' \otimes \mathbf{Z}_t\boldsymbol{\varepsilon}_t)\, \text{vec}((\tilde{\boldsymbol{\beta}}_n - \boldsymbol{\beta}_o)') \xrightarrow{p} \mathbf{0}.
\end{aligned}$$

For the final term, use $\text{vec}(\mathbf{ABC}) = (\mathbf{C}' \otimes \mathbf{A})\text{vec}(\mathbf{B})$ to write

$$\begin{aligned}
&\text{vec}\left((n-\tau)^{-1} \sum_{t=\tau+1}^{n} \mathbf{Z}_t\mathbf{X}_t'(\tilde{\boldsymbol{\beta}}_n - \boldsymbol{\beta}_o)(\tilde{\boldsymbol{\beta}}_n - \boldsymbol{\beta}_o)'\mathbf{X}_{t-\tau}\mathbf{Z}_{t-\tau}'\right) \\
&= (n-\tau)^{-1} \sum_{t=\tau+1}^{n} (\mathbf{Z}_{t-\tau}\mathbf{X}_{t-\tau}' \otimes \mathbf{Z}_t\mathbf{X}_t')\,\text{vec}((\tilde{\boldsymbol{\beta}}_n - \boldsymbol{\beta}_o)(\tilde{\boldsymbol{\beta}}_n - \boldsymbol{\beta}_o)').
\end{aligned}$$

The conditions of the theorem ensure $\tilde{\boldsymbol{\beta}}_n \xrightarrow{p} \boldsymbol{\beta}_o$, while conditions (*ii*) and (*iv.a*) ensure that the ergodic theorem applies, which implies

$$(n-\tau)^{-1} \sum_{t=\tau+1}^{n} (\mathbf{Z}_{t-\tau}\mathbf{X}_{t-\tau}' \otimes \mathbf{Z}_t\mathbf{X}_t') = O_p(1).$$

The final term thus vanishes by Corollary 2.36 and the proof is complete. ∎

Results analogous to Corollaries 6.4 and 6.5 also follow similarly.

Corollary 6.10 *Suppose conditions (i)–(iv) of Theorem 6.9 hold. Then* $\mathbf{D}^{-1/2}\sqrt{n}(\tilde{\boldsymbol{\beta}}_n - \boldsymbol{\beta}_o) \overset{A}{\sim} N(\mathbf{0}, \mathbf{I})$, *where*

$$\mathbf{D} \equiv (\mathbf{Q}'\mathbf{P}\mathbf{Q})^{-1}\mathbf{Q}'\mathbf{P}\mathbf{V}\mathbf{P}\mathbf{Q}(\mathbf{Q}'\mathbf{P}\mathbf{Q})^{-1}.$$

Further, $\hat{\mathbf{D}}_n - \mathbf{D} \xrightarrow{p} \mathbf{0}$, *where*

$$\hat{\mathbf{D}}_n = (\mathbf{X}'\mathbf{Z}\hat{\mathbf{P}}_n\mathbf{Z}'\mathbf{X}/n^2)^{-1}(\mathbf{X}'\mathbf{Z}/n)\hat{\mathbf{P}}_n\hat{\mathbf{V}}_n\hat{\mathbf{P}}_n(\mathbf{Z}'\mathbf{X}/n)(\mathbf{X}'\mathbf{Z}\hat{\mathbf{P}}_n\mathbf{Z}'\mathbf{X}/n^2)^{-1}.$$

Proof. Immediate from Exercise 5.19 and Theorem 6.9. ∎

Corollary 6.11 *Suppose that*

(*i*) $\mathbf{Y}_t = \mathbf{X}_t'\beta_0 + \varepsilon_t, \quad t = 1, 2, \ldots, \quad \boldsymbol{\beta}_o \in \mathbb{R}^k$;

(*ii*) $\{(\mathbf{Z}_t', \mathbf{X}_t', \varepsilon_t)\}$ *is a stationary ergodic sequence;*

(*iii*) (*a*) $E(\mathbf{Z}_t\varepsilon_t|\mathcal{F}_{t-\tau}) = \mathbf{0}$ *for* $\tau = m+1 < \infty$ *and adapted* σ*-fields* $\mathcal{F}_t$;

(*b*) $E|Z_{thi}\varepsilon_{th}|^2 < \infty$, $h = 1, \ldots, p$, $i = 1, \ldots, l$;

(*c*) $\mathbf{V}_n \equiv \text{var}(n^{-1/2}\mathbf{Z}'\boldsymbol{\varepsilon}) = \mathbf{V}$ *is positive definite;*

(*iv*) (*a*) $E|Z_{thi}X_{thj}|^2 < \infty$, $h = 1, \ldots, p$, $i = 1, \ldots, l$, $j = 1, \ldots, k$, *and* $E|Z_{thi}|^2 < \infty$, $h = 1, \ldots, p$, $i = 1, \ldots, l$;

(*b*) $\mathbf{Q} \equiv E(\mathbf{Z}_t\mathbf{X}_t')$ *has full column rank;*

(*c*) $\mathbf{L} \equiv E(\mathbf{Z}_t\mathbf{Z}_t')$ *is positive definite.*

Define

$$\hat{\mathbf{V}}_n \equiv n^{-1}\sum_{t=1}^{n}\mathbf{Z}_t\tilde{\varepsilon}_t\tilde{\varepsilon}_t'\mathbf{Z}_t' + \sum_{\tau=1}^{m}\sum_{t=\tau+1}^{n}\mathbf{Z}_t\tilde{\varepsilon}_t\tilde{\varepsilon}_{t-\tau}'\mathbf{Z}_{t-\tau}' + \mathbf{Z}_{t-\tau}\tilde{\varepsilon}_{t-\tau}\tilde{\varepsilon}_t'\mathbf{Z}_t',$$

where $\tilde{\varepsilon}_t \equiv \mathbf{Y}_t - \mathbf{X}_t'\tilde{\boldsymbol{\beta}}_n$, $\tilde{\boldsymbol{\beta}}_n \equiv (\mathbf{X}'\mathbf{Z}(\mathbf{Z}'\mathbf{Z})^{-1}\mathbf{Z}'\mathbf{X})^{-1}\mathbf{X}'\mathbf{Z}(\mathbf{Z}'\mathbf{Z})^{-1}\mathbf{Z}'\mathbf{Y}$, and define

$$\boldsymbol{\beta}_n^* \equiv (\mathbf{X}'\mathbf{Z}\hat{\mathbf{V}}_n^{-1}\mathbf{Z}'\mathbf{X})^{-1}\mathbf{X}'\mathbf{Z}\hat{\mathbf{V}}_n^{-1}\mathbf{Z}'\mathbf{Y}.$$

Then $\mathbf{D}^{-1/2}\sqrt{n}(\boldsymbol{\beta}_n^* - \boldsymbol{\beta}_o) \overset{A}{\sim} N(\mathbf{0}, \mathbf{I})$, where

$$\mathbf{D} = (\mathbf{Q}'\mathbf{V}^{-1}\mathbf{Q})^{-1}.$$

Further, $\hat{\mathbf{D}}_n - \mathbf{D} \xrightarrow{p} \mathbf{0}$, where

$$\hat{\mathbf{D}}_n = (\mathbf{X}'\mathbf{Z}\hat{\mathbf{V}}_n^{-1}\mathbf{Z}'\mathbf{X}/n^2)^{-1}.$$

Proof. Conditions (i)–(iv) ensure that Theorem 6.9 holds for $\tilde{\boldsymbol{\beta}}_n$. Set $\hat{\mathbf{P}}_n = \hat{\mathbf{V}}_n^{-1}$ in Corollary 6.10. Then $\hat{\mathbf{P}}_n = \hat{\mathbf{V}}_n^{-1}$ and the result follows. ∎

Results for mixing sequences parallel those of Exercises 6.6–6.8.

Exercise 6.12 *Prove the following result. Suppose*

(*i*) $\mathbf{Y}_t = \mathbf{X}_t'\boldsymbol{\beta}_o + \varepsilon_t, \quad t = 1, 2, \ldots, \quad \boldsymbol{\beta}_o \in \mathbb{R}^k$;

(*ii*) $\{(\mathbf{Z}_t', \mathbf{X}_t', \varepsilon_t)\}$ *is a mixing sequence with either* ϕ *of size* $-r/(2r-2)$, $r \geq 2$, *or* α *of size* $-r/(r-2)$, $r > 2$;

(*iii*) (*a*) $E(\mathbf{Z}_t\varepsilon_t|\mathcal{F}_{t-\tau}) = \mathbf{0}$, *for* $\tau = m+1 < \infty$ *and adapted* σ*-fields* $\mathcal{F}_t$, $t = 1, 2, \ldots$;

(*b*) $E|Z_{thi}\varepsilon_{th}|^{r+\delta} < \Delta < \infty$ *for some* $\delta > 0$ *and all* $h = l, \ldots, p$, $i = 1, \ldots, l$, *and* $t = 1, 2, \ldots$;

(*c*) $\mathbf{V}_n \equiv \text{var}(n^{-1/2}\sum_{t=1}^{n}\mathbf{Z}_t\varepsilon_t)$ *is uniformly positive definite*;

(*iv*) (*a*) $E|Z_{thi}X_{thj}|^{r+\delta} < \Delta < \infty$ *for some* $\delta > 0$ *and all* $h = 1, \ldots, p$, $i = 1, \ldots, l$, $j = 1, \ldots, k$, *and* $t = 1, 2, \ldots$;

(*b*) $\mathbf{Q}_n \equiv E(\mathbf{Z}'\mathbf{X}/n)$ *has uniformly full column rank*;

(*c*) $\hat{\mathbf{P}}_n - \mathbf{P}_n \xrightarrow{p} \mathbf{0}$, *where* $\mathbf{P}_n = O(1)$ *is symmetric and uniformly positive definite.*

Then $\hat{\mathbf{V}}_n - \mathbf{V}_n \xrightarrow{p} \mathbf{0}$ *and* $\hat{\mathbf{V}}_n^{-1} - \mathbf{V}_n^{-1} \xrightarrow{p} \mathbf{0}$.

(Hint: be careful to handle r properly to ensure the proper mixing size requirements.)

Exercise 6.13 *Prove the following result. Suppose conditions (i)–(iv) of Exercise 6.12 hold. Then* $\mathbf{D}_n^{-1/2}\sqrt{n}(\tilde{\boldsymbol{\beta}}_n - \boldsymbol{\beta}_o) \overset{A}{\sim} N(\mathbf{0}, \mathbf{I})$, *where*

$$\mathbf{D}_n \equiv (\mathbf{Q}_n'\mathbf{P}_n\mathbf{Q}_n)^{-1}\mathbf{Q}_n'\mathbf{P}_n\mathbf{V}_n\mathbf{P}_n\mathbf{Q}_n(\mathbf{Q}_n'\mathbf{P}_n\mathbf{Q}_n)^{-1}.$$

Further, $\hat{\mathbf{D}}_n - \mathbf{D}_n \xrightarrow{p} \mathbf{0}$, *where*

$$\hat{\mathbf{D}}_n = (\mathbf{X}'\mathbf{Z}\hat{\mathbf{P}}_n\mathbf{Z}'\mathbf{X}/n^2)^{-1}(\mathbf{X}'\mathbf{Z}/n)\hat{\mathbf{P}}_n\hat{\mathbf{V}}_n\hat{\mathbf{P}}_n(\mathbf{Z}'\mathbf{X}/n)(\mathbf{X}'\mathbf{Z}\hat{\mathbf{P}}_n\mathbf{Z}'\mathbf{X}/n^2)^{-1}.$$

(Hint: apply Theorem 5.23.)

Exercise 6.14 *Prove the following result. Suppose*

(i) $\mathbf{Y}_t = \mathbf{X}_t'\boldsymbol{\beta}_o + \varepsilon_t, \quad t = 1, 2, \ldots, \quad \boldsymbol{\beta}_o \in \mathbb{R}^k$;

(ii) $\{(\mathbf{Z}_t', \mathbf{X}_t', \varepsilon_t)\}$ *is a mixing sequence with either* ϕ *of size* $-r/(2r-2)$, $r \geq 2$, *or* α *of size* $-r/(r-2)$, $r > 2$;

(iii) (a) $E(\mathbf{Z}_t\varepsilon_t|\mathcal{F}_{t-\tau}) = \mathbf{0}$ *for* $\tau = m + 1 < \infty$ *and adapted* σ-*fields* $\mathcal{F}_t$, $t = 1, 2, \ldots$;
(b) $E|Z_{thi}\varepsilon_{th}|^{r+\delta} < \Delta < \infty$ *for some* $\delta > 0$ *and all* $h = 1, \ldots, p$, $i = 1, \ldots, l$, *and* $t = 1, 2, \ldots$;
(c) $\mathbf{V}_n \equiv \text{var}(n^{-1/2}\sum_{t=1}^n \mathbf{Z}_t\varepsilon_t)$ *is uniformly positive definite;*

(iv) (a) $E|Z_{thi}X_{thj}|^{r+\delta} < \Delta < \infty$ *for some* $\delta > 0$ *and all* $h = 1, \ldots, p$, $i = 1, \ldots, l$, $j = 1, \ldots, k$, *and* $t = 1, 2, \ldots$;
(b) $\mathbf{Q}_n \equiv E(\mathbf{Z}'\mathbf{X}/n)$ *has uniformly full column rank;*
(c) $\mathbf{L}_n \equiv E(\mathbf{Z}'\mathbf{Z}/n)$ *is uniformly positive definite.*

Define

$$\begin{aligned}\hat{\mathbf{V}}_n &= n^{-1}\sum_{t=1}^n \mathbf{Z}_t\tilde{\varepsilon}_t\tilde{\varepsilon}_t'\mathbf{Z}_t' \\ &\quad + n^{-1}\sum_{\tau=1}^m \sum_{t=\tau+1}^n \mathbf{Z}_t\tilde{\varepsilon}_t\tilde{\varepsilon}_{t-\tau}'\mathbf{Z}_{t-\tau}' + \mathbf{Z}_{t-\tau}\tilde{\varepsilon}_{t-\tau}\tilde{\varepsilon}_t'\mathbf{Z}_t',\end{aligned}$$

where $\tilde{\varepsilon}_t \equiv \mathbf{Y}_t - \mathbf{X}_t'\tilde{\boldsymbol{\beta}}_n$, $\tilde{\boldsymbol{\beta}}_n \equiv (\mathbf{X}'\mathbf{Z}(\mathbf{Z}'\mathbf{Z})^{-1}\mathbf{Z}'\mathbf{X})^{-1}\mathbf{X}'\mathbf{Z}(\mathbf{Z}'\mathbf{Z})^{-1}\mathbf{Z}'\mathbf{Y}$, *and define*

$$\boldsymbol{\beta}_n^* \equiv (\mathbf{X}'\mathbf{Z}\hat{\mathbf{V}}_n\mathbf{Z}'\mathbf{X})^{-1}\mathbf{X}'\mathbf{Z}\hat{\mathbf{V}}_n^{-1}\mathbf{Z}'\mathbf{Y}.$$

Then $\mathbf{D}_n^{-1/2}\sqrt{n}(\boldsymbol{\beta}_n^* - \boldsymbol{\beta}_o) \overset{A}{\sim} N(\mathbf{0}, \mathbf{I})$, *where*

$$\mathbf{D}_n = (\mathbf{Q}_n'\mathbf{V}_n^{-1}\mathbf{Q}_n)^{-1}.$$

Further, $\hat{\mathbf{D}}_n - \mathbf{D}_n \xrightarrow{p} \mathbf{0}$, *where*

$$\hat{\mathbf{D}}_n = (\mathbf{X}'\mathbf{Z}\hat{\mathbf{V}}_n^{-1}\mathbf{Z}'\mathbf{X}/n^2)^{-1}.$$

Because $\hat{\mathbf{V}}_n - \mathbf{V}_n \xrightarrow{p} \mathbf{0}$ and $\mathbf{V}_n$ is assumed uniformly positive definite, it follows that $\hat{\mathbf{V}}_n$ is positive definite with probability approaching one as $n \to \infty$. In fact, as the proofs of the theorems demonstrate, the convergence is almost sure (provided $\hat{\mathbf{P}}_n - \mathbf{P}_n \xrightarrow{a.s.} \mathbf{0}$), so $\hat{\mathbf{V}}_n$ will then be positive definite for all n sufficiently large almost surely.

Nevertheless, for given n and particular samples, $\hat{\mathbf{V}}_n$ as just analyzed can fail to be positive definite. In fact, not only can it be positive semidefinite, but it can be indefinite. This is clearly inconvenient, as negative variance estimates can lead to results that are utterly useless for testing hypotheses or for any other purpose where variance estimates are required.

What can be done? A simple but effective strategy is to consider the following weighted version of $\hat{\mathbf{V}}_n$,

$$\begin{aligned}\tilde{\mathbf{V}}_n &= n^{-1}\sum_{t=1}^{n}\mathbf{Z}_t\tilde{\varepsilon}_t\tilde{\varepsilon}_t'\mathbf{Z}_t' \\ &\quad + n^{-1}\sum_{\tau=1}^{m} w_{n\tau}\sum_{t=\tau+1}^{n}\mathbf{Z}_t\tilde{\varepsilon}_t\tilde{\varepsilon}_{t-\tau}'\mathbf{Z}_{t-\tau}' + \mathbf{Z}_{t-\tau}\tilde{\varepsilon}_{t-\tau}\tilde{\varepsilon}_t'\mathbf{Z}_t'.\end{aligned}$$

The estimator $\hat{\mathbf{V}}_n$ obtains when $w_{n\tau} = 1$ for all n and τ. Moreover, consistency of $\tilde{\mathbf{V}}_n$ is straightforward to ensure, as the following exercise asks you to verify.

Exercise 6.15 *Show that under the conditions of Theorem 6.9 or Exercise 6.12 a sufficient condition to ensure* $\tilde{\mathbf{V}}_n - \mathbf{V}_n \xrightarrow{p} \mathbf{0}$ *is that* $w_{n\tau} \xrightarrow{p} 1$ *for each* $\tau = 1, \ldots, m$.

Subject to this requirement, we can then manipulate $w_{n\tau}$ to ensure the positive definiteness of $\tilde{\mathbf{V}}_n$ in finite samples. One natural way to proceed is to let the properties of $\hat{\mathbf{V}}_n$ suggest how to choose $w_{n\tau}$. In particular, if $\hat{\mathbf{V}}_n$ is positive definite (as evidenced by having all positive eigenvalues), then set $w_{n\tau} = 1$. (As is trivially verified, this ensures $w_{n\tau} \xrightarrow{p} 1$.) Otherwise, choose $w_{n\tau}$ to enforce positive definiteness in some principled way. For example, choose $w_{n\tau} = f(\tau, \theta_n)$ and adjust θ_n to the extent needed to achieve positive definite $\tilde{\mathbf{V}}_n$. For example, one might choose $w_{n\tau} = 1 - \theta_n \tau$ $(\theta_n > 0)$, $w_{n\tau} = (\theta_n)^\tau$ $(\theta_n < 1)$, or $w_{n\tau} = \exp(-\theta_n \tau)$ $(\theta_n > 0)$. More sophisticated methods are available, but as a practical matter, this simple approach will often suffice.

6.4 Case 3: $\{\mathbf{Z}_t \varepsilon_t\}$ Asymptotically Uncorrelated

In this section we consider the general case in which

$$\begin{aligned}\mathbf{V}_n &= n^{-1}\sum_{t=1}^{n} E(\mathbf{Z}_t \varepsilon_t \varepsilon_t' \mathbf{Z}_t') \\ &\quad + n^{-1}\sum_{\tau=1}^{n-1}\sum_{t=\tau+1}^{n} E(\mathbf{Z}_t \varepsilon_t \varepsilon_{t-\tau}' \mathbf{Z}_{t-\tau}') + E(\mathbf{Z}_{t-\tau} \varepsilon_{t-\tau} \varepsilon_t' \mathbf{Z}_t').\end{aligned}$$

The essential restriction we impose is that as $\tau \to \infty$ the covariance (correlation) between $\mathbf{Z}_t \varepsilon_t$ and $\mathbf{Z}_{t-\tau} \varepsilon_{t-\tau}$ goes to zero. We ensure this behavior by assuming that $\{(\mathbf{Z}_t', \mathbf{X}_t', \varepsilon_t)\}$ is a mixing sequence. In the stationary case, we replace ergodicity with mixing, which, as we saw in Chapter 3, implies ergodicity. Mixing is not the weakest possible requirement. Mixingale conditions can also be used in the present context. Nevertheless, to keep our analysis tractable we restrict attention to mixing processes.

The fact that mixing sequences are asymptotically uncorrelated is a consequence of the following lemma.

Lemma 6.16 *Let $\mathcal{Z}$ be a random variable measurable with respect to $\mathcal{F}_{n+\tau}^{\infty}$, $0 < \tau < \infty$, such that $\|\mathcal{Z}\|_q \equiv [E|\mathcal{Z}|^q]^{1/q} < \infty$ for some $q > 1$, and let $1 \le r \le q$. Then*

$$\left\| E(\mathcal{Z}|\mathcal{F}_{-\infty}^{n}) - E(\mathcal{Z}) \right\|_r \le 2[\phi(\tau)]^{1-1/q} \left\|\mathcal{Z}\right\|_q$$

and

$$\left\| E(\mathcal{Z}|\mathcal{F}_{-\infty}^{n}) - E(\mathcal{Z}) \right\|_r \le 2(2^{1/r}+1)[\alpha(\tau)]^{1/r-1/q} \left\|\mathcal{Z}\right\|_q .$$

Proof. This follows immediately from Lemma 2.1 of McLeish (1975). ∎

For mixing sequences, $\phi(\tau)$ or $\alpha(\tau)$ goes to zero as $\tau \to \infty$, so this result imposes bounds on the rate that the conditional expectation of $\mathcal{Z}$, given the past up to period n, converges to the unconditional expectation as the time separation τ gets larger and larger.

By setting $r = 2$, we obtain the following result.

Corollary 6.17 *Let* $E(\mathcal{Z}_n) = E(\mathcal{Z}_{n+\tau}) = 0$ *and suppose* $\text{var}(\mathcal{Z}_n) < \infty$, *and for some* $q \geq 2$, $E|\mathcal{Z}_{n+\tau}|^q < \infty$, $0 < \tau < \infty$. *Then*

$$|E(\mathcal{Z}_n\mathcal{Z}_{n+\tau})| \leq 2\phi(\tau)^{1-1/q}(\text{var}(\mathcal{Z}_n))^{1/2}\left\|\mathcal{Z}_{n+\tau}\right\|_q$$

and

$$\begin{aligned}|E(\mathcal{Z}_n\mathcal{Z}_{n+\tau})| &\leq 2(2^{1/2}+1)\alpha(\tau)^{1/2-1/q}(\text{var}(\mathcal{Z}_n))^{1/2} \\ &\quad \times \left\|\mathcal{Z}_{n+\tau}\right\|_q.\end{aligned}$$

Proof. Put $\mathcal{F}_{-\infty}^n = \sigma(\ldots, \mathcal{Z}_n)$ and $\mathcal{F}_{n+\tau}^{\infty} = \sigma(\mathcal{Z}_{n+\tau}, \ldots)$. By the law of iterated expectations,

$$\begin{aligned}E(\mathcal{Z}_n\mathcal{Z}_{n+\tau}) &= E(E(\mathcal{Z}_n\mathcal{Z}_{n+\tau}|\mathcal{F}_{-\infty}^n)) \\ &= E(\mathcal{Z}_nE(\mathcal{Z}_{n+\tau}|\mathcal{F}_{-\infty}^n))\end{aligned}$$

by Proposition 3.65. It follows from the Cauchy-Schwarz inequality and Jensen's inequality that

$$|E(\mathcal{Z}_n\mathcal{Z}_{n+\tau})| \leq E(\mathcal{Z}_n^2)^{1/2}E(E(\mathcal{Z}_{n+\tau}|\mathcal{F}_{-\infty}^n)^2)^{1/2}.$$

By Lemma 6.16, we have

$$E(E(\mathcal{Z}_{n+\tau}|\mathcal{F}_{-\infty}^n)^2)^{1/2} \leq 2\phi(\tau)^{1-1/q}\left\|\mathcal{Z}_{n+\tau}\right\|_q$$

and

$$E(E(\mathcal{Z}_{n+\tau}|\mathcal{F}_{-\infty}^n)^2)^{1/2} \leq 2(2^{1/2}+1)\alpha(\tau)^{1/2-1/q}\left\|\mathcal{Z}_{n+\tau}\right\|_q,$$

where we set $r = 2$ in Lemma 6.16. Combining these inequalities yields the final results,

$$|E(\mathcal{Z}_n\mathcal{Z}_{n+\tau})| \leq 2\phi(\tau)^{1-1/q}(\text{var}(\mathcal{Z}_n))^{1/2}\left\|\mathcal{Z}_{n+\tau}\right\|_q,$$

and

$$|E(\mathcal{Z}_n\mathcal{Z}_{n+\tau})| \leq 2(2^{1/2}+1)\alpha(\tau)^{1/2-1/q}(\text{var}(\mathcal{Z}_n))^{1/2}\left\|\mathcal{Z}_{n+\tau}\right\|_q.$$

■

The direct implication of this result is that mixing sequences are asymptotically uncorrelated, because $\phi(\tau) \to 0$ $(q \geq 2)$ or $\alpha(\tau) \to 0$ $(q > 2)$

implies $|E(\mathcal{Z}_n \mathcal{Z}_{n+\tau})| \to 0$ as $\tau \to \infty$. For mixing sequences, it follows that $\mathbf{V}_n$ might be well approximated by

$$\begin{aligned}\bar{\mathbf{V}}_n \equiv\ & w_{n0}\, n^{-1} \sum_{t=1}^{n} E(\mathbf{Z}_t \varepsilon_t \varepsilon_t' \mathbf{Z}_t') \\ & + n^{-1} \sum_{\tau=1}^{m} w_{n\tau} \sum_{t=\tau+1}^{n} E(\mathbf{Z}_t \varepsilon_t \varepsilon_{t-\tau}' \mathbf{Z}_{t-\tau}') + E(\mathbf{Z}_{t-\tau} \varepsilon_{t-\tau} \varepsilon_t' \mathbf{Z}_t')\end{aligned}$$

for some value m, because the neglected terms (those with $m < \tau \leq n$) will be small in absolute value if m is sufficiently large. Note, however, that if m is simply kept fixed as n grows, the number of neglected terms grows, and may grow in such a way that the sum of the neglected terms does not remain negligible. This suggests that m will have to grow with n, so that the terms in $\mathbf{V}_n$ ignored by $\bar{\mathbf{V}}_n$ remain negligible. We will write m_n to make this dependence explicit.

Note that in $\bar{\mathbf{V}}_n$ we have introduced weights $w_{n\tau}$ analogous to those appearing in $\tilde{\mathbf{V}}_n$ of the previous section. This facilitates our analysis of an extension of that estimator, which we now define as

$$\begin{aligned}\tilde{\mathbf{V}}_n \equiv\ & w_{n0}\, n^{-1} \sum_{t=1}^{n} \mathbf{Z}_t \tilde{\varepsilon}_t \tilde{\varepsilon}_t' \mathbf{Z}_t' \\ & + n^{-1} \sum_{\tau=1}^{m_n} w_{n\tau} \sum_{t=\tau+1}^{n} \mathbf{Z}_t \tilde{\varepsilon}_t \tilde{\varepsilon}_{t-\tau}' \mathbf{Z}_{t-\tau}' + \mathbf{Z}_{t-\tau} \tilde{\varepsilon}_{t-\tau} \tilde{\varepsilon}_t' \mathbf{Z}_t'.\end{aligned}$$

We establish the consistency of $\tilde{\mathbf{V}}_n$ for $\mathbf{V}_n$ by first showing that under suitable conditions $\bar{\mathbf{V}}_n - \mathbf{V}_n \xrightarrow{p} \mathbf{0}$ and then showing that $\tilde{\mathbf{V}}_n - \bar{\mathbf{V}}_n \xrightarrow{p} \mathbf{0}$.

Now, however, it will not be enough for consistency just to require $w_{n\tau} \xrightarrow{p} 1$, as we also have to properly treat $m_n \to \infty$. For simplicity, we consider only nonstochastic weights $w_{n\tau}$ in what follows. Stochastic weights can be treated straightforwardly in a similar manner. Our next result provides conditions under which $\bar{\mathbf{V}}_n - \mathbf{V}_n \to \mathbf{0}$.

Lemma 6.18 *Let $\{\mathcal{Z}_{nt}\}$ be a double array of random $k \times 1$ vectors such that $E(|\mathcal{Z}_{nt}' \mathcal{Z}_{nt}|^{r/2}) \leq \Delta < \infty$ for some $r > 2$, $E(\mathcal{Z}_{nt}) = \mathbf{0}$, $n, t = 1, 2, \ldots$, and $\{\mathcal{Z}_{nt}\}$ is mixing with ϕ of size $-r/(r-1)$ or α of size $-2r/(r-2)$. Define*

$$\mathbf{V}_n \equiv \text{var}(n^{-1/2} \sum_{t=1}^{n} \mathcal{Z}_{nt}),$$

and for any sequence $\{m_n\}$ of integers and any triangular array $\{w_{n\tau} : n = 1, 2, \ldots ; \tau = 1, \ldots, m_n\}$ define

$$\begin{aligned}\bar{\mathbf{V}}_n &\equiv w_{n0}\, n^{-1} \sum_{t=1}^{n} E(\mathcal{Z}_{nt}\mathcal{Z}_{nt}') \\ &\quad + n^{-1}\sum_{\tau=1}^{m_n} w_{n\tau} \sum_{t=\tau+1}^{n} E(\mathcal{Z}_{nt}\mathcal{Z}_{n,t-\tau}') + E(\mathcal{Z}_{n,t-\tau}\mathcal{Z}_{nt}').\end{aligned}$$

If $m_n \to \infty$ as $n \to \infty$, if $|w_{n\tau}| \leq \Delta$, $n = 1, 2, \ldots$, $\tau = 1, \ldots, m_n$, and if for each τ, $w_{n\tau} \to 1$ as $n \to \infty$ then $\bar{\mathbf{V}}_n - \mathbf{V}_n \to \mathbf{0}$.

Proof. See Gallant and White (1988, Lemma 6.6). ∎

Here we see the explicit requirements that $m_n \to \infty$ and $w_{n\tau} \to 1$ for each τ.

Our next result is an intermediate lemma related to Lemma 6.19 of White (1984). That result, however, contained an error, as pointed out by Phillips (1985) and Newey and West (1987), that resulted in an incorrect rate for m_n. The following result gives a correct rate.

Lemma 6.19 *Let $\{\mathcal{Z}_{nt}\}$ be a double array of random $k \times 1$ vectors such that $E(|\mathcal{Z}_{nt}'\mathcal{Z}_{nt}|^r) \leq \Delta < \infty$ for some $r > 2$, $E(\mathcal{Z}_{nt}) = \mathbf{0}$, $n, t = 1, 2, \ldots$ and $\{\mathcal{Z}_{nt}\}$ is mixing with ϕ of size $-r/(r-1)$ or α of size $-2r/(r-2)$. Define*

$$\zeta_{nt\tau}^{ij} = \mathcal{Z}_{nti}\mathcal{Z}_{n,t-\tau,j} - E(\mathcal{Z}_{nti}\mathcal{Z}_{n,t-\tau,j}).$$

If $m_n = o(n^{1/4})$ and $|w_{n\tau}| \leq \Delta$, $n = 1, 2, \ldots$, $\tau = 1, \ldots, m_n$, then for all $i, j = 1, \ldots, k$

$$n^{-1}\sum_{\tau=1}^{m_n} w_{n\tau} \sum_{t=\tau+1}^{n} \zeta_{nt\tau}^{ij} \xrightarrow{p} 0.$$

Proof. See Gallant and White (1988, Lemma 6.7 (*d*)). ∎

We now have the results we need to establish the consistency of a generally useful estimator for $\text{var}(n^{-1}\sum_{t=1}^{n}\mathcal{Z}_{nt})$.

Theorem 6.20 *Let $\{\mathcal{Z}_{nt}\}$ be a double array of random $k \times 1$ vectors such that $E(|\mathcal{Z}_{nt}'\mathcal{Z}_{nt}|^r) \leq \Delta < \infty$ for some $r > 2$, $E(\mathcal{Z}_{nt}) = \mathbf{0}$, $n, t = 1, 2, \ldots$ and $\{\mathcal{Z}_{nt}\}$ is mixing with ϕ of size $-r/(r-1)$ or α of size $-2r/(r-2)$. Define*

$$\mathbf{V}_n \equiv \text{var}(n^{-1}\sum_{t=1}^{n}\mathcal{Z}_{nt}),$$

and for any sequence $\{m_n\}$ *of integers and any triangular array* $\{w_{n\tau} : n = 1, 2, \ldots ; \tau = 1, \ldots, m_n\}$ *define*

$$\begin{aligned} \tilde{\mathbf{V}}_n &\equiv w_{n0}\, n^{-1} \sum_{t=1}^{n} \mathcal{Z}_{nt} \mathcal{Z}'_{nt} \\ &\quad + n^{-1} \sum_{\tau=1}^{m_n} w_{n\tau} \sum_{t=\tau+1}^{n} \mathcal{Z}_{nt} \mathcal{Z}'_{n,t-\tau} + \mathcal{Z}_{n,t-\tau} \mathcal{Z}'_{nt}. \end{aligned}$$

If $m_n \to \infty$ *as* $n \to \infty$, $m_n = o(n^{1/4})$, *and if* $|w_{n\tau}| \leq \Delta$, $n = 1, 2, \ldots$, $\tau = 1, \ldots, m_n$, *and if for each* τ, $w_{n\tau} \to 1$ *as* $n \to \infty$, *then* $\tilde{\mathbf{V}}_n - \mathbf{V}_n \xrightarrow{p} \mathbf{0}$.

Proof. For $\bar{\mathbf{V}}_n$ as defined in Lemma 6.18 we have

$$\tilde{\mathbf{V}}_n - \mathbf{V}_n = (\tilde{\mathbf{V}}_n - \bar{\mathbf{V}}_n) + (\bar{\mathbf{V}}_n - \mathbf{V}_n).$$

By Lemma 6.18 it follows that $\bar{\mathbf{V}}_n - \mathbf{V}_n \to \mathbf{0}$ so the result holds if $\tilde{\mathbf{V}}_n - \bar{\mathbf{V}}_n \xrightarrow{p} \mathbf{0}$.

Now

$$\begin{aligned} \tilde{\mathbf{V}}_n - \bar{\mathbf{V}}_n &= w_{n0}\, n^{-1} \sum_{t=1}^{n} \mathcal{Z}_{nt} \mathcal{Z}'_{nt} - E(\mathcal{Z}_{nt} \mathcal{Z}'_{nt}) \\ &\quad + n^{-1} \sum_{\tau=1}^{m_n} w_{n\tau} \sum_{t=\tau+1}^{n} \mathcal{Z}_{nt} \mathcal{Z}'_{n,t-\tau} - E(\mathcal{Z}_{nt} \mathcal{Z}'_{n,t-\tau}) \\ &\quad + n^{-1} \sum_{\tau=1}^{m_n} w_{n\tau} \sum_{t=\tau+1}^{n} \mathcal{Z}_{n,t-\tau} \mathcal{Z}'_{nt} - E(\mathcal{Z}_{n,t-\tau} \mathcal{Z}'_{nt}). \end{aligned}$$

The first term converges almost surely to zero by the mixing law of large numbers Corollary 3.48, while the next term, which has i, j element

$$n^{-1} \sum_{\tau=1}^{m_n} w_{n\tau} \sum_{t=\tau+1}^{n} \mathcal{Z}_{nti} \mathcal{Z}_{n,t-\tau,j} - E(\mathcal{Z}_{nti} \mathcal{Z}_{n,t-\tau,j})$$

converges in probability to zero by Lemma 6.19. The final term is the transpose of the preceding term so it too vanishes in probability, and the result follows. ■

With this result, we can establish the consistency of $\hat{\mathbf{V}}_n$ for the instrumental variables estimator by setting $\mathcal{Z}_{nt} = \mathbf{Z}_t \varepsilon_t$ and handling the additional terms that arise from the presence of $\tilde{\varepsilon}_t$ in place of ε_t with an application of Lemma 6.19.

Because the results for stationary mixing sequences follow as corollaries to the results for general mixing sequences, we state only the results for general mixing sequences.

Theorem 6.21 *Suppose*

(*i*) $\mathbf{Y}_t = \mathbf{X}_t'\boldsymbol{\beta}_o + \varepsilon_t, \quad t = 1, 2, \ldots, \quad \boldsymbol{\beta}_o \in \mathbb{R}^k$;

(*ii*) $\{(\mathbf{Z}_t', \mathbf{X}_t', \varepsilon_t)\}$ *is a mixing sequence with either* ϕ *of size* $-r/(r-1)$ *or* α *of size* $-2r/(r-2)$, $r > 2$;

(*iii*) (*a*) $E(\mathbf{Z}_t\varepsilon_t) = \mathbf{0}, \quad t = 1, 2, \ldots$;
(*b*) $E|Z_{thi}\varepsilon_{th}|^{2(r+\delta)} < \Delta < \infty$ *for some* $\delta > 0$, $h = 1, \ldots, p$, $i = 1, \ldots, l$, *and all* t;
(*c*) $\mathbf{V}_n \equiv \text{var}(n^{-1/2}\sum_{t=1}^n \mathbf{Z}_t\varepsilon_t)$ *is uniformly positive definite;*

(*iv*) (*a*) $E|Z_{thi}X_{thj}|^{2(r+\delta)} < \Delta < \infty$ *for some* $\delta > 0$ *and all* $h = 1, \ldots, p$, $i = 1, \ldots, l$, $j = 1, \ldots, k$, *and* $t = 1, 2, \ldots$;
(*b*) $\mathbf{Q}_n \equiv E(\mathbf{Z}'\mathbf{X}/n)$ *has uniformly full column rank;*
(*c*) $\hat{\mathbf{P}}_n - \mathbf{P}_n \xrightarrow{p} \mathbf{0}$, *where* $\mathbf{P}_n = O(1)$ *and is symmetric and uniformly positive definite.*

Define $\tilde{\mathbf{V}}_n$ *as above. If* $m_n \to \infty$ *as* $n \to \infty$ *such that* $m_n = o(n^{1/4})$, *and if* $|w_{n\tau}| \le \Delta$, $n = 1, 2, \ldots$, $\tau = 1, \ldots, m_n$ *such that* $w_{n\tau} \to 1$ *as* $n \to \infty$ *for each* τ, *then* $\tilde{\mathbf{V}}_n - \mathbf{V}_n \xrightarrow{p} \mathbf{0}$ *and* $\tilde{\mathbf{V}}_n^{-1} - \mathbf{V}_n^{-1} \xrightarrow{p} \mathbf{0}$.

Proof. By definition

$$\begin{aligned}\tilde{\mathbf{V}}_n - \mathbf{V}_n = {} & w_{n0}n^{-1}\sum_{t=1}^n \mathbf{Z}_t\tilde{\varepsilon}_t\tilde{\varepsilon}_t'\mathbf{Z}_t' \\ & + n^{-1}\sum_{\tau=1}^{m_n} w_{n\tau} \sum_{t=\tau+1}^n \mathbf{Z}_t\tilde{\varepsilon}_t\tilde{\varepsilon}_{t-\tau}'\mathbf{Z}_{t-\tau}' + \mathbf{Z}_{t-\tau}\tilde{\varepsilon}_{t-\tau}\tilde{\varepsilon}_t'\mathbf{Z}_t' - \mathbf{V}_n.\end{aligned}$$

Substituting $\tilde{\varepsilon}_t = \varepsilon_t - \mathbf{X}_t'(\tilde{\boldsymbol{\beta}}_n - \boldsymbol{\beta}_o)$ gives

$$\begin{aligned}\tilde{\mathbf{V}}_n - \mathbf{V}_n = {} & w_{n0}\, n^{-1}\sum_{t=1}^n \mathbf{Z}_t\varepsilon_t\varepsilon_t'\mathbf{Z}_t' \\ & + n^{-1}\sum_{\tau=1}^{m_n} w_{n\tau} \sum_{t=\tau+1}^n \mathbf{Z}_t\varepsilon_t\varepsilon_{t-\tau}'\mathbf{Z}_{t-\tau}' + \mathbf{Z}_{t-\tau}\varepsilon_{t-\tau}\varepsilon_t'\mathbf{Z}_t' - \mathbf{V}_n + \mathbf{A}_n,\end{aligned}$$

where

$$\begin{aligned}
\mathbf{A}_n &= -w_{n0}\, n^{-1} \sum_{t=1}^{n} \mathbf{Z}_t \varepsilon_t (\tilde{\boldsymbol{\beta}}_n - \boldsymbol{\beta}_o)' \mathbf{X}_t \mathbf{Z}_t' \\
&\quad - w_{n0}\, n^{-1} \sum_{t=1}^{n} \mathbf{Z}_t \mathbf{X}_t' (\tilde{\boldsymbol{\beta}}_n - \boldsymbol{\beta}_o) \varepsilon_t' \mathbf{Z}_t' \\
&\quad + w_{n0}\, n^{-1} \sum_{t=1}^{n} \mathbf{Z}_t \mathbf{X}_t' (\tilde{\boldsymbol{\beta}}_n - \boldsymbol{\beta}_o)(\tilde{\boldsymbol{\beta}}_n - \boldsymbol{\beta}_o)' \mathbf{X}_t \mathbf{Z}_t' \\
&\quad - n^{-1} \sum_{\tau=1}^{m_n} w_{n\tau} \sum_{t=\tau+1}^{n} \mathbf{Z}_t \varepsilon_t (\tilde{\boldsymbol{\beta}}_n - \boldsymbol{\beta}_o)' \mathbf{X}_{t-\tau} \mathbf{Z}_{t-\tau}' \\
&\quad - n^{-1} \sum_{\tau=1}^{m_n} w_{n\tau} \sum_{t=\tau+1}^{n} \mathbf{Z}_t \mathbf{X}_t' (\tilde{\boldsymbol{\beta}}_n - \boldsymbol{\beta}_o) \varepsilon_{t-\tau}' \mathbf{Z}_{t-\tau}' \\
&\quad + n^{-1} \sum_{\tau=1}^{m_n} w_{n\tau} \sum_{t=\tau+1}^{n} \mathbf{Z}_t \mathbf{X}_t' (\tilde{\boldsymbol{\beta}}_n - \boldsymbol{\beta}_o)(\tilde{\boldsymbol{\beta}}_n - \boldsymbol{\beta}_o)' \mathbf{X}_{t-\tau} \mathbf{Z}_{t-\tau}' \\
&\quad - n^{-1} \sum_{\tau=1}^{m_n} w_{n\tau} \sum_{t=\tau+1}^{n} \mathbf{Z}_{t-\tau} \varepsilon_{t-\tau} (\tilde{\boldsymbol{\beta}}_n - \boldsymbol{\beta}_o)' \mathbf{X}_t \mathbf{Z}_t' \\
&\quad - n^{-1} \sum_{\tau=1}^{m_n} w_{n\tau} \sum_{t=\tau+1}^{n} \mathbf{Z}_{t-\tau} \mathbf{X}_{t-\tau} (\tilde{\boldsymbol{\beta}}_n - \boldsymbol{\beta}_o) \varepsilon_t' \mathbf{Z}_t' \\
&\quad + n^{-1} \sum_{\tau=1}^{m_n} w_{n\tau} \sum_{t=\tau+1}^{n} \mathbf{Z}_{t-\tau} \mathbf{X}_{t-\tau} (\tilde{\boldsymbol{\beta}}_n - \boldsymbol{\beta}_o)(\tilde{\boldsymbol{\beta}}_n - \boldsymbol{\beta}_o)' \mathbf{X}_t \mathbf{Z}_t'.
\end{aligned}$$

The conditions of the theorem ensure that the conditions of Theorem 6.20 hold for $\mathcal{Z}_{nt} = \mathbf{Z}_t \varepsilon_t$, so that

$$w_{n0}\, n^{-1} \sum_{t=1}^{n} \mathbf{Z}_t \varepsilon_t \varepsilon_t' \mathbf{Z}_t' + n^{-1} \sum_{\tau=1}^{m_n} w_{n\tau} \sum_{t=\tau+1}^{n} \mathbf{Z}_t \varepsilon_t \varepsilon_{t-\tau}' \mathbf{Z}_{t-\tau}' + \mathbf{Z}_{t-\tau} \varepsilon_{t-\tau} \varepsilon_t' \mathbf{Z}_t' \\ - \mathbf{V}_n \xrightarrow{p} \mathbf{0}.$$

The desired result then follows provided that all remaining terms (in $\mathbf{A}_n$) vanish in probability.

The mixing and moment conditions imposed are more than enough to ensure that the terms involving w_{n0} vanish in probability, by arguments identical to those used in the proof of Exercise 6.6. Thus, consider the term

$$\begin{aligned}
&\operatorname{vec}\left(n^{-1}\sum_{\tau=1}^{m_n} w_{n\tau}\sum_{t=\tau+1}^{n}\mathbf{Z}_t\varepsilon_t(\tilde{\boldsymbol{\beta}}_n-\boldsymbol{\beta}_o)'\mathbf{X}_{t-\tau}\mathbf{Z}_{t-\tau}'\right)\\
&\quad= n^{-1}\sum_{\tau=1}^{m_n} w_{n\tau}\sum_{t=\tau+1}^{n}\left(\mathbf{Z}_{t-\tau}\mathbf{X}_{t-\tau}'\otimes\mathbf{Z}_t\varepsilon_t\right)\operatorname{vec}((\tilde{\boldsymbol{\beta}}_n-\boldsymbol{\beta}_o)')\\
&\qquad= n^{-1}\sum_{\tau=1}^{m_n} w_{n\tau}\sum_{t=\tau+1}^{n}[(\mathbf{Z}_{t-\tau}\mathbf{X}_{t-\tau}'\otimes\mathbf{Z}_t\varepsilon_t)\\
&\qquad\quad - E(\mathbf{Z}_{t-\tau}\mathbf{X}_{t-\tau}'\otimes\mathbf{Z}_t\varepsilon_t)]\operatorname{vec}((\tilde{\boldsymbol{\beta}}_n-\boldsymbol{\beta}_o)')\\
&\qquad + n^{-1}\sum_{\tau=1}^{m_n} w_{n\tau}\sum_{t=\tau+1}^{n}E\left(\mathbf{Z}_{t-\tau}\mathbf{X}_{t-\tau}'\otimes\mathbf{Z}_t\varepsilon_t\right)\operatorname{vec}((\tilde{\boldsymbol{\beta}}_n-\boldsymbol{\beta}_o)').
\end{aligned}$$

Applying Lemma 6.19 with $\mathcal{Z}_{nt}=\operatorname{vec}(\mathbf{Z}_t\mathbf{X}_t'\otimes\mathbf{Z}_t\varepsilon_t)$ we have that

$$n^{-1}\sum_{\tau=1}^{m_n} w_{n\tau}\sum_{t=\tau+1}^{n}\left(\mathbf{Z}_{t-\tau}\mathbf{X}_{t-\tau}'\otimes\mathbf{Z}_t\varepsilon_t\right)-E(\mathbf{Z}_{t-\tau}\mathbf{X}_{t-\tau}'\otimes\mathbf{Z}_t\varepsilon_t)\xrightarrow{p}\mathbf{0}.$$

This together with the fact that $\tilde{\boldsymbol{\beta}}_n-\boldsymbol{\beta}_o\xrightarrow{p}\mathbf{0}$ ensures that the first of the two terms above vanishes. It therefore suffices to show that

$$n^{-1}\sum_{\tau=1}^{m_n} w_{n\tau}\sum_{t=\tau+1}^{n}E\left(\mathbf{Z}_{t-\tau}\mathbf{X}_{t-\tau}'\otimes\mathbf{Z}_t\varepsilon_t\right)\operatorname{vec}((\tilde{\boldsymbol{\beta}}_n-\boldsymbol{\beta}_o)')$$

vanishes in probability.

Under the conditions of the theorem, we have $\sqrt{n}(\tilde{\boldsymbol{\beta}}_n-\boldsymbol{\beta}_o)=O_p(1)$ (by asymptotic normality, Theorem 5.23) so it will suffice that

$$n^{-3/2}\sum_{\tau=1}^{m_n} w_{n\tau}\sum_{t=\tau+1}^{n}E\left(\mathbf{Z}_{t-\tau}\mathbf{X}_{t-\tau}'\otimes\mathbf{Z}_t\varepsilon_t\right)=o(1).$$

Applying the triangle inequality and Jensen's inequality we have

$$\begin{aligned}
&|n^{-3/2}\sum_{\tau=1}^{m_n} w_{n\tau}\sum_{t=\tau+1}^{n}E\left(\mathbf{Z}_{t-\tau}\mathbf{X}_{t-\tau}'\otimes\mathbf{Z}_t\varepsilon_t\right)|\\
&\qquad\qquad\leq n^{-3/2}\sum_{\tau=1}^{m_n}|w_{n\tau}|\sum_{t=\tau+1}^{n}E|\mathbf{Z}_{t-\tau}\mathbf{X}_{t-\tau}'\otimes\mathbf{Z}_t\varepsilon_t|,
\end{aligned}$$

where the absolute value and inequality are understood to hold element by element. Because second moments of $\mathbf{Z}_t\mathbf{X}_t'$ and $\mathbf{Z}_t\varepsilon_t$ are uniformly bounded, the Minkowski and Cauchy-Schwarz inequalities ensure the existence of a finite matrix $\boldsymbol{\Delta}$ such that $E|\mathbf{Z}_{t-\tau}\mathbf{X}_{t-\tau}' \otimes \mathbf{Z}_t\varepsilon_t| \leq \boldsymbol{\Delta}$. Further $|w_{n\tau}| \leq \Delta$ for all n and τ, so that

$$\begin{aligned} n^{-3/2}\sum_{\tau=1}^{m_n} w_{n\tau} & \sum_{t=\tau+1}^{n} E|\mathbf{Z}_{t-\tau}\mathbf{X}_{t-\tau}' \otimes \mathbf{Z}_t\varepsilon_t| \\ & \leq \quad n^{-3/2}\sum_{\tau=1}^{m_n} |w_{n\tau}|(n-\tau)\boldsymbol{\Delta} \\ & \leq \quad n^{-3/2} m_n \Delta (n-\tau)\boldsymbol{\Delta} \\ & \leq \quad n^{-1/2} m_n \Delta\boldsymbol{\Delta}. \end{aligned}$$

But $m_n = o(n^{1/4})$, so $n^{-1/2}m_n \to 0$, which implies

$$n^{-3/2}\sum_{\tau=1}^{m_n} w_{n\tau} \sum_{t=\tau+1}^{n} E(\mathbf{Z}_{t-\tau}\mathbf{X}_{t-\tau}' \otimes \mathbf{Z}_t\varepsilon_t) = o(1)$$

as we needed.

The same argument works for all of the other terms under the conditions given, so the result follows. ∎

Comparing the conditions of this result to the asymptotic normality result, Theorem 5.23, we see that the memory conditions here are twice as strong as in Theorem 5.23. The moment conditions on $\mathbf{Z}_t\varepsilon_t$ are roughly twice as strong as in Theorem 5.23, while those on $\mathbf{Z}_t\mathbf{X}_t'$ are roughly four times as strong.

The rate $m_n = o(n^{1/4})$ is not necessarily the optimal rate, and other methods of proof can deliver faster rates for m_n. (See, e.g., Andrews, 1991.) For discussion on methods relevant for choosing m_n, see Den Haan and Levin (1997).

Gallant and White (1988, Lemma 6.5) provide the following conditions on $w_{n\tau}$ guaranteeing the positive definiteness of $\tilde{\mathbf{V}}_n$.

Lemma 6.22 *Let $\{Z_{nt}\}$ be an arbitrary double array and let $\{a_{ni}\}$, $n = 1, 2, \ldots$, $i = 1, \ldots, m_n + 1$ be a triangular array of real numbers. Then for any triangular array of weights*

$$w_{n\tau} = \sum_{i=\tau+1}^{m_n+1} a_{ni}a_{n,i-\tau}, \quad n = 1, 2, \ldots, \quad \tau = 1, \ldots, m_n$$

we have

$$\mathcal{Y}_n = w_{n0}\sum_{t=1}^{n}\mathcal{Z}_{nt}^2 + 2\sum_{\tau=1}^{m_n} w_{n\tau}\sum_{t=1}^{n}\mathcal{Z}_{nt}\mathcal{Z}_{n,t-\tau} \geq 0.$$

Proof. See Gallant and White (1988, Lemma 6.5). ■

For example, choosing $a_{ni} = (m_n+1)^{1/2}$ for all $i = 1, \ldots, m_n+1$ delivers

$$w_{n\tau} = 1 - \tau/(m_n + 1), \quad \tau = 1, \ldots, m_n,$$

which are the Bartlett (1950) weights given by Newey and West (1987). Other choices for a_{ni} lead to other choices of weights that arise in the problem of estimating the *spectrum of a time series at zero frequency*. (See Anderson (1971, Ch. 8) for further discussion.) This is quite natural, as $\mathbf{V}_n$ can be interpreted precisely as the value of the spectrum of $\mathbf{Z}_t\varepsilon_t$ at zero frequency.

Corollary 6.23 *Suppose the conditions of Theorem 6.21 hold. Then*

$$\mathbf{D}_n^{-1/2}\sqrt{n}(\tilde{\boldsymbol{\beta}}_n - \boldsymbol{\beta}_o) \stackrel{A}{\sim} N(\mathbf{0}, \mathbf{I}),$$

where

$$\mathbf{D}_n \equiv (\mathbf{Q}_n'\mathbf{P}_n\mathbf{Q}_n)^{-1}\mathbf{Q}_n'\mathbf{P}_n\mathbf{V}_n\mathbf{P}_n\mathbf{Q}_n(\mathbf{Q}_n'\mathbf{P}_n\mathbf{Q}_n)^{-1}.$$

Further, $\hat{\mathbf{D}}_n - \mathbf{D}_n \xrightarrow{p} \mathbf{0}$*, where*

$$\hat{\mathbf{D}}_n = (\mathbf{X}'\mathbf{Z}\hat{\mathbf{P}}_n\mathbf{Z}'\mathbf{X}/n^2)^{-1}(\mathbf{X}'\mathbf{Z}/n)\hat{\mathbf{P}}_n\tilde{\mathbf{V}}_n\hat{\mathbf{P}}_n(\mathbf{Z}'\mathbf{Z}/n)(\mathbf{X}'\mathbf{Z}\hat{\mathbf{P}}_n\mathbf{Z}'\mathbf{X}/n^2)^{-1}.$$

Proof. Immediate from Theorem 5.23 and Theorem 6.21. ■

This result contains versions of all preceding asymptotic normality results as special cases while making minimal assumptions on the error covariance structure.

Finally, we state a general result for the 2SIV estimator.

Corollary 6.24 *Suppose*

(*i*) $\mathbf{Y}_t = \mathbf{X}_t'\boldsymbol{\beta}_o + \varepsilon_t, \quad t = 1, 2, \ldots, \quad \boldsymbol{\beta}_o \in \mathbb{R}^k$;

(*ii*) $\{(\mathbf{Z}_t', \mathbf{X}_t', \varepsilon_t)\}$ *is a mixing sequence with either* ϕ *of size* $-r/(r-1)$ *or* α *of size* $-2r/(r-2)$, $r > 2$;

(*iii*) (*a*) $E(\mathbf{Z}_t\varepsilon_t) = \mathbf{0}, \quad t = 1, 2, \ldots$;

(*b*) $E|Z_{thi}\varepsilon_{th}|^{2(r+\delta)} < \Delta < \infty$ *for some* $\delta > 0$ *and all* $h = 1, \ldots, p$, $i = 1, \ldots, l$, *and* $t = 1, 2, \ldots$;

(*c*) $\mathbf{V}_n \equiv \text{var}(n^{-1/2}\sum_{t=1}^{n}\mathbf{Z}_t\varepsilon_t)$ *is uniformly positive definite;*

(iv) *(a)* $E|Z_{thi}X_{thj}|^{2(r+\delta)} < \Delta < \infty$ *and* $E|Z_{thi}|^{(r+\delta)} < \Delta < \infty$ *for some* $\delta > 0$ *and all* $h = 1, \ldots, p$, $i = 1, \ldots, l$, $j = 1, \ldots, k$, *and* $t = 1, 2, \ldots$;

(b) $\mathbf{Q}_n \equiv E(\mathbf{Z}'\mathbf{X}/n)$ *has uniformly full column rank;*

(c) $\mathbf{L}_n \equiv E(\mathbf{Z}'\mathbf{Z}/n)$ *is uniformly positive definite.*

Define

$$\begin{aligned}\tilde{\mathbf{V}}_n &\equiv w_{n0}\, n^{-1} \sum_{t=1}^{n} \mathbf{Z}_t \tilde{\boldsymbol{\varepsilon}}_t \tilde{\boldsymbol{\varepsilon}}_t' \mathbf{Z}_t' \\ &\quad + n^{-1} \sum_{\tau=1}^{m_n} w_{n\tau} \sum_{t=\tau+1}^{n} \mathbf{Z}_t \tilde{\boldsymbol{\varepsilon}}_t \tilde{\boldsymbol{\varepsilon}}_{t-\tau}' \mathbf{Z}_{t-\tau}' + \mathbf{Z}_{t-\tau} \tilde{\boldsymbol{\varepsilon}}_{t-\tau} \tilde{\boldsymbol{\varepsilon}}_t' \mathbf{Z}_t',\end{aligned}$$

where $\tilde{\boldsymbol{\varepsilon}}_t \equiv \mathbf{Y}_t - \mathbf{X}_t'\tilde{\boldsymbol{\beta}}_n$, $\tilde{\boldsymbol{\beta}}_n \equiv (\mathbf{X}'\mathbf{Z}(\mathbf{Z}'\mathbf{Z})^{-1}\mathbf{Z}'\mathbf{X})^{-1}\mathbf{X}'\mathbf{Z}(\mathbf{Z}'\mathbf{Z})^{-1}\mathbf{Z}'\mathbf{Y}$, *and define*

$$\boldsymbol{\beta}_n^* \equiv (\mathbf{X}'\mathbf{Z}\tilde{\mathbf{V}}_n^{-1}\mathbf{Z}'\mathbf{X})^{-1}\mathbf{X}'\mathbf{Z}\tilde{\mathbf{V}}_n^{-1}\mathbf{Z}'\mathbf{Y}.$$

If $m_n \to \infty$ *as* $n \to \infty$ *such that* $m_n = o(n^{1/4})$ *and if* $|w_{n\tau}| \leq \Delta$, $n = 1, 2, \ldots$, $\tau = 1, \ldots, m_n$ *such that* $w_{n\tau} \to 1$ *as* $n \to \infty$ *for each* τ, *then* $\mathbf{D}_n^{-1/2}\sqrt{n}(\boldsymbol{\beta}_n^* - \boldsymbol{\beta}_o) \overset{A}{\sim} N(\mathbf{0}, \mathbf{I})$, *where*

$$\mathbf{D}_n = (\mathbf{Q}_n'\mathbf{V}_n^{-1}\mathbf{Q}_n)^{-1}.$$

Further, $\tilde{\mathbf{D}}_n - \mathbf{D}_n \xrightarrow{p} \mathbf{0}$, *where*

$$\tilde{\mathbf{D}}_n = (\mathbf{X}'\mathbf{Z}\tilde{\mathbf{V}}_n^{-1}\mathbf{Z}'\mathbf{X}/n^2)^{-1}.$$

Proof. Conditions *(i)*–*(iv)* ensure that Theorem 6.21 holds for $\tilde{\boldsymbol{\beta}}_n$. Set $\hat{\mathbf{P}}_n = \tilde{\mathbf{V}}_n^{-1}$ in Corollary 6.23. Then $\mathbf{P}_n = \mathbf{V}_n^{-1}$, and the result follows. ∎

References

Anderson, T. W. (1971). *The Statistical Analysis of Time Series.* Wiley, New York.

Andrews, D. W. K. (1991). "Heteroskedasticity and autocorrelation consistent covariance matrix estimation." *Econometrica*, 59, 817–858.

Bartlett, M. S. (1950). "Periodogram analysis and continuous spectra." *Biometrika*, 37, 1–16.

Den Haan, W. J. and A. T. Levin (1997). "A practitioner's guide to robust covariance matrix estimation." In *Handbook of Statistics*, vol. 15, G. S. Maddala and C. R. Rao, eds., pp. 309–327. Elsevier, Amsterdam.

Gallant, A. R. and H. White (1988). *A Unified Theory of Estimation and Inference for Nonlinear Dynamic Models.* Basil Blackwell, Oxford.

McLeish, D. L. (1975). "A maximal inequality and dependent strong laws." *Annals of Probability*, 3, 826–836.

Newey, W. and K. West (1987). "A simple positive semi-definite, heteroskedasticity and autocorrelation consistent covariance matrix." *Econometrica*, 55, 703–708.

Phillips, P. C. B. (1985). Personal communication.

White, H. (1980). "A heteroskedasticity-consistent covariance matrix estimator and a direct test for heteroskedasticity." *Econometrica*, 48, 817–838.

——— (1982). "Instrumental variables regression with independent observations." *Econometrica*, 50, 483–500.

——— (1984). *Asymptotic Theory for Econometricians.* Academic Press, Orlando.

CHAPTER 7

Functional Central Limit Theory and Applications

The conditions imposed on the random elements of $\mathbf{X}_t$, $\mathbf{Y}_t$, and $\mathbf{Z}_t$ appearing in the previous chapters have required that certain moments be bounded, e.g., $E|X_{thi}^2|^{1+\delta} < \Delta < \infty$ for some $\delta > 0$ and for all t (Exercise 5.12 (*iv.a*)). In fact, many economic time-series processes, especially those relevant for macroeconomics or finance violate this restriction. In this chapter, we develop tools to handle such processes.

7.1 Random Walks and Wiener Processes

We begin by considering the random walk, defined as follows.

Definition 7.1 (Random walk) *Let $\{\mathcal{X}_t\}$ be generated according to $\mathcal{X}_t = \mathcal{X}_{t-1} + \mathcal{Z}_t$, $t = 1, 2, \ldots$, where $\mathcal{X}_0 = 0$ and $\{\mathcal{Z}_t\}$ is i.i.d. with $E(\mathcal{Z}_t) = 0$ and $0 < \sigma^2 \equiv \text{var}(\mathcal{Z}_t) < \infty$. Then $\{\mathcal{X}_t\}$ is a* random walk.

By repeated substitution we have

$$\begin{aligned}
\mathcal{X}_t &= \mathcal{X}_{t-1} + \mathcal{Z}_t = \mathcal{X}_{t-2} + \mathcal{Z}_{t-1} + \mathcal{Z}_t \\
&= \mathcal{X}_0 + \sum_{s=1}^{t} \mathcal{Z}_s \\
&= \sum_{s=1}^{t} \mathcal{Z}_s,
\end{aligned}$$

as we have assumed $\mathcal{X}_0 = 0$. It is straightforward to establish the following fact.

Exercise 7.2 *If* $\{\mathcal{X}_t\}$ *is a random walk, then* $E(\mathcal{X}_t) = 0$ *and* $\text{var}(\mathcal{X}_t) = t\sigma^2$, $t = 1, 2, \ldots$.

Because $E(\mathcal{X}_t^2)^{1/2} \leq E(|\mathcal{X}_t|^r)^{\frac{1}{r}}$ for all $r \geq 2$ (Jensen's Inequality), a random walk $\mathcal{X}_t$ cannot satisfy $E|\mathcal{X}_t^2|^{1+\delta} < \Delta < \infty$ for all t (set $r = 2(1+\delta)$). Thus when $\mathbf{X}_t$, $\mathbf{Y}_t$, or $\mathbf{Z}_t$ contain random walks, the results of the previous chapters do not apply.

One way to handle such situations is to transform the process so that it *does* satisfy conditions of the sort previously imposed. For example, we can take the "first difference" of a random walk to get $\mathcal{Z}_t = \mathcal{X}_t - \mathcal{X}_{t-1}$ (which is i.i.d.) and base subsequent analysis on $\mathcal{Z}_t$.

Nevertheless, it is frequently of interest to examine the behavior of estimators that do not make use of such transformations, but that instead directly involve random walks or similar processes. For example, consider the least squares estimator $\hat{\beta}_n = (\mathbf{X}'\mathbf{X})^{-1}\mathbf{X}'\mathbf{Y}$, where $\mathbf{X}$ is $n \times 1$ with $X_t = Y_{t-1}$, and Y_t is a random walk. To study the behavior of such estimators, we make use of *Functional* Central Limit Theorems (FCLTs), which extend the Central Limit Theorems (CLTs) studied previously in just the right way.

Before we can study the behavior of estimators based on random walks or similar processes, we must understand in more detail the behavior of the processes themselves. This also directly enables us to understand the way in which the FCLT extends the CLT

Thus, consider the random walk $\{\mathcal{X}_t\}$. We can write

$$\mathcal{X}_n = \sum_{t=1}^{n} \mathcal{Z}_t.$$

Rescaling, we have

$$n^{-1/2}\mathcal{X}_n/\sigma = n^{-1/2}\sum_{t=1}^{n} \mathcal{Z}_t/\sigma.$$

According to the Lindeberg-Lévy central limit theorem, we have

$$n^{-1/2}\mathcal{X}_n/\sigma \xrightarrow{d} N(0,1).$$

Thus, when n is large, outcomes of the random walk process are drawn from a distribution that is approximately normally distributed.

Next, consider the behavior of the *partial sum*

$$\mathcal{X}_{[an]} = \sum_{t=1}^{[an]} \mathcal{Z}_t,$$

where $1/n \leq a < \infty$ and $[an]$ represents the largest integer less than or equal to an. For $0 \leq a < 1/n$, define $\mathcal{X}_{[an]} = \mathcal{X}_0 = 0$, so the partial sum is now defined for all $0 \leq a < \infty$. Applying the same rescaling, we define

$$\begin{aligned} \mathcal{W}_n(a) &\equiv n^{-1/2}\mathcal{X}_{[an]}/\sigma \\ &= n^{-1/2}\sum_{t=1}^{[an]} \mathcal{Z}_t/\sigma. \end{aligned}$$

Now

$$\mathcal{W}_n(a) = n^{-1/2}\,[an]^{1/2}\left\{[an]^{-1/2}\sum_{t=1}^{[an]}\mathcal{Z}_t/\sigma\right\},$$

and for given a, the term in the brackets $\{\cdot\}$ again obeys the CLT and converges in distribution to $N(0,1)$, whereas $n^{-1/2}\,[an]^{1/2}$ converges to $a^{1/2}$. It follows from now standard arguments that $\mathcal{W}_n(a)$ converges in distribution to $N(0,a)$.

We have written $\mathcal{W}_n(a)$ so that it is clear that $\mathcal{W}_n$ can be considered to be a function of a. Also, because $\mathcal{W}_n(a)$ depends on the $\mathcal{Z}_t$'s, it is random. Therefore, we can think of $\mathcal{W}_n(a)$ as defining a *random function* of a, which we write $\mathcal{W}_n$. Just as the CLT provides conditions ensuring that the rescaled random walk $n^{-1/2}\mathcal{X}_n/\sigma$ (which we can now write as $\mathcal{W}_n(1)$) converges, as n becomes large, to a well-defined limiting random variable (the standard normal), the FCLT provides conditions ensuring that the random function $\mathcal{W}_n$ converges, as n becomes large, to a well-defined limiting random function, say $\mathcal{W}$. The word "Functional" in Functional Central Limit Theorem appears because this limit is a function of a.

The limiting random function specified by the FCLT is, as we should expect, a generalization of the standard normal random variable. This limit is called a Wiener process or a Brownian motion in honor of Norbert Wiener (1923, 1924), who provided the mathematical foundation for the theory of random motions observed and described by nineteenth century botanist Robert Brown in 1827. Of further historical interest is the fact that in his dissertation, Bachelier (1900) proposed the Brownian motion as a model for stock prices.

Before we formally characterize the Wiener process, we note some further properties of random walks, suitably rescaled.

Exercise 7.3 *If* $\{\mathcal{X}_t\}$ *is a random walk, then* $\mathcal{X}_{t_4} - \mathcal{X}_{t_3}$ *is independent of* $\mathcal{X}_{t_2} - \mathcal{X}_{t_1}$ *for all* $t_1 < t_2 < t_3 < t_4$. *Consequently,* $\mathcal{W}_n(a_4) - \mathcal{W}_n(a_3)$ *is independent of* $\mathcal{W}_n(a_2) - \mathcal{W}_n(a_1)$ *for all* a_i *such that* $[a_i n] = t_i$, $i = 1, \ldots, 4$.

Exercise 7.4 *For given* $0 \leq a < b < \infty$, $\mathcal{W}_n(b) - \mathcal{W}_n(a) \xrightarrow{d} N(0, b-a)$ *as* $n \to \infty$.

In words, the random walk has *independent increments* (Exercise 7.3) and those increments have a limiting normal distribution, with a variance reflecting the size of the interval $(b-a)$ over which the increment is taken (Exercise 7.4).

It should not be surprising, therefore, that the limit of the sequence of functions $\{\mathcal{W}_n\}$ constructed from the random walk preserves these properties in the limit in an appropriate sense. In fact, these properties form the basis of the definition of the Wiener process.

Definition 7.5 (Wiener process) *Let* $(\Omega, \mathcal{F}, P)$ *be a complete probability space. Then* $\mathcal{W} : [0, \infty) \times \Omega \to \mathbb{R}$ *is a* Wiener process *if for each* $a \in [0, \infty)$, $\mathcal{W}(a, \cdot)$ *is measurable-*$\mathcal{F}$, *and in addition*

(*i*) *The process starts at zero:* $P[\mathcal{W}(0, \cdot) = 0] = 1$.

(*ii*) *The increments are independent: If* $0 \leq a_0 \leq a_1 \leq \ldots \leq a_k < \infty$, *then* $\mathcal{W}(a_i, \cdot) - \mathcal{W}(a_{i-1}, \cdot)$ *is independent of* $\mathcal{W}(a_j, \cdot) - \mathcal{W}(a_{j-1}, \cdot)$, $j = 1, \ldots, k$, $j \neq i$ *for all* $i = 1, \ldots, k$.

(*iii*) *The increments are normally distributed: For* $0 \leq a \leq b < \infty$ *the increment* $\mathcal{W}(b, \cdot) - \mathcal{W}(a, \cdot)$ *is distributed as* $N(0, b-a)$.

In the definition, we have written $\mathcal{W}(a, \cdot)$ for explicitness; whenever convenient, however, we will write $\mathcal{W}(a)$ instead of $\mathcal{W}(a, \cdot)$, analogous to our notation elsewhere.

Fundamental facts about the Wiener process are simple to state, but somewhat involved to prove. The interested reader may consult Billingsley (1979, Section 37) or Davidson (1994, Chapter 27) for further background and details. We record the following facts.

Proposition 7.6 *The Wiener process* $\mathcal{W}$ *exists; that is, there exists a function* $\mathcal{W}$ *satisfying the conditions of Definition 7.5.*

Proof. See Billingsley (1979, pp. 443–444). ∎

Proposition 7.7 *There exists a Wiener process $\mathcal{W}$ such that for all $\omega \in \Omega$, $\mathcal{W}(0, \omega) = 0$ and $\mathcal{W}(\cdot, \omega) : [0, \infty) \to \mathbb{R}$ is continuous on $[0, \infty)$.*

Proof. See Billingsley (1979, pp. 444–447). ∎

When $\mathcal{W}$ has the properties established in Proposition 7.7 we say that $\mathcal{W}$ has *continuous sample paths*. ($\mathcal{W}(\cdot, \omega)$ is a *sample path*.) From now on, when we speak of a Wiener process, we shall have in mind one with continuous sample paths.

Even though $\mathcal{W}$ has continuous sample paths, these paths are highly irregular: they wiggle extravagantly, as the next result makes precise.

Proposition 7.8 *For $\omega \in F$, $P(F) = 1$, $\mathcal{W}(\cdot, \omega)$ is nowhere differentiable.*

Proof. See Billingsley (1979, pp. 450–451). ∎

With these basic facts in place, we can now consider the sense in which $\mathcal{W}_n$ converges to $\mathcal{W}$. Because $\mathcal{W}_n$ is a random function, our available notions of stochastic convergence for random variables are inadequate. Nevertheless, we can extend these notions naturally in a way that enables the extension to adequately treat the convergence of $\mathcal{W}_n$. Our main tool will be an extension of the notion of convergence in distribution known as *weak convergence*.

7.2 Weak Convergence

To obtain the right notion for weak convergence of $\mathcal{W}_n$, we need to consider what sort of function $\mathcal{W}_n$ is. Recall that by definition

$$\mathcal{W}_n(a) \equiv n^{-1/2} \sum_{s=1}^{[an]} \mathcal{Z}_s / \sigma.$$

Fix a realization $\omega \in \Omega$, and suppose that we first choose a so that for some integer t, $an = t$ (i.e., $a = t/n$). Then we will consider what happens as a increases to the value $(t+1)/n$. With $a = t/n$ we have $[an] = t$, so

$$\mathcal{W}_n(a, \omega) = n^{-1/2} \sum_{s=1}^{t} \mathcal{Z}_s(\omega)/\sigma, \quad a = t/n.$$

For $t/n < a < (t+1)/n$, we still have $[an] = t$, so

$$\mathcal{W}_n(a, \omega) = n^{-1/2} \sum_{s=1}^{t} \mathcal{Z}_s(\omega)/\sigma, \quad t/n < a < (t+1)/n.$$

That is, $\mathcal{W}_n(a, \omega)$ is constant for $t/n \leq a < (t+1)/n$. When a hits $(t+1)/n$, we see that $\mathcal{W}_n(a, \omega)$ jumps to

$$\mathcal{W}_n(a, \omega) = n^{-1/2} \sum_{s=1}^{t+1} \mathcal{Z}_s(\omega)/\sigma, \quad a = (t+1)/n.$$

Thus, for given ω, $\mathcal{W}_n(\cdot, \omega)$ is a piecewise constant function that jumps to a new value whenever $a = t/n$ for integer t. This is a simple example of a function that is said to be *right continuous with left limit* (*rcll*), also referred to as *cadlag* (*continue à droite, limites à gauche*). It follows that we need a notion of convergence that applies to functions $\mathcal{W}_n(\cdot, \omega)$ that are rcll on $[0, \infty)$ for each ω in Ω.

Formally, we define the rcll functions on $[0, \infty)$ as follows.

Definition 7.9 (rcll) *$D[0, \infty)$ is the space of functions $f : [0, \infty) \to \mathbb{R}$ that (i) are* right continuous *and (ii) have* left limits *(rcll):*

(i) For $0 \leq a < \infty$, $f(a^+) \equiv \lim_{b \downarrow a} f(b)$ exists and $f(a^+) = f(a)$.

(ii) For $0 < a < \infty$, $f(a^-) \equiv \lim_{b \uparrow a} f(b)$ exists.

In this definition, the notation $\lim_{b \downarrow a}$ means the limit as b approaches a from the right ($a < b$) while $\lim_{b \uparrow a}$ means the limit as b approaches a from the left ($b < a$).

The space $C[0, \infty)$ of continuous functions on $[0, \infty)$ is a subspace of the space $D[0, \infty)$. By Proposition 7.7, $\mathcal{W}(\cdot, \omega)$ belongs to $C[0, \infty)$ (and therefore $D[0, \infty)$) for all $\omega \in \Omega$, whereas $\mathcal{W}_n(\cdot, \omega)$ belongs to $D[0, \infty)$ for all $\omega \in \Omega$.

Thus, we need an appropriate notion for weak convergence of a sequence of random elements of $D[0, \infty)$ analogous to our notion of convergence in distribution to a random element of $\mathbb{R}$.

To this end, recall that if $\{\mathcal{X}_n\}$ is a sequence of real-valued random numbers then $\mathcal{X}_n \xrightarrow{d} \mathcal{X}$ if $F_n(x) \to F(x)$ for every continuity point x of F, where F_n is the c.d.f. of $\mathcal{X}_n$ and F is the c.d.f. of $\mathcal{X}$ (Definition 4.1). By definition,

$$\begin{aligned} F_n(x) &\equiv P\{\omega : \mathcal{X}_n(\omega) \leq x\} \\ &= P\{\omega : \mathcal{X}_n(\omega) \in B_x\} \end{aligned}$$

and

$$\begin{aligned} F(x) &\equiv P\{\omega : \mathcal{X}(\omega) \leq x\} \\ &= P\{\omega : \mathcal{X}(\omega) \in B_x\}, \end{aligned}$$

where $B_x \equiv (-\infty, x]$ (a Borel set). Let $\mu_n(B_x) \equiv P\{\omega : \mathcal{X}_n(\omega) \in B_x\}$ and $\mu(B_x) \equiv P\{\omega : \mathcal{X}(\omega) \in B_x\}$. Then convergence in distribution holds if $\mu_n(B_x) \to \mu(B_x)$ for all sets B_x such that x is a continuity point of F.

Observe that x is a continuity point of F if and only if $\mu(\{x\}) = 0$, that is, the probability that $\mathcal{X} = x$ is zero. Also note that x is distinctive because it lies on the boundary of the set B_x. Formally, the *boundary* of a set B, denoted ∂B, is the set of all points not interior to B. For B_x, we have $\partial B_x = \{x\}$. Thus, when x is a continuity point of F, we have $\mu(\partial B_x) = 0$, and we call B_x a *continuity set* of μ; in general, any Borel set B such that $\mu(\partial B) = 0$ is called a continuity set of μ, or a *μ-continuity set.*

Thus, convergence in distribution occurs whenever

$$\mu_n(B) \to \mu(B)$$

for all continuity sets B. Clearly, this implies the original Definition 4.1, because that definition can be restated as

$$\mu_n(B_x) \to \mu(B_x)$$

for all continuity sets of the form $B_x = (-\infty, x]$. It turns out, however, that these two requirements are equivalent. Either can serve as a definition of convergence in distribution.

In fact, the formulation in terms of generic continuity sets B is ideally suited for direct extension from real valued random variables $\mathcal{X}_n$ and Borel sets B (subsets of $\mathbb{R}$) not only to $D[0,\infty)$-valued random functions $\mathcal{W}_n$ and suitable Borel subsets of $D[0,\infty)$, but also to random elements of metric spaces generally and their Borel subsets. This latter fact is not just of abstract interest — it plays a key role in the analysis of spurious regression and cointegration, as we shall see next.

The required Borel subsets of $D[0,\infty)$ can be generated from the open sets of $D[0,\infty)$ in a manner precisely analogous to that in which we can generate the Borel subsets of $\mathbb{R}$ from the open sets of $\mathbb{R}$ (recall Definition 3.18 and the following comments). However, because of the richness of the set $D[0,\infty)$ we have considerable latitude in defining what we mean by an open set, and we will therefore need to exercise care in defining what an open set is. For our purposes, it is useful to define open sets using a metric d on $D[0,\infty)$.

Let S be a set (e.g., $S = D[0,\infty)$ or $S = \mathbb{R}$). A *metric* is a mapping $d : S \times S \to \mathbb{R}$ with the properties (*i*) (*nonnegativity*) $d(x,y) \geq 0$ for all $x, y \in S$, and $d(x,y) = 0$ if and only if $x = y$; (*ii*) (*symmetry*) $d(x,y) = d(y,x)$ for all $x, y \in S$; (*iii*) (*triangle inequality*) $d(x,y) \leq d(x,z) + d(z,y)$ for all $x, y, z \in S$. We call the pair (S, d) a *metric space*. For example, $d_{|\cdot|}(x,y) = |x - y|$ defines a metric on $\mathbb{R}$, and $(\mathbb{R}, d_{|\cdot|})$ is a metric space.

By definition, a subset A of S is *open in the metric* d (*d-open*) if every point x of A is an interior point; that is, for some $\varepsilon > 0$, the ε-neighborhood of x, $\{y \in S : d(x,y) < \varepsilon\}$, is a subset of A. We can now define the Borel sets of S.

Definition 7.10 *Let d be a metric on S. The Borel σ-field $\mathcal{S}_d = \mathcal{B}(S,d)$ is the smallest collection of sets (the Borel sets of S with respect to d) that includes*

(*i*) *all d-open subsets of S;*

(*ii*) *the complement B^c of any set B in $\mathcal{S}_d$;*

(*iii*) *the union $\bigcup_{i=1}^{\infty} B_i$ of any sequence $\{B_i\}$ in $\mathcal{S}_d$.*

Observe that different choices for the metric d may generate different Borel σ-fields. When the metric d is understood implicitly, we suppress explicit reference and just write $\mathcal{S} = \mathcal{S}_d$.

Putting $S = \mathbb{R}$ or $S = \mathbb{R}^k$ and letting d be the Euclidean metric ($d(x,y) = \|x - y\| = ((x-y)'(x-y))^{1/2}$) gives the Borel σ-fields $\mathcal{B}(\mathbb{R})$ or $\mathcal{B}(\mathbb{R}^k)$ introduced in Chapter 3. Putting $S = D[0,\infty)$ and choosing d suitably will give us the needed Borel sets of $D[0,\infty)$, denoted $\mathcal{D}_{\infty,d} \equiv \mathcal{B}(D[0,\infty),d)$.

The pair $(S, \mathcal{S}_d)$ is a *metrized measurable space.* We obtain a *metrized probability space* $(S, \mathcal{S}_d, \mu)$ by requiring that μ be a probability measure on $(S, \mathcal{S}_d)$.

We can now give the desired definition of weak convergence.

Definition 7.11 (Weak convergence) *Let μ, μ_n, $n = 1, 2, \ldots$, be probability measures on the metrized measurable space $(S, \mathcal{S})$. Then μ_n* converges weakly *to μ, written $\mu_n \Rightarrow \mu$ or $\mu_n \xrightarrow{d} \mu$ if $\mu_n(A) \to \mu(A)$ as $n \to \infty$ for all μ-continuity sets A of $\mathcal{S}$.*

The parallel with the case of real-valued random variables $\mathcal{X}_n$ is now clear from this definition and our discussion following Definition 7.9. Indeed, Definition 4.1 is equivalent to Definition 7.11 when $(S, \mathcal{S}) = (\mathbb{R}, \mathcal{B})$.

An equivalent definition can be posed in terms of suitably defined integrals of real-valued functions. Specifically $\mu_n \Rightarrow \mu$ if and only if

$$\int f d\mu_n \to \int f d\mu \quad \text{as } n \to \infty$$

for all bounded uniformly continuous functions $f : S \to \mathbb{R}$. (See Billingsley, 1968, pp. 11–14). We use Definition 7.11 because of its straightforward relation to Definition 4.1.

Convergence of random elements on $(S, \mathcal{S})$ is covered by our next definition.

Definition 7.12 *Let $\mathcal{V}_n$ and $\mathcal{V}$ be random elements on $(S, \mathcal{S})$; that is $\mathcal{V}_n : \Omega \to S$ and $\mathcal{V} : \Omega \to S$ are measurable functions on a probability space $(\Omega, \mathcal{F}, P)$. Then we say that $\mathcal{V}_n$* converges weakly *to $\mathcal{V}$, denoted $\mathcal{V}_n \Rightarrow \mathcal{V}$, provided that $\mu_n \Rightarrow \mu$, where $\mu_n(A) \equiv P\{\omega : \mathcal{V}_n(\omega) \in A\}$ and $\mu(A) \equiv P\{\omega : \mathcal{V}(\omega) \in A\}$ for $A \in \mathcal{S}$.*

7.3 Functional Central Limit Theorems

In previous sections we have defined the functions $\mathcal{W}_n$ and the Wiener process $\mathcal{W}$ in the natural and usual way as functions mapping $[0, \infty) \times \Omega$ to the real line, $\mathbb{R}$. Typically, however, the Functional Central Limit Theorem (FCLT) and our applications of the FCLT, to which we now turn our attention, are concerned with the convergence of a restricted version of $\mathcal{W}_n$, defined by

$$\mathcal{W}_n(a, \omega) = n^{-1/2} \sum_{s=1}^{[an]} \mathcal{Z}_s(\omega)/\sigma, \quad 0 \leq a \leq 1.$$

For convenience, we continue to use the same notation, but now we have $\mathcal{W}_n : [0, 1] \times \Omega \to \mathbb{R}$ and we view $\mathcal{W}_n(a)$ as defining a random element of $D[0, 1]$, the functions on $[0, 1]$ that are right continuous with left limits.

The FCLT provides conditions under which $\mathcal{W}_n$ converges to the Wiener process restricted to $[0, 1]$, which we continue to write as $\mathcal{W}$. We now view $\mathcal{W}(a)$ as defining a random element of $C[0, 1]$, the continuous functions on the unit interval.

In treating the FCLT, we will always be dealing with $D[0, 1]$ and $C[0, 1]$. Accordingly, in this context we write $D = D[0, 1]$ and $C = C[0, 1]$ to keep the notation simple. No confusion will arise from this shorthand.

The measures whose convergence are the subject of the Functional Central Limit Theorem (FCLT) can be defined as

$$\mu_n(A) \equiv P\{\omega : \mathcal{W}_n(\cdot, \omega) \in A\},$$

where $A \in \mathcal{D} = \mathcal{D}_d$ for a suitable choice of metric d on D.

A study of the precise properties of the metrics typically used in this context cannot adequately be pursued here. Suffice it to say that excellent treatments can be found in Billingsley (1968, Chapter 3) and Davidson

(1994, Chapter 28), where Billingsley's modification d_B of the Skorokhod metric d_S is shown to be ideally suited for studying the FCLT. The Skorokhod metric d_S is itself a modification of the uniform metric d_u such that $d_u(\mathcal{U}, \mathcal{V}) = \sup_{a \in [0,1]} |\mathcal{U}(a) - \mathcal{V}(a)|$, $\mathcal{U}, \mathcal{V} \in D$.

The fact that $\mathcal{W}_n(a, \cdot)$ is measurable for each a is enough to ensure that the set $\{\omega : \mathcal{W}_n(\cdot, \omega) \in A\}$ is a measurable set, so that the probability defining μ_n is well-defined. This is a consequence of Theorem 14.5 of Billingsley (1968, p. 121).

The Functional Central Limit Theorem provides conditions under which μ_n converges weakly to the *Wiener measure* $\mu_{\mathcal{W}}$, defined as

$$\mu_{\mathcal{W}}(A) \equiv P\{\omega : \mathcal{W}(\cdot, \omega) \in A \cap C\},$$

where $A \in \mathcal{D}$ and $C = C[0,1]$. When $\mu_n \Rightarrow \mu_{\mathcal{W}}$ for μ_n and $\mu_{\mathcal{W}}$ as just defined, we say that $\mathcal{W}_n$ *obeys the FCLT.*

The simplest FCLT is a generalization of the Lindeberg-Lévy CLT, known as Donsker's theorem (Donsker, 1951).

Theorem 7.13 (Donsker) *Let $\{\mathcal{Z}_t\}$ be a sequence of i.i.d. random scalars with mean zero. If $\sigma^2 \equiv \text{var}(\mathcal{Z}_t) < \infty$, $\sigma^2 \neq 0$, then $\mathcal{W}_n \Rightarrow \mathcal{W}$.*

Proof. See the proof given by Billingsley (1968, Theorem 16.1, pp. 137–138). ∎

Because pointwise convergence in distribution $\mathcal{W}_n(a, \cdot) \xrightarrow{d} \mathcal{W}(a, \cdot)$ for each $a \in [0,1]$ is necessary (but not sufficient) for weak convergence ($\mathcal{W}_n \Rightarrow \mathcal{W}$), the Lindeberg-Lévy Central Limit Theorem ($\mathcal{W}_n(1, \cdot) \xrightarrow{d} \mathcal{W}(1, \cdot)$) follows immediately from Donsker's theorem. Donsker's theorem is strictly stronger than Lindeberg-Lévy however, as both use identical assumptions, but Donsker's theorem delivers a much stronger conclusion.

Donsker called his result an *invariance principle*. Consequently, the FCLT is often referred to as an invariance principle.

So far, we have assumed that the sequence $\{\mathcal{Z}_t\}$ used to construct $\mathcal{W}_n$ is i.i.d. Nevertheless, just as we can obtain central limit theorems when $\{\mathcal{Z}_t\}$ is not necessarily i.i.d., so also can we obtain functional central limit theorems when $\{\mathcal{Z}_t\}$ is not necessarily i.i.d. In fact, versions of the FCLT hold for each CLT previously given.

To make the statements of our FCLTs less cumbersome than they would otherwise be, we use the following condition.

Definition 7.14 (Global covariance stationarity) *Let $\{\boldsymbol{\mathcal{Z}}_t\}$ be a sequence of $k \times 1$ random vectors such that $E(\boldsymbol{\mathcal{Z}}_t' \boldsymbol{\mathcal{Z}}_t) < \infty$, $t = 1, 2, \ldots$, and define $\boldsymbol{\Sigma}_n \equiv \text{var}(n^{-1/2} \sum_{t=1}^n \boldsymbol{\mathcal{Z}}_t)$. If $\boldsymbol{\Sigma} \equiv \lim_{n \to \infty} \boldsymbol{\Sigma}_n$ exists and is finite,* *then we say that* $\{\mathcal{Z}_t\}$ *is* globally covariance stationary. *We call* $\mathbf{\Sigma}$ *the* global covariance matrix.

For our CLTs, we have required only that $\mathbf{\Sigma}_n = O(1)$. FCLTs can be given under this weaker requirement, but both the conditions and conclusions are more complicated to state. (See for example Wooldridge and White, 1988, and Davidson, 1994, Ch. 29.) Imposing the global covariance stationarity requirement gains us clarity at the cost of a mild restriction on the allowed heterogeneity. Note that global covariance stationarity does *not* require us to assume that $E(\mathcal{Z}_t\mathcal{Z}'_{t-\tau}) = E(\mathcal{Z}_s\mathcal{Z}'_{s-\tau})$ for all t, s, and τ (covariance stationarity).

We give the following FCLTs.

Theorem 7.15 (Lindeberg-Feller i.n.i.d. FCLT) *Suppose* $\{\mathcal{Z}_t\}$ *satisfies the conditions of the Lindeberg-Feller central limit theorem (Theorem 5.6), and suppose that* $\{\mathcal{Z}_t\}$ *is globally covariance stationary. If* $\sigma^2 \equiv \lim_{n\to\infty} \text{var}(\mathcal{W}_n(1)) > 0$, *then* $\mathcal{W}_n \Rightarrow \mathcal{W}$.

Proof. This is a straightforward consequence of Theorem 15.4 of Billingsley (1968). ■

Theorem 7.16 (Liapounov i.n.i.d. FCLT) *Suppose* $\{\mathcal{Z}_t\}$ *satisfies the conditions of the Liapounov central limit theorem (Theorem 5.10) and suppose that* $\{\mathcal{Z}_t\}$ *is globally covariance stationary. If* $\sigma^2 \equiv \lim_{n\to\infty} \text{var}(\mathcal{W}_n(1)) > 0$, *then* $\mathcal{W}_n \Rightarrow \mathcal{W}$.

Proof. This follows immediately from Theorem 7.15, as the Liapounov moment condition implies the Lindeberg-Feller condition. ■

Theorem 7.17 (Stationary ergodic FCLT) *Suppose* $\{\mathcal{Z}_t\}$ *satisfies the conditions of the stationary ergodic CLT (Theorem 5.16). If* $\sigma^2 \equiv \lim_{n\to\infty} \text{var}(\mathcal{W}_n(1)) > 0$, *then* $\mathcal{W}_n \Rightarrow \mathcal{W}$.

Proof. This follows from Theorem 3 of Scott (1973). ■

Note that the conditions of the stationary ergodic CLT already impose global covariance stationarity, so we do not require an explicit statement of this condition.

Theorem 7.18 (Heterogeneous mixing FCLT) *Suppose* $\{\mathcal{Z}_t\}$ *satisfies the conditions of the heterogeneous mixing CLT (Theorem 5.20) and suppose that* $\{\mathcal{Z}_t\}$ *is globally covariance stationary. If* $\sigma^2 \equiv \lim_{n\to\infty} \text{var}(\mathcal{W}_n(1)) > 0$, *then* $\mathcal{W}_n \Rightarrow \mathcal{W}$.

Proof. See Wooldridge and White (1988, Theorem 2.11) ∎

Theorem 7.19 (Martingale difference FCLT) *Suppose $\{\mathcal{Z}_t\}$ satisfies the conditions of the martingale difference central limit theorem (Theorem 5.24 or Corollary 5.26) and suppose that $\{\mathcal{Z}_t\}$ is globally covariance stationary. If $\sigma^2 \equiv \lim_{n\to\infty} \text{var}(\mathcal{W}_n(1)) > 0$, then $\mathcal{W}_n \Rightarrow \mathcal{W}$.*

Proof. See McLeish (1974). See also Hall (1977). ∎

Whenever $\{\mathcal{Z}_t\}$ satisfies conditions sufficient to ensure $\mathcal{W}_n \Rightarrow \mathcal{W}$, we say $\{\mathcal{Z}_t\}$ *obeys the FCLT*. The dependence and moment conditions under which $\{\mathcal{Z}_t\}$ obeys the FCLT can be relaxed further. For example, Wooldridge and White (1988) give results that do not require global covariance stationarity and that apply to infinite histories of mixing sequences with possibly trending moments. Davidson (1994) contains an excellent exposition of these and related results.

7.4 Regression with a Unit Root

The FCLT and the following extension of Lemma 4.27 give us the tools needed to study regression for "unit root" processes. Our treatment here follows that of Phillips (1987). We begin with an extension of Lemma 4.27.

Theorem 7.20 (Continuous mapping theorem) *Let the pair $(S, \mathcal{S})$ be a metrized measurable space and let μ, μ_n be probability measures on $(S, \mathcal{S})$ corresponding to $\mathcal{V}$, $\mathcal{V}_n$, random elements of S, $n = 1, 2, \ldots$. (i) Let $h : S \to \mathbb{R}$ be a continuous mapping. If $\mathcal{V}_n \Rightarrow \mathcal{V}$, then $h(\mathcal{V}_n) \Rightarrow h(\mathcal{V})$. (ii) Let $h : S \to \mathbb{R}$ be a mapping such that the set of discontinuities of h, $D_h \equiv \{s \in S : \lim_{r\to s} h(r) \neq h(s)\}$ has $\mu(D_h) = 0$. If $\mathcal{V}_n \Rightarrow \mathcal{V}$, then $h(\mathcal{V}_n) \Rightarrow h(\mathcal{V})$.*

Proof. See Billingsley (1968, pp. 29–31). ∎

Using this result, we can now prove an asymptotic distribution result for the least squares estimator with unit root regressors, analogous to Theorem 4.25.

Theorem 7.21 (Unit root regression) *Suppose*

(i) $Y_t = X_t\beta_o + \varepsilon_t$, $t = 1, 2, \ldots$, *where* $X_t = Y_{t-1}$, $\beta_o = 1$, *and* $Y_0 = 0$;

(ii) $\mathcal{W}_n \Rightarrow \mathcal{W}$, *where* $\mathcal{W}_n$ *is defined by* $\mathcal{W}_n(a) \equiv n^{-1/2} \sum_{t=1}^{[an]} \varepsilon_t/\sigma$, $0 \leq a \leq 1$, *where* $\sigma^2 \equiv \lim_{n\to\infty} \text{var}(n^{-1/2} \sum_{t=1}^{n} \varepsilon_t)$ *is finite and nonzero.*

Then

(*a*) $n^{-2}\sum_{t=1}^{n} Y_{t-1}^2 \Rightarrow \sigma^2 \int_0^1 \mathcal{W}(a)^2 da$.

If in addition

(*iii*) $n^{-1}\sum_{t=1}^{n} \varepsilon_t^2 \xrightarrow{p} \tau^2$, $0 < \tau^2 < \infty$,

then

(*b*) $n^{-1}\sum_{t=1}^{n} Y_{t-1}\varepsilon_t \Rightarrow (\sigma^2/2)\left(\mathcal{W}(1)^2 - \tau^2/\sigma^2\right)$;

(*c*) $n(\hat{\beta}_n - 1) \Rightarrow \left[\int_0^1 \mathcal{W}(a)^2 da\right]^{-1} (1/2)\left(\mathcal{W}(1)^2 - \tau^2/\sigma^2\right)$;

and

(*d*) $\hat{\beta}_n \xrightarrow{p} 1$.

Before proceeding to the proof, it is helpful to make some comments concerning both the assumptions and the conclusions.

First, when $\{Y_t\}$ is generated according to assumptions (*i*) and (*ii*) of Theorem 7.21, we will say that $\{Y_t\}$ is an *integrated process*. This nomenclature arises because we can view $Y_n = \sum_{t=1}^{n} \varepsilon_t$ as an "integral" of ε_t, where $\{\varepsilon_t\}$ obeys the FCLT. Integrated processes are also commonly called "unit root" processes. The "unit" root is that of the lag polynomial $B(L)$ ensuring the good behavior of $\varepsilon_t = B(L)Y_t$; see Hamilton (1994) for background and further details. The good behavior of ε_t in this context is often heuristically specified to be stationarity. Nevertheless, the good behavior relevant for us is precisely that $\{\varepsilon_t\}$ obeys the FCLT. Stationarity is neither necessary nor sufficient for the FCLT. For example, if $\{\varepsilon_t\}$ is i.i.d., then $\{\varepsilon_t - \varepsilon_{t-1}\}$ is stationary but does not obey the FCLT. (See Davidson, 1998, for further discussion.)

The unit root process is an extension of the random walk, as we do not require that $\{\varepsilon_t\}$ be i.i.d. Instead, we just require that $\{\varepsilon_t\}$ obeys the FCLT. Donsker's theorem establishes that $\{\varepsilon_t\}$ i.i.d. is sufficient for this, but Theorems 7.15 through 7.19 show that this is not necessary.

In (*i*), we have assumed $Y_0 = 0$. A common alternate assumption is that Y_0 is some random variable; but (*i*) implies instead that Y_1 is some random variable (i.e., ε_1), so, after a reassignment of indexes, the situation is identical either way. In applications, some statistics may be sensitive to the initial value, especially if this is far from zero. A simple way to avoid this sensitivity is to reset the process to zero by subtracting the initial value from all observations and working with the shifted series $\tilde{Y}_t = Y_t - Y_0$, $t = 0, 1, \ldots$, conditional on Y_0.

In conclusion (a), the integral $\int_0^1 \mathcal{W}(a)^2 da$ appears. We interpret this as that random variable, say $\mathcal{M}$, defined by $\mathcal{M}(\omega) \equiv \int_0^1 \mathcal{W}(a,\omega)^2 da$, $\omega \in \Omega$. For fixed ω, this is just a standard (Riemann) integral, so no new integral concept is involved. We now have a situation quite unlike that studied previously. Before, $n^{-1}\sum_{t=1}^n X_t X_t' - M_n$ converged to zero, where $\{M_n\}$ is not random. Here, $n^{-2}\sum_{t=1}^n X_t X_t' = n^{-2}\sum_{t=1}^n Y_{t-1}^2$ converges to a random variable, $\sigma^2 \mathcal{M}$.

In conclusion (b), something similar happens. We have $n^{-1}\sum_{t=1}^n X_t\varepsilon_t = n^{-1}\sum_{t=1}^n Y_{t-1}\varepsilon_t$ converging to a random variable, $(\sigma^2/2)\left(\mathcal{W}(1)^2 - \tau^2/\sigma^2\right)$, whereas in previous chapters we had $n^{-1}\sum_{t=1}^n X_t\varepsilon_t$ converging stochastically to zero. Note that $\mathcal{W}(1)^2$ is χ_1^2 (chi-squared with one degree of freedom) so the expectation of this limiting random variable is

$$E\left((\sigma^2/2)\left(\mathcal{W}(1)^2 - \tau^2/\sigma^2\right)\right) = (\sigma^2/2)\left(1 - \tau^2/\sigma^2\right),$$

from which we see that the expectation is not necessarily zero unless $\tau^2 = \sigma^2$, as happens for the cases in which $\{\varepsilon_t\}$ is an independent or martingale difference sequence.

Together, (a) and (b) imply the asymptotic distribution results for the least squares estimator, conclusion (c). Several things are noteworthy. First, note that the scale factor here is n, not $\sqrt{n}$ as it previously has been. Thus, $\hat{\beta}_n$ is "collapsing" to its limit at a much faster rate than before. This is sometimes called *superconsistency*. Next, note that the limiting distribution is no longer normal; instead, we have a distribution that is a somewhat complicated function of a Wiener process. When $\tau^2 = \sigma^2$ (independent or martingale difference case) we have the distribution of J. S. White (1958, p. 1196), apart from an incorrect scaling there, as noted by Phillips (1987). For $\tau^2 = \sigma^2$, this distribution is also that tabulated by Dickey and Fuller (1979, 1981) in their famous work on testing for unit roots.

In the regression setting studied in previous chapters the existence of serial correlation in ε_t in the presence of a lagged dependent variable regressor leads to the inconsistency of $\hat{\beta}_n$ for β_o, as discussed in earlier chapters. Here, however, the situation is quite different. Even though the regressor is a lagged dependent variable, $\hat{\beta}_n$ is consistent for $\beta_o = 1$ (conclusion (d)) despite the fact that conditions 7.21 (ii) and (iii) permit $\{\varepsilon_t\}$ to display considerable serial correlation.

The effect of the serial correlation is that $\tau^2 \neq \sigma^2$. This results in a shift of the location of the asymptotic distribution away from zero, relative to the $\tau^2 = \sigma^2$ case (no serial correlation). Despite this effect of the serial correlation in $\{\varepsilon_t\}$, we no longer have the serious adverse consequence of inconsistency of $\hat{\beta}_n$.

One way of understanding why this is so is succinctly expressed by Phillips (1987, p. 283):

> Intuitively, when the [data generating process] has a unit root, the strength of the signal (as measured by the sample variation of the regressor Y_{t-1}) dominates the noise by a factor of $O(n)$, so that the effects of any regressor-error correlation are annihilated in the regression as $n \to \infty$. [Notation changed to correspond.]

Note, however, that even when $\tau^2 = \sigma^2$ the asymptotic distribution given in (*c*) is not centered about zero, so an asymptotic bias is still present. The reason for this is that there generally exists a strong (negative) correlation between $\mathcal{W}(1)^2$ and $[\int_0^1 \mathcal{W}(a)^2 da]^{-1}$, resulting from the fact that $\mathcal{W}(1)^2$ and $\mathcal{W}(a)^2$ are highly correlated for each a. Thus, even though $E(\mathcal{W}(1)^2 - \tau^2/\sigma^2) = 0$ with $\tau^2 = \sigma^2$ we do *not* have

$$E\left([\int_0^1 \mathcal{W}(a)^2 da]^{-1}(1/2)(\mathcal{W}(1)^2 - \tau^2/\sigma^2)\right) = 0.$$

See Abadir (1995) for further details.

We are now ready to prove Theorem 7.21, using what is essentially the proof of Phillips (1987, Theorem 3.1).

Proof of Theorem 7.21. (*a*) First rewrite $n^{-2}\sum_{t=1}^n Y_{t-1}^2$ in terms of $\mathcal{W}_n(a_{t-1}) \equiv n^{-1/2}Y_{t-1}/\sigma = n^{-1/2}\sum_{s=1}^{t-1}\varepsilon_s/\sigma$, where $a_{t-1} = (t-1)/n$, so that $n^{-2}\sum_{t=1}^n Y_{t-1}^2 = \sigma^2 n^{-1}\sum_{t=1}^n \mathcal{W}_n(a_{t-1})^2$. Because $\mathcal{W}_n(a)$ is constant for $(t-1)/n \leq a < t/n$, we have

$$\begin{aligned} n^{-1}\sum_{t=1}^n \mathcal{W}_n(a_{t-1})^2 &= \sum_{t=1}^n \int_{(t-1)/n}^{t/n} \mathcal{W}_n(a)^2 da \\ &= \int_0^1 \mathcal{W}_n(a)^2 da. \end{aligned}$$

The continuous mapping theorem applies to $h(\mathcal{W}_n) = \int_0^1 \mathcal{W}_n(a)^2 da$. It follows that $h(\mathcal{W}_n) \Rightarrow h(\mathcal{W})$, so that $n^{-2}\sum_{t=1}^n Y_{t-1}^2 \Rightarrow \sigma^2\int_0^1 \mathcal{W}(a)^2 da$, as claimed.

(*b*) Because $Y_{t-1} = \sigma n^{1/2}\mathcal{W}_n(a_{t-1})$, we have

$$n^{-1}\sum_{t=1}^n Y_{t-1}\varepsilon_t = \sigma n^{-1/2}\sum_{t=1}^n \mathcal{W}_n(a_{t-1})\varepsilon_t.$$

Now $\mathcal{W}_n(a_t) = \mathcal{W}_n(a_{t-1}) + n^{-1/2}\varepsilon_t/\sigma$, so

$$\mathcal{W}_n(a_t)^2 = \mathcal{W}_n(a_{t-1})^2 + n^{-1}\varepsilon_t^2/\sigma^2 + 2n^{-1/2}\mathcal{W}_n(a_{t-1})\varepsilon_t/\sigma.$$

Thus $\sigma n^{-1/2}\mathcal{W}_n(a_{t-1})\varepsilon_t = (1/2)\sigma^2\left(\mathcal{W}_n(a_t)^2 - \mathcal{W}_n(a_{t-1})^2\right) - (1/2)n^{-1}\varepsilon_t^2$. Substituting and summing, we have

$$\begin{aligned} n^{-1}\sum_{t=1}^n Y_{t-1}\varepsilon_t &= (\sigma^2/2)\sum_{t=1}^n \mathcal{W}_n(a_t)^2 - \mathcal{W}_n(a_{t-1})^2 \\ &\quad -(1/2)n^{-1}\sum_{t=1}^n \varepsilon_t^2 \\ &= (\sigma^2/2)\,\mathcal{W}_n(1)^2 - (1/2)n^{-1}\sum_{t=1}^n \varepsilon_t^2. \end{aligned}$$

By Lemma 4.27 and the FCLT (condition 7.21 (*ii*)), we have $\mathcal{W}_n(1)^2 \Rightarrow \mathcal{W}(1)^2$; by condition 7.21 (*iii*) we have $n^{-1}\sum_{t=1}^n \varepsilon_t^2 \xrightarrow{p} \tau^2$. It follows by Lemma 4.27 that

$$\begin{aligned} n^{-1}\sum_{t=1}^n Y_{t-1}\varepsilon_t &\Rightarrow (\sigma^2/2)\mathcal{W}(1)^2 - \tau^2/2 \\ &= (\sigma^2/2)\left(\mathcal{W}(1)^2 - \tau^2/\sigma^2\right). \end{aligned}$$

(*c*) We have

$$\begin{aligned} n(\hat{\beta}_n - 1) &= n\left[\left(\sum_{t=1}^n Y_{t-1}^2\right)^{-1}\sum_{t=1}^n Y_{t-1}Y_t - \left(\sum_{t=1}^n Y_{t-1}^2\right)^{-1}\sum_{t=1}^n Y_{t-1}^2\right] \\ &= n\left(\sum_{t=1}^n Y_{t-1}^2\right)^{-1}\left[\sum_{t=1}^n Y_{t-1}(Y_t - Y_{t-1})\right] \\ &= \left(n^{-2}\sum_{t=1}^n Y_{t-1}^2\right)^{-1} n^{-1}\sum_{t=1}^n Y_{t-1}\varepsilon_t. \end{aligned}$$

Conclusions (*a*) and (*b*) and Lemma 4.27 then give the desired result:

$$\begin{aligned} n(\hat{\beta}_n - 1) &= \left(n^{-2}\sum_{t=1}^n Y_{t-1}^2\right)^{-1} n^{-1}\sum_{t=1}^n Y_{t-1}\varepsilon_t \\ &\Rightarrow \left(\int_0^1 \mathcal{W}(a)^2 da\right)^{-1}(1/2)\left(\mathcal{W}(1)^2 - \tau^2/\sigma^2\right). \end{aligned}$$

(*d*) From (*c*), we have $n(\hat{\beta}_n - 1) = O_p(1)$. Thus, $\hat{\beta}_n - 1 = n^{-1}(n(\hat{\beta}_n - 1)) = o(1)O_p(1) = o_p(1)$, as claimed. ∎

In the proof of (a), we appealed to the continuous mapping theorem to establish that $\int_0^1 \mathcal{W}_n(a)^2 da \Rightarrow \int_0^1 \mathcal{W}(a)^2 da$. The next exercise asks you to verify this and then gives a situation where the continuous mapping theorem does not apply.

Exercise 7.22 *For $\mathcal{U}, \mathcal{V} \in D$, put $d_u(\mathcal{U}, \mathcal{V}) = \sup_{a \in [0,1]} |\mathcal{U}(a) - \mathcal{V}(a)|$, and consider the metrized measurable spaces (D, d_u) and $(\mathbb{R}, |\cdot|)$, the mapping $M_1(\mathcal{U}) = \mathcal{U}^2$, and the two functionals $M_2(\mathcal{U}) = \int_0^1 \mathcal{U}(a)^2 da$ and $M_3(\mathcal{U}) = \int_0^1 \log |\mathcal{U}(a)| da$.*

(i) Show that $M_1 : (D, d_u) \to (D, d_u)$ is continuous at $\mathcal{U}$ for any $\mathcal{U} \in C$, but not everywhere in D.

(ii) Show that $M_2 : (D, d_u) \to (\mathbb{R}, |\cdot|)$ is continuous at $\mathcal{U}$ for any $\mathcal{U} \in C$, so that $\int_0^1 \mathcal{W}_n(a)^2 da \Rightarrow \int_0^1 \mathcal{W}(a)^2 da$.

(iii) Show that $M_3 : (D, d_u) \to (\mathbb{R}, |\cdot|)$ is not continuous everywhere in C, and $\int_0^1 \log(|\mathcal{W}_n(a)|) da \not\Rightarrow \int_0^1 \log(|\mathcal{W}(a)|) da$.

Phillips (1987, Theorem 3.1) states a version of Theorem 7.21 with specific conditions corresponding to those of Theorem 7.18 (heterogeneous mixing FCLT) ensuring that conditions 7.21 (ii) and (iii) hold. Clearly, however, many alternate versions can be stated. The following exercise asks you to complete the details for Phillips's result.

Exercise 7.23 *Use Theorem 7.18 and a corresponding law of large numbers to state conditions on $\{\varepsilon_t\}$ ensuring that 7.21 (ii) and 7.21 (iii) hold, with conclusions 7.21 (a) – (d) holding in consequence. What conditions suffice for $\tau^2 = \sigma^2$?*

Phillips also gives a limiting distribution for the standard t-statistic centered appropriately for testing the hypothesis $\beta_o = 1$ (the "unit root hypothesis"). Not surprisingly, this statistic no longer has the Student-t distribution nor is it asymptotically normal; instead, the t-statistic limiting distribution is a function of $\mathcal{W}$, similar in form to that for $n(\hat{\beta}_n - 1)$.

Although the nonstandard distribution of the t-statistic makes it awkward to use to test the unit root hypothesis (H_o: $\beta_o = 1$), a simple rearrangement leads to a convenient χ_1^2 statistic, first given by Phillips and Durlauf (1986, Lemma 3.1 (d)). From 7.21 (b) we have that

$$\begin{aligned} \left(n^{-1} \sum_{t=1}^{n} Y_{t-1}^2 \right) (\hat{\beta}_n - 1) &= n^{-1} \sum_{t=1}^{n} Y_{t-1} \varepsilon_t \\ &\Rightarrow (\sigma^2/2) \left(\mathcal{W}(1)^2 - \tau^2/\sigma^2 \right). \end{aligned}$$

Thus when $\beta_o = 1$

$$(2/\sigma^2)\left(n^{-1}\sum_{t=1}^{n} Y_{t-1}^2\right)(\hat{\beta}_n - 1) + \tau^2/\sigma^2 \Rightarrow \mathcal{W}(1)^2 = \chi_1^2.$$

This statistic depends on the unknown quantities σ^2 and τ^2, but estimators $\hat{\sigma}_n^2$ and $\hat{\tau}_n^2$ consistent for σ^2 and τ^2, respectively, under the unit root null hypothesis can be straightforwardly constructed using $\varepsilon_t = Y_t - Y_{t-1}$. In particular, set $\hat{\tau}_n^2 = n^{-1}\sum_{t=1}^{n}\varepsilon_t^2$ and form $\hat{\sigma}_n^2$ using Theorem 6.20. We then have

$$(2/\hat{\sigma}_n^2)\left(n^{-1}\sum_{t=1}^{n} Y_{t-1}^2\right)(\hat{\beta}_n - 1) + \hat{\tau}_n^2/\hat{\sigma}_n^2 \Rightarrow \chi_1^2,$$

under the unit root null hypothesis, providing a simple unit root test procedure.

Despite the convenience of the Phillips–Durlauf statistic, it turns out to have disappointing power properties, even though it can be shown to represent the locally best invariant test (see Tanaka, 1996, pp. 324–336). The difficulty is that its optimality is typically highly localized. In fact as Elliott, Rothenberg, and Stock (1996) note, there is no uniformly most powerful test in the present context, in sharp contrast to the typical situation of earlier chapters, where we could rely on asymptotic normality. Here, the limiting distribution is nonnormal. In consequence, there is a plethora of plausible unit root tests in the literature, and our discussion in this section has done no more than scratch the surface. Nevertheless, the basic results just given should assist the reader interested in exploring this literature. An overview of the literature is given by Phillips and Xiao (1998); of particular interest are the articles by Dickey and Fuller (1979, 1981), Elliott *et al.* (1996), Johansen (1988, 1991), Phillips (1987), Phillips and Durlauf (1986), and Stock (1994, 1999).

7.5 Spurious Regression, Multivariate Wiener Processes, and Multivariate FCLTs

Now consider what happens when we regress a unit root process $Y_t = Y_{t-1} + \varepsilon_t$ not on its own lagged value Y_{t-1}, but on another unit root process, say $X_t = X_{t-1} + \eta_t$. For simplicity, assume that $\{\eta_t\}$ is i.i.d. and independent of the i.i.d. sequence $\{\varepsilon_t\}$ so that $\{Y_t\}$ and $\{X_t\}$ are independent random walks, and as before we set $X_0 = Y_0 = 0$. We can write a regression equation for Y_t in terms of X_t formally as

$$Y_t = X_t \beta_o + u_t,$$

where $\beta_o = 0$ and $u_t = Y_t$, reflecting the lack of any relation between Y_t and X_t.

We then ask how the ordinary least squares estimator

$$\hat{\beta}_n = \left(\sum_{t=1}^{n} X_t^2 \right)^{-1} \sum_{t=1}^{n} X_t Y_t$$

behaves as n becomes large. As we will see, $\hat{\beta}_n$ is not consistent for $\beta_o = 0$ but instead converges to a particular random variable. Because there is truly no relation between Y_t and X_t, and because $\hat{\beta}_n$ is incapable of revealing this, we call this a case of "spurious regression." This situation was first considered by Yule (1926), and the dangers of spurious regression were forcefully brought to the attention of economists by the Monte Carlo studies of Granger and Newbold (1974).

To proceed, we write

$$\begin{aligned}
\mathcal{W}_{1n}(a_t) &\equiv n^{-1/2} X_t / \sigma_1 = n^{-1/2} \sum_{s=1}^{t} \eta_s / \sigma_1, \\
\mathcal{W}_{2n}(a_t) &\equiv n^{-1/2} Y_t / \sigma_2 = n^{-1/2} \sum_{s=1}^{t} \varepsilon_s / \sigma_2,
\end{aligned}$$

where $\sigma_1^2 \equiv \lim_{n \to \infty} \text{var}(n^{-1/2} \sum_{t=1}^{n} \eta_t)$ and $\sigma_2^2 \equiv \lim_{n \to \infty} \text{var}(n^{-1/2} \sum_{t=1}^{n} \varepsilon_t)$, and $a_t = t/n$ as before. Substituting for X_t and Y_t and, for convenience, treating $\hat{\beta}_{n-1}$ instead of $\hat{\beta}_n$ we can write

$$\begin{aligned}
\hat{\beta}_{n-1} &= \left(\sum_{t=1}^{n} X_{t-1}^2 \right)^{-1} \sum_{t=1}^{n} X_{t-1} Y_{t-1} \\
&= \left(\sigma_1^2 \, n \sum_{t=1}^{n} \mathcal{W}_{1n}(a_{t-1})^2 \right)^{-1} \sigma_1 \sigma_2 \, n \sum_{t=1}^{n} \mathcal{W}_{1n}(a_{t-1}) \mathcal{W}_{2n}(a_{t-1}) \\
&= (\sigma_2/\sigma_1) \left(n^{-1} \sum_{t=1}^{n} \mathcal{W}_{1n}(a_{t-1})^2 \right)^{-1} n^{-1} \sum_{t=1}^{n} \mathcal{W}_{1n}(a_{t-1}) \mathcal{W}_{2n}(a_{t-1}).
\end{aligned}$$

From the proof of Theorem 7.21 (a), we have that

$$n^{-1}\sum_{t=1}^{n}\mathcal{W}_{1n}(a_{t-1})^2 \Rightarrow \int_0^1 \mathcal{W}_1(a)^2 da,$$

where $\mathcal{W}_1$ is a Wiener process. We also have

$$n^{-1}\sum_{t=1}^{n}\mathcal{W}_{1n}(a_{t-1})\mathcal{W}_{2n}(a_{t-1}) = \sum_{t=1}^{n}\int_{(t-1)/n}^{t/n}\mathcal{W}_{1n}(a)\mathcal{W}_{2n}(a)da,$$

because $\mathcal{W}_{1n}(a)\mathcal{W}_{2n}(a)$ is constant for $(t-1)/n \leq a < t/n$. Thus

$$n^{-1}\sum_{t=1}^{n}\mathcal{W}_{1n}(a_{t-1})\mathcal{W}_{2n}(a_{t-1}) = \int_0^1 \mathcal{W}_{1n}(a)\mathcal{W}_{2n}(a)da.$$

We might expect this to converge in distribution to $\int_0^1 \mathcal{W}_1(a)\mathcal{W}_2(a)da$, where $\mathcal{W}_1$ and $\mathcal{W}_2$ are independent Wiener processes. (Why?) If so, then we have

$$\hat{\beta}_n \Rightarrow (\sigma_2/\sigma_1)\left[\int_0^1 \mathcal{W}_1(a)^2 da\right]^{-1}\int_0^1 \mathcal{W}_1(a)\mathcal{W}_2(a)da,$$

which is a nondegenerate random variable. $\hat{\beta}_n$ is then not consistent for $\beta_o = 0$, so the regression is "spurious."

Nevertheless, we do not yet have all the tools needed to draw this conclusion formally. In particular, we need to extend the notion of a univariate Wiener process to that of a multivariate Wiener process, and for this we need to extend the spaces of functions we consider from $C[0,\infty)$ or $D[0,\infty)$ to Cartesian product spaces $C^k[0,\infty) \equiv \times_{j=1}^{k} C[0,\infty)$ and $D^k[0,\infty) \equiv \times_{j=1}^{k} D[0,\infty)$.

Definition 7.24 (Multivariate Wiener process) $\boldsymbol{\mathcal{W}} = (\mathcal{W}_1, \ldots, \mathcal{W}_k)'$ *is a* multivariate (k-dimensional) Wiener process *if* $\mathcal{W}_1, \ldots, \mathcal{W}_k$ *are independent* ($\mathbb{R}$*-valued*) *Wiener processes.*

The multivariate Wiener process exists (e.g., Breiman, 1992, Ch. 12), has independent increments, and has increments $\boldsymbol{\mathcal{W}}(a,\cdot) - \boldsymbol{\mathcal{W}}(b,\cdot)$ distributed as multivariate normal $N(\mathbf{0},(a-b)\mathbf{I})$, $0 \leq b \leq a < \infty$, as is straightforwardly shown. Further, there is a version such that for all $\omega \in \Omega$, $\boldsymbol{\mathcal{W}}(0,\omega) = \mathbf{0}$ and $\boldsymbol{\mathcal{W}}(\cdot,\omega) : [0,\infty) \to \mathbb{R}^k$ is continuous, a consequence of Proposition 7.7 and the fact that $\boldsymbol{\mathcal{W}}$ is continuous if and only if its components are continuous. Thus, there is a version of the multivariate Wiener process taking values in $C^k[0,\infty)$, so that $\mathcal{W}$ is a random element of $C^k[0,\infty)$. As in the univariate case, when we speak of a multivariate Wiener process, we shall have in mind one with continuous sample paths. When dealing with multivariate FCLTs it will suffice here to restrict attention to functions defined on $[0,1]$. We thus write $C^k \equiv \times_{j=1}^k C[0,1]$ and $D^k \equiv \times_{j=1}^k D[0,1]$.

Analogous to the univariate case, we can define a multivariate random walk as follows.

Definition 7.25 (Multivariate random walk) *Let* $\boldsymbol{\mathcal{X}}_t = \boldsymbol{\mathcal{X}}_{t-1} + \boldsymbol{\mathcal{Z}}_t$, $t = 1, 2, \ldots$, *where* $\boldsymbol{\mathcal{X}}_0 = \mathbf{0}$ $(k \times 1)$ *and* $\{\boldsymbol{\mathcal{Z}}_t\}$ *is a sequence of i.i.d.* $k \times 1$ *vectors* $\boldsymbol{\mathcal{Z}}_t = (\mathcal{Z}_{t1}, \ldots , \mathcal{Z}_{tk})'$ *such that* $E(\boldsymbol{\mathcal{Z}}_t) = 0$ *and* $E(\boldsymbol{\mathcal{Z}}_t\boldsymbol{\mathcal{Z}}_t') = \boldsymbol{\Sigma}$, *a finite positive definite matrix. Then* $\{\boldsymbol{\mathcal{X}}_t\}$ *is a* multivariate (k-dimensional) random walk.

We form the rescaled partial sums as

$$\boldsymbol{\mathcal{W}}_n(a) \equiv \boldsymbol{\Sigma}^{-1/2} n^{-1/2} \sum_{t=1}^{[an]} \boldsymbol{\mathcal{Z}}_t.$$

The components of $\boldsymbol{\mathcal{W}}_n$ are the individual partial sums

$$\mathcal{W}_{nj}(a) = n^{-1/2} \sum_{t=1}^{[an]} \tilde{\mathcal{Z}}_{tj}, \quad j = 1, \ldots , k,$$

where $\tilde{\mathcal{Z}}_{tj}$ is the jth element of $\boldsymbol{\Sigma}^{-1/2}\boldsymbol{\mathcal{Z}}_t$. For given ω, the components $\mathcal{W}_{nj}(\cdot, \omega)$ are piecewise constant, so $\boldsymbol{\mathcal{W}}_n$ is a random element of D^k.

We expect that a multivariate version of Donsker's theorem should hold, analogous to the multivariate CLT, so that $\boldsymbol{\mathcal{W}}_n \Rightarrow \boldsymbol{\mathcal{W}}$. To establish this formally, we study the weak convergence of the measures μ_n, defined by

$$\mu_n(A) = P\{\omega : \boldsymbol{\mathcal{W}}_n(\cdot, \omega) \in A\},$$

where now $A \in \mathcal{B}(D^k, d)$ for a suitable choice of metric d on D^k. For example, we can choose $d(x, y) = \sum_{j=1}^k d_B(x_j, y_j)$ for $x = (x_1, \ldots , x_k)'$, $y = (y_1, \ldots , y_k)'$, $x_j, y_j \in D$ with d_B the Billingsley metric on D.

The multivariate FCLT provides conditions under which μ_n converges to the multivariate Wiener measure $\mu_{\mathcal{W}}$ defined by

$$\mu_{\mathcal{W}}(A) = P\{\omega : \boldsymbol{\mathcal{W}}(\cdot, \omega) \in A \cap C^k\},$$

where $A \in \mathcal{B}(D^k, d)$. When $\mu_n \Rightarrow \mu_{\mathcal{W}}$ we say that $\mathcal{W}_n \Rightarrow \mathcal{W}$ and that $\mathcal{W}_n$ obeys the multivariate FCLT, or that $\{\mathcal{Z}_t\}$ obeys the multivariate FCLT.

To establish the multivariate FCLT it is often convenient to apply an analog of the Cramér-Wold device (e.g., Wooldridge and White, 1988).

Proposition 7.26 (Functional Cramér-Wold device) *Let $\{\mathcal{V}_n\}$ be a sequence of random elements of D^k and let $\mathcal{V}$ be a random element of D^k (not necessarily the Wiener process). Then $\mathcal{V}_n \Rightarrow \mathcal{V}$ if and only if $\boldsymbol{\lambda}'\mathcal{V}_n \Rightarrow \boldsymbol{\lambda}'\mathcal{V}$ for all $\boldsymbol{\lambda} \in \mathbb{R}^k$, $\boldsymbol{\lambda}'\boldsymbol{\lambda} = 1$.*

Proof. See Wooldridge and White (1988), proof of Proposition 4.1. ∎

Applying the functional Cramér-Wold device makes it straightforward to establish multivariate versions of Theorems 7.13 and 7.15 through 7.19. To complete our discussion of spurious regression, we state the multivariate Donsker Theorem.

Theorem 7.27 (Multivariate Donsker) *Let $\{\mathcal{Z}_t\}$ be a sequence of i.i.d. $k \times 1$ vectors $\mathcal{Z}_t = (\mathcal{Z}_{t1}, \dots, \mathcal{Z}_{tk})'$ such that $E(\mathcal{Z}_t) = \mathbf{0}$ and $E(\mathcal{Z}_t\mathcal{Z}_t') = \boldsymbol{\Sigma}$, a finite nonsingular matrix. Then $\mathcal{W}_n \Rightarrow \mathcal{W}$.*

Proof. Fix $\boldsymbol{\lambda} \in \mathbb{R}^k$, $\boldsymbol{\lambda}'\boldsymbol{\lambda} = 1$. Then $\boldsymbol{\lambda}'\mathcal{W}_n(a) = n^{-1/2}\sum_{t=1}^{[an]} \boldsymbol{\lambda}'\boldsymbol{\Sigma}^{-1/2}\mathcal{Z}_t$, where $\{\boldsymbol{\lambda}'\boldsymbol{\Sigma}^{-1/2}\mathcal{Z}_t\}$ is i.i.d. with $E(\boldsymbol{\lambda}'\boldsymbol{\Sigma}^{-1/2}\mathcal{Z}_t) = 0$ and

$$\begin{aligned}\operatorname{var}(\boldsymbol{\lambda}'\boldsymbol{\Sigma}^{-1/2}\mathcal{Z}_t) &= \boldsymbol{\lambda}'\boldsymbol{\Sigma}^{-1/2}E(\mathcal{Z}_t\mathcal{Z}_t')\boldsymbol{\Sigma}^{-1/2}\boldsymbol{\lambda} \\ &= \boldsymbol{\lambda}'\boldsymbol{\Sigma}^{-1/2}\boldsymbol{\Sigma}\boldsymbol{\Sigma}^{-1/2}\boldsymbol{\lambda} = \boldsymbol{\lambda}'\boldsymbol{\lambda} = 1.\end{aligned}$$

The conditions of Donsker's Theorem 7.13 hold, so $\boldsymbol{\lambda}'\mathcal{W}_n \Rightarrow \mathcal{W}$, the univariate Wiener process. Now $\mathcal{W} = \boldsymbol{\lambda}'\mathcal{W}$ and this holds for all $\boldsymbol{\lambda} \in \mathbb{R}^k$, $\boldsymbol{\lambda}'\boldsymbol{\lambda} = 1$. The result then follows by the functional Cramér-Wold device. ∎

At last we have what we need to state a formal result for spurious regression. We leave the proof as an exercise.

Exercise 7.28 (Spurious regression) *Let $\{X_t\}$ and $\{Y_t\}$ be independent random walks, $X_t = X_{t-1} + \eta_t$ and $Y_t = Y_{t-1} + \varepsilon_t$, where $\sigma_1^2 \equiv E(\eta_t^2)$ and $\sigma_2^2 \equiv E(\varepsilon_t^2)$. Then $\hat{\beta}_n \Rightarrow (\sigma_2/\sigma_1)\left[\int_0^1 \mathcal{W}_1(a)^2 da\right]^{-1} \int_0^1 \mathcal{W}_1(a)\mathcal{W}_2(a)da$, where $\mathcal{W} = (\mathcal{W}_1, \mathcal{W}_2)'$ is a bivariate Wiener process. (Hint: apply the multivariate Donsker Theorem and the continuous mapping theorem with $S = D^2$.)*

Not only does $\hat{\beta}_n$ not converge to zero (the true value of β_o) in this case, but it can be shown that the usual t-statistic tends to ∞, giving the misleading impression that $\hat{\beta}_n$ is highly statistically significant. See Watson (1994, p. 2863) for a nice discussion and Phillips (1986) for further details.

For each univariate FCLT, there is an analogous multivariate FCLT. This follows from the following result.

Theorem 7.29 (Multivariate FCLT) *Suppose that $\{\mathcal{Z}_t\}$ is globally covariance stationary with mean zero and nonsingular global covariance matrix $\mathbf{\Sigma}$ such that for each $\boldsymbol{\lambda} \in \mathbb{R}^k$, $\boldsymbol{\lambda}'\boldsymbol{\lambda} = 1$, $\{\boldsymbol{\lambda}'\mathbf{\Sigma}^{-1/2}\mathcal{Z}_t\}$ obeys the FCLT. Then $\mathcal{W}_n \Rightarrow \mathcal{W}$.*

Proof. Fix $\boldsymbol{\lambda} \in \mathbb{R}^k$, $\boldsymbol{\lambda}'\boldsymbol{\lambda} = 1$. Then $\boldsymbol{\lambda}'\mathcal{W}_n(a) = n^{-1/2}\sum_{t=1}^{[an]} \boldsymbol{\lambda}'\mathbf{\Sigma}^{-1/2}\mathcal{Z}_t$. Now $E(\boldsymbol{\lambda}'\mathbf{\Sigma}^{-1/2}\mathcal{Z}_t) = 0$ and $\text{var}(\boldsymbol{\lambda}'\mathcal{W}_n(1)) \to 1$ as $n \to \infty$. Because $\{\boldsymbol{\lambda}'\mathbf{\Sigma}^{-1/2}\mathcal{Z}_t\}$ satisfies the FCLT, we have $\boldsymbol{\lambda}'\mathcal{W}_n \Rightarrow \mathcal{W} = \boldsymbol{\lambda}'\mathcal{W}$. This follows for all $\boldsymbol{\lambda} \in \mathbb{R}^k$, $\boldsymbol{\lambda}'\boldsymbol{\lambda} = 1$, so the conclusion follows by the functional Cramér-Wold device. ∎

Quite general multivariate FCLTs are available. See Wooldridge and White (1988) and Davidson (1994, Ch. 29) for some further results and discussion. For example, here is a useful multivariate FCLT for heterogeneous mixing processes, which follows as an immediate corollary to Wooldridge and White (1988, Corollary 4.2).

Theorem 7.30 (Heterogeneous mixing multivariate FCLT) *Let $\{\mathcal{Z}_{nt}\}$ be a double array of $k \times 1$ random vectors $\mathcal{Z}_{nt} = (Z_{nt1}, \ldots, Z_{ntk})'$ such that $\{\mathcal{Z}_{nt}\}$ is mixing with ϕ of size $-r/(2r-2)$ or α of size $-r/(r-2)$, $r > 2$. Suppose further that $E|Z_{ntj}| < \Delta < \infty$, $E(Z_{ntj}) = 0$, $n, t = 1, 2, \ldots$, $j = 1, \ldots, k$. If $\{\mathcal{Z}_{nt}\}$ is globally covariance stationary with nonsingular global covariance matrix $\mathbf{\Sigma} = \lim_{n\to\infty} \text{var}(n^{-1/2}\sum_{t=1}^{n} \mathcal{Z}_{nt})$, then $\mathcal{W}_n \Rightarrow \mathcal{W}$.*

Proof. Under the conditions given, $\boldsymbol{\lambda}'\mathbf{\Sigma}^{-1/2}\mathcal{Z}_{nt}$ obeys the heterogeneous mixing FCLT, Theorem 7.18. As $\mathcal{Z}_{nt}$ is globally covariance stationary, the result follows from Theorem 7.29. See also Wooldridge and White (1988, Corollary 4.2). ∎

Our next exercise is an application of this result.

Exercise 7.31 *Determine the behavior of the least squares estimator $\hat{\beta}_n$ when the unit root process $Y_t = Y_{t-1} + \varepsilon_t$ is regressed on the unit root process $X_t = X_{t-1} + \eta_t$, where $\{\eta_t\}$ is independent of $\{\varepsilon_t\}$, and $\{\eta_t, \varepsilon_t\}$ satisfies the conditions of Theorem 7.30.*

7.6 Cointegration and Stochastic Integrals

Continuing with the spurious regression setup in which $\{X_t\}$ and $\{Y_t\}$ are independent random walks, consider what happens if we take a nontrivial linear combination of X_t and Y_t:

$$a_1 Y_t + a_2 X_t = a_1 Y_{t-1} + a_2 X_{t-1} + a_1 \varepsilon_t + a_2 \eta_t,$$

where a_1 and a_2 are not both zero. We can write this as

$$Z_t = Z_{t-1} + v_t,$$

where $Z_t = a_1 Y_t + a_2 X_t$ and $v_t = a_1 \varepsilon_t + a_2 \eta_t$. Thus, Z_t is again a random walk process, as $\{v_t\}$ is i.i.d. with mean zero and finite variance, given that $\{\varepsilon_t\}$ and $\{\eta_t\}$ each are i.i.d. with mean zero and finite variance. No matter what coefficients a_1 and a_2 we choose, the resulting linear combination is again a random walk, hence an integrated or unit root process.

Now consider what happens when $\{X_t\}$ is a random walk (hence integrated) as before, but $\{Y_t\}$ is instead generated according to $Y_t = X_t \beta_o + \varepsilon_t$, with $\{\varepsilon_t\}$ again i.i.d. By itself, $\{Y_t\}$ is an integrated process, because

$$Y_t - Y_{t-1} = (X_t - X_{t-1})\beta_o + \varepsilon_t - \varepsilon_{t-1}$$

so that

$$\begin{aligned} Y_t &= Y_{t-1} + \eta_t \beta_o + \varepsilon_t - \varepsilon_{t-1} \\ &= Y_{t-1} + \zeta_t, \end{aligned}$$

where $\zeta_t = \eta_t \beta_o + \varepsilon_t - \varepsilon_{t-1}$ is readily verified to obey the FCLT.

Despite the fact that both $\{X_t\}$ and $\{Y_t\}$ are integrated processes, the situation is very different from that considered at the outset of this section. Here, there is indeed a linear combination of X_t and Y_t that is *not* an integrated process: putting $a_1 = 1$ and $a_2 = -\beta_o$ we have

$$a_1 Y_t + a_2 X_t = Y_t - \beta_o X_t = \varepsilon_t,$$

which is i.i.d. This is an example of a pair $\{X_t, Y_t\}$ of *cointegrated processes*.

Definition 7.32 (Cointegrated processes) *Let $\mathcal{X}_t = (\mathcal{X}_{t1}, \ldots, \mathcal{X}_{tk})'$ be a vector of integrated processes. If there exists a $k \times 1$ vector $\mathbf{a}$ such that the linear combination $\{Z_t = \mathbf{a}'\mathcal{X}_t\}$ obeys the FCLT, then $\mathcal{X}_t$ is a* vector of cointegrated processes.

Cointegrated processes were introduced by Granger (1981). This paper and that of Engle and Granger (1987) have had a major impact on modern econometrics, and there is now a voluminous literature on the theory and application of cointegration. Excellent treatments can be found in Johansen (1988, 1991, 1996), Phillips (1991), Sims, Stock, and Watson (1990) and Stock and Watson (1993).

Our purpose here is not to pursue the various aspects of the theory of cointegration. Instead, we restrict our attention to developing the tools necessary to analyze the behavior of the least squares estimator $\hat{\boldsymbol{\beta}}_n = (\sum_{t=1}^n \mathbf{X}_t\mathbf{X}_t')^{-1}\sum_{t=1}^n \mathbf{X}_t\mathbf{Y}_t$, when $(\mathbf{X}_t, \mathbf{Y}_t)$ is a vector of cointegrated processes.

For the case of scalar X_t,

$$\begin{aligned}\hat{\beta}_n &= (\sum_{t=1}^n X_t^2)^{-1}\sum_{t=1}^n X_t(X_t\beta_o + \varepsilon_t)\\ &= \beta_o + (\sum_{t=1}^n X_t^2)^{-1}\sum_{t=1}^n X_t\varepsilon_t.\end{aligned}$$

For now, we maintain the assumption that $\{X_t\}$ is a random walk and that $\{\varepsilon_t\}$ is i.i.d., independent of $\{\eta_t\}$ (which underlies $\{X_t\}$). We later relax these requirements.

From the expression above, we see that the behavior of $\hat{\beta}_n$ is determined by that of $\sum_{t=1}^n X_t^2$ and $\sum_{t=1}^n X_t\varepsilon_t$, so we consider each of these in turn.

First consider $\sum_{t=1}^n X_t^2$. From Theorem 7.21 (*a*) we know that

$$n^{-2}\sum_{t=1}^n X_t^2 \Rightarrow \sigma_1^2\int_0^1 \mathcal{W}_1(a)^2 da,$$

where $\sigma_1^2 = E(\eta_t^2)$.

Next, consider $\sum_{t=1}^n X_t\varepsilon_t$. Substituting $X_t = X_{t-1} + \eta_t$ we have

$$n^{-1}\sum_{t=1}^n X_t\varepsilon_t = n^{-1}\sum_{t=1}^n X_{t-1}\varepsilon_t + n^{-1}\sum_{t=1}^n \eta_t\varepsilon_t.$$

Under our assumptions, $\{\eta_t\varepsilon_t\}$ obeys a law of large numbers, so the last term converges to $E(\eta_t\varepsilon_t) = 0$. We thus focus on $n^{-1}\sum_{t=1}^n X_{t-1}\varepsilon_t$. If we write

$$\begin{aligned} \mathcal{W}_{1n}(a_t) &= n^{-1/2}\sum_{s=1}^{t}\eta_s/\sigma_1 \\ \mathcal{W}_{2n}(a_t) &= n^{-1/2}\sum_{s=1}^{t}\varepsilon_s/\sigma_2, \end{aligned}$$

where, as before, we set $a_t = t/n$, we have $X_{t-1} = n^{1/2}\sigma_1\mathcal{W}_{1n}(a_{t-1})$ and $\varepsilon_t = n^{1/2}\sigma_2\left(\mathcal{W}_{2n}(a_t) - \mathcal{W}_{2n}(a_{t-1})\right)$. Substituting these expressions we obtain

$$\begin{aligned} n^{-1}\sum_{t=1}^{n}X_{t-1}\varepsilon_t &= n^{-1}\sum_{t=1}^{n}n^{1/2}\sigma_1\mathcal{W}_{1n}(a_{t-1}) \\ &\quad \times n^{1/2}\sigma_2\left(\mathcal{W}_{2n}(a_t) - \mathcal{W}_{2n}(a_{t-1})\right) \\ &= \sigma_1\sigma_2\sum_{t=1}^{n}\mathcal{W}_{1n}(a_{t-1})\left(\mathcal{W}_{2n}(a_t) - \mathcal{W}_{2n}(a_{t-1})\right). \end{aligned}$$

The summation appearing in the expression immediately above has a prototypical form that plays a central role not only in the estimation of the parameters of cointegration models, but in a range of other contexts as well.

The analysis of such expressions is facilitated by defining a *stochastic integral* as

$$\int_0^1 \mathcal{W}_{1n}d\mathcal{W}_{2n} \equiv \sum_{t=1}^{n}\mathcal{W}_{1n}(a_{t-1})\left(\mathcal{W}_{2n}(a_t) - \mathcal{W}_{2n}(a_{t-1})\right).$$

Writing the expression in this way and noting that $\boldsymbol{\mathcal{W}}_n = (\mathcal{W}_{1n}, \mathcal{W}_{2n})' \Rightarrow \boldsymbol{\mathcal{W}} = (\mathcal{W}_1, \mathcal{W}_2)'$ suggest that we might expect that

$$\int_0^1 \mathcal{W}_{1n}d\mathcal{W}_{2n} \Rightarrow \int_0^1 \mathcal{W}_1 d\mathcal{W}_2,$$

where the integral on the right, involving the stochastic differential $d\mathcal{W}_2$, will have to be given a suitable meaning, as this expression does not correspond to any of the standard integrals familiar from elementary calculus.

Under certain conditions this convergence does hold. Chan and Wei (1988) were the first to establish a result of this sort. Nevertheless, this result is not generally valid. Instead, as we describe in more detail below, a recentering may be needed to accommodate dependence in the increments of $\mathcal{W}_{1n}$ or $\mathcal{W}_{2n}$ not present in the increments of $\mathcal{W}_1$ and $\mathcal{W}_2$. As it turns out, the generic result is that

$$\int_0^1 \mathcal{W}_{1n} d\mathcal{W}_{2n} - \Lambda_n \Rightarrow \int_0^1 \mathcal{W}_1 d\mathcal{W}_2,$$

where Λ_n performs the recentering.

We proceed by first making sense of the integral on the right, using the phenomenally successful theory of stochastic integration developed by Ito in the 1940's; see Ito (1944). We then discuss the issues involved in establishing the limiting behavior of $\int_0^1 \mathcal{W}_{1n} d\mathcal{W}_{2n}$.

To ensure that the stochastic integrals defined below are properly behaved, we make use of the notion of the *filtration generated by* $\boldsymbol{\mathcal{W}}$.

Definition 7.33 (Filtration generated by $\boldsymbol{\mathcal{W}}$) *Let $\boldsymbol{\mathcal{W}}$ be a standard multivariate Wiener process. The* filtration generated by $\boldsymbol{\mathcal{W}}$ *is the sequence of σ-fields $\{\mathcal{F}_t,\ t \in [0, \infty)\}$, where $\mathcal{F}_t = \sigma(\boldsymbol{\mathcal{W}}(a),\ 0 \leq a \leq t)$.*

Note that $\{\mathcal{F}_t\}$ is an increasing sequence of σ-fields ($\mathcal{F}_a \subset \mathcal{F}_t$, $a < t$). In what follows, the σ-field $\mathcal{F}_t$ will always denote that just defined.

We can now define the random step functions that provide the foundation for Ito's stochastic integral, parallel to the construction of the familiar Riemann integral.

Definition 7.34 (Random step function) *Suppose there is a finite sequence of real numbers $0 = a_0 < a_1 < \cdots < a_n$ and a sequence of random variables η_t, with $E(\eta_t^2) < \infty$, where η_t is adapted to $\mathcal{F}_t$, $t = 0, \ldots, n-1$. Let $f : [0, \infty) \times \Omega \to \mathbb{R}$ be defined so that $f(a, \cdot) = \eta_t$ for $a_t \leq a < a_{t+1}$. Then f is a* random step function.

The Ito stochastic integral is straightforward to define for random step functions.

Definition 7.35 *Let $\mathcal{W}$ be a component of $\boldsymbol{\mathcal{W}}$. The* Ito stochastic integral of a random step function *f is defined as*

$$\mathcal{I}(f) \equiv \sum_{t=1}^{n} \eta_{t-1}(\mathcal{W}(a_t) - \mathcal{W}(a_{t-1})).$$

We also write $\mathcal{I}(f) = \int_0^\infty f d\mathcal{W}$ or $\mathcal{I}(f) = \int_0^\infty f(a) d\mathcal{W}(a)$ in this case.

The Ito stochastic integral of a random step function has finite second moment:

Proposition 7.36 *If f is a random step function, then*

$$E(\mathcal{I}(f)^2) = E(\int_0^\infty f(a)^2 da) < \infty.$$

Proof. See Brzeźniak and Zastawniak (1999, pp. 182–183). ∎

To extend the definition of the Ito stochastic integral to a class of functions wider than the random step functions, we use the random step functions as approximations, analogous to the construction of the Riemann integral. Specifically, we define the Ito stochastic integral for functions well approximated by random step functions in mean square. We first define the class of square integrable stochastic functions.

Definition 7.37 (Square integrable (adapted) stochastic function) *Let $f : [0, \infty) \times \Omega \to \mathbb{R}$ be such that $f(a, \cdot)$ is measurable for each $a \in [0, \infty)$. If $E\left(\int_0^\infty f(a)^2 da\right) < \infty$, then f is a* square integrable stochastic function. *If in addition $f(a, \cdot)$ is measurable-$\mathcal{F}_a$ for each $a \in [0, \infty)$ then f is a* square integrable adapted stochastic function.

For square integrable stochastic functions, we have $E\left(\int_0^\infty f(a)^2 da\right) = \int_0^\infty E\left(f(a)^2\right) da$. (Why?)

Definition 7.38 (Approximatable stochastic function) *Let f be a square integrable adapted stochastic function such that there is a sequence $\{f_n\}$ of random step functions such that*

$$\lim_{n\to\infty} E\left(\int_0^\infty |f(a) - f_n(a)|^2 da\right) = 0.$$

Then f is an approximatable stochastic function *and $\{f_n\}$ is a* sequence of approximating step functions for f.

A general definition of the Ito stochastic integral can now be given.

Definition 7.39 (Ito stochastic integral) *Suppose f is an approximatable stochastic function. If for any sequence $\{f_n\}$ of approximating step functions for f there exists a random variable $\mathcal{I}(f)$ with $E(\mathcal{I}(f)) < \infty$ and such that $\lim_{n\to\infty} E\left(|\mathcal{I}(f) - \mathcal{I}(f_n)|^2\right) = 0$, then we call $\mathcal{I}(f)$ the* Ito stochastic integral *and write*

$$\mathcal{I}(f) = \int_0^\infty f(a)\, d\mathcal{W}(a) = \int_0^\infty f d\mathcal{W}.$$

Proposition 7.40 *For every approximatable stochastic function the Ito stochastic integral exists, is unique (to within equality, a.s.), and satisfies*

$$E\left(\mathcal{I}(f)^2\right) = E\left(\int_0^\infty f(a)^2 da\right).$$

Proof. See Brzeźniak and Zastawniak (1999, pp. 184–185). ∎

In the light of this result, if f is an approximatable stochastic function, we shall also call f a *stochastically integrable* function.

If $1_{[b,c)}f$ is stochastically integrable, we can define

$$\begin{aligned}\int_b^c f(a)d\mathcal{W}(a) &\equiv \int_0^\infty 1_{[b,c)}(a)f(a)d\mathcal{W}(a)\\ &= \mathcal{I}(1_{[b,c)}f),\end{aligned}$$

where $1_{[b,c)}(a) = 1$ if $b \leq a < c$ and is zero otherwise. We also write $\mathcal{I}(1_{[b,c)}f) = \int_b^c f d\mathcal{W}$.

It is not always easy to check that a function f is stochastically integrable. The next result establishes that f is stochastically integrable if it is continuous almost surely and properly adapted.

Proposition 7.41 *Let f be a stochastic function with continuous sample paths almost surely such that $f(a,\cdot)$ is measurable-$\mathcal{F}_a$ for all $a \in [0,\infty)$. Then*

(*i*) *if f is a square integrable stochastic function, then f is stochastically integrable;*

(*ii*) *if $1_{[b,c)}f$ is a square integrable stochastic function, then $1_{[b,c)}f$ is stochastically integrable.*

Proof. See Brzeźniak and Zastawniak (1999, pp. 187–188). ∎

We can now make sense of the integral $\int_0^1 \mathcal{W}_1 d\mathcal{W}_2$ that led to the foregoing discussion. Put $\boldsymbol{\mathcal{W}} = (\mathcal{W}_1, \mathcal{W}_2)$, $f = \mathcal{W}_1$ and $\mathcal{W} = \mathcal{W}_2$, and apply Proposition 7.41. By definition, $f = \mathcal{W}_1$ is a stochastic function with continuous sample paths, with $\mathcal{W}_1(a)$ measurable-$\mathcal{F}_a$, $a \in [0,\infty)$. To verify that $1_{[0,1]}f = 1_{[0,1]}\mathcal{W}_1$ is square integrable, as required for Proposition 7.41 (*ii*), we write $E\left[\int 1_{[0,1]}(a)\mathcal{W}_1(a)^2 da\right] = E\int_0^1 \mathcal{W}_1(a)^2 da = \int_0^1 E(\mathcal{W}_1(a)^2)da = \int_0^1 a da = \left[a^2/2\right]_0^1 = 1/2 < \infty$. $f = \mathcal{W}_1$ is therefore stochastically integrable on $[0,1]$, ensuring that $\int_0^1 \mathcal{W}_1 d\mathcal{W}_2$ is well defined.

We can extend the notion of Ito stochastic integral to vector- or matrix-valued integrals; these forms appear commonly in applications. Specifically, let $\mathbf{f}$ be $m \times 1$, let $\mathbf{F}$ be $m \times k$ and let $\mathcal{W}$ be $k \times 1$. Then

$$\int_b^c \mathbf{f}\, d\mathcal{W}'$$

is an $m \times k$ matrix with elements

$$\int_b^c f_i\, d\mathcal{W}_j, \quad i = 1, \ldots, m, \ j = 1, \ldots, k,$$

and

$$\int_b^c \mathbf{F}\, d\mathcal{W}$$

is an $m \times 1$ vector with elements

$$\sum_{j=1}^k \int_b^c F_{ij}\, d\mathcal{W}_j, \quad i = 1, \ldots, m.$$

For example, the matrix

$$\int_b^c \mathcal{W} d\mathcal{W}'$$

is the $k \times k$ matrix of random variables with elements $\int_b^c \mathcal{W}_i\, d\mathcal{W}_j$, $i, j = 1, \ldots, k$.

We now turn our attention to the limiting behavior of $\int_0^1 \mathcal{W}_{1n} d\mathcal{W}_{2n}$. For this, consider a more general setup in which we have $(\mathcal{U}_n, \mathcal{V}_n) \Rightarrow (\mathcal{U}, \mathcal{V})$, and consider the limiting behavior of

$$\int_0^1 \mathcal{U}_n d\mathcal{V}_n'.$$

Contrary to what one might at first expect it is not true in general that $\int_0^1 \mathcal{U}_n d\mathcal{V}_n' \Rightarrow \int_0^1 \mathcal{U} d\mathcal{V}'$.

To see this, recall from Theorem 7.21 (*b*) that $n^{-1} \sum_{t=1}^n Y_{t-1}\varepsilon_t \Rightarrow (\sigma^2/2)$ $(\mathcal{W}(1)^2 - \tau^2/\sigma^2)$, where $\tau^2 = \text{plim}\, n^{-1} \sum_{t=1}^n \varepsilon_t^2$. Writing $\mathcal{W}_n(a_{t-1}) = n^{-1/2}$ $\sum_{s=1}^{t-1} \varepsilon_s/\sigma$, we have

$$\begin{aligned} n^{-1} \sum_{t=1}^n Y_{t-1}\varepsilon_t &= \sigma n^{-1/2} \sum_{t=1}^n \mathcal{W}_n(a_{t-1})\varepsilon_t \\ &= \sigma^2 \sum_{t=1}^n \mathcal{W}_n(a_{t-1})(\mathcal{W}_n(a_t) - \mathcal{W}_n(a_{t-1})) \\ &= \sigma^2 \int_0^1 \mathcal{W}_n d\mathcal{W}_n, \end{aligned}$$

where the first equality is taken from the proof of Theorem 7.21(*b*), the second uses the fact that $\varepsilon_t = \sigma n^{1/2}(\mathcal{W}_n(a_t) - \mathcal{W}_n(a_{t-1}))$, and the third uses the definition of a stochastic integral.

Now if $(\mathcal{U}_n, \mathcal{V}_n) \Rightarrow (\mathcal{U}, \mathcal{V})$ were to imply

$$\int_0^1 \mathcal{U}_n d\mathcal{V}_n' \Rightarrow \int_0^1 \mathcal{U} d\mathcal{V}',$$

then $\mathcal{W}_n \Rightarrow \mathcal{W}$ (as assumed in conditions 7.21(*ii*)) would imply that

$$\int_0^1 \mathcal{W}_n d\mathcal{W}_n \Rightarrow \int_0^1 \mathcal{W} d\mathcal{W}.$$

(Set $\mathcal{U}_n = \mathcal{V}_n = \mathcal{W}_n$ and $\mathcal{U} = \mathcal{V} = \mathcal{W}$.) It is a standard exercise in stochastic integration to show that

$$\int_0^1 \mathcal{W} d\mathcal{W} = (1/2)(\mathcal{W}(1)^2 - 1),$$

so we would then have

$$n^{-1} \sum_{t=1}^{n} Y_{t-1}\varepsilon_t \Rightarrow (\sigma^2/2)(\mathcal{W}(1)^2 - 1).$$

But we have already seen that

$$\begin{aligned} n^{-1} \sum_{t=1}^{n} Y_{t-1}\varepsilon_t &= \sigma^2 \int_0^1 \mathcal{W}_n d\mathcal{W}_n \\ &\Rightarrow (\sigma^2/2)(\mathcal{W}(1)^2 - \tau^2/\sigma^2). \end{aligned}$$

We now see that the convergence we might have naively expected does not hold in general, because we can have $\tau^2 \neq \sigma^2$. Clearly, more is going on than might appear at first glance.

To see what this is, let $\{\eta_t\}$ and $\{\varepsilon_t\}$ each obey the FCLT, and write

$$\begin{aligned} \mathcal{U}_n(a_t) &= n^{-1/2} \sum_{s=1}^{t} \eta_s/\sigma_1 \\ \mathcal{V}_n(a_t) &= n^{-1/2} \sum_{s=1}^{t} \varepsilon_s/\sigma_2, \end{aligned}$$

with $a_t = t/n$ and the definitions $\sigma_1^2 \equiv \lim_{n\to\infty} \text{var}(n^{-1/2}\sum_{t=1}^{n}\eta_t)$, and $\sigma_2^2 \equiv \lim_{n\to\infty} \text{var}(n^{-1/2}\sum_{t=1}^{n}\varepsilon_t)$. Then

$$\begin{aligned}\int_0^1 \mathcal{U}_n d\mathcal{V}_n &= \sum_{t=1}^{n} \mathcal{U}_n(a_{t-1})(\mathcal{V}_n(a_t) - \mathcal{V}_n(a_{t-1})) \\ &= n^{-1/2}\sum_{t=1}^{n} \mathcal{U}_n(a_{t-1})\varepsilon_t/\sigma_2 \\ &= n^{-1}\sum_{t=2}^{n}\sum_{s=1}^{t-1} \eta_s\varepsilon_t/(\sigma_1\sigma_2).\end{aligned}$$

Taking expectations, we have, say,

$$\begin{aligned}E\left(\int_0^1 \mathcal{U}_n d\mathcal{V}_n\right) &= E\left(n^{-1}\sum_{t=2}^{n}\sum_{s=1}^{t-1} \eta_s\varepsilon_t/(\sigma_1\sigma_2)\right) \\ &= n^{-1}\sum_{t=2}^{n}\sum_{s=1}^{t-1} E\left(\eta_s\varepsilon_t\right)/(\sigma_1\sigma_2) \\ &\equiv \Lambda_n.\end{aligned}$$

The value of Λ_n depends on the covariances $E(\eta_s\varepsilon_t)$, $s = 1,\ldots,t-1$, $t = 1,\ldots,n$. If these are all zero, as happens, for example, when $\eta_t = \varepsilon_t$ and $\{\varepsilon_t\}$ is either independent or a martingale difference sequence, then Λ_n is zero. If, however, ε_t is correlated with past values η_s, $s = 1,\ldots,t-1$, then Λ_n need not be zero.

By assumption, we have that $\mathcal{U}_n \Rightarrow \mathcal{U}$ and $\mathcal{V}_n \Rightarrow \mathcal{V}$, where $\mathcal{U}$ and $\mathcal{V}$ are both standard Wiener processes (not necessarily independent of each other). Now the expectation of $\int_0^1 \mathcal{U}\, d\mathcal{V}$ depends not at all on the covariance properties of $\{\varepsilon_t\}$ and $\{\eta_t\}$. In fact, it can be shown that $E(\int_0^1 \mathcal{U}\, d\mathcal{V}) = 0$. Thus, at a minimum, we must recenter $\int_0^1 \mathcal{U}_n d\mathcal{V}_n$ to

$$\int_0^1 \mathcal{U}_n d\mathcal{V}_n - \Lambda_n,$$

to ensure that its expectation matches that of $\int_0^1 \mathcal{U} d\mathcal{V}$.

In fact, for the stochastic processes we study, this recentering is enough to give us what we want. Conditions ensuring that $\{\varepsilon_t\}$ and $\{\eta_t\}$ obey the FCLT together with the assumption that $\Lambda_n \to \Lambda$ are sufficient to deliver

$$\int_0^1 \mathcal{U}_n d\mathcal{V}_n - \Lambda_n \Rightarrow \int_0^1 \mathcal{U}\, d\mathcal{V},$$

a consequence of Theorem 4.1 of DeJong and Davidson (2000). DeJong and Davidson's proof is sophisticated and involved. We therefore content ourselves with stating corollaries to DeJong and Davidson's (2000) Theorem 4.1 that deliver the desired results for our cointegration setup.

For this, we let $\{\boldsymbol{\eta}_t\}$ and $\{\boldsymbol{\varepsilon}_t\}$ be $m \times 1$ and $k \times 1$ vectors, respectively, and define

$$\begin{aligned}\mathcal{U}_n(a) &= \boldsymbol{\Sigma}_1^{-1/2} n^{-1/2} \sum_{t=1}^{[an]} \boldsymbol{\eta}_t \\ \mathcal{V}_n(a) &= \boldsymbol{\Sigma}_2^{-1/2} n^{-1/2} \sum_{t=1}^{[an]} \boldsymbol{\varepsilon}_t,\end{aligned}$$

where $\boldsymbol{\Sigma}_1 \equiv \lim_{n\to\infty} \text{var}(n^{-1/2} \sum_{t=1}^n \boldsymbol{\eta}_t)$ and $\boldsymbol{\Sigma}_2 \equiv \lim_{n\to\infty} \text{var}(n^{-1/2} \sum_{t=1}^n \boldsymbol{\varepsilon}_t)$. We also define

$$\boldsymbol{\Lambda}_n \equiv \boldsymbol{\Sigma}_1^{-1/2} n^{-1} \sum_{t=2}^{n} \sum_{s=1}^{t-1} E(\boldsymbol{\eta}_s \boldsymbol{\varepsilon}_t') \boldsymbol{\Sigma}_2^{-1/2\prime}.$$

Theorem 7.42 (i.i.d. stochastic integral convergence) *Suppose that* $\{\boldsymbol{\eta}_t\}$ *and* $\{\boldsymbol{\varepsilon}_t\}$ *are i.i.d. sequences each satisfying the conditions of the multivariate Donsker theorem. Suppose also that* $\boldsymbol{\Lambda}_n \to \boldsymbol{\Lambda}$, *a finite matrix. Then*

$$(\mathcal{U}_n, \mathcal{V}_n, \int_0^1 \mathcal{U}_n d\mathcal{V}_n' - \boldsymbol{\Lambda}_n) \Rightarrow (\mathcal{U}, \mathcal{V}, \int_0^1 \mathcal{U} d\mathcal{V}').$$

Proof. The argument of the proof of DeJong and Davidson (2000, Theorem 4.1) specialized to the i.i.d. case delivers the result. ∎

Note that we have stated the conclusion in terms of the joint convergence of $\mathcal{U}_n$, $\mathcal{V}_n$ and $\int_0^1 \mathcal{U}_n d\mathcal{V}_n' - \boldsymbol{\Lambda}_n$. This is convenient because it permits easy application of the continuous mapping theorem, as DeJong and Davidson (2000) note.

Exercise 7.43 (*i*) *Verify that* $\boldsymbol{\Lambda} = \mathbf{0}$ *when* $\{\boldsymbol{\eta}_t\}$ *and* $\{\boldsymbol{\varepsilon}_t\}$ *are independent and the conditions of Theorem 7.42 hold, so that* $\int_0^1 \mathcal{U}_n d\mathcal{V}_n' \Rightarrow \int_0^1 \mathcal{U} d\mathcal{V}'$.
(*ii*) *Find the value of* $\boldsymbol{\Lambda}$ *when* $\boldsymbol{\eta}_t = \boldsymbol{\varepsilon}_{t-1}$.

We now have what we need to establish the limiting distribution of the least squares estimator for cointegrated random walks.

Exercise 7.44 (Cointegrated regression with random walk) *Suppose the following two conditions hold.*

(*i*) $\{\varepsilon_t\}$ *and* $\{\eta_t\}$ *are independent i.i.d. processes with* $E(\varepsilon_t) = E(\eta_t) = 0$, $0 < \sigma_1^2 \equiv \text{var}(\eta_t) < \infty$ *and* $0 < \sigma_2^2 \equiv \text{var}(\varepsilon_t) < \infty$.

(*ii*) $Y_t = X_t\beta_o + \varepsilon_t$, $t = 1, \ldots$, *where* $X_t = X_{t-1} + \eta_t$, $t = 1, \ldots$, *and* $X_0 = 0$, *with* $\beta_o \in \mathbb{R}$.

Then for independent standard Wiener processes $\mathcal{W}_1$, $\mathcal{W}_2$,

(*a*) $n^{-2}\sum_{t=1}^n X_t^2 \Rightarrow \sigma_1^2 \int_0^1 \mathcal{W}_1(a)^2 da$;

(*b*) $n^{-1}\sum_{t=1}^n X_t\varepsilon_t \Rightarrow \sigma_1\sigma_2 \int_0^1 \mathcal{W}_1(a)\, d\mathcal{W}_2(a)$;

(*c*) $n(\hat{\beta}_n - \beta_o) \Rightarrow \sigma_2/\sigma_1 \left[\int_0^1 \mathcal{W}_1(a)da\right]^{-1} \int_0^1 \mathcal{W}_1(a)\, d\mathcal{W}_2(a)$;

(*d*) $\hat{\beta}_n \xrightarrow{p} \beta_o$.

Now suppose that $\mathbf{X}_t$ is a $k \times 1$ vector of integrated processes, $\mathbf{X}_t = \mathbf{X}_{t-1} + \boldsymbol{\eta}_t$ and that $Y_t = \mathbf{X}_t'\boldsymbol{\beta}_o + \varepsilon_t$. Further let $\boldsymbol{\zeta}_t \equiv (\boldsymbol{\eta}_t', \varepsilon_t)'$ obey the multivariate FCLT. $\{\mathbf{X}_t\}$ and $\{Y_t\}$ will then be integrated though not necessarily random walk processes. To handle this case, let

$$\boldsymbol{\Sigma} \equiv \lim_{n\to\infty} \text{var}(n^{-1/2}\sum_{t=1}^n \boldsymbol{\zeta}_t),$$

and define the $(k+1) \times 1$ vector

$$\boldsymbol{\xi}_t = \boldsymbol{\Sigma}^{-1/2}\boldsymbol{\zeta}_t,$$

so that $\boldsymbol{\zeta}_t = \boldsymbol{\Sigma}^{1/2}\boldsymbol{\xi}_t$. Using this, we can write

$$\begin{aligned} \mathbf{X}_t &= \mathbf{X}_{t-1} + \boldsymbol{\eta}_t \\ &= \mathbf{X}_{t-1} + \mathbf{D}_1'\boldsymbol{\Sigma}^{1/2}\boldsymbol{\xi}_t, \end{aligned}$$

where $\mathbf{D}_1'$ is the $k \times (k+1)$ selection matrix such that $\mathbf{D}_1'\boldsymbol{\zeta}_t = \boldsymbol{\eta}_t$. Similarly, we can write

$$\begin{aligned} Y_t &= \mathbf{X}_t'\boldsymbol{\beta}_o + \varepsilon_t \\ &= \mathbf{X}_t'\boldsymbol{\beta}_o + \mathbf{D}_2'\boldsymbol{\Sigma}^{1/2}\boldsymbol{\xi}_t, \end{aligned}$$

where $\mathbf{D}_2'$ is the $1 \times (k+1)$ selection vector such that $\mathbf{D}_2'\boldsymbol{\zeta}_t = \varepsilon_t$.

Next, we write

$$\mathcal{W}_n(a_t) = n^{-1/2}\sum_{s=1}^t \boldsymbol{\xi}_s, \quad a_t = t/n.$$

With this notation we have

$$n^{-2}\sum_{t=1}^{n}\mathbf{X}_t\mathbf{X}_t' = n^{-1}\sum_{t=1}^{n}\mathbf{D}_1'\boldsymbol{\Sigma}^{1/2}\mathcal{W}_n(a_t)\mathcal{W}_n(a_t)'\boldsymbol{\Sigma}^{1/2\prime}\mathbf{D}_1.$$

Provided that $\{\boldsymbol{\xi}_t\}$ obeys the multivariate FCLT, we have

$$n^{-2}\sum_{t=1}^{n}\mathbf{X}_t\mathbf{X}_t' \Rightarrow \mathbf{D}_1'\boldsymbol{\Sigma}^{1/2}\int_0^1 \mathcal{W}(a)\mathcal{W}(a)'da\ \boldsymbol{\Sigma}^{1/2\prime}\mathbf{D}_1.$$

We also have

$$\begin{aligned} n^{-1}\sum_{t=1}^{n}\mathbf{X}_t\varepsilon_t &= n^{-1}\sum_{t=1}^{n}\mathbf{X}_{t-1}\varepsilon_t + n^{-1}\sum_{t=1}^{n}\boldsymbol{\eta}_t\varepsilon_t \\ &= \sum_{t=1}^{n}\mathbf{D}_1'\boldsymbol{\Sigma}^{1/2}\mathcal{W}_n(a_{t-1})(\mathcal{W}_n(a_t)-\mathcal{W}_n(a_{t-1}))'\boldsymbol{\Sigma}^{1/2\prime}\mathbf{D}_2 \\ &\quad + n^{-1}\sum_{t=1}^{n}\boldsymbol{\eta}_t\varepsilon_t \\ &= \mathbf{D}_1'\boldsymbol{\Sigma}^{1/2}\int_0^1 \mathcal{W}_n d\mathcal{W}_n'\ \boldsymbol{\Sigma}^{1/2\prime}\mathbf{D}_2 + n^{-1}\sum_{t=1}^{n}\boldsymbol{\eta}_t\varepsilon_t. \end{aligned}$$

The second term, $n^{-1}\sum_{t=1}^{n}\boldsymbol{\eta}_t\varepsilon_t$, can be handled with a law of large numbers. To handle the first term, we apply the following corollary of Theorem 4.1 of DeJong and Davidson (2000).

Theorem 7.45 (Heterogeneous mixing stochastic integral convergence) *Suppose that $\{\boldsymbol{\eta}_t\}$ and $\{\boldsymbol{\varepsilon}_t\}$ are vector-valued mixing sequences each satisfying the conditions of the heterogeneous mixing multivariate FCLT (Theorem 7.30). Suppose also that $\boldsymbol{\Lambda}_n \to \boldsymbol{\Lambda}$, a finite matrix. Then*

$$(\mathcal{U}_n, \mathcal{V}_n, \int_0^1 \mathcal{U}_n d\mathcal{V}_n' - \boldsymbol{\Lambda}_n) \Rightarrow (\mathcal{U}, \mathcal{V}, \int_0^1 \mathcal{U}d\mathcal{V}').$$

Proof. This is an immediate corollary of Theorem 4.1 of DeJong and Davidson (2000). ∎

Theorem 7.46 (Cointegrating regression with mixing innovations) *Suppose*

(*i*) *$\{\boldsymbol{\zeta}_t = (\boldsymbol{\eta}_t', \varepsilon_t)'\}$ is a globally covariance stationary mixing process of $(k+1)\times 1$ vectors with ϕ of size $-r/(2r-2)$ or α of size $-r/(r-2)$,*

$r > 2$, such that $E(\zeta_t) = \mathbf{0}$, $E(|\zeta_{ti}|^r) < \Delta < \infty$, $i = 1, \ldots, k+1$ and for all t. Suppose further that $\mathbf{\Sigma} \equiv \lim_{n\to\infty} \text{var}(n^{-1/2} \sum_{t=1}^n \zeta_t)$ is finite and nonsingular.

(*ii*) *$Y_t = \mathbf{X}_t'\boldsymbol{\beta}_o + \varepsilon_t$, $t = 1, 2, \ldots$, where $\mathbf{X}_t = \mathbf{X}_{t-1} + \boldsymbol{\eta}_t$, $t = 1, 2, \ldots$, and $\mathbf{X}_0 = \mathbf{0}$, with $\boldsymbol{\beta}_o \in \mathbb{R}^k$.*

Let $\mathcal{W}$ denote a standard multivariate Wiener process, let $\mathbf{D}_1'$ be the $k \times (k+1)$ selection matrix such that $\mathbf{D}_1'\zeta_t = \boldsymbol{\eta}_t$, let $\mathbf{D}_2'$ be the $1 \times (k+1)$ selection vector such that $\mathbf{D}_2'\zeta_t = \varepsilon_t$, let

$$\mathbf{\Lambda} \equiv \lim_{n\to\infty} \mathbf{\Sigma}^{-1/2} n^{-1} \sum_{t=2}^{n} \sum_{s=1}^{t} E(\zeta_s \zeta_t') \mathbf{\Sigma}^{-1/2\prime},$$

and let $\mathbf{\Gamma} \equiv \lim_{n\to\infty} n^{-1} \sum_{t=1}^n E(\zeta_t \varepsilon_t)$.

Then $\mathbf{\Lambda}$ and $\mathbf{\Gamma}$ are finite and

(*a*) $n^{-2} \sum_{t=1}^n \mathbf{X}_t \mathbf{X}_t' \Rightarrow \mathbf{D}_1'\mathbf{\Sigma}^{1/2} \left[\int_0^1 \mathcal{W}(a)\mathcal{W}(a)'da\right] \mathbf{\Sigma}^{1/2\prime}\mathbf{D}_1$.

(*b*) $n^{-1} \sum_{t=1}^n \mathbf{X}_t \varepsilon_t \Rightarrow \mathbf{D}_1'\mathbf{\Sigma}^{1/2} \left[\int_0^1 \mathcal{W}d\mathcal{W}' + \mathbf{\Lambda}\right] \mathbf{\Sigma}^{1/2\prime}\mathbf{D}_2 + \mathbf{\Gamma}$.

(*c*)

$$\begin{aligned} n(\hat{\boldsymbol{\beta}}_n - \boldsymbol{\beta}_o) \;\Rightarrow\; & \left[\mathbf{D}_1'\mathbf{\Sigma}^{1/2} \left[\int_0^1 \mathcal{W}(a)\mathcal{W}(a)'da\right] \mathbf{\Sigma}^{1/2\prime}\mathbf{D}_1\right]^{-1} \\ & \times \left[\mathbf{D}_1'\mathbf{\Sigma}^{1/2} \left[\int_0^1 \mathcal{W}d\mathcal{W}' + \mathbf{\Lambda}\right] \mathbf{\Sigma}^{1/2\prime}\mathbf{D}_2 + \mathbf{\Gamma}\right]. \end{aligned}$$

(*d*) $\hat{\boldsymbol{\beta}}_n \xrightarrow{p} \boldsymbol{\beta}_o$.

Proof. The mixing and moment conditions ensure the finiteness of $\mathbf{\Lambda}$ and $\mathbf{\Gamma}$. (*a*) Under the mixing conditions of (*i*) $\{\boldsymbol{\xi}_t = \mathbf{\Sigma}^{-1/2}\zeta_t\}$ obeys the heterogeneous mixing multivariate FCLT, so the result follows from the argument preceding the statement of the theorem.

(*b*) As we wrote above,

$$n^{-1} \sum_{t=1}^{n} \mathbf{X}_t \varepsilon_t = \mathbf{D}_1'\mathbf{\Sigma}^{1/2} \int_0^1 \mathcal{W}_n d\mathcal{W}_n' \mathbf{\Sigma}^{1/2}\mathbf{D}_2 + n^{-1} \sum_{t=1}^{n} \boldsymbol{\eta}_t \varepsilon_t.$$

Under the mixing conditions of (*i*) $\{\boldsymbol{\eta}_t', \varepsilon_t\}$ obeys the law of large numbers, so $n^{-1} \sum_{t=1}^n \boldsymbol{\eta}_t \varepsilon_t \xrightarrow{p} \mathbf{\Gamma}$. Theorem 7.45 applies given (*i*) to ensure $\int_0^1 \mathcal{W}_n d\mathcal{W}_n' \Rightarrow \int_0^1 \mathcal{W}d\mathcal{W}' + \mathbf{\Lambda}$. The result follows by Lemma 4.27.

(*c*) The results of (*a*) and (*b*), together with Lemma 4.27 deliver the conclusion, as $n(\hat{\boldsymbol{\beta}}_n - \boldsymbol{\beta}_o) = \left(n^{-2}\sum_{t=1}^n \mathbf{X}_t\mathbf{X}_t'\right)^{-1} n^{-1}\sum_{t=1}^n \mathbf{X}_t\varepsilon_t$.

(*d*) $\hat{\boldsymbol{\beta}}_n - \boldsymbol{\beta}_o = n^{-1}\left(n(\hat{\boldsymbol{\beta}}_n - \boldsymbol{\beta}_o)\right) = o(1)O_p(1) = o_p(1)$. ■

Observe that the conclusions here extend those of Exercise 7.44 in a natural way.

The statement of the results can be somewhat simplified by making use of the notion of a *Brownian motion with covariance* $\boldsymbol{\Sigma}$, defined as $\boldsymbol{\mathcal{B}} = \boldsymbol{\Sigma}^{1/2}\boldsymbol{\mathcal{W}}$, denoted BM($\boldsymbol{\Sigma}$), where $\boldsymbol{\mathcal{W}}$ is a standard Wiener process (Brownian motion). With this notation we have

$$n(\hat{\boldsymbol{\beta}}_n - \boldsymbol{\beta}_o) \Rightarrow \left[\mathbf{D}_1'\left[\int_0^1 \boldsymbol{\mathcal{B}}(a)\boldsymbol{\mathcal{B}}(a)'da\right]\mathbf{D}_1\right]^{-1} \times \left[\mathbf{D}_1'\left[\int_0^1 \boldsymbol{\mathcal{B}}d\boldsymbol{\mathcal{B}}' + \boldsymbol{\Sigma}^{1/2}\boldsymbol{\Lambda}\boldsymbol{\Sigma}^{1/2\prime}\right]\mathbf{D}_2 + \boldsymbol{\Gamma}\right].$$

In conclusion (*c*), we observe the presence of the term

$$\left[\mathbf{D}_1'\left[\int_0^1 \boldsymbol{\mathcal{B}}(a)\boldsymbol{\mathcal{B}}(a)'da\right]\mathbf{D}_1\right]^{-1}(\mathbf{D}_1'\boldsymbol{\Sigma}^{1/2}\boldsymbol{\Lambda}\boldsymbol{\Sigma}^{1/2\prime}\mathbf{D}_2 + \boldsymbol{\Gamma}).$$

The component involving $\boldsymbol{\Lambda}$ arises from serial correlation in $\boldsymbol{\zeta}_t$; the component involving $\boldsymbol{\Gamma}$ arises from correlation between $\boldsymbol{\eta}_t$ and ε_t. As in the case of a unit root regression, the effect of serial correlation in the errors is not to induce inconsistency of $\hat{\boldsymbol{\beta}}_n$; instead, the asymptotic distribution exhibits a bias. Similarly, the correlation between the regressors $\mathbf{X}_t$ and the errors ε_t also does not result in inconsistency of $\hat{\boldsymbol{\beta}}_n$, as it does in the results of previous chapters. Instead, the effect is again the more modest effect of an asymptotic bias in $\hat{\boldsymbol{\beta}}_n$. As in the case of regression with a unit root, we note that even when $\boldsymbol{\Lambda}$ and $\boldsymbol{\Gamma}$ vanish, the asymptotic distribution still is not centered around zero, due to the presence of correlation between $\int_0^1 \boldsymbol{\mathcal{B}}(a)\boldsymbol{\mathcal{B}}(a)'da$ and $\int_0^1 \boldsymbol{\mathcal{B}}d\boldsymbol{\mathcal{B}}'$. Asymptotic bias thus remains, although inconsistency does not arise.

The least squares estimator $\hat{\boldsymbol{\beta}}_n$ is only the simplest of a fascinating array of estimators proposed for cointegrating regressions, and the results depend heavily on the placement of the unit roots and the nature of the cointegrating relationships. We cannot address these issues here; rather, our intent is that the material presented will provide basic understanding and useful tools for the reader interested in delving more deeply into that literature. For further reading, the reader is directed to the works of Hansen (1992a,b), Johansen (1988, 1991, 1996), Park and Phillips (1988,

1989), Phillips (1987), Saikkonen (1992), Sims, Stock, and Watson (1990), and Wooldridge (1994).

References

Abadir, K. M. (1995). "The joint density of two functionals of a Brownian motion." *Mathematical Methods of Statistics*, 4, 449–462.

Bachelier, L. B. J. A. (1900). *Théorie de la spéculation*, Thèse–Faculté des sciences de Paris. Gauthier-Villars, Paris.

Billingsley, P. (1968). *Convergence of Probability Measures.* Wiley, New York.

——— (1979). *Probability and Measure.* Wiley, New York.

Breiman, L. (1992). *Probability.* Siam, Philadelphia.

Brzeźniak, Z. and T. Zastawniak (1999). *Basic Stochastic Processes: A Course Through Exercises.* Springer-Verlag, New York.

Chan, N. H. and C. Z. Wei (1988). "Limiting distributions of least squares estimates of unstable autoregressive processes." *Annals of Statistics*, 16, 367–401.

Davidson, J. (1994). *Stochastic Limit Theory.* Oxford University Press, New York.

——— (1998). "When is a time series $I(0)$? Evaluating the memory properties of nonlinear dynamic models." Cardiff University Discussion Paper.

DeJong R. M. and J. Davidson (2000). "The functional central limit theorem and weak convegence to stochastic integrals I: Weakly dependent processes," forthcoming in *Econometric Theory*, 16.

Dickey, D. A. and W. A. Fuller (1979). "Distribution of the estimators for autoregressive time series with a unit root." *Journal of the American Statistical Association*, 74, 427–431.

——— and ——— (1981). "Likelihood ratio statistics for autoregressive time series with a unit root." *Econometrica*, 49, 1057–1072.

Donsker, M. D. (1951). "An invariance principle for certain probability limit theorems." *Memoirs of the American Mathematical Society*, 6, 1–12.

Elliott, G., T. J. Rothenberg and J. H. Stock (1996). "Efficient tests for an autoregressive unit root." *Econometrica*, 64, 813–836.

Engle, R. F. and C. W. J. Granger (1987). "Cointegration and error correction: representation, estimation and testing." *Econometrica*, 55, 251–276.

Granger, C. W. J. (1981). "Some properties of time series data and their use in econometric model specification." *Journal of Econometrics*, 16, 121–130.

——— and P. Newbold (1974). "Spurious regressions in econometrics." *Journal of Econometrics*, 2, 111–120.

Hall, P. (1977). "Martingale invariance principles." *Annals of Probability*, 5, 875–877.

Hamilton, J. D. (1994). *Time Series Analysis*, Princeton University Press, Princeton.

Hansen, B. E. (1992a). "Efficient estimation and testing of cointegrating vectors in the presence of deterministic trends." *Journal of Econometrics*, 53, 87-121.

——— (1992b). "Heteroskedastic cointegration." *Journal of Econometrics*, 54, 139–158.

Ito, K. (1944). "Stochastic integral." *Proc. Imperial Acad. Tokyo*, 20, 519–524.

Johansen, S. (1988). "Statistical analysis of cointegration vectors." *Journal of Economic Dynamics and Control*, 12, 231–254.

——— (1991). "Estimation and hypothesis testing of cointegration vectors in Gaussian vector autoregressive models." *Econometrica*, 59, 1551–1580.

——— (1996). *Likelihood-Based Inference in Cointegrated Vector Autoregressive Models*. 2nd ed. Oxford University Press, Oxford.

McLeish, D. L. (1974). "Dependent central limit theorems and invariance principles." *Annals of Probability*, 2, 620–628.

Park, J. Y. and P. C. B. Phillips (1988). "Statistical inference in regressions with integrated processes: Part 1." *Econometric Theory*, 4, 468–497.

——— and ——— (1989). "Statistical inference in regressions with integrated processes: Part 2." *Econometric Theory*, 5, 95-132.

Phillips, P. C. B. (1986). "Understanding spurious regressions in econometrics." *Journal of Econometrics*, 33, 311–340.

——— (1987). "Time series regression with a unit root." *Econometrica*, 55, 277–301.

——— (1991). "Optimal inference in cointegrated systems." *Econometrica*, 59, 283–306.

——— and S. N. Durlauf (1986). "Multiple time series regression with integrated processes." *Review of Economic Studies*, 53, 473–496.

——— and Z. Xiao (1998). "A primer on unit root testing." Cowles Foundation Discussion Papers No. 1189.

Saikkonen, P. (1992). "Estimation and testing of cointegrated systems by an autoregressive approximation." *Econometric Theory*, 8, 1–27.

Sims, C. A., J. H. Stock, and M. W. Watson (1990). "Inference in linear time series models with some unit roots." *Econometrica*, 58, 113–144.

Stock, J. H. (1994). "Unit roots, structural breaks and trends." In *Handbook of Econometrics*, vol. 4, R. F. Engle and D. McFadden eds., pp. 2739–2841. North-Holland, Amsterdam.

——— (1999). "A class of tests for integration and cointegration." In *Cointegration, Causality, and Forecasting*, R. F. Engle and H. White eds., pp. 135–167. Oxford University Press, New York.

——— and M. W. Watson (1993). "A simple estimator of cointegrating vectors in higher order integrated systems." *Econometrica*, 61, 783–820.

Tanaka, K. (1996). *Time Series Analysis: Nonstationary and Noninvertible Distribution Theory.* John Wiley, New York.

Watson, M. W. (1994). "Vector autoregressions and cointegration." In *Handbook of Econometrics*, vol. 4, R. F. Engle and D. McFadden eds., pp. 2843–2915. North-Holland, Amsterdam.

White, J. S. (1958). "The limiting distribution of the serial correlation coefficient in the explosive case." *Annals of Mathematical Statistics*, 29, 1188–1197.

Wiener, N. (1923). "Differential space." *Journal of Mathematics and Physics*, 58, 131–174.

——— (1924). "Un probléme de probabilités dénombrables." *Bull. Soc. Math., France*, 52, 569–578.

Wooldridge, J. M. (1994). "Estimation and inference for dependent processes." In *Handbook of Econometrics*, vol. 4, R. F. Engle and D. McFadden eds., pp. 2639–2738. North-Holland, Amsterdam.

——— and H. White (1988). "Some invariance principles and central limit theorems for dependent heterogeneous processes." *Econometric Theory*, 4, 210–230.

Yule, G. U. (1926). "Why do we sometimes get nonsense correlations between time series? – a study in sampling and the nature of time series." *Journal of the Royal Statistical Society*, 89, 1–64.

CHAPTER 8

Directions for Further Study

Although the results of the previous chapters cover a considerable range of the possibilities of interest to economists, they also constitute but a modest entry into the rich realm of modern econometrics. We may view the territory before us as extending in a number of different though related directions. Among these are more general data generating processes (DGPs); more general specifications for the models used to analyze these DGPs; estimation procedures alternative to least squares and instrumental variables; and consideration of the consequences and detection of model misspecification.

8.1 Extending the Data Generating Process

Loosely speaking, there are three dimensions in which the data generating processes we consider can be extended: moments, memory, and heterogeneity. For example, although we consider unit root DGPs, we have not discussed DGPs that involve deterministic time trends. Nevertheless, the Markov law of large numbers (Theorem 3.7) or the McLeish law of large numbers (Theorem 3.47) can be useful in establishing consistency in models with trending explanatory or instrumental variables. In fact, consistency may happen "faster" in models with these variables because the error variance may become quite negligible in comparison to the magnitude of the regression function $\mathbf{X}_t'\boldsymbol{\beta}_o$. Asymptotic normality can be established with the help of the Lindeberg or Martingale-Lindeberg central limit theorems (Theorems 5.6 or 5.24). In fact, conditions ensuring asymptotic normality in models with nonstochastic and possibly trending variables were the subject of careful attention very early on (Grenander, 1954) and there is a well-developed general theory now available (e.g., Crowder, 1980).

Deterministic time trends as usually considered constitute a growth in the first moment of the dependent variable. Trends may occur in higher moments as well. The key to handling such cases is to have available laws of large numbers, central limit theorems and/or functional central limit theorems that permit such possibilities. For example, Wooldridge and White (1988) give FCLT results for processes with possibly trending moments of higher order.

We have considered DGPs satisfying the memory requirements of ergodicity and mixing. Recall also that we imposed the mixingale memory requirement to establish the stationary ergodic CLT and FCLT. Although it constitutes a restriction for stationary ergodic processes, the mixingale notion can also be used to relax the memory conditions in the mixing context. Specifically, by considering stochastic processes that depend on an infinite history of an underlying mixing process, but which depend primarily on the "near epoch" of the mixing process, we can obtain processes that have longer memory than a simple mixing process but which inherit enough of the properties of the underlying mixing process to satisfy the mixingale condition. In fact, it can be shown that such "near epoch dependent" functions of a mixing process are mixingales that are sufficiently well behaved so as to satisfy laws of large numbers, CLTs and FCLTs.

Such conditions were introduced by Ibragimov (1962) and treated by Billingsley (1968). McLeish (1975a,b) used these conditions in developing laws of large numbers, CLTs and FCLTs, which were introduced to econometrics by Gallant and White (1988). See Gallant and White (1988) and Davidson (1994) for further discussion and details.

In Chapter 7, we considered integrated (unit root) processes, which exhibit considerably more dependence than mixing, mixingales, or ergodicity permit. We see, however, that the large sample behavior of our estimators in these cases depends on the FCLT, whose validity is based on the memory properties of the innovations to the integrated process. A memory requirement intermediate to the mixingale and integrated processes considered here is that of fractional integration, a generalization of the notion of integrated processes. A review of such processes is given by Sowell (1992) and Baillie (1996). The tools required to study the large sample properties of estimators associated with fractionally integrated DGPs are extensions of the FCLT and the other tools of Chapter 7. With fractional integration, the FCLT analogs deliver convergence to "fractional Brownian motion." See, e.g., Taqqu (1975) for further discussion.

To keep our discussion of the FCLT in Chapter 7 relatively simple, we impose the global covariance stationarity assumption, restricting the heterogeneity of the DGP more than is necessary to deliver the FCLT or analogous results. See Wooldridge and White (1988), Davidson (1994), and DeJong and Davidson (2000) for results that do not require global covariance stationarity.

8.2 Nonlinear Models

Throughout, we have restricted attention to models linear in the parameters, although we have allowed nonlinear restrictions among the parameters to hold. A more general model that contains many situations of interest to economists can be written as $\mathbf{q}_t(\mathbf{X}_t, \mathbf{Y}_t, \boldsymbol{\beta})$, where for some $\boldsymbol{\beta}_o$ it is assumed that $\mathbf{q}_t(\mathbf{X}_t, \mathbf{Y}_t, \boldsymbol{\beta}_o) = \boldsymbol{\varepsilon}_t$.

In the particular case we studied, the model has the form

$$\mathbf{q}_t(\mathbf{X}_t, \mathbf{Y}_t, \boldsymbol{\beta}) = \mathbf{Y}_t - \mathbf{X}_t'\boldsymbol{\beta}.$$

Situations in which the elements of the dependent variable $\mathbf{Y}_t$ take values in a restricted subset of the real line are often of considerable interest. For example, suppose Y_t is a scalar that can take only the values 0 or 1 (the "limited dependent variable" case). In this case a relevant model is given by

$$q(\mathbf{X}_t, Y_t, \boldsymbol{\beta}) = Y_t - F(\mathbf{X}_t'\boldsymbol{\beta}),$$

where F is a cumulative distribution function (e.g., the normal or logistic c.d.f.). We interpret $F(\mathbf{X}_t'\boldsymbol{\beta})$ as a model for $E(Y_t|\mathbf{X}_t) = P[Y_t = 1|\mathbf{X}_t]$.

There is a vast range of other possibilities of which the linear model is merely a simple and convenient special case. Further, the nature of the model adopted and the other knowledge available about the DGP can play a determining role in the estimation procedures one employs.

8.3 Other Estimation Techniques

To estimate parameters of the model $\mathbf{q}_t(\mathbf{X}_t, \mathbf{Y}_t, \boldsymbol{\beta})$ just discussed, we can employ the method of moments introduced and described briefly in Chapter

4. Specifically, if we have instrumental variables $\mathbf{Z}_t$ available such that $E(\mathbf{Z}_t\boldsymbol{\varepsilon}_t) = \mathbf{0}$, then we can attempt to estimate $\boldsymbol{\beta}_o$ by solving the problem

$$\min_{\boldsymbol{\beta}} \mathbf{q}(\boldsymbol{\beta})'\mathbf{Z}\hat{\mathbf{P}}_n\mathbf{Z}'\mathbf{q}(\boldsymbol{\beta}),$$

where $\mathbf{q}(\boldsymbol{\beta})$ is the $np \times 1$ vector with tth block $\mathbf{q}_t(\mathbf{X}_t, \mathbf{Y}_t, \boldsymbol{\beta})$, so

$$\mathbf{Z}'\mathbf{q}(\boldsymbol{\beta}) = \sum_{t=1}^{n} \mathbf{Z}_t\mathbf{q}_t(\mathbf{X}_t, \mathbf{Y}_t, \boldsymbol{\beta}).$$

This corresponds to the method of moments procedure with $\mathbf{g}(\mathbf{X}_t, \mathbf{Y}_t, \mathbf{Z}_t, \boldsymbol{\beta}) = \mathbf{Z}_t\mathbf{q}_t(\mathbf{X}_t, \mathbf{Y}_t, \boldsymbol{\beta})$.

The properties of this method of moments estimator have been studied by Amemiya (1977), Burguete, Gallant, and Souza (1982), and Hansen (1982), among others.

To establish properties for estimators of nonlinear models analogous to those obtained here, we need somewhat more powerful tools than those given. In particular, repeated use is made of uniform laws of large numbers and the mean value theorem for random functions (e.g., see Jennrich, 1969, and White, 1994).

A leading alternative to the method of instrumental variables studied here is the method of maximum likelihood. In fact, if one assumes that the disturbances $\boldsymbol{\varepsilon}_t$ are independent and identically distributed as multivariate normal with unknown covariance matrix, then the optimal IV estimators of Chapter 4 can be shown to be asymptotically equivalent to the maximum likelihood estimator under general conditions. There is a broad range of situations where maximum likelihood and instrumental variables are asymptotically equivalent (see Hausman, 1975, and Amemiya, 1977), although this equivalence fails for the general case of nonlinear models previously mentioned. In that case, maximum likelihood can be shown to be more efficient than instrumental variables (Amemiya, 1977).

Use of the method of maximum likelihood requires an assumption about the distribution of the errors, whereas the instrumental variables method does not. Thus, the method of instrumental variables is available in situations where a knowledge of the error distribution is absent or suspect. Nevertheless, maximum likelihood estimation can be conducted as if the errors have the assumed distribution, whether this assumption is valid or not. This procedure is known as quasi-maximum likelihood estimation, a member of the class of M-estimators (Huber, 1967), which contains a wealth of useful and interesting estimators. By selecting an M-estimator appropriately, it is possible to obtain estimators that are robust to failure of distributional assumptions or to certain plausible kinds of data errors.

Again, the study of these estimators requires, among other things, use of uniform laws of large numbers and mean value theorems for random functions. A general treatment of these estimators that also highlights the parallels with IV estimators is that of Gallant and White (1988).

8.4 Model Misspecification

Throughout this book, we have maintained the assumption that the data generating relationship is known to be

$$\mathbf{Y}_t = \mathbf{X}_t'\boldsymbol{\beta}_o + \varepsilon_t, \quad t = 1, 2, \ldots .$$

It would indeed be fortunate if the relationship between $\mathbf{X}_t$ and $\mathbf{Y}_t$ were ever truly "known." Owing to the complexity of economic phenomena, it is perhaps more realistic to suppose that the relationship between $\mathbf{X}_t$ and $\mathbf{Y}_t$ is unknown. In this case, a linear relationship such as that just given can be viewed as a convenient approximation but not necessarily as a definitive description of the relationship between $\mathbf{X}_t$ and $\mathbf{Y}_t$. It then becomes important to consider questions such as "How is this approximation to be interpreted?"; "What are the properties of the estimated parameters of the approximation?"; "How can the approximation be improved?"; and "How can we tell if our approximation is exact?".

For a discussion of these issues that builds on the material in this book in a framework encompassing several of the extensions discussed in this chapter, the reader is referred to *Estimation, Inference, and Specification Analysis* (White, 1994).

References

Amemiya, T. (1977). "The maximum likelihood estimator and the nonlinear three-stage least squares estimator in the general nonlinear simultaneous equation model." *Econometrica*, 45, 955–968.

Baillie, R. T. (1996). "Long memory processes and fractional integration in econometrics." *Journal of Econometrics*, 73, 5–59.

Billingsley, P. (1968). *Convergence of Probability Measures.* Wiley, New York.

Burguete, J. F., A. R. Gallant, and G. Souza (1982). "On unification of the asymptotic theory of nonlinear econometric models." *Econometric Reviews*, 1, 151–212.

Crowder, M. J. (1980). "On the asymptotic properties of least-squares estimators in autoregression." *Annals of Statistics*, 8, 132–146.

Davidson, J. (1994). *Stochastic Limit Theory*. Oxford University Press, New York.

DeJong R. M. and J. Davidson (2000). "The functional central limit theorem and weak convegence to stochastic integrals I: Weakly dependent processes," forthcoming in *Econometric Theory*, 16.

Gallant, A. R. and H. White (1988). *A Unified Theory of Estimation and Inference for Nonlinear Dynamic Models*. Basil Blackwell, Oxford.

Grenander, U. (1954). "On the estimation of regression coefficients in the case of an autocorrelated disturbance." *Annals of Mathematical Statistics*, 25, 252–272.

Hansen, L. P. (1982). "Large sample properties of generalized method of moments estimators." *Econometrica*, 50, 1029–1054.

Hausman, J. A. (1975). "An instrumental variable approach to full information estimators for linear and certain nonlinear structural models." *Econometrica*, 43, 727–738.

Huber, P. J. (1967). "The behavior of maximum likelihood estimates under nonstandard conditions." In *Proceedings of the Fifth Berkeley Symposium on Mathematical Statistics and Probability*, vol. 1, pp. 221–233. University of California Press, Berkeley, California.

Ibragimov, I. A. (1962). "Some limit theorems for stationary processes." *Theory of Probability and Its Applications*, 7, 349–382.

Jennrich, R. I. (1969). "Asymptotic properties of nonlinear least squares estimators." *Annals of Mathematical Statistics*, 40, 633–643.

McLeish, D. L. (1975a). "A maximal inequality and dependent strong laws." *Annals of Probability*, 3, 826–836.

——— (1975b). "Invariance principles for dependent variables." *Zeitschrift für Wahrscheinlichkeitstheorie und Verwandte Gebiete*, 32, 165–178

Sowell, F. (1992). "Maximum-likelihood-estimation of stationary univariate fractionally integrated time-series models." *Journal of Econometrics*, 53, 165–188.

Taqqu, M. S. (1975). "Weak convergence to fractional Brownian motion and to the Rosenblatt process." *Zeitschrift für Wahrscheinlichkeitstheorie und Verwandte Gebiete*, 31, 287–302.

White, H. (1994). *Estimation, Inference and Specification Analysis*. Cambridge University Press, New York.

Wooldridge, J. M. and H. White (1988). "Some invariance principles and central limit theorems for dependent heterogeneous processes." *Econometric Theory*, 4, 210–230.

Solution Set

Exercise 2.8

Proof. Let $\mathbf{a}_n = \mathbf{A}_n\mathbf{b}_n$, where $\mathbf{A}_n = [A_{nij}]$ and $\mathbf{b}_n = (b_{n1}, b_{n2}, \ldots, b_{nk})'$. Then $a_{ni} = \sum_{j=1}^{k} A_{nij}b_{nj}$. Since $A_{nij} = o(1)$ and $b_{nj} = O(1)$, $A_{nij}b_{nj} = o(1)$ by Proposition 2.7 (*iii*). By Proposition 2.7 (*ii*), $a_{ni} = o(1)$ because it is the sum of k terms, each of which is $O(1)$. It follows that $\mathbf{a}_n \equiv \mathbf{A}_n\mathbf{b}_n = o(1)$. ■

Exercise 2.13

Proof. Since $\mathbf{Z}'\mathbf{X}/n \xrightarrow{a.s.} \mathbf{Q}$ and $\hat{\mathbf{P}}_n \xrightarrow{a.s.} \mathbf{P}$, it follows from Proposition 2.11 that $\det(\mathbf{X}'\mathbf{Z}\hat{\mathbf{P}}_n\mathbf{Z}'\mathbf{X}/n^2) \xrightarrow{a.s.} \det(\mathbf{Q}'\mathbf{P}\mathbf{Q})$. Since $\mathbf{Q}$ has full column rank and $\mathbf{P}$ is nonsingular by (*iii*), $\det(\mathbf{Q}'\mathbf{P}\mathbf{Q}) > 0$. It follows that $\det(\mathbf{X}'\mathbf{Z}\hat{\mathbf{P}}_n\mathbf{Z}'\mathbf{X}/n^2) > 0$ for all n sufficiently large almost surely, so that $(\mathbf{X}'\mathbf{Z}\hat{\mathbf{P}}_n\mathbf{Z}'\mathbf{X}/n^2)^{-1}$exists for all n sufficiently large $a.s.$ Hence

$$\tilde{\boldsymbol{\beta}}_n \equiv (\mathbf{X}'\mathbf{Z}\hat{\mathbf{P}}_n\mathbf{Z}'\mathbf{X}/n^2)^{-1}\mathbf{X}'\mathbf{Z}\hat{\mathbf{P}}_n\mathbf{Z}'\mathbf{Y}/n^2$$

exists for all n sufficiently large $a.s.$ Given (*i*),

$$\tilde{\boldsymbol{\beta}}_n = \boldsymbol{\beta}_o + (\mathbf{X}'\mathbf{Z}\hat{\mathbf{P}}_n\mathbf{Z}'\mathbf{X}/n^2)^{-1}\mathbf{X}'\mathbf{Z}\hat{\mathbf{P}}_n\mathbf{Z}'\boldsymbol{\varepsilon}/n^2.$$

It follows from Proposition 2.11 that

$$\tilde{\boldsymbol{\beta}}_n \xrightarrow{a.s.} \boldsymbol{\beta}_o + (\mathbf{Q}'\mathbf{P}\mathbf{Q})^{-1}\mathbf{Q}'\mathbf{P}\cdot\mathbf{0} = \boldsymbol{\beta}_o$$

given (*ii*) and (*iii*). ■

Exercise 2.20

Proof. Since $\mathbf{Q}_n = O(1)$ and $\mathbf{P}_n = O(1)$, it follows from Proposition 2.16 that $\det(\mathbf{X}'\mathbf{Z}\hat{\mathbf{P}}_n\mathbf{Z}'\mathbf{X}/n^2) - \det(\mathbf{Q}_n'\mathbf{P}_n\mathbf{Q}_n) \xrightarrow{a.s.} 0$. Given (iii), it follows from Lemma 2.19 that $\{\mathbf{Q}_n'\mathbf{P}_n\mathbf{Q}_n\}$ is uniformly positive definite, so

$$\det(\mathbf{Q}_n'\mathbf{P}_n\mathbf{Q}_n) > \delta > 0$$

for all n sufficiently large. It follows that $\det(\mathbf{X}'\mathbf{Z}\hat{\mathbf{P}}_n\mathbf{Z}'\mathbf{X}/n^2) > \delta/2 > 0$ for all n sufficiently large almost surely. Hence

$$\tilde{\boldsymbol{\beta}}_n = (\mathbf{X}'\mathbf{Z}\hat{\mathbf{P}}_n\mathbf{Z}'\mathbf{X}/n^2)^{-1}\mathbf{X}'\mathbf{Z}\hat{\mathbf{P}}_n\mathbf{Z}'\mathbf{Y}/n^2$$

exists for all n sufficiently large almost surely. Given (i), $\tilde{\boldsymbol{\beta}}_n = \boldsymbol{\beta}_o + (\mathbf{X}'\mathbf{Z}\hat{\mathbf{P}}_n\mathbf{Z}'\mathbf{X}/n^2)^{-1}\mathbf{X}'\mathbf{Z}\hat{\mathbf{P}}_n\mathbf{Z}'\boldsymbol{\varepsilon}/n^2$. Given (ii) and (iii) it follows from Proposition 2.16 that $\tilde{\boldsymbol{\beta}}_n - (\boldsymbol{\beta}_o + (\mathbf{Q}_n'\mathbf{P}_n\mathbf{Q}_n)^{-1}\mathbf{Q}_n'\mathbf{P}_n \times \mathbf{0}) \xrightarrow{a.s.} \mathbf{0}$, that is, $\tilde{\boldsymbol{\beta}}_n \xrightarrow{a.s.} \boldsymbol{\beta}_o$. ■

Exercise 2.22

Proof.

(i) By definition, there exist sets F, $G \subset \Omega$ with $P(F) = P(G) = 1$, where for all $\omega \in F$ it holds that $|a_n(\omega)n^{-\lambda}| < \Delta_a$ for all $n \geq N_a$, and for all $\omega \in G$ it holds that $|b_n(\omega)n^{-\mu}| < \Delta_b$ for all $n \geq N_b$. Set $\Delta = \Delta_a\Delta_b$ and $N = \max(N_a, N_b)$, then for all $\omega \in F \cap G$ it holds that $|a_n(\omega)b_n(\omega)n^{-\lambda}n^{-\mu}| < \Delta$ for all $n \geq N$. Since $P(F \cap G) = 1$ the first result follows. To obtain the second result, let $\Delta = \Delta_a + \Delta_b$, and set N as before. Then for all $\omega \in F \cap G$ it holds that $|(a_n(\omega) + b_n(\omega))n^{-\kappa}| \leq |a_n(\omega)n^{-\kappa} + b_n(\omega)n^{-\kappa}| \leq |a_n(\omega)n^{-\lambda}| + |b_n(\omega)n^{-\mu}| < \Delta_a + \Delta_b = \Delta$ for all $n \geq N$.

(ii) By definition, there exist sets F, $G \subset \Omega$ with $P(F) = P(G) = 1$, where for all $\omega \in F$ it holds that $a_n(\omega) = o(n^{\lambda})$ and for all $\omega \in G$ it holds that $b_n(\omega) = o(n^{\mu})$. By Proposition 2.7, $a_n(\omega)b_n(\omega) = o(n^{\lambda+\mu})$ and $a_n(\omega) + b_n(\omega) = o(n^{\kappa})$ on $F \cap G$. Since $P(F \cap G) = 1$ the results follow.

(iii) Define F as in (i) and G as in (ii). The result follows immediately by Proposition 2.7 and the fact that $P(F \cap G) = 1$.

■

Exercise 2.29

Proof. The proof is identical to that of Exercise 2.13 except that Proposition 2.27 is used instead of Proposition 2.11 and convergence in probability replaces convergence almost surely. ■

Exercise 2.32

Proof. The proof is identical to that of Exercise 2.20 except that Proposition 2.30 is used in place of Proposition 2.16 and convergence in probability replaces convergence almost surely. ■

Exercise 2.35

Proof.

(*i*) Since $a_n = O_p(n^\lambda)$ and $b_n = O_p(n^\mu)$, we know that for a given $\varepsilon > 0$ there exist $\Delta_{a,\varepsilon}$, $\Delta_{b,\varepsilon}$, $N_{a,\varepsilon}$, and $N_{b,\varepsilon}$ such that $P(\omega : |n^{-\lambda}a_n| > \Delta_{a,\varepsilon}) < \varepsilon/2$ for $n \geq N_{a,\varepsilon}$ and $P(\omega : |n^{-\mu}b_n| > \Delta_{b,\varepsilon}) < \varepsilon/2$ for $n \geq N_{b,\varepsilon}$. Define $N = \max(N_{a,\varepsilon}, N_{b,\varepsilon})$ and $\Delta_\varepsilon = \Delta_{a,\varepsilon}\Delta_{b,\varepsilon}$. Now if

$$|n^{-\lambda-\mu}a_n(\omega)b_n(\omega)| = |n^{-\lambda}a_n(\omega)||n^{-\mu}b_n(\omega)| > \Delta_\varepsilon = \Delta_{a,\varepsilon}\Delta_{b,\varepsilon}$$

then $|n^{-\lambda}a_n(\omega)| > \Delta_{a,\varepsilon}$ or $|n^{-\mu}b_n(\omega)| > \Delta_{b,\varepsilon}$. So

$$\begin{aligned} P(\omega : |n^{-\lambda-\mu}a_n(\omega)b_n(\omega)| > \Delta_\varepsilon) &\leq P(\omega : |n^{-\lambda}a_n(\omega)| > \Delta_{a,\varepsilon}) \\ &\quad + P(\omega : |n^{-\mu}b_n(\omega)| > \Delta_{b,\varepsilon}) \\ &< \varepsilon/2 + \varepsilon/2 = \varepsilon \end{aligned}$$

for $n \geq N$, which proves that $a_n b_n = O_p(n^{\lambda+\mu})$.
Next, let $\Delta'_\varepsilon = \Delta_{a,\varepsilon} + \Delta_{b,\varepsilon}$. Since $n^{-\lambda}, n^{-\mu} \geq n^\kappa$ it follows that

$$\begin{aligned} P(|n^{-\kappa}(a_n + b_n)| > \Delta'_\varepsilon) &\leq P(|(n^{-\lambda}a_n + n^{-\mu}b_n)| > \Delta'_\varepsilon) \\ &\leq P(|(n^{-\lambda}a_n| + |n^{-\mu}b_n| > \Delta'_\varepsilon) \\ &\leq P(|(n^{-\lambda}a_n| > \Delta_{a,\varepsilon}) + P(|n^{-\mu}b_n| > \Delta_{b,\varepsilon}) \\ &< \varepsilon/2 + \varepsilon/2 = \varepsilon. \end{aligned}$$

for $n \geq N$, which proves that $a_n + b_n = O_p(n^\kappa)$.

(*ii*) We have $n^{-\lambda}a_n \xrightarrow{p} 0$, $n^{-\mu}b_n \xrightarrow{p} 0$. It follows from Proposition 2.30 that $n^{-\lambda}a_n n^{-\mu}b_n = n^{-(\lambda+\mu)}a_n b_n \xrightarrow{p} 0$ so that $a_n b_n = o_p(n^{\lambda+\mu})$. Consider $\{a_n + b_n\}$. Since $\{a_n\}$ and $\{b_n\}$ are $o_p(n^\kappa)$, we again apply Proposition 2.30 and obtain $n^{-\kappa}a_n + n^{-\kappa}b_n = n^{-\kappa}(a_n + b_n) \xrightarrow{p} 0$.

(*iii*) We need to prove that for any $\varepsilon > 0$, there exist $\delta_\varepsilon > 0$ and $N_\varepsilon \in \mathbb{N}$ such that

$$P(|n^{-\lambda-\mu}a_n b_n| > \delta_\varepsilon) < \varepsilon$$

for all $n \geq N$. By definition there exist $N_{a,\varepsilon} \in \mathbb{N}$ and $\Delta_{a,\varepsilon} < \infty$ such that $P(\omega : |n^{-\lambda}a_n| > \Delta_{a,\varepsilon}) < \varepsilon/2$ for all $n \geq N_{a,\varepsilon}$. Define $\delta_{b,\varepsilon} \equiv$

$\delta_\varepsilon/\Delta_{a,\varepsilon} > 0$; then by the definition of convergence in probability, there exists $N_{b,\varepsilon}$ such that $P(|n^{-\mu}b_n| > \delta_{b,\varepsilon}) < \varepsilon/2$ for all $n \geq N_{b,\varepsilon}$. As in (i) we have that

$$P(|n^{-\lambda-\mu}a_n b_n| > \delta_\varepsilon) \leq P(|n^{-\lambda}a_n| > \Delta_{a,\varepsilon}) + P(|n^{-\mu}b_n| > \delta_{b,\varepsilon}) < \varepsilon.$$

Since this holds for arbitrary choice of $\varepsilon > 0$, we have shown that $a_n b_n = o_p(n^{\lambda+\mu})$.

Consider $\{a_n + b_n\}$. Since $\{b_n\}$ is also $O_p(n^\mu)$, it follows from (i) that $a_n + b_n = O_p(n^\kappa)$.

■

Exercise 3.6

Proof. We verify the conditions of Exercise 2.13. Given (ii), the elements of $\{\mathbf{Z}_t\boldsymbol{\varepsilon}_t\}$ and $\{\mathbf{Z}_t\mathbf{X}_t'\}$ are i.i.d. sequences by Proposition 3.3. The elements of $\{\mathbf{Z}_t\boldsymbol{\varepsilon}_t\}$ and $\{\mathbf{Z}_t\mathbf{X}_t'\}$ have finite expected absolute values given $(iii.b)$ and $(iv.a)$. By Theorem 3.1,

$$\mathbf{Z}'\boldsymbol{\varepsilon}/n = n^{-1}\sum_{t=1}^{n}\mathbf{Z}_t\boldsymbol{\varepsilon}_t \xrightarrow{a.s.} \mathbf{0}$$

and

$$\mathbf{Z}'\mathbf{X}/n = n^{-1}\sum_{t=1}^{n}\mathbf{Z}_t\mathbf{X}_t' \xrightarrow{a.s.} \mathbf{Q},$$

finite with full column rank. Since $(iv.c)$ is also given, the conditions of Exercise 2.13 are satisfied and the result follows. ■

Exercise 3.13

Proof. By Minkowski's inequality,

$$\begin{aligned} E\left|\sum_{h=1}^{p} X_{thi}\varepsilon_{th}\right|^{1+\delta} &\leq \left[\sum_{h=1}^{p}(E|X_{thi}\varepsilon_{th}|^{1+\delta})^{1/(1+\delta)}\right]^{1+\delta} \\ &< \left[\sum_{h=1}^{p}\Delta^{1/(1+\delta)}\right]^{1+\delta} = p^{1+\delta}\Delta \equiv \Delta'. \end{aligned}$$

■

Exercise 3.14

Proof. We verify the conditions of Theorem 2.18. By Proposition 3.10, $\{\mathbf{X}_t\varepsilon_t\}$ and $\{\mathbf{X}_t\mathbf{X}_t'\}$ are independent sequences with elements satisfying the moment condition of Corollary 3.9 given (*iii.b*), (*iv.a*), and using the results of Corollary 3.12 and Exercise 3.13. It follows from Corollary 3.9 that

$$\mathbf{X}'\varepsilon/n = n^{-1}\sum_{t=1}^{n}\mathbf{X}_t\varepsilon_t \xrightarrow{a.s.} \mathbf{0}$$

and

$$\mathbf{X}'\mathbf{X}/n - \mathbf{M}_n = n^{-1}\sum_{t=1}^{n}\mathbf{X}_t\mathbf{X}_t' - \mathbf{M}_n \xrightarrow{a.s.} \mathbf{0}.$$

$\mathbf{M}_n = O(1)$ given (*iv.a*) as a consequence of Jensen's inequality and the Cauchy-Schwarz inequality. To show this, consider the i, jth element of $\mathbf{M}_n$,

$$n^{-1}\sum_{t=1}^{n}\sum_{h=1}^{p}E(X_{thi}X_{thj}).$$

Now

$$\begin{aligned}
\left|n^{-1}\sum_{t=1}^{n}\sum_{h=1}^{p}E(X_{thi}X_{thj})\right| &\leq n^{-1}\sum_{t=1}^{n}\sum_{h=1}^{p}|E(X_{thi}X_{thj})| \\
&\leq n^{-1}\sum_{t=1}^{n}\sum_{h=1}^{p}E\left|X_{thi}X_{thj}\right| \\
&\leq n^{-1}\sum_{t=1}^{n}\sum_{h=1}^{p}\left(E\left|X_{thi}\right|^2 E\left|X_{thj}\right|^2\right)^{1/2} \\
&< n^{-1}\sum_{t=1}^{n}\sum_{h=1}^{p}\Delta' \\
&= p\Delta' < \infty
\end{aligned}$$

given (*iv.a*). Hence, the conditions of Theorem 2.18 are satisfied and the result follows. ∎

Exercise 3.38

Proof. We verify the conditions of Exercise 2.13. Given (*ii*), $\{\mathbf{Z}_t\varepsilon_t\}$ and $\{\mathbf{Z}_t\mathbf{X}_t'\}$ are stationary ergodic sequences by Proposition 3.36, with elements having finite expected absolute values given (*iii.b*) and (*iv.a*). By the ergodic theorem (Theorem 3.34),

$$\mathbf{Z}'\varepsilon/n = n^{-1}\sum_{t=1}^{n}\mathbf{Z}_t\varepsilon_t \xrightarrow{a.s.} \mathbf{0}$$

and

$$\mathbf{Z}'\mathbf{X}/n = n^{-1}\sum_{t=1}^{n}\mathbf{Z}_t\mathbf{X}_t' \xrightarrow{a.s.} \mathbf{Q},$$

finite with full column rank. Since $(iv.c)$ is also given, the conditions of Exercise 2.13 are satisfied and the result follows. ∎

Exercise 3.51

Proof. We verify the conditions of Theorem 2.18. Given (ii), $\{\mathbf{X}_t\varepsilon_t\}$ and $\{\mathbf{X}_t\mathbf{X}_t'\}$ are mixing sequences with ϕ of size $-r/(2r-1)$, $r \geq 1$, or α of size $-r/(r-1)$, $r > 1$, by Proposition 3.50. Given $(iii.b)$ and $(iv.a)$ the elements of $\{\mathbf{X}_t\varepsilon_t\}$ and $\{\mathbf{X}_t\mathbf{X}_t'\}$ satisfy the moment condition of Corollary 3.48 by Minkowski's inequality and the Cauchy-Schwarz inequality. It follows that $\mathbf{X}'\varepsilon/n \xrightarrow{a.s.} \mathbf{0}$ and $\mathbf{X}'\mathbf{X}/n - \mathbf{M}_n \xrightarrow{a.s.} \mathbf{0}$. $\mathbf{M}_n = O(1)$ by Jensen's inequality given $(iv.a)$. Hence the conditions of Theorem 2.18 are satisfied and the result follows. ∎

Exercise 3.53

Proof. (i) The following conditions are sufficient:

- (i) $Y_t = \alpha_o Y_{t-1} + \beta_o X_t + \varepsilon_t$, $|\alpha_o| < 1$, $|\beta_o| < \infty$;
- (ii) $\{(Y_t, X_t)\}$ is a mixing sequence with ϕ of size $-r/(2r-1)$, $r \geq 1$, or α of size $-r/(r-1)$, $r > 1$;
- (iii) (a) $E(X_{t-j}\varepsilon_t) = 0$, $j = 0, 1, \ldots$ and all t;
  - (b) $E(\varepsilon_t\varepsilon_{t-j}) = 0$, $j = 1, 2, \ldots$ and all t;
- (iv) (a) $E|X_t^2|^{r+\delta} < \Delta < \infty$ and $E|\varepsilon_t^2|^{r+\delta} < \Delta < \infty$ for some $0 < \delta \leq r$ and all t;
  - (b) $\mathbf{M}_n \equiv E(\mathbf{X}'\mathbf{X}/n)$ has $\det(\mathbf{M}_n) > \gamma > 0$ for all n sufficiently large, where $\mathbf{X}_t \equiv (Y_{t-1}, X_t)'$.

First, we verify the hint (see Laha and Rohatgi, 1979, p. 53). We are given that

$$\sum_{t=1}^{n}(E|\mathcal{Z}_t|^p)^{1/p} < \infty.$$

By Minkowski's inequality for finite sums,

$$E\left|\sum_{t=1}^{n}|\mathcal{Z}_t|\right|^p \leq \left(\sum_{t=1}^{n}(E|\mathcal{Z}_t|^p)^{1/p}\right)^p$$

for all $n \geq 1$. Hence

$$\begin{aligned}\lim_{n\to\infty} E\left|\sum_{t=1}^{n}|\mathcal{Z}_t|\right|^p &\leq \lim_{n\to\infty}\left(\sum_{t=1}^{n}(E|\mathcal{Z}_t|^p)^{1/p}\right)^p \\ &= \left(\sum_{t=1}^{\infty}(E|\mathcal{Z}_t|^p)^{1/p}\right)^p\end{aligned}$$

by continuity of the function $g(x) \equiv x^p$. Consequently,

$$\begin{aligned}E\left|\sum_{t=1}^{\infty}\mathcal{Z}_t\right|^p &= E\left|\lim_{n\to\infty}\sum_{t=1}^{n}\mathcal{Z}_t\right|^p \\ &\leq E\left|\lim_{n\to\infty}\sum_{t=1}^{n}|\mathcal{Z}_t|\right|^p \\ &= \lim_{n\to\infty} E\left|\sum_{t=1}^{n}|\mathcal{Z}_t|\right|^p \\ &\leq \left(\sum_{t=1}^{\infty}(E|\mathcal{Z}_t|^p)^{1/p})\right)^p,\end{aligned}$$

where we have applied the monotone convergence theorem to the function $f_n = |\sum_{t=1}^{n}|\mathcal{Z}_t||^p$ with limit $f = |\sum_{t=1}^{\infty}|\mathcal{Z}_t||^p$ $(0 \leq f_1 \leq f_2 \leq \ldots \leq f_n \rightarrow f)$. Thus we obtain the desired result.

Next, we verify the conditions of Exercise 3.51. First $\{(Y_t, X_t)\}$ mixing implies $\{(\mathbf{X}_t', \varepsilon_t)\} \equiv \{(Y_{t-1}, X_t, \varepsilon_t)\}$ is mixing and of the same sizes, given (*i*) and (*ii*) by Theorem 3.49.

Next, by repeated substitution we can write Y_t as

$$Y_t = \beta_o \sum_{j=0}^{\infty}\alpha_o^j X_{t-j} + \sum_{j=0}^{\infty}\alpha_o^j \varepsilon_{t-j},$$

so that

$$Y_{t-1}\varepsilon_t = \beta_o \sum_{j=0}^{\infty} \alpha_o^j X_{t-j-1}\varepsilon_t + \sum_{j=0}^{\infty} \alpha_o^j \varepsilon_{t-j-1}\varepsilon_t.$$

Consider $Z_t = |\beta_o| \sum_{j=0}^{\infty} |\alpha_o|^j |X_{t-j-1}\varepsilon_t| + \sum_{j=0}^{\infty} |\alpha_o|^j |\varepsilon_{t-j-1}\varepsilon_t|$. Since the elements $E|X_{t-j-1}\varepsilon_t| < \Delta_{x\varepsilon} < \infty$ and $E|\varepsilon_{t-j-1}\varepsilon_t| < \Delta_\varepsilon < \infty$ (apply Cauchy-Schwarz inequality and (*iv*)), we have that $E(Z_t) \leq \frac{|\beta_o|}{1-|\alpha_o|}\Delta_{x\varepsilon} + \frac{1}{1-|\alpha_o|}\Delta_\varepsilon < \infty$. So by Proposition 3.52 we can interchange the summation and expectation operators. Hence

$$E(Y_{t-1}\varepsilon_t) = \beta_o \sum_{j=0}^{\infty} \alpha_o^j E(X_{t-j-1}\varepsilon_t) + \sum_{j=0}^{\infty} \alpha_o^j E(\varepsilon_{t-j-1}\varepsilon_t) = 0,$$

given (*iii.a*) and (*iii.b*). Therefore

$$E(\mathbf{X}_t\varepsilon_t) \equiv (E(Y_{t-1}\varepsilon_t), E(X_t\varepsilon_t))' = \mathbf{0}$$

so that condition (*iii.a*) of Exercise 3.51 is satisfied.

Now consider condition (*iii.b*). By the Cauchy-Schwarz inequality,

$$E|X_t\varepsilon_t|^{r+\delta} \leq (E|X_t^2|^{r+\delta} E|\varepsilon_t^2|^{r+\delta})^{1/2} < \Delta < \infty$$

given (*iv.a*). Further,

$$E|Y_{t-1}\varepsilon_t|^{r+\delta} \leq (E|Y_{t-1}^2|^{r+\delta} E|\varepsilon_t^2|^{r+\delta})^{1/2} < (\Delta'\Delta)^{1/2} < \infty,$$

provided $E|Y_{t-1}^2|^{r+\delta} < \Delta' < \infty$ for some Δ'. To show this, we write Y_t as above and apply Minkowski's inequality:

$$E|Y_{t-1}^2|^{r+\delta} = E\left|\beta_o \sum_{j=0}^{\infty} \alpha_o^j X_{t-j} + \sum_{j=0}^{\infty} \alpha_o^j \varepsilon_{t-j}\right|^{2(r+\delta)}$$

$$\leq \left[\sum_{j=0}^{\infty} \left(E\left[\left(\alpha_o^j \beta_o X_{t-j}\right)^{2(r+\delta)}\right]\right)^{\frac{1}{2(r+\delta)}} + \left(E\left[\left(\alpha_o^j \varepsilon_{t-j}\right)^{2(r+\delta)}\right]\right)^{\frac{1}{2(r+\delta)}}\right]^{2(r+\delta)}$$

$$= \left[\sum_{j=0}^{\infty} \alpha_o^j \beta_o \left(E\left[X_{t-j}^{2(r+\delta)}\right]\right)^{\frac{1}{2(r+\delta)}} + \alpha_o^j \left(E\left[\varepsilon_{t-j}^{2(r+\delta)}\right]\right)^{\frac{1}{2(r+\delta)}}\right]^{2(r+\delta)}$$

$$< \left[\sum_{j=0}^{\infty} \alpha_o^j \beta_o (\Delta)^{\frac{1}{2(r+\delta)}} + \alpha_o^j (\Delta)^{\frac{1}{2(r+\delta)}}\right]^{2(r+\delta)}$$

$$= \left[\frac{\beta_o + 1}{1 - \alpha_o} (\Delta)^{\frac{1}{2(r+\delta)}}\right]^{2(r+\delta)} \leq \left|\frac{\beta_o + 1}{1 - \alpha_o}\right|^{2(r+\delta)} \Delta < \infty.$$

if and only if $|\alpha_o| < 1$, where we have again used Proposition 3.52 to pass the expectation operator through the summation operator. Therefore (i) and $(iv.a)$ ensure that $(iii.b)$ is satisfied. We now see that all the conditions of Exercise 3.51 hold, so that the OLS estimate of (α_o, β_o) is consistent.
(ii) Consider the following data generating process:

$$\begin{aligned} Y_t &= \alpha_o Y_{t-1} + \varepsilon_t \\ \varepsilon_t &= \rho_o \varepsilon_{t-1} + v_t, \end{aligned}$$

where we set $\beta_o = 0$ and assume $E(Y_{t-1} v_t) = 0$, $E(Y_{t-1}\varepsilon_{t-1}) = E(Y_t \varepsilon_t)$, and $E(\varepsilon_t^2) = \text{var}(\varepsilon_t) = \sigma_o^2$. Then from Chapter 1 we know that

$$E(Y_{t-1}\varepsilon_t) = \sigma_o^2 \rho_o / (1 - \rho_o \alpha_o).$$

Therefore, if $\sigma_o^2 \neq 0$ and $\rho_o \neq 0$, condition $(iii.a)$ of Exercise 3.51 is violated.
■

Exercise 3.77

Proof. We verify the moment condition of Theorem 3.76. Since $E|\mathcal{Z}_t|^{2r} < \Delta < \infty$ for all t, it follows that

$$\begin{aligned}\sum_{t=1}^{\infty} E|\mathcal{Z}_t|^{2r}/t^{1+r} &< \sum_{t=1}^{\infty} \Delta/t^{1+r} \\ &= \Delta \sum_{t=1}^{\infty} t^{-(1+r)} < \infty.\end{aligned}$$

since $\sum_{t=1}^{\infty} t^{-(1+r)} < \infty$ for any $r > 0$. The result follows from Theorem 3.76. ■

Exercise 3.79

Proof. We verify the conditions of Exercise 2.20. First, note that $\mathbf{Z}'\varepsilon/n = n^{-1}\sum_{h=1}^{p} \mathbf{Z}_h \varepsilon_h$, where $\mathbf{Z}_h$ is the $n \times l$ matrix with rows $\mathbf{Z}_{th}$ and ε_h is the $n \times 1$ error vector with elements ε_{th}. By assumption $(iii.a)$, $\{Z_{thi}\varepsilon_{th}, \mathcal{F}_t\}$ is a martingale difference sequence. Given $(iii.b)$, the moment conditions of Exercise 3.77 are satisfied so that $n^{-1}\sum_{t=1}^{n} Z_{thi}\varepsilon_{th} \xrightarrow{a.s.} 0$, $h = 1, \ldots, p$, $i = 1, \ldots, l$, and therefore $\mathbf{Z}'\varepsilon/n \xrightarrow{a.s.} \mathbf{0}$ by Proposition 2.11.

Next, Proposition 3.50 ensures that $\{\mathbf{Z}_t\mathbf{X}_t'\}$ is a mixing sequence given (ii), which satisfies the conditions of Corollary 3.48 given $(iv.a)$. It follows from Corollary 3.48 that $\mathbf{Z}'\mathbf{X}/n - \mathbf{Q}_n \xrightarrow{a.s.} \mathbf{0}$, and $\mathbf{Q}_n = O(1)$ given $(iv.a)$ by Jensen's inequality. Hence the conditions of Exercise 2.20 are satisfied and the result follows. ■

Exercise 4.18

Proof. Let $\mathbf{V}$ be $k \times k$ with eigenvalues $\lambda_1, \ldots, \lambda_k$. Since $\mathbf{V}$ is real and symmetric it can be diagonalized by $\mathbf{V} = \mathbf{Q}'\mathbf{D}\mathbf{Q}$, where $\mathbf{D} = \text{diag}(\lambda_1, \ldots, \lambda_k)$ is the matrix with the eigenvalues of $\mathbf{V}$ along its diagonal and zeros elsewhere, and $\mathbf{Q}$ is an orthogonal matrix that has as its rows the standardized eigenvectors of $\mathbf{V}$ corresponding to $\lambda_1, \ldots, \lambda_k$. Furthermore, since $\mathbf{V}$ is positive (semi) definite its eigenvalues satisfy $\lambda_i > 0$ ($\lambda_i \geq 0$), $i = 1, \ldots, k$. Hence, defining $\mathbf{D}^{1/2} \equiv \text{diag}(\lambda_1^{1/2}, \ldots, \lambda_k^{1/2})$, we can define the square root of $\mathbf{V}$ as

$$\mathbf{V}^{1/2} = \mathbf{Q}'\mathbf{D}^{1/2}\mathbf{Q},$$

which is clearly positive (semi) definite. From

$$(\mathbf{V}^{1/2})' = \mathbf{Q}'(\mathbf{D}^{1/2})'(\mathbf{Q}')' = \mathbf{V}^{1/2}$$

we see that $\mathbf{V}^{1/2}$ is symmetric, and we verify that

$$\begin{aligned}\mathbf{V}^{1/2}\mathbf{V}^{1/2} &= \mathbf{Q}'\mathbf{D}^{1/2}\mathbf{Q}\mathbf{Q}'\mathbf{D}^{1/2}\mathbf{Q} \\ &= \mathbf{Q}'\mathbf{D}^{1/2}\mathbf{D}^{1/2}\mathbf{Q} \\ &= \mathbf{V},\end{aligned}$$

where we used the fact that $\mathbf{Q}$ is orthogonal.

The mapping $\mathbf{V} \longmapsto (\mathbf{Q}, \mathbf{D})$ is continuous because for any matrix with $\lim_{n\to\infty} \mathbf{H}_n = \mathbf{0}$, it holds that $\lim_{n\to\infty} \mathbf{Q}(\mathbf{V} + \mathbf{H}_n)\mathbf{Q}' = \mathbf{D}$, thus

$$\lim_{n\to\infty} (\mathbf{V} + \mathbf{H}_n) = \mathbf{Q}'\mathbf{D}\mathbf{Q}.$$

Since also $\lambda \mapsto \sqrt{\lambda}$ is continuous $(\lambda \geq 0)$ then it follows that $\mathbf{V} \mapsto \mathbf{V}^{1/2}$ is continuous. ■

Exercise 4.19

Proof. If $\mathcal{Z} \sim N(\mathbf{0}, \mathbf{V})$ it follows from Example 4.12 that

$$\mathbf{V}^{-1/2}\mathcal{Z} \sim N(\mathbf{0}, \mathbf{I}),$$

since $\mathbf{V}^{-1/2}\mathbf{V}\mathbf{V}^{-1/2} = \mathbf{I}$. ■

Exercise 4.26

Proof. Since $\mathbf{Z}'\mathbf{X}/n - \mathbf{Q}_n \xrightarrow{p} \mathbf{0}$, where $\mathbf{Q}_n$ is finite and has full column rank for all n sufficiently large, and $\hat{\mathbf{P}}_n - \mathbf{P}_n \xrightarrow{p} \mathbf{0}$, where $\mathbf{P}_n$ is finite and nonsingular for all n sufficiently large, it follows from Proposition 2.30 that

$$\mathbf{X}'\mathbf{Z}\hat{\mathbf{P}}_n\mathbf{Z}'\mathbf{X}/n^2 - \mathbf{Q}_n'\mathbf{P}_n\mathbf{Q}_n \xrightarrow{p} \mathbf{0}.$$

Also since $\mathbf{Q}_n'\mathbf{P}_n\mathbf{Q}_n$ is nonsingular for all n sufficiently large by Lemma 2.19 given (iii), $(\mathbf{X}'\mathbf{Z}\hat{\mathbf{P}}_n\mathbf{Z}'\mathbf{X}/n^2)^{-1}$ and $\tilde{\boldsymbol{\beta}}_n$ exist in probability. So given (i)

$$\sqrt{n}(\tilde{\boldsymbol{\beta}}_n - \boldsymbol{\beta}_o) = (\mathbf{X}'\mathbf{Z}\hat{\mathbf{P}}_n\mathbf{Z}'\mathbf{X}/n^2)^{-1}(\mathbf{X}'\mathbf{Z}/n)\hat{\mathbf{P}}_n n^{-1/2}\mathbf{Z}'\boldsymbol{\varepsilon}.$$

Hence, given (ii),

$$\begin{aligned}&\sqrt{n}(\tilde{\boldsymbol{\beta}}_n - \boldsymbol{\beta}_o) - (\mathbf{Q}_n'\mathbf{P}_n\mathbf{Q}_n)^{-1}\mathbf{Q}_n'\mathbf{P}_n n^{-1/2}\mathbf{Z}'\boldsymbol{\varepsilon} \\ &\qquad = [(\mathbf{X}'\mathbf{Z}\hat{\mathbf{P}}_n\mathbf{Z}'\mathbf{X}/n^2)^{-1}(\mathbf{X}'\mathbf{Z}/n)\hat{\mathbf{P}}_n \\ &\qquad\qquad - (\mathbf{Q}_n'\mathbf{P}_n\mathbf{Q}_n)^{-1}\mathbf{Q}_n'\mathbf{P}_n]\mathbf{V}_n^{1/2}\mathbf{V}_n^{-1/2}n^{-1/2}\mathbf{Z}'\boldsymbol{\varepsilon}.\end{aligned}$$

Premultiplying by $\mathbf{D}_n^{-1/2}$ yields

$$\begin{aligned}
&\mathbf{D}_n^{-1/2}\sqrt{n}(\tilde{\boldsymbol{\beta}}_n - \boldsymbol{\beta}_o) - \mathbf{D}_n^{-1/2}(\mathbf{Q}_n'\mathbf{P}_n\mathbf{Q})^{-1}\mathbf{Q}_n'\mathbf{P}_n n^{-1/2}\mathbf{Z}'\boldsymbol{\varepsilon} \\
&\quad = \mathbf{D}_n^{-1/2}[(\mathbf{X}'\mathbf{Z}\hat{\mathbf{P}}_n\mathbf{Z}'\mathbf{X}/n^2)^{-1}(\mathbf{X}'\mathbf{Z}/n)\hat{\mathbf{P}}_n - (\mathbf{Q}\mathbf{P}_n\mathbf{Q})^{-1}\mathbf{Q}_n'\mathbf{P}_n] \\
&\qquad\qquad \times \mathbf{V}_n^{1/2}\mathbf{V}_n^{-1/2}n^{-1/2}\mathbf{Z}'\boldsymbol{\varepsilon}.
\end{aligned}$$

Now $\mathbf{V}_n^{-1/2}n^{-1/2}\mathbf{Z}'\boldsymbol{\varepsilon} \overset{A}{\sim} N(\mathbf{0}, \mathbf{I})$ given (ii) and

$$\mathbf{D}_n^{-1/2}[(\mathbf{X}'\mathbf{Z}\hat{\mathbf{P}}_n\mathbf{Z}'\mathbf{X}/n^2)^{-1}(\mathbf{X}'\mathbf{Z}/n)\hat{\mathbf{P}}_n - (\mathbf{Q}_n'\mathbf{P}_n\mathbf{Q}_n)^{-1}\mathbf{Q}_n'\mathbf{P}_n]\mathbf{V}_n^{1/2} = o_p(1)$$

since $\mathbf{D}_n^{-1/2} = O(1)$ and $\mathbf{V}_n^{1/2} = O(1)$ given (ii) and (iii), and

$$(\mathbf{X}'\mathbf{Z}\hat{\mathbf{P}}_n\mathbf{Z}'\mathbf{X}/n^2)^{-1}(\mathbf{X}'\mathbf{Z}/n)\hat{\mathbf{P}}_n - (\mathbf{Q}_n'\mathbf{P}_n\mathbf{Q}_n)^{-1}\mathbf{Q}_n'\mathbf{P}_n = o_p(1),$$

given (iii) by Proposition 2.30. Hence, by Lemma 4.6,

$$\mathbf{D}_n^{-1/2}\sqrt{n}(\tilde{\boldsymbol{\beta}}_n - \boldsymbol{\beta}_0) - \mathbf{D}_n^{-1/2}(\mathbf{Q}_n'\mathbf{P}_n\mathbf{Q}_n)^{-1}\mathbf{Q}_n'\mathbf{P}_n n^{-1/2}\mathbf{Z}'\boldsymbol{\varepsilon} \xrightarrow{p} \mathbf{0}.$$

By Lemma 4.7, $\mathbf{D}_n^{-1/2}\sqrt{n}(\tilde{\boldsymbol{\beta}}_n - \boldsymbol{\beta}_o)$ has the same limiting distribution as

$$\mathbf{D}_n^{-1/2}(\mathbf{Q}_n'\mathbf{P}_n\mathbf{Q}_n)^{-1}\mathbf{Q}_n'\mathbf{P}_n n^{-1/2}\mathbf{Z}'\boldsymbol{\varepsilon}.$$

We find the asymptotic distribution of this random vector by applying Corollary 4.24 with $\mathbf{A}_n' \equiv (\mathbf{Q}_n'\mathbf{P}_n\mathbf{Q}_n)^{-1}\mathbf{Q}_n'\mathbf{P}_n$ and $\boldsymbol{\Gamma}_n \equiv \mathbf{D}_n$, which immediately yields

$$\mathbf{D}_n^{-1/2}(\mathbf{Q}_n'\mathbf{P}_n\mathbf{Q}_n)^{-1}\mathbf{Q}_n'\mathbf{P}_n n^{-1/2}\mathbf{Z}'\boldsymbol{\varepsilon} \overset{A}{\sim} N(\mathbf{0}, \mathbf{I}).$$

Since (ii), (iii) and (iv) hold, $\hat{\mathbf{D}}_n - \mathbf{D}_n \xrightarrow{p} \mathbf{0}$ as an immediate consequence of Proposition 2.30. ■

Exercise 4.33

Proof. Given that $\hat{\mathbf{V}}_n - \mathbf{V}_n \xrightarrow{p} \mathbf{0}$ and $\ddot{\mathbf{V}}_n - \mathbf{V}_n \xrightarrow{p} \mathbf{0}$, it follows from Proposition 2.30 that $\hat{\mathbf{V}}_n - \ddot{\mathbf{V}}_n = (\hat{\mathbf{V}}_n - \mathbf{V}_n) - (\ddot{\mathbf{V}}_n - \mathbf{V}_n) \xrightarrow{p} \mathbf{0}$. It immediately follows from Proposition 2.30 that $\mathcal{W}_n - \mathcal{LM}_n \xrightarrow{p} 0$. ■

Exercise 4.34

Proof. From the solution to the constrained minimization problem we know that

$$\ddot{\boldsymbol{\lambda}}_n = 2(\mathbf{R}(\mathbf{X}'\mathbf{X}/n)^{-1}\mathbf{R}')^{-1}(\mathbf{R}\ddot{\boldsymbol{\beta}}_n - \mathbf{r})$$

and applying the hint,

$$\ddot{\lambda}_n = 2(\mathbf{R}(\mathbf{X}'\mathbf{X}/n)^{-1}\mathbf{R}')^{-1}\mathbf{R}(\mathbf{X}'\mathbf{X}/n)^{-1}\mathbf{X}'(\mathbf{Y} - \mathbf{X}\ddot{\boldsymbol{\beta}}_n)/n.$$

Now $\mathbf{Y} - \mathbf{X}\ddot{\boldsymbol{\beta}}_n = \mathbf{Y} - \mathbf{X}_1\ddot{\boldsymbol{\beta}}_{1n} - \mathbf{X}_2\ddot{\boldsymbol{\beta}}_{2n} = \mathbf{Y} - \mathbf{X}_1\ddot{\boldsymbol{\beta}}_{1n} = \ddot{\varepsilon}$ so that

$$\ddot{\lambda}_n = 2(\mathbf{R}(\mathbf{X}'\mathbf{X})^{-1}\mathbf{R}')^{-1}\mathbf{R}(\mathbf{X}'\mathbf{X})^{-1}\mathbf{X}'\varepsilon/n.$$

Partitioning $\mathbf{R}$ as $[\mathbf{0}, \mathbf{I}_q]$ and $\mathbf{X}'\mathbf{X}$ as

$$\mathbf{X}'\mathbf{X} = \begin{bmatrix} \mathbf{X}_1'\mathbf{X}_1 & \mathbf{X}_1'\mathbf{X}_2 \\ \mathbf{X}_2'\mathbf{X}_1 & \mathbf{X}_2'\mathbf{X}_2 \end{bmatrix}$$

and applying the formula for a partitioned inverse gives

$$\mathbf{R}(\mathbf{X}'\mathbf{X})^{-1}\mathbf{R}' = (\mathbf{X}_2'(\mathbf{I} - \mathbf{X}_1(\mathbf{X}_1'\mathbf{X}_1)^{-1}\mathbf{X}_1')\mathbf{X}_2)^{-1}$$

and

$$\mathbf{R}(\mathbf{X}'\mathbf{X})^{-1}\mathbf{X}' = (\mathbf{X}_2'(\mathbf{I} - \mathbf{X}_1(\mathbf{X}_1'\mathbf{X}_1)^{-1}\mathbf{X}_1')\mathbf{X}_2)^{-1}\mathbf{X}_2'(\mathbf{I} - \mathbf{X}_1(\mathbf{X}_1'\mathbf{X}_1)^{-1}\mathbf{X}_1').$$

Hence by substitution

$$\ddot{\lambda}_n = 2\mathbf{X}_2'(\mathbf{I} - \mathbf{X}_1(\mathbf{X}_1'\mathbf{X}_1)^{-1}\mathbf{X}_1')\ddot{\varepsilon}/n = 2\mathbf{X}_2'\ddot{\varepsilon}/n$$

since $\ddot{\varepsilon} = (\mathbf{I} - \mathbf{X}_1(\mathbf{X}_1'\mathbf{X}_1)^{-1}\mathbf{X}_1')\mathbf{Y}$ and $\mathbf{I} - \mathbf{X}_1(\mathbf{X}_1'\mathbf{X}_1)^{-1}\mathbf{X}_1'$ is idempotent. ■

Exercise 4.35

Proof. Substituting $\hat{\mathbf{V}}_n = \ddot{\sigma}_n^2(\mathbf{X}'\mathbf{X}/n)$ into the Lagrange multiplier statistic of Theorem 4.32 yields

$$\mathcal{LM}_n = n\ddot{\lambda}_n'\mathbf{R}[\ddot{\varepsilon}'\ddot{\varepsilon}/n(\mathbf{X}'\mathbf{X}/n)]^{-1}\mathbf{R}'\ddot{\lambda}_n/4.$$

From Exercise 4.34, $\ddot{\lambda}_n = 2\mathbf{X}_2'\ddot{\varepsilon}/n$ under $H_0 : \boldsymbol{\beta}_2 = \mathbf{0}$. Substituting this into the above expression and rearranging gives

$$\mathcal{LM}_n = n\ddot{\varepsilon}'\mathbf{X}_2\mathbf{R}(\mathbf{X}'\mathbf{X})^{-1}\mathbf{R}'\mathbf{X}_2'\ddot{\varepsilon}/(\ddot{\varepsilon}'\ddot{\varepsilon}).$$

Recalling that $\mathbf{X}_2\mathbf{R} = (\mathbf{0}, \mathbf{X}_2)$ and $\ddot{\varepsilon}'\mathbf{X}_1 = \mathbf{0}$ we can write

$$\ddot{\varepsilon}'\mathbf{X}_2\mathbf{R} = \ddot{\varepsilon}'(\mathbf{0}, \mathbf{X}_2) = \ddot{\varepsilon}'(\mathbf{X}_1, \mathbf{X}_2) = \ddot{\varepsilon}'\mathbf{X},$$

which upon substitution immediately yields the result. ■

Exercise 4.40

Proof. We are given that $s(\boldsymbol{\beta}) = \beta_3 - \beta_1\beta_2$. Hence $\nabla s(\boldsymbol{\beta}) = (-\beta_2, -\beta_1, 1)'$. Substituting $s(\hat{\boldsymbol{\beta}}_n)$ and $\nabla \mathrm{s}(\hat{\boldsymbol{\beta}}_n)$ into the Wald statistic of Theorem 4.39 yields

$$\mathcal{W}_n = n(\hat{\beta}_{3n} - \hat{\beta}_{1n}\hat{\beta}_{2n})^2/\hat{\Gamma}_n,$$

where

$$\hat{\Gamma}_n = (-\hat{\beta}_{2n}, -\hat{\beta}_{1n}, 1)(\mathbf{X}'\mathbf{X}/n)^{-1}\hat{\mathbf{V}}_n(\mathbf{X}'\mathbf{X}/n)^{-1}(-\hat{\beta}_{2n}, -\hat{\beta}_{1n}, 1)'.$$

Note that $\mathcal{W}_n \stackrel{A}{\sim} \chi_1^2$ in this case. ■

Exercise 4.41

Proof. The Lagrange multiplier statistic is motivated by the constrained minimization problem

$$\min_{\boldsymbol{\beta}}(\mathbf{Y} - \mathbf{X}\boldsymbol{\beta})'(\mathbf{Y} - \mathbf{X}\boldsymbol{\beta})/n \quad \text{s.t. } \mathbf{s}(\boldsymbol{\beta}) = \mathbf{0}.$$

The Lagrangian for the problem is

$$\mathcal{L} = (\mathbf{Y} - \mathbf{X}\boldsymbol{\beta})'(\mathbf{Y} - \mathbf{X}\boldsymbol{\beta})/n + \mathbf{s}(\boldsymbol{\beta})'\boldsymbol{\lambda}$$

and the first order conditions are

$$\begin{aligned} \partial\mathcal{L}/\partial\boldsymbol{\beta} &= 2(\mathbf{X}'\mathbf{X}/n)\boldsymbol{\beta} - 2\mathbf{X}'\mathbf{Y}/n + \nabla\mathbf{s}(\boldsymbol{\beta})'\boldsymbol{\lambda} = \mathbf{0} \\ \partial\mathcal{L}/\partial\lambda &= \mathbf{s}(\boldsymbol{\beta}) = \mathbf{0}. \end{aligned}$$

Setting $\hat{\boldsymbol{\beta}}_n = (\mathbf{X}'\mathbf{X}/n)^{-1}\mathbf{X}'\mathbf{Y}/n$ and taking a mean value expansion of $\mathbf{s}(\boldsymbol{\beta})$ around $\hat{\boldsymbol{\beta}}_n$ gives

$$\begin{aligned} \partial\mathcal{L}/\partial\boldsymbol{\beta} &= 2(\mathbf{X}'\mathbf{X}/n)(\boldsymbol{\beta} - \hat{\boldsymbol{\beta}}_n) + \nabla\mathbf{s}(\boldsymbol{\beta})'\boldsymbol{\lambda} = \mathbf{0} \\ \partial\mathcal{L}/\partial\lambda &= \mathbf{s}(\hat{\boldsymbol{\beta}}_n) + \nabla\bar{\mathbf{s}}'(\boldsymbol{\beta} - \hat{\boldsymbol{\beta}}_n) = \mathbf{0}, \end{aligned}$$

where $\nabla\bar{\mathbf{s}}'$ is the $q \times k$ Jacobian of $\mathbf{s}$ with ith row evaluated at a mean value $\bar{\boldsymbol{\beta}}_n^{(i)}$. Premultiplying the first equation by $\nabla\bar{\mathbf{s}}'(\mathbf{X}'\mathbf{X}/n)^{-1}$ and substituting $-\mathbf{s}(\hat{\boldsymbol{\beta}}_n) = \nabla\bar{\mathbf{s}}'(\boldsymbol{\beta} - \hat{\boldsymbol{\beta}}_n)$ gives

$$\ddot{\boldsymbol{\lambda}}_n = 2[\nabla\bar{\mathbf{s}}'(\mathbf{X}'\mathbf{X}/n)^{-1}\nabla\mathbf{s}(\hat{\boldsymbol{\beta}}_n)]^{-1}\mathbf{s}(\hat{\boldsymbol{\beta}}_n).$$

Thus, following the procedures of Theorems 4.32 and 4.39 we could propose the statistic

$$\mathcal{LM}_n = n\ddot{\boldsymbol{\lambda}}_n'\hat{\boldsymbol{\Lambda}}_n^{-1}\ddot{\boldsymbol{\lambda}}_n,$$

where

$$\begin{aligned}\hat{\mathbf{\Lambda}}_n &\equiv 4(\nabla\bar{\mathbf{s}}'(\mathbf{X}'\mathbf{X}/n)^{-1}\nabla\mathbf{s}(\hat{\boldsymbol{\beta}}_n))^{-1}\nabla\mathbf{s}(\hat{\boldsymbol{\beta}}_n)'(\mathbf{X}'\mathbf{X}/n)^{-1}\ddot{\mathbf{V}}_n \\ &\quad\times(\mathbf{X}'\mathbf{X}/n)^{-1}\nabla\mathbf{s}(\hat{\boldsymbol{\beta}}_n)(\nabla\bar{\mathbf{s}}'(\mathbf{X}'\mathbf{X}/n)^{-1}\nabla\mathbf{s}(\hat{\boldsymbol{\beta}}_n))^{-1}.\end{aligned}$$

The preceding statistic, however, is not very useful because it depends on generally unknown mean values and also on the unconstrained estimate $\hat{\boldsymbol{\beta}}_n$. An asymptotically equivalent statistic replaces $\nabla\bar{\mathbf{s}}'$ by $\nabla\mathbf{s}(\ddot{\boldsymbol{\beta}}_n)'$ and $\hat{\boldsymbol{\beta}}_n$ by $\ddot{\boldsymbol{\beta}}_n$:

$$\mathcal{LM}_n = n\ddot{\boldsymbol{\lambda}}_n'\ddot{\mathbf{\Lambda}}_n^{-1}\ddot{\boldsymbol{\lambda}}_n,$$

where

$$\ddot{\boldsymbol{\lambda}}_n = 2[\nabla\mathbf{s}(\ddot{\boldsymbol{\beta}}_n)'(\mathbf{X}'\mathbf{X}/n)^{-1}\nabla\mathbf{s}(\ddot{\boldsymbol{\beta}}_n)]^{-1}\mathbf{s}(\ddot{\boldsymbol{\beta}}_n)$$

and

$$\begin{aligned}\ddot{\mathbf{\Lambda}}_n &= 4(\nabla\mathbf{s}(\ddot{\boldsymbol{\beta}}_n)'(\mathbf{X}'\mathbf{X}/n)^{-1}\nabla\mathbf{s}(\ddot{\boldsymbol{\beta}}_n))^{-1}\nabla\mathbf{s}(\ddot{\boldsymbol{\beta}}_n)'(\mathbf{X}'\mathbf{X}/n)^{-1} \\ &\quad\times\ddot{\mathbf{V}}_n(\mathbf{X}'\mathbf{X}/n)^{-1}\nabla\mathbf{s}(\ddot{\boldsymbol{\beta}}_n)(\nabla\mathbf{s}(\ddot{\boldsymbol{\beta}}_n)'(\mathbf{X}'\mathbf{X}/n)^{-1}\nabla\mathbf{s}(\ddot{\boldsymbol{\beta}}_n))^{-1}.\end{aligned}$$

To show that $\mathcal{LM}_n \overset{A}{\sim} \chi^2_q$ under H_0 we note that $\mathcal{LM}_n$ differs from $\mathcal{W}_n$ only in that $\ddot{\mathbf{V}}_n$ is used in place of $\hat{\mathbf{V}}_n$ and $\ddot{\boldsymbol{\beta}}_n$ replaces $\hat{\boldsymbol{\beta}}_n$. Since $\ddot{\boldsymbol{\beta}}_n - \hat{\boldsymbol{\beta}}_n \xrightarrow{p} \mathbf{0}$ and $\ddot{\mathbf{V}}_n - \hat{\mathbf{V}}_n \xrightarrow{p} \mathbf{0}$ under H_0 given the conditions of Theorem 4.25, it follows from Proposition 2.30 that

$$\mathcal{LM}_n - \mathcal{W}_n \xrightarrow{p} 0$$

given that $\nabla\mathbf{s}$ is continuous. Hence $\mathcal{LM}_n \overset{A}{\sim} \chi^2_q$ by Lemma 4.7. ■

Exercise 4.42

Proof. First consider testing the hypothesis $\mathbf{R}\boldsymbol{\beta}_o = \mathbf{r}$. Analogous to Theorem 4.31 the Wald statistic is

$$\mathcal{W}_n \equiv n(\mathbf{R}\tilde{\boldsymbol{\beta}}_n - \mathbf{r})'\hat{\mathbf{\Gamma}}_n^{-1}(\mathbf{R}\tilde{\boldsymbol{\beta}}_n - \mathbf{r}) \xrightarrow{d} \chi^2_q$$

under H_0, where

$$\begin{aligned}\hat{\mathbf{\Gamma}}_n &\equiv \mathbf{R}\hat{\mathbf{D}}_n\mathbf{R}' \\ &= \mathbf{R}(\mathbf{X}'\mathbf{Z}\hat{\mathbf{P}}_n\mathbf{Z}'\mathbf{X}/n^2)^{-1}(\mathbf{X}'\mathbf{Z}/n)\hat{\mathbf{P}}_n\hat{\mathbf{V}}_n\hat{\mathbf{P}}_n(\mathbf{Z}'\mathbf{X}/n) \\ &\quad\times(\mathbf{X}'\mathbf{Z}\hat{\mathbf{P}}_n\mathbf{Z}'\mathbf{X}/n^2)^{-1}\mathbf{R}'.\end{aligned}$$

To prove $\mathcal{W}_n$ has an asymptotic χ_q^2 distribution under H_0, we note that

$$\mathbf{R}\tilde{\boldsymbol{\beta}}_n - \mathbf{r} = \mathbf{R}(\tilde{\boldsymbol{\beta}}_n - \boldsymbol{\beta}_o)$$

so

$$\boldsymbol{\Gamma}_n^{-1/2}\sqrt{n}(\mathbf{R}\tilde{\boldsymbol{\beta}}_n - \mathbf{r}) = \boldsymbol{\Gamma}_n^{-1/2}\mathbf{R}\sqrt{n}(\tilde{\boldsymbol{\beta}}_n - \boldsymbol{\beta}_o),$$

where

$$\boldsymbol{\Gamma}_n = \mathbf{R}(\mathbf{Q}_n'\mathbf{P}_n\mathbf{Q}_n)^{-1}\mathbf{Q}_n'\mathbf{P}_n\mathbf{V}_n\mathbf{P}_n\mathbf{Q}_n(\mathbf{Q}_n'\mathbf{P}_n\mathbf{Q}_n)^{-1}\mathbf{R}'.$$

It follows from Corollary 4.24 that $\boldsymbol{\Gamma}_n^{-1/2}\mathbf{R}\sqrt{n}(\tilde{\boldsymbol{\beta}}_n - \boldsymbol{\beta}_o) \overset{A}{\sim} N(\mathbf{0}, \mathbf{I})$ so that $\boldsymbol{\Gamma}_n^{-1/2}\sqrt{n}(\mathbf{R}\tilde{\boldsymbol{\beta}}_n - \mathbf{r}) \overset{A}{\sim} N(\mathbf{0}, \mathbf{I})$. Since $\hat{\mathbf{D}}_n - \mathbf{D}_n \xrightarrow{p} \mathbf{0}$ from Exercise 4.26 it follows that $\hat{\boldsymbol{\Lambda}}_n - \boldsymbol{\Lambda}_n \xrightarrow{p} \mathbf{0}$ by Proposition 2.30. Hence $\mathcal{W}_n \overset{A}{\sim} \chi_q^2$ by Theorem 4.30.

We can derive the Lagrange multiplier statistic from the constrained minimization problem:

$$\min_{\boldsymbol{\beta}} (\mathbf{Y} - \mathbf{X}\boldsymbol{\beta})'\mathbf{Z}\hat{\mathbf{P}}_n\mathbf{Z}'(\mathbf{Y} - \mathbf{X}\boldsymbol{\beta})/n^2 \quad \text{s.t. } \mathbf{R}\boldsymbol{\beta} = \mathbf{r}.$$

The first-order conditions are

$$\begin{aligned}
\partial\mathcal{L}/\partial\boldsymbol{\beta} &= 2(\mathbf{X}'\mathbf{Z}\hat{\mathbf{P}}_n\mathbf{Z}'\mathbf{X}/n^2)\boldsymbol{\beta} - 2(\mathbf{X}'\mathbf{Z}/n)\hat{\mathbf{P}}_n\mathbf{Z}'\mathbf{Y}/n + \mathbf{R}\boldsymbol{\lambda} = \mathbf{0} \\
\partial\mathcal{L}/\partial\boldsymbol{\lambda} &= \mathbf{R}\boldsymbol{\beta} - \mathbf{r} = \mathbf{0},
\end{aligned}$$

where $\boldsymbol{\lambda}$ is the vector of Lagrange multipliers. It follows that

$$\begin{aligned}
\ddot{\boldsymbol{\lambda}}_n &= 2(\mathbf{R}(\mathbf{X}'\mathbf{Z}\hat{\mathbf{P}}_n\mathbf{Z}'\mathbf{X}/n^2)^{-1}\mathbf{R}')^{-1}(\mathbf{R}\ddot{\boldsymbol{\beta}}_n - \mathbf{r}) \\
\ddot{\boldsymbol{\beta}}_n &= \tilde{\boldsymbol{\beta}}_n - (\mathbf{X}'\mathbf{Z}\hat{\mathbf{P}}_n\mathbf{Z}'\mathbf{X}/n^2)^{-1}\mathbf{R}'\ddot{\boldsymbol{\lambda}}_n/2.
\end{aligned}$$

Hence, analogous to Theorem 4.32, $\mathcal{LM}_n \equiv n\ddot{\boldsymbol{\lambda}}_n'\hat{\boldsymbol{\Lambda}}_n^{-1}\ddot{\boldsymbol{\lambda}}_n \overset{A}{\sim} \chi_q^2$ under H_0, where

$$\begin{aligned}
\hat{\boldsymbol{\Lambda}}_n \equiv\ & 4(\mathbf{R}(\mathbf{X}'\mathbf{Z}\hat{\mathbf{P}}_n\mathbf{Z}'\mathbf{X}/n^2)^{-1}\mathbf{R}')^{-1}\mathbf{R}(\mathbf{X}'\mathbf{Z}\hat{\mathbf{P}}_n\mathbf{Z}'\mathbf{X}/n^2)^{-1} \\
& \times(\mathbf{X}'\mathbf{Z}/n)\hat{\mathbf{P}}_n\ddot{\mathbf{V}}_n\hat{\mathbf{P}}_n(\mathbf{Z}'\mathbf{X}/n)(\mathbf{X}'\mathbf{Z}\hat{\mathbf{P}}_n\mathbf{Z}'\mathbf{X}/n^2)^{-1} \\
& \times\mathbf{R}'(\mathbf{R}(\mathbf{X}'\mathbf{Z}\hat{\mathbf{P}}_n\mathbf{Z}'\mathbf{X}/n^2)^{-1}\mathbf{R}')^{-1}
\end{aligned}$$

and $\ddot{\mathbf{V}}_n$ is computed under the constrained regression such that $\ddot{\mathbf{V}}_n - \hat{\mathbf{V}}_n \xrightarrow{p} \mathbf{0}$ under H_0. If we can show that $\mathcal{LM}_n - \mathcal{W}_n \xrightarrow{p} \mathbf{0}$, then we can apply Lemma 4.7 to conclude $\mathcal{LM}_n \overset{A}{\sim} \chi_q^2$. Note that $\mathcal{LM}_n$ differs from

$\mathcal{W}_n$ in that $\ddot{\mathbf{V}}_n$ is used in place of $\hat{\mathbf{V}}_n$. Since $\ddot{\mathbf{V}}_n - \hat{\mathbf{V}}_n \xrightarrow{p} \mathbf{0}$ under H_0, it follows from Proposition 2.30 that $\mathcal{LM}_n - \mathcal{W}_n \xrightarrow{p} \mathbf{0}$.

Next, consider the nonlinear hypothesis $\mathbf{s}(\boldsymbol{\beta}_o) = \mathbf{0}$. The Wald statistic is easily seen to be

$$\mathcal{W}_n \equiv n\mathbf{s}(\tilde{\boldsymbol{\beta}}_n)'\hat{\boldsymbol{\Gamma}}_n^{-1}\mathbf{s}(\tilde{\boldsymbol{\beta}}_n),$$

where

$$\hat{\boldsymbol{\Gamma}}_n^{-1} \equiv \nabla\mathbf{s}(\tilde{\boldsymbol{\beta}}_n)'\hat{\mathbf{D}}_n\nabla\mathbf{s}(\tilde{\boldsymbol{\beta}}_n)$$

and $\hat{\mathbf{D}}_n$ is given in Exercise 4.26. The proof that $\mathcal{W}_n \overset{A}{\sim} \chi^2_q$ under H_0 is identical to that of Theorem 4.39 except that $\tilde{\boldsymbol{\beta}}_n$ replaces $\hat{\boldsymbol{\beta}}_n$, $\hat{\mathbf{D}}_n$ is appropriately defined, and the results of Exercise 4.26 are used in place of those of Theorem 4.25.

The Lagrange Multiplier statistic can be derived in a manner analogous to Exercise 4.41, and the result is that the Lagrange multiplier statistic has the form of the Wald statistic with the constrained estimates $\ddot{\boldsymbol{\beta}}_n$ and $\ddot{\mathbf{V}}_n$ replacing $\hat{\boldsymbol{\beta}}_n$ and $\hat{\mathbf{V}}_n$. Thus

$$\mathcal{LM}_n = n\ddot{\boldsymbol{\lambda}}_n'\hat{\boldsymbol{\Lambda}}_n^{-1}\ddot{\boldsymbol{\lambda}}_n,$$

where

$$\boldsymbol{\lambda}_n = 2[\nabla\mathbf{s}(\ddot{\boldsymbol{\beta}}_n)'(\mathbf{X}'\mathbf{Z}\hat{\mathbf{P}}_n\mathbf{Z}'\mathbf{X}/n^2)^{-1}\nabla\mathbf{s}(\ddot{\boldsymbol{\beta}}_n)]^{-1}\mathbf{s}(\ddot{\boldsymbol{\beta}}_n)$$

and

$$\begin{aligned}\hat{\boldsymbol{\Lambda}}_n \quad = \quad & 4[\nabla\mathbf{s}(\ddot{\boldsymbol{\beta}}_n)'(\mathbf{X}'\mathbf{Z}\hat{\mathbf{P}}_n\mathbf{Z}'\mathbf{X}/n^2)^{-1}\nabla\mathbf{s}(\ddot{\boldsymbol{\beta}}_n)]^{-1} \\ & \times\nabla\mathbf{s}(\boldsymbol{\beta}_n)'(\mathbf{X}'\mathbf{Z}\hat{\mathbf{P}}_n\mathbf{Z}'\mathbf{X}/n^2)^{-1}(\mathbf{X}'\mathbf{Z}/n)\hat{\mathbf{P}}_n\ddot{\mathbf{V}}_n\hat{\mathbf{P}}_n(\mathbf{Z}'\mathbf{X}/n) \\ & \times(\mathbf{X}'\mathbf{Z}\hat{\mathbf{P}}_n\mathbf{Z}'\mathbf{X}/n^2)^{-1}\nabla\mathbf{s}(\ddot{\boldsymbol{\beta}}_n)[\nabla\mathbf{s}(\ddot{\boldsymbol{\beta}}_n)' \\ & \times(\mathbf{X}'\mathbf{Z}\hat{\mathbf{P}}_n\mathbf{Z}'\mathbf{X}/n^2)^{-1}\nabla\mathbf{s}(\ddot{\boldsymbol{\beta}}_n)]^{-1}.\end{aligned}$$

Now $\ddot{\mathbf{V}}_n - \mathbf{V}_n \xrightarrow{p} \mathbf{0}$ and $\nabla\mathbf{s}(\ddot{\boldsymbol{\beta}}_n) - \nabla\mathbf{s}(\hat{\boldsymbol{\beta}}_n) \xrightarrow{p} \mathbf{0}$ given that $\nabla\mathbf{s}(\boldsymbol{\beta})$ is continuous. It follows from Proposition 2.30 that $\mathcal{LM}_n - \mathcal{W}_n \xrightarrow{p} 0$, so that $\mathcal{LM}_n \overset{A}{\sim} \chi^2_q$ by Lemma 4.7. ■

Exercise 4.46

Proof. Under the conditions of Exercise 4.26, Proposition 4.45 tells us that the asymptotically efficient estimator is

$$\begin{aligned}\boldsymbol{\beta}_n^* &= (\mathbf{X}'\mathbf{X}\hat{\mathbf{V}}_n^{-1}\mathbf{X}'\mathbf{X})^{-1}\mathbf{X}'\mathbf{X}\hat{\mathbf{V}}_n^{-1}\mathbf{X}'\mathbf{Y}\\ &= (\mathbf{X}'\mathbf{X})^{-1}\hat{\mathbf{V}}_n(\mathbf{X}'\mathbf{X})^{-1}\mathbf{X}'\mathbf{X}\hat{\mathbf{V}}_n^{-1}\mathbf{X}'\mathbf{Y}\\ &= (\mathbf{X}'\mathbf{X})^{-1}\mathbf{X}'\mathbf{Y} = \hat{\boldsymbol{\beta}}_n,\end{aligned}$$

where we substituted $\mathbf{X}'\mathbf{X} = \hat{\mathbf{V}}_n$. ∎

Exercise 4.47

Proof. We assume that the conditions of Exercise 4.26 are satisfied. In addition, we assume $\tilde{\sigma}_n^2(\mathbf{Z}'\mathbf{Z}/n) - \sigma_o^2\mathbf{L}_n \xrightarrow{p} \mathbf{0}$ so that $\hat{\mathbf{V}}_n = \tilde{\sigma}_n^2(\mathbf{Z}'\mathbf{Z}/n)$. (This follows from a law of large numbers.) Then from Proposition 4.45 it follows that the asymptotically efficient estimator is

$$\begin{aligned}\boldsymbol{\beta}_n^* &= (\mathbf{X}'\mathbf{Z}(\tilde{\sigma}_n^2(\mathbf{Z}'\mathbf{Z}/n))^{-1}\mathbf{Z}'\mathbf{X})^{-1}\mathbf{X}'\mathbf{Z}(\tilde{\sigma}_n^2(\mathbf{Z}'\mathbf{Z}/n))^{-1}\mathbf{Z}'\mathbf{Y}\\ &= (\mathbf{X}'\mathbf{Z}(\mathbf{Z}'\mathbf{Z})^{-1}\mathbf{Z}'\mathbf{X})^{-1}\mathbf{X}'\mathbf{Z}(\mathbf{Z}'\mathbf{Z})^{-1}\mathbf{Z}'\mathbf{Y}\\ &= \tilde{\boldsymbol{\beta}}_{2SLS}.\end{aligned}$$

∎

Exercise 4.48

Proof. From the definition

$$\begin{aligned}\sqrt{n}(\boldsymbol{\beta}_n^{**} - \boldsymbol{\beta}_n^*) &= (\mathbf{X}'\mathbf{Z}\hat{\mathbf{P}}_n\mathbf{Z}'\mathbf{X}/n^2)^{-1}\nabla \mathbf{s}(\boldsymbol{\beta}_n^*)\\ &\quad\times[\nabla \mathbf{s}(\boldsymbol{\beta}_n^*)'(\mathbf{X}'\mathbf{Z}\hat{\mathbf{P}}_n\mathbf{Z}'\mathbf{X}/n^2)^{-1}\nabla \mathbf{s}(\boldsymbol{\beta}_n^*)]^{-1}\sqrt{n}\mathbf{s}(\boldsymbol{\beta}_n^*)\end{aligned}$$

it follows that $\sqrt{n}(\boldsymbol{\beta}_n^{**} - \boldsymbol{\beta}_n^*) \xrightarrow{p} \mathbf{0}$ provided that $(\mathbf{X}'\mathbf{Z}\hat{\mathbf{P}}_n\mathbf{Z}'\mathbf{X}/n^2)^{-1} = O_p(1)$, $\nabla \mathbf{s}(\boldsymbol{\beta}_n^*) = O_p(1)$, and $\sqrt{n}\mathbf{s}(\boldsymbol{\beta}_n^*) = o_p(1)$. The first two are easy to show, so we just show that $\sqrt{n}\mathbf{s}(\boldsymbol{\beta}_n^*) = o_p(1)$. Taking a mean value expansion and substituting the definition of $\boldsymbol{\beta}_n^*$ gives

$$\begin{aligned}\sqrt{n}\,\mathbf{s}(\boldsymbol{\beta}_n^*) &= \sqrt{n}\,\mathbf{s}(\tilde{\boldsymbol{\beta}}_n) + \sqrt{n}\nabla\bar{\mathbf{s}}_n'(\boldsymbol{\beta}_n^* - \tilde{\boldsymbol{\beta}}_n)\\ &= \sqrt{n}\,\mathbf{s}(\tilde{\boldsymbol{\beta}}_n) - \nabla\bar{\mathbf{s}}_n'(\mathbf{X}'\mathbf{Z}\hat{\mathbf{P}}_n\mathbf{Z}'\mathbf{X})^{-1}\nabla \mathbf{s}(\tilde{\boldsymbol{\beta}}_n)\\ &\quad\times[\nabla \mathbf{s}(\tilde{\boldsymbol{\beta}}_n)'(\mathbf{X}'\mathbf{Z}\hat{\mathbf{P}}_n\mathbf{Z}'\mathbf{X})^{-1}\nabla \mathbf{s}(\tilde{\boldsymbol{\beta}}_n)]^{-1}\sqrt{n}\mathbf{s}(\tilde{\boldsymbol{\beta}}_n)\\ &= \Big(\mathbf{I} - \nabla\bar{\mathbf{s}}_n'(\mathbf{X}'\mathbf{Z}\hat{\mathbf{P}}_n\mathbf{Z}'\mathbf{X})^{-1}\nabla \mathbf{s}(\tilde{\boldsymbol{\beta}}_n)\\ &\quad\times[\nabla \mathbf{s}(\tilde{\boldsymbol{\beta}}_n)'(\mathbf{X}'\mathbf{Z}\hat{\mathbf{P}}_n\mathbf{Z}'\mathbf{X})^{-1}\nabla \mathbf{s}(\tilde{\boldsymbol{\beta}}_n)]^{-1}\Big)\,\sqrt{n}\mathbf{s}(\tilde{\boldsymbol{\beta}}_n).\end{aligned}$$

Now

$$\mathbf{I} - \nabla\bar{\mathbf{s}}_n'(\mathbf{X}'\mathbf{Z}\hat{\mathbf{P}}_n\mathbf{Z}'\mathbf{X})^{-1}\nabla\mathbf{s}(\tilde{\boldsymbol{\beta}}_n)[\nabla\mathbf{s}(\tilde{\boldsymbol{\beta}}_n)'(\mathbf{X}'\mathbf{Z}\hat{\mathbf{P}}_n\mathbf{Z}'\mathbf{X})^{-1}\nabla\mathbf{s}(\tilde{\boldsymbol{\beta}}_n)]^{-1} = o_p(1)$$

since $\nabla\bar{\mathbf{s}}_n - \nabla\mathbf{s}(\tilde{\boldsymbol{\beta}}_n) = o_p(1)$, and $\sqrt{n}\,\mathbf{s}(\tilde{\boldsymbol{\beta}}_n) = \sqrt{n}\,\mathbf{s}(\boldsymbol{\beta}_o) + \nabla\ddot{\mathbf{s}}_n'\sqrt{n}(\tilde{\boldsymbol{\beta}}_n - \boldsymbol{\beta}_o) = \mathbf{0} + O_p(1)O_p(1) = O_p(1)$ by Lemma 4.6, and the result follows. ■

Exercise 4.56

Proof. Since $\mathbf{X}_t^o$ is $\mathcal{F}_{t-1}$-measurable then so is $\mathbf{Z}_t^o(\gamma^*) = \mathbf{X}_t^o\boldsymbol{\Omega}_t^{-1}$. For brevity, we write $\mathbf{Z}_t^o = \mathbf{Z}_t^o(\gamma^*)$ in the following.

We have

$$\begin{aligned} E^o(n^{-1}\sum_{t=1}^n \mathbf{Z}_t^o\varepsilon_t) &= E^o(n^{-1}\sum_{t=1}^n E^o(\mathbf{Z}_t^o\varepsilon_t|\mathcal{F}_{t-1})) \\ &= E^o(n^{-1}\sum_{t=1}^n \mathbf{Z}_t^o E^o(\varepsilon_t|\mathcal{F}_{t-1})) \\ &= \mathbf{0}, \end{aligned}$$

and by the martingale difference property

$$\begin{aligned} \mathbf{V}_n &= \text{var}^o(n^{-1}\sum_{t=1}^n \mathbf{Z}_t^o\varepsilon_t) \\ &= E^o(n^{-1}\sum_{t=1}^n \mathbf{Z}_t^o\varepsilon_t\varepsilon_t'\mathbf{Z}_t'^o) \\ &= E^o(n^{-1}\sum_{t=1}^n \mathbf{Z}_t^o E^o(\varepsilon_t\varepsilon_t'|\mathcal{F}_{t-1})\mathbf{Z}_t'^o) \\ &= E^o(n^{-1}\sum_{t=1}^n \mathbf{Z}_t^o\boldsymbol{\Omega}_t\mathbf{Z}_t'^o) \\ &= E^o(n^{-1}\sum_{t=1}^n \mathbf{X}_t^o\boldsymbol{\Omega}_t^{-1}\mathbf{X}_t'^o). \end{aligned}$$

Set $\hat{\mathbf{V}}_n = n^{-1}\sum_{t=1}^n \mathbf{X}_t^o\boldsymbol{\Omega}_t^{-1}\mathbf{X}_t'^o$.

With $\mathbf{Z}_t^o = \mathbf{X}_t^o \boldsymbol{\Omega}_t^{-1}$ we have

$$\begin{aligned}\boldsymbol{\beta}_n^* &= \left(\sum_{t=1}^n \mathbf{X}_t^o \mathbf{Z}_t^{\prime o} \hat{\mathbf{V}}_n^{-1} \sum_{t=1}^n \mathbf{Z}_t^o \mathbf{X}_t^{\prime o}\right)^{-1} \sum_{t=1}^n \mathbf{X}_t^o \mathbf{Z}_t^{\prime o} \hat{\mathbf{V}}_n^{-1} \sum_{t=1}^n \mathbf{Z}_t^o \mathbf{Y}_t^{\prime o} \\ &= \left(\sum_{t=1}^n \mathbf{X}_t^o \boldsymbol{\Omega}_t^{-1} \mathbf{X}_t^{\prime o}\right)^{-1} \sum_{t=1}^n \mathbf{X}_t^o \boldsymbol{\Omega}_t^{-1} \mathbf{Y}_t^{\prime o} \\ &= \left(\mathbf{X}'\boldsymbol{\Omega}^{-1}\mathbf{X}\right)^{-1} \mathbf{X}'\boldsymbol{\Omega}^{-1}\mathbf{Y}.\end{aligned}$$

■

Exercise 4.58
Proof. We have

$$\begin{aligned}\boldsymbol{\beta}_n^* &= \left(\sum_{t=1}^n \mathbf{X}_t^o \boldsymbol{\Omega}_t^{-1} \mathbf{X}_t^{o\prime}\right)^{-1} \sum_{t=1}^n \mathbf{X}_t^o \boldsymbol{\Omega}_t^{-1} \mathbf{Y}_t^o \\ &= \left(\sum_{t=1}^n \mathbf{X}_t^o \boldsymbol{\Omega}_t^{-1} \mathbf{X}_t^{o\prime}\right)^{-1} \sum_{t=1}^n \mathbf{X}_t^o \boldsymbol{\Omega}_t^{-1} (\mathbf{X}_t^{o\prime}\boldsymbol{\beta}^o + \boldsymbol{\varepsilon}_t) \\ &= \boldsymbol{\beta}^o + \left(\sum_{t=1}^n \mathbf{X}_t^o \boldsymbol{\Omega}_t^{-1} \mathbf{X}_t^{o\prime}\right)^{-1} \sum_{t=1}^n \mathbf{X}_t^o \boldsymbol{\Omega}_t^{-1} \boldsymbol{\varepsilon}_t.\end{aligned}$$

Set

$$\mathbf{m}_n^o(\boldsymbol{\gamma}^*) = n^{-1} \sum_{t=1}^n \mathbf{X}_t^o \boldsymbol{\Omega}_t^{-1} \boldsymbol{\varepsilon}_t$$

and we have

$$\begin{aligned}\sqrt{n}(\boldsymbol{\beta}_n^* - \boldsymbol{\beta}^o) &= \left(n^{-1} \sum_{t=1}^n \mathbf{X}_t^o \boldsymbol{\Omega}_t^{-1} \mathbf{X}_t^{o\prime}\right)^{-1} n^{1/2} \mathbf{m}_n^o(\boldsymbol{\gamma}^*) \\ &= \mathbf{Q}_n^o(\boldsymbol{\gamma}^*)^{-1} n^{1/2} \mathbf{m}_n^o(\boldsymbol{\gamma}^*) \\ &\quad + \left[\left(n^{-1} \sum_{t=1}^n \mathbf{X}_t^o \boldsymbol{\Omega}_t^{-1} \mathbf{X}_t^{o\prime}\right)^{-1} - \mathbf{Q}_n^o(\boldsymbol{\gamma}^*)^{-1}\right] n^{1/2} \mathbf{m}_n^o(\boldsymbol{\gamma}^*) \\ &= \mathbf{Q}_n^o(\boldsymbol{\gamma}^*)^{-1} n^{1/2} \mathbf{m}_n^o(\boldsymbol{\gamma}^*) + o_{p^o}(1)\end{aligned}$$

using Theorem 4.54 (*iii.a*) and (*ii*). So

$$\text{avar}^o(\boldsymbol{\beta}_n^*) = \mathbf{Q}_n^o(\boldsymbol{\gamma}^*)^{-1} \mathbf{V}_n^o(\boldsymbol{\gamma}^*) \mathbf{Q}_n^o(\boldsymbol{\gamma}^*)^{-1},$$

where

$$\begin{aligned}
\mathbf{V}_n^o(\boldsymbol{\gamma}^*) &= E^o\left(n^{-1}\sum_{t=1}^{n}\mathbf{X}_t^o\boldsymbol{\Omega}_t^{-1}\boldsymbol{\varepsilon}_t\boldsymbol{\varepsilon}_t'\boldsymbol{\Omega}_t^{-1}\mathbf{X}_t^{o\prime}\right)\\
&= n^{-1}\sum_{t=1}^{n}E^o(\mathbf{X}_t^o\boldsymbol{\Omega}_t^{-1}\boldsymbol{\varepsilon}_t\boldsymbol{\varepsilon}_t'\boldsymbol{\Omega}_t^{-1}\mathbf{X}_t^{o\prime})\\
&= n^{-1}\sum_{t=1}^{n}E^o(\mathbf{X}_t^o\boldsymbol{\Omega}_t^{-1}E^o(\boldsymbol{\varepsilon}_t\boldsymbol{\varepsilon}_t'|\mathcal{F}_{t-1})\boldsymbol{\Omega}_t^{-1}\mathbf{X}_t^{o\prime})\\
&= n^{-1}\sum_{t=1}^{n}E^o(\mathbf{X}_t^o\boldsymbol{\Omega}_t^{-1}\mathbf{X}_t^{o\prime})
\end{aligned}$$

using the law of iterated expectations.

By assumption, $\mathbf{Q}_n^o(\boldsymbol{\gamma}^*) = n^{-1}\sum_{t=1}^{n}E^o(\mathbf{X}_t^o\boldsymbol{\Omega}_t^{-1}\mathbf{X}_t^{o\prime})$, so

$$\text{avar}^o(\boldsymbol{\beta}_n^*) = \left[n^{-1}\sum_{t=1}^{n}E^o(\mathbf{X}_t^o\boldsymbol{\Omega}_t^{-1}\mathbf{X}_t^{o\prime})\right]^{-1}$$

Consistency of $\hat{\mathbf{D}}_n$ follows given Theorem 4.54 (*iii.a*) and the assumption that $\mathbf{Q}_n^o(\boldsymbol{\gamma}^*) = n^{-1}\sum_{t=1}^{n}E^o(\mathbf{X}_t^o\boldsymbol{\Omega}_t^{-1}\mathbf{X}_t^{o\prime})$ by the continuity of the inverse function and given that $\mathbf{Q}_n^o(\boldsymbol{\gamma}^*) = \mathbf{V}_n^o(\boldsymbol{\gamma}^*)$ is uniformly positive definite. ∎

Exercise 4.60

Proof. Similar to Exercise 4.58 we have that

$$\begin{aligned}
\sqrt{n}(\boldsymbol{\beta}_n^* - \boldsymbol{\beta}^o) &= \left(n^{-1}\sum_{t=1}^{n}\mathbf{X}_t^o\hat{\boldsymbol{\Omega}}_{nt}^{-1}\mathbf{X}_t^{o\prime}\right)^{-1} n^{-1/2}\sum_{t=1}^{n}\mathbf{X}_t^o\hat{\boldsymbol{\Omega}}_{nt}^{-1}\boldsymbol{\varepsilon}_t\\
&= \left(n^{-1}\sum_{t=1}^{n}E^o(\mathbf{X}_t^o\boldsymbol{\Omega}_t^{o-1}\mathbf{X}_t^{o\prime})\right)^{-1} n^{-1/2}\sum_{t=1}^{n}\mathbf{X}_t^o\boldsymbol{\Omega}_t^{o-1}\boldsymbol{\varepsilon}_t
\end{aligned}$$

$$+[\left(n^{-1}\sum_{t=1}^{n}\mathbf{X}_t^o\hat{\mathbf{\Omega}}_{nt}^{-1}\mathbf{X}_t^{o\prime}\right)^{-1} - \left(n^{-1}\sum_{t=1}^{n}E^o(\mathbf{X}_t^o\mathbf{\Omega}_t^{o-1}\mathbf{X}_t^{o\prime})\right)^{-1}]$$
$$\times n^{-1/2}\sum_{t=1}^{n}\mathbf{X}_t^o\mathbf{\Omega}_t^{o-1}\varepsilon_t$$
$$+\left(n^{-1}\sum_{t=1}^{n}E^o(\mathbf{X}_t^o\mathbf{\Omega}_t^{o-1}\mathbf{X}_t^{o\prime})\right)^{-1}$$
$$\times[n^{-1/2}\sum_{t=1}^{n}\mathbf{X}_t^o\hat{\mathbf{\Omega}}_{nt}^{-1}\varepsilon_t - n^{-1/2}\sum_{t=1}^{n}\mathbf{X}_t^o\mathbf{\Omega}_t^{o-1}\varepsilon_t]$$
$$+[\left(n^{-1}\sum_{t=1}^{n}\mathbf{X}_t^o\hat{\mathbf{\Omega}}_{nt}^{-1}\mathbf{X}_t^{o\prime}\right)^{-1} - \left(n^{-1}\sum_{t=1}^{n}E^o(\mathbf{X}_t^o\mathbf{\Omega}_t^{o-1}\mathbf{X}_t^{o\prime})\right)^{-1}]$$
$$\times[n^{-1/2}\sum_{t=1}^{n}\mathbf{X}_t^o\hat{\mathbf{\Omega}}_{nt}^{-1}\varepsilon_t - n^{-1/2}\sum_{t=1}^{n}\mathbf{X}_t^o\mathbf{\Omega}_t^{o-1}\varepsilon_t]$$
$$= \left(n^{-1}\sum_{t=1}^{n}E^o(\mathbf{X}_t^o\mathbf{\Omega}_t^{o-1}\mathbf{X}_t^{o\prime})\right)^{-1} n^{-1/2}\sum_{t=1}^{n}\mathbf{X}_t^o\mathbf{\Omega}_t^{o-1}\varepsilon_t$$
$$+o_{p^o}(1)O_{p^o}(1) + O(1)o_{p^o}(1) + o_{p^o}(1)o_{p^o}(1)$$

using Theorem 4.54 conditions (*iii.a*) and (*ii*) on the second, third, and fourth terms.

It follows that

$$\text{avar}^o(\boldsymbol{\beta}_n^*) = \left(n^{-1}\sum_{t=1}^{n}E^o(\mathbf{X}_t^o\mathbf{\Omega}_t^{o-1}\mathbf{X}_t^{o\prime})\right)^{-1},$$

which is consistently estimated by

$$\hat{\mathbf{D}}_n = \left(n^{-1}\sum_{t=1}^{n}\mathbf{X}_t^o\hat{\mathbf{\Omega}}_{nt}^{-1}\mathbf{X}_t^{o\prime}\right)^{-1},$$

given Theorem 4.54 (*iii.a*). ∎

Exercise 4.61

Proof. (*i*) Let $\tilde{\mathbf{W}}_t^o = (1, W_t^o)'$; then

$$\begin{aligned}
\hat{\alpha}_n &= \left(n^{-1}\sum_{t=1}^n \tilde{\mathbf{W}}_t^o \tilde{\mathbf{W}}_t^{o\prime}\right)^{-1} n^{-1}\sum_{t=1}^n \tilde{\mathbf{W}}_t^o \hat{\varepsilon}_t^2 \\
&= \left(n^{-1}\sum_{t=1}^n \tilde{\mathbf{W}}_t^o \tilde{\mathbf{W}}_t^{o\prime}\right)^{-1} n^{-1}\sum_{t=1}^n \tilde{\mathbf{W}}_t^o (\varepsilon_t - \mathbf{X}_t^{o\prime}(\hat{\boldsymbol{\beta}}_n - \boldsymbol{\beta}^o))^2 \\
&= \left(n^{-1}\sum_{t=1}^n \tilde{\mathbf{W}}_t^o \tilde{\mathbf{W}}_t^{o\prime}\right)^{-1} n^{-1}\sum_{t=1}^n \tilde{\mathbf{W}}_t^o \varepsilon_t^2 \\
&\quad -2\left(n^{-1}\sum_{t=1}^n \tilde{\mathbf{W}}_t^o \tilde{\mathbf{W}}_t^{o\prime}\right)^{-1} n^{-1}\sum_{t=1}^n \tilde{\mathbf{W}}_t^o \varepsilon_t \mathbf{X}_t^{o\prime}(\hat{\boldsymbol{\beta}}_n - \boldsymbol{\beta}^o) \\
&\quad +\left(n^{-1}\sum_{t=1}^n \tilde{\mathbf{W}}_t^o \tilde{\mathbf{W}}_t^{o\prime}\right)^{-1} n^{-1}\sum_{t=1}^n \tilde{\mathbf{W}}_t^o (\mathbf{X}_t^{o\prime}(\hat{\boldsymbol{\beta}}_n - \boldsymbol{\beta}^o))^2 \\
&= \left(n^{-1}\sum_{t=1}^n \tilde{\mathbf{W}}_t^o \tilde{\mathbf{W}}_t^{o\prime}\right)^{-1} n^{-1}\sum_{t=1}^n \tilde{\mathbf{W}}_t^o \tilde{\mathbf{W}}_t^o \boldsymbol{\alpha}_o + o_{p^o}(1) + o_{p^o}(1) \\
&= \boldsymbol{\alpha}_o + o_{p^o}(1),
\end{aligned}$$

provided that

$$\begin{aligned}
\left(n^{-1}\sum_{t=1}^n \tilde{\mathbf{W}}_t^o \tilde{\mathbf{W}}_t^{o\prime}\right)^{-1} &= O_{p^o}(1), \\
n^{-1}\sum_{t=1}^n \tilde{\mathbf{W}}_t^o \varepsilon_t \mathbf{X}_t^{o\prime} &= O_{p^o}(1), \\
n^{-1}\sum_{t=1}^n \tilde{\mathbf{W}}_t^o (\mathbf{X}_t^{o\prime} \otimes \mathbf{X}_t^{o\prime}) &= O_{p^o}(1),
\end{aligned}$$

and $(\hat{\boldsymbol{\beta}}_n - \boldsymbol{\beta}^o) = o_{p^o}(1)$.

The third condition enables us to verify

$$n^{-1}\sum_{t=1}^n \tilde{\mathbf{W}}_t^o (\mathbf{X}_t^{o\prime}(\hat{\boldsymbol{\beta}}_n - \boldsymbol{\beta}^o)) = n^{-1}\sum_{t=1}^n \tilde{\mathbf{W}}_t^o \mathbf{X}_t^{o\prime}(\hat{\boldsymbol{\beta}}_n - \boldsymbol{\beta}^o)(\hat{\boldsymbol{\beta}}_n - \boldsymbol{\beta}^o)'\mathbf{X}_t^o$$

$$= n^{-1}\sum_{t=1}^{n}\tilde{\mathbf{W}}_t^o(\mathbf{X}_t^{o\prime}\otimes\mathbf{X}_t^{o\prime})\mathrm{vec}((\hat{\boldsymbol{\beta}}_n-\boldsymbol{\beta}^o)(\hat{\boldsymbol{\beta}}_n-\boldsymbol{\beta}^o)')$$
$$= O_{p^o}(1)o_{p^o}(1)=o_{p^o}(1).$$

The first condition holds quite generally since W_t^o is bounded. Set $\bar{W}_n^o \equiv n^{-1}\sum_{t=1}^n W_t^o$ then

$$n^{-1}\sum_{t=1}^{n}\tilde{\mathbf{W}}_t^o\tilde{\mathbf{W}}_t^{o\prime}=\begin{pmatrix}1 & \bar{W}_n^o\\ \bar{W}_n^o & n^{-1}\sum_{t=1}^n W_t^{o2}\end{pmatrix}.$$

If this matrix is uniformly nonsingular, its inverse is $O_{p^o}(1)$, and for that it suffices that $\bar{W}_n^o$ is bounded away from zero and one.

(*ii*) Consider

$$n^{-1/2}\sum_{t=1}^{n}\mathbf{X}_t^o\hat{\Omega}_{nt}^{-1}\varepsilon_t-n^{-1/2}\sum_{t=1}^{n}\mathbf{X}_t^o\Omega_t^{o-1}\varepsilon_t$$
$$= n^{-1/2}\sum_{t=1}^{n}\mathbf{X}_t^o(\hat{\Omega}_{nt}^{-1}-\Omega_t^{o-1})\varepsilon_t$$
$$= n^{-1/2}\sum_{t=1}^{n}\mathbf{X}_t^o((\tilde{\mathbf{W}}_t^{o\prime}\hat{\boldsymbol{\alpha}}_n)^{-1}-(\tilde{\mathbf{W}}_t^{o\prime}\boldsymbol{\alpha}^o)^{-1})\varepsilon_t$$
$$= n^{-1/2}\sum_{t=1}^{n}\mathbf{X}_t^o((\hat{\alpha}_{1n})^{-1}-(\alpha_1^o)^{-1})\varepsilon_t 1[W_t^o=0]$$
$$+n^{-1/2}\sum_{t=1}^{n}\mathbf{X}_t^o((\hat{\alpha}_{1n}+\hat{\alpha}_{2n})^{-1}-(\alpha_1^o+\alpha_2^o)^{-1})\varepsilon_t 1[W_t^o=1]$$
$$= ((\hat{\alpha}_{1n})^{-1}-(\alpha_1^o)^{-1})n^{-1/2}\sum_{t=1}^{n}\mathbf{X}_t^o\varepsilon_t 1[W_t^o=0]$$
$$+((\hat{\alpha}_{1n}+\hat{\alpha}_{2n})^{-1}-(\alpha_1^o+\alpha_2^o)^{-1})n^{-1/2}\sum_{t=1}^{n}\mathbf{X}_t^o\varepsilon_t 1[W_t^o=1]$$
$$= o_{p^o}(1)O_{p^o}(1)+o_{p^o}(1)O_{p^o}(1)$$

To obtain the final equality, we apply the martingale difference central limit theorem to the terms $n^{-1/2}\sum_{t=1}^n \mathbf{X}_t^o\varepsilon_t 1[W_t^o=j]$, $j=0,1$, and require that α_1^o and $\alpha_1^o+\alpha_2^o$ are different from zero.

Similarly

$$
\begin{aligned}
& n^{-1}\sum_{t=1}^{n}\mathbf{X}_t^o\hat{\Omega}_{nt}^{-1}\mathbf{X}_t^{o\prime} - n^{-1}\sum_{t=1}^{n}\mathbf{X}_t^o\Omega_t^{o-1}\mathbf{X}_t^{o\prime} \\
= & ((\hat{\alpha}_{1n})^{-1} - (\alpha_1^o)^{-1})n^{-1}\sum_{t=1}^{n}\mathbf{X}_t^o\mathbf{X}_t^{o\prime}1[W_t^o = 0] \\
& + ((\hat{\alpha}_{1n} + \hat{\alpha}_{2n})^{-1} - (\alpha_1^o + \alpha_2^o)^{-1})n^{-1}\sum_{t=1}^{n}\mathbf{X}_t^o\mathbf{X}_t^{o\prime}1[W_t^o = 1] \\
= & o_{p^o}(1)O_{p^o}(1) + o_{p^o}(1)O_{p^o}(1).
\end{aligned}
$$

■

Exercise 4.63
Proof. Similar to Exercise 4.60 we have

$$
\begin{aligned}
\sqrt{n}(\beta_n^* - \beta^o) = & \left(n^{-1}\sum_{t=1}^{n}\hat{\mathbf{X}}_t^o\hat{\mathbf{\Omega}}_{nt}^{-1}\hat{\mathbf{X}}_t^{o\prime}\right)^{-1} n^{-1/2}\sum_{t=1}^{n}\hat{\mathbf{X}}_t^o\hat{\mathbf{\Omega}}_{nt}^{-1}\varepsilon_t \\
= & \left(n^{-1}\sum_{t=1}^{n}E^o(\tilde{\mathbf{X}}_t^o\mathbf{\Omega}_t^{o-1}\mathbf{X}_t^{o\prime})\right)^{-1} n^{-1/2}\sum_{t=1}^{n}\tilde{\mathbf{X}}_t^o\mathbf{\Omega}_t^{o-1}\varepsilon_t \\
& + \left[\left(n^{-1}\sum_{t=1}^{n}\hat{\mathbf{X}}_t^o\hat{\mathbf{\Omega}}_{nt}^{-1}\mathbf{X}_t^{o\prime}\right)^{-1} - \left(n^{-1}\sum_{t=1}^{n}E^o(\tilde{\mathbf{X}}_t^o\mathbf{\Omega}_t^{o-1}\mathbf{X}_t^{o\prime})\right)^{-1}\right] \\
& \times n^{-1/2}\sum_{t=1}^{n}\tilde{\mathbf{X}}_t^o\mathbf{\Omega}_t^{o-1}\varepsilon_t \\
& + \left(n^{-1}\sum_{t=1}^{n}E^o(\tilde{\mathbf{X}}_t^o\mathbf{\Omega}_t^{o-1}\mathbf{X}_t^{o\prime})\right)^{-1} \\
& \times [n^{-1/2}\sum_{t=1}^{n}\hat{\mathbf{X}}_t^o\hat{\mathbf{\Omega}}_{nt}^{-1}\varepsilon_t - n^{-1/2}\sum_{t=1}^{n}\tilde{\mathbf{X}}_t^o\mathbf{\Omega}_t^{o-1}\varepsilon_t] \\
& + \left[\left(n^{-1}\sum_{t=1}^{n}\hat{\mathbf{X}}_t^o\hat{\mathbf{\Omega}}_{nt}^{-1}\mathbf{X}_t^{o\prime}\right)^{-1} - \left(n^{-1}\sum_{t=1}^{n}E^o(\tilde{\mathbf{X}}_t^o\mathbf{\Omega}_t^{o-1}\mathbf{X}_t^{o\prime})\right)^{-1}\right] \\
& \times [n^{-1/2}\sum_{t=1}^{n}\hat{\mathbf{X}}_t^o\hat{\mathbf{\Omega}}_{nt}^{-1}\varepsilon_t - n^{-1/2}\sum_{t=1}^{n}\tilde{\mathbf{X}}_t^o\mathbf{\Omega}_t^{o-1}\varepsilon_t]
\end{aligned}
$$

$$= \left(n^{-1} \sum_{t=1}^{n} E^o(\tilde{\mathbf{X}}_t^o \boldsymbol{\Omega}_t^{o-1} \mathbf{X}_t^{o\prime}) \right)^{-1} n^{-1/2} \sum_{t=1}^{n} \tilde{\mathbf{X}}_t^o \boldsymbol{\Omega}_t^{o-1} \varepsilon_t$$
$$+ o_{p^o}(1) O_{p^o}(1) + O(1) o_{p^o}(1) + o_{p^o}(1) o_{p^o}(1)$$

applying Theorem 4.54 conditions (*iii.a*) and (*ii*) to the second, third, and fourth terms.

Since

$$\begin{aligned} E^o(\tilde{\mathbf{X}}_t^o \boldsymbol{\Omega}_t^{o-1} \mathbf{X}_t^{o\prime}) &= E^o(E^o(\tilde{\mathbf{X}}_t^o \boldsymbol{\Omega}_t^{o-1} \mathbf{X}_t^{o\prime}) | \mathcal{F}_{t-1}) \\ &= E^o(\tilde{\mathbf{X}}_t^o \boldsymbol{\Omega}_t^{o-1} \tilde{\mathbf{X}}_t^{o\prime}) \end{aligned}$$

by the law of iterated expectations, we have

$$\text{avar}^o(\boldsymbol{\beta}_n^*) = \left(n^{-1} \sum_{t=1}^{n} E^o(\tilde{\mathbf{X}}_t^o \boldsymbol{\Omega}_t^{o-1} \tilde{\mathbf{X}}_t^{o\prime}) \right)^{-1}.$$

To show that the matrix is consistently estimated by

$$\hat{\mathbf{D}}_n = 2 \left(n^{-1} \sum_{t=1}^{n} \hat{\mathbf{X}}_t^o \hat{\boldsymbol{\Omega}}_{nt}^{-1} \mathbf{X}_t^{o\prime} + n^{-1} \sum_{t=1}^{n} \mathbf{X}_t^o \hat{\boldsymbol{\Omega}}_{nt}^{-1} \hat{\mathbf{X}}_t^{o\prime} \right)^{-1},$$

it suffices that $\hat{\mathbf{D}}_n^{-1} - \text{avar}^o(\boldsymbol{\beta}_n^*)^{-1} = o_{p^o}(1)$. We have

$$\begin{aligned} &\hat{\mathbf{D}}_n^{-1} - \text{avar}^o(\boldsymbol{\beta}_n^*)^{-1} \\ = \; & (1/2)(n^{-1} \sum_{t=1}^{n} \hat{\mathbf{X}}_t^o \hat{\boldsymbol{\Omega}}_{nt}^{-1} \mathbf{X}_t^{o\prime} + n^{-1} \sum_{t=1}^{n} \mathbf{X}_t^o \hat{\boldsymbol{\Omega}}_{nt}^{-1} \hat{\mathbf{X}}_t^{o\prime}) \\ & - n^{-1} \sum_{t=1}^{n} E^o(\tilde{\mathbf{X}}_t^o \boldsymbol{\Omega}_t^{o-1} \tilde{\mathbf{X}}_t^{o\prime}) \\ = \; & (1/2)(n^{-1} \sum_{t=1}^{n} \hat{\mathbf{X}}_t^o \hat{\boldsymbol{\Omega}}_{nt}^{-1} \mathbf{X}_t^{o\prime} - n^{-1} \sum_{t=1}^{n} E^o(\tilde{\mathbf{X}}_t^o \boldsymbol{\Omega}_t^{o-1} \mathbf{X}_t^{o\prime})) \\ & + (1/2)(n^{-1} \sum_{t=1}^{n} \mathbf{X}_t^o \hat{\boldsymbol{\Omega}}_{nt}^{-1} \hat{\mathbf{X}}_t^{o\prime} - n^{-1} \sum_{t=1}^{n} E^o(\mathbf{X}_t^o \boldsymbol{\Omega}_t^{o-1} \tilde{\mathbf{X}}_t^{o\prime})), \end{aligned}$$

again using the law of iterated expectations.

Now

$$n^{-1} \sum_{t=1}^{n} \hat{\mathbf{X}}_t^o \hat{\boldsymbol{\Omega}}_{nt}^{-1} \mathbf{X}_t^{o\prime} - n^{-1} \sum_{t=1}^{n} E^o(\tilde{\mathbf{X}}_t^o \boldsymbol{\Omega}_t^{o-1} \mathbf{X}_t^{o\prime}) \xrightarrow{p^o} 0$$

by Theorem 4.54 condition (*iii*) and Theorem 4.62 condition (*iii*) and the result follows. ■

Exercise 4.64

Proof. (*i*)(*a*) Set $\boldsymbol{v}_t = \mathbf{X}_t^{\prime o} - E(\mathbf{X}_t^{\prime o}|\mathcal{F}_{t-1})$ so that $\mathbf{X}_t^{\prime o} = \mathbf{Z}_t^{o\prime}\boldsymbol{\pi}_o + \boldsymbol{v}_t$. Then

$$\begin{aligned}\hat{\boldsymbol{\pi}}_n &= \left(n^{-1}\sum_{t=1}^n \mathbf{Z}_t^o\mathbf{Z}_t^{o\prime}\right)^{-1} n^{-1}\sum_{t=1}^n \mathbf{Z}_t^o\mathbf{X}_t^{o\prime} \\ &= \boldsymbol{\pi}_o + (n^{-1}\sum_{t=1}^n \mathbf{Z}_t^o\mathbf{Z}_t^{o\prime})^{-1} n^{-1}\sum_{t=1}^n \mathbf{Z}_t^o\boldsymbol{v}_t \\ &= \boldsymbol{\pi}_o + o_{p^o}(1)\end{aligned}$$

given $n^{-1}\sum_{t=1}^n \mathbf{Z}_t^o\mathbf{Z}_t^{o\prime} = O_{p^o}(1)$ and $n^{-1}\sum_{t=1}^n \mathbf{Z}_t^o\boldsymbol{v}_t = o_{p^o}(1)$; the latter follows by the martingale difference weak law of large numbers.

(*b*) Substituting

$$\hat{\boldsymbol{\varepsilon}}_t = \boldsymbol{\varepsilon}_t + \mathbf{X}_t^{o\prime}(\boldsymbol{\beta}^o - \tilde{\boldsymbol{\beta}}_n)$$

we have that

$$\begin{aligned}\hat{\boldsymbol{\Sigma}}_n &= n^{-1}\sum_{t=1}^n \hat{\boldsymbol{\varepsilon}}_t\hat{\boldsymbol{\varepsilon}}_t' \\ &= n^{-1}\sum_{t=1}^n \boldsymbol{\varepsilon}_t\boldsymbol{\varepsilon}_t' \\ &\quad + n^{-1}\sum_{t=1}^n \boldsymbol{\varepsilon}_t(\boldsymbol{\beta}^o - \tilde{\boldsymbol{\beta}}_n)'\mathbf{X}_t^o + n^{-1}\sum_{t=1}^n \mathbf{X}_t^{o\prime}(\boldsymbol{\beta}^o - \tilde{\boldsymbol{\beta}}_n)\boldsymbol{\varepsilon}_t' \\ &\quad + n^{-1}\sum_{t=1}^n \mathbf{X}_t^{o\prime}(\boldsymbol{\beta}^o - \tilde{\boldsymbol{\beta}}_n)(\boldsymbol{\beta}^o - \tilde{\boldsymbol{\beta}}_n)'\mathbf{X}_t^o.\end{aligned}$$

Given that $n^{-1}\sum_{t=1}^n \boldsymbol{\varepsilon}_t\mathbf{X}_t^o$ and $n^{-1}\sum_{t=1}^n \mathbf{X}_t^{o\prime}\mathbf{X}_t^o$ are $O_{p^o}(1)$, that

$$\begin{aligned}n^{-1}\sum_{t=1}^n \mathbf{Z}_t^{o\prime}\mathbf{Z}_t^o &= O_{p^o}(1) \\ n^{-1}\sum_{t=1}^n \mathbf{Z}_t^{o\prime}\boldsymbol{\varepsilon}_t &= o_{p^o}(1),\end{aligned}$$

so that $(\boldsymbol{\beta}^o - \tilde{\boldsymbol{\beta}}_n) = o_{p^o}(1)$, it follows that the last three terms vanish in probability. To see this, apply the rule $\text{vec}(ABC) = (C'\otimes A)\text{vec}(B)$ to each of terms, for example:

$$\begin{aligned}\mathrm{vec}(n^{-1}\sum_{t=1}^{n}\varepsilon_t(\boldsymbol{\beta}^o-\tilde{\boldsymbol{\beta}}_n)'\mathbf{X}_t^o) &= n^{-1}\sum_{t=1}^{n}(\mathbf{X}_t^{o\prime}\otimes\varepsilon_t)\mathrm{vec}((\boldsymbol{\beta}^o-\tilde{\boldsymbol{\beta}}_n)') \\ &= O_{p^o}(1)o_{p^o}(1)=o_{p^o}(1).\end{aligned}$$

Given $n^{-1}\sum_{t=1}^{n}\varepsilon_t\varepsilon_t' \xrightarrow{p^o} \boldsymbol{\Sigma}^o$ it then follows that $\hat{\boldsymbol{\Sigma}}_n=\boldsymbol{\Sigma}^o+o_{p^o}(1)$.

(*ii*) To verify condition (*iii*) of Theorem 4.62 we write

$$\begin{aligned}& n^{-1/2}\sum_{t=1}^{n}\hat{\boldsymbol{\pi}}_n'\mathbf{Z}_t^o\hat{\boldsymbol{\Sigma}}_n^{-1}\varepsilon_t - n^{-1/2}\sum_{t=1}^{n}\boldsymbol{\pi}_o'\mathbf{Z}_t^o\boldsymbol{\Sigma}^{o-1}\varepsilon_t \\ =\ & \hat{\boldsymbol{\pi}}_n' n^{-1/2}\sum_{t=1}^{n}\mathbf{Z}_t^o\hat{\boldsymbol{\Sigma}}_n^{-1}\varepsilon_t - \boldsymbol{\pi}_o' n^{-1/2}\sum_{t=1}^{n}\mathbf{Z}_t^o\boldsymbol{\Sigma}^{o-1}\varepsilon_t \\ =\ & \hat{\boldsymbol{\pi}}_n' n^{-1/2}\sum_{t=1}^{n}\mathbf{Z}_t^o(\hat{\boldsymbol{\Sigma}}_n^{-1}-\boldsymbol{\Sigma}^{o-1})\varepsilon_t \\ & +\hat{\boldsymbol{\pi}}_n' n^{-1/2}\sum_{t=1}^{n}\mathbf{Z}_t^o\boldsymbol{\Sigma}^{o-1}\varepsilon_t - \boldsymbol{\pi}_o' n^{-1/2}\sum_{t=1}^{n}\mathbf{Z}_t^o\boldsymbol{\Sigma}^{o-1}\varepsilon_t \\ =\ & \hat{\boldsymbol{\pi}}_n' n^{-1/2}\sum_{t=1}^{n}(\varepsilon_t'\otimes\mathbf{Z}_t^o)\mathrm{vec}(\hat{\boldsymbol{\Sigma}}_n^{-1}-\boldsymbol{\Sigma}^{o-1}) \\ & +(\hat{\boldsymbol{\pi}}_n'-\boldsymbol{\pi}_o')n^{-1/2}\sum_{t=1}^{n}\mathbf{Z}_t^o\boldsymbol{\Sigma}^{o-1}\varepsilon_t \\ =\ & O_{p^o}(1)O_{p^o}(1)o_{p^o}(1)+o_{p^o}(1)O_{p^o}(1)=o_{p^o}(1).\end{aligned}$$

Similarly, to verify condition (*vi*) of Theorem 4.62 we write

$$\begin{aligned}& n^{-1}\sum_{t=1}^{n}\hat{\boldsymbol{\pi}}_n'\mathbf{Z}_t^o\hat{\boldsymbol{\Sigma}}_n^{-1}\mathbf{X}_t^o - n^{-1}\sum_{t=1}^{n}\boldsymbol{\pi}_o'\mathbf{Z}_t^o\boldsymbol{\Sigma}^{o-1}\mathbf{X}_t^o \\ =\ & \hat{\boldsymbol{\pi}}_n' n^{-1}\sum_{t=1}^{n}(\mathbf{X}_t'\otimes\mathbf{Z}_t^o)\mathrm{vec}(\hat{\boldsymbol{\Sigma}}_n^{-1}-\boldsymbol{\Sigma}^{o-1}) \\ & +(\hat{\boldsymbol{\pi}}_n'-\boldsymbol{\pi}_o')n^{-1}\sum_{t=1}^{n}\mathbf{Z}_t^o\boldsymbol{\Sigma}^{o-1}\mathbf{X}_t \\ =\ & O_{p^o}(1)O_{p^o}(1)o_{p^o}(1)+o_{p^o}(1)O_{p^o}(1)=o_{p^o}(1).\end{aligned}$$

■

Exercise 5.4

Proof. We verify the conditions of Exercise 4.26. To apply Theorem 5.2 let $\mathcal{Z}_t \equiv \boldsymbol{\lambda}'\mathbf{V}^{-1/2}\mathbf{Z}_t\varepsilon_t$, where $\boldsymbol{\lambda}'\boldsymbol{\lambda} = 1$ and consider

$$n^{-1/2}\sum_{t=1}^{n}\boldsymbol{\lambda}'\mathbf{V}^{-1/2}\mathbf{Z}_t\varepsilon_t = n^{-1/2}\sum_{t=1}^{n}\mathcal{Z}_t.$$

The summands $\mathcal{Z}_t$ are i.i.d. by Proposition 3.2 given (*ii*) with $E(\mathcal{Z}_t) = 0$ given (*iii.a*) and $\text{var}(\mathcal{Z}_t) = \boldsymbol{\lambda}'\mathbf{V}^{-1/2}\mathbf{V}\mathbf{V}^{-1/2}\boldsymbol{\lambda} = 1$ given (*iii.b*) and (*iii.c*). Therefore

$$n^{-1/2}\sum_{t=1}^{n}\mathcal{Z}_t = n^{-1/2}\sum_{t=1}^{n}\boldsymbol{\lambda}'\mathbf{V}^{-1/2}\mathbf{Z}'\varepsilon = \lambda'\mathbf{V}^{-1/2}n^{-1/2}\mathbf{Z}'\varepsilon \overset{A}{\sim} N(0,1)$$

by Theorem 5.2. It follows from Proposition 5.1 that $\mathbf{V}^{-1/2}n^{-1/2}\mathbf{Z}'\varepsilon \overset{A}{\sim} N(\mathbf{0},\mathbf{I})$ since if $\mathcal{Y} \sim N(\mathbf{0},\mathbf{I})$ then $\boldsymbol{\lambda}'\mathcal{Y} \sim N(0,1)$, for all $\boldsymbol{\lambda}$, $\boldsymbol{\lambda}'\boldsymbol{\lambda} = 1$. By (*iii.b*) and (*iii.c*) we have that $\mathbf{V}$ is $O(1)$ and nonsingular. It follows from Theorem 3.1 and Theorem 2.24 that $\mathbf{Z}'\mathbf{X}/n - \mathbf{Q} \xrightarrow{p} \mathbf{0}$ given (*ii*), (*iv.a*), and (*iv.b*). Since the remaining conditions of Exercise 4.26 are satisfied by assumption, the result follows. ∎

Exercise 5.5

Proof. Given the i.i.d. assumption of Exercise 5.4 it follows that

$$\mathbf{V} = n^{-1}\sum_{t=1}^{n}E(\varepsilon_t^2\mathbf{Z}_t\mathbf{Z}_t') = E(\varepsilon_t^2\mathbf{Z}_t\mathbf{Z}_t').$$

Now

$$\begin{aligned} E(\varepsilon_t^2\mathbf{Z}_t'\mathbf{Z}_t) &= E(E(\varepsilon_t^2\mathbf{Z}_t\mathbf{Z}_t'|\mathbf{Z}_t)) \\ &= E(E(\varepsilon_t^2|\mathbf{Z}_t)\mathbf{Z}_t\mathbf{Z}_t') \\ &= \sigma_o^2 E(\mathbf{Z}_t\mathbf{Z}_t') = \sigma_o^2\mathbf{L}. \end{aligned}$$

Hence $\mathbf{V} = \sigma_o^2\mathbf{L}$. It follows from Exercise 4.47 that the efficient IV estimator chooses $\mathbf{P} = \mathbf{V}^{-1}$ to yield the two stage least squares estimator,

$$\tilde{\beta}_{2SLS} = (\mathbf{X}'\mathbf{Z}(\mathbf{Z}'\mathbf{Z})^{-1}\mathbf{Z}'\mathbf{X})^{-1}\mathbf{X}'\mathbf{Z}(\mathbf{Z}'\mathbf{Z})^{-1}\mathbf{Z}'\mathbf{Y}.$$

The natural estimator for $\mathbf{V}$ is $\hat{\mathbf{V}}_n = \tilde{\sigma}_n^2(\mathbf{Z}'\mathbf{Z}/n)$, where

$$\tilde{\sigma}_n^2 = (\mathbf{Y} - \mathbf{X}\tilde{\beta}_{2SLS})'(\mathbf{Y} - \mathbf{X}\tilde{\beta}_{2SLS})/n.$$

The conditions of Exercise 5.4 are not quite strong enough to ensure $\hat{\mathbf{V}}_n$ is consistent for $\mathbf{V}$. It suffices that we add

(i') $E|\varepsilon_t^2| < \infty$

(ii') (a) $E\ |Z_{ti}^2| < \infty$, $i = 1, \ldots, l$;

(b) $E|X_{tj}^2| < \infty$, $j = 1, \ldots, k$;

(c) $\mathbf{L} \equiv E(\mathbf{Z}_t\mathbf{Z}_t')$ is nonsingular.

Note that $(ii'.a)$ and $(ii'.b)$ together imply $(iv.a)$ by the Cauchy-Schwarz inequality.

We show that $\mathbf{Z}'\mathbf{Z}/n \xrightarrow{p} \mathbf{L}$ and $\tilde{\sigma}_n^2 \xrightarrow{p} \sigma_o^2$. Since $\{\mathbf{Z}_t\mathbf{Z}_t'\}$ is an i.i.d. sequence given (ii), it follows that $\mathbf{Z}'\mathbf{Z}/n = n^{-1}\sum_{t=1}^n \mathbf{Z}_t\mathbf{Z}_t' \xrightarrow{p} \mathbf{L}$ by Theorem 3.1 and Theorem 2.24 given $(ii'.a)$. Next consider

$$\tilde{\sigma}_n^2 = n^{-1}(\boldsymbol{\varepsilon} - \mathbf{X}(\tilde{\boldsymbol{\beta}}_{2SLS} - \boldsymbol{\beta}_o))'(\boldsymbol{\varepsilon} - \mathbf{X}(\tilde{\boldsymbol{\beta}}_{2SLS} - \boldsymbol{\beta}_o))$$
$$= \boldsymbol{\varepsilon}'\boldsymbol{\varepsilon}/n - 2(\tilde{\boldsymbol{\beta}}_{2SLS} - \boldsymbol{\beta}_o)'\mathbf{X}'\boldsymbol{\varepsilon}/n + (\tilde{\boldsymbol{\beta}}_{2SLS} - \boldsymbol{\beta}_o)'(\mathbf{X}'\mathbf{X}/n)(\tilde{\boldsymbol{\beta}}_{2SLS} - \boldsymbol{\beta}_o).$$

Now $\tilde{\boldsymbol{\beta}}_{2SLS} - \boldsymbol{\beta}_o \xrightarrow{a.s.} \mathbf{0}$. The elements of $\mathbf{X}_t\boldsymbol{\varepsilon}_t$ have finite expected absolute value given (i') and $(ii'.b)$. Hence $\mathbf{X}'\boldsymbol{\varepsilon}/n = O_{a.s.}(1)$ by Theorem 3.1. Similarly, $\mathbf{X}_t\mathbf{X}_t'$ has finite expected absolute value given $(ii'.b)$. Since $\{\mathbf{X}_t\mathbf{X}_t'\}$ is an i.i.d. sequence it follows from Theorem 3.1 that $\mathbf{X}'\mathbf{X}/n = O_{a.s.}(1)$. Therefore

$$2(\tilde{\boldsymbol{\beta}}_{2SLS} - \boldsymbol{\beta}_o)\mathbf{X}'\boldsymbol{\varepsilon}/n \xrightarrow{p} \mathbf{0}$$

and

$$(\tilde{\boldsymbol{\beta}}_{2SLS} - \boldsymbol{\beta}_o)'(\mathbf{X}'\mathbf{X}/n)(\tilde{\boldsymbol{\beta}}_{2SLS} - \boldsymbol{\beta}_o) \xrightarrow{p} \mathbf{0}$$

by Theorem 2.24 and Proposition 2.30. Finally, consider

$$\boldsymbol{\varepsilon}'\boldsymbol{\varepsilon}/n = n^{-1}\sum_{t=1}^{n} \varepsilon_t^2.$$

Now $\{\varepsilon_t^2\}$ is an i.i.d. sequence given (ii) with finite expected absolute value given (i'). It follows from Theorem 3.1 that $n^{-1}\sum_{t=1}^n \varepsilon_t^2 - E(\varepsilon_t^2) = n^{-1}\sum_{t=1}^n \varepsilon_t^2 - \sigma_o^2 \xrightarrow{a.s.} 0$.

Hence $\hat{\mathbf{V}}_n - \mathbf{V} = \tilde{\sigma}_n^2(\mathbf{Z}'\mathbf{Z}/n) - \sigma_o^2\mathbf{L} \xrightarrow{p} \mathbf{0}$ by Proposition 2.30. Given that $\sigma_o^2 > 0$ and $\mathbf{L}$ is nonsingular it follows from Proposition 2.30 that

$$\hat{\mathbf{P}}_n - \mathbf{P} = \hat{\mathbf{V}}_n^{-1} - \mathbf{V}^{-1} = (\tilde{\sigma}_n^2(\mathbf{Z}'\mathbf{Z}/n))^{-1} - (\sigma_o^2\mathbf{L})^{-1} \xrightarrow{p} \mathbf{0}.$$

This completes the exercise. ■

Exercise 5.9

Proof. For an identically distributed sequence $\{\mathcal{Z}_t\}$ with $E(\mathcal{Z}_t) = \mu$, $\text{var}(\mathcal{Z}_t) = \sigma^2 < \infty$, the Lindeberg condition reduces to

$$\lim_{n\to\infty} \sigma^{-2} \int_{(z-\mu)^2 > \varepsilon n \sigma^2} (z-\mu)^2 dF(z) = 0.$$

Now let

$$g_n(z) = (z-\mu)^2 1_{\{(z-\mu)^2 \leq \varepsilon n \sigma^2\}}(z).$$

Then $\{g_n\}$ is a increasing sequence of functions that converges to the function $g(z) = (z-\mu)^2$. The monotone convergence theorem (see Rao, 1973, p. 135) allows us to interchange limit and integral

$$\begin{aligned} \lim_{n\to\infty} \int_{(z-\mu)^2 \leq \varepsilon n \sigma^2} (z-\mu)^2 dF(z) &= \lim_{n\to\infty} \int_{-\infty}^{\infty} g_n(z) dF(z) \\ &= \int_{-\infty}^{\infty} \lim_{n\to\infty} g_n(z) dF(z) \\ &= \int_{-\infty}^{\infty} (z-\mu)^2 dF(z) = \sigma^2. \end{aligned}$$

Now

$$\begin{aligned} &\lim_{n\to\infty} \sigma^{-2} \int_{(z-\mu)^2 > \varepsilon n \sigma^2} (z-\mu)^2 dF(z) \\ =\ & \lim_{n\to\infty} \sigma^{-2} \left[\sigma^2 - \int_{(z-\mu)^2 \leq \varepsilon n \sigma^2} (z-\mu)^2 dF(z) \right] \\ =\ & \sigma^{-2} \left[\sigma^2 - \lim_{n\to\infty} \int_{-\infty}^{\infty} g_n(z) dF(z) \right] \\ =\ & \sigma^{-2} \left[\sigma^2 - \sigma^2 \right] = 0. \end{aligned}$$

■

Exercise 5.12

Proof. We verify the conditions of Theorem 4.25. To apply Theorem 5.11, let $\mathcal{Z}_{nt} \equiv \boldsymbol{\lambda}' \mathbf{V}_n^{-1/2} \mathbf{X}_t' \varepsilon_t$ and consider

$$n^{-1/2} \sum_{t=1}^{n} \boldsymbol{\lambda}' \mathbf{V}_n^{-1/2} \mathbf{X}_t \varepsilon_t = n^{-1/2} \sum_{t=1}^{n} \mathcal{Z}_{nt}.$$

The summands $\mathcal{Z}_{nt}$ are independent by Proposition 3.3 given (ii), with $E(\mathcal{Z}_{nt}) = 0$ given $(iii.a)$, and

$$\begin{aligned}\bar{\sigma}_n^2 &\equiv \text{var}(\sqrt{n}\mathcal{Z}) = \boldsymbol{\lambda}'\mathbf{V}_n^{-1/2}\text{var}(n^{-1/2}\mathbf{X}'\boldsymbol{\varepsilon})\mathbf{V}_n^{-1/2}\boldsymbol{\lambda} \\ &= \boldsymbol{\lambda}'\mathbf{V}_n^{-1/2}\mathbf{V}_n\mathbf{V}_n^{-1/2}\boldsymbol{\lambda} = 1\end{aligned}$$

given $(iii.c)$. By $(iii.b)$ $E|\mathcal{Z}_{nt}|^{2+\delta}$ is uniformly bounded (apply Minkowski's inequality). Hence, for all $\boldsymbol{\lambda}$, $\boldsymbol{\lambda}'\boldsymbol{\lambda} = 1$,

$$n^{-1/2}\sum_{t=1}^{n}\mathcal{Z}_{nt} = n^{-1/2}\sum_{t=1}^{n}\mathbf{V}_n^{-1/2}\mathbf{X}_t\varepsilon_t = \boldsymbol{\lambda}'\mathbf{V}_n^{-1/2}n^{-1/2}\mathbf{X}'\boldsymbol{\varepsilon} \overset{A}{\sim} N(0,1)$$

and therefore $\mathbf{V}_n^{-1/2}n^{-1/2}\mathbf{X}'\boldsymbol{\varepsilon} \overset{A}{\sim} N(\mathbf{0},\mathbf{I})$ by Proposition 5.1.

Assumptions (ii), $(iv.a)$, and $(iv.b)$ ensure that $\mathbf{X}'\mathbf{X}/n - \mathbf{M}_n \xrightarrow{p} \mathbf{0}$ by Corollary 3.9 and Theorem 2.24. Given $(iv.a)$ $\mathbf{M}_n = O(1)$ and uniformly positive definite given $(iv.b)$. Since (v) also holds, the result follows from Theorem 4.25. ■

Exercise 5.18

Proof. The following conditions are sufficient for asymptotic normality:

(i') (a) $Y_t = \beta_{o1}Y_{t-1} + \beta_{o2}Y_{t-2} + \varepsilon_t$;
(b) $-1 < \beta_{o2} < 1$;
$\beta_{o2} - \beta_{o1} < 1$;
$\beta_{o1} + \beta_{o2} < 1$;

(ii') (a) $\{\varepsilon_t\}$ is a stationary, ergodic sequence;
(b) $\{\varepsilon_t, \mathcal{F}_t\}$ is a martingale difference sequence, where

$$\mathcal{F}_t = \sigma(\ldots, \varepsilon_{t-1}, \varepsilon_t);$$

(iii') (a) $E(\varepsilon_t^2|\mathcal{F}_{t-1}) = \sigma_o^2 > 0$.
(b) $E|\varepsilon_t|^4 = \Delta < \infty$.

We verify the conditions of Theorem 5.17.

(i) is implied by (i')

(ii) $\{(\mathbf{X}_t', \varepsilon_t)\} \equiv \{(Y_{t-1}, Y_{t-2}, \varepsilon_t)\}$ is a stationary ergodic sequence by Theorem 3.35,

$(iii.a)$ The data generating process given in $(i'.a)$ is an $AR(2)$ time series process and condition $(i'.b)$ is the familiar stationarity condition that the roots of the polynomial $1-\beta_{o1}z-\beta_{o2}z^2$ lie outside the unit disk. Given

$(i'.b)$ we can write Y_t as an infinite moving average, $Y_t = \sum_{j=0}^{\infty} c_j \varepsilon_{t-j}$, where $c_j = (|\beta_{o2}|^{1/2})^j a(j)$ and $|a(j)| < \Delta' < \infty$ for all $j \geq 0$ (see Dhrymes, 1980, pp. 394–395.) Since $|\beta_{o2}| < 1$ it follows that $\sum_{j=0}^{\infty} |c_j| < \infty$. Thus, Y_t is $\mathcal{F}_t$-measurable and

$$\begin{aligned} E(Y_{t-1}\varepsilon_t|\mathcal{F}_{t-1}) &= Y_{t-1}E(E(\varepsilon_t|\mathcal{F}_{t-1})) = 0 \\ E(Y_{t-2}\varepsilon_t|\mathcal{F}_{t-1}) &= Y_{t-2}E(E(\varepsilon_t|\mathcal{F}_{t-1})) = 0. \end{aligned}$$

Given $(ii'.a)$ $\{\mathbf{X}_t\varepsilon_t, \mathcal{F}_t\}$ is a martingale difference sequence and hence a mixingale. Therefore Theorem 5.17 $(iii.a)$ holds.

$(iii.b)$ We have that $E|Y_{t-1}\varepsilon_t|^2 \leq (E|Y_{t-1}|^4)^{1/2}(E|\varepsilon_t|^4)^{1/2}$ by the Cauchy-Schwarz inequality. Hence, if we can show $E|Y_{t-1}|^4 < \infty$, then condition $(iii.b)$ is verified. Now by Minkowski's inequality (see Exercise 3.53),

$$\begin{aligned} E|Y_t|^4 &= E\left|\sum_{j=0}^{\infty} c_j\varepsilon_{t-j}\right|^4 \\ &\leq \left(\sum_{j=0}^{\infty} |c_j| \left(E\,|\varepsilon_{t-j}|^4\right)^{1/4}\right)^4 \\ &< \Delta\left(\sum_{j=0}^{\infty} |c_j|\right)^4 < \infty. \end{aligned}$$

$(iii.c)$ By the martingale difference assumption and by stationarity we have that

$$\begin{aligned} \mathbf{V}_n &= n^{-1}\sum_{t=1}^{n} E(\mathbf{X}_t\varepsilon_t\varepsilon_t\mathbf{X}_t') = \sigma_o^2 E(\mathbf{X}_t\mathbf{X}_t') \\ &= \sigma_o^2 \begin{pmatrix} E(Y_{t-1}^2) & E(Y_{t-1}Y_{t-2}) \\ E(Y_{t-2}Y_{t-1}) & E(Y_{t-2}^2) \end{pmatrix} = \sigma_o^2\mathbf{M}, \end{aligned}$$

which is positive definite if $E(Y_{t-1}^2)^2 - E(Y_{t-2}Y_{t-1})^2 > 0$ or equivalently, if $E(Y_t^2) > E(|Y_tY_{t-1}|)$. Now

$$\begin{aligned} E(Y_t^2) &= \sigma_o^2(1-\beta_{o2})[(1+\beta_{o2})(1-\beta_{o2}) - \beta_{o1}^2]^{-1} \\ E(Y_tY_{t-1}) &= \sigma_o^2\beta_{o1}[(1+\beta_{o2})(1-\beta_{o2}) - \beta_{o1}^2]^{-1}, \end{aligned}$$

(see Granger and Newbold, 1977, Ch. 1) so $E(Y_t^2) > E(|Y_tY_{t-1}|)$ holds if and only if $(1-\beta_{o2}) > |\beta_{o1}|$. This is ensured by $(i'.b)$, and the condition holds.

(*iv.a*) $E|Y_{t-i}^2| < \infty$ is directly implied by $E|Y_{t-i}^4| < \Delta$ using Jensen's inequality.

(*iv.b*) That $\mathbf{M}$ is positive definite was proven in (*iii.c*).

■

Exercise 5.19

Proof. We verify the conditions of Exercise 4.26. The proof that

$$\mathbf{V}_n^{-1/2} n^{-1/2} \mathbf{Z}'\boldsymbol{\varepsilon} \overset{A}{\sim} N(\mathbf{0}, \mathbf{I})$$

is exactly parallel to the proof that

$$\mathbf{V}_n^{-1/2} n^{-1/2} \mathbf{X}'\boldsymbol{\varepsilon} \overset{A}{\sim} N(\mathbf{0}, \mathbf{I})$$

in Theorem 5.17 with $\mathbf{Z}$ replacing $\mathbf{X}$ everywhere. Next, $\mathbf{Z}'\mathbf{X}/n - \mathbf{Q} \xrightarrow{p} \mathbf{0}$ by the ergodic theorem (Theorem 3.34) given (*ii*), (*iv.a*), and (*iv.b*), where $\mathbf{Q}$ is finite with full column rank. Since the conditions of Exercise 4.26 are satisfied, it follows that

$$\mathbf{D}_n^{-1/2} \sqrt{n}(\tilde{\boldsymbol{\beta}}_n - \boldsymbol{\beta}_o) \overset{A}{\sim} N(\mathbf{0}, \mathbf{I}),$$

where

$$\mathbf{D}_n \equiv (\mathbf{Q}'\mathbf{P}\mathbf{Q})^{-1}\mathbf{Q}'\mathbf{P}\mathbf{V}_n\mathbf{P}\mathbf{Q}(\mathbf{Q}'\mathbf{P}\mathbf{Q})^{-1}.$$

Since $\mathbf{D}_n - \mathbf{D} \to \mathbf{0}$ it follows that

$$\begin{aligned}\mathbf{D}^{-1/2}\sqrt{n}(\tilde{\boldsymbol{\beta}}_n - \boldsymbol{\beta}_o) &- \mathbf{D}_n^{-1/2}\sqrt{n}(\tilde{\boldsymbol{\beta}}_n - \boldsymbol{\beta}_o) \\ &= (\mathbf{D}^{-1/2}\mathbf{D}_n^{1/2} - \mathbf{I})\mathbf{D}_n^{-1/2}\sqrt{n}(\tilde{\boldsymbol{\beta}}_n - \boldsymbol{\beta}_o) \xrightarrow{p} \mathbf{0}\end{aligned}$$

by Lemma 4.6. Therefore, by Lemma 4.7, $\mathbf{D}^{-1/2}\sqrt{n}(\tilde{\boldsymbol{\beta}}_n - \boldsymbol{\beta}_o) \overset{A}{\sim} N(\mathbf{0}, \mathbf{I})$.

■

Exercise 5.21

Proof. We verify the conditions of Theorem 4.25. First we apply Theorem 5.20 and Proposition 5.1 to show that $\mathbf{V}_n^{-1/2} n^{-1/2} \mathbf{X}'\boldsymbol{\varepsilon} \overset{A}{\sim} N(\mathbf{0}, \mathbf{I})$. Consider

$$\boldsymbol{\lambda}'\mathbf{V}_n^{-1/2} n^{-1/2} \mathbf{X}'\boldsymbol{\varepsilon} = n^{-1/2}\sum_{t=1}^{n} \boldsymbol{\lambda}'\mathbf{V}_n^{-1/2}\mathbf{X}_t\varepsilon_t.$$

By Theorem 3.49, $\{\boldsymbol{\lambda}'\mathbf{V}_n^{-1/2}\mathbf{X}_t\varepsilon_t\}$ is a mixing sequence, with either ϕ of size $-r/(2r-1)$, $r \geq 2$, or α of size $-r/(r-2)$, $r > 2$, given (ii). Further, $E(\boldsymbol{\lambda}'\mathbf{V}_n^{-1/2}\mathbf{X}_t\varepsilon_t) = \mathbf{0}$ given $(iii.a)$, and application of Minkowski's inequality gives

$$E(|\boldsymbol{\lambda}'\mathbf{V}_n^{-1/2}\mathbf{X}_t\varepsilon_t|^{r+\delta}) < \Delta < \infty$$

for some $\delta > 0$ and for all t given $(iii.b)$.

It follows from Theorem 5.20 that for all $\boldsymbol{\lambda}$, $\boldsymbol{\lambda}'\boldsymbol{\lambda} = 1$, we have

$$n^{-1/2}\sum_{t=1}^{n}\boldsymbol{\lambda}'\mathbf{V}_n^{-1/2}\mathbf{X}_t\varepsilon_t = \boldsymbol{\lambda}'\mathbf{V}_n^{-1/2}n^{-1/2}\mathbf{X}'\boldsymbol{\varepsilon} \overset{A}{\sim} N(0,1).$$

Hence, by Proposition 5.1, $\mathbf{V}_n^{-1/2}n^{-1/2}\mathbf{X}'\boldsymbol{\varepsilon} \overset{A}{\sim} N(\mathbf{0},\mathbf{I})$, so Theorem 4.25 (ii) holds.

Next, $\mathbf{X}'\mathbf{X}/n - \mathbf{M}_n \xrightarrow{p} \mathbf{0}$ by Corollary 3.48 and Theorem 2.24 given $(iv.a)$. Given $(iv.a)$ $\mathbf{M}_n = O(1)$ and $\det(\mathbf{M}_n) > \delta > 0$ for all n sufficiently large given $(iv.b)$. Hence, the conditions of Theorem 4.25 are satisfied and the result follows. ∎

Exercise 5.22

Proof. The following conditions are sufficient for asymptotic normality:

(i') (a) $Y_t = \beta_{o1}Y_{t-1} + \beta_{o2}W_t + \varepsilon_t$;

(b) $|\beta_{o1}| < 1$, $|\beta_{o2}| < \infty$;

(ii') $\{Y_t\}$ is a mixing sequence with either ϕ of size $-r/2(r-1)$, $r \geq 2$, or α of size $-r/(r-2)$, $r > 2$; $\{W_t\}$ is a bounded nonstochastic sequence.

(iii') (a) $E(\varepsilon_t|\mathcal{F}_{t-1}) = 0$, $\quad t = 1, 2, \ldots$, where $\mathcal{F}_t = \sigma(Y_t, Y_{t-1}, \ldots)$;

(b) $E|\varepsilon_t|^{2r} < \Delta < \infty$, $\quad t = 1, 2, \ldots$;

(c) $\mathbf{V}_n \equiv \text{var}(n^{-1/2}\sum_{t=1}^{n}\mathbf{X}_t\varepsilon_t)$ is uniformly positive definite, where $\mathbf{X}_t \equiv (Y_{t-1}, W_t)$;

(iv') (a) $\mathbf{M}_n \equiv E(\mathbf{X}'\mathbf{X}/n)$ has $\det(\mathbf{M}_n) > \delta > 0$ for all n sufficiently large.

We verify the conditions of Exercise 5.21. Since $\varepsilon_t = Y_t - \beta_{o1}Y_{t-1} - \beta_{o2}W_t$, it follows from Theorem 3.49 that $\{(\mathbf{X}_t, \varepsilon_t)\} = \{(Y_{t-1}, W_t, \varepsilon_t)\}$ is mixing with either ϕ of size $-r/2(r-1)$, $r \geq 2$, or α of size $-r/(r-2)$, $r > 2$, given (ii'). Thus, condition (ii) of Exercise 5.21 is satisfied.

Next consider condition (iii). Now $E(W_t\varepsilon_t) = W_tE(\varepsilon_t) = 0$ given $(iii'.a)$. Also, by repeated substitution we can express Y_t as

$$Y_t = \beta_{o2}\sum_{j=0}^{\infty}\beta_{o1}^{j}W_{t-j} + \sum_{j=0}^{\infty}\beta_{o1}^{j}\varepsilon_{t-j}.$$

By Proposition 3.52 it follows that $E(Y_{t-1}\varepsilon_t) = 0$ given $(iii'.a)$ and $(iii'.c)$. Hence, $E(\mathbf{X}_t\varepsilon_t) = (E(Y_{t-1}\varepsilon_t), E(W_t\varepsilon_t))' = 0$ so that $(iii.a)$ is satisfied. Turning to condition $(iii.b)$ we have $E|W_t\varepsilon_t|^r = \Delta' E|\varepsilon_t|^r < \Delta'\Delta < \infty$ given $(iii'.b)$, where $|W_t| < \Delta' < \infty$. Also

$$E|Y_{t-1}\varepsilon_t|^r \leq (E|Y_{t-1}|^{2r})^{1/2}(E|\varepsilon_t|^{2r})^{1/2}$$

by the Cauchy-Schwarz inequality. Since $E|\varepsilon_t|^{2r} < \Delta < \infty$ given $(iii'.b)$, it remains to be shown that $E|Y_t|^{2r} < \infty$. Applying Minkowski's inequality (see Exercise 3.53),

$$\begin{aligned} E|Y_t|^{2r} &= E\left|\beta_{o2}\sum_{j=0}^{\infty}\beta_{o1}^j W_{t-j} + \sum_{j=0}^{\infty}\beta_{o1}^j\varepsilon_{t-j}\right|^{2r} \\ &\leq \left(|\beta_{o2}|\sum_{j=0}^{\infty}|\beta_{o1}^j||W_{t-j}| + \sum_{j=0}^{\infty}|\beta_{o1}^j|\left(E|\varepsilon_{t-j}|^{2r}\right)^{1/(2r)}\right)^{2r} \\ &< \left(|\beta_{o2}|\Delta' + \Delta^{1/(2r)}\sum_{j=0}^{\infty}|\beta_{o1}^j|\right)^{2r} < \infty \end{aligned}$$

if and only if $|\beta_{o1}| < 1$. Therefore, $E|Y_{t-1}\varepsilon_t|^r < \infty$ given (i') and $(iv'.a)$ so that condition $(iii.b)$ is satisfied. Next, condition 5.21 $(iii.c)$ is imposed by 5.22 $(iii'.c)$. It remains to verify condition 5.21 $(iv.a)$. Now $E|W_t^2|^r = |W_t|^{2r} < \Delta'^{2r}$ given $(iv.a)$ and $E|Y_t^2|^{r/2} < \infty$ as shown previously. Hence, all conditions of Exercise 5.21 are satisfied so that the OLS estimate of (β_{o1}, β_{o2}) is consistent and asymptotically normal. ■

Exercise 5.27

Proof. First, we apply Corollary 5.26 and Proposition 5.1 to show that

$$\mathbf{V}_n^{-1/2}n^{-1/2}\mathbf{Z}'\boldsymbol{\varepsilon} \overset{A}{\sim} N(\mathbf{0}, \mathbf{I}).$$

Given $(iii'.a)$, $\{\mathbf{Z}_t\varepsilon_t\}$ is a martingale difference sequence with $\text{var}(n^{-1/2}\mathbf{Z}'\boldsymbol{\varepsilon}) = \mathbf{V}_n$ finite by $(iii'.b)$ with $\det(\mathbf{V}_n) > \delta > 0$ for all n sufficiently large given $(iii'.c)$. Hence, consider

$$\boldsymbol{\lambda}'\mathbf{V}_n^{-1/2}n^{-1/2}\mathbf{Z}'\boldsymbol{\varepsilon} = n^{-1/2}\sum_{t=1}^{n}\boldsymbol{\lambda}'\mathbf{V}_n^{-1/2}\mathbf{Z}_t\varepsilon_t.$$

By writing

$$\boldsymbol{\lambda}'\mathbf{V}_n^{-1/2}\mathbf{Z}_t\varepsilon_t = \sum_{h=1}^{p}\sum_{i=1}^{k}\tilde{\lambda}_{in}Z_{thi}\varepsilon_{th},$$

we see that the additivity of conditional expectations implies

$$E(\boldsymbol{\lambda}'\mathbf{V}_n^{-1/2}\mathbf{Z}_t\boldsymbol{\varepsilon}_t|\mathcal{F}_{t-1}) = \sum_{h=1}^{p}\sum_{i=1}^{k}\tilde{\lambda}_{in}E(Z_{thi}\varepsilon_{th}|\mathcal{F}_{t-1}) = 0,$$

as $E(Z_{thi}\varepsilon_{th}|\mathcal{F}_{t-1}) = 0$ given (*iii.a*). Applying Minkowski's inequality yields

$$\begin{aligned} E|\boldsymbol{\lambda}'\mathbf{V}_n^{-1/2}\mathbf{Z}_t\boldsymbol{\varepsilon}_t|^r &= E\left|\sum_{h=1}^{p}\sum_{i=1}^{k}\tilde{\lambda}_{in}Z_{thi}\varepsilon_{th}\right|^r \\ &\leq \left[\sum_{h=1}^{p}\sum_{i=1}^{k}\tilde{\lambda}_{in}\left(E\left|Z_{thi}\varepsilon_{th}\right|^r\right)^{1/r)}\right]^r \\ &< \left[\Delta\sum_{h=1}^{p}\sum_{i=1}^{k}\Delta^{1/r}\right]^r < \infty \end{aligned}$$

given (*iii'.b*). Further,

$$\begin{aligned} \bar{\sigma}_n^2 &= \text{var}(\boldsymbol{\lambda}'\mathbf{V}_n^{-1/2}n^{-1/2}\mathbf{Z}'\boldsymbol{\varepsilon}) \\ &= \boldsymbol{\lambda}'\mathbf{V}_n^{-1/2}\text{var}(n^{-1/2}\mathbf{Z}'\boldsymbol{\varepsilon})\mathbf{V}_n^{-1/2}\boldsymbol{\lambda} = 1 \end{aligned}$$

for all n sufficiently large.

Next, consider

$$n^{-1}\sum_{t=1}^{n}\boldsymbol{\lambda}'\mathbf{V}_n^{-1/2}\mathbf{Z}_t\boldsymbol{\varepsilon}_t\boldsymbol{\varepsilon}_t'\mathbf{Z}_t'\mathbf{V}_n^{-1/2}\boldsymbol{\lambda}.$$

Since $\{\mathbf{Z}_t\boldsymbol{\varepsilon}_t\boldsymbol{\varepsilon}_t'\mathbf{Z}_t'\}$ is a mixing sequence with either ϕ of size $-r/2(r-1)$, $r \geq 2$, or α of size $-r/(r-2)$, $r > 2$, by Theorem 3.49 it follows that $n^{-1}\sum_{t=1}^{n}\mathbf{Z}_t\boldsymbol{\varepsilon}_t\boldsymbol{\varepsilon}_t'\mathbf{Z}_t' - \mathbf{V}_n \xrightarrow{p} \mathbf{0}$ given (*iii'.b*). By Proposition 2.30,

$$\begin{aligned} n^{-1}\sum_{t=1}^{n}&\boldsymbol{\lambda}'\mathbf{V}_n^{-1/2}\mathbf{Z}_t\boldsymbol{\varepsilon}_t\boldsymbol{\varepsilon}_t'\mathbf{Z}_t'\mathbf{V}_n^{-1/2}\boldsymbol{\lambda} - \boldsymbol{\lambda}'\mathbf{V}_n^{-1/2}\mathbf{V}_n\mathbf{V}_n^{-1/2}\boldsymbol{\lambda} \\ &= n^{-1}\sum_{t=1}^{n}\boldsymbol{\lambda}'\mathbf{V}_n^{-1/2}\mathbf{Z}_t\boldsymbol{\varepsilon}_t\boldsymbol{\varepsilon}_t'\mathbf{Z}_t'\mathbf{V}_n^{-1/2}\boldsymbol{\lambda} - 1 \xrightarrow{p} 0. \end{aligned}$$

Hence, the sequence $\{\boldsymbol{\lambda}'\mathbf{V}_n^{-1/2}\mathbf{Z}_t\boldsymbol{\varepsilon}_t\}$ satisfies the conditions of Corollary 5.26, and it follows that $\boldsymbol{\lambda}\mathbf{V}_n^{-1/2}n^{-1/2}\sum_{t=1}^{n}\mathbf{Z}_t\boldsymbol{\varepsilon}_t = \boldsymbol{\lambda}'\mathbf{V}_n^{-1/2}n^{-1/2}\mathbf{Z}'\boldsymbol{\varepsilon} \overset{A}{\sim} N(0,1)$. By Proposition 5.1, $\mathbf{V}_n^{-1/2}n^{-1/2}\mathbf{Z}'\boldsymbol{\varepsilon} \overset{A}{\sim} N(\mathbf{0},\mathbf{I})$.

Now, given (ii'), $(iv.a)$, and $(iv.b)$, $\mathbf{Z}'\mathbf{X}/n - \mathbf{Q}_n \xrightarrow{p} \mathbf{0}$ by Corollary 3.48 and Theorem 2.24. The remaining results follow as before. ∎

Exercise 6.2

Proof. The following conditions are sufficient:

(*i*) $\mathbf{Y}_t = \mathbf{X}_t'\boldsymbol{\beta}_o + \boldsymbol{\varepsilon}_t, \quad t = 1, 2, \ldots, \ \boldsymbol{\beta}_o \in \mathbb{R}^k$;

(*ii*) $\{(\mathbf{Z}_t', \mathbf{X}_t', \boldsymbol{\varepsilon}_t)\}$ is a mixing sequence with either ϕ of size $-r/2(r-1)$, $r \geq 2$, or α of size $-r/(r-2)$, $r > 2$;

(*iii*) (*a*) $E(Z_{tgi}\varepsilon_{th}|\mathcal{F}_{t-1}) = 0$ for all t, where $\{\mathcal{F}_t\}$ is adapted to $\{Z_{tgi}\varepsilon_{th}\}$, $g, h = 1, \ldots, p$, $i = 1, \ldots, l$;

(*b*) $E|Z_{tgi}\varepsilon_{th}|^{r+\delta} < \Delta < \infty$ and $E|\varepsilon_{th}|^{r+\delta} < \Delta < \infty$ for some $\delta > 0$, $g, h = 1, \ldots, p$, $i = 1, \ldots, l$, and all t;

(*c*) $E(\boldsymbol{\varepsilon}_t\boldsymbol{\varepsilon}_t'|\mathbf{Z}_t) = \sigma_o^2\mathbf{I}_p$, $t = 1, \ldots, n$;

(*iv*) (*a*) $E|Z_{thi}|^{r+\delta} < \Delta < \infty$ and $E|X_{thj}|^{r+\delta} < \Delta < \infty$ for some $\delta > 0$, $h = 1, \ldots, p$, $i = 1, \ldots, l$, $j = 1, \ldots k$, and all t;

(*b*) $\mathbf{Q}_n \equiv E(\mathbf{Z}'\mathbf{X}/n)$ has full column rank uniformly in n for all n sufficiently large;

(*c*) $\mathbf{L}_n \equiv E(\mathbf{Z}'\mathbf{Z}/n)$ has $\det(\mathbf{L}_n) > \delta > 0$ for all n sufficiently large.

Given conditions (*i*)–(*iv*), the asymptotically efficient estimator is

$$\tilde{\boldsymbol{\beta}}_n = \tilde{\boldsymbol{\beta}}_{2SLS} = (\mathbf{X}'\mathbf{Z}(\mathbf{Z}'\mathbf{Z})^{-1}\mathbf{Z}'\mathbf{X})^{-1}\mathbf{X}'\mathbf{Z}(\mathbf{Z}'\mathbf{Z})^{-1}\mathbf{Z}'\mathbf{Y}$$

by Exercise 4.47. First, consider $\mathbf{Z}'\mathbf{Z}/n$. Now $\{\mathbf{Z}_t\mathbf{Z}_t'\}$ is a mixing sequence with the same size as $\{(\mathbf{Z}_t', \mathbf{X}_t', \boldsymbol{\varepsilon}_t)\}$ by Proposition 3.50. Hence, by Corollary 3.48, $\mathbf{Z}'\mathbf{Z}/n - \mathbf{L}_n = n^{-1}\sum_{t=1}^n \mathbf{Z}_t\mathbf{Z}_t' - n^{-1}\sum_{t=1}^n E(\mathbf{Z}_t\mathbf{Z}_t') \xrightarrow{a.s.} \mathbf{0}$ given $(iv.a)$ and $\mathbf{Z}'\mathbf{Z}/n - \mathbf{L}_n \xrightarrow{p} \mathbf{0}$ by Theorem 2.24.

Next consider

$$\begin{aligned}
\tilde{\sigma}_n^2 &\equiv (np)^{-1}(\mathbf{Y} - \mathbf{X}\tilde{\boldsymbol{\beta}}_n)'(\mathbf{Y} - \mathbf{X}\tilde{\boldsymbol{\beta}}_n) \\
&= (\boldsymbol{\varepsilon} - \mathbf{X}(\tilde{\boldsymbol{\beta}}_n - \boldsymbol{\beta}_o))'(\boldsymbol{\varepsilon} - \mathbf{X}(\tilde{\boldsymbol{\beta}}_n - \boldsymbol{\beta}_o))/(np) \\
&= \boldsymbol{\varepsilon}'\boldsymbol{\varepsilon}/(np) - 2(\tilde{\boldsymbol{\beta}}_n - \boldsymbol{\beta}_o)'\mathbf{X}'\boldsymbol{\varepsilon}/(np) \\
&\quad + (\tilde{\boldsymbol{\beta}}_n - \boldsymbol{\beta}_o)'(\mathbf{X}'\mathbf{X}/n)(\tilde{\boldsymbol{\beta}}_n - \boldsymbol{\beta}_o)/p.
\end{aligned}$$

As the conditions of Exercise 3.79 are satisfied, it follows that $\tilde{\boldsymbol{\beta}}_n - \boldsymbol{\beta}_o \xrightarrow{a.s.} \mathbf{0}$. Also, $\mathbf{X}'\boldsymbol{\varepsilon}/n = O_{a.s.}(1)$ by Corollary 3.48 given (*ii*), $(iii.b)$, and $(iv.a)$. Hence $(\tilde{\boldsymbol{\beta}}_n - \boldsymbol{\beta}_o)\mathbf{X}'\boldsymbol{\varepsilon}/n \xrightarrow{p} \mathbf{0}$ by Exercise 2.22 and Theorem 2.24. Similarly, $\{\mathbf{X}_t\mathbf{X}_t'\}$ a mixing sequence with size given in (*ii*) with elements satisfying the moment condition of Corollary 3.48 given (*iv.a*), so that $\mathbf{X}'\mathbf{X}/n = O_{a.s.}(1)$ and therefore $(\tilde{\boldsymbol{\beta}}_n - \boldsymbol{\beta}_o)'(\mathbf{X}'\mathbf{X}/n)(\tilde{\boldsymbol{\beta}}_n - \boldsymbol{\beta}_o) \xrightarrow{p} 0$. Finally, consider

$$\boldsymbol{\varepsilon}'\boldsymbol{\varepsilon}/(np) = p^{-1}\sum_{h=1}^{p} n^{-1}\sum_{t=1}^{n} \varepsilon_{th}^2.$$

Now for any $h = 1, \ldots, p$, $\{\varepsilon_{th}^2\}$ is a mixing sequence with ϕ of size $-r/2(r-1)$, $r \geq 2$, or α of size $-r/(r-2)$, $r > 2$. As $\{\varepsilon_{th}^2\}$ satisfies the moment condition of Corollary 3.48 given (*iii.b*) and $E(\varepsilon_{th}^2) = \sigma_o^2$ given (*iii.c*), it follows that

$$n^{-1}\sum_{t=1}^{n} \varepsilon_{th}^2 - n^{-1}\sum_{t=1}^{n} E(\varepsilon_{th}^2) = n^{-1}\sum_{t=1}^{n} \varepsilon_{th}^2 - \sigma_o^2 \xrightarrow{p} 0,$$

Hence, $\boldsymbol{\varepsilon}'\boldsymbol{\varepsilon}/(np) \xrightarrow{p} \sigma_o^2$, and it follows that $\tilde{\sigma}_n^2 \xrightarrow{p} \sigma_o^2$ by Exercise 2.35. ∎

Exercise 6.6

Proof. The proof is analogous to that of Theorem 6.3. Consider for simplicity the case $p = 1$. We decompose $\hat{\mathbf{V}}_n - \mathbf{V}_n$ as follows:

$$\begin{aligned}\hat{\mathbf{V}}_n - \mathbf{V}_n &= n^{-1}\sum_{t=1}^{n} \varepsilon_t^2 \mathbf{Z}_t\mathbf{Z}_t' - n^{-1}\sum_{t=1}^{n} E(\varepsilon_t^2 \mathbf{Z}_t\mathbf{Z}_t') \\ &\quad -2n^{-1}\sum_{t=1}^{n} (\tilde{\boldsymbol{\beta}}_n - \boldsymbol{\beta}_o)'\mathbf{X}_t'\varepsilon_t\mathbf{Z}_t\mathbf{Z}_t' \\ &\quad +n^{-1}\sum (\tilde{\boldsymbol{\beta}}_n - \boldsymbol{\beta}_o)'\mathbf{X}_t\mathbf{X}_t'(\tilde{\boldsymbol{\beta}}_n - \boldsymbol{\beta}_o)\mathbf{Z}_t\mathbf{Z}_t'.\end{aligned}$$

Now $\{\varepsilon_t^2\mathbf{Z}_t\mathbf{Z}_t'\}$ is a mixing sequence with either ϕ of size $-r/(2r-1)$, $r \geq 1$, or α of size $-r/(r-1)$, $r > 1$, given (*ii*) with elements satisfying the moment condition of Corollary 3.48 given (*iii.b*). Hence

$$n^{-1}\sum_{t=1}^{n} \varepsilon_t^2\mathbf{Z}_t\mathbf{Z}_t' - n^{-1}\sum_{t=1}^{n} E(\varepsilon_t^2\mathbf{Z}_t\mathbf{Z}_t') \xrightarrow{p} \mathbf{0}.$$

The remaining terms converge to zero in probability as in Theorem 6.3, where we now use results on mixing sequences in place of results on stationary, ergodic sequences. For example, by the Cauchy-Schwarz inequality,

$$E|X_{t\kappa}Z_{ti}Z_{tj}\varepsilon_t|^{r+\delta} < \left(E|X_{t\kappa}Z_{ti}|^{2(r+\delta)}\right)^{1/2}\left(E|Z_{tj}\varepsilon_t|^{2(r+\delta)}\right)^{1/2} < \Delta < \infty$$

given $(iii.b)$ and $(iv.a)$. As $\{X_{t\kappa} Z_{ti} Z_{tj} \varepsilon_t\}$ is a mixing sequence with size given in (ii) and it satisfies the moment condition of Corollary 3.48, it follows that

$$n^{-1} \sum_{t=1}^{n} X_{t\kappa} Z_{ti} Z_{tj} \varepsilon_t - n^{-1} \sum_{t=1}^{n} E(X_{t\kappa} Z_{ti} Z_{tj} \varepsilon_t) \xrightarrow{p} 0.$$

Since $\tilde{\boldsymbol{\beta}}_n - \boldsymbol{\beta}_o \xrightarrow{p} \mathbf{0}$ under the conditions given, we have

$$n^{-1} \sum_{t=1}^{n} (\tilde{\boldsymbol{\beta}}_n - \boldsymbol{\beta}_o)' \mathbf{X}_t \varepsilon_t \mathbf{Z}_t \mathbf{Z}_t' \xrightarrow{p} \mathbf{0}$$

by Exercise 2.35. Finally, consider the third term. The Cauchy-Schwarz inequality gives $E|X_{t\kappa} X_{t\lambda} Z_{ti} Z_{tj}|^{r+\delta} < \infty$ so that

$$n^{-1} \sum_{t=1}^{n} X_{t\kappa} X_{t\lambda} Z_{ti} Z_{tj} - n^{-1} \sum_{t=1}^{n} E(X_{t\kappa} X_{t\lambda} Z_{ti} Z_{tj}) \xrightarrow{p} 0$$

by Corollary 3.48. Thus the third term vanishes in probability and application of Exercise 2.35 yields $\hat{\mathbf{V}}_n - \mathbf{V}_n \xrightarrow{p} \mathbf{0}$. ∎

Exercise 6.7
Proof. The proof is immediate from Exercise 5.27 and Exercise 6.6. ∎

Exercise 6.8
Proof. Conditions (i)–(iv) ensure that Exercise 6.6 holds for $\tilde{\boldsymbol{\beta}}_n$ and $\hat{\mathbf{V}}_n - \mathbf{V}_n \xrightarrow{p} \mathbf{0}$. Next set $\hat{\mathbf{P}}_n = \mathbf{V}_n^{-1}$ in Exercise 6.7. Then $\mathbf{P}_n = \mathbf{V}_n^{-1}$ and the result follows. ∎

Exercise 6.12
Proof. Exactly as in the proof of Theorem 6.9, all the terms

$$\begin{aligned}
&(n-\tau)^{-1} \sum_{t=\tau+1}^{n} \mathbf{Z}_t \varepsilon_t \varepsilon_{t-\tau} \mathbf{Z}_{t-\tau}' - E(\mathbf{Z}_t \varepsilon_t \varepsilon_{t-\tau} \mathbf{Z}_{t-\tau}') \\
&-(n-\tau)^{-1} \sum_{t=\tau+1}^{n} \mathbf{Z}_t \mathbf{X}_t' (\tilde{\boldsymbol{\beta}}_n - \boldsymbol{\beta}_o) \varepsilon_{t-\tau} \mathbf{Z}_{t-\tau}' \\
&-(n-\tau)^{-1} \sum_{t=\tau+1}^{n} \mathbf{Z}_t \varepsilon_t (\tilde{\boldsymbol{\beta}}_n - \boldsymbol{\beta}_o)' \mathbf{X}_{t-\tau} \mathbf{Z}_{t-\tau}' \\
&+(n-\tau)^{-1} \sum_{t=\tau+1}^{n} \mathbf{Z}_t \mathbf{X}_t' (\tilde{\boldsymbol{\beta}}_n - \boldsymbol{\beta}_o)(\tilde{\boldsymbol{\beta}}_n - \boldsymbol{\beta}_o)' \mathbf{X}_{t-\tau} \mathbf{Z}_{t-\tau}'.
\end{aligned}$$

converge to zero in probability. Note that Theorem 3.49 is invoked to guarantee the summands are mixing sequences with size given in (*ii*), and the Cauchy-Schwarz inequality is used to verify the moment condition of Corollary 3.48. For example, given (*ii*) $\{\mathbf{Z}_t\varepsilon_t\varepsilon_{t-\tau}\mathbf{Z}'_{t-\tau}\}$ is a mixing sequence with either ϕ of size $-r/(2r-2)$, $r \geq 2$, or α of size $-r/(r-2)$, $r > 2$, with elements satisfying the moment condition of Corollary 3.48 given (*iii.b*).

Hence

$$(n-\tau)^{-1}\sum_{t=\tau+1}^{n}\mathbf{Z}_t\varepsilon_t\varepsilon_{t-\tau}\mathbf{Z}'_{t-\tau} - (n-\tau)^{-1}\sum_{t=\tau+1}^{n}E(\mathbf{Z}_t\varepsilon_t\varepsilon_{t-\tau}\mathbf{Z}'_{t-\tau}) \xrightarrow{p} \mathbf{0}.$$

The remaining terms can be shown to converge to zero in probability in a manner similar to Theorem 6.3. ■

Exercise 6.13

Proof. Immediate from Theorem 5.22 and Exercise 6.12. ■

Exercise 6.14

Proof. Conditions (*i*)-(*iv*) ensure that Exercise 6.12 holds for $\tilde{\boldsymbol{\beta}}_n$ and $\hat{\mathbf{V}}_n - \mathbf{V}_n \xrightarrow{p} \mathbf{0}$. Next set $\hat{\mathbf{P}}_n = \hat{\mathbf{V}}_n^{-1}$ in Exercise 6.13. Then $\mathbf{P}_n = \mathbf{V}_n^{-1}$ and the result follows. ■

Exercise 6.15

Proof. Under the conditions of Theorem 6.9 or Exercise 6.12 it holds that $\hat{\mathbf{V}}_n - \mathbf{V}_n \xrightarrow{p} \mathbf{0}$, so the result will follow if also $\tilde{\mathbf{V}}_n - \hat{\mathbf{V}}_n \xrightarrow{p} \mathbf{0}$. Now

$$\tilde{\mathbf{V}}_n - \hat{\mathbf{V}}_n = \sum_{\tau=1}^{m}(w_{n\tau}-1)n^{-1}\sum_{t=\tau+1}^{n}\mathbf{Z}\tilde{\varepsilon}_t\tilde{\varepsilon}'_{t-\tau}\mathbf{Z}'_{t-\tau} + \mathbf{Z}_{t-\tau}\tilde{\varepsilon}_{t-\tau}\tilde{\varepsilon}'_t\mathbf{Z}'_t.$$

Since for each $\tau = 1, \ldots, m$ we have

$$n^{-1}\sum_{t=\tau+1}^{n}\mathbf{Z}_t\tilde{\varepsilon}_t\tilde{\varepsilon}'_{t-\tau}\mathbf{Z}'_{t-\tau} + \mathbf{Z}_{t-\tau}\tilde{\varepsilon}_{t-\tau}\tilde{\varepsilon}'_t\mathbf{Z}'_t = O_p(1)$$

it follows that

$$\begin{aligned}\tilde{\mathbf{V}}_n - \hat{\mathbf{V}}_n &= \sum_{\tau=1}^{m}(w_{n\tau}-1)O_p(1)\\ &= \sum_{\tau=1}^{m}o_p(1)O_p(1) = o_p(1),\end{aligned}$$

where we used that $w_{n\tau} \xrightarrow{p} 1$. ■

Exercise 7.2

Proof. Since $\mathcal{X}_t = \mathcal{X}_0 + \sum_{s=1}^{t} \mathcal{Z}_s$, we have

$$\begin{aligned} E(\mathcal{X}_t) &= E(\mathcal{X}_0 + \sum_{s=1}^{t} \mathcal{Z}_s) \\ &= 0 + \sum_{s=1}^{t} E(\mathcal{Z}_s) = 0, \end{aligned}$$

and

$$\begin{aligned} \text{var}(\mathcal{X}_t) &= \text{var}(\mathcal{X}_0 + \sum_{s=1}^{t} \mathcal{Z}_s) \\ &= 0 + \sum_{s=1}^{t} \text{var}(\mathcal{Z}_s) = t\sigma^2, \end{aligned}$$

using the independence between $\mathcal{Z}_r$ and $\mathcal{Z}_s$ for $r \neq s$. ∎

Exercise 7.3

Proof. Note that

$$\begin{aligned} \mathcal{X}_{t_4} - \mathcal{X}_{t_3} &= \mathcal{Z}_{t_4} + \mathcal{Z}_{t_4-1} + \cdots + \mathcal{Z}_{t_3+1}, \\ \mathcal{X}_{t_2} - \mathcal{X}_{t_1} &= \mathcal{Z}_{t_2} + \mathcal{Z}_{t_2-1} + \cdots + \mathcal{Z}_{t_1+1}. \end{aligned}$$

Since $(\mathcal{Z}_{t_1+1}, \ldots, \mathcal{Z}_{t_2})$ is independent of $(\mathcal{Z}_{t_3+1}, \ldots, \mathcal{Z}_{t_4})$ it follows from Proposition 3.2 (*ii*) that $\mathcal{X}_{t_4} - \mathcal{X}_{t_3}$ and $\mathcal{X}_{t_2} - \mathcal{X}_{t_1}$ are independent. ∎

Exercise 7.4

Proof. By definition

$$\begin{aligned} \mathcal{W}_n(b) - \mathcal{W}_n(a) &= n^{-1/2} \sum_{t=[na]+1}^{[nb]} \mathcal{Z}_t \\ &= n^{-1/2}([nb] - [na])^{1/2} \\ &\quad \times([nb] - [na])^{-1/2} \sum_{t=[na]+1}^{[nb]} \mathcal{Z}_t. \end{aligned}$$

The last term $([nb] - [na])^{-1/2} \sum_{t=[na]+1}^{[nb]} \mathcal{Z}_t \xrightarrow{d} N(0,1)$ by the central limit theorem, and $n^{-1/2}([nb] - [na])^{1/2} = (([nb] - [na])/n)^{1/2} \to (b-a)^{1/2}$ as $n \to \infty$. Hence $\mathcal{W}_n(b) - \mathcal{W}_n(a) \xrightarrow{d} N(0, b-a)$. ∎

Exercise 7.22

Proof. (*i*) Let $\mathcal{U} \in C$, and let $\mathcal{U}_n$ be a sequence of mappings in D such that $\mathcal{U}_n \to \mathcal{U}$, i.e., $b_n \equiv d_u(\mathcal{U}_n, \mathcal{U}) = \sup_{a\in[0,1]} |\mathcal{U}_n(a) - \mathcal{U}(a)| \to 0$ as $n \to \infty$. We have

$$\begin{aligned} d_u(\mathcal{U}_n^2, \mathcal{U}^2) &= \sup_{a\in[0,1]} |\mathcal{U}_n(a)^2 - \mathcal{U}(a)^2| \\ &= \sup_{a\in[0,1]} |\mathcal{U}_n(a) - \mathcal{U}(a)||\mathcal{U}_n(a) + \mathcal{U}(a)| \\ &\leq b_n \sup_{a\in[0,1]} |\mathcal{U}_n(a) + \mathcal{U}(a)|, \end{aligned}$$

where $b_n \equiv d_u(\mathcal{U}_n, \mathcal{U})$. The boundedness of $\mathcal{U}$ and the fact that $b_n \to 0$ imply that for all n sufficiently large, $\mathcal{U}_n$ is bounded on $[0, 1]$. Hence, $\sup_{a\in[0,1]} |\mathcal{U}_n(a) + \mathcal{U}(a)| = O(1)$ and it follows that $d_u(\mathcal{U}_n^2, \mathcal{U}^2) \to 0$, which proves that M_1 is continuous at $\mathcal{U}$.

Now consider the function on $[0, 1]$ given by

$$\mathcal{V}(a) = \begin{cases} \text{int}(\frac{1}{1-a}), & \text{for } 0 \leq a < 1 \\ 0, & \text{for } a = 1. \end{cases}$$

For $0 \leq a < 1/2$, this function is 1, then jumps to 2 for $a = 1/2$, to 3 for $a = 2/3$, and so forth. Clearly $\mathcal{V}(a)$ is continuous from the right and has left limits everywhere, so $\mathcal{V} \in D = D[0, 1]$.

Next, define the sequence of functions $\mathcal{V}_n(a) = \mathcal{V}(a) + \varepsilon/n$, for some $\varepsilon > 0$. Then $\mathcal{V}_n \in D$ and $\mathcal{V}_n \to \mathcal{V}$.

Since

$$\begin{aligned} d_u(\mathcal{V}_n^2, \mathcal{V}^2) &= \sup_{a\in[0,1]} |\mathcal{V}_n(a)^2 - \mathcal{V}(a)^2| \\ &= \sup_{a\in[0,1]} |(\mathcal{V}_n(a) - \mathcal{V}(a))(\mathcal{V}_n(a) + \mathcal{V}(a))| \\ &= (\varepsilon/n) \sup_{a\in[0,1]} |\mathcal{V}_n(a) + \mathcal{V}(a)| \end{aligned}$$

is infinite for all n, we conclude that $\mathcal{V}_n^2 \nrightarrow \mathcal{V}^2$. Hence, M_1 is not continuous everywhere in D.

(*ii*) Let $\mathcal{U} \in C$; then $\mathcal{U}$ is bounded and $\int_0^1 |\mathcal{U}(a)|da < \infty$. Let $\{\mathcal{U}_n\}$ be a sequence of functions in D such that $\mathcal{U}_n \to \mathcal{U}$. Define $b_n \equiv d_u(\mathcal{U}_n, \mathcal{U})$; then $b_n \to 0$ and $\int_0^1 |\mathcal{U}_n(a)|da \leq \int_0^1 |\mathcal{U}(a)|da + b_n$.

Since

$$\begin{aligned}|\int_0^1 \mathcal{U}_n(a)^2 da - \int_0^1 \mathcal{U}(a)^2 da| &\leq \int_0^1 |\mathcal{U}_n(a)^2 - \mathcal{U}(a)^2| da \\ &= \int_0^1 |\mathcal{U}_n(a) - \mathcal{U}(a)||\mathcal{U}_n(a) + \mathcal{U}(a)| da \\ &\leq b_n \int_0^1 |\mathcal{U}_n(a) + \mathcal{U}(a)| da \\ &\leq b_n(b_n + 2\int_0^1 |\mathcal{U}(a)| da) \to 0\end{aligned}$$

M_2 is continuous at $\mathcal{U} \in C$.

(*iii*) Let $\mathcal{V}(a) = a$ for all $a \in [0,1]$ and let $\mathcal{V}_n(a) = 0$ for $0 \leq a < 1/n$ and $\mathcal{V}_n = \mathcal{V}(a)$ for $a \geq 1/n$. Thus $d_u(\mathcal{V}, \mathcal{V}_n) = 1/n$ and $\mathcal{V}_n \to \mathcal{V}$; however, $\int_0^1 \log(|\mathcal{V}_n(a)|)da \nrightarrow \int_0^1 \log(|\mathcal{V}(a)|)da$, since $\int_0^1 \log(|\mathcal{V}(a)|)da = -1$ whereas $\int_0^1 \log(|\mathcal{V}_n(a)|)da = -\infty$ for all n. Hence, it follows that M_3 is not continuous. ■

Exercise 7.23

Proof. If $\{\varepsilon_t\}$ satisfies the conditions of the heterogeneous mixing CLT and is globally covariance stationary, then (*ii*) of Theorem 7.21 follows directly from Theorem 7.18. Since $\{\varepsilon_t\}$ is assumed to be mixing, then $\{\varepsilon_t^2\}$ is also mixing of the same size (see Proposition 3.50). By Corollary 3.48 it also then follows that $n^{-1}\sum_{t=1}^n \varepsilon_t^2 - n^{-1}\sum_{t=1}^n E(\varepsilon_t^2) = o_p(1)$. So if $n^{-1}\sum_{t=1}^n E(\varepsilon_t^2)$ converges as $n \to \infty$, then (*iii*) of Theorem 7.21 holds.

For $\sigma^2 = \tau^2$ it is required that $\lim n^{-1}\sum_{t=2}^n \sum_{s=1}^{t-1} E(\varepsilon_{t-s}\varepsilon_t) = 0$. It suffices that $\{\varepsilon_t\}$ is independent or that $\{\varepsilon_t, \mathcal{F}_t\}$ is a martingale difference sequence. ■

Exercise 7.28

Proof. From Donsker's theorem and the continuous mapping theorem we have that $n^{-2}\sum_{t=1}^n X_t^2 \Rightarrow \sigma_1^2 \int \mathcal{W}_1(a)^2 da$. The multivariate version of Donsker's theorem states that

$$(n^{-1/2}X_{[na]}, n^{-1/2}Y_{[na]}) \Rightarrow (\sigma_1\mathcal{W}_1(a), \sigma_2\mathcal{W}_2(a)).$$

Applying the continuous mapping theorem to the mapping

$$(x, y) \mapsto \int_0^1 x(a)y(a)da,$$

we have that

$$\begin{aligned} n^{-2}\sum_{t=1}^{n} X_t Y_t &= n^{-1}\sum_{t=1}^{n}\sigma_1 \mathcal{W}_{1n}(a_{t-1})\sigma_2 \mathcal{W}_{2n}(a_{t-1}) \\ &= \sigma_1\sigma_2 \int_0^1 \mathcal{W}_{1n}(a)\mathcal{W}_{2n}(a)da \\ &\Rightarrow \sigma_1\sigma_2 \int_0^1 \mathcal{W}_1(a)\mathcal{W}_2(a)da. \end{aligned}$$

Hence

$$\begin{aligned} \hat{\beta}_n &= \left(n^{-2}\sum_{t=1}^{n} X_t^2\right)^{-1} n^{-2}\sum_{t=1}^{n} X_t Y_t \\ &\Rightarrow \left(\sigma_1^2 \int_0^1 \mathcal{W}_1(a)^2 da\right)^{-1} \sigma_1\sigma_2 \int_0^1 \mathcal{W}_1(a)\mathcal{W}_2(a)da \\ &= (\sigma_2/\sigma_1)\left(\int_0^1 \mathcal{W}_1(a)^2 da\right)^{-1} \int_0^1 \mathcal{W}_1(a)\mathcal{W}_2(a)da. \end{aligned}$$

■

Exercise 7.31

Proof. Since $\{\eta_t, \varepsilon_t\}$ satisfies the conditions of Theorem 7.30, it holds that

$$\begin{aligned} (n^{-1/2}X_{[na]}, n^{-1/2}Y_{[na]}) &= (\sigma_1 \mathcal{W}_{1n}(a_{t-1}), \sigma_2 \mathcal{W}_{2n}(a_{t-1})) \\ &\Rightarrow (\sigma_1 \mathcal{W}_1(a), \sigma_2 \mathcal{W}_2(a)), \end{aligned}$$

where σ_1^2 and σ_2^2 are the diagonal elements of $\mathbf{\Sigma}$ (the off diagonal elements are zero, due to the independence of η_t and ε_t). Applying the continuous mapping theorem, we find $\hat{\beta}_n$ to have the same limiting distribution as we found in Exercise 7.28. ■

Exercise 7.43

Proof. (*i*) If $\{\boldsymbol{\eta}_t\}$ and $\{\boldsymbol{\varepsilon}_t\}$ are independent, then $E(\boldsymbol{\eta}_s \boldsymbol{\varepsilon}_t') = \mathbf{0}$ for all s and t. So

$$\begin{aligned} \mathbf{\Lambda}_n &\equiv \mathbf{\Sigma}_1^{-1/2} n^{-1} \sum_{t=2}^{n}\sum_{s=1}^{t-1} E(\boldsymbol{\eta}_s \boldsymbol{\varepsilon}_t')\mathbf{\Sigma}_2^{-1/2\prime} \\ &= \mathbf{0}, \end{aligned}$$

and clearly $\mathbf{\Lambda}_n \to \mathbf{\Lambda} = \mathbf{0}$.

(*ii*) If $\eta_t = \varepsilon_{t-1}$, then

$$\begin{aligned}\Lambda_n &\equiv \Sigma_1^{-1/2} n^{-1} \sum_{t=2}^{n} \sum_{s=1}^{t-1} E(\eta_s \varepsilon_t') \Sigma_2^{-1/2\prime} \\ &= \Sigma_1^{-1/2} n^{-1} \sum_{t=2}^{n} \sum_{s=1}^{t-1} E(\varepsilon_{s-1} \varepsilon_t') \Sigma_1^{-1/2\prime}.\end{aligned}$$

If the sequence $\{\varepsilon_t\}$ is covariance stationary such that $\rho_h \equiv E(\varepsilon_t \varepsilon_{t-h}')$ is well defined, then

$$\begin{aligned}n^{-1} \sum_{t=2}^{n} \sum_{s=1}^{t-1} E(\varepsilon_{s-1} \varepsilon_t') &= n^{-1} \sum_{t=2}^{n} \sum_{s=2}^{t} E(\varepsilon_{t-s} \varepsilon_t') \\ &= n^{-1} \sum_{t=2}^{n} \sum_{s=2}^{t} \rho_s' \\ &= \sum_{s=2}^{n} \frac{(n+1-s)}{n} \rho_s',\end{aligned}$$

so that

$$\Lambda_n \equiv \Sigma_1^{-1/2} \left(\sum_{s=2}^{n} \frac{(n+1-s)}{n} \rho_s \right) \Sigma_1^{-1/2\prime} \to \Lambda,$$

where in this situation we have

$$\Sigma_1 = \Sigma_2 = \lim_{n\to\infty} n^{-1} \sum_{t=1}^{n} \sum_{s=1}^{n} \rho_{t-s} = \rho_0 + \lim_{n\to\infty} \sum_{s=1}^{n-1} \frac{(n-s)}{n} (\rho_s + \rho_s').$$

Notice that when $\{\varepsilon_t\}$ is a sequence of independent variables such that $\rho_s = \mathbf{0}$ for $s \geq 1$, then $\text{var}(\varepsilon_t) = \rho_0 = \Sigma_1$ and $\Lambda = \mathbf{0}$. This remains true for the case where $\eta_t = \varepsilon_t$, which is assumed in the likelihood analysis of cointegrated processes by Johansen (1988, 1991). ∎

Exercise 7.44
Proof.

(*a*) This follows from Theorem 7.21 (*a*), or we have directly

$$n^{-2} \sum_{t=1}^{n} X_t^2 = \sigma_1^2 \int_0^1 \mathcal{W}_{1n}(a) \mathcal{W}_{1n}(a) da \Rightarrow \sigma_1^2 \int_0^1 \mathcal{W}_1(a)^2 da.$$

(*b*) Similarly,

$$n^{-1}\sum_{t=1}^{n} X_t\varepsilon_t = \sigma_1 \int_0^1 \mathcal{W}_{1n}(a)d\mathcal{W}_{2n}(a)\sigma_2 \Rightarrow \sigma_1\sigma_2 \int_0^1 \mathcal{W}_1(a)\, d\mathcal{W}_2(a),$$

by Theorem 7.42 and using that $\Lambda = 0$ since $\{\varepsilon_t\}$ and $\{\eta_t\}$ are independent (see Exercise 7.43).

(*c*)

$$\begin{aligned} n(\hat{\beta}_n - \beta_o) &= \left(n^{-2}\sum_{t=1}^{n} X_t^2\right)^{-1}\left(n^{-1}\sum_{t=1}^{n} X_t\varepsilon_t\right) \\ &\Rightarrow (\sigma_2/\sigma_1)\left[\int_0^1 \mathcal{W}_1(a)da\right]^{-1} \int_0^1 \mathcal{W}_1(a)\, d\mathcal{W}_2(a). \end{aligned}$$

(*d*) From (*c*) we have that $n(\hat{\beta}_n - \beta_o) = O_p(1)$, and by Exercise 2.35 we have that $(\hat{\beta}_n - \beta_o) = n^{-1}n(\hat{\beta}_n - \beta_o) = o_p(1)O_p(1) = o_p(1)$. So $\hat{\beta}_n \xrightarrow{p} \beta_o$.

■

References

Dhrymes, P. (1980). *Econometrics*. Springer-Verlag, New York.

Granger, C. W. J. and P. Newbold (1977). *Forecasting Economic Time Series*. Academic Press, New York.

Johansen, S. (1988). "Statistical analysis of cointegration vectors." *Journal of Economic Dynamics and Control*, 12, 231–254.

——— (1991). "Estimation and hypothesis testing of cointegration vectors in Gaussian vector autoregressive models." *Econometrica*, 59, 1551–80.

Laha, R. G. and V. K. Rohatgi (1979). *Probability Theory*. Wiley, New York.

Rao, C. R. (1973). *Linear Statistical Inference and Its Applications*. Wiley, New York.

Index

Adapted mixingale, 124
Adapted stochastic sequence, 58
Approximatable stochastic function, 194
AR(1), 48, 49
ARCH(q), 102
ARMA, 49
Asymptotic covariance matrix, 70, 73
  estimator, 137
    heteroskedasticity consistent, 139–146
    heteroskedasticity/autocorrelation consistent, 154–164
    heteroskedasticity/moving average consistent, 147–154
  Newey-West estimator, 163
Asymptotic distribution, 66
Asymptotic efficiency, 83
  Bates and White framework, 93
  IV estimator, 84
  two-stage least squares, 86
Asymptotic equivalence, 67
Asymptotic normality, 71
  of $\hat{\beta}_n$, 71
  of $\tilde{\beta}_n$, 73
Asymptotically uncorrelated process, 52, 139, 154
avar, 70, 83

Backshift operator, 42
Best linear unbiased estimator, 3
Borel
  sets, 41
  σ-field, 40
Boundary of a set, 173
Bounded in probability, 28
Brownian motion, 169
  BM($\mathbf{\Sigma}$), 203
  definition, 170

$C[0,1]$, 175
$C[0,\infty)$, 172
$C^k[0,1]$, 187
$C^k[0,\infty)$, 186
Cadlag function, 172
Cauchy-Schwarz inequality, 33
Central limit theorem, 113
  functional, 175
  Liapounov, 118
  Lindeberg-Feller, 117
  Lindeberg-Lévy, 114
  martingale difference, 133
  mixing, 130
  stationary ergodic adapted mixingale, 125
  Wooldridge-White, 130

Characteristic function, 67–71
continuity theorem, 69
uniqueness theorem, 68
Chebyshev inequality, 30
generalized, 29
Classical assumptions of least squares, 2
generalized, 5
Classical linear model, 1–8
Cointegrated processes, 190
likelihood analysis, 258
Cointegrated regression, 199, 201
Conditional expectation, 54–59
linearity of, 55
Consistency
strong, 19
super, 180
weak, 24
Continuity
uniform, 21
Continuity set, 173
Continuous function, 16
Continuous mapping theorem, 178
Convergence
almost sure, 18
in distribution, 65
in probability, 24
in rth mean, 28
of stochastic integral, 199, 201
weak, 171
Covariance stationary process, 52
globally, 177
Cramér-Wold device, 114
functional, 188

$D[0,1]$, 175
$D[0,\infty)$, 172
$D^k[0,1]$, 187
$D^k[0,\infty)$, 186
Data generating process, 94, 207
Dickey-Fuller distribution, 180
Dispersion matrix, 73
Donsker's theorem, 176
multivariate, 188

Ergodic
process, 44
theorem, 44

Estimator
asymptotic covariance matrix, 137
heteroskedasticity consistent, 139–146
heteroskedasticity/autocorrelation consistent, 154–164
heteroskedasticity/moving average consistent, 147–154
generalized least squares, 5, 100
efficiency, 101
feasible, 102
feasible and efficient, 105
generalized method of moments, 85
instrumental variables, 9
constrained, 86
efficient, 109
M-, 210
maximum likelihood, 3, 210
method of moments, 85
ordinary least squares, 2
three-stage least squares, 111
two-stage instrumental variables, 144, 163
two-stage least squares, 10, 144
asymptotically efficient, 86
efficient, 111
Events, 39

Filtration, 58, 193
Finitely correlated process, 138, 147
Fractionally integrated process, 208
Functional central limit theorem, 175
Donsker, 176
heterogeneous mixing, 177
multivariate, 189
Liapounov, 177
Lindeberg-Feller, 177
martingale difference, 178
multivariate, 189
stationary ergodic, 177

GARCH(1,1), 102
Gaussian AR(1), 48

Generalized least squares, 5
estimator, 5
efficiency, 101
feasible estimator, 102
efficient, 105
Generalized method of moments, 85

Heteroskedasticity, 3, 38, 143
ARCH, 102
conditional, 130
GARCH, 102
unconditional, 130
Hölder inequality, 33
Hypothesis testing, 74–83

Implication rule, 25
Inequalities
Cauchy-Schwarz, 33
Chebyshev, 30
c_r, 35
Hölder, 33
Jensen, 29
conditional, 56
Markov, 30
Minkowski, 36
Instrumental variables, 8
estimator, 9
asymptotic normality, 74, 143, 145, 150, 152
consistency, 21, 23, 26, 27, 34, 38, 46, 51, 61
constrained, 86
definition, 9
efficient, 109
Integrated process, 179
fractionally, 208
Invariance principle, 176
Ito stochastic integral, 194
for random step functions, 193

Jensen inequality, 29
conditional, 56

Lagged dependent variable, 7
Lagrange multiplier test, 77
Law of iterated expectations, 57
Law of large numbers
martingale difference, 60
Laws of large numbers, 31
ergodic theorem, 44
i.i.d., 32
i.n.i.d., 35
mixing, 49
Lévy device, 58
Likelihood analysis, 210
cointegrated processes, 258
Likelihood ratio test, 80
Limit, 15
almost sure, 19
in mean square, 29
in probability, 24
Limited dependent variable, 209
Limiting distribution, 66
Lindeberg condition, 117

M-estimator, 210
Markov condition, 35
Markov inequality, 30
Martingale difference sequence, 53, 58
Maximum likelihood estimator, 210
Mean value theorem, 80
Measurable
function, 41
one-to-one transformation, 42
space, 39
Measure preserving transformation, 42
Measurement errors, 6
Method of moments estimator, 9
Metric, 173
space, 173
Metrized measurable space, 174
Metrized probability space, 174
Minkowski inequality, 36
Misspecification, 207
Mixing, 47
coefficients, 47
conditions, 46
size, 49
strong, (α-mixing), 47
uniform, (ϕ-mixing), 47
Mixingale, 125

Nonlinear model, 209

$O(n^\lambda)$, 16
$o(n^\lambda)$, 16

$O_{a.s.}(n^{\lambda})$, 23
$o_{a.s.}(n^{\lambda})$, 23
$O_p(n^{\lambda})$, 28
$o_p(n^{\lambda})$, 28
Ordinary least squares, 2
estimator, 2
definition, 72
asymptotic normality, 72
consistency, 20, 22, 26, 27, 33, 38, 45, 50, 61
definition, 2

Panel data, 11
Partial sum, 169
Probability
measure, 39
space, 39
Product rule, 28

Quasi-maximum likelihood estimator, 79, 210

Random function, 169
step function, 193
Random walk, 167
multivariate, 187
Rcll function, 172

Serially correlated errors, 7
Shift operator, 42
σ-algebra, 39
σ-field, 39
Borel, 40
σ-fields
increasing sequence, 58
Simultaneous systems, 11
for panel data, 12
Spurious regression, 185, 188
Stationary process, 43
covariance stationary, 52
Stochastic function
approximatable, 194
square integrable, 194
Stochastic integral, 192
Strong mixing, 47
Sum of squared residuals, 2
Superconsistency, 180

Test statistics
Lagrange multiplier, 77
Likelihood ratio, 80
Wald, 76, 81
Three-stage least squares
estimator, 111
Two-stage instrumental variables
estimator, 144, 163
Two-stage instrumental variables estimator
asymptotic normality, 146, 151, 153, 164
Two-stage least squares, 10
estimator, 144
efficient, 111

Uncorrelated process, 138, 139
asymptotically, 139, 154
Uniform asymptotic negligibility, 118
Uniform continuity, 21
theorem, 21
Uniform mixing, 47
Uniform nonsingularity, 22
Uniform positive definiteness, 22
Uniformly full column rank, 22
Uniqueness theorem, 68
Unit root, 179
regression, 178

Vec operator, 142

Wald test, 76, 81
Weak convergence, 171
definition, 174
Wiener measure, 176
Wiener process, 170
definition, 170
multivariate, 186
sample path, 171